One Year through the Bible

Keepin'
It
Real

Lighthouse

Keepin'

It

Real

Lighthouse

ONE YEAR
THROUGH THE
BIBLE

with devotionals by
David R. Veerman and Daryl J. Lucas

Tyndale House Publishers, Inc.   Wheaton, Illinois

Visit Tyndale's exciting Web site at www.tyndale.com

Copyright © 2000 by the Livingstone Corporation. All rights reserved.

Cover photograph copyright © 2000 by Michael Hudson. All rights reserved.

One Year is a registered trademark of Tyndale House Publishers, Inc.

Scripture quotations are taken from the *Holy Bible,* New Living Translation, copyright © 1996.
Used by permission of Tyndale House Publishers, Inc., Wheaton, Illinois 60189. All rights reserved.

Edited by S. Harrison

Designed by Julie Chen

Library of Congress Cataloging-in-Publication Data

Veerman, David.
     One year through the Bible : with devotionals / by David R. Veerman and Daryl J. Lucas.
         p. cm.
     ISBN 0-8423-3553-6 (pbk.)
     1. Bible—Reading. 2. Bible—Devotional literature. 3. Devotional calendars.   I. Lucas, Daryl.
II. Title.

BS617 .V44 2000
242'.2—dc21   00-044704

Printed in the United States of America

06   05   04
9   8   7   6   5

Centuries ago, the apostle Paul wrote to his young protégé, Timothy: "All Scripture is inspired by God and is useful to teach us what is true and to make us realize what is wrong in our lives" (2 Timothy 3:16). Note that Paul said "*all* Scripture"—not a part or some, but all. "All" means all of the Bible, every part and every type of literature—law, history, poetry, prophecy, gospel, epistle, and apocalypse.

That short passage in Paul's letter also emphasizes what Scripture does: "It straightens us out and teaches us to do what is right. It is God's way of preparing us in every way, fully equipped for every good thing God wants us to do" (2 Timothy 3:16-17). In other words, the Bible tells us how to live by showing us what God wants. As we read Scripture we need to think about what God is revealing about himself and what he is telling us to do—what actions to take and what changes to make.

This book helps you do just that—read and apply the Bible. Here's how it works.

Each day features a daily reading, highlighted at the top of the right-hand page. If you read all these passages from your Bible, you will read the entire Bible in a year.

From each of those daily reading passages we have selected a short "Bible Reading," which is included on the same page. If you read only those smaller passages each day, you will get a sampling of the whole Bible, hitting the highlighted stories and teachings.

Each selected reading also ties to a devotional on the preceding page. The purpose of each devotional is to help you understand the passage and apply it to your life.

You can read the entire Bible alongside the devotionals, or just the excerpted "Bible Readings." Either way, I suggest that you read the "Preview" section of the devotional first, then the "Bible Reading," and finally the "Personal Application" section of the devotional.

I pray that God will use this book to impact your life, giving you a deeper appreciation and understanding of "all Scripture."

Dave Veerman

*T*HAT LOOKS TEMPTING

PREVIEW

Diets can be maddening because they make it so difficult to stick to your convictions. The plan looks great, with a limit on calories or grams of fat per day and a list of prohibited or acceptable edibles. But when offered a piece of pie, you give in to the temptation, forgetting your diet and your resolution to lose weight. This struggle is real. It's war.

This passage right at the beginning of the Bible tells all about the origin of the world, life, people, and work. It also covers husband-wife relationships. Closest to home, it explains how a perfect world went wrong and why human beings have struggled since then against all sorts of evil. It tells about temptation.

PERSONAL APPLICATION

Everyone struggles with temptation. We are tempted to lie, to cheat, to steal, and to indulge ourselves in countless ways that God has forbidden. We give in because of Satan (Genesis 3:1-6). Temptation is Satan's invitation to live his kind of life and give up on God's. Satan tempted Eve and succeeded in getting her to sin; soon after, Adam yielded to the pull of Satan's tempting offer. So sin entered the world, and every person since has been born a sinner. Today, Satan is busy trying to get us to give in to his temptations.

Eve and Adam could have resisted temptation by remembering what God had commanded them. We must realize that being tempted is not sin. We have not sinned until we give in to the temptation. To resist temptation, we must (1) pray for strength to resist (see Matthew 6:13), (2) say no when confronted with what we know is wrong (see James 4:7), and (3) run away from the temptation, sometimes literally (see Genesis 39:12). James 1:12 tells of the blessings and rewards for those who don't give in when tempted.

As you read about the tragic fall of our perfect ancestors, watch the progression of temptation and sin. Then determine to obey God rather than believe Satan's lies. Resist Satan and his temptations, and live.

BIBLE READING

¹Now the serpent was the shrewdest of all the creatures the LORD God had made. "Really?" he asked the woman. "Did God really say you must not eat any of the fruit in the garden?"

²"Of course we may eat it," the woman told him. ³"It's only the fruit from the tree at the center of the garden that we are not allowed to eat. God says we must not eat it or even touch it, or we will die."

⁴"You won't die!" the serpent hissed. ⁵"God knows that your eyes will be opened when you eat it. You will become just like God, knowing everything, both good and evil."

⁶The woman was convinced. The fruit looked so fresh and delicious, and it would make her so wise! So she ate some of the fruit. She also gave some to her husband, who was with her. Then he ate it, too. ⁷At that moment, their eyes were opened, and they suddenly felt shame at their nakedness. So they strung fig leaves together around their hips to cover themselves.   GENESIS 3:1-7

BROTHERLY HATE

PREVIEW

How do you react when someone suggests that you have done something wrong? Do you move to correct the mistake, or do you deny that you have a problem or need to do anything? What about when the critic is someone in your family?

This reading describes Adam and Eve's immediate family. It focuses mostly on Cain, the first son—his choices and what God thought of them. Don't read too fast or you will miss important details—but it's all there, including the most horrifying fact of all: Cain killed his brother, Abel. Our experiences today mirror what occurred between these two brothers, however horrifying, because theirs is the story of what can happen when anger and jealousy rule.

Tangles in the ties that bind—reacting to criticism, jealousy, sibling rivalry—all appear in this passage. The lessons bear remembering, so you'd better go slow.

PERSONAL APPLICATION

Cain's failures hinged on his reaction to God's rebuke (Genesis 4:6-7). We don't know why God rejected Cain's sacrifice. But instead of listening to God, learning, and changing his ways, he reacted impulsively. Cain was wrong, yet he would not accept responsibility for or deal with it. He countered God's correction with anger and denial.

After Cain's sacrifice was rejected, God gave him the chance to right his wrong and try again. God even encouraged him to do so, but Cain proudly refused. The rest of Cain's life is a startling example of what happens to those who refuse to admit their mistakes. It also shows what happens when we blame others for our problems and allow anger to build.

As you read this passage, learn from Cain's mistakes. Then the next time someone suggests you are wrong, especially God, take an honest look at yourself, and make the necessary changes.

BIBLE READING

¹Now Adam slept with his wife, Eve, and she became pregnant. When the time came, she gave birth to Cain, and she said, "With the Lord's help, I have brought forth a man!" ²Later she gave birth to a second son and named him Abel.

When they grew up, Abel became a shepherd, while Cain was a farmer. ³At harvesttime Cain brought to the LORD a gift of his farm produce, ⁴while Abel brought several choice lambs from the best of his flock. The LORD accepted Abel and his offering, ⁵but he did not accept Cain and his offering. This made Cain very angry and dejected.

⁶"Why are you so angry?" the LORD asked him. "Why do you look so dejected? ⁷You will be accepted if you respond in the right way. But if you refuse to respond correctly, then watch out! Sin is waiting to attack and destroy you, and you must subdue it."

⁸Later Cain suggested to his brother, Abel, "Let's go out into the fields." And while they were there, Cain attacked and killed his brother.

⁹Afterward the LORD asked Cain, "Where is your brother? Where is Abel?"

"I don't know!" Cain retorted. "Am I supposed to keep track of him wherever he goes?"

¹⁰But the LORD said, "What have you done? Listen—your brother's blood cries out to me from the ground! ¹¹You are hereby banished from the ground you have defiled with your brother's blood. ¹²No longer will it yield abundant crops for you, no matter how hard you work! From now on you will be a homeless fugitive on the earth, constantly wandering from place to place."   GENESIS 4:1-12

WARNING!

PREVIEW

The end of the world is always near, according to somebody. This person's placard states that we had better change our ways—or die. That group proclaims that the Lord will return one hundred days after the next presidential election. Each week brings numerous alarms from environmental and nutritional activists or religious and political zealots. Most people stopped listening long ago to the warnings of these "kooks" or "extremists," as they are labeled.

That's probably how people responded to Noah. This passage tells the story of the Flood, how Noah and his family built an ark in obedience to God, in response to his warning that the earth would be destroyed. Only a few generations had passed since Adam and Eve, yet Noah was the only righteous living person. The Bible doesn't state that people mocked Noah, but it certainly shows that no one listened to him or to God. This familiar story pictures God's mercy and the consequences when people forget (or stop caring) about their Creator.

The story also gives a snapshot of patience (living in an ark for over a year); doing what is right in the face of criticism and ridicule ("Why would you build an ark now and here?"); and gratitude (for God's mercy).

PERSONAL APPLICATION

Noah got right to work when God told him to build the ark (Genesis 6:22). It seems that other people had been warned about the coming disaster (see 1 Peter 3:20) but, apparently, did not expect it to happen. This is how people today often react to warnings, even warnings from God. Each day, thousands are told of God's inevitable judgment, yet most don't really believe it will occur. Don't expect people to welcome or accept your message of God's coming judgment on sin. Those who don't believe in God will scoff at his judgment and try to get you to deny God as well.

As you read this passage, note God's covenant with Noah to keep him safe and God's promise to the world. Then determine to do what God tells you to do, despite opposition, trusting him to bring you through the flood.

BIBLE READING

⁹This is the history of Noah and his family. Noah was a righteous man, the only blameless man living on earth at the time. He consistently followed God's will and enjoyed a close relationship with him. ¹⁰Noah had three sons: Shem, Ham, and Japheth.

¹¹Now the earth had become corrupt in God's sight, and it was filled with violence. ¹²God observed all this corruption in the world, and he saw violence and depravity everywhere. ¹³So God said to Noah, "I have decided to destroy all living creatures, for the earth is filled with violence because of them. Yes, I will wipe them all from the face of the earth!

¹⁴"Make a boat from resinous wood and seal it with tar, inside and out. Then construct decks and stalls throughout its interior. ¹⁵Make it 450 feet long, 75 feet wide, and 45 feet high. ¹⁶Construct an opening all the way around the boat, 18 inches below the roof. Then put three decks inside the boat—bottom, middle, and upper—and put a door in the side.

¹⁷"Look! I am about to cover the earth with a flood that will destroy every living thing. Everything on earth will die! ¹⁸But I solemnly swear to keep you safe in the boat, with your wife and your sons and their wives. ¹⁹Bring a pair of every kind of animal—a male and a female—into the boat with you to keep them alive during the flood. ²⁰Pairs of each kind of bird and each kind of animal, large and small alike, will come to you to be kept alive. ²¹And remember, take enough food for your family and for all the animals."

²²So Noah did everything exactly as God had commanded him.

GENESIS 6:9-22

$\mathscr{S}$HINE THE SPOTLIGHT

PREVIEW

We build monuments to great moments and great people. "Lest we forget" is etched on the bronze plates of more than one statue. But monuments are more than just memory aids; in building them we want, above all, to glorify something. We want to honor a person or idealize an event.

Shortly after the Flood, God made a covenant (or agreement) with Noah and his descendants. But soon the people forgot God, his goodness, his deliverance, his judgment, and his promise. And they became impressed with themselves, so much so that they decided to erect a monument—to themselves. They built their tower to glorify their greatness; it became, instead, a memorial to their (and our) greatest foolishness—human arrogance.

We can learn several lessons in this passage: (1) God is good and merciful to us. (2) God is greater than we are. (3) All humans are connected by sin.

PERSONAL APPLICATION

The people in this story built the Tower of Babel for the whole world to see (Genesis 11:3-4). This tower was most likely a *ziggurat*, a common structure in Babylonia at the time. Usually built as temples, ziggurats looked like pyramids with steps or ramps leading up the sides. Standing as high as three hundred feet and often just as wide, a ziggurat would stand out as the focal point of a city.

Today, people may not build statues, temples, or pyramids, but they still erect monuments (achievements, expensive clothes, big houses, fancy cars, important jobs) to call attention to themselves. When used to give personal identity and self-worth, these otherwise worthy pursuits take God's place. God gives us freedom to develop in many areas, but not the freedom to replace him.

As you read, check out the attitudes of the builders in the story, and consider any "towers" that you may be building. Tear down anything that stands in God's place.

BIBLE READING

[1]At one time the whole world spoke a single language and used the same words. [2]As the people migrated eastward, they found a plain in the land of Babylonia and settled there. [3]They began to talk about construction projects. "Come," they said, "let's make great piles of burnt brick and collect natural asphalt to use as mortar. [4]Let's build a great city with a tower that reaches to the skies—a monument to our greatness! This will bring us together and keep us from scattering all over the world."

[5]But the LORD came down to see the city and the tower the people were building. [6]"Look!" he said. "If they can accomplish this when they have just begun to take advantage of their common language and political unity, just think of what they will do later. Nothing will be impossible for them! [7]Come, let's go down and give them different languages. Then they won't be able to under-stand each other."

[8]In that way, the LORD scattered them all over the earth; and that ended the building of the city. [9]That is why the city was called Babel, because it was there that the LORD confused the people by giving them many languages, thus scattering them across the earth.   GENESIS 11:1-9

$\mathcal{D}$O YOU TRUST ME?

PREVIEW

No close relationship can function without trust. Like a huge diamond, hope is the largest, most precious, most irreplaceable component of every relationship. It is so difficult to get and yet so easy to lose.

This passage opens with one of the most significant events in the Bible—Abram receiving God's call. Abram's calling established the covenant (or agreement) by which God created the nation of Israel, his chosen people. Abram's move to Canaan and the challenges he faced living there with his nephew Lot stretched his faith the way life's challenges often stretch ours. With this calling God posed the question to Abram: Do you trust me?

This story also includes lessons about selfishness; generosity; helping out family; taking risks; and honoring God.

PERSONAL APPLICATION

God promised to bless Abram and to make him great. There was one condition to this promise, however: Abram had to do what God wanted him to do (Genesis 12:2). This meant leaving his home and friends and traveling to a new land, where God promised to build a great nation from Abram's family. Abram obeyed, walking away from his home, his comfort zone, accepting God's promise of even greater blessings in the future. Abram believed God, and he demonstrated his trust through his actions.

It's difficult to step out in faith. We know the past, and can feel secure in the present—the future, though, is unknown and risky. But when God leads we can follow, confident that his way is best.

As you read this passage, watch Abram live by faith. And think of where God may be trying to lead you to better serve him. Don't let the comfort and security of your present position make you miss God's plan for you. Be flexible and willing to change.

BIBLE READING

¹Then the LORD told Abram, "Leave your country, your relatives, and your father's house, and go to the land that I will show you. ²I will cause you to become the father of a great nation. I will bless you and make you famous, and I will make you a blessing to others. ³I will bless those who bless you and curse those who curse you. All the families of the earth will be blessed through you."

⁴So Abram departed as the LORD had instructed him, and Lot went with him. Abram was seventy-five years old when he left Haran. ⁵He took his wife, Sarai, his nephew Lot, and all his wealth—his livestock and all the people who had joined his household at Haran—and finally arrived in Canaan. ⁶Traveling through Canaan, they came to a place near Shechem and set up camp beside the oak at Moreh. At that time, the area was inhabited by Canaanites.

⁷Then the LORD appeared to Abram and said, "I am going to give this land to your offspring." And Abram built an altar there to commemorate the Lord's visit. ⁸After that, Abram traveled southward and set up camp in the hill country between Bethel on the west and Ai on the east. There he built an altar and worshiped the LORD. ⁹Then Abram traveled south by stages toward the Negev. GENESIS 12:1-9

PLEASE WAIT. . . .

PREVIEW

Right turns on red, your keyboard's escape key, and speeding tickets all testify to our hatred for waiting. More often than not, when we hear "Please wait," we want to say, "No, thank you." We are often asked to wait, and are often not good at complying.

It's small wonder, then, that Abram and Sarai stopped waiting for God. We see their faith weaken and fail when Sarai and Abram agree to bring Hagar into the process of starting a family. As a result, Ishmael is born. Despite Abram and Sarai's impulsive decision, God reaffirms his promise and establishes the covenant of circumcision—a permanent sign of his relationship with Abram's descendants.

As you read, watch for other lessons on patience; trusting God to do what he promises; and not taking matters into your own hands.

PERSONAL APPLICATION

Abram and Sarai had trouble believing God's promise and began thinking up creative ways to manipulate events and have a child (Genesis 16:1-3). A married woman who could not have children was shamed by her peers and was often required to give a female servant to her husband in order to produce an heir. The children born to the servant woman were considered the children of the wife.

When Sarai gave Hagar to Abram, they were acting in line with the custom of the day, but this action revealed their lack of faith that God would fulfill his promise. Consequently, a series of problems arose. This invariably happens when we take over for God and try to fulfill his promises through efforts that are not in line with his specific directions. In this case, time provided the greatest test of Abram and Sarai's faith and their willingness to let God work in their lives. Sometimes, we, too, must simply wait. When we ask God for something and have to wait, we are tempted to take matters into our own hands and interfere with God's plans.

Do your continual prayers seem to go unanswered? Do you feel yourself getting impatient with God as you wait for him to fulfill his promise and meet your need? Consider what God might be teaching you in the process. Obey God, and trust him for the outcome.

BIBLE READING

[1]But Sarai, Abram's wife, had no children. So Sarai took her servant, an Egyptian woman named Hagar, [2]and gave her to Abram so she could bear his children. "The LORD has kept me from having any children," Sarai said to Abram. "Go and sleep with my servant. Perhaps I can have children through her." And Abram agreed. [3]So Sarai, Abram's wife, took Hagar the Egyptian servant and gave her to Abram as a wife. (This happened ten years after Abram first arrived in the land of Canaan.)

[4]So Abram slept with Hagar, and she became pregnant. When Hagar knew she was pregnant, she began to treat her mistress Sarai with contempt. [5]Then Sarai said to Abram, "It's all your fault! Now this servant of mine is pregnant, and she despises me, though I myself gave her the privilege of sleeping with you. The LORD will make you pay for doing this to me!"

[6]Abram replied, "Since she is your servant, you may deal with her as you see fit." So Sarai treated her harshly, and Hagar ran away.   GENESIS 16:1-6

[15]Then God added, "Regarding Sarai, your wife—her name will no longer be Sarai; from now on you will call her Sarah. [16]And I will bless her and give you a son from her! Yes, I will bless her richly, and she will become the mother of many nations. Kings will be among her descendants!"

[17]Then Abraham bowed down to the ground, but he laughed to himself in disbelief. "How could I become a father at the age of one hundred?" he wondered. "Besides, Sarah is ninety; how could she have a baby?" [18]And Abraham said to God, "Yes, may Ishmael enjoy your special blessing!"

[19]But God replied, "Sarah, your wife, will bear you a son. You will name him Isaac, and I will confirm my everlasting covenant with him and his descendants.   GENESIS 17:15-19

S GOD FAIR?

PREVIEW

When was the last time you heard "It's not fair!" Perhaps that familiar phrase was uttered two minutes ago by a child, or maybe you can remember saying it yourself not long ago. Most people have a keen sensitivity to how the scales are tipped, especially when we think that we are being treated unfairly.

This reading shows us three kinds of belief and unbelief. Abraham and Sarah struggled to believe as three angels repeated another of God's specific promises. In contrast, the unbelief of Sodom and Gomorrah was so absolute that the entire population was destroyed. In between, stood Lot, a man who seemed to think mainly of himself and who stretched the meaning of the term *righteous*. Notice how God dealt differently with each one.

Look for other lessons as you read: on hospitality; not compromising with the world around you; and the dangers of desperation.

PERSONAL APPLICATION

Was God being unfair to the people of Sodom and Gomorrah (Genesis 19:27-28)? Actually, God's fairness stands out: (1) he agreed to spare them if only ten righteous people lived there (18:32); (2) he showed great mercy toward Lot, apparently the only man in either city who had any kind of relationship with him (19:12); and (3) he showed great patience with Lot, almost forcing him to leave Sodom before destroying the wicked city (19:16).

Remember God's patience when you are tempted to think he is unfair. All people, even the most godly, deserve his justice. We should be glad that God doesn't direct his justice toward us as he did toward Sodom and Gomorrah. As we grow spiritually, we should find ourselves developing a deeper respect for God because of his anger toward sin, and a deeper love for God because of his patience when we sin.

Take time today to recount God's acts of mercy and love for you. Thank him for *not* giving you what you deserve and, instead, giving you what you don't deserve—forgiveness and eternal life through Christ. It certainly isn't "fair"—but isn't that great!

BIBLE READING

[15]At dawn the next morning the angels became insistent. "Hurry," they said to Lot. "Take your wife and your two daughters who are here. Get out of here right now, or you will be caught in the destruction of the city."

[16]When Lot still hesitated, the angels seized his hand and the hands of his wife and two daughters and rushed them to safety outside the city, for the LORD was merciful. [17]"Run for your lives!" the angels warned. "Do not stop anywhere in the valley. And don't look back! Escape to the mountains, or you will die."

[18]"Oh no, my lords, please," Lot begged. [19]"You have been so kind to me and saved my life, and you have granted me such mercy. But I cannot go to the mountains. Disaster would catch up to me there, and I would soon die. [20]See, there is a small village nearby. Please let me go there instead; don't you see how small it is? Then my life will be saved."

[21]"All right," the angel said, "I will grant your request. I will not destroy that little village. [22]But hurry! For I can do nothing until you are there." From that time on, that village was known as Zoar.

[23]The sun was rising as Lot reached the village. [24]Then the LORD rained down fire and burning sulfur from the heavens on Sodom and Gomorrah. [25]He utterly destroyed them, along with the other cities and villages of the plain, eliminating all life— people, plants, and animals alike. [26]But Lot's wife looked back as she was following along behind him, and she became a pillar of salt.

[27]The next morning Abraham was up early and hurried out to the place where he had stood in the Lord's presence. [28]He looked out across the plain to Sodom and Gomorrah and saw columns of smoke and fumes, as from a furnace, rising from the cities there. [29]But God had listened to Abraham's request and kept Lot safe, removing him from the disaster that engulfed the cities on the plain.   GENESIS 19:15-29

GIVING TILL IT HURTS

PREVIEW

What comes to mind when you hear the word *children*? Small children can take everything out of us, yet they can also brighten our lives with a cute action, a smile, or a loving word.

After years of waiting and several tests of faith, at last Sarah conceives and has a baby— Isaac, or "Laughter"—the promised son. But Abraham's faith must undergo one more test.

Tests of faith share the spotlight in this passage with other important lessons. As you read, note also what Abraham and others learn about the seriousness of sin; the importance of mourning; and the effect of a good reputation.

PERSONAL APPLICATION

Through the years, Abraham had learned many tough lessons about the importance of obeying God—when he was called out of Ur, when he went to Egypt, and when he had to wait for Isaac's birth. Initially, Abraham did not always show that he trusted or believed God; but through each test, he saw God's willingness and ability to keep his promises, even if it took a miracle.

That is why God asked Abraham to sacrifice Isaac (Genesis 22:1-2), to kill his beloved, only son—his miracle child—on an altar. God did not want Isaac to die, but he wanted Abraham to sacrifice Isaac in his heart so that he could learn to trust God completely (see Hebrews 11:19). Imagine what Abraham must have felt as he walked with Isaac up the mountain, each torturous step leading him painfully closer to unspeakable grief. Yet Abraham obeyed, and God honored his faith.

Obeying God may often be quite a struggle because it may mean giving up something that we truly want. We should not expect our obedience to God to be easy or to come naturally. Just as fire refines ore to extract precious metals, God refines us through difficult circumstances. When tested, we can complain or we can obey, trusting God as we try to see how he is teaching us.

In what ways might God be testing your faith? What steps of faith do you need to take today to obey him?

BIBLE READING

"Abraham!" God called. . . . ²"Take your son, your only son—yes, Isaac, whom you love so much—and go to the land of Moriah. Sacrifice him there as a burnt offering on one of the mountains, which I will point out to you."

³The next morning Abraham got up early. He saddled his donkey and took two of his servants with him, along with his son Isaac. Then he chopped wood to build a fire for a burnt offering and set out for the place where God had told him to go. ⁴On the third day of the journey, Abraham saw the place in the distance. ⁵"Stay here with the donkey," Abraham told the young men. "The boy and I will travel a little farther. We will worship there, and then we will come right back."

⁶Abraham placed the wood for the burnt offering on Isaac's shoulders, while he himself carried the knife and the fire. As the two of them went on together, ⁷Isaac said, "Father?"

"Yes, my son," Abraham replied.

"We have the wood and the fire," said the boy, "but where is the lamb for the sacrifice?"

⁸"God will provide a lamb, my son," Abraham answered. And they both went on together.

⁹When they arrived at the place where God had told Abraham to go, he built an altar and placed the wood on it. Then he tied Isaac up and laid him on the altar over the wood. ¹⁰And Abraham took the knife and lifted it up to kill his son as a sacrifice to the LORD. ¹¹At that moment the angel of the LORD shouted to him from heaven, "Abraham! Abraham!"

"Yes," he answered. "I'm listening."

¹²"Lay down the knife," the angel said. "Do not hurt the boy in any way, for now I know that you truly fear God. You have not withheld even your beloved son from me."

¹³Then Abraham looked up and saw a ram caught by its horns in a bush. So he took the ram and sacrificed it as a burnt offering on the altar in place of his son. ¹⁴Abraham named the place "The LORD Will Provide." This name has now become a proverb: "On the mountain of the LORD it will be provided."

GENESIS 22:1-14

OMENTS OF WEAKNESS

PREVIEW

Have you ever let a salesperson talk you into a dumb purchase? Have you ever given away a valuable possession and later regretted it? Looking back on these experiences, you probably realize that you made those choices under pressure. At the time, resistance seemed impossible. In such a moment of weakness, an otherwise honest business owner might cheat on his or her taxes, a faithful wife might cheat on her husband, or a safe driver might drive recklessly. Sudden crises test our convictions.

Just ask Esau. In this reading, Isaac grows up and gets married; soon thereafter, Isaac and Rebekah have twins, Esau and Jacob. God had told Abraham that he would become a great nation, and here we see the promise continue to unfold. But the age-old stain of sin remains: within this chosen family of four are one shortsighted hothead and two skilled liars. Keep your eye on Esau's "moments of weakness."

There are many lessons in this passage—on being a servant; seeking God's guidance; staying faithful to our tasks; resisting the temptation to scheme; and working hard.

PERSONAL APPLICATION

A birthright was a special honor given to the firstborn son (Genesis 25:31). It included a double portion of the family inheritance along with the honor of one day becoming the family's leader. Birthrights were priceless. In Isaac's family, the birthright belonged to Esau, the older of the twin boys. But because of Esau's shortsightedness, he did not hold on to it. When Esau happened to be hungry and Jacob had some food, Esau could not see beyond his exaggerated sense of need. "Look, I'm dying of starvation!" he said (25:32). That was probably not true; it merely reflected how he felt. Esau acted on impulse, satisfying his immediate desires without pausing to consider the long-range consequences of what he was about to do. Esau did not need to eat the meal he so desperately wanted, but the pressure of the moment distorted his perspective and made his decision seem urgent.

People often experience similar pressures and face similar decisions. When feeling sexual temptation, for example, a marriage vow may seem unimportant. A person might feel such great pressure in one area that nothing else seems to matter and the person loses his or her perspective.

What pressures do you face? You can avoid making Esau's mistake by comparing an action's short-term satisfaction with its long-range consequences before you act. Getting through that short, pressure-filled moment is often the most difficult—and most important—part of overcoming a temptation.

BIBLE READING

[27]As the boys grew up, Esau became a skillful hunter, a man of the open fields, while Jacob was the kind of person who liked to stay at home. [28]Isaac loved Esau in particular because of the wild game he brought home, but Rebekah favored Jacob.

[29]One day when Jacob was cooking some stew, Esau arrived home exhausted and hungry from a hunt. [30]Esau said to Jacob, "I'm starved! Give me some of that red stew you've made." (This was how Esau got his other name, Edom—"Red.")

[31]Jacob replied, "All right, but trade me your birthright for it."

[32]"Look, I'm dying of starvation!" said Esau. "What good is my birthright to me now?"

[33]So Jacob insisted, "Well then, swear to me right now that it is mine." So Esau swore an oath, thereby selling all his rights as the firstborn to his younger brother. [34]Then Jacob gave Esau some bread and lentil stew. Esau ate and drank and went on about his business, indifferent to the fact that he had given up his birthright. GENESIS 25:27-34

OOMERANG TIME

PREVIEW

Have you ever had a bad choice come back to haunt you? Who hasn't? No medicine goes down more bitterly than your own.

Here begins the story of Jacob, three generations after Abraham. Through no merit of Jacob's, God renews his covenant with Abraham's descendants to him in a dream, and Jacob heads for his uncle Laban's home. This is a forced move, one that he has brought on himself. Jacob is shrewd, and he has proved it. Now he has to prove that he's resourceful as well.

As you read, look for these themes: personalizing faith; being patient; dealing with injustice; struggling with childlessness; resolving sibling rivalry; and taking matters into your own hands.

PERSONAL APPLICATION

Laban could scheme just like Jacob. It was the custom of the day for a man to present a dowry, or substantial gift, to the family of his future wife (Genesis 29:18-27). Jacob's dowry was not a material possession, for he had none to offer. Instead, he agreed to work seven years for Laban. But there was another custom of the land that Laban did not tell Jacob: the older daughter had to be married first. By giving Jacob Leah and not Rachel, Laban tricked him into promising another seven years of hard work.

Jacob was enraged when he learned that Laban had tricked him (29:23-25). The deceiver of Esau was now deceived himself. We quickly become upset at an injustice done to us, yet we excuse, justify, or ignore the injustices that we do to others. Be careful how you treat others, because poor choices have a way of coming back to haunt you.

Think of a recent time when you felt cheated. How would God have you respond to the person who cheated you? And think of how you might have acted unjustly toward someone else. What should you do to make that situation right?

BIBLE READING

¹⁵Laban said to him, "You shouldn't work for me without pay just because we are relatives. How much do you want?"

¹⁶Now Laban had two daughters: Leah, who was the oldest, and her younger sister, Rachel. ¹⁷Leah had pretty eyes, but Rachel was beautiful in every way, with a lovely face and shapely figure. ¹⁸Since Jacob was in love with Rachel, he told her father, "I'll work for you seven years if you'll give me Rachel, your younger daughter, as my wife."

¹⁹"Agreed!" Laban replied. "I'd rather give her to you than to someone outside the family."

²⁰So Jacob spent the next seven years working to pay for Rachel. But his love for her was so strong that it seemed to him but a few days. ²¹Finally, the time came for him to marry her. "I have fulfilled my contract," Jacob said to Laban. "Now give me my wife so we can be married."

²²So Laban invited everyone in the neighborhood to celebrate with Jacob at a wedding feast. ²³That night, when it was dark, Laban took Leah to Jacob, and he slept with her. ²⁴And Laban gave Leah a servant, Zilpah, to be her maid.

²⁵But when Jacob woke up in the morning—it was Leah! "What sort of trick is this?" Jacob raged at Laban. "I worked seven years for Rachel. What do you mean by this trickery?"

²⁶"It's not our custom to marry off a younger daughter ahead of the firstborn," Laban replied. ²⁷"Wait until the bridal week is over, and you can have Rachel, too—that is, if you promise to work another seven years for me."   GENESIS 29:15-27

ITTER PILLS

PREVIEW

Next week's family reunion has you wrestling with a couple of conflict-ing emotions. You'll love seeing Erica—it seems that no matter how long it's been, you just pick up where you left off. But it's just the oppo-site with Cousin Dale. He's still bitter. Has he forgiven you? Or will it be awkward . . . again?

This is the last part of Jacob's story, and much has changed. Having fled *to* Laban, Jacob now flees *from* him. Having exploited Esau, Jacob now seeks to be reconciled. Having left home single and poor, he now returns with a family and wealth. The only constant from the past is his uncertainty: Jacob wonders what Esau will do—whether he still harbors anger and will seek revenge. But Jacob has learned to trust in God.

This story has much to say about everyday life and relationships. Look for lessons on dealing with jealousy; working hard; releasing chil-dren; letting go of bitterness; reconciling; and forgiving.

PERSONAL APPLICATION

When the two brothers meet again, the bitterness over losing his birth-right and blessing (Genesis 25:29-34, 27:1-40) seems to have been forgotten by Esau. He greets his brother, Jacob, with a great hug (33:1-11). Imagine how difficult this must have been for a man who once had actually plotted to kill his brother (27:41). Instead of being consumed by thoughts of vengeance, however, Esau is content with what he has and is eager to reconcile. Time away from Jacob has allowed Esau's bitter wounds to heal. Jacob even exclaims how great it is to see his brother, obviously pleased with him (33:10).

Life can bring struggle and pain; we may even feel cheated, as Esau did. But we don't have to hold on to the past and remain bitter. We can remove our bitterness by honestly expressing our feelings to God, forgiv-ing those who have wronged us, and being content with what we have.

What grudges have you been nursing? Whom are you refusing to forgive? What revengeful scenarios have you been imagining? Confess your thoughts and feelings to God and allow him to heal your memo-ries. Be *better*, not *bitter*.

BIBLE READING

[1]Then, in the distance, Jacob saw Esau coming with his four hundred men. [2]Jacob now arranged his family into a column, with his two concubines and their children at the front, Leah and her children next, and Rachel and Joseph last. [3]Then Jacob went on ahead. As he approached his brother, he bowed low seven times before him. [4]Then Esau ran to meet him and embraced him affectionately and kissed him. Both of them were in tears.

[5]Then Esau looked at the women and children and asked, "Who are these people with you?"

"These are the children God has graciously given to me," Jacob replied. [6]Then the concubines came forward with their children and bowed low before him. [7]Next Leah came with her children, and they bowed down. Finally, Rachel and Joseph came and made their bows.

[8]"And what were all the flocks and herds I met as I came?" Esau asked.

Jacob replied, "They are gifts, my lord, to ensure your good-will."

[9]"Brother, I have plenty," Esau answered. "Keep what you have."

[10]"No, please accept them," Jacob said, "for what a relief it is to see your friendly smile. It is like seeing the smile of God! [11]Please take my gifts, for God has been very generous to me. I have more than enough." Jacob continued to insist, so Esau finally accepted them.   GENESIS 33:1-11

REFINED BY THE GRIND

PREVIEW

What are some of your most menial chores? No matter which ones you select (or how long the list), you doubtless have responsibilities that you would not miss if you never did them again.

Joseph, son of Jacob, dreams of being ruler of all, but is sold into slavery and is put in prison. Then he interprets the pharaoh's dreams and rises to power in Egypt. We see (as Joseph learns) that God rules over every circumstance, even the menial ones.

Sibling rivalry, lust, shame, despair, shattered hopes, and sudden success all play a part in this piece of Joseph's drama. As you read, look for lessons in each of these themes.

PERSONAL APPLICATION

As a prisoner and slave, Joseph could have seen his situation as hopeless (Genesis 39:20). Prisons were grim places with vile conditions. They were used to house convicted criminals, forced laborers, or, like Joseph, the accused who were awaiting trial. Prisoners were guilty until proven innocent and had no right to a speedy trial. In addition, Joseph's accuser was a very prominent member of society who would certainly be believed sooner than Joseph, a slave, would be. Joseph had every reason to despair.

Instead, Joseph did his best with each small task given him. His diligence and positive attitude were soon noticed by the warden, who promoted him to prison administrator (39:21-22). And even during these dark prison days, Joseph faithfully served his Lord. Eventually, Joseph rose to the top—from prison cell to Pharaoh's palace (41:39-40).

What predicament at work, at home, or at school seems at best, daunting, and at worst, hopeless? Follow Joseph's example by taking each small task and doing your best. Whatever your situation, no matter how undesirable, consider it part of your training for serving the Lord. Remember how God turned Joseph's situation around. Be assured that God sees your efforts, and remember that he can reverse desperate predicaments and overcome overwhelming odds.

BIBLE READING

[1]Now when Joseph arrived in Egypt with the Ishmaelite traders, he was purchased by Potiphar, . . . the captain of the palace guard.

[2]The LORD was with Joseph and blessed him greatly as he served in the home of his Egyptian master. [3]Potiphar noticed this. . . . [4]So Joseph naturally became quite a favorite with him. Potiphar soon put Joseph in charge of his entire household and entrusted him with all his business dealings. . . . [7]About this time, Potiphar's wife began to desire him and invited him to sleep with her. [8]But Joseph refused. . . . [9]"How could I ever do such a wicked thing? It would be a great sin against God."

. . . [11]"One day, however, no one else was around when he was doing his work inside the house. [12]She came and grabbed him by his shirt, demanding, "Sleep with me!" Joseph tore himself away, but as he did, his shirt came off. She was left holding it as he ran from the house.

[13]When she saw that she had his shirt and that he had fled, [14]she began screaming. Soon all the men around the place came running. "My husband has brought this Hebrew slave here to insult us!" she sobbed. "He tried to rape me, but I screamed. [15]When he heard my loud cries, he ran and left his shirt behind with me." . . .

[19]After hearing his wife's story, Potiphar was furious! [20]He took Joseph and threw him into the prison where the king's prisoners were held. [21]But the LORD was with Joseph there, too, and he granted Joseph favor with the chief jailer. [22]Before long, the jailer put Joseph in charge of all the other prisoners and over everything that happened in the prison. [23]The chief jailer had no more worries after that, because Joseph took care of everything. The LORD was with him, making everything run smoothly and successfully.   GENESIS 39:1-15, 19-23

E'LL NEVER CHANGE

PREVIEW

High school reunions can be eye-opening experiences. The guy who was voted "most likely to succeed"—did he make it? The girl who was homecoming queen—what became of her? What about others? Have any of them turned out as expected? People change dramatically, and the changes catch us by surprise.

In this part of Joseph's story, his dreams come true, literally. Joseph discovers that his brothers (especially Judah) have changed—and so has he.

Don't miss the implications in this story for family relationships: mistakes don't have to be permanent. There's peace in this once-volatile family, and it's all in spite of, and *because of,* mistakes and tragic events.

PERSONAL APPLICATION

Joseph wanted to see if his brothers' attitudes had changed for the better, so he tested the way they treated each other (Genesis 44:16-34). When Judah was younger, he had shown no regard for his brother, Joseph, or for his father, Jacob. First, Judah convinced his brothers to sell Joseph as a slave (37:27); then he joined his brothers in lying to his father about Joseph's fate (37:32). But what a change had taken place in this man! Having promised Jacob that he would guarantee young Benjamin's safety (43:9), Judah now had a chance to keep that promise. Becoming a slave was a terrible fate, but Judah was determined to keep his word to his father. The man who had sold one favored little brother into slavery now offered to become a slave to save another favored little brother.

When you are ready to give up hope on yourself or others, remem-ber that God can work a complete change in even the most selfish personality. Think of the self-centered people in your life. Pray for them to understand and experience God's love and power. Think also about your own self-centeredness, and ask God to forgive and change you as well. God changes lives!

BIBLE READING

[18]Then Judah stepped forward and said, "My lord, let me say just this one word to you. . . . [30]I cannot go back to my father without the boy. Our father's life is bound up in the boy's life. [31]When he sees that the boy is not with us, our father will die. We will be responsible for bringing his gray head down to the grave in sorrow. [32]My lord, I made a pledge to my father that I would take care of the boy. I told him, 'If I don't bring him back to you, I will bear the blame forever.' [33]Please, my lord, let me stay here as a slave instead of the boy, and let the boy return with his brothers. [34]For how can I return to my father if the boy is not with me? I cannot bear to see what this would do to him."

[45:1]Joseph could stand it no longer. "Out, all of you!" he cried out to his attendants. He wanted to be alone with his brothers when he told them who he was. [2]Then he broke down and wept aloud. His sobs could be heard throughout the palace, and the news was quickly carried to Pharaoh's palace.

[3]"I am Joseph!" he said to his brothers. "Is my father still alive?" But his brothers were speechless! They were stunned to realize that Joseph was standing there in front of them. [4]"Come over here," he said. So they came closer. And he said again, "I am Joseph, your brother whom you sold into Egypt. [5]But don't be angry with yourselves that you did this to me, for God did it. He sent me here ahead of you to preserve your lives. . . . [8]Yes, it was God who sent me here, not you! And he has made me a counselor to Pharaoh—manager of his entire household and ruler over all Egypt. . . . [13]Tell my father how I am honored here in Egypt. Tell him about everything you have seen, and bring him to me quickly." [14]Weeping with joy, he embraced Benjamin, and Benjamin also began to weep. [15]Then Joseph kissed each of his brothers and wept over them, and then they began talking freely with him.   GENESIS 44:18–45:15

UCH!

PREVIEW

Bad news never comes at a good time. Whether it's a flat tire or the death of a close relative, negative and tragic experiences happen all too often. Can anything good come of these events?

The final events of Jacob's life play out in this section of Scripture. We learn of his family's move to Egypt. The famine in Egypt continues. Joseph's sons, Manasseh and Ephraim, become Jacob's, and Jacob blesses them. The passage of time has proven Joseph right. Now what?

As you read this story's ending, note the lessons available to each of the key people: to Joseph (choosing forgiveness instead of revenge, knowing that God is in control, and finding blessing in tragedy); to Jacob (seeing God keep his promises, depending on God); and even to Pharaoh (learning that God is great). And imagine how Manasseh, Ephraim, and Judah must have felt.

PERSONAL APPLICATION

When Joseph became a slave, Jacob thought he was dead and wept in despair (Genesis 37:33-35). Eventually God's plan allowed Jacob to regain not only his son, but his grandchildren as well. Circumstances are never so bad that they are beyond God's help. Jacob regained his son. Job got a new family (see Job 42:10-17). Mary regained her brother Lazarus (see John 11:1-44). We need never despair, because we belong to a loving God. We never know what good he will bring out of a seemingly hopeless situation.

God brought good from many bad circumstances in Joseph's life— his brothers' evil deed, Potiphar's wife's false accusation, the cup bearer's neglect, and seven years of famine. The experiences in Joseph's life taught him that God brings good from evil for those who trust him.

What difficult circumstances are you enduring? Do you trust God enough to wait patiently for him to bring good out of bad situations? You can trust him because, as Joseph learned, God can overrule people's evil intentions to bring about his intended results.

BIBLE READING

[14]Then Joseph returned to Egypt with his brothers and all who had accompanied him to his father's funeral. [15]But now that their father was dead, Joseph's brothers became afraid. "Now Joseph will pay us back for all the evil we did to him," they said. [16]So they sent this message to Joseph: "Before your father died, he instructed us [17]to say to you: 'Forgive your brothers for the great evil they did to you.' So we, the servants of the God of your father, beg you to forgive us." When Joseph received the message, he broke down and wept. [18]Then his brothers came and bowed low before him. "We are your slaves," they said.

[19]But Joseph told them, "Don't be afraid of me. Am I God, to judge and punish you? [20]As far as I am concerned, God turned into good what you meant for evil. He brought me to the high position I have today so I could save the lives of many people. [21]No, don't be afraid. Indeed, I myself will take care of you and your families." And he spoke very kindly to them, reassuring them. GENESIS 50:14-21

EXCUSES, EXCUSES

PREVIEW

Don't you just hate it when people make excuses? Excuses mean that somebody is trying to avoid responsibility—some job or task that rightly belongs to that person but which he or she considers too inconvenient to do. On the surface the excuse looks right, but closer examination reveals major flaws in the argument.

This reading begins a new chapter in Israel's history. The small, privileged family of Joseph has become a large nation of oppressed Hebrew slaves. Moses will be their deliverer. After fleeing to Midian, Moses meets God at the burning bush, is given his assignment, and returns to Egypt. Moses is not qualified for the job.

Look for other lessons, including the dual excuse-busters *be courageous* (the Hebrew midwives) and *don't run from your problems* (Moses).

PERSONAL APPLICATION

Moses made excuses because he felt inadequate for the job that God asked him to do (Exodus 3:10–4:17). It was natural for him to feel that way, because he *was* inadequate all by himself. But God wasn't asking Moses to work alone. He offered other resources to help (God himself, Aaron, and the ability to do miracles). God often calls us to perform tasks that seem too difficult, but he doesn't ask us to do them alone. God offers us his resources, just as he did to Moses. We should not hide behind our inadequacies, as Moses did, but look beyond ourselves to God's great available resources. Then we can allow him to empower our unique contributions.

What has God asked you to do? What excuses are you using to avoid this responsibility and work? Obey God by stepping out in faith. He will give you the resources to do his work.

BIBLE READING

¹But Moses protested again, "Look, they won't believe me! They won't do what I tell them. They'll just say, 'The LORD never appeared to you.' "

²Then the LORD asked him, "What do you have there in your hand?"

"A shepherd's staff," Moses replied.

³"Throw it down on the ground," the LORD told him. So Moses threw it down, and it became a snake! Moses was terrified, so he turned and ran away.

⁴Then the LORD told him, "Take hold of its tail." So Moses reached out and grabbed it, and it became a shepherd's staff again.

⁵"Perform this sign, and they will believe you," the LORD told him. "Then they will realize that the LORD, the God of their ancestors—the God of Abraham, the God of Isaac, and the God of Jacob—really has appeared to you."

⁶Then the LORD said to Moses, "Put your hand inside your robe." Moses did so, and when he took it out again, his hand was white as snow with leprosy. ⁷"Now put your hand back into your robe again," the LORD said. Moses did, and when he took it out this time, it was as healthy as the rest of his body.

⁸"If they do not believe the first miraculous sign, they will believe the second," the LORD said. ⁹"And if they do not believe you even after these two signs, then take some water from the Nile River and pour it out on the dry ground. When you do, it will turn into blood."

¹⁰But Moses pleaded with the LORD, "O Lord, I'm just not a good speaker. I never have been, and I'm not now, even after you have spoken to me. I'm clumsy with words."

¹¹"Who makes mouths?" the LORD asked him. "Who makes people so they can speak or not speak, hear or not hear, see or not see? Is it not I, the LORD? ¹²Now go, and do as I have told you. I will help you speak well, and I will tell you what to say."

¹³But Moses again pleaded, "Lord, please! Send someone else." EXODUS 4:1-13

GOD SENDS MOSES TO PHARAOH

PREVIEW

If you've ever had to learn something you didn't want to learn, you know how much discipline it takes. No matter what the subject, you have to do some digging and some hard work. Learning isn't a downhill ride, it's more of a mountain climb. It takes *work*.

In this part of the story of the Exodus, God sends Moses to confront Pharaoh. Pharaoh's response is to make the Hebrews work even harder. Moses complains, God promises deliverance, and a showdown begins. Here we see the grand effects of feeble steps of faith (a tough lesson for anyone to learn).

Here's the lesson: Enduring rejection for our faith and trusting God when he seems to be ignoring our prayers are part of God's curriculum for us. As you read this passage, learn, with Moses, God's profound lessons.

PERSONAL APPLICATION

Moses did not like God's methods. Despite God's message—indeed, because of it—Pharaoh increased the Hebrews' workload. Moses protested that God was not rescuing his people (Exodus 5:22-23). Moses expected faster results and fewer problems. When God is at work, suffering, setbacks, and hardship may still occur. We can be sure, however, that each hardship has a purpose—to teach, discipline, punish, or accomplish another work of God. In James 1:2-4, we are encouraged to be joyful when difficulties come our way. Problems teach us to (1) trust God to do what is best for us; (2) look for ways to honor God in our present situation; (3) remember that God will not abandon us; and (4) watch for God's plan for us.

What tough lesson is God teaching you today? Think of what you can do to honor him through your attitude, words, and actions.

BIBLE READING

[17]But Pharaoh replied, "You're just lazy! You obviously don't have enough to do. If you did, you wouldn't be saying, 'Let us go, so we can offer sacrifices to the LORD.' [18]Now, get back to work! No straw will be given to you, but you must still deliver the regular quota of bricks."

[19]Since Pharaoh would not let up on his demands, the Israelite foremen could see that they were in serious trouble. [20]As they left Pharaoh's court, they met Moses and Aaron, who were waiting outside for them. [21]The foremen said to them, "May the LORD judge you for getting us into this terrible situation with Pharaoh and his officials. You have given them an excuse to kill us!"

[22]So Moses went back to the LORD and protested, "Why have you mistreated your own people like this, Lord? Why did you send me? [23]Since I gave Pharaoh your message, he has been even more brutal to your people. You have not even begun to rescue them!"   EXODUS 5:17-23

STUBBORN AS A MULE

PREVIEW

Perhaps you have heard people joke about "the terrible twos." In case you're not a parent or haven't heard before, they're speaking of how tenacious and stubborn two-year-old children can be. Mules have nothing on these determined individuals. Their displays of *stubbornness*—often culminating in a temper tantrum—test the resolve and endurance of the saintliest adults.

In this part of the story of the Exodus, God strikes Egypt with ten plagues: blood, frogs, gnats, flies, sick livestock, boils, hail, locusts, darkness, and (finally) the death of Egypt's firstborn sons. Each is a message to Pharaoh (and the world) that God rules. Unfortunately for Pharaoh, he doesn't get the point until it costs him his son. Stubbornness can be fatal.

These crucial chapters contain many other lessons. As we watch God free his people, we also learn about (1) not compromising with God; (2) persisting in doing right; (3) paying attention to God's message; and (4) being thankful for God's grace.

PERSONAL APPLICATION

Although he received many warnings, Pharaoh refused to obey God (Exodus 7:22; 8:15, 19, 32; 9:7, 12, 35; 10:20, 27). Before the ten plagues began, Moses and Aaron announced what God would do if Pharaoh didn't let the people go. But Pharaoh refused to listen and hardened his heart. Through the first six plagues, Pharaoh dug in a little more each time. Pharaoh wouldn't change, so God confirmed Pharaoh's arrogant decision, hardening his heart permanently (11:10) and setting the painful consequences of his actions in motion. This brought suffering upon Pharaoh and on his entire country.

God gave Pharaoh every opportunity to change his mind; it was Pharaoh's stubbornness that prevented it from changing. Stubbornness against God leads to disobedience. When you stop stubbornly insisting on your own way and begin submitting to God, you may be surprised by the work he will do in your life.

BIBLE READING

[1]Then the LORD said to Moses, "I will send just one more disaster on Pharaoh and the land of Egypt. After that, Pharaoh will let you go. In fact, he will be so anxious to get rid of you that he will practically force you to leave the country. [2]Tell all the Israelite men and women to ask their Egyptian neighbors for articles of silver and gold."

[3](Now the LORD had caused the Egyptians to look favorably on the people of Israel, and Moses was considered a very great man in the land of Egypt. He was respected by Pharaoh's officials and the Egyptian people alike.)

[4]So Moses announced to Pharaoh, "This is what the LORD says: About midnight I will pass through Egypt. [5]All the firstborn sons will die in every family in Egypt, from the oldest son of Pharaoh, who sits on the throne, to the oldest son of his lowliest slave. Even the firstborn of the animals will die. [6]Then a loud wail will be heard throughout the land of Egypt; there has never been such wailing before, and there never will be again. [7]But among the Israelites it will be so peaceful that not even a dog will bark. Then you will know that the LORD makes a distinction between the Egyptians and the Israelites. [8]All the officials of Egypt will come running to me, bowing low. 'Please leave!' they will beg. 'Hurry! And take all your followers with you.' Only then will I go!" Then, burning with anger, Moses left Pharaoh's presence.

[9]Now the LORD had told Moses, "Pharaoh will not listen to you. But this will give me the opportunity to do even more mighty miracles in the land of Egypt." [10]Although Moses and Aaron did these miracles in Pharaoh's presence, the LORD hardened his heart so he wouldn't let the Israelites leave the country.

EXODUS 11:1-10

OF SPINACH AND LIMA BEANS

PREVIEW

When you were a child, what foods did your family serve that you absolutely refused to eat? You know, the foods that you *hated*—foods you would go to war over, feed to the dog, or otherwise reject. It seems that everybody has one of these in his or her past. Food can evoke such emotion!

In this part of the story of the Exodus, the Israelites finally leave Egypt. Moses and Miriam celebrate with a song. The people complain about lack of food and water, but God provides. Enemies attack, but the Israelites defeat them. Moses and his father-in-law have a reunion. Finally, God's people worship in peace. Everything happens just as God had predicted. Did the Israelites understand and appreciate that fact?

In this passage, we also learn that celebration is good; that God keeps his promises; provides what we need; and always vindicates his people.

PERSONAL APPLICATION

As the Israelites encountered dangers, shortages, and inconveniences, they complained bitterly and whined about going back to Egypt. This happened often, but God still provided for them. They forgot, or did not believe, that God had promised to meet their needs if they would obey his instructions. These hardships were a test of faith; their complaining proved they were failing the test.

Difficult circumstances often lead to stress, and complaining is a natural response. But these circumstances are also a test of our faith. The question is this: Can we trust God to meet our needs in his own time and in his own way? The Israelites didn't really want to be back in Egypt—they just wanted life to be easier. In the pressure of the moment, they did not focus on trusting God; they could only think about escaping their circumstances.

When pressure comes your way, resist the temptation to complain or to seek an immediate escape. Instead, focus on God's power and wisdom to help you deal with the cause of your stress. Don't be a problem; be a solution.

BIBLE READING

¹Then they left Elim and journeyed into the Sin Desert, between Elim and Mount Sinai. They arrived there a month after leaving Egypt. ²There, too, the whole community of Israel spoke bitterly against Moses and Aaron.

³"Oh, that we were back in Egypt," they moaned. "It would have been better if the LORD had killed us there! At least there we had plenty to eat. But now you have brought us into this desert to starve us to death."

⁴Then the LORD said to Moses, "Look, I'm going to rain down food from heaven for you. The people can go out each day and pick up as much food as they need for that day. I will test them in this to see whether they will follow my instructions. ⁵Tell them to pick up twice as much as usual on the sixth day of each week."

⁶Then Moses and Aaron called a meeting of all the people of Israel and told them, "In the evening you will realize that it was the LORD who brought you out of the land of Egypt. ⁷In the morning you will see the glorious presence of the LORD. He has heard your complaints, which are against the LORD and not against us. ⁸The LORD will give you meat to eat in the evening and bread in the morning, for he has heard all your complaints against him. Yes, your complaints are against the LORD, not against us."   EXODUS 16:1-8

AGAINST THE LAW

PREVIEW

What sorts of rules do you have in your house? They don't have to be written down—many firm rules never make it to paper or poster board, though sometimes they feel more official that way. Parents usually start with this one: "Mom and Dad are in charge," and go on from there. Whenever two or more people gather together, there can be chaos; rules help us get organized.

This is the story of when God's people are given God's laws, including the Ten Commandments. The laws cover worship, servants, personal injuries, property, social responsibility, justice, the Sabbath, and three annual festivals. Israel encamps at Mt. Sinai for a year, giving them time to soak in God's commands.

These chapters also highlight the importance of keeping commitments; preparing for worship; honoring God above all else; being fair to others; making restitution; and being kind to the poor. Is there any area of your life that the list doesn't touch?

PERSONAL APPLICATION

Why did God give the Ten Commandments (Exodus 20:1-17)? Israel was God's people, and the commandments gave them a blueprint for a life of practical holiness, life as a people belonging to God. In these laws, the people could see God's nature and his plan for how they should live. The commands and guidelines were intended to direct the community to meet the needs of each individual in a loving and responsible manner. If we love God, we will love his will. We show our love by responding obediently to what God wants. The Ten Commandments tell us what God wants.

Take a fresh look at these familiar commandments; look at them from the positive side. For example, the commandment against adultery really means that you should honor the sanctity of marriage. And the commandment against murder means that you should respect all human beings as valuable creations of our loving God. Which commandments cause you the most difficulty? Does anything compete for God's place in your life? Do you show honor and respect to others?

BIBLE READING

[2]"I am the LORD your God, who rescued you from slavery in Egypt.

[3]"Do not worship any other gods besides me.

[4]"Do not make idols of any kind, whether in the shape of birds or animals or fish. [5]You must never worship or bow down to them, for I, the LORD your God, am a jealous God who will not share your affection with any other god! I do not leave unpunished the sins of those who hate me, but I punish the children for the sins of their parents to the third and fourth generations. [6]But I lavish my love on those who love me and obey my commands, even for a thousand generations.

[7]"Do not misuse the name of the LORD your God. The LORD will not let you go unpunished if you misuse his name.

[8]"Remember to observe the Sabbath day by keeping it holy. [9]Six days a week are set apart for your daily duties and regular work, [10]but the seventh day is a day of rest dedicated to the LORD your God. On that day no one in your household may do any kind of work. This includes you, your sons and daughters, your male and female servants, your livestock, and any foreigners living among you. [11]For in six days the LORD made the heavens, the earth, the sea, and everything in them; then he rested on the seventh day. That is why the LORD blessed the Sabbath day and set it apart as holy.

[12]"Honor your father and mother. Then you will live a long, full life in the land the LORD your God will give you.

[13]"Do not murder.

[14]"Do not commit adultery.

[15]"Do not steal.

[16]"Do not testify falsely against your neighbor.   EXODUS 20:2-16

So CLOSE AND YET SO FAR

PREVIEW

Does someone you know seem distant? It's amazing how two people can be in the same room physically and yet be miles apart relationally. It's one thing to be together in the same room; it's quite another to be together in mind and spirit.

Do you feel close to God? It's possible to be together in the same room and yet not together with him in mind and spirit. We come close to him through worship.

Some of the laws that God gave Israel regulated their worship. This passage records God's directions for building the tabernacle—the tent and surrounding structures that would house God's place of worship during Israel's time in the wilderness. These detailed instructions leave little doubt about the importance that God places on our worship.

Other lessons in this section include the importance of respecting God's appointed teachers; God's holiness; and our need for holy rest. Take this passage in small bites, and chew slowly.

PERSONAL APPLICATION

One of the tabernacle curtains separated two sacred rooms—the Holy Place and the Most Holy Place (Exodus 26:31-33). A priest would enter the Holy Place each day to commune with God and tend to the altar of incense, the lampstand, and the table with the Bread of the Presence. The Most Holy Place was where God himself resided, his presence resting on the atonement cover covering the ark of the covenant. Only the high priest could enter the Most Holy Place. Even he could do so only on the Day of Atonement, once a year, to make atonement for the sins of the whole nation. Without these vivid reminders, it is easy for us to forget the vast gulf between us and God's perfect holiness. Because of Christ, this barrier has been torn down forever. Now we can approach God's throne with confidence that he sympathizes with our weaknesses (see Hebrews 4:16). What a privilege!

Make worship a holy celebration of your relationship with your loving Lord. God, the Holy One of Israel, invites you to come close.

BIBLE READING

[8]"I want the people of Israel to build me a sacred residence where I can live among them. [9]You must make this Tabernacle and its furnishings exactly according to the plans I will show you. . . . [40]"Be sure that you make everything according to the pattern I have shown you here on the mountain.

[30]"Set up this Tabernacle according to the design you were shown on the mountain.

[31]"Across the inside of the Tabernacle hang a special curtain made of fine linen, with cherubim skillfully embroidered into the cloth using blue, purple, and scarlet yarn. [32]Hang this inner curtain on gold hooks set into four posts made from acacia wood and overlaid with gold. The posts will fit into silver bases. [33]When the inner curtain is in place, put the Ark of the Covenant behind it. This curtain will separate the Holy Place from the Most Holy Place.

[34]"Then put the Ark's cover—the place of atonement—on top of the Ark of the Covenant inside the Most Holy Place. [35]Place the table and lampstand across the room from each other outside the inner curtain. The lampstand must be placed on the south side, and the table must be set toward the north.

[36]"Make another curtain from fine linen for the entrance of the sacred tent, and embroider exquisite designs into it, using blue, purple, and scarlet yarn. [37]Hang this curtain on gold hooks set into five posts made from acacia wood and overlaid with gold. The posts will fit into five bronze bases.

EXODUS 25:8-9, 40; 26:30-37

ONE SIZE FITS ALL

PREVIEW

Bill is a Hindu. Sandy is a Muslim. You're a Christian. Your friend Rich says you're all pretty much the same. "You're all religious," he says. "You all believe in God." Is he right, or does it make a difference what a person believes—in *whom* a person believes?

Israel is still at Sinai after receiving many of God's laws on holy living and worship. Moses periodically brings God's words to them from the mountain. But the Israelites tire of waiting for Moses, so they sculpt and worship a golden calf instead. Here is a perfect example of the human tendency to remake God into something other than who he is.

Also watch for two other lessons in this passage: from the people, we learn that it's never too late to seek God's forgiveness; from Aaron, we learn that leading with integrity really does matter.

PERSONAL APPLICATION

Even though the Israelites had seen the invisible God in action, they still wanted gods they could see and shape into whatever image they desired (Exodus 32:1-10). Two popular Egyptian gods, Hapi (Apis) and Hathor, were thought of as a bull and a heifer (32:4-5). The Canaanites around them worshiped Baal, pictured as a bull. No doubt the Israelites, fresh from Egypt, found it quite natural to make a golden calf to represent the God that had just delivered them from their oppressors. They were weary of a God without a face. But they were ignoring the command God had just given them: "You shall not make for yourself an idol in the form of anything in heaven above or on the earth beneath or in the waters below" (20:4). How much like the Israelites we are—wanting to shape God to our liking, and make him into a thing for which we merely perform rituals, while we live as we please. Yet we, too, know that there is only one God, and he alone deserves to be worshiped. The gods we create blind us to reality and to the love that God wants to shower on us. God cannot work in us when we elevate anyone or anything above him.

BIBLE READING

¹When Moses failed to come back down the mountain right away, the people went to Aaron. "Look," they said, "make us some gods who can lead us. This man Moses, who brought us here from Egypt, has disappeared. We don't know what has happened to him."

²So Aaron said, "Tell your wives and sons and daughters to take off their gold earrings, and then bring them to me."

³All the people obeyed Aaron and brought him their gold earrings. ⁴Then Aaron took the gold, melted it down, and molded and tooled it into the shape of a calf. The people exclaimed, "O Israel, these are the gods who brought you out of Egypt!"

⁵When Aaron saw how excited the people were about it, he built an altar in front of the calf and announced, "Tomorrow there will be a festival to the LORD!"

⁶So the people got up early the next morning to sacrifice burnt offerings and peace offerings. After this, they celebrated with feasting and drinking, and indulged themselves in pagan revelry.

⁷Then the LORD told Moses, "Quick! Go down the mountain! The people you brought from Egypt have defiled themselves. ⁸They have already turned from the way I commanded them to live. They have made an idol shaped like a calf, and they have worshiped and sacrificed to it. They are saying, 'These are your gods, O Israel, who brought you out of Egypt.'" EXODUS 32:1-8

$\mathscr{S}$KILLED LABOR

PREVIEW

I can (check all that apply): ☐ paint, ☐ talk to people, ☐ make something out of cloth, paper, wood, metal, or plastic, ☐ mow grass, ☐ cut hair, ☐ grocery shop, ☐ hammer nails, ☐ vacuum, ☐ pick up trash, ☐ rearrange tables and chairs, ☐ read aloud. If you checked even one of those abilities, you can serve God in the church.

This section of Scripture tells how the Israelites carried out God's instructions for building the tabernacle, God's mobile house of worship. The passage includes some Sabbath regulations, descriptions of materials used for the tabernacle, and many miscellaneous anecdotes. Everyone pitches in.

As you read, you will learn about giving freely and generously, being helpful, and delegating responsibilities to others—a whole host of practical advice for ordinary believers who are ready to use their skills for God.

PERSONAL APPLICATION

Moses asked people with various abilities to help with the tabernacle (Exodus 35:10-19). Those who could spin cloth made an important contribution—cloth. Bezalel and Oholiab, men with artistic skills, lent their expertise in cutting jewels, carving wood, and other areas (36:1-2). Moses laid out the steps, while Ithamar served as scribe for the project. God didn't ask Moses to build the tabernacle alone, but to motivate others to do it. Once the tabernacle was built, its physical care required a long list of important tasks (40:17-33).

Every one of God's people has been given special talents and gifts. We are responsible to develop these abilities—even those not considered religious—and use them for God's glory. This principle is important to remember today, when God's house is not a building but a body of people—the *real* church. Many seemingly unimportant tasks must be done to keep your local church functioning. Washing dishes, painting walls, or printing bulletins may not seem very spiritual, but these tasks are vital to the ministry of the church and have an important role in worship.

BIBLE READING

³⁰And Moses told them, "The LORD has chosen Bezalel son of Uri, grandson of Hur, of the tribe of Judah. ³¹The LORD has filled Bezalel with the Spirit of God, giving him great wisdom, intelligence, and skill in all kinds of crafts. ³²He is able to create beautiful objects from gold, silver, and bronze. ³³He is skilled in cutting and setting gemstones and in carving wood. In fact, he has every necessary skill. ³⁴And the LORD has given both him and Oholiab son of Ahisamach, of the tribe of Dan, the ability to teach their skills to others. ³⁵The LORD has given them special skills as jewelers, designers, weavers, and embroiderers in blue, purple, and scarlet yarn on fine linen cloth. They excel in all the crafts needed for the work.

³⁶:¹"Bezalel, Oholiab, and the other craftsmen whom the LORD has gifted with wisdom, skill, and intelligence will construct and furnish the Tabernacle, just as the LORD has commanded."

²So Moses told Bezalel and Oholiab to begin the work, along with all those who were specially gifted by the LORD.

EXODUS 35:30—36:2

THE PRICE IS NOT RIGHT

PREVIEW

Surely everyone has uttered the words, "I can't afford it." Some things are just too expensive. You simply can't pay for them. You can save up or borrow enough for some items, but others will always command a higher price than you can pay. For those things, you don't have enough now, and you probably never will.

The opening verse of Leviticus says, "The Lord called to Moses from the Tabernacle" (1:1). The next seven chapters (1:1–7:38) contain what God said. Included in this account is the first set of instructions for worship and rules regarding the sacrifices (or offerings). From then on, it's quite clear that sin carries a very steep price.

As you read, note the benefits of giving to God; being aware of sin in your life; and reconciling with others whom you have hurt.

PERSONAL APPLICATION

Since Creation, God has made it clear that sin separates people from him, and that those who sin deserve to die. But because everyone has sinned (see Romans 3:23), God designed sacrifice as a way to seek forgiveness and to restore a relationship with him. Because God is filled with love and mercy, he decided from the very beginning that he would come into our world and die to pay sin's penalty (death). This he did through his Son, who, while still God, became a human being. In the meantime, before God made this ultimate sacrifice of his Son, he instructed people to kill animals as sacrifices for sin. That's why when God taught his people to worship him, he placed great emphasis on sacrifices (Leviticus 1:2). Sacrifices were God's Old Testament way for people to ask forgiveness for their sins.

Animal sacrifice accomplished two purposes: (1) the animal symbolically took the sinner's place and paid the penalty for sin; and (2) the animal's death represented one life given so that another life could be saved. This method, picturing what Jesus would do on the cross, continued throughout Old Testament times. It was effective in teaching saved. This method, picturing what Jesus would do on the cross, continued throughout Old Testament times. It was effective in teaching and guiding the people and bringing them back to God. In New Testament times, however, Christ's death became the last sacrifice needed. He took the punishment once and for all for those who trust in him. Animal sacrifice is no longer required. Now, all people can be freed from the penalty of sin by turning away from their sin, trusting in Jesus, and accepting the forgiveness he offers.

Thank God for sacrificing his only Son for you. Then tell someone the Good News about God and his salvation.

BIBLE READING

[27]"If any of the citizens of Israel do something forbidden by the LORD, they will be guilty even if they sinned unintentionally. [28]When they become aware of their sin, they must bring as their offering a female goat with no physical defects. It will be offered for their sin. [29]They are to lay a hand on the head of the sin offering and slaughter it at the place where burnt offerings are slaughtered. [30]The priest will then dip his finger into the blood, put the blood on the horns of the altar of burnt offerings, and pour out the rest of the blood at the base of the altar. [31]Those who are guilty must remove all the goat's fat, just as is done with the peace offering. Then the priest will burn the fat on the altar, and it will be very pleasing to the LORD. In this way, the priest will make atonement for them, and they will be forgiven.

LEVITICUS 4:27-31

 QUEAKY CLEAN

PREVIEW

Have you ever seen a one-year-old eat? It's amazing how much indifference a young child can show toward the location of his or her food. The child will tolerate food on the face and hands, inside the clothes, on the hair, anywhere. Cleanliness? What's that? Thankfully, most of us outgrow this form of apathy.

This section continues the instructions for worshiping God, with rules for the priests. It details the ordination of Aaron and his sons, the beginning of the priests' ministry, and the death of the priests Nadab and Abihu when they disregarded God's instructions. They paid for their apathy toward God. The story vividly reminds us that approaching God is a serious business.

You may not be a priest, but these chapters are for you, too. In fact, they have much to say to anyone interested in approaching God; obeying God in everyday routines; staying close to the truth when teaching; and avoiding drunkenness.

PERSONAL APPLICATION

God required that Aaron and his sons be cleansed and set apart for their duties as priests (Leviticus 8:1–9:24). Although all the men from the tribe of Levi were dedicated for service to God, only Aaron's descendants could be priests. They alone had the honor and responsibility of performing the sacrifices. These priests had to cleanse and dedicate themselves before they could help the people do the same.

Leviticus chapters 8 and 9 describe the priests' ordination ceremony. It showed that holiness came from God alone, not from the priestly role. Similarly, we are not spiritually cleansed just because we have a religious position or come from a religious family. Spiritual cleansing comes only from God. No matter how high our position or how long we have held it, we must depend on God for forgiveness and a relationship with him.

Don't take your relationship with God for granted and slip into apathy or mindless routine. Stay close to the Father; he wants to be close to you.

BIBLE READING

¹The LORD said to Moses, ²"Now bring Aaron and his sons, along with their special clothing, the anointing oil, the bull for the sin offering, the two rams, and the basket of unleavened bread ³to the entrance of the Tabernacle. Then call the entire community of Israel to meet you there."

⁴So Moses followed the Lord's instructions, and all the people assembled at the Tabernacle entrance. ⁵Moses announced to them, "The LORD has commanded what I am now going to do!" ⁶Then he presented Aaron and his sons and washed them with water. ⁷He clothed Aaron with the embroidered tunic and tied the sash around his waist. He dressed him in the robe of the ephod, along with the ephod itself, and attached the ephod with its decorative sash. ⁸Then Moses placed the chestpiece on Aaron and put the Urim and the Thummim inside it. ⁹He placed on Aaron's head the turban with the gold medallion at its front, just as the LORD had commanded him.

¹⁰Then Moses took the anointing oil and anointed the Tabernacle and everything in it, thus making them holy. ¹¹He sprinkled the altar seven times, anointing it and all its utensils and the washbasin and its pedestal, making them holy. ¹²Then he poured some of the anointing oil on Aaron's head, thus anointing him and making him holy for his work.   LEVITICUS 8:1-12

*E*VERYDAY MYSTERIES

PREVIEW

How much do you understand about the inner workings of your television? How about your car? your municipal government? your spouse? your kids? A wonderful fact of life is that we can enjoy many things without understanding how they work. We may satisfy our curiosity by understanding them, but we don't have to.

This is the final section of instructions for worshiping God (Leviticus 1:1–17:16). It includes instructions about food, childbirth, infectious skin diseases, mildew, bodily discharges, the Day of Atonement, and handling blood. There is more to this set of instructions than rules about eating, treating wounds, and personal hygiene. In them we see God's love and care for his people.

That's a good reason to study the other rules in this section, too— preparing for worship, practicing good health and hygiene, and keeping sex pure. What evidence of God's love and care do you see in these areas? Read on.

PERSONAL APPLICATION

God wanted his people to be holy (set apart, different, unique), just as he is holy. That is why he designed laws to separate them—both socially and spiritually—from the wicked pagan nations they would encounter in Canaan.

These laws also had an immediate practical benefit. God told the Israelites how to diagnose infectious skin diseases and mildew so that they could avoid and treat them (Leviticus 13:1–14:57). These laws helped the Israelites avoid diseases that were serious threats in that time and place. Although the people would not have understood the medical reasons for some of these laws, their obedience to them made them healthier. Many of God's laws must have seemed strange to the Israelites. His laws, however, helped them avoid not only physical contamination, but also moral and spiritual infection.

We do not always understand why God commands us to do this or to avoid that. But his expressed will is for our good, even when we don't understand exactly how.

BIBLE READING

¹And the LORD said to Moses, ²"The following instructions must be followed by those seeking purification from a contagious skin disease. Those who have been healed must be brought to the priest, ³who will examine them at a place outside the camp. If the priest finds that someone has been healed of the skin disease, ⁴he will perform a purification ceremony . . .

⁸"The people being purified must complete the cleansing ceremony by washing their clothes, shaving off all their hair, and bathing themselves in water. Then they will be ceremonially clean and may return to live inside the camp. However, they must still remain outside their tents for seven days. ⁹On the seventh day, they must again shave off all their hair, including the hair of the beard and eyebrows, and wash their clothes and bathe themselves in water. Then they will be pronounced ceremonially clean.

⁵⁴"These are the instructions for dealing with the various kinds of contagious skin disease and infectious mildew, ⁵⁵whether in clothing, in a house, ⁵⁶in a swollen area of skin, in a skin rash, or in a shiny patch of skin. ⁵⁷These instructions must be followed when dealing with any contagious skin disease or infectious mildew, to determine when something is ceremonially clean or unclean." LEVITICUS 14:1-9, 54-57

CHECKING THE MAP

PREVIEW

Where would we be without maps? We can't see too far ahead, we can't see too far behind, and we certainly can't see around the corner. Maps come to the rescue when our two-dimensional perspective of the road keeps us from being able to see where we are going. If we ignore maps in these situations, we will be lost.

This section of Scripture begins a set of instructions for everyday life—some for the people and some for the priests. It covers sexual relations, punishments for sin, rules for priests, and unacceptable sacrifices. These are God's expressed desires for his people—his map for our life's travels.

The landscape includes several highways: resisting the negative influence and immorality of the culture around us; showing mercy to those in need; avoiding occult practices; and giving our best efforts and gifts to God.

PERSONAL APPLICATION

God gave many rules to his people, each for a reason. He did not withhold good from them; he prohibited those acts that would bring them to ruin and commanded those acts that would benefit them. All of us can see God's physical laws of nature. Jumping off a ten-story building will result in grave injuries or death because of the law of gravity. Eating healthy foods means fueling the body with what it needs. But some of us don't understand how God's spiritual laws work. God forbids us to do certain things because he wants to keep us from self-destruction. He commands us to do other acts because he knows what we need to flourish.

The next time you are drawn to a forbidden physical activity or emotional response, remember that it may lead to suffering and separation from the God who is trying to help you. The next time a good act seems unpleasant or inconvenient, remember that God has only the best planned for you.

BIBLE READING

²⁴"Do not defile yourselves in any of these ways, because this is how the people I am expelling from the Promised Land have defiled themselves. ²⁵As a result, the entire land has become defiled. That is why I am punishing the people who live there, and the land will soon vomit them out. ²⁶You must strictly obey all of my laws and regulations, and you must not do any of these detestable things. This applies both to you who are Israelites by birth and to the foreigners living among you.

²⁷"All these detestable activities are practiced by the people of the land where I am taking you, and the land has become defiled. ²⁸Do not give the land a reason to vomit you out for defiling it, as it will vomit out the people who live there now. ²⁹Whoever does any of these detestable things will be cut off from the community of Israel. ³⁰So be careful to obey my laws, and do not practice any of these detestable activities. Do not defile yourselves by doing any of them, for I, the LORD, am your God."

LEVITICUS 18:24-30

*L*ET'S CELEBRATE!

PREVIEW

What is your favorite holiday or time of year? What do you do to prepare for it? What are some of the ways that you observe it? How do you feel after the holiday has passed?

Here, through Moses, God provides more instructions for everyday life through the establishment of feasts, seasons, and festivals. There are seven annual "holidays" plus the Sabbath year and the Year of Jubilee. God also presents rules for honoring him in the tabernacle and for maintaining justice. God says that observing these holidays will make a big difference.

We can learn other, more specific lessons from these chapters as well: giving God the "firstfruits" of our labors; not using God's name in vain; and having mercy on others (Jubilee). Consider all this a priority check.

PERSONAL APPLICATION

Feasts played a major role in God's plan for Israel (Leviticus 23:1-44). These feasts were different from those of any other nation, because being ordained by God, they were times of celebrating with him, not times of moral depravity, drunkenness, or indulgence. God wanted to set aside special days for the people to come together for rest and refreshment, and to remember with thanksgiving all he had done for them. They celebrated God's goodness.

Much can be learned about people by observing what and how they celebrate. Consider your holidays and the traditions you observe: what do they say about your values? How do you celebrate? When do you take time to rest, refresh yourself, and remember God? Include in your calendar feasts and traditions that celebrate God's goodness, rejoice in your fellowship with other believers, and honor the Lord.

BIBLE READING

[1]The LORD said to Moses, [2]"Give the Israelites instructions regarding the LORD's appointed festivals, the days when all of you will be summoned to worship me. [3]You may work for six days each week, but on the seventh day all work must come to a complete stop. It is the LORD's Sabbath day of complete rest, a holy day to assemble for worship. . . . [4]In addition to the Sabbath, the LORD has established festivals, the holy occasions to be observed at the proper time each year.

[5]"First comes the LORD's Passover. . . . [6]Then the day after the Passover celebration, the Festival of Unleavened Bread begins. This festival to the LORD continues for seven days, and during that time all the bread you eat must be made without yeast. [7]On the first day of the festival, all the people must stop their regular work and gather for a sacred assembly. [8]On each of the next seven days, the people must present an offering to the LORD by fire. On the seventh day, the people must again stop all their regular work to hold a sacred assembly.

[24]"On the appointed day in early autumn, you are to celebrate a day of complete rest. All your work must stop on that day. You will call the people to a sacred assembly—the Festival of Trumpets—with loud blasts from a trumpet. [25]You must do no regular work on that day. Instead, you are to present offerings to the LORD by fire."

. . . [27]"Remember that the Day of Atonement is to be celebrated on the ninth day after the Festival of Trumpets. On that day you must humble yourselves, gather for a sacred assembly, and present offerings to the LORD by fire. . . . [32]This will be a Sabbath day of total rest for you, and on that day you must humble yourselves." LEVITICUS 23:1-8, 24-32

OOK OUT!

PREVIEW

Parents issue a lot of warnings. To outsiders these warnings can seem harsh. Sometimes they seem harsh to the insiders too—thus the famous question, "*Why?*" But loving parents issue them anyway. They know that the world's dangers are real.

This reading completes God's instructions for Israel's everyday living (Leviticus 18:1–27:34) by summarizing the rewards for obedience to God, the consequences of disobedience, and by telling how to dedicate something to the Lord. It's a clear statement of why we should obey God.

The point: There is only one true and living God, so it doesn't make sense to live for money, possessions, or other idols. Not only that, such living is dangerous.

PERSONAL APPLICATION

Some people think that the Old Testament portrays God as harsh, pointing to passages like Leviticus 26:14-39 as an example. But this passage shows what God really wanted to accomplish with such warnings, and also what God meant when he said that he is slow to anger (see Exodus 34:6). God warned his people of sin's consequences for the same reason a parent warns a child of danger—to protect and provide for them out of love. God wanted his people to prosper through their compliance to his design for life. And he wanted it so much that he promised to reward them if they obeyed (Leviticus 26:3-13). Even if the Israelites chose to disobey God and were scattered among their enemies, God would still give them the opportunity to repent and return to him (26:40-45). God did not want to destroy the Israelites, but to help them grow. That is the purpose of his harsh warnings.

Our day-to-day experiences and hardships can sometimes seem overwhelming. God allows these events to happen to help us grow, not to curse us. We need to see that God's purposes are to help us live as he designed us to live and to bring about continual growth in us. Jeremiah 29:11 puts it this way: "'For I know the plans I have for you,' says the LORD. 'They are plans for good and not for disaster, to give you a future and a hope.'" To retain hope while we suffer shows that we understand God's merciful ways of relating to his people.

With what are you struggling these days? What stresses and problems do you face? Endure hardship as God's teaching tool; ask God to teach you through every difficulty.

BIBLE READING

9"I will look favorably upon you and multiply your people and fulfill my covenant with you. 10You will have such a surplus of crops that you will need to get rid of the leftovers from the previous year to make room for each new harvest. 11I will live among you, and I will not despise you. 12I will walk among you; I will be your God, and you will be my people. 13I, the LORD, am your God, who brought you from the land of Egypt so you would no longer be slaves. I have lifted the yoke of slavery from your neck so you can walk free with your heads held high.

14"However, if you do not listen to me or obey my commands, 15and if you break my covenant by rejecting my laws and treating my regulations with contempt, 16I will punish you. You will suffer from sudden terrors, with wasting diseases, and with burning fevers, causing your eyes to fail and your life to ebb away. You will plant your crops in vain because your enemies will eat them. 17I will turn against you, and you will be defeated by all your enemies. They will rule over you, and you will run even when no one is chasing you! LEVITICUS 26:9-17

ON YOUR MARK, GET SET . . .

PREVIEW

"You're not old enough!" or, "Sorry, you don't have enough experience." Either response can be disheartening, even when it's true. It means you will have to go through a frustrating, perhaps tiresome, time of growing up or acquiring experience.

The Israelites know what this is like. After the Lord delivered them out of Egypt, he led them to Mount Sinai. Here they've been encamped for more than a year, receiving God's laws and learning how to relate to him. But at the beginning of Numbers things begin to change. God isn't just giving the Israelites laws to live by anymore. In fact, the instructions he gives to Moses in the first two chapters seem a bit strange. But God always has a good reason for everything he does, and the instructions he gives here are for the Israelites' benefit.

PERSONAL APPLICATION

The Israelites were at a transition point in their journey, and taking a census was an important task (Numbers 1:2-15). The fighting men had to be counted to determine Israel's military strength before entering the Promised Land, and the tribes had to be organized to determine the amount of land each would need and to provide genealogical records. Without such a census, the task of conquering and organizing the Promised Land would have been more difficult.

At every transition point in life it is important to take inventory of our resources and count the cost of each alternative (see Proverbs 13:16). We will serve more effectively if, before plunging in, we set aside time to take stock of all we have—possessions, relationships, spiritual condition, time, goals, and so forth. While God does not want us to trust in our material resources, he does want us to use well what we have.

Before your next move or major decision, analyze your resources and count the cost. Then use what God has given you for his glory.

BIBLE READING

[1]One day in midspring, during the second year after Israel's departure from Egypt, the LORD spoke to Moses in the Tabernacle in the wilderness of Sinai. He said, [2]"Take a census of the whole community of Israel by their clans and families. List the names of all the men [3]twenty years old or older who are able to go to war. You and Aaron are to direct the project, [4]assisted by one family leader from each tribe."

[17]Now Moses and Aaron and the chosen leaders [18]called together the whole community of Israel on that very day. All the people were registered according to their ancestry by their clans and families. The men of Israel twenty years old or older were registered, one by one, [19]just as the LORD had commanded Moses. So Moses counted the people there in the wilderness of Sinai.

[47]But this total did not include the Levites. [48]For the LORD had said to Moses, [49]"Exempt the tribe of Levi from the census; do not include them when you count the rest of the Israelites. [50]You must put the Levites in charge of the Tabernacle of the Covenant, along with its furnishings and equipment. They must carry the Tabernacle and its equipment as you travel, and they must care for it and camp around it. [51]Whenever the Tabernacle is moved, the Levites will take it down and set it up again. Anyone else who goes too near the Tabernacle will be executed. [52]Each tribe of Israel will have a designated camping area with its own family banner. [53]But the Levites will camp around the Tabernacle of the Covenant to offer the people of Israel protection from the LORD's fierce anger. The Levites are responsible to stand guard around the Tabernacle."

[54]So the Israelites did everything just as the LORD had commanded Moses.   NUMBERS 1:1-4, 17-19, 47-54

WELL, WE'RE OFF . . . ALMOST!

PREVIEW

Preparing for a vacation can be more stressful than actually going on the trip, but there's no escaping it. Without preparation, the trip will probably not go smoothly—or worse, it may not happen at all.

In this reading, the Israelites continue their preparations for entering the Promised Land. God gives them numerous instructions. Moses and Aaron bless them. The people dedicate the tabernacle and celebrate Passover. Then God provides guidance for the journey. As you read, learn that especially at the onset of great plans, a right relationship with God comes first.

In this passage, you will find these lessons as well: making restitution; dealing with suspicion in marriage; avoiding foolish vows; pitching in to help; and doing what is right when compromise is necessary.

PERSONAL APPLICATION

As part of Israel's preparation for entering the Promised Land, Moses instructed Aaron to bless the people. A blessing was one way of asking for God's divine favor to rest upon others, and that's what Aaron and his sons did for the people of Israel here (Numbers 6:24-26). This blessing's five parts conveyed hope that God would (1) bless and protect them; (2) smile upon them (be pleased); (3) be gracious (merciful and compassionate); (4) show them his favor (give his approval); and (5) give peace.

When you ask God to bless others or yourself, you are asking him to grant these five requests. The blessing you offer will not only help the ones receiving it, it will also demonstrate love, encourage them, and provide a model of caring for them. You can bless others through prayer and in person, face-to-face. Who can you bless in this way today?

BIBLE READING

²²Then the LORD said to Moses, ²³"Instruct Aaron and his sons to bless the people of Israel with this special blessing:

²⁴ 'May the LORD bless you
   and protect you.
²⁵ May the LORD smile on you
   and be gracious to you.
²⁶ May the LORD show you his favor
   and give you his peace.'

²⁷This is how Aaron and his sons will designate the Israelites as my people, and I myself will bless them."

⁷:¹On the day Moses set up the Tabernacle, he anointed it and set it apart as holy, along with all its furnishings and the altar with its utensils. ²Then the leaders of Israel—the tribal leaders who had organized the census—came and brought their offerings. ³Together they brought six carts and twelve oxen. There was a cart for every two leaders and an ox for each leader. They presented these to the LORD in front of the Tabernacle.

NUMBERS 6:22–7:3

$\mathcal{A}$H, THOSE WERE THE DAYS

PREVIEW

What do you miss most about the past? What, for you, are "the good old days"? Is there a time of life you wish you could revisit? Is there a period of time that you remember as full of joy and wonder?

The Israelites find themselves doing this shortly after they leave Mount Sinai—only they take it too far. This is the story of Israel's first approach to the land God wanted to give them, and it's a disaster. From the food, to the leadership, to the Promised Land itself, the people cannot seem to find enough to complain about— despite God's faithfulness—and want to go back to the "good life" in Egypt!

There are too many lessons here to list, but here are a few key concepts to grasp in this passage: the Lord will provide for our needs; it's not wise to put the Lord to the test; and the Lord hears the cries of the faithful and answers their prayers.

PERSONAL APPLICATION

God became angry with the Israelites because they complained (Numbers 11:1-3, 10). They were grumbling because they didn't seem to notice what God was doing for them—setting them free, making them a nation, giving them a new land—because they were so wrapped up in what God *wasn't* doing for them (11:4-6). They could think of nothing but the delicious Egyptian food that they had left behind. Somehow they forgot that the price of that food was the brutal whip of Egyptian slavery.

Before we judge the Israelites too harshly, it's helpful to think about what occupies our attention most of the time. Dissatisfaction comes when our attention shifts from what we have to what we don't have.

Are you grateful for what God has given you, or are you always thinking about what you would like to have? Don't allow your unfulfilled desires to cause you to forget God's gifts of life, food, health, work, and friends.

BIBLE READING

[4]Then the foreign rabble who were traveling with the Israelites began to crave the good things of Egypt, and the people of Israel also began to complain. "Oh, for some meat!" they exclaimed. [5]"We remember all the fish we used to eat for free in Egypt. And we had all the cucumbers, melons, leeks, onions, and garlic that we wanted. [6]But now our appetites are gone, and day after day we have nothing to eat but this manna!"

[7]The manna looked like small coriander seeds, pale yellow in color. [8]The people gathered it from the ground and made flour by grinding it with hand mills or pounding it in mortars. Then they boiled it in a pot and made it into flat cakes. These cakes tasted like they had been cooked in olive oil. [9]The manna came down on the camp with the dew during the night.

[10]Moses heard all the families standing in front of their tents weeping, and the LORD became extremely angry. Moses was also very aggravated. [11]And Moses said to the LORD, "Why are you treating me, your servant, so miserably? What did I do to deserve the burden of a people like this? [12]Are they my children? Am I their father? Is that why you have told me to carry them in my arms—like a nurse carries a baby—to the land you swore to give their ancestors? [13]Where am I supposed to get meat for all these people? They keep complaining and saying, 'Give us meat!' [14]I can't carry all these people by myself! The load is far too heavy! [15]I'd rather you killed me than treat me like this. Please spare me this misery!"   NUMBERS 11:4-15

WET BLANKETS ON THE MOVE

PREVIEW

The most negative person you know is probably not your favorite person. We are so averse to negative people that we have a small arsenal of verbal flyswatters devoted to shooing them away: "One bad apple spoils the whole bunch." "Don't rain on my parade." "Don't be a party pooper." "Don't be a stick in the mud." "You're such a wet blanket."

Many of the Israelites in this reading are "wet blankets." They struggle with bad attitudes that eventually lead to drastic and devastating consequences. Here you can see the enormous damage that negative attitudes can do.

There are other lessons in this passage on (1) ambition (good or bad?); (2) tithing; and (3) recognizing when we ourselves are at fault.

PERSONAL APPLICATION

After witnessing spectacular miracles and experiencing the actual presence of God, the Israelites still grumbled and rebelled against the Lord (Numbers 14:1-10; 20:2-5). We may wonder how they could be so blind and ignorant, yet aren't we just like them? Despite centuries of evidence, scores of Bible translations, and the convincing results of archaeological and historical studies, people today continue to grumble against God and go their own way.

Rebellion against God begins with dissatisfaction and skepticism, with grumbling about God and present circumstances. Then follows bitterness and resentment, and lastly, open hostility and rebellion.

If you are often dissatisfied, skeptical, complaining, or bitter—beware! These attitudes color your perspective and bias you against God. You can escape this trap by choosing a better attitude. Has God guided and protected you? Has he answered your prayers? Do you know people who have experienced remarkable blessings and healings? Do you know Bible stories about the way God has led his people? Focus your thoughts on what God has done.

Bible Reading

²There was no water for the people to drink at that place, so they rebelled against Moses and Aaron. ³The people blamed Moses and said, "We wish we had died in the Lord's presence with our brothers! ⁴Did you bring the Lord's people into this wilderness to die, along with all our livestock? ⁵Why did you make us leave Egypt and bring us here to this terrible place? This land has no grain, figs, grapes, or pomegranates. And there is no water to drink!"

⁶Moses and Aaron turned away from the people and went to the entrance of the Tabernacle, where they fell face down on the ground. Then the glorious presence of the LORD appeared to them, ⁷and the LORD said to Moses, ⁸"You and Aaron must take the staff and assemble the entire community. As the people watch, command the rock over there to pour out its water. You will get enough water from the rock to satisfy all the people and their livestock."

⁹So Moses did as he was told. He took the staff from the place where it was kept before the LORD. ¹⁰Then he and Aaron summoned the people to come and gather at the rock. "Listen, you rebels!" he shouted. "Must we bring you water from this rock?" ¹¹Then Moses raised his hand and struck the rock twice with the staff, and water gushed out. So all the people and their livestock drank their fill. NUMBERS 20:2-11

BRAKE FOR ANGELS

PREVIEW

Most people have mixed reactions around animals. But no one—even those who *love* animals—would say that animals should run our lives.

After wandering in the desert for disobeying God's command to enter Canaan, a new generation of Israelites has grown up. Now they are poised to enter the land, but the Moabites stand in the way. Their king, Balak, tries to get Balaam, a sorcerer, to stop them. Can he do it? Well, yes and no—Balaam's donkey has it right.

This section of Scripture is brimming with wisdom found by seeing what *not* to do.

PERSONAL APPLICATION

Balaam was a sorcerer, a person called upon to place curses on others (Numbers 22:4-6). The king of Moab wanted Balaam to use his powers with the God of Israel to place a curse on Israel—hoping that, by magic, God would turn against his people. Neither Balaam nor Balak had any idea whom they were dealing with!

Why would God speak through a sorcerer like Balaam (22:9)? God wanted to give a message to the Moabites, who had already chosen to employ Balaam. So Balaam was available for God to use. Balaam's devotion and motives were mixed. He had some knowledge of God, but not enough to quit his magic and turn wholeheartedly to God. Later passages in the Bible show that Balaam couldn't resist the tempting pull of money and idolatry (2 Peter 2:15; Jude 11).

Do not take good feelings and apparent positive results as a sign of God's blessing on your life. A popular following, a track record of success, a speech about respecting God—Balaam had all of these, yet he still lacked a relationship with God. God was not blessing Balaam but using him in spite of his duplicitous heart.

What will it take to give your whole heart to God? Get rid of anything that would distract you from him.

BIBLE READING

²¹So the next morning Balaam saddled his donkey and started off with the Moabite officials. ²²But God was furious that Balaam was going, so he sent the angel of the LORD to stand in the road to block his way. As Balaam and two servants were riding along, ²³Balaam's donkey suddenly saw the angel of the LORD standing in the road with a drawn sword in his hand. The donkey bolted off the road into a field, but Balaam beat it and turned it back onto the road. ²⁴Then the angel of the LORD stood at a place where the road narrowed between two vineyard walls. ²⁵When the donkey saw the angel of the LORD standing there, it tried to squeeze by and crushed Balaam's foot against the wall. So Balaam beat the donkey again. ²⁶Then the angel of the LORD moved farther down the road and stood in a place so narrow that the donkey could not get by at all. ²⁷This time when the donkey saw the angel, it lay down under Balaam. In a fit of rage Balaam beat it again with his staff.

³²"Why did you beat your donkey those three times?" the angel of the LORD demanded. "I have come to block your way because you are stubbornly resisting me. ³³Three times the donkey saw me and shied away; otherwise, I would certainly have killed you by now and spared the donkey."

³⁴Then Balaam confessed to the angel of the LORD, "I have sinned. I did not realize you were standing in the road to block my way. I will go back home if you are against my going."

³⁵But the angel of the LORD told him, "Go with these men, but you may say only what I tell you to say." So Balaam went on with Balak's officials.   NUMBERS 22:21-27, 32-35

CAPTAIN, MY CAPTAIN!

PREVIEW

If you ever played kickball at recess, you know what a difference having the right team captain can make. If you end up on the wrong team, it can be a long game.

Leaders who continually make bad decisions cause anxiety and anguish for those they lead. That's why it's important to choose leaders carefully.

Moses knew the value of good leadership. In this reading, he asks God to appoint a successor to lead the Israelites. But Moses doesn't ask for just anyone, he asks the Lord for someone who will care for the Israelites. As you read this passage, notice whom God appoints as Moses' successor.

Also look for lessons on preparing for worship; taking holidays; and safeguarding against making foolish vows.

PERSONAL APPLICATION

Moses asked God to appoint a leader, one who could lead the people in battle but who would also care for their needs. The Lord responded by appointing Joshua, a man "who has the Spirit in him" (27:18). Moses then presented Joshua to the people and commissioned him to serve as God had commanded. Moses also clearly told the people that Joshua had the authority and the ability to lead the nation.

Most of us are in the position of developing and choosing leaders. Leaders are important, and the kind of people we choose and the way we choose them matters a great deal. Whenever we see a change in leadership coming or we influence the choice of a leader, we should do as Moses did—first, ask God for a person who is both able and compassionate; then, commission and support the person in his or her new position.

In what ways are you developing leaders at home? at work? at church? in the community? What can you do to influence them to lead God's way?

\

BIBLE READING

¹⁵Then Moses said to the LORD, ¹⁶"O LORD, the God of the spirits of all living things, please appoint a new leader for the community. ¹⁷Give them someone who will lead them into battle, so the people of the LORD will not be like sheep without a shepherd."

¹⁸The LORD replied, "Take Joshua son of Nun, who has the Spirit in him, and lay your hands on him. ¹⁹Present him to Eleazar the priest before the whole community, and publicly commission him with the responsibility of leading the people. ²⁰Transfer your authority to him so the whole community of Israel will obey him. ²¹When direction from the LORD is needed, Joshua will stand before Eleazar the priest, who will determine the Lord's will by means of sacred lots. This is how Joshua and the rest of the community of Israel will discover what they should do."

²²So Moses did as the LORD commanded and presented Joshua to Eleazar the priest and the whole community. ²³Moses laid his hands on him and commissioned him to his responsibilities, just as the LORD had commanded through Moses.

NUMBERS 27:15-23

JUMPING TO CONCLUSIONS

PREVIEW

How easy it is to assume we know what others are thinking. We easily come up with our own reasons for why people do this or that. When we feel unsure about others' motives, we tend to assume the worst of them.

The Israelites are no different. Having finally entered the land of God's promise—the part that lies east of the Jordan River—a misunderstanding arises between Moses and three of the tribes of Israel. That leads to the age-old squabble over fairness. As you read, look for a lesson about communication and the problem with making wrong assumptions.

Other gems lie hidden in these chapters: a technique for avoiding past mistakes, and knowing when to be harsh.

PERSONAL APPLICATION

Three tribes (Reuben, Gad, and half of Manasseh) told Moses that they wanted to live on the land that was east of the Jordan River (Numbers 32:1-5). This land had been already been conquered; the hard work had been done by all of the tribes together. When Moses heard the request of the three tribes, he immediately assumed that they had selfish motives and were trying to avoid helping the others fight for the land across the river (32:6-15). Moses jumped to the wrong conclusion. These tribes fully intended to continue the fight and promised to keep working with the others until everyone's land was conquered (32:16-19).

Don't automatically assume that others have wrong motives, even if their plans sound suspicious. With any person, take time to let the facts surface before making up your mind.

BIBLE READING

¹Now the tribes of Reuben and Gad owned vast numbers of live-stock. So when they saw that the lands of Jazer and Gilead were ideally suited for their flocks and herds, ²they came to Moses, Eleazar the priest, and the other leaders of the people. They said, ³"Ataroth, Dibon, Jazer, Nimrah, Heshbon, Elealeh, Sebam, Nebo, and Beon—⁴the LORD has conquered this whole area for the people of Israel. It is ideally suited for all our flocks and herds. ⁵If we have found favor with you, please let us have this land as our property instead of giving us land across the Jordan River."

⁶"Do you mean you want to stay back here while your brothers go across and do all the fighting?" Moses asked the Reubenites and Gadites. ⁷"Are you trying to discourage the rest of the people of Israel from going across to the land the LORD has given them?"

¹⁶But they responded to Moses, "We simply want to build sheepfolds for our flocks and fortified cities for our wives and children. ¹⁷Then we will arm ourselves and lead our fellow Israel-ites into battle until we have brought them safely to their inheri-tance. Meanwhile, our families will stay in the fortified cities we build here, so they will be safe from any attacks by the local people. ¹⁸We will not return to our homes until all the people of Israel have received their inheritance of land. ¹⁹But we do not want any of the land on the other side of the Jordan. We would rather live here on the east side where we have received our inheritance."   NUMBERS 32:1-7, 16-19

$\mathscr{B}$EWARE OF THE HOTHEADED RESPONSE

PREVIEW

Suppose you were accused of murder. Wouldn't *you* want an impartial jury and a fair trial?

This reading concludes the story of Israel's campaign to take the land east of the Jordan River. Having defeated the Midianites and divided the land, all that remains is to give some towns to the Levites. Six of these are designated cities of refuge to serve as important safeguards on personal revenge and hotheaded lynch mobs. Doing justice isn't easy, as the anecdote about discrimination shows at the very end.

Also in this passage, look for lessons on the value of human life; a humane system of justice; and the importance of family.

PERSONAL APPLICATION

Of the forty-eight cities given to the Levites, six were cities of refuge (Numbers 35:6). Such cities were needed because the ancient customs of justice called for revenge in the event of any death, accidental or otherwise, by the hand of another person (see, for example, 2 Samuel 14:7). The Levites would hold a preliminary hearing outside the gates while the accused person was kept in the city until the time of his or her trial. If the killing was judged to be accidental, the person would stay in the city until the death of the high priest. At that time, he or she would be allowed to go free and could start a new life without worrying about revenge. If it was not accidental, the person would be handed over to the slain person's avengers for execution.

This shows how important God considers both justice and mercy. God wanted the people to be intolerant of the sin, yet impartial so the accused could have a fair trial.

It is unjust both to overlook wrongdoing and to jump to conclusions about guilt. When someone is accused of wrongdoing, stand up for justice, protect those not yet proven guilty, and listen carefully to all sides of the story.

BIBLE READING

¹⁰"When you cross the Jordan into the land of Canaan, ¹¹designate cities of refuge for people to flee to if they have killed someone accidentally. ¹²These cities will be places of protection from a dead person's relatives who want to avenge the death. The slayer must not be killed before being tried by the community. . . . ¹⁵These cities are for the protection of Israelites, resident foreigners, and traveling merchants. Anyone who accidentally kills someone may flee there for safety.

¹⁶"But if someone strikes and kills another person with a piece of iron, it must be presumed to be murder, and the murderer must be executed. . . . ¹⁹The victim's nearest relative is responsible for putting the murderer to death. When they meet, the avenger must execute the murderer. . . . ²²"But suppose someone pushes another person without premeditated hostility, or throws something that unintentionally hits another person, ²³or accidentally drops a stone on someone, though they were not enemies, and the person dies. ²⁴If this should happen, the assembly must follow these regulations in making a judgment between the slayer and the avenger, the victim's nearest relative. ²⁵They must protect the slayer from the avenger, and they must send the slayer back to live in a city of refuge until the death of the high priest.

²⁶"But if the slayer leaves the city of refuge, ²⁷and the victim's nearest relative finds him outside the city limits and kills him, it will not be considered murder. ²⁸The slayer should have stayed inside the city of refuge until the death of the high priest. But after the death of the high priest, the slayer may return to his own property. ²⁹These are permanent laws for you to observe from generation to generation, wherever you may live.

NUMBERS 35:10-29

T'S THE LAW

PREVIEW

If you were to give a slide show reviewing the last twenty years of your life, what would you highlight? The fun times? The disasters? The family outings? The struggles and pain? The brushes with greatness?

The book of Deuteronomy is where Israel gets to sit down for a little reminiscing—both good and bad. Moses highlights God's laws and how well (or poorly) Israel obeyed those laws along the way.

As you relive the history of Moses and the Israelites, watch for other important insights for God's people: understanding the qualities of good leaders; knowing when not to fight; and overcoming insurmountable obstacles.

PERSONAL APPLICATION

God gave Israel many laws, and he commanded that the people remember those laws and then teach them to their children (Deuteronomy 4:8-9). Do these laws apply to Christians today? God designed his laws to guide his people in honoring and worshiping him and to help them see their sin and the proper way to deal with that sin. God's law is the perfect expression of who God is and how he wants his people to live.

God's laws always have a purpose, but in some cases the purpose has been finished. For example, God told Israel to practice animal sacrifice in worship to receive forgiveness and to express thanks. But Christ made the ultimate, final sacrifice for sin—we must now come to him for forgiveness. The principle (coming to God for forgiveness and thanking him), not the form (animal sacrifice), still applies.

Whenever you come upon a law directed specifically to Israel in its own time, look for the principle behind it. Look for ways to obey God; don't search for loopholes in his commandments.

BIBLE READING

¹"And now, Israel, listen carefully to these laws and regulations that I am about to teach you. Obey them so that you may live, so you may enter and occupy the land the LORD, the God of your ancestors, is giving you. ²Do not add to or subtract from these commands I am giving you from the LORD your God. Just obey them. ³You saw what the LORD did to you at Baal-peor, where the LORD your God destroyed everyone who had worshiped the god Baal of Peor. ⁴But all of you who were faithful to the LORD your God are still alive today.

⁵"You must obey these laws and regulations when you arrive in the land you are about to enter and occupy. The LORD my God gave them to me and commanded me to pass them on to you. ⁶If you obey them carefully, you will display your wisdom and intelligence to the surrounding nations. When they hear about these laws, they will exclaim, 'What other nation is as wise and prudent as this!' ⁷For what great nation has a god as near to them as the LORD our God is near to us whenever we call on him? ⁸And what great nation has laws and regulations as fair as this body of laws that I am giving you today?

⁹"But watch out! Be very careful never to forget what you have seen the LORD do for you. Do not let these things escape from your mind as long as you live! And be sure to pass them on to your children and grandchildren." DEUTERONOMY 4:1-9

O SATISFACTION

PREVIEW

"I'm starving!" we often say in deliberate exaggeration. It's just a signal to those nearby that we're *really* hungry and open to devoting great energy to getting access to food as soon as possible.

In this reminiscence by Moses, God reminds the Israelites that he allowed them to experience hunger for a purpose, to help them learn something about finding satisfaction. As you read, look for the lesson on where to find *spiritual* nourishment.

There's plenty more to learn in this passage: seeing God's place in everyday experiences; responding whenever success strikes; heeding warnings; and reading God's Word.

PERSONAL APPLICATION

Jesus quoted Deuteronomy 8:3 when the devil tempted him to turn stones into bread (see Matthew 4:4). God's Word is the ultimate source of nourishment, and we should be much more concerned about feeding our spirits than feeding our bodies.

Many people think that life consists of satisfying physical appetites and indulging their desires. If they can earn enough money to dress, eat, and play in high style, they think they are living the good life. But indulging such desires does not satisfy a person's deepest longings. Instead, satisfaction comes from total commitment to God, the one who created life itself. This means relying on God and feeding on his Word. It requires discipline, sacrifice, and hard work—which is why most people never find it.

Be careful not to equate *indulgence* with *satisfaction*. When are you tempted to place your physical desires above your spiritual needs? Keep your focus on the Lord, and find your satisfaction in him.

BIBLE READING

[1]"Be careful to obey all the commands I am giving you today. Then you will live and multiply, and you will enter and occupy the land the LORD swore to give your ancestors. [2]Remember how the LORD your God led you through the wilderness for forty years, humbling you and testing you to prove your character, and to find out whether or not you would really obey his commands. [3]Yes, he humbled you by letting you go hungry and then feeding you with manna, a food previously unknown to you and your ancestors. He did it to teach you that people need more than bread for their life; real life comes by feeding on every word of the LORD. [4]For all these forty years your clothes didn't wear out, and your feet didn't blister or swell. [5]So you should realize that just as a parent disciplines a child, the LORD your God disciplines you to help you.

[6]"So obey the commands of the LORD your God by walking in his ways and fearing him. [7]For the LORD your God is bringing you into a good land of flowing streams and pools of water, with springs that gush forth in the valleys and hills. [8]It is a land of wheat and barley, of grapevines, fig trees, pomegranates, olives, and honey. [9]It is a land where food is plentiful and nothing is lacking. It is a land where iron is as common as stone, and copper is abundant in the hills. [10]When you have eaten your fill, praise the LORD your God for the good land he has given you."

DEUTERONOMY 8:1-10

EW AND IMPROVED–NOT

PREVIEW

New math. New philosophy. A new theory. New and improved. It seems as though everyone has something to sell, and they have to make it "new and improved" to make the sale. This approach is used in selling religion too—false gods and phony worship can be packaged as brightly and promoted as aggressively as soap and cereal.

This may be one reason why God warns his people about false prophets and teachers. Moses explains how God's people can approach God. Many of these instructions have much to say to *all* worshipers who care about worshiping God properly.

As you read, be on the lookout for other areas that affect your worship: resisting temptations that lure you away from God; worshiping together as a family; giving to God's work; and helping the poor.

PERSONAL APPLICATION

Moses warned the Israelites against false prophets who encouraged worship of other gods (Deut. 13:1-3). New ideas from inspiring people may sound good, but we must judge them by whether or not they are consistent with God's Word. Some people speak the truth while directing people toward God, but others speak persuasively while directing followers toward themselves. It is even possible to say the right words but still lead people in the wrong direction. False prophets are still around today. The wise person will carefully test ideas against the truth of God's Word.

When people claim to speak for God today, check them in these areas: Are they telling the truth? Is their focus on God? Are their words consistent with what you already know to be true? When you hear a new, attractive idea, examine it carefully before getting too excited.

BIBLE READING

¹"Suppose there are prophets among you, or those who have dreams about the future, and they promise you signs or miracles, ²and the predicted signs or miracles take place. If the prophets then say, 'Come, let us worship the gods of foreign nations,' ³do not listen to them. The LORD your God is testing you to see if you love him with all your heart and soul. ⁴Serve only the LORD your God and fear him alone. Obey his commands, listen to his voice, and cling to him. ⁵The false prophets or dreamers who try to lead you astray must be put to death, for they encourage rebellion against the LORD your God, who brought you out of slavery in the land of Egypt. Since they try to keep you from following the LORD your God, you must execute them to remove the evil from among you.

⁶"Suppose your brother, son, daughter, beloved wife, or closest friend comes to you secretly and says, 'Let us go worship other gods'—gods that neither you nor your ancestors have known. ⁷They might suggest that you worship the gods of peoples who live nearby or who come from the ends of the earth. ⁸If they do this, do not give in or listen, and have no pity. Do not spare or protect them. ⁹You must put them to death! You must be the one to initiate the execution; then all the people must join in. ¹⁰Stone the guilty ones to death because they have tried to draw you away from the LORD your God, who rescued you from the land of Egypt, the place of slavery. ¹¹Then all Israel will hear about it and be afraid, and such wickedness will never again be done among you."   DEUTERONOMY 13:1-11

FUTURE LOOK

PREVIEW

People want to know the future. Most newspapers carry horoscopes and predictions by self-proclaimed future-tellers. There are even "psychic hot lines" to call. These people make a living because there's a market.

This section of Scripture highlights laws for ruling the nation of Israel. It covers the usual civil regulations, such as instructions on judges, the courts, and the king. But right smack in the middle are guidelines about the occult.

All citizens will find something here: responsibility to vote; responsibility of leaders; and balancing justice with mercy.

PERSONAL APPLICATION

The Israelites were naturally curious about the occult practices of the Canaanite religions. They may have thought, "What's wrong with checking it out?" or "It won't hurt to dabble in it just a little." But Satan is behind the occult, and God flatly forbade Israel to have anything to do with it (Deuteronomy 18:9-14).

Today, people are still fascinated by horoscopes, fortune-telling, Ouija boards, witchcraft, and even satanic cults. Often their interest arises from a desire to know and control the future. "What's the harm?" they may think. But Satan is no less dangerous today than he was in Moses' time. God tells us all we need to know about what is going to happen. We don't need to turn to occult sources for faulty information; instead we should seek the trustworthy guidance of the Holy Spirit through the Bible and the church.

BIBLE READING

[9]"When you arrive in the land the LORD your God is giving you, be very careful not to imitate the detestable customs of the nations living there. [10]For example, never sacrifice your son or daughter as a burnt offering. And do not let your people practice fortune-telling or sorcery, or allow them to interpret omens, or engage in witchcraft, [11]or cast spells, or function as mediums or psychics, or call forth the spirits of the dead. [12]Anyone who does these things is an object of horror and disgust to the LORD. It is because the other nations have done these things that the LORD your God will drive them out ahead of you. [13]You must be blameless before the LORD your God. [14]The people you are about to displace consult with sorcerers and fortune-tellers, but the LORD your God forbids you to do such things.

[15]"The LORD your God will raise up for you a prophet like me from among your fellow Israelites, and you must listen to that prophet. [16]For this is what you yourselves requested of the LORD your God when you were assembled at Mount Sinai. You begged that you might never again have to listen to the voice of the LORD your God or see this blazing fire for fear you would die.

[20]But any prophet who claims to give a message from another god or who falsely claims to speak for me must die.' [21]You may wonder, 'How will we know whether the prophecy is from the LORD or not?' [22]If the prophet predicts something in the LORD's name and it does not happen, the LORD did not give the message. That prophet has spoken on his own and need not be feared.

DEUTERONOMY 18:9-16, 20-22

PRICELESS COMMODITY

PREVIEW

It's called the world's oldest profession because it's been around for a long, long time indeed. Many people reason, therefore, that if prostitution is so persistent, that if it has survived this long, what's wrong with it?

The answer is here, among many other laws that God gives to his people at this crucial time in their history. They are receiving God's laws on human relationships, and one of the top areas of God's concern is the sexual one. It's too important to ignore.

Other laws in this section cover community responsibility; practical benefits in God's laws; kindness to the poor; discipline; and remembering what God has done.

PERSONAL APPLICATION

Prostitution was not overlooked in God's law—it was strictly forbidden (Deuteronomy 23:17-18). Almost every other religion known to the Israelites included prostitution as a part of its worship services. But prostitution makes a mockery of God's original idea for sex, treating it as an isolated physical experience rather than an act of commitment to another person. Outside of marriage, sex destroys relationships. Within marriage, if approached with the right attitude, it can be a relationship builder. God frequently had to warn the people against the practice of extramarital sex. Today we still need to hear his warnings; young people need to be reminded about the dangers of premarital sex, and adults need to be reminded about the importance of sexual fidelity.

Don't be taken in by the cheapening of sex through self-indulgent, recreational sexual encounters portrayed in television shows, movies, books, music, and magazines. Sex was God's idea. He created it for procreation, for expressing love, and for enjoyment *within marriage*. Celebrate your sexuality God's way!

BIBLE READING

[17]"No Israelite man or woman may ever become a temple prostitute. [18]Do not bring to the house of the LORD your God any offering from the earnings of a prostitute, whether a man or a woman, for both are detestable to the LORD your God.

[19]"Do not charge interest on the loans you make to a fellow Israelite, whether it is money, food, or anything else that may be loaned with interest. [20]You may charge interest to foreigners, but not to Israelites, so the LORD your God may bless you in everything you do in the land you are about to enter and occupy.

[21]"When you make a vow to the LORD your God, be prompt in doing whatever you promised him. For the LORD your God demands that you promptly fulfill all your vows. If you don't, you will be guilty of sin. [22]However, it is not a sin to refrain from making a vow. [23]But once you have voluntarily made a vow, be careful to do as you have said, for you have made a vow to the LORD your God.

[24]"You may eat your fill of grapes from your neighbor's vineyard, but do not take any away in a basket. [25]And you may pluck a few heads of your neighbor's grain by hand, but you may not harvest it with a sickle."   DEUTERONOMY 23:17–18, 19–25

FLUORESCENT ORANGE CONES

PREVIEW

Picture this: You're driving along at fifty miles per hour on a cloudy day. The road ahead is suddenly narrow, with deep, unforgiving ditches on both sides. But the two endless lines of fluorescent orange cones that line the road on either side keep you out of trouble.

If you think of the curses in this reading as fluorescent orange cones, you come pretty close to their meaning. If you understand that those cones are really doing you a favor, you can't help but be happy about them. The cones help everyone. The other chapters in this section of Deuteronomy are proof enough of that.

There are other road signs in today's reading: something to remember when it looks as if the world is falling apart; seeking God with all your heart, soul, and strength; and following a plan of action no matter how badly you've sinned.

PERSONAL APPLICATION

The curses God wanted his people to remember were a series of oaths, spoken by the priests and affirmed by those listening, by which the people promised to stay away from wrong actions (Deuteronomy 27:15-26). Those saying *Amen,* "So be it," were taking responsibility for their actions.

Sometimes looking at a list of curses like this gives us the idea that God has a bad temper and is out to crush anyone who steps out of line. But we need to see these restrictions not as threats but as loving warnings about the plain facts of life. Wrongdoing toward others or God has tragic consequences, and God is merciful enough to tell us this truth plainly. His strong words help us avoid the serious consequences that result from neglecting God or wronging others. Just as we warn children to stay away from hot stoves and busy streets, God warns us to stay away from dangerous actions.

BIBLE READING

[16]"'Cursed is anyone who despises father or mother.'
And all the people will reply, 'Amen.'

[17]'Cursed is anyone who steals property from a neighbor by moving a boundary marker.'
And all the people will reply, 'Amen.'

[18]'Cursed is anyone who leads a blind person astray on the road.'
And all the people will reply, 'Amen.'

[19]'Cursed is anyone who is unjust to foreigners, orphans, and widows.'
And all the people will reply, 'Amen.'

[24]'Cursed is anyone who kills another person in secret.'
And all the people will reply, 'Amen.'

[25]'Cursed is anyone who accepts payment to kill an innocent person.'
And all the people will reply, 'Amen.'

[26]'Cursed is anyone who does not affirm the terms of this law by obeying them.'
And all the people will reply, 'Amen.'"

DEUTERONOMY 27:16-19, 24-26

HE BOOK

PREVIEW

Books can entertain, educate, edify, and enrage. Well-written books draw us along, page by page, till the end. What memories do you have of books? What feelings do you have toward books?

This section constitutes Moses' last words of advice, and includes several points about reading (even singing) God's Book aloud. This isn't mere formality; it's a necessity.

Changes in leadership are sensitive times. Don't miss what happens here because it's Moses' last opportunity to impart God's word.

This passage touches on at least two additional topics to be aware of: music as a part of life with God, and differences in God's blessings to different people.

PERSONAL APPLICATION

Moses commanded the Israelites to read God's laws to the whole assembly so that everyone, including the children, could hear them (Deuteronomy 31:10-13). Every seven years the entire nation would gather together and listen as a priest read the law to them. There were no books or Bibles to pass around, so the people had to rely on word of mouth and an accurate memory. Memorization was an important part of worship, because if everyone knew the law, ignorance would be no excuse for breaking the law.

To fulfill God's purpose and will in our lives, we need the content and substance of his Word in our hearts and minds. For the Hebrews, this process began in childhood.

If you are resistant or feel awkward about leading family devotions, simply read the Bible to your children. There are Bibles available in English for all ages—storybooks for the youngest children, simple translations for early readers, and Bibles designed especially for young people and teenagers. Teaching your children (and new believers) should be one of your top priorities.

BIBLE READING

[9]So Moses wrote down this law and gave it to the priests, who carried the Ark of the Lord's covenant, and to the leaders of Israel. [10]Then Moses gave them this command: "At the end of every seventh year, the Year of Release, during the Festival of Shelters, [11]you must read this law to all the people of Israel when they assemble before the LORD your God at the place he chooses. [12]Call them all together—men, women, children, and the foreigners living in your towns—so they may listen and learn to fear the LORD your God and carefully obey all the terms of this law. [13]Do this so that your children who have not known these laws will hear them and will learn to fear the LORD your God. Do this as long as you live in the land you are crossing the Jordan to occupy."

[45]When Moses had finished reciting these words to Israel, [46]he added: "Take to heart all the words I have given you today. Pass them on as a command to your children so they will obey every word of this law. [47]These instructions are not mere words—they are your life! By obeying them you will enjoy a long life in the land you are crossing the Jordan River to occupy."

DEUTERONOMY 31:9-13, 45-47

FIRST DAY ON THE JOB

PREVIEW

Think back to your first day on the job. Like most people, you probably felt a little overwhelmed by all the challenges ahead of you: new names and faces to learn, responsibilities, procedures, and high hopes.

The book of Joshua opens with the anticipation of a new job for Joshua, the new leader of Israel. No sooner does he get the job than he must deal with an unpleasant situation—calling upon the tribes of Gad, Reuben, and Manasseh to keep the promise they made to Moses. In addition, Joshua must follow God's orders and carry out a painful and possibly humiliating task. But he is capable and willing to do what the Lord desires of him as the leader of Israel.

This portion of the book of Joshua helps answer several other questions: (1) Is it ever right to lie? (2) How important is a pure heart? (3) What should a person do in the face of great opposition?

PERSONAL APPLICATION

Joshua's new job responsibilities included leading more than two million people into a strange new land and conquering it. What a challenge—even for a man of Joshua's caliber!

Every new job is a challenge. Without God it can be frightening. With God it can be a great adventure. Just as God was with Joshua, he is with us as we face our new challenges.

You may not conquer nations, but every day you face tough situations, difficult people, and strong temptations. However, God promises that he will never abandon you or fail to help you (see Deuteronomy 4:31). Ask God to direct your ways, and you will be able to conquer many of life's challenges.

BIBLE READING

¹⁰Joshua then commanded the leaders of Israel, ¹¹"Go through the camp and tell the people to get their provisions ready. In three days you will cross the Jordan River and take possession of the land the LORD your God has given you."

¹²Then Joshua called together the tribes of Reuben, Gad, and the half-tribe of Manasseh. He told them, ¹³"Remember what Moses, the servant of the LORD, commanded you: 'The LORD your God is giving you rest and has given you this land.' ¹⁴Your wives, children, and cattle may remain here on the east side of the Jordan River, but your warriors, fully armed, must lead the other tribes across the Jordan to help them conquer their territory. Stay with them ¹⁵until the LORD gives rest to them as he has given rest to you, and until they, too, possess the land the LORD your God is giving them. Only then may you settle here on the east side of the Jordan River in the land that Moses, the servant of the LORD, gave you."

¹⁶They answered Joshua, "We will do whatever you command us, and we will go wherever you send us. ¹⁷We will obey you just as we obeyed Moses. And may the LORD your God be with you as he was with Moses. ¹⁸Anyone who rebels against your word and does not obey your every command will be put to death. So be strong and courageous!"   JOSHUA 1:10-18

AGAINST ALL ODDS

PREVIEW

There's something beautiful about a well-executed military strategy. Think of the Trojan Horse or Operation Desert Storm. The operation totally surprises the enemy and leaves hardly any casualties on your side. The victory is swift and sure. Generals who design these plans earn the reputation as geniuses because clean victories are so difficult to achieve.

It's good that the Israelites had God as their general because this passage is one long string of military engagements. The people find out who the real genius is. Fortunately, Joshua goes along with God's program too.

In this passage, we also learn about the possible negative effects of sin and about the responsibilities of family members.

PERSONAL APPLICATION

Why did God give Joshua so many complicated instructions for the battle (Joshua 6:3-5)? First, God was making it clear that the battle would depend on him and not on Israel's weapons and expertise. This is why priests, not soldiers, carrying the ark led the Israelites into battle. Second, God's method of taking the city accentuated the terror already felt in Jericho (2:9). Finally, this strange military maneuver was a test of the Israelites' faith and their willingness to follow God completely.

It must have seemed strange to the Israelites that, instead of going directly to battle, they would march around the city for a week (6:3-20). But that was God's plan, and the Israelites had a guaranteed victory if they would follow it (6:2). As strange as the plan sounded, it worked.

God's instructions may require you to take actions that don't make sense at first. Even as you follow him, you may wonder how things can possibly work out. Like the Israelites, take one day at a time and follow step-by-step. You may not see the logic of God's plan until after you have obeyed.

BIBLE READING

[1]Now the gates of Jericho were tightly shut because the people were afraid of the Israelites. No one was allowed to go in or out. [2]But the LORD said to Joshua, "I have given you Jericho, its king, and all its mighty warriors. [3]Your entire army is to march around the city once a day for six days. [4]Seven priests will walk ahead of the Ark, each carrying a ram's horn. On the seventh day you are to march around the city seven times, with the priests blowing the horns. [5]When you hear the priests give one long blast on the horns, have all the people give a mighty shout. Then the walls of the city will collapse, and the people can charge straight into the city."

[6]So Joshua called together the priests and said, "Take up the Ark of the Covenant, and assign seven priests to walk in front of it, each carrying a ram's horn." [7]Then he gave orders to the people: "March around the city, and the armed men will lead the way in front of the Ark of the LORD."

[14]They followed this pattern for six days. [15]On the seventh day the Israelites got up at dawn and marched around the city as they had done before. But this time they went around the city seven times. [16]The seventh time around, as the priests sounded the long blast on their horns, Joshua commanded the people, "Shout! For the LORD has given you the city! [17]. . . Only Rahab the prostitute and the others in her house will be spared, for she protected our spies." . . . [20]When the people heard the sound of the horns, they shouted as loud as they could. Suddenly, the walls of Jericho collapsed, and the Israelites charged straight into the city from every side and captured it. [21]They completely destroyed everything in it—men and women, young and old, cattle, sheep, donkeys—everything.   JOSHUA 6:1-7, 14-21

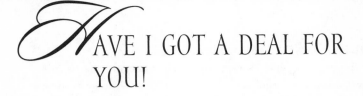AVE I GOT A DEAL FOR YOU!

PREVIEW

To be an American is to be a connoisseur of sales pitches. We can't go to the store or even answer the telephone without someone trying to sell us something. They keep coming because they know we're vulnerable—many people cave in to the salesperson's pressure.

Shortly into their campaign to take over Canaan, Israel falls prey to something very similar. The sales pitch that does them in comes knocking door-to-door, the old-fashioned way. Observe their folly and learn from it.

You'll find other lessons here too, on keeping your word and overcoming overwhelming odds.

PERSONAL APPLICATION

Israel's leaders got fooled (Joshua 9:3-17). When they sampled these men's provisions, they saw that the bread was dry and moldy, the wineskins were cracked, and the clothes and sandals worn out. But they did not see through the deception. After the promise had been made and the treaty ratified, the facts came out—Israel's leaders had been deceived. God had told Israel to make no treaties with the inhabitants of Canaan (Exodus 23:32; 34:12; Numbers 33:55; Deuteronomy 7:2; 20:17-18). As a strategist, Joshua knew enough to talk to God before leading his troops into battle. But the peace treaty seemed innocent enough, so Joshua and the leaders made this decision on their own. By failing to seek God's guidance and wisdom and rushing ahead with their own plans, they had to deal with angry people and an awkward alliance.

Take the time, and have the courage, to consult God before making important decisions—especially when those decisions affect others. Read the Bible daily so that you will know what God wants.

BIBLE READING

³When the people of Gibeon heard what had happened to Jericho and Ai, ⁴they resorted to deception to save themselves. They sent ambassadors to Joshua, loading their donkeys with weathered saddlebags and old patched wineskins. ⁵They put on ragged clothes and worn-out, patched sandals. And they took along dry, moldy bread for provisions. ⁶When they arrived at the camp of Israel at Gilgal, they told Joshua and the men of Israel, "We have come from a distant land to ask you to make a peace treaty with us."

⁸ᵇ . . ."But who are you?" Joshua demanded. "Where do you come from?"

⁹They answered, "We are from a very distant country. We have heard of the might of the LORD your God and of all he did in Egypt. . . . "So our leaders and our people instructed us, 'Prepare for a long journey. Go meet with the people of Israel and declare our people to be their servants, and ask for peace.'

¹²"This bread was hot from the ovens when we left. But now, as you can see, it is dry and moldy. ¹³These wineskins were new when we filled them, but now they are old and cracked. And our clothing and sandals are worn out from our long, hard trip."

¹⁴So the Israelite leaders examined their bread, but they did not consult the LORD. ¹⁵Then Joshua went ahead and signed a peace treaty with them, and the leaders of Israel ratified their agreement with a binding oath.

¹⁶Three days later, the facts came out—these people of Gibeon lived nearby! ¹⁷The Israelites set out at once to investigate and reached their towns in three days. The names of these towns were Gibeon, Kephirah, Beeroth, and Kiriath-jearim.

JOSHUA 9:3-17

*C*HOOSING YOUR BATTLES

PREVIEW

If you could change one thing about the world, what would you change? Don't worry about how it would happen, whether it's realistic, or whether anyone would ever go for it—just dream. Imagine that it *could* happen. What would you change?

This period of time in Israel's history is their opportunity to change their world. Much of what God wants done is theirs to do, and their list of tasks lies before them like an agenda for change. But it means setting priorities.

In this passage, also look for the lessons about the rewards of faith in God, when to break with tradition, and hazards along the path of least resistance.

PERSONAL APPLICATION

Much of the Promised Land was unconquered at this point, but God's plan was to go ahead and include it in the divisions among the tribes (Joshua 13:7). God's desire was that it would eventually be conquered by the Israelites.

God knows the future, and as he leads us, he already knows about the victories that lie ahead. Just as the Israelites still had to go to battle and fight, so we must still face the trials and fight the battles of our unconquered land.

What are our unconquered lands? They may be overseas missionary territories, new languages in which to translate the Bible, new missionary areas in our neighborhoods, interest groups or institutions that need to change, unchallenged public problems or ethical issues, unconfessed sin in our lives, or underdeveloped talents and resources.

What territory has God given you to conquer? This territory is *your* promised land. Trust God and take the land. Your inheritance will be a new heaven and a new earth (see Revelation 21:1).

BIBLE READING

[1]When Joshua was an old man, the LORD said to him, "You are growing old, and much land remains to be conquered. [2]The people still need to occupy the land of the Philistines and the Geshurites—[3]territory that belongs to the Canaanites. This land extends from the stream of Shihor, which is on the boundary of Egypt, northward to the boundary of Ekron, [4]and includes the five Philistine cities of Gaza, Ashdod, Ashkelon, Gath, and Ekron. The land of the Avvites in the south also remains to be conquered. In the north, this area has not yet been conquered: all the land of the Canaanites, including Mearah (which belongs to the Sidonians), stretching northward to Aphek on the border of the Amorites; [5]the land of the Gebalites and all of the Lebanon mountain area to the east, from Baal-gad beneath Mount Hermon to Lebo-hamath; [6]and all the hill country from Lebanon to Misrephoth-maim, including all the land of the Sidonians.

"I will drive these people out of the land for the Israelites. So be sure to give this land to Israel as a special possession, just as I have commanded you. [7]Include all this territory as Israel's inheritance when you divide the land among the nine tribes and the half-tribe of Manasseh."   JOSHUA 13:1-7

DON'T FORGET . . .

PREVIEW

You don't have to be old to forget something of great importance. It happens to people all the time. It's happened to you, hasn't it? Or can't you remember?

Israel is quite forgetful throughout this time in their history. "Now what was that God we were serving? Oh bother, I can't remember quite why I've got this book of the Law in my hands"—or something like that.

In this section, you will see the Israelites forgetting their heritage and lessons learned in the past, and you will see God reminding them.

Don't forget to note some of the other lessons: following through on your promises and responsibilities; knowing your weaknesses; and realizing the truth of the maxim, "Talk is cheap."

PERSONAL APPLICATION

The covenant between Israel and God was that the people would worship and obey the Lord alone. Their purpose was to become a holy nation that would influence the rest of the world for God. The conquest of Canaan was a means to achieve this purpose, but Israel became preoccupied with the land and lost sight of the Lord God.

The same can happen in our lives. We can spend so much time on the means or methods that we forget the end—to glorify God. Churches may make this mistake as well. For example, the congregation may pour all of its energies into a new facility, only to become self-satisfied or fearful of letting certain groups use it. If this happens, they have focused on the building and lost sight of its purpose—to bring others to God.

What is your purpose at work? at home? Make your actions there a part of fulfilling God's highest purposes. Remember what God has called you to do and your promises to him.

BIBLE READING

[1]"Honor the LORD and serve him wholeheartedly. Put away forever the idols your ancestors worshiped when they lived beyond the Euphrates River and in Egypt. Serve the LORD alone. [15]But if you are unwilling to serve the LORD, then choose today whom you will serve. Would you prefer the gods your ancestors served beyond the Euphrates? Or will it be the gods of the Amorites in whose land you now live? But as for me and my family, we will serve the LORD."

[16]The people replied, "We would never forsake the LORD and worship other gods. [17]For the LORD our God is the one who rescued us and our ancestors from slavery in the land of Egypt. He performed mighty miracles before our very eyes. As we traveled through the wilderness among our enemies, he preserved us. [18]It was the LORD who drove out the Amorites and the other nations living here in the land. So we, too, will serve the LORD, for he alone is our God."

[19]Then Joshua said to the people, "You are not able to serve the LORD, for he is a holy and jealous God. He will not forgive your rebellion and sins. [20]If you forsake the LORD and serve other gods, he will turn against you and destroy you, even though he has been so good to you."

[21]But the people answered Joshua, saying, "No, we are determined to serve the LORD!"

[22]"You are accountable for this decision," Joshua said. "You have chosen to serve the LORD."

"Yes," they replied, "we are accountable."

[23]"All right then," Joshua said, "destroy the idols among you, and turn your hearts to the LORD, the God of Israel."

[24]The people said to Joshua, "We will serve the LORD our God. We will obey him alone." JOSHUA 24:1-24

HOO! SHOO!

PREVIEW

Pest control is a multi-billion dollar national industry. Is this due to an irrational obsession with bugs? Not at all. Termites and carpenter ants can do serious damage to a home. Rats and many insects carry diseases. Bee stings can be life-threatening to people who are allergic to them.

Did the Israelites understand this? In this reading, evidence mounts that they did not. But their pests bring a different kind of threat than to house and health; this time, compassion and convenience go too far, and it costs God's people dearly.

As you read this passage, you will also find other lessons: conditions on claiming God's promises, peer pressure, and the value of obstacles and problems.

PERSONAL APPLICATION

God's people failed to drive the evil Canaanites from their land (Judges 1:21, 27-36). Why didn't they follow through and completely obey God's commands? First, they had been fighting for a long time and were tired. Although the goal was in sight, they lacked the discipline and energy to reach it. Second, they were afraid the enemy was too strong—the iron chariots seemed invincible. Third, since Joshua's death, power and authority had been decentralized to the tribal leaders, and the tribes were no longer unified in purpose. Fourth, spiritual decay had infected them from within. They thought they could handle the temptation of doing business with the Canaanites.

Don't coddle sin. Know that God has given you the means to do what he commands—whether you are tired, apathetic, confused, or just lazy. Victory comes from pressing on to do God's will today. Drive out those pesky sins!

BIBLE READING

⁶After Joshua sent the people away, each of the tribes left to take possession of the land allotted to them. ⁷And the Israelites served the LORD throughout the lifetime of Joshua and the leaders who outlived him—those who had seen all the great things the LORD had done for Israel.

⁸Then Joshua son of Nun, the servant of the LORD, died at the age of 110. ⁹They buried him in the land he had inherited, at Timnath-serah in the hill country of Ephraim, north of Mount Gaash.

¹⁰After that generation died, another generation grew up who did not acknowledge the LORD or remember the mighty things he had done for Israel. ¹¹Then the Israelites did what was evil in the Lord's sight and worshiped the images of Baal. ¹²They abandoned the LORD, the God of their ancestors, who had brought them out of Egypt. They chased after other gods, worshiping the gods of the people around them. And they angered the LORD. ¹³They abandoned the LORD to serve Baal and the images of Ashtoreth. ¹⁴This made the LORD burn with anger against Israel, so he handed them over to marauders who stole their possessions. He sold them to their enemies all around, and they were no longer able to resist them. ¹⁵Every time Israel went out to battle, the LORD fought against them, bringing them defeat, just as he promised. And the people were very distressed.   JUDGES 2:6-15

ON CASE OF EMERGENCY . . .

PREVIEW

What provisions for emergencies have you made in your home? Syrup of ipecac, fire extinguishers, smoke alarms, emergency phone numbers by the phone, a planned escape route in case of fire—do any of these sound familiar?

This time of the judges is full of emergencies and chaos, brought on by Eglon king of Moab, Jabin king of Canaan, the Midianites, and the ever annoying Philistines. Read this passage to see if the Israelites learn anything from all this chaos.

Don't miss other lessons about God's use of "handicaps"; leadership; when to take risks; finding courage; and some thoughts on jewelry.

PERSONAL APPLICATION

The Israelites had a habit of hitting rock bottom and staying there, then trying to dig out of the hole by themselves. In one case, they endured twenty years of being oppressed by the Canaanites before crying to God for help (Judges 4:3). You would think one such emergency would teach them, but it didn't. The formula the Israelites applied was this: When in deep trouble, call on God as a last resort.

God should be the *first* place we turn when we are facing struggles or dilemmas. How much suffering the Israelites could have avoided if they had turned to God right away!

We, too, often try to control our own lives without God's help. When struggles come our way, God wants us to come to him first, seeking his strength and guidance.

Turn to God first for help each day, not as a last resort. Then turn to others for help as God directs. About what problem or struggle should you talk to God right now?

BIBLE READING

[1]Again the Israelites did what was evil in the Lord's sight. So the LORD handed them over to the Midianites for seven years. [2]The Midianites were so cruel that the Israelites fled to the mountains, where they made hiding places for themselves in caves and dens. [3]Whenever the Israelites planted their crops, marauders from Midian, Amalek, and the people of the east would attack Israel, [4]camping in the land and destroying crops as far away as Gaza. They left the Israelites with nothing to eat, taking all the sheep, oxen, and donkeys. [5]These enemy hordes, coming with their cattle and tents as thick as locusts, arrived on droves of camels too numerous to count. And they stayed until the land was stripped bare. [6]So Israel was reduced to starvation by the Midianites. Then the Israelites cried out to the LORD for help.

[7]When they cried out to the LORD because of Midian, [8]the LORD sent a prophet to the Israelites. He said, "This is what the LORD, the God of Israel, says: I brought you up out of slavery in Egypt [9]and rescued you from the Egyptians and from all who oppressed you. I drove out your enemies and gave you their land. [10]I told you, 'I am the LORD your God. You must not worship the gods of the Amorites, in whose land you now live.' But you have not listened to me."   JUDGES 6:1-10

HURRY IT UP, WILL YOU?

PREVIEW

We do an awful lot of waiting, don't we? There's waiting at the doctor's office, at traffic lights, and at home. And then we wait for rides, for kids to come home, for kids to leave, and for the weekend. Waiting can be frustrating.

This passage contains a particularly poignant story about waiting. Jotham has to do it. Ask yourself whether you think *he* enjoys it, because his experience is much like everybody else's in some ways.

While you're pondering that, also read about when to call on God; making (and keeping) promises; and how *not* to respond when you feel left out.

PERSONAL APPLICATION

Abimelech was the opposite of what God wanted in a judge, but it was three years before God moved against him, fulfilling Jotham's parable (Judges 9:22-24). Those three years must have seemed like forever to Jotham. And he must have wondered why Abimelech wasn't punished sooner for his evil ways.

We are not alone when we wonder why evil seems to prevail— many others have also wondered (Job 10:3; Job 21:1-18; Jeremiah 12:1; Habakkuk 1:2-4, 12-17). God promises to deal with sin, but in his time, not ours. Actually, it is good that God doesn't punish us immediately, because we, too, deserve God's punishment for our sins. When we demand that God punish evil *now*, we are demanding that he punish us, too, and he's more merciful than that. In his mercy, God often spares us from immediate punishment and allows us time to turn from our sins and turn to him in repentance.

Understand that trusting God for justice means waiting for his timing. First, you must recognize your own sins, turn from them, and ask for God's forgiveness. You may face a difficult time of waiting for the wicked to be punished, but know that in God's time, all evil will be destroyed.

BIBLE READING

¹One day Gideon's son Abimelech went to Shechem to visit his mother's brothers. He said to them and to the rest of his mother's family, ²"Ask the people of Shechem whether they want to be ruled by all seventy of Gideon's sons or by one man. And remember, I am your own flesh and blood!"

³So Abimelech's uncles spoke to all the people of Shechem on his behalf. And after listening to their proposal, they decided in favor of Abimelech because he was their relative. ⁴They gave him seventy silver coins from the temple of Baal-berith, which he used to hire some soldiers who agreed to follow him. ⁵He took the soldiers to his father's home at Ophrah, and there, on one stone, they killed all seventy of his half brothers. But the youngest brother, Jotham, escaped and hid. ⁶Then the people of Shechem and Beth-millo called a meeting under the oak beside the pillar at Shechem and made Abimelech their king.

JUDGES 9:1-6

LUST IS BLIND

PREVIEW

Do you remember your first crush? At the time, you thought there was no one else quite like that special person. You daydreamed, you wished, and you hoped.

Samson is experienced with crushes. Despite his many opportunities, he never quite learns. Or does he?

As you read, see what you can learn about relationships with the opposite sex and about keeping your focus on God.

In this section of Scripture, there are also lessons on the kinds of people God uses; on how to use God's gifts; and on taking revenge. All courtesy of Samson.

PERSONAL APPLICATION

Samson was deceived because Delilah flattered him and indulged his sexual appetite (Judges 16:15-19). Although Samson could strangle a lion, he could not smother his burning lust or his vanity. As a result, Delilah took advantage of him again and again. If Samson didn't realize what was happening after the first or second incident, surely he should have understood the situation by the fourth time! Yet his sexual appetite and weakness controlled him.

How can you keep your desire for love and sexual pleasure from deceiving you? First, decide what kind of a person you will love *before* passion takes over. Determine whether a person's character and faith in God are as desirable as his or her physical appearance. Second, look for what is truly important in a potential husband or wife. Because most of the time you spend with your spouse will *not* involve sex, your companion's personality, temperament, and commitment to solve problems must be as gratifying as his or her kisses. Third, you should be patient. Time often reveals what is beneath a pleasant appearance and attentive touch.

BIBLE READING

[4]Later Samson fell in love with a woman named Delilah, who lived in the valley of Sorek. [5]The leaders of the Philistines went to her and said, "Find out from Samson what makes him so strong and how he can be overpowered and tied up securely. Then each of us will give you eleven hundred pieces of silver."

[6]So Delilah said to Samson, "Please tell me what makes you so strong and what it would take to tie you up securely."

[7]Samson replied, "If I am tied up with seven new bowstrings that have not yet been dried, I will be as weak as anyone else."

[8]So the Philistine leaders brought Delilah seven new bowstrings, and she tied Samson up with them. [9]She had hidden some men in one of the rooms of her house, and she cried out, "Samson! The Philistines have come to capture you!" But Samson snapped the bowstrings as if they were string that had been burned in a fire. So the secret of his strength was not discovered.

[10]Afterward Delilah said to him, "You made fun of me and told me a lie! Now please tell me how you can be tied up securely."

[11]Samson replied, "If I am tied up with brand-new ropes that have never been used, I will be as weak as anyone else."

[12]So Delilah took new ropes and tied him up with them. The men were hiding in the room as before, and again Delilah cried out, "Samson! The Philistines have come to capture you!" But Samson snapped the ropes from his arms as if they were thread.

[13]Then Delilah said, "You have been making fun of me and telling me lies! Won't you please tell me how you can be tied up securely?"

Samson replied, "If you weave the seven braids of my hair into the fabric on your loom and tighten it with the loom shuttle, I will be as weak as anyone else." JUDGES 16:4-13

WHO'S THE BOSS?

PREVIEW

If you have ever ridden in an airplane, you know how much depends on workers' actions. Suppose the flight attendants decided to watch the movie instead of serve the meals? Or the copilot counteracted every move the captain made? Or the captain ignored the air traffic controllers?

Life in Israel at this time of the judges looks a lot like a trip on just such an airplane. They make idols, make war, and make points with cruel and violent visual aids (all against the rules). And why? Look for the very, very strong hint near the end of the story.

PERSONAL APPLICATION

During the time of the judges, the people of Israel experienced great trouble because everyone became their own authority and acted on their own opinions of right and wrong (Judges 21:25). If they didn't like God's rules, they simply disregarded them.

Our world is similar. Individuals, groups, and societies have made themselves the final authorities without reference to God.

Some of the judges whom God sent to rescue Israel were little better. Men like Gideon, Jephthah, and Samson are known for their heroism in battle; but in their personal lives, they lacked deep commitment to obeying the God for whom they fought.

To be truly heroic, we must go into battle each day in our home, job, church, and society to make God's kingdom a reality. Our weapons are the standards and convictions we receive from God's Word. We need to do what is right in his eyes, not ours.

BIBLE READING

¹Now in those days Israel had no king. There was a man from the tribe of Levi living in a remote area of the hill country of Ephraim. One day he brought home a woman from Bethlehem in Judah to be his concubine. ²But she was unfaithful to him and returned to her father's home in Bethlehem. . . . ³Her husband took a servant and an extra donkey to Bethlehem to persuade her to come back. . . .¹⁰ He took his two saddled donkeys and his concubine and headed in the direction of Jebus (that is, Jerusalem). . . . ¹⁴They came to Gibeah, a town in the land of Benjamin, ¹⁵so they stopped there to spend the night. They rested in the town square, but no one took them in for the night.

¹⁶That evening an old man came home from his work in the fields. . . . ¹⁷When he saw the travelers sitting in the town square, . . . ²¹he took them home with him and fed their donkeys. . . . ²²While they were enjoying themselves, some of the wicked men in the town surrounded the house. They began beating at the door and shouting to the old man, "Bring out the man who is staying with you so we can have sex with him. . . . "

²⁵Then the Levite took his concubine and pushed her out the door. The men of the town abused her all night. . . .

²⁷When her husband opened the door to leave, he found her there. She was lying face down, with her hands on the threshold. ²⁸He said, "Get up! Let's go!" But there was no answer. So he put her body on his donkey and took her home.

²⁹When he got home, he took a knife and cut his concubine's body into twelve pieces. Then he sent one piece to each tribe of Israel. ³⁰Everyone who saw it said, "Such a horrible crime has not been committed since Israel left Egypt. Shouldn't we speak up and do something about this?"

²¹:²⁵In those days Israel had no king, so the people did whatever seemed right in their own eyes.   JUDGES 19:1-30; 21:25

VISION THAT IMPROVES WITH AGE

PREVIEW

When you're immersed in a problem, it can be difficult to see exactly what to do. But afterward, when you look back on the situation, you can see it all perfectly, and the solution seems obvious. You can see what you couldn't see before. As the saying goes, hindsight is 20/20.

The book of Ruth has that rare quality of showing us how the past has affected today. How could Naomi have seen, while feeling the pain of her bitter losses, that her future would hold more than ten times the good? She couldn't—she could only trust God—and that's a crucial lesson to learn.

You will find many other lessons in this book: on selflessness; praying honestly; gaining a good reputation (Ruth knows the secret); taking advice; and trusting God to bring good out of tragedy.

PERSONAL APPLICATION

To some people, the book of Ruth appears to be little more than a nice story about a fortunate young woman. This small book, however, records the birth of a man named Obed (Ruth 4:16-17). His birth and the other events recorded in Ruth were part of God's preparation for the births of David and Jesus. Ruth could not have guessed that her actions would lead to such a glorious future event—just as we, today, have no idea of how our lives will affect others years from now.

It's easy to make decisions based totally on our present, limited perspective. Instead, we should consider God's eternal values as we make our choices. Although Ruth's perspective was limited, she faithfully obeyed God—and she left a significant legacy.

Live in faithfulness to God, knowing that the significance of your life will extend beyond your lifetime. God's rewards will outweigh any sacrifice you make.

BIBLE READING

¹So Boaz went to the town gate and took a seat there. When the family redeemer he had mentioned came by, Boaz called out to him, "Come over here, friend. I want to talk to you." So they sat down together. ²Then Boaz called ten leaders from the town and asked them to sit as witnesses. ³And Boaz said to the family redeemer, "You know Naomi, who came back from Moab. She is selling the land that belonged to our relative Elimelech. . . . ⁵Of course, your purchase of the land from Naomi also requires that you marry Ruth, the Moabite widow. That way, she can have children who will carry on her husband's name and keep the land in the family."

⁶"Then I can't redeem it," the family redeemer replied, "because this might endanger my own estate. You redeem the land; I cannot do it."

¹³So Boaz married Ruth and took her home to live with him. When he slept with her, the LORD enabled her to become pregnant, and she gave birth to a son. ¹⁴And the women of the town said to Naomi, "Praise the LORD who has given you a family redeemer today! May he be famous in Israel. ¹⁵May this child restore your youth and care for you in your old age. For he is the son of your daughter-in-law who loves you so much and who has been better to you than seven sons!"

¹⁶Naomi took care of the baby and cared for him as if he were her own. ¹⁷The neighbor women said, "Now at last Naomi has a son again!" And they named him Obed. He became the father of Jesse and the grandfather of David.   RUTH 4:1-6, 13-17

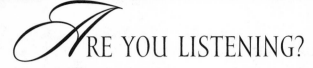RE YOU LISTENING?

PREVIEW

It's frustrating to talk to someone who only pretends to listen. You want to shout, "I'm talking, but you're not listening!" You may be talking about something very important to you, but the person seems to be daydreaming or appears distracted. People can be close—even talking—and yet not communicate.

That problem characterized Israel for many years. God would speak, but Israel wouldn't listen. The birth of Samuel opens a new chapter in Israel's history. Decades have passed since a prophet of God has spoken; Samuel will reopen the lines of communication. As you read, learn about what it means to listen carefully to God.

This piece of Israel's grand story has other lessons as well: bringing the right kinds of gifts to God; praising God for his gifts to us; and knowing when to stop others from doing evil.

PERSONAL APPLICATION

God had spoken directly and audibly with Moses and Joshua, but his word had become rare during the three centuries of rule by the judges. During this time, no prophets were speaking God's messages to Israel (1 Samuel 3:1). The attitude of Eli's sons provides the reason for the silence. They refused to listen to God, and they allowed greed to block their communication with him. Instead of listening to God, Israel had turned to other sources of wisdom. But when God spoke to Samuel, the young boy responded, "Yes, your servant is listening" (3:10).

God does not always use the sound of a human voice, but he always speaks clearly through his Word. To receive his messages, we must be ready to listen and to act upon what he tells us. We must be open to God if we are going to hear and understand him. We must make a conscious choice to read his Word, to respond with prayer, and to be open to the prompting of his Spirit. Listening and responding are vital in a relationship with God.

Have you heard God lately? He's speaking to you. Like Samuel, be ready to say, "Here I am," when God gives you a message.

BIBLE READING

¹Meanwhile, the boy Samuel was serving the LORD by assisting Eli. Now in those days messages from the LORD were very rare, and visions were quite uncommon.

²One night Eli, who was almost blind by now, had just gone to bed. ³The lamp of God had not yet gone out, and Samuel was sleeping in the Tabernacle near the Ark of God. ⁴Suddenly, the LORD called out, "Samuel! Samuel!"

"Yes?" Samuel replied. "What is it?" ⁵He jumped up and ran to Eli. "Here I am. What do you need?"

"I didn't call you," Eli replied. "Go on back to bed." So he did.

⁶Then the LORD called out again, "Samuel!"

Again Samuel jumped up and ran to Eli. "Here I am," he said. "What do you need?"

"I didn't call you, my son," Eli said. "Go on back to bed."

⁷Samuel did not yet know the LORD because he had never had a message from the LORD before. ⁸So now the LORD called a third time, and once more Samuel jumped up and ran to Eli. "Here I am," he said. "What do you need?"

Then Eli realized it was the LORD who was calling the boy. ⁹So he said to Samuel, "Go and lie down again, and if someone calls again, say, 'Yes, LORD, your servant is listening.'" So Samuel went back to bed.

¹⁰And the LORD came and called as before, "Samuel! Samuel!"

And Samuel replied, "Yes, your servant is listening."

¹¹Then the LORD said to Samuel, "I am about to do a shocking thing in Israel. ¹²I am going to carry out all my threats against Eli and his family. ¹³I have warned him continually that judgment is coming for his family, because his sons are blaspheming God and he hasn't disciplined them. ¹⁴So I have vowed that the sins of Eli and his sons will never be forgiven by sacrifices or offerings."

1 SAMUEL 3:1–14

ALL I GOT WAS THIS LOUSY T-SHIRT

PREVIEW

Tourists and travelers purchase memorable souvenirs from the places they visit. What are your favorites? Souvenirs connect us to a place and an experience; they become hooks for our memories. Souvenirs also prove that we've been to a specific place, and they can be excellent discussion starters.

This reading highlights a bit of souvenir collecting—the Philistines grab a priceless Israelite treasure, and the Israelites build a collection of choice Canaanite items. In neither case are the souvenirs harmless, as you'll soon see. The Israelites took their collectibles from the inhabitants that they were to have driven from Canaan, clearly violating God's command. As you read, look for God's lesson about collecting the wrong kind of souvenirs.

This passage also has a lesson about listening to God, and contains reminders about God's power.

PERSONAL APPLICATION

As the Israelites began to inhabit Canaan, they were supposed to destroy all the idols they found. Instead, many people collected the idols, brought them home, and included them in their worship. They were clearly disobeying God because he had warned them to avoid idols (Exodus 20:4). Samuel saw the Israelites' sin and urged them to get rid of their foreign gods (1 Samuel 7:3).

Today's idols don't look like the ancient gods of wood and stone, but they endanger us just as much. Whatever holds first place in a person's life is, in fact, that person's god. Money, success, material goods, pride, or anything else can be an idol if it takes God's place.

The Lord alone is worthy of our service and worship, and we must let nothing rival him. If we have "foreign gods," we need to dethrone them, giving the true God his rightful place.

What idols vie for control of your life? What should you do to keep God in first place?

BIBLE READING

[19]But the LORD killed seventy men from Beth-shemesh because they looked into the Ark of the LORD. And the people mourned greatly because of what the LORD had done. [20]"Who is able to stand in the presence of the LORD, this holy God?" they cried out. "Where can we send the Ark from here?" [21]So they sent messengers to the people at Kiriath-jearim and told them, "The Philistines have returned the Ark of the LORD. Please come here and get it!"

[7:1]So the men of Kiriath-jearim came to get the Ark of the LORD. They took it to the hillside home of Abinadab and ordained Eleazar, his son, to be in charge of it. [2]The Ark remained in Kiriath-jearim for a long time—twenty years in all. During that time, all Israel mourned because it seemed that the LORD had abandoned them.

[3]Then Samuel said to all the people of Israel, "If you are really serious about wanting to return to the LORD, get rid of your foreign gods and your images of Ashtoreth. Determine to obey only the LORD; then he will rescue you from the Philistines." [4]So the Israelites destroyed their images of Baal and Ashtoreth and worshiped only the LORD.

[5]Then Samuel told them, "Come to Mizpah, all of you. I will pray to the LORD for you." [6]So they gathered there and, in a great ceremony, drew water from a well and poured it out before the LORD. They also went without food all day and confessed that they had sinned against the LORD. So it was at Mizpah that Samuel became Israel's judge.   1 SAMUEL 6:19—7:6

FITTING IN

PREVIEW

Many people take steps to fit in with the people around them—they say the right phrases, socialize at known establishments, walk a special way, show off important possessions, or are seen in the right places. Being accepted and fitting in matter a great deal.

In this reading, Israel finally gets a king—Saul. Remember, the nation has been in the process of conquering the land of Canaan, as God had commanded them. But they haven't felt comfortable with the unique identity they have in contrast to their neighbors. They want to fit in. By having a king, now they do—at least they think so. As you read this story, learn a lesson about what is more important than fitting in.

This passage, and the example of Saul, have much to teach us about seeing God's purposes in every circumstance; handling feelings of inadequacy; and channeling anger to constructive uses.

PERSONAL APPLICATION

Israel wanted a king for several reasons (1 Samuel 8:4-9): (1) Samuel's sons were not fit to lead Israel. (2) The twelve tribes of Israel had continual problems working together because each tribe had its own leader and territory; they hoped that a king would unite the tribes. (3) The people wanted to be like the neighboring nations. This last reason, especially, was exactly what God didn't want. Having a king would make it easy for Israel to forget that God was their real leader. It was not wrong for Israel to want a king; God had mentioned the possibility (see Deuteronomy 17:14-20). What they really wanted, however, was to be just like all the other nations around them (1 Samuel 8:19-20). This was in total opposition to God's original intent for them. In reality, the people were rejecting God as their leader.

Often we let others' values and actions dictate our attitudes and behavior. Have you ever made a wrong choice because you wanted to be like everyone else? Be careful that the values of your friends or heroes don't pull you away from what God says is right. Trying to be like unbelievers is a recipe for spiritual disaster.

BIBLE READING

¹As Samuel grew old, he appointed his sons to be judges over Israel. ²Joel and Abijah, his oldest sons, held court in Beersheba. ³But they were not like their father, for they were greedy for money. They accepted bribes and perverted justice.

⁴Finally, the leaders of Israel met at Ramah to discuss the matter with Samuel. ⁵"Look," they told him, "you are now old, and your sons are not like you. Give us a king like all the other nations have."

⁶Samuel was very upset with their request and went to the LORD for advice. ⁷"Do as they say," the LORD replied, "for it is me they are rejecting, not you. They don't want me to be their king any longer. ⁸Ever since I brought them from Egypt they have continually forsaken me and followed other gods. And now they are giving you the same treatment. ⁹Do as they ask, but solemnly warn them about how a king will treat them."

¹⁹But the people refused to listen to Samuel's warning. "Even so, we still want a king," they said. ²⁰"We want to be like the nations around us. Our king will govern us and lead us into battle."

²¹So Samuel told the LORD what the people had said, ²²and the LORD replied, "Do as they say, and give them a king." Then Samuel agreed and sent the people home.

1 SAMUEL 8:1-9, 19-22

ALL THE SIGNS ARE THERE

PREVIEW

Joe can tell that Susan and Steve are Christians. They go to church, wear crosses and other religious jewelry, give to charity, and even serve on a committee at church. All the outward signs are there—they are Christians, all right.

Saul thought that outward appearances made all the difference. In fact, in this account he's got the outward signs covered. He's religious—you can tell just by looking (or so he thinks). As you read, note the difference between external religious signs and true, internal spirituality.

Other lessons in this section include, taking (and giving) credit where it is due; doing God's work when you don't have the tools; and knowing how not to lead (hint: watch Saul).

PERSONAL APPLICATION

This is the first of numerous places in the Bible that states the theme "Obedience is far better than sacrifice" (1 Samuel 15:22-23; see also Psalm 40:6-8; 51:16-17; Proverbs 21:3; Isaiah 1:11-17; Jeremiah 7:21-23; Hosea 6:6; Micah 6:6-8; Matthew 12:7; Mark 12:33; Hebrews 10:8-9). Samuel wasn't saying that sacrifice was not important; he was urging Saul to look at his *reasons* for making the sacrifice. A sacrifice involved giving to God a special gift, usually a lamb or a dove. It was a ritual exchange between a person and God that demonstrated the relationship between them. If the sacrificing person's heart was not truly repentant, or if he or she did not in fact love God, the sacrifice had no meaning.

Religious ceremonies mean nothing unless we perform them with a desire to love and obey God. He isn't impressed with the external signs of religion—going to church, displaying a bumper sticker, wearing a cross or witness T-shirt, serving on a committee, giving to charity, and so forth. What God wants are actions flowing out of devotion and obedience to him.

Do a spiritual inventory. You may look good on the outside, like Saul, but it's what's on the inside that counts with God. Determine to be *his* kind of person.

BIBLE READING

¹²Early the next morning Samuel went to find Saul. Someone told him, "Saul went to Carmel to set up a monument to himself; then he went on to Gilgal."

¹³When Samuel finally found him, Saul greeted him cheerfully. "May the LORD bless you," he said. "I have carried out the Lord's command!"

¹⁴"Then what is all the bleating of sheep and lowing of cattle I hear?" Samuel demanded.

¹⁵"It's true that the army spared the best of the sheep and cattle," Saul admitted. "But they are going to sacrifice them to the LORD your God. We have destroyed everything else."

¹⁶Then Samuel said to Saul, "Stop! Listen to what the LORD told me last night!"

"What was it?" Saul asked.

¹⁷And Samuel told him, "Although you may think little of yourself, are you not the leader of the tribes of Israel? The LORD has anointed you king of Israel. ¹⁸And the LORD sent you on a mission and told you, 'Go and completely destroy the sinners, the Amalekites, until they are all dead.' ¹⁹Why haven't you obeyed the LORD? Why did you rush for the plunder and do exactly what the LORD said not to do?"

²⁰"But I did obey the LORD," Saul insisted. "I carried out the mission he gave me. I brought back King Agag, but I destroyed everyone else. ²¹Then my troops brought in the best of the sheep and cattle and plunder to sacrifice to the LORD your God in Gilgal."

²²But Samuel replied, "What is more pleasing to the LORD: your burnt offerings and sacrifices or your obedience to his voice? Obedience is far better than sacrifice. Listening to him is much better than offering the fat of rams. ²³Rebellion is as bad as the sin of witchcraft, and stubbornness is as bad as worshiping idols. So because you have rejected the word of the LORD, he has rejected you from being king."   1 SAMUEL 15:12-23

BEAUTIFUL PEOPLE

PREVIEW

The world loves beautiful people. Teachers are more likely to call on attractive students in class and more likely to give them positive feedback. Employers are more likely to promote handsome or pretty employees. And people are more likely to like good-looking *anybodies*, to want their friendship, and even to envy them. They say that "Beauty is only skin deep," but that's as deep as most people seem to go.

This section of Scripture records a very significant event, the choosing of Israel's second king. It raises the beauty question directly. At first, Samuel gets it wrong, but then God shows him a better way. As you read, learn how God looks at people.

This passage is home to other great lessons too—when to put plans on hold, and fighting "giants."

PERSONAL APPLICATION

Saul was tall and handsome; he was an impressive-looking man. Samuel may have been trying to find someone who looked like Saul to be Israel's next king, but God warned him against judging by appearance alone (1 Samuel 16:7). God judges by faith and character, not appearances. And because only God can see on the inside, only he can accurately judge people. When people judge by outward appearances, they may overlook quality individuals who lack the particular physical characteristics that society admires. Appearance doesn't reveal what people are really like, or what their true value is.

Most people spend hours each week maintaining their outward appearances. There's nothing wrong with trying to look your best, but do you do as much to develop your inner character? While everyone can see your face, only your character determines how you will live and work and enjoy life. What steps can you take to improve your character?

BIBLE READING

¹Finally, the LORD said to Samuel, "You have mourned long enough for Saul. I have rejected him as king of Israel. Now fill your horn with olive oil and go to Bethlehem. Find a man named Jesse who lives there, for I have selected one of his sons to be my new king."

⁴So Samuel did as the LORD instructed him. When he arrived at Bethlehem, the leaders of the town became afraid. "What's wrong?" they asked. "Do you come in peace?"

⁵"Yes," Samuel replied. "I have come to sacrifice to the LORD. Purify yourselves and come with me to the sacrifice." Then Samuel performed the purification rite for Jesse and his sons and invited them, too.

⁶When they arrived, Samuel took one look at Eliab and thought, "Surely this is the Lord's anointed!" ⁷But the LORD said to Samuel, "Don't judge by his appearance or height, for I have rejected him. The LORD doesn't make decisions the way you do! People judge by outward appearance, but the LORD looks at a person's thoughts and intentions."

¹⁰ . . . all seven of Jesse's sons were presented to Samuel. But Samuel said to Jesse, "The LORD has not chosen any of these." ¹¹Then Samuel asked, "Are these all the sons you have?"

"There is still the youngest," Jesse replied. "But he's out in the fields watching the sheep."

"Send for him at once," Samuel said. "We will not sit down to eat until he arrives."

¹²So Jesse sent for him. He was ruddy and handsome, with pleasant eyes. And the LORD said, "This is the one; anoint him."

¹³So as David stood there among his brothers, Samuel took the olive oil he had brought and poured it on David's head. And the Spirit of the LORD came mightily upon him from that day on. Then Samuel returned to Ramah.   1 SAMUEL 16:1, 4–13

CLOSE FRIENDS

PREVIEW

Do you have any close friends? That's a tough question for many people. Everyone has *acquaintances*. Most have *friends*, too. But many cannot say that they have a *close* friend, someone who will sacrifice for them. Such friends don't come along every day.

In this reading, the young and popular warrior David meets young prince Jonathan, and they immediately become close friends. This friendship is good for them and for Israel, but it quickly becomes tested, as most friendships do. As you read, look for what makes a quality friendship.

In addition, each main character in this passage illustrates something else: how to handle popularity (David); obedience to parents (Jonathan); and the futility of trying to resist God's will (Saul).

PERSONAL APPLICATION

When David and Jonathan met, they became close friends right away (1 Samuel 18:1-4). Jonathan, the prince of Israel, later realized that David, and not he, would be the next king (1 Samuel 23:17). But that did not weaken his love for David. Jonathan would much rather lose the throne of Israel than lose his closest friend. They stayed loyal to each other throughout their lives.

Their friendship is one of the deepest and closest recorded in the Bible: (1) they based their friendship on commitment to God, not just each other; (2) they let nothing come between them, not even career or family problems; (3) they drew closer together when their friendship was tested; and (4) they remained friends to the end.

What can you do to be that kind of friend to another?

BIBLE READING

¹After David had finished talking with Saul, he met Jonathan, the king's son. There was an immediate bond of love between them, and they became the best of friends. ²From that day on Saul kept David with him at the palace and wouldn't let him return home. ³And Jonathan made a special vow to be David's friend, ⁴and he sealed the pact by giving him his robe, tunic, sword, bow, and belt.

⁵Whatever Saul asked David to do, David did it successfully. So Saul made him a commander in his army, an appointment that was applauded by the fighting men and officers alike. ⁶But something happened when the victorious Israelite army was returning home after David had killed Goliath. Women came out from all the towns along the way to celebrate and to cheer for King Saul, and they sang and danced for joy with tambourines and cymbals. ⁷This was their song:

> "Saul has killed his thousands,
>   and David his ten thousands!"

⁸This made Saul very angry. "What's this?" he said. "They credit David with ten thousands and me with only thousands. Next they'll be making him their king!" ⁹So from that time on Saul kept a jealous eye on David.

¹⁰The very next day, in fact, a tormenting spirit from God overwhelmed Saul, and he began to rave like a madman. David began to play the harp, as he did whenever this happened. But Saul, who had a spear in his hand, ¹¹suddenly hurled it at David, intending to pin him to the wall. But David jumped aside and escaped. This happened another time, too, ¹²for Saul was afraid of him, and he was jealous because the LORD had left him and was now with David. ¹³Finally, Saul banned him from his presence and appointed him commander over only a thousand men, but David faithfully led his troops into battle.   1 SAMUEL 18:1-13

POLITICAL INACTION

PREVIEW

Finding fault with the government is a national pastime. Some say the government controls us too little, others say it controls us too much. Everybody thinks it spends too little on this and not enough on that. Standard rules of etiquette say you shouldn't discuss politics in polite company—and for good reason.

This portion of Scripture shows us David (still) running for his life from Saul. We can plainly see that David has more reasons than most to find fault with his government. His example for dealing with these gripes has something to say to us all.

Along the way, David also teaches several other valuable lessons, such as applying God's laws with compassion; suffering and its source (evil people); marks of true friendship; being fair to those who help us; having courage; and showing mercy.

PERSONAL APPLICATION

David showed respect for Saul, despite the fact that Saul was trying to kill him (1 Samuel 24:5-6). Although Saul was sinning and rebelling against God, David still respected the position he held as God's appointed authority. David knew that one day he would be king; he also knew it was not right to strike down the man whom God had placed on the throne. By assassinating Saul, David would be setting a precedent for his opponents to remove *him* someday.

Romans 13:1-7 teaches that God has placed the government and its leaders in power. We may not know why, but, like David, we are to respect the positions and roles of those to whom God has given authority. There is one exception, however—because God is our highest authority, we should never allow any earthly leader to pressure us to violate God's law.

Do you respect your political leaders? What can you do to be a better citizen?

BIBLE READING

¹²David took the spear and jug of water that were near Saul's head. Then he and Abishai got away without anyone seeing them or even waking up, because the LORD had put Saul's men into a deep sleep. ¹³David climbed the hill opposite the camp until he was at a safe distance. ¹⁴Then he shouted down to Abner and Saul, "Wake up, Abner!"

"Who is it?" Abner demanded.

¹⁵"Well, Abner, you're a great man, aren't you?" David taunted. "Where in all Israel is there anyone as mighty? So why haven't you guarded your master the king when someone came to kill him? ¹⁶This isn't good at all! I swear by the LORD that you and your men deserve to die, because you failed to protect your master, the Lord's anointed! Look around! Where are the king's spear and the jug of water that were beside his head?"

¹⁷Saul recognized David's voice and called out, "Is that you, my son David?"

And David replied, "Yes, my lord the king. ¹⁸Why are you chasing me? What have I done? What is my crime? ¹⁹But now let my lord the king listen to his servant. If the LORD has stirred you up against me, then let him accept my offering. But if this is simply a human scheme, then may those involved be cursed by the LORD. For you have driven me from my home, so I can no longer live among the Lord's people and worship as I should. ²⁰Must I die on foreign soil, far from the presence of the LORD? Why has the king of Israel come out to search for a single flea? Why does he hunt me down like a partridge on the mountains?"

²¹Then Saul confessed, "I have sinned. Come back home, my son, and I will no longer try to harm you, for you valued my life today. I have been a fool and very, very wrong."

1 SAMUEL 26:12–21

MY WAY

PREVIEW

Most American heroes wear the label "rugged individualist." These macho types set a sort of standard—an American ideal. And while we may argue about the details, most of us would agree that these heroes live by three rules: they blaze their own trail; they don't take orders (they give them); and they apologize to no one.

This is the story of Saul's death, and it's a dark time in Israel's history. Saul has tried to be a rugged individualist, and this portion of the Scriptures passes judgment on that experiment in living. Given the similarities to the way we're urged to live today, we'd do well to pay attention.

As you read, you'll find these other lessons: being patient; avoiding the occult; and remembering that those who do unglamorous, behind-the-scenes jobs to support the efforts of others are important too.

PERSONAL APPLICATION

In Saul's death (1 Samuel 31:4-13) an ideal also died. Israel could no longer believe that having a king like the other nations would solve all their troubles. The real problem was not the form of government, but the sinful king. Saul tried to please God with spurts of religiosity; real spirituality takes a lifetime of consistent obedience. Saul didn't have it; he really was a "rugged individualist."

Heroic spiritual lives take a different approach. They are built by stacking days of obedience, one on top of the other. Like a brick, each obedient act is small in itself, but in time the acts pile up, and a huge wall of strong character results—a great defense against temptation. This strategy doesn't concern itself with trailblazing, calling the shots, or never saying, "Oops!" Rather, it concerns itself with striving for consistent obedience to God—doing it *his* way—each day.

Which kind of hero are *you* trying to be?

BIBLE READING

¹Now the Philistines attacked Israel, forcing the Israelites to flee. Many were slaughtered on the slopes of Mount Gilboa. ²The Philistines closed in on Saul and his sons, and they killed three of his sons—Jonathan, Abinadab, and Malkishua. ³The fighting grew very fierce around Saul, and the Philistine archers caught up with him and wounded him severely. ⁴Saul groaned to his armor bearer, "Take your sword and kill me before these pagan Philistines run me through and humiliate me." But his armor bearer was afraid and would not do it. So Saul took his own sword and fell on it. ⁵When his armor bearer realized that Saul was dead, he fell on his own sword and died beside the king. ⁶So Saul, three of his sons, his armor bearer, and his troops all died together that same day.

⁷When the Israelites on the other side of the Jezreel Valley and beyond the Jordan saw that their army had been routed and that Saul and his sons were dead, they abandoned their towns and fled. So the Philistines moved in and occupied their towns.

1 SAMUEL 31:1-7

*B*IG BOYS DON'T CRY

PREVIEW

Kids of playground age can make merciless fun of a boy for crying. Some fathers will too. If you had a son and he tended to show emotion, especially by shedding tears, what would you say to him?

In this reading, David and his men first hear of Saul's death and the death of David's close friend, Jonathan. Nobody among David's men takes it well. Some might say that they should rejoice because now David can take his rightful place as king. But celebrating isn't part of their reaction. You'll learn a valuable lesson from their response.

As you read, note also how to tell the difference between persistence (good) and stubbornness (bad), how revenge can backfire, and how important it is to do justice to others.

PERSONAL APPLICATION

When David and his men learned of Saul and Jonathan's deaths, "they mourned and wept and fasted all day" (2 Samuel 1:12). David and his men were visibly shaken over the tragic news. Their actions showed their genuine sorrow over the loss of their king, their friend Jonathan, and the other soldiers of Israel who had died that day. They were not ashamed to grieve. Today, some people consider expressing emotions to be a sign of weakness. Those who wish to appear strong try to hide their feelings. But expressing our grief can help us deal with our intense sorrow when a loved one dies.

Do you tend to keep your feelings inside? Because "sadness has a refining influence on us" (Ecclesiastes 7:3), find ways to express sorrow when you feel it. Tell God exactly how you feel—he understands. And share your feelings with a close friend.

BIBLE READING

¹After the death of Saul, David returned from his victory over the Amalekites and spent two days in Ziklag. ²On the third day after David's return, a man arrived from the Israelite battlefront. He had torn his clothes and put dirt on his head to show that he was in mourning. He fell to the ground before David in deep respect.

³"Where have you come from?" David asked.

"I escaped from the Israelite camp," the man replied.

⁴"What happened?" David demanded. "Tell me how the battle went."

The man replied, "Our entire army fled. Many men are dead and wounded on the battlefield, and Saul and his son Jonathan have been killed."

⁵"How do you know that Saul and Jonathan are dead?" David demanded.

⁶The young man answered, "I happened to be on Mount Gilboa. I saw Saul there leaning on his spear with the enemy chariots closing in on him. ⁷When he turned and saw me, he cried out for me to come to him. 'How can I help?' I asked him. ⁸And he said to me, 'Who are you?' I replied, 'I am an Amalekite.' ⁹Then he begged me, 'Come over here and put me out of my misery, for I am in terrible pain and want to die.'

¹⁰"So I killed him," the Amalekite told David, "for I knew he couldn't live. Then I took his crown and one of his bracelets so I could bring them to you, my lord."

¹¹David and his men tore their clothes in sorrow when they heard the news. ¹²They mourned and wept and fasted all day for Saul and his son Jonathan, and for the Lord's army and the nation of Israel, because so many had died that day.

2 SAMUEL 1:1-12

$\mathcal{T}$HOROUGHLY EMBARRASSED

PREVIEW

Being embarrassed by someone you love ranks as one of life's most inevitable experiences. No matter how carefully you guard against it, it's bound to happen. Has it happened to you lately?

This is the story of David's consolidation of power. He takes Jerusalem, defeats some of his enemies, and brings the ark of the covenant back to Jerusalem (it had been captured by the Philistines). Now it's time to celebrate, and David dances before the Lord. But Michal, David's wife, is too embarrassed by David to enjoy the festivities. How could he *do* such a thing?

Look for important lessons in this passage on waiting for the fulfillment of God's promises; how to fight; and why God sometimes says no to our requests.

PERSONAL APPLICATION

Michal was so concerned about David's undignified actions that she did not rejoice in the ark's return to the city (2 Samuel 6:16-20). Her contempt for David probably did not start with David's grand entrance into the city. She may have resented David's taking her from her former husband, Paltiel (see 2 Samuel 3:13-14). Whatever her reason, this contempt that Michal felt toward David escalated into a difficult confrontation.

Close friends and married couples know each other extremely well, including each other's faults, weaknesses, and annoying habits. Minor irritations can lead to anger, and bitterness can lead to hatred. Unchecked feelings of resentment will destroy any relationship. Deal with your negative emotions before they escalate into open warfare.

Michal focused on appearances while David emphasized the condition of his heart before God. David was willing to look foolish in order to worship God fully and honestly. Don't be afraid to express *your* feelings toward God, even when others are present.

BIBLE READING

[16]But as the Ark of the LORD entered the City of David, Michal, the daughter of Saul, looked down from her window. When she saw King David leaping and dancing before the LORD, she was filled with contempt for him.

[17]The Ark of the LORD was placed inside the special tent that David had prepared for it. And David sacrificed burnt offerings and peace offerings to the LORD. [18]When he had finished, David blessed the people in the name of the LORD Almighty. [19]Then he gave a gift of food to every man and woman in Israel: a loaf of bread, a cake of dates, and a cake of raisins. Then everyone went home.

[20]When David returned home to bless his family, Michal came out to meet him and said in disgust, "How glorious the king of Israel looked today! He exposed himself to the servant girls like any indecent person might do!"

[21]David retorted to Michal, "I was dancing before the LORD, who chose me above your father and his family! He appointed me as the leader of Israel, the people of the LORD. So I am willing to act like a fool in order to show my joy in the LORD. [22]Yes, and I am willing to look even more foolish than this, but I will be held in honor by the girls of whom you have spoken!" [23]So Michal, the daughter of Saul, remained childless throughout her life.

2 SAMUEL 6:16-23

LOSING THE GOOD FIGHT

PREVIEW

You decided to take up a just cause. You knew it was right—that God was for it. But then you lost the fight, and you wonder what happened.

In the process of consolidating his power, David conquers the surrounding nations. His general, Joab, gives advice to David's men that can teach us a lot about the fights we take up for God.

Watching David in this section of Scripture will also teach us that God keeps his promises, and that we need to show kindness even when it isn't what other people are doing.

PERSONAL APPLICATION

David and his men fought many battles as they established their control over Israel. As they prepared to attack the Ammonites, David's general, Joab, said, "Let us fight bravely" (2 Samuel 10:12). He was urging the men to do the best they could by using their minds to figure out the best techniques and using their resources strategically. But in the very same breath Joab also said, "May the Lord's will be done." Joab knew that God would determine the outcome of the battle.

We need to keep our actions and our faith in God in balance. Some seem to think that all believers need to do is to sit passively and wait for God to act. Others seem to think that everything depends on them, on their cleverness and effort. In reality, God expects us to use our minds and our muscles *while* we depend on him. We use our resources to obey God, while at the same time trusting him for the outcome.

The next time you have a task to accomplish or a problem to solve, turn it over to God and then do your best. Trust God for the result and then accept what he brings.

BIBLE READING

⁶Now the people of Ammon realized how seriously they had angered David, so they hired twenty thousand Aramean mercenaries from the lands of Beth-rehob and Zobah, one thousand from the king of Maacah, and twelve thousand from the land of Tob. ⁷When David heard about this, he sent Joab and the entire Israelite army to fight them. ⁸The Ammonite troops drew up their battle lines at the entrance of the city gates, while the Arameans from Zobah and Rehob and the men from Tob and Maacah positioned themselves to fight in the open fields.

⁹When Joab saw that he would have to fight on two fronts, he chose the best troops in his army. He placed them under his personal command and led them out to fight the Arameans in the fields. ¹⁰He left the rest of the army under the command of his brother Abishai, who was to attack the Ammonites. ¹¹"If the Arameans are too strong for me, then come over and help me," Joab told his brother. "And if the Ammonites are too strong for you, I will come and help you. ¹²Be courageous! Let us fight bravely to save our people and the cities of our God. May the LORD's will be done."

¹³When Joab and his troops attacked, the Arameans began to run away. ¹⁴And when the Ammonites saw the Arameans running, they ran from Abishai and retreated into the city. After the battle was over, Joab returned to Jerusalem.   2 SAMUEL 10:6-14

RRESISTIBLE?

PREVIEW

Temptations seldom appear as ugly or dangerous as they really are. Think of it from a fish's perspective, or from that of a mouse approaching a trap. They bite the worm and pounce on the cheese that seem so good and harmless—until they have done their damage. People do the same.

This is the tragic story of David and Bathsheba. David sees her (the "bait"), makes a choice, and he's "hooked." The results are devastating to David, to Bathsheba, to Uriah, and to the nation. As you read this passage, ask yourself: What could David have done to prevent this?

This story also teaches the futility of trying to cover up a sin; the importance of correcting a friend; and the best way to respond when you get caught.

PERSONAL APPLICATION

As David looked from the roof of the palace, he saw a beautiful woman bathing (2 Samuel 11:2-4). He didn't see a dangerous situation that could damage the rest of his life. As his heart filled with lust, he pushed aside the cautions that must have filled his head and asked about Bathsheba. David should have left the roof and fled the temptation; instead, he entertained it. As a result, David succumbed to temptation and committed adultery and murder.

To escape temptation, (1) ask God to help you stay away from people, places, and situations that may strongly tempt you. (2) Memorize and meditate on portions of Scripture that combat your specific weaknesses. At the root of most temptation is a real need or desire that God can fill, but we must trust in his timing. (3) Find another believer with whom you can openly share your struggles, and call this person for help when temptation strikes.

When tempted, move away from the temptation and toward a good place or safe activity. Fight the temptation, don't just stay there and look into the possibilities.

BIBLE READING

²Late one afternoon David got out of bed after taking a nap and went for a stroll on the roof of the palace. As he looked out over the city, he noticed a woman of unusual beauty taking a bath. ³He sent someone to find out who she was, and he was told, "She is Bathsheba, the daughter of Eliam and the wife of Uriah the Hittite." ⁴Then David sent for her; and when she came to the palace, he slept with her. (She had just completed the purification rites after having her menstrual period.) Then she returned home. ⁵Later, when Bathsheba discovered that she was pregnant, she sent a message to inform David.

⁶So David sent word to Joab: "Send me Uriah the Hittite." ⁷When Uriah arrived, David asked him how Joab and the army were getting along and how the war was progressing. ⁸Then he told Uriah, "Go on home and relax." David even sent a gift to Uriah after he had left the palace. ⁹But Uriah wouldn't go home. He stayed that night at the palace entrance with some of the king's other servants.

¹⁰When David heard what Uriah had done, he summoned him and asked, "What's the matter with you? Why didn't you go home last night after being away for so long?"

¹¹Uriah replied, "The Ark and the armies of Israel and Judah are living in tents, and Joab and his officers are camping in the open fields. How could I go home to wine and dine and sleep with my wife? I swear that I will never be guilty of acting like that."

¹²"Well, stay here tonight," David told him, "and tomorrow you may return to the army." So Uriah stayed in Jerusalem that day and the next. ¹³Then David invited him to dinner and got him drunk. But even then he couldn't get Uriah to go home to his wife. Again he slept at the palace entrance.

¹⁴So the next morning David wrote a letter to Joab and gave it to Uriah to deliver. ¹⁵The letter instructed Joab, "Station Uriah on the front lines where the battle is fiercest. Then pull back so that he will be killed."   2 SAMUEL 11:2-15

LIKE FATHER, LIKE SON

PREVIEW

As you get older, do you notice how much you are becoming like your parents? You may think, "I'm just like my father or mother." It's funny how we leave adolescence eager to be *unlike* our parents, and then the plan goes afoul. There's a part of Mom and Dad that we just can't escape.

David's kids are all grown up now, and his sons are bringing him a lot of grief. Unfortunately, by this time there's little he can do about it—indeed he does little. In this way, David sees his own sins come back to haunt him. As you read this passage, think of the parenting implications David's actions have brought (disciplining, being a good role model, spending time together).

In this section of Scripture, you will also see the difference between love and lust, and the damage that can result from a rebellious attitude.

PERSONAL APPLICATION

David faced sins in his own family similar to those that he had committed earlier. David's son, Amnon, raped his half-sister Tamar. Amnon was then murdered by another of David's sons, Tamar's brother, Absalom (2 Samuel 13:1-29). David's sin was magnified in the lives of his children. David was angry with Amnon for raping Tamar, but he did not punish this wayward son (13:21-22). David probably hesitated because he didn't want to cross Amnon, who was his firstborn son (1 Chronicles 3:1), and next in line to be king. David was guilty of a similar sin, himself, in his adultery with Bathsheba. While unsurpassed as a king and military leader, David had problems as a husband and father.

If you are a parent, you can't always control what your children will do. You can, however, live by God's standards and give them a good example to follow. What changes should you make in order to be a better mother or father?

BIBLE READING

[11]"But as she was feeding him, he grabbed her and demanded, "Come to bed with me, my darling sister."

[12]"No, my brother!" she cried. "Don't be foolish! Don't do this to me! You know what a serious crime it is to do such a thing in Israel. [13]Where could I go in my shame? And you would be called one of the greatest fools in Israel. Please, just speak to the king about it, and he will let you marry me."

[14]But Amnon wouldn't listen to her, and since he was stronger than she was, he raped her. [15]Then suddenly Amnon's love turned to hate, and he hated her even more than he had loved her. "Get out of here!" he snarled at her.

[16]"No, no!" Tamar cried. "To reject me now is a greater wrong than what you have already done to me."

But Amnon wouldn't listen to her. [17]He shouted for his servant and demanded, "Throw this woman out, and lock the door behind her!"

[18]So the servant put her out. She was wearing a long, beautiful robe, as was the custom in those days for the king's virgin daughters. [19]But now Tamar tore her robe and put ashes on her head. And then, with her face in her hands, she went away crying.

[20]Her brother Absalom saw her and asked, "Is it true that Amnon has been with you? Well, don't be so upset. Since he's your brother anyway, don't worry about it." So Tamar lived as a desolate woman in Absalom's house. [21]When King David heard what had happened, he was very angry.   2 SAMUEL 13:11-21

$\mathcal{T}$HE POLLS ARE IN

PREVIEW

Public opinion polls give solid proof that public opinion changes faster than a traffic light. They tell minute by minute what people are thinking—which is good, because people change their minds just as fast.

Absalom knows that aspect of human nature all too well. In this story of national rebellion against David, Absalom is the chief perpetrator, appealing directly to the crowds. His rebellion is popular, showing that the crowd will follow just about anybody. Learn from the fickle nature of the crowds.

Other lessons in this passage include: evaluating leaders (making sure they're not schemers); ignoring unjustified criticism; avoiding flattery; thinking before acting; and using diplomacy and tact.

PERSONAL APPLICATION

For a short time, most of Israel was supporting the rebel ruler, Absalom. Soon, however, the people wanted David back as their king (2 Samuel 19:8-10).

Crowds are often fickle, changing their minds with the wind. That's just one of the reasons we need to live by a higher moral code than the pleasure of the majority. One day the people will want this, the next day they will want that. What the crowd wants, and what people pressure us to do, will rarely conform to what God wants.

Although there is much pressure to conform to the world, rather than trying to be popular and acceptable to the crowd, guide your life by the moral principles given in God's Word. God never changes, and he knows and wants what is best for you.

BIBLE READING

[1]After this, Absalom bought a chariot and horses, and he hired fifty footmen to run ahead of him. [2]He got up early every morning and went out to the gate of the city. When people brought a case to the king for judgment, Absalom would ask where they were from, and they would tell him their tribe. [3]Then Absalom would say, "You've really got a strong case here! It's too bad the king doesn't have anyone to hear it. [4]I wish I were the judge. Then people could bring their problems to me, and I would give them justice!" [5]And when people tried to bow before him, Absalom wouldn't let them. Instead, he took them by the hand and embraced them. [6]So in this way, Absalom stole the hearts of all the people of Israel.

[7]After four years, Absalom said to the king, "Let me go to Hebron to offer a sacrifice to the LORD in fulfillment of a vow I made to him. [8]For while I was at Geshur, I promised to sacrifice to him in Hebron if he would bring me back to Jerusalem."

[9]"All right," the king told him. "Go and fulfill your vow."

So Absalom went to Hebron. [10]But while he was there, he sent secret messengers to every part of Israel to stir up a rebellion against the king. "As soon as you hear the trumpets," his message read, "you will know that Absalom has been crowned king in Hebron." [11]He took two hundred men from Jerusalem with him as guests, but they knew nothing of his intentions. [12]While he was offering the sacrifices, he sent for Ahithophel, one of David's counselors who lived in Giloh. Soon many others also joined Absalom, and the conspiracy gained momentum.

2 SAMUEL 15:1-12

T'S ALL RIGHT

PREVIEW

"It's all right," Billy said forgivingly, and you couldn't help but smile. You had accused him of conspiring to keep you out of the clubhouse, but that wasn't what was truly going on. In fact, Billy had been decorating the clubhouse for your surprise birthday party. Now the truth was out, and so was your sheepish apology.

These are the later years of David's rule, a song of praise that David wrote, and some of David's last words. In this song, David brings up the subject of his own guilt. It's a telling speech. As you read, you will see that, to paraphrase, "forgiveness is cool."

You'll find other lessons too, about bringing justice to others and placing our security in God instead of money.

PERSONAL APPLICATION

"I am blameless before God; I have kept myself from sin" (2 Samuel 22:24). With these words, David was not denying that he had *ever* sinned. Psalm 51 shows his tremendous anguish over his sins against Uriah and Bathsheba. But David understood God's faithfulness and was writing this hymn from God's perspective. He knew that God had made him pure again—"whiter than snow," with a "clean heart" (Psalm 51:7, 10).

God will forgive our sins if we bring them to him in sorrow and repentance. Through the death and resurrection of Jesus Christ, we can be cleansed and made perfect in God's eyes. God replaces our sin with his purity—he sees us as forgiven and clean.

Stop right now and confess your sins to your loving heavenly Father. Accept his total forgiveness through Christ.

BIBLE READING

¹⁷ "He reached down from heaven and rescued me;
    he drew me out of deep waters.
¹⁸ He delivered me from my powerful enemies,
    from those who hated me and were too strong for me.
¹⁹ They attacked me at a moment when I was weakest,
    but the LORD upheld me.
²⁰ He led me to a place of safety;
    he rescued me because he delights in me.

²⁶ "To the faithful you show yourself faithful;
    to those with integrity you show integrity.
²⁷ To the pure you show yourself pure,
    but to the wicked you show yourself hostile.
²⁸ You rescue those who are humble,
    but your eyes are on the proud to humiliate them.
²⁹ O LORD, you are my light;
    yes, LORD, you light up my darkness.
³⁰ In your strength I can crush an army;
    with my God I can scale any wall.

³¹ "As for God, his way is perfect.
    All the Lord's promises prove true.
    He is a shield for all who look to him for protection.
³² For who is God except the LORD?
    Who but our God is a solid rock?
³³ God is my strong fortress;
    he has made my way safe.
³⁴ He makes me as surefooted as a deer,
    leading me safely along the mountain heights."

2 SAMUEL 22:17-20, 26-34

HAT WOULD YOU DO?

PREVIEW

When was the last time someone asked you for advice and you didn't know what to say? It happens to everyone. Life throws some awful curve balls—problems that we've never seen before and have no idea how to confront.

Here we read where Solomon becomes king (after a conspiracy against him is quashed) and first gains his great wisdom. He already shows some wisdom, but he's wise enough to know that he doesn't know enough. Solomon's humility serves him well. As you read, carefully watch this ultimate advice-giver in action.

Other lessons in this passage include: parenting (in retrospect); interfering when someone is about to do an injustice; putting God at the center (even of government); and getting organized.

PERSONAL APPLICATION

When given a chance to have anything in the world, Solomon asked for wisdom—"an understanding mind"—in order to lead well and to make right decisions (1 Kings 3:6-9). This, in itself, showed wisdom, and God honored Solomon's request. Solomon became the wisest man ever (3:12) and, at the moving of God's Spirit, recorded much of his God-given insight in the book of Proverbs.

God wants to work *through* us, not *for* us. Notice that Solomon asked for understanding to carry out his job; he did not ask God to do the job for him.

Ask God to give you the wisdom to know what to do and the courage to follow through on it. And remember, if you ask for wisdom, God has promised to give you all you need (see James 1:5).

BIBLE READING

[5]That night the LORD appeared to Solomon in a dream, and God said, "What do you want? Ask, and I will give it to you!"

[6]Solomon replied, "You were wonderfully kind to my father, David, because he was honest and true and faithful to you. And you have continued this great kindness to him today by giving him a son to succeed him. [7]O LORD my God, now you have made me king instead of my father, David, but I am like a little child who doesn't know his way around. [8]And here I am among your own chosen people, a nation so great they are too numerous to count! [9]Give me an understanding mind so that I can govern your people well and know the difference between right and wrong. For who by himself is able to govern this great nation of yours?"

[10]The Lord was pleased with Solomon's reply and was glad that he had asked for wisdom. [11]So God replied, "Because you have asked for wisdom in governing my people and have not asked for a long life or riches for yourself or the death of your enemies—[12]I will give you what you asked for! I will give you a wise and understanding mind such as no one else has ever had or ever will have! [13]And I will also give you what you did not ask for—riches and honor! No other king in all the world will be compared to you for the rest of your life! [14]And if you follow me and obey my commands as your father, David, did, I will give you a long life."

1 KINGS 3:5-14

CATHEDRALS AND CHARACTER

PREVIEW

"What church do you attend?" Usually when asked that question, a person will respond with "Community Congregational," "First Presbyterian," or another church name. When pressed for more information, the person might describe the building. The building where the church meets is also important, makes a public statement about the church, and provides a focal point for a particular body of believers.

In this passage, at long last, Solomon gets to build the temple. What a grand structure! David wanted to do it but couldn't. More than most people, David understood the temple's significance. That's why it mattered so much to him and why God wouldn't let him build it. See what you can learn from this massive, monumental project.

Note in Solomon's foremanship two more lessons: balancing work and family life, and dedicating ourselves to God's service.

PERSONAL APPLICATION

For four hundred and eighty years after Israel's escape from Egypt, God did not ask his people, the Jews, to build a temple for him (1 Kings 8:15-21). Instead, he emphasized the importance of his presence among them and their need for spiritual leaders.

It is easy to think of a building as the focus of God's presence and power, but God chooses and uses *people* to do his work. He can use you more than he can use any building of wood and stone. Building or enlarging our place of worship may be necessary, but it should never take priority over developing spiritual leaders.

Remember that God's church is a community of believers, not a building of stone, brick, and wood. Do you worry more about the carpet in the hallway than about the people walking on it? Do you find yourself overly concerned about wear and tear on the building, while neglecting the people using it? While it is good to maintain the church building (as a responsible church member and good steward of God's resources), remember that people are infinitely more important.

BIBLE READING

[12]Then Solomon prayed, "O LORD, you have said that you would live in thick darkness. [13]But I have built a glorious Temple for you, where you can live forever!"

[14]Then the king turned around to the entire community of Israel standing before him and gave this blessing: [15]"Blessed be the LORD, the God of Israel, who has kept the promise he made to my father, David. [16]For he told my father, 'From the day I brought my people Israel out of Egypt, I have never chosen a city among the tribes of Israel as the place where a temple should be built to honor my name. But now I have chosen David to be king over my people.' "

[17]Then Solomon said, "My father, David, wanted to build this Temple to honor the name of the LORD, the God of Israel. [18]But the LORD told him, 'It is right for you to want to build the Temple to honor my name, [19]but you are not the one to do it. One of your sons will build it instead.'

[20]"And now the LORD has done what he promised, for I have become king in my father's place. I have built this Temple to honor the name of the LORD, the God of Israel. [21]And I have prepared a place there for the Ark, which contains the covenant that the LORD made with our ancestors when he brought them out of Egypt."   1 KINGS 8:12-21

GETTING TOO CLOSE

PREVIEW

Dagwood is always making a sandwich or taking a nap. Blondie is always hoping he will do something more productive—like fixing the sink. We laugh at the comic strip because it mirrors life. And we know that two people coming to marriage from two different directions can lead to bumps and even collisions.

This passage tells of Solomon's greatness and his downfall. His greatness was asking God to be with him and the people, and to bless them. Solomon's downfall involves a domestic problem—marriage doesn't work for him at all. As you read, determine to emulate Solomon's good decisions and to avoid the ones that led to disaster. You will also find cautions about indulging in luxuries and about flirting with false gods.

PERSONAL APPLICATION

Solomon had hundreds of wives. Most of these he married for political reasons, but eventually they exerted significant influence on Solomon and changed him. Unfortunately, most of Solomon's wives worshiped idols, and this put tremendous pressure on Solomon to do the same. Faced with such pressure, at first he *resisted* it, maintaining his own purity of faith while tolerating his wives' private preferences. Then Solomon *tolerated* a more widespread practice of idolatry throughout Israel. Finally, he involved himself in the idolatrous worship, *rationalizing* away the potential dangers to himself and to the kingdom. Solomon could handle great pressures in running the government, but he could not handle the pressure from his wives (1 Kings 11:4).

In marriage and in close friendships, it is difficult to resist pressure to compromise. Our love leads us to identify with the desires of those we care about. Because of this strong desire to please our loved ones, God tells his people not to marry those who do not share a commitment to him. Build your closest relationships with those who share your faith and values.

Bible Reading

[1]Now King Solomon loved many foreign women. Besides
Pharaoh's daughter, he married women from Moab, Ammon,
Edom, Sidon, and from among the Hittites. [2]The Lord had
clearly instructed his people not to intermarry with those
nations, because the women they married would lead them to
worship their gods. Yet Solomon insisted on loving them anyway.
[3]He had seven hundred wives and three hundred concubines.
And sure enough, they led his heart away from the Lord. [4]In
Solomon's old age, they turned his heart to worship their gods
instead of trusting only in the Lord his God, as his father,
David, had done. [5]Solomon worshiped Ashtoreth, the goddess of
the Sidonians, and Molech, the detestable god of the
Ammonites. [6]Thus, Solomon did what was evil in the Lord's
sight; he refused to follow the Lord completely, as his father,
David, had done. [7]On the Mount of Olives, east of Jerusalem, he
even built a shrine for Chemosh, the detestable god of Moab,
and another for Molech, the detestable god of the Ammonites.
[8]Solomon built such shrines for all his foreign wives to use for
burning incense and sacrificing to their gods.

[9]The Lord was very angry with Solomon, for his heart had
turned away from the Lord, the God of Israel, who had appeared
to him twice. [10]He had warned Solomon specifically about
worshiping other gods, but Solomon did not listen to the Lord's
command. [11]So now the Lord said to him, "Since you have not
kept my covenant and have disobeyed my laws, I will surely tear
the kingdom away from you and give it to one of your servants.
[12]But for the sake of your father, David, I will not do this while
you are still alive. I will take the kingdom away from your son.
[13]And even so, I will let him be king of one tribe, for the sake of
my servant David and for the sake of Jerusalem, my chosen city."

1 Kings 11:1-13

# BAD ADVICE

PREVIEW

When was the last time you got some bad advice? Did you have any clue that the counsel had cracks in it? Or was it your own foolish fault for listening in the first place?

In this reading, Solomon's death brings about a national crisis. After Solomon's successor, Rehoboam, listens to the bad advice of poor counselors, he makes unwise and unpopular decrees. The northern tribes of Israel then revolt and set up their own kingdom under Jeroboam. Only the southern tribes of Judah and Benjamin remain loyal to Rehoboam. We can't entirely blame the northern rebels for their actions—Rehoboam helps them along, whether he realizes it or not. As you read this passage, look for the strong lesson about seeking wise counsel and rejecting bad advice.

Other lessons in this section of Scripture include being careful in what you accept as messages from God; how *not* to pick church leaders; the consequences of flagrant disregard for God's commands; and what happens to those who don't learn from the mistakes of their parents (Baasha).

PERSONAL APPLICATION

At a time when he really needed it, Rehoboam asked for advice. That was a great idea, but he didn't carefully evaluate what he was told, nor did he weigh the quality of the advisors (1 Kings 12:6-14). It's no wonder that Rehoboam rejected the greater wisdom of his elders in favor of that of his peers. It's often difficult for those who are younger to listen to those who are older. The young may think that the old don't understand them, the current times, or anything, well enough. Or perhaps they just lack the humility to submit to their elders even though they see the wisdom of their counsel.

When receiving advice, carefully evaluate it, asking if it is realistic, workable, and consistent with biblical principles. The next time you ask for advice, determine if the results of following it will make improvements and give a positive solution or direction. Seek counsel from those who are wiser and more experienced. Advice is helpful only if it is consistent with God's standards.

BIBLE READING

¹Rehoboam went to Shechem, where all Israel had gathered to make him king. ²When Jeroboam son of Nebat heard of Solomon's death, he returned from Egypt, for he had fled to Egypt to escape from King Solomon. ³The leaders of Israel sent for Jeroboam, and the whole assembly of Israel went to speak with Rehoboam. ⁴"Your father was a hard master," they said. "Lighten the harsh labor demands and heavy taxes that your father imposed on us. Then we will be your loyal subjects."

⁵Rehoboam replied, "Give me three days to think this over. Then come back for my answer." So the people went away.

⁶Then King Rehoboam went to discuss the matter with the older men who had counseled his father, Solomon. "What is your advice?" he asked. "How should I answer these people?"

⁷The older counselors replied, "If you are willing to serve the people today and give them a favorable answer, they will always be your loyal subjects."

⁸But Rehoboam rejected the advice of the elders and instead asked the opinion of the young men who had grown up with him and who were now his advisers. ⁹"What is your advice?" he asked them. "How should I answer these people who want me to lighten the burdens imposed by my father?"

¹⁰The young men replied, "This is what you should tell those complainers: 'My little finger is thicker than my father's waist—if you think he was hard on you, just wait and see what I'll be like! ¹¹Yes, my father was harsh on you, but I'll be even harsher! My father used whips on you, but I'll use scorpions!' "

¹²Three days later, Jeroboam and all the people returned to hear Rehoboam's decision, just as the king had requested. ¹³But Rehoboam spoke harshly to them, for he rejected the advice of the older counselors ¹⁴and followed the counsel of his younger advisers. He told the people, "My father was harsh on you, but I'll be even harsher! My father used whips on you, but I'll use scorpions!"

1 KINGS 12:1-14

LET DOWN

PREVIEW

Sally is ready to quit her job. Her coworkers have shut her out, and she feels as if she gets no support from her boss. She has tried to endure the isolation and do her best, but after three years, the situation has not improved. She's thoroughly discouraged.

This is the first half of the story of Elijah's ministry. Elijah is one of Israel's most significant prophets, yet he fights great discouragement. In fact, it's more like depression or despair. "It's all over," he moans, and he really believes it. But God has a cure for Elijah's ills—check it out.

In this passage you will learn that God sends rescuers when they're needed, and that God's people can always get the resources to do what God commands them to do.

PERSONAL APPLICATION

Elijah fell into the depths of fatigue and discouragement immediately following two of his great spiritual triumphs: the defeat of the prophets of Baal and the answered prayer for rain. After experiencing God's astounding victory at Mount Carmel, Elijah ran for his life. Then, tired, lonely, and discouraged, he felt sorry for himself, believing that he was the only person left who was still true to God (1 Kings 19:10). To lead Elijah out of depression, God first allowed him to rest and to eat. Then God confronted Elijah with the need to return to his mission—to speak God's words in Israel. Elijah's battles were not over; there was still work for him to do (1 Kings 19:15-18).

Often discouragement sets in after great spiritual experiences, especially those requiring physical effort or involving great emotion. When you feel let down after a great spiritual experience, remember that God's purpose for your life is not yet over. When you are tempted to think that you are the only one remaining faithful to a task, don't wallow in self-pity—it will only dilute the good you are doing. Be assured that even if you don't know who they are, others are faithfully obeying God and fulfilling their duties as well. God is at work in the world as well as in your life.

BIBLE READING

³Elijah . . . went . . . ⁴alone into the desert, traveling all day. He sat down under a solitary broom tree and prayed that he might die. "I have had enough, LORD," he said. "Take my life, for I am no better than my ancestors."

⁷Then the angel of the LORD came again and touched him and said, "Get up and eat some more, for there is a long journey ahead of you."

⁸So he got up and ate and drank, and the food gave him enough strength to travel forty days and forty nights to Mount Sinai, the mountain of God. ⁹There he came to a cave, where he spent the night.

¹¹"Go out and stand before me on the mountain," the LORD told him. And as Elijah stood there, the LORD passed by, and a mighty windstorm hit the mountain. It was such a terrible blast that the rocks were torn loose, but the LORD was not in the wind. After the wind there was an earthquake, but the LORD was not in the earthquake. ¹²And after the earthquake there was a fire, but the LORD was not in the fire. And after the fire there was the sound of a gentle whisper. ¹³When Elijah heard it, he wrapped his face in his cloak and went out and stood at the entrance of the cave.

¹⁵Then the LORD told him, "Go back the way you came, and travel to the wilderness of Damascus. When you arrive there, anoint Hazael to be king of Aram. ¹⁶Then anoint Jehu son of Nimshi to be king of Israel, and anoint Elisha son of Shaphat from Abel-meholah to replace you as my prophet. ¹⁷Anyone who escapes from Hazael will be killed by Jehu, and those who escape Jehu will be killed by Elisha! ¹⁸Yet I will preserve seven thousand others in Israel who have never bowed to Baal or kissed him!"

1 KINGS 19:3-9, 11-18

$\mathscr{P}$OLITE CONVERSATION

PREVIEW

Polite conversation is designed to insulate us from certain forms of the truth. How many cashiers, for example, total strangers to you, really need to know how you are doing that day? But most people confine polite conversation to contacts with the public. Only close friends get to hear—and tell—the truth.

There's precious little polite conversation here in Micaiah's prophesies against Ahab. This is truth straight from God to Ahab—no glossy public coating in sight. If Ahab really knew God, he would realize that he's hearing from a friend. Instead he takes offense, and the warnings have no effect. For us, this story means "CAUTION, Negative Examples Here."

Also, don't miss the point of the judgments in this passage: things can get rough when we refuse to listen to God, and they can get downright deadly when we keep it up.

PERSONAL APPLICATION

"I will go out and inspire all Ahab's prophets to speak lies" (1 Kings 22:20-22). Does God allow angels to entice people to do evil? No. What Micaiah saw was either a picture of a real incident in heaven, or a parable of what was happening on earth—illustrating that the seductive influence of the false prophets would be part of God's judgment upon Ahab (22:23). Whether or not God sent an angel in disguise, he used the system of false prophets to snare Ahab in his sin. The lying spirit (22:22) symbolized the mind-set of these prophets who told the king only what he wanted to hear.

Don't be like Ahab! Don't surround yourself with people who only tell you what you want to hear, or you may make it impossible to hear the truth from anyone. The very people you trust with your life may lead you right into a dead end. Instead, seek out people who will be honest with you. Then when they tell you the hard truth, accept it graciously.

BIBLE READING

¹³Meanwhile, the messenger who went to get Micaiah said to him, "Look, all the prophets are promising victory for the king. Be sure that you agree with them and promise success."

¹⁴But Micaiah replied, "As surely as the LORD lives, I will say only what the LORD tells me to say."

¹⁵When Micaiah arrived before the king, Ahab asked him, "Micaiah, should we go to war against Ramoth-gilead or not?"

And Micaiah replied, "Go right ahead! The LORD will give the king a glorious victory!"

¹⁶But the king replied sharply, "How many times must I demand that you speak only the truth when you speak for the LORD?"

¹⁷So Micaiah told him, "In a vision I saw all Israel scattered on the mountains, like sheep without a shepherd. And the LORD said, 'Their master has been killed. Send them home in peace.' "

¹⁸"Didn't I tell you?" the king of Israel said to Jehoshaphat. "He does it every time. He never prophesies anything but bad news for me."

¹⁹Then Micaiah continued, "Listen to what the LORD says! I saw the LORD sitting on his throne with all the armies of heaven around him, on his right and on his left. ²⁰And the LORD said, 'Who can entice Ahab to go into battle against Ramoth-gilead so that he can be killed there?' There were many suggestions, ²¹until finally a spirit approached the LORD and said, 'I can do it!'

²²" 'How will you do this?' the LORD asked.

"And the spirit replied, 'I will go out and inspire all Ahab's prophets to speak lies.'

" 'You will succeed,' said the LORD. 'Go ahead and do it.'

²³"So you see, the LORD has put a lying spirit in the mouths of your prophets. For the LORD has determined disaster for you."

1 KINGS 22:13-23

DEMANDING SOME RESPECT

PREVIEW

Cures are seldom pleasant. Usually they involve taking pills, getting stuck by needles, having surgery, enduring nauseating side effects, or getting into embarrassing positions. It's no wonder our aversion to doctors and dentists can be as strong as our dependence on them.

In this reading, Naaman has great trouble with the cure offered to him, even though his disease is terminal, not to mention degrading. The problem is not needles or side effects—it's something else. As you read, learn a lesson about obeying God and finding his sure cures.

This section of Scripture is loaded with other lessons, such as talking about your faith; making fun of God's appointed messengers; listening to God's appointed messengers; showing concern for hurting people; blaming others; and sharing good news with others.

PERSONAL APPLICATION

Naaman, a great military hero, was used to getting respect and was outraged when Elisha treated him like an ordinary person (2 Kings 5:9-15). A proud man, he expected royal treatment. To wash in a great river would be one thing, but the Jordan was small and dirty. To wash there, Naaman thought, was beneath a man of his position. But Naaman had to humble himself and obey Elisha's commands in order to be healed.

Obedience to God begins with humility. We must believe that his way is better than our own. We may not always understand his ways, but by humbly obeying, we will receive his blessings.

When confronted with a choice of doing something God's way (that may seem unusual or could prove to be embarrassing) or your way (that may seem logical and would certainly be easier), remember that (1) God's ways are best; (2) God wants your obedience more than anything else; and (3) God can use anything to accomplish his purposes.

BIBLE READING

⁹So Naaman went with his horses and chariots and waited at the door of Elisha's house. ¹⁰But Elisha sent a messenger out to him with this message: "Go and wash yourself seven times in the Jordan River. Then your skin will be restored, and you will be healed of leprosy."

¹¹But Naaman became angry and stalked away. "I thought he would surely come out to meet me!" he said. "I expected him to wave his hand over the leprosy and call on the name of the LORD his God and heal me! ¹²Aren't the Abana River and Pharpar River of Damascus better than all the rivers of Israel put together? Why shouldn't I wash in them and be healed?" So Naaman turned and went away in a rage.

¹³But his officers tried to reason with him and said, "Sir, if the prophet had told you to do some great thing, wouldn't you have done it? So you should certainly obey him when he says simply to go and wash and be cured!" ¹⁴So Naaman went down to the Jordan River and dipped himself seven times, as the man of God had instructed him. And his flesh became as healthy as a young child's, and he was healed!

¹⁵Then Naaman and his entire party went back to find the man of God. They stood before him, and Naaman said, "I know at last that there is no God in all the world except in Israel. Now please accept my gifts." 2 KINGS 5:9-15

OLERANCE

PREVIEW

In 1908, Israel Zangwill, a British Jew, published *The Melting Pot,* a play about America that portrayed it as, well, a huge melting pot. He observed that people from all over the world go to America, rub shoulders with each other, and mix until their individual ways of life disappear. What ends up inside the vat bears no resemblance to what went in. It's a whole new concoction—like a cake mix.

People try to do that with religion, too, melting and stirring until the result is a personal belief system that looks nothing like any of the original ingredients. This reading is about several of the kings of Israel and Judah: Jehoram, Ahaziah, Jehu, Joram, and Ahab. They have a lot in common—most notably that they become experts on cooking up new religions in the name of tolerance. Are these really God's people? Learn from their bad examples.

The other lessons in this passage fall into two categories: when to seek peace and when to seek war.

PERSONAL APPLICATION

Israel was supposed to be intolerant of any religion that did not worship the true God. The religions of surrounding nations were evil and corrupt. They were designed to destroy life, not uphold it. Israel was God's special nation, chosen to be an example of what was right. Instead of obeying God, however, Israel's kings, priests, and elders first tolerated and then incorporated surrounding pagan beliefs. This led to their becoming apathetic and even hostile toward God's way (2 Kings 10:31).

Be completely intolerant of any sin—especially false religion. You should always be tolerant of *people* who hold differing views, but you should never tolerate or follow any belief or practice that is contrary to God's Word. It will lead you away from God and his standards for living.

BIBLE READING

²⁰Then Jehu ordered, "Prepare a solemn assembly to worship Baal!" So they did. ²¹He sent messengers throughout all Israel summoning those who worshiped Baal. They all came and filled the temple of Baal from one end to the other. ²²And Jehu instructed the keeper of the wardrobe, "Be sure that every worshiper of Baal wears one of these robes." So robes were given to them.

²³Then Jehu went into the temple of Baal with Jehonadab son of Recab. Jehu said to the worshipers of Baal, "Make sure that only those who worship Baal are here. Don't let anyone in who worships the LORD!" ²⁴So they were all inside the temple to offer sacrifices and burnt offerings. Now Jehu had surrounded the building with eighty of his men and had warned them, "If you let anyone escape, you will pay for it with your own life."

²⁵As soon as Jehu had finished sacrificing the burnt offering, he commanded his guards and officers, "Go in and kill all of them. Don't let a single one escape!" So they killed them all with their swords, and the guards and officers dragged their bodies outside. Then Jehu's men went into the fortress of the temple of Baal. ²⁶They dragged out the sacred pillar used in the worship of Baal and destroyed it. ²⁷They broke down the sacred pillar of Baal and wrecked the temple of Baal, converting it into a public toilet. That is what it is used for to this day. ²⁸Thus, Jehu destroyed every trace of Baal worship from Israel. ²⁹He did not, however, destroy the gold calves at Bethel and Dan, the great sin that Jeroboam son of Nebat had led Israel to commit.

³⁰Nonetheless the LORD said to Jehu, "You have done well in following my instructions to destroy the family of Ahab. Because of this I will cause your descendants to be the kings of Israel down to the fourth generation." ³¹But Jehu did not obey the law of the LORD, the God of Israel, with all his heart. He refused to turn from the sins of idolatry that Jeroboam had led Israel to commit.   2 KINGS 10:20-31

*F*INISHING THE WORK

PREVIEW

It seems that every workplace depends on a humming core of border-line workaholics. These people have a true devotion to their work. Both master and slave to their jobs, they work because they *want* to. Who do you know like that?

You will find out more about the kings of Israel and Judah in this reading. The most notable is King Joash—an actual good king (there weren't many)—who sets out to finish repairing the temple. His crew can't find the time to do their jobs, however, so Joash has to make some new assignments. Read this passage and learn about the importance of doing God's work.

See if you can find insights on going far enough when making changes.

PERSONAL APPLICATION

Much had to be done to repair the temple, but many years had gone by without progress. The priests simply hadn't done any of the work. So King Joash took them off the task and gave the assignment to laypeople. As it turns out, these people proved to be exceedingly honest and dedicated—to the point of not having to account for the money given to them for the job. What a contrast between these workmen and the priests (2 Kings 12:8, 15)! As trained men of God, the priests should have been responsible and concerned, for the temple was their life's work. But they did not have the necessary commitment.

God's work is best accomplished by people devoted to it. Don't let your lack of training or position stop you from making a solid contribution to God's kingdom. Give your energy wherever it can be used to carry out his work. What task does God have for you to do today?

BIBLE READING

⁴One day King Joash said to the priests, "Collect all the money brought as a sacred offering to the Lord's Temple, whether it is a regular assessment, a payment of vows, or a voluntary gift. ⁵Let the priests take some of that money to pay for whatever repairs are needed at the Temple."

⁶But by the twenty-third year of Joash's reign, the priests still had not repaired the Temple. ⁷So King Joash called for Jehoiada and the other priests and asked them, "Why haven't you repaired the Temple? Don't use any more gifts for your own needs. From now on, it must all be spent on getting the Temple into good condition." ⁸So the priests agreed not to collect any more money from the people, and they also agreed not to undertake the repairs of the Temple themselves.

⁹Then Jehoiada the priest bored a hole in the lid of a large chest and set it on the right-hand side of the altar at the entrance of the Temple of the LORD. The priests guarding the entrance put all of the people's contributions into the chest. ¹⁰Whenever the chest became full, the court secretary and the high priest counted the money that had been brought to the Lord's Temple and put it into bags. ¹¹Then they gave the money to the construction supervisors, who used it to pay the people working on the Lord's Temple—the carpenters, the builders, ¹²the masons, and the stonecutters. They also used the money to buy timber and cut stone for repairing the Lord's Temple, and they paid any other expenses related to the Temple's restoration.

¹³The money brought to the Temple was not used for making silver cups, lamp snuffers, basins, trumpets, or other articles of gold or silver for the Temple of the LORD. ¹⁴It was paid out to the workmen, who used it for the Temple repairs. ¹⁵No accounting was required from the construction supervisors, because they were honest and faithful workers.   2 KINGS 12:4-15

ONEY EQUALS POWER

PREVIEW

If you have enough money, you can go places, buy things, hire lawyers, and protect yourself in ways that others can't. In our society, it seems as though money is power. In what ways have you seen this to be true? How has that been frustrating to you?

This reading continues the (mostly) sad story of the kings of Israel and Judah. Here the spotlight falls on Jeroboam II, who gets extremely rich. Success is his middle name. Yet in this passage, we see the pitfalls of money and power.

You will also notice these other cautions: the problem of overrating oneself; the difference it can make when leaders love and obey God; remaking God to suit our preferences; and discerning when imitation is *not* flattering.

PERSONAL APPLICATION

Jeroboam II had no devotion to God, yet under his warlike policies and skillful administration, Israel enjoyed more national power and material prosperity than at any time since the days of Solomon (2 Kings 14:28). God's prophets, Amos and Hosea, however, tell us what was really happening within the kingdom (Hosea 13:4-8; Amos 6:11-14). Because Jeroboam's administration ignored the policies of justice and fairness, the rich became richer and the poor, poorer. The people became self-centered, relying more on their power, security, and possessions than on God. The poor were so oppressed that they found it difficult to believe God cared about their plight.

Material prosperity is not always an indication of God's blessing; it can also be a result of self-centeredness. If you are experiencing prosperity, remember that God holds you accountable for how you attain success and how you use your wealth. Everything you have belongs to him. Use God's gifts with his interests in mind.

BIBLE READING

²³Jeroboam II, the son of Jehoash, began to rule over Israel in the fifteenth year of King Amaziah's reign in Judah. Jeroboam reigned in Samaria forty-one years. ²⁴He did what was evil in the Lord's sight. He refused to turn from the sins of idolatry that Jeroboam son of Nebat had led Israel to commit. ²⁵Jeroboam II recovered the territories of Israel between Lebo-hamath and the Dead Sea, just as the LORD, the God of Israel, had promised through Jonah son of Amittai, the prophet from Gath-hepher. ²⁶For the LORD saw the bitter suffering of everyone in Israel, and how they had absolutely no one to help them. ²⁷And because the LORD had not said he would blot out the name of Israel completely, he used Jeroboam II, the son of Jehoash, to save them.

²⁸The rest of the events in the reign of Jeroboam II and all his deeds, including the extent of his power, his wars, and how he recovered for Israel both Damascus and Hamath, which had belonged to Judah, are recorded in The Book of the History of the Kings of Israel. ²⁹When Jeroboam II died, he was buried with his ancestors, the kings of Israel. Then his son Zechariah became the next king. 2 KINGS 14:23-29

OUNTERFEITS

PREVIEW

How do you know that the money in your wallet isn't counterfeit? You probably don't—that's the genius of counterfeits; they can pass for the real thing, fooling all but the most determined experts.

This section of Scripture focuses on kings of Judah, mostly Hezekiah and Manasseh. King Manasseh makes up his own religion and passes it off as legitimate. But this just means that Israel is going spiritually bankrupt. As you read, look for the differences between true and false religions.

In this passage, you will also find positive lessons from Hezekiah: standing up to bullies and people who try to intimidate you; an object lesson for the arrogant; and the difference one person can make.

PERSONAL APPLICATION

Manasseh was an evil king, and he angered God with his sin (2 Kings 21:6). Listed among his sins are occult practices, sorcery, divination, and consulting mediums and spiritists. These acts were strictly forbidden by God (Leviticus 19:31; Deuteronomy 18:9-13) because they demonstrated a lack of faith in him, involved sinful actions, and opened the door to demonic influences.

Today, many books, television shows, and games emphasize fortune-telling, seances, and other occult practices. Some people seem almost obsessed with knowing and controlling the future. Instead of trusting God, they read their horoscopes or consult their personal psychic. Others actually seek power through seances, black magic, and mysterious satanic rituals.

Don't let the desire to know what will happen to you lead you toward the occult. And don't believe that superstition is harmless. Occult practices are counterfeits of God's power and are based on a system of beliefs totally opposed to him.

BIBLE READING

¹Manasseh . . . ²did what was evil in the Lord's sight, imitating the detestable practices of the pagan nations whom the LORD had driven from the land ahead of the Israelites. ³He rebuilt the pagan shrines his father, Hezekiah, had destroyed. He constructed altars for Baal and set up an Asherah pole, just as King Ahab of Israel had done. He also bowed before all the forces of heaven and worshiped them. ⁴He even built pagan altars in the Temple of the LORD, the place where the LORD had said his name should be honored. ⁵He built these altars for all the forces of heaven in both courtyards of the Lord's Temple. ⁶Manasseh even sacrificed his own son in the fire. He practiced sorcery and divination, and he consulted with mediums and psychics. He did much that was evil in the Lord's sight, arousing his anger.

⁷Manasseh even took an Asherah pole he had made and set it up in the Temple, the very place where the LORD had told David and his son Solomon: "My name will be honored here forever in this Temple and in Jerusalem—the city I have chosen from among all the other tribes of Israel. ⁸If the Israelites will obey my commands—the whole law that was given through my servant Moses—I will not send them into exile from this land that I gave their ancestors." ⁹But the people refused to listen, and Manasseh led them to do even more evil than the pagan nations whom the LORD had destroyed when the Israelites entered the land.

¹⁰Then the LORD said through his servants the prophets: ¹¹"King Manasseh of Judah has done many detestable things. He is even more wicked than the Amorites, who lived in this land before Israel. He has led the people of Judah into idolatry. ¹²So this is what the LORD, the God of Israel, says: I will bring such disaster on Jerusalem and Judah that the ears of those who hear about it will tingle with horror."   2 KINGS 21:1-12

CELEBRATION

PREVIEW

The lights go out and everybody sings the familiar song as the cake enters the room. Then the partygoers gather around the center of attention. "Make a wish!" somebody says, and during a brief pause the birthday girl stares at the candles and thinks, then takes a deep breath and blows. Soon the room is a paradise of cake and ice cream.

This reading concludes the focus on Judah's kings. It's like a sandwich, with Judah's celebration right in the middle. From facing up to their sins at the beginning to getting hauled off into captivity, it's quite exciting at both ends.

In this passage, you will also learn that grief isn't all bad—sometimes it's the best thing that can happen to you; how to start over; and the painful consequences of poor choices.

PERSONAL APPLICATION

When Josiah rediscovered the meaning and significance of the Passover celebration in the Book of the Covenant, he ordered everyone to observe the ceremonies exactly as they were prescribed (2 Kings 23:21-23). The Passover was to have been celebrated yearly in remembrance of the nation's deliverance from slavery in Egypt (see Exodus 12), but it had not been celebrated "since the time when the judges ruled in Israel, throughout all the years of the kings of Israel and Judah" (23:22).

One common misconception holds that God is against celebration and parties, and that he wants to take all the fun out of life. In reality, God wants to give us life in its fullness (see John 10:10), and those who love him have the most to celebrate—especially when we remember all that he has done for us.

Make Christian holidays special. And look for other ways to celebrate God's goodness and blessings with your family and loved ones.

BIBLE READING

¹Then the king summoned all the leaders of Judah and Jerusalem. ²And the king went up to the Temple of the LORD with all the people of Judah and Jerusalem, and the priests, and the prophets—all the people from the least to the greatest. There the king read to them the entire Book of the Covenant that had been found in the Lord's Temple. ³The king took his place of authority beside the pillar and renewed the covenant in the Lord's presence. He pledged to obey the LORD by keeping all his commands, regulations, and laws with all his heart and soul. In this way, he confirmed all the terms of the covenant that were written in the scroll, and all the people pledged themselves to the covenant.

²¹King Josiah then issued this order to all the people: "You must celebrate the Passover to the LORD your God, as it is written in the Book of the Covenant." ²²There had not been a Passover celebration like that since the time when the judges ruled in Israel, throughout all the years of the kings of Israel and Judah. ²³This Passover was celebrated to the LORD in Jerusalem during the eighteenth year of King Josiah's reign.

²⁴Josiah also exterminated the mediums and psychics, the household gods, and every other kind of idol worship, both in Jerusalem and throughout the land of Judah. He did this in obedience to all the laws written in the scroll that Hilkiah the priest had found in the Lord's Temple. ²⁵Never before had there been a king like Josiah, who turned to the LORD with all his heart and soul and strength, obeying all the laws of Moses. And there has never been a king like him since.   2 KINGS 23:1-3, 21-25

N MEMORY

PREVIEW

Everyone leaves behind at least one legacy at death—the memories that others have of him or her. Each person leaves a name and a face, plus some experiences that a few close friends will remember long afterward. What would you want your loved ones to memorialize about you? How would you like to be remembered?

In this dateless family tree of mostly unpronounceable names, very few people are remembered for anything more than their name. But here and there, a note surfaces about a particular person. Jabez, for example, left an impression on the author of Chronicles, and to be recognized in this way in such a massive genealogy says something important—there's a lesson to learn here.

This list contains other lessons from history as well: some people make a mark for good; some leave a trail of wreckage; and all leave behind a reputation—even if it's a blank one.

PERSONAL APPLICATION

The Bible records many heroes in Israel's history. Yet Jabez is remembered for a prayer request rather than a heroic act (1 Chronicles 4:9-10). In his prayer, Jabez asked God to do four things: (1) bless him, (2) help him in his work ("extend my lands"), (3) be with him in all he did, and (4) protect him from evil and harm. Jabez acknowledged God as the true center of his work and the protector of his life.

When we pray for God's blessing, we should also pray that we will rightfully regard him as Lord over everything we do—our work, our family time, and our recreation.

Do you want God's blessing on your life? Do you want to be remembered as a "hero"? Obey God in your daily responsibilities. That is heroic living, and it's something worth being remembered for.

BIBLE READING

⁷Achan son of Carmi, one of Zerah's descendants, brought disaster on Israel by taking plunder that had been set apart for the LORD.

⁴:⁹There was a man named Jabez who was more distinguished than any of his brothers. His mother named him Jabez because his birth had been so painful. ¹⁰He was the one who prayed to the God of Israel, "Oh, that you would bless me and extend my lands! Please be with me in all that I do, and keep me from all trouble and pain!" And God granted him his request.

⁵:¹The oldest son of Israel was Reuben. But since he dishonored his father by sleeping with one of his father's concubines, his birthright was given to the sons of his brother Joseph. For this reason, Reuben is not listed in the genealogy as the firstborn son. ²It was the descendants of Judah that became the most powerful tribe and provided a ruler for the nation, but the birthright belonged to Joseph.

¹⁸There were 44,760 skilled warriors in the armies of Reuben, Gad, and the half-tribe of Manasseh. They were all skilled in combat and armed with shields, swords, and bows. ¹⁹They waged war against the Hagrites, the Jeturites, the Naphishites, and the Nodabites. ²⁰They cried out to God during the battle, and he answered their prayer because they trusted in him. So the Hagrites and all their allies were defeated.

1 CHRONICLES 1:7; 4:9-10; 5:1-2, 18-20

HALF EMPTY, HALF FULL

PREVIEW

When you see a glass filled to its halfway mark, is it half empty or half full? In fairness, the answer probably has more to do with how thirsty you are. And whether you see the glass as half empty or half full, you're still only getting half a glass of water.

This reading tells us about the death of King Saul, the halfway man. Even in dying Saul makes a bad choice. Was Saul half empty or half full? You decide.

What matters here is that his devotion to God is halfhearted. As you read, note how Saul's lackluster devotion influences his actions and leadership as king—in the end leading to severe consequences for himself and his family.

PERSONAL APPLICATION

Saul made two mistakes in the way he lived—he actively did wrong, and he failed to do right (1 Chronicles 10:13-14). He actively did wrong by disobeying God's instructions (see 1 Samuel 13:1-14; 15:1-23). He passively failed to do right by neglecting to ask God for guidance as he ran the kingdom.

Our responsibility to obey God is much the same—both passive and active. It is not enough just to avoid what is wrong; we need to actively pursue what is right. How can we do this? We can avoid doing wrong by keeping God's commandments—worshiping God alone, telling the truth, being faithful to a husband or wife, being content with what we have, loving our enemies. We can actively pursue what is right by seeking God's guidance through prayer and his Word. In addition, we should take advantage of opportunities to serve God and others.

Bible Reading

¹Now the Philistines attacked Israel, forcing the Israelites to flee. Many were slaughtered on the slopes of Mount Gilboa. ²The Philistines closed in on Saul and his sons, and they killed three of his sons—Jonathan, Abinadab, and Malkishua. ³The fighting grew very fierce around Saul, and the Philistine archers caught up with him and wounded him severely. ⁴Saul groaned to his armor bearer, "Take your sword and run me through before these pagan Philistines come and humiliate me." But his armor bearer was afraid and would not do it. So Saul took his own sword and fell on it. ⁵When his armor bearer realized that Saul was dead, he fell on his own sword and died. ⁶So Saul and his three sons died there together, bringing his dynasty to an end.

⁷When the Israelites in the Jezreel Valley saw that their army had been routed and that Saul and his sons were dead, they abandoned their towns and fled. So the Philistines moved in and occupied their towns.

⁸The next day when the Philistines went out to strip the dead, they found the bodies of Saul and his sons on Mount Gilboa. ⁹So they stripped off Saul's armor and cut off his head. Then they proclaimed the news of Saul's death before their idols and to the people throughout the land of Philistia. ¹⁰They placed his armor in the temple of their gods, and they fastened his head to the wall in the temple of Dagon.

¹¹But when the people of Jabesh-gilead heard what the Philistines had done to Saul, ¹²their warriors went out and brought the bodies of Saul and his three sons back to Jabesh. Then they buried their remains beneath the oak tree at Jabesh, and they fasted for seven days.

¹³So Saul died because he was unfaithful to the LORD. He failed to obey the Lord's command, and he even consulted a medium ¹⁴instead of asking the LORD for guidance. So the LORD killed him and turned his kingdom over to David son of Jesse.

1 Chronicles 10:1-14

CELEBRATION TIME!

PREVIEW

Marguerite can't understand Robert's enthusiasm for football; he cannot understand her passion for reading. That's the way it often is from person to person—each individual gets excited over different experiences and for different reasons. What gets you excited?

In this reading, bringing the ark of the covenant to Jerusalem is cause for great excitement and celebration, and David dances for joy! But not everyone gets excited about the ark's debut in Jerusalem. In fact, one person is more preoccupied with despising David and his enthusiasm than in celebrating the ark's arrival. As you read this passage, think about worship and consider how you might celebrate God's entrance into your life.

There are other things besides the debut of the ark to get excited about in this reading. Note, for example, David's victories over the Philistines and his prayer of thanks to God for his goodness and mercy.

PERSONAL APPLICATION

David worshiped God with music and exuberant dancing (1 Chronicles 13:8; 15:29). Because of his enthusiasm, David's wife, Michal, was disgusted with him. Today, some people may think that those who are more expressive in their worship of God look foolish. At the same time, those who are reserved in their worship may appear uninspired or somber.

Whether we fall into one of these categories or strike a balance between the two, we should not be critical of how others worship God, for we do not know their hearts like God does. On the other hand, we should not be concerned with what others think of us as we worship. We should instead use whatever expressions seem appropriate in pouring out our heartfelt praise and worship to God.

Don't be afraid to worship God with whatever expressions seem appropriate. What do you need in your life, more serious reflection or more joyous celebration?

BIBLE READING

²⁵Then David and the leaders of Israel and the generals of the army went to the home of Obed-edom to bring the Ark of the Lord's covenant up to Jerusalem with a great celebration. ²⁶And because God was clearly helping the Levites as they carried the Ark of the Lord's covenant, they sacrificed seven bulls and seven lambs. ²⁷David was dressed in a robe of fine linen, as were the Levites who carried the Ark, the singers, and Kenaniah the song leader. David was also wearing a priestly tunic. ²⁸So all Israel brought up the Ark of the Lord's covenant to Jerusalem with shouts of joy, the blowing of horns and trumpets, the crashing of cymbals, and loud playing on harps and lyres.

²⁹But as the Ark of the Lord's covenant entered the City of David, Michal, the daughter of Saul, looked down from her window. When she saw King David dancing and leaping for joy, she was filled with contempt for him.   1 CHRONICLES 15:25-29

CREDIT WHERE CREDIT IS DUE

PREVIEW

Think of the people who have helped you get where you are today—those who have helped you succeed or who have taught you the skills you use every day. Who are they? How did they help you?

This is the story of some of David's military exploits. He's at war with the surrounding nations, including the Moabites, the Arameans, the Ammonites, and the Philistines. He's very successful, indeed, and that calls for handing out some accolades to the people who have helped him get there. See what you can learn about giving credit and expressing gratitude to the One who gives every success.

In this passage, David also shows us ways we need to show restraint—not being overly suspicious of others and avoiding overconfidence in ourselves.

PERSONAL APPLICATION

When David received gifts from King Toi for successfully defeating King Hadadezer's army, he dedicated them to God, realizing that all of the gifts had come from God and were to be used for him (1 Chronicles 18:9-11). In a similar way, the list of battles in this chapter makes it clear that *God* had given David victory after victory (18:13).

It is easy to think that our successes and material blessings are the result of our abilities and hard work rather than gifts coming from a loving God (see James 1:17). Unbelieving people think that victory and success come from their own skills and a little luck. But David acknowledged God's role in his success and prosperity, and so should we.

What has God given you? Dedicate all your gifts and resources to him, and use them for his service. He will lead you in the method you should use. The first step is to be willing. Don't take credit for the work God does.

BIBLE READING

¹After this, David subdued and humbled the Philistines by conquering Gath and its surrounding towns. ²David also conquered the land of Moab, and the Moabites became David's subjects and brought him tribute money.

³Then David destroyed the forces of King Hadadezer of Zobah, as far as Hamath, when Hadadezer marched out to strengthen his control along the Euphrates River. ⁴David captured one thousand chariots, seven thousand charioteers, and twenty thousand foot soldiers. Then he crippled all but one hundred of the chariot horses.

⁵When Arameans from Damascus arrived to help Hadadezer, David killed twenty-two thousand of them. ⁶Then he placed several army garrisons in Damascus, the Aramean capital, and the Arameans became David's subjects and brought him tribute money. So the LORD gave David victory wherever he went. ⁷David brought the gold shields of Hadadezer's officers to Jerusalem, ⁸along with a large amount of bronze from Hadadezer's cities of Tebah and Cun. Later Solomon melted the bronze and used it for the Temple. He molded it into the bronze Sea, the pillars, and the various bronze utensils used at the Temple.

⁹When King Toi of Hamath heard that David had destroyed the army of King Hadadezer of Zobah, ¹⁰he sent his son Joram to congratulate David on his success. Hadadezer and Toi had long been enemies, and there had been many wars between them. Joram presented David with many gifts of gold, silver, and bronze. ¹¹King David dedicated all these gifts to the LORD, along with the silver and gold he had taken from the other nations he had subdued—Edom, Moab, Ammon, Philistia, and Amalek.

1 CHRONICLES 18:1-11

A WORTHY CAUSE

PREVIEW

Just about everyone is willing to share their money and time with others—with a church, a charity, or even a relative in need. Charitable organizations count on these donations. But most people have one kind of need to which they are sensitive and will give a little more, a little extra; the kind of need for which a person will *sacrifice* and not just give a token amount. What sort of need gets that kind of response from you?

In this reading, David arranges for the building of the temple. Many of David's military officers show grand support of this effort by giving generously from their own pockets. They've worked hard for their money. They deserve it. They don't have to do this. But they're not thinking of their pocketbooks, because this isn't just any other fund-raising drive. As you read this passage, learn a lesson about giving.

This portion of Scripture also teaches about preparing the way for our children and appreciating the different roles in God's work.

PERSONAL APPLICATION

As David went about securing his place as king, his victories meant there were spoils of war to divide among his soldiers. War plunder rightfully belonged to the victorious army, but some of the Israelite military commanders expressed their dedication to God by generously donating a portion of their plunder to help pay for the repair of the temple (1 Chronicles 26:27).

Some people give a token amount to church and other worthy causes—as though they are tipping God. Gifts like that come out of a feeling of obligation, and not out of love and devotion. Like these commanders, God's people today should think of what we *can* give, rather than only what we are obligated to give.

Is your giving a matter of rejoicing rather than duty? Consider all that God has given to you. Then give to his work as a response of joy and love for him.

BIBLE READING

²⁰Other Levites, led by Ahijah, were in charge of the treasuries of the house of God and the storerooms. ²¹From the family of Libni in the clan of Gershon, Jehiel was the leader. ²²The sons of Jehiel, Zetham and his brother Joel, were in charge of the treasuries of the house of the LORD.

²³These are the leaders that descended from Amram, Izhar, Hebron, and Uzziel:

²⁴From the clan of Amram, Shebuel was a descendant of Gershom son of Moses. He was the chief officer of the treasuries. ²⁵His relatives through Eliezer were Rehabiah, Jeshaiah, Joram, Zicri, and Shelomoth.

²⁶Shelomoth and his relatives were in charge of the treasuries that held all the things dedicated to the LORD by King David, the family leaders, and the generals and captains and other officers of the army. ²⁷These men had dedicated some of the plunder they had gained in battle to maintain the house of the LORD. ²⁸Shelomoth and his relatives also cared for the items dedicated to the LORD by Samuel the seer, Saul son of Kish, Abner son of Ner, and Joab son of Zeruiah. All the other dedicated items were in their care, too.

1 CHRONICLES 26:20-28

T'S A SECRET

PREVIEW

Who knows you better than anybody else? In answer to that question, some people would name a parent; others a spouse or a friend. Perhaps you have managed to escape that kind of scrutiny, so *nobody* really knows you well—your motives, desires, thoughts, feelings, and dreams.

Whether you've opened your life up to someone or have kept it a secret from others, there is one person that knows you intimately—God. In this reading, David reminds his son Solomon of this and cautions him to be open and honest with the Lord.

Nobody knows us better than God, David reminds his son, so why try to hide? His advice to Solomon is also great advice to us.

Other lessons in David's speech include the connections between present obedience to God and the future; how to give; and humility.

PERSONAL APPLICATION

David pointed out to his son Solomon that "the Lord sees every heart" (1 Chronicles 28:9). In other words, nothing can be hidden from God. He sees and understands everything: our desires, thoughts, motives, feelings, and dreams. David had found this out the hard way when God sent Nathan to expose David's sins of adultery and murder (see 2 Samuel 12). Out of this experience, David told Solomon to be completely open with God and dedicated to him.

God's total knowledge of us can cause us fear and dread because we cannot hide our sinful thoughts and actions from him—we are totally vulnerable. But his knowledge of us can also cause great comfort and joy because he loves us—the *real* us—and wants the very best for us.

Rejoice in the fact that God knows your deepest needs and longings, and that he desires a better life for you than you could ever imagine. Be honest with him—express your doubts and questions, confess your sinful thoughts and actions, pour out your feelings and ask him for help.

BIBLE READING

¹David summoned all his officials to Jerusalem—the leaders of the tribes, the commanders of the twelve army divisions, the other generals and captains, the overseers of the royal property and livestock, the palace officials, the mighty men, and all the other warriors in the kingdom. ²David rose and stood before them and addressed them as follows: "My brothers and my people! It was my desire to build a temple where the Ark of the Lord's covenant, God's footstool, could rest permanently. I made the necessary preparations for building it, ³but God said to me, 'You must not build a temple to honor my name, for you are a warrior and have shed much blood.'

⁴"Yet the LORD, the God of Israel, has chosen me from among all my father's family to be king over Israel forever. For he has chosen the tribe of Judah to rule, and from among the families of Judah, he chose my father's family. And from among my father's sons, the LORD was pleased to make me king over all Israel. ⁵And from among my sons—for the LORD has given me many children—he chose Solomon to succeed me on the throne of his kingdom of Israel. ⁶He said to me, 'Your son Solomon will build my Temple and its courtyards, for I have chosen him as my son, and I will be his father. ⁷And if he continues to obey my commands and regulations as he does now, I will make his kingdom last forever.' ⁸So now, with God as our witness, I give you this charge for all Israel, the Lord's assembly: Be careful to obey all the commands of the LORD your God, so that you may possess this good land and leave it to your children as a permanent inheritance.

⁹"And Solomon, my son, get to know the God of your ancestors. Worship and serve him with your whole heart and with a willing mind. For the LORD sees every heart and understands and knows every plan and thought. If you seek him, you will find him. But if you forsake him, he will reject you forever. ¹⁰So take this seriously. The LORD has chosen you to build a Temple as his sanctuary. Be strong, and do the work." 1 CHRONICLES 28:1-10

ORE THAN A DAY OFF

PREVIEW

New Year's Day, Easter, Thanksgiving, and Christmas are just a few of the holidays marked on our calendars. Most of our holidays exist for a significant reason. The Fourth of July, for instance, is celebrated as the birthday of our nation.

The Israelites also celebrated holidays of great significance. To aid in their celebration, Solomon wants to establish a central place to observe these holidays. So, he begins to carry out his responsibility of building the temple. But before construction can begin, Solomon has to find craftsmen skilled enough to work on God's house. As you read, think of possible celebrations you could include in your schedule.

Also in this passage you will find the kind of wish God will grant; decorations suitable for a place of worship; and the importance of following instructions.

PERSONAL APPLICATION

A celebration is an occasion of joy, and remembering God's goodness to his people was certainly a reason to be joyful (2 Chronicles 2:4). God wanted Israel to celebrate certain historical events regularly because the people were so forgetful, so quick to turn to other gods, so quick to find more important actions to do than to worship him. The celebrations were designed to turn their attention and their hearts to the Lord.

Today, our church celebrations recall God's goodness. Because, like the people of Israel, we also have short memories, Christmas, Easter, and other special occasions help us remember what God has done for us. To some people, these holidays are just an excuse to have some fun. They should be much more than that—they should help us remember God's work in the world and in our lives.

Use Christian holidays and traditional church celebrations to remember God's goodness to you. And create your own celebrations that commemorate special days in your walk with the Savior.

BIBLE READING

[1]Solomon now decided that the time had come to build a Temple for the LORD and a royal palace for himself. [2]He enlisted a force of 70,000 common laborers, 80,000 stonecutters in the hill country, and 3,600 foremen. [3]Solomon also sent this message to King Hiram at Tyre:

"Send me cedar logs like the ones that were supplied to my father, David, when he was building his palace. [4]I am about to build a Temple to honor the name of the LORD my God. It will be a place set apart to burn incense and sweet spices before him, to display the special sacrificial bread, and to sacrifice burnt offerings each morning and evening, on the Sabbaths, at new moon celebrations, and at the other appointed festivals of the LORD our God. He has commanded Israel to do these things forever.

[5]"This will be a magnificent Temple because our God is an awesome God, greater than any other. [6]But who can really build him a worthy home? Not even the highest heavens can contain him! So who am I to consider building a Temple for him, except as a place to burn sacrifices to him?"

2 CHRONICLES 2:1-6

POSITIONING

PREVIEW

Getting up in front of an audience strikes fear in the hearts of most people. "That's not my idea of a good time," they might say. It's a big responsibility to be in the spotlight—being observed by everybody, critiqued by some, and copied by others.

Solomon is one of the few who can stand in front of an audience and not be stricken with fear. As he dedicates the recently-finished temple, he stands in front of the people—on a platform—and blesses them.

This is the second part of Solomon's story. After seven years of construction, Solomon's work crews finally finish the temple. Solomon dedicates the magnificent edifice to God and inaugurates it into service. He brings the ark of the covenant into the Holy of Holies, prays a prayer of dedication, and God appears to him. Then we read of Solomon's riches and wisdom and of his many building projects. Follow closely—the best part is the prayer.

There's a lot here: the importance of the Old Testament temple; what to pray about; what it means to dedicate ourselves to God; consequences of turning away from God; and the power of example.

PERSONAL APPLICATION

As the people received Solomon's blessing, they stood (2 Chronicles 6:3). As Solomon prayed, he knelt (6:12-13). Solomon showed love and respect for God by kneeling before him as the people of Israel looked on. His action wasn't just for public display, though. It showed that he acknowledged God as the ultimate king and authority, and it encouraged the people to do the same.

When you stand or kneel in church or at prayer, make these actions reflect more than mere changes in posture. Let them indicate your love for God.

BIBLE READING

[12]Then Solomon stood with his hands spread out before the altar of the LORD in front of the entire community of Israel. [13]He had made a bronze platform $7\frac{1}{2}$ feet long, $7\frac{1}{2}$ feet wide, and $7\frac{1}{2}$ feet high and had placed it at the center of the Temple's outer courtyard. He stood on the platform before the entire assembly, and then he knelt down and lifted his hands toward heaven. [14]He prayed, "O LORD, God of Israel, there is no God like you in all of heaven and earth. You keep your promises and show unfailing love to all who obey you and are eager to do your will. [15]You have kept your promise to your servant David, my father. You made that promise with your own mouth, and today you have fulfilled it with your own hands. [16]And now, O LORD, God of Israel, carry out your further promise to your servant David, my father. For you said to him, 'If your descendants guard their behavior and obey my law as you have done, they will always reign over Israel.' [17]Now, O LORD, God of Israel, fulfill this promise to your servant David."   2 CHRONICLES 6:12-17

$\mathcal{T}$HE RIGHT PERSON FOR THE JOB

PREVIEW

There's more to baby-sitting than preventing food fights and keeping the kids alive. That's why when parents need a baby-sitter, they want someone who will care for the children the way they themselves would.

Kings are similar to baby-sitters—they're both in charge of caring for people and keeping order. In this reading, the Jews of the northern tribes of Israel need to choose a king because they have decided not to put up with the current tyrant. Unfortunately, they aren't careful as to who they choose. As you read this story, note especially Abijah's advice to Jeroboam, and learn God's lesson there.

In this passage, you also will find these lessons: how to avoid bad advice; trappings of greed and power; confession and repentance; and a source of peace.

PERSONAL APPLICATION

In setting up his own religion, Jeroboam discarded the worship of God and made idols. He appointed priests to serve in his new religion, but he tossed out the standards that God had set for the priesthood of his people. Literally anyone could qualify to be a priest—all the person had to do was to present a prescribed offering, much like paying a fee.

Abijah criticized Jeroboam for this (2 Chronicles 13:9). He wanted Jeroboam to follow the instructions of the Lord (13:11), because a priest is a representative of God. Anyone can represent a worthless god; but to represent the Lord God Almighty, a person must live by God's standards.

Those appointed to positions of responsibility in your church should not be selected merely because they are influential or are highly educated. Instead they should demonstrate sound doctrine, dedication to God, and strong spiritual character (see 1 Timothy 3; Titus 1). It matters who leads you in worship, so don't choose just anybody.

Bible Reading

⁶Yet Jeroboam son of Nebat, who was a mere servant of David's son Solomon, became a traitor to his master. ⁷Then a whole gang of scoundrels joined him, defying Solomon's son Rehoboam when he was young and inexperienced and could not stand up to them. ⁸Do you really think you can stand against the kingdom of the LORD that is led by the descendants of David? Your army is vast indeed, but with you are those gold calves that Jeroboam made as your gods! ⁹And you have chased away the priests of the LORD and the Levites and have appointed your own priests, just like the pagan nations. You let anyone become a priest these days! Whoever comes to be dedicated with a young bull and seven rams can become a priest of these so-called gods of yours!

¹⁰"But as for us, the LORD is our God, and we have not abandoned him. Only the descendants of Aaron serve the LORD as priests, and the Levites alone may help them in their work. ¹¹They present burnt offerings and fragrant incense to the LORD every morning and evening. They place the Bread of the Presence on the holy table, and they light the gold lampstand every evening. We are following the instructions of the LORD our God, but you have abandoned him. ¹²So you see, God is with us. He is our leader. His priests blow their trumpets and lead us into battle against you. O people of Israel, do not fight against the LORD, the God of your ancestors, for you will not succeed!"

2 Chronicles 13:6-12

PREPARING FOR WAR IN TIMES OF PEACE

PREVIEW

Suppose you suddenly had two hours to do whatever you wanted. This was *your* time—no one else could call or interrupt you, no one could lay claim to your priorities, no one could tell you to get up and start washing the dishes. What would you most like to do with that time?

For some good tips, read the story of Asa, king of Judah. Asa is a good king. He loves God and does what is right. And this has a wonderful, positive effect on his nation—peace. As you read, note how Asa uses free time.

In this passage, Asa shows us other good examples—like the importance of removing sin and corrupt practices from our lives, as well as listening to and following through on godly counsel.

PERSONAL APPLICATION

This passage notes that the nation of Judah had been given rest from its enemies, meaning that they had peace with all their neighbors (2 Chronicles 14:7). King Asa wisely used this time to build his defenses, fortifying the cities with walls and battlements. Times of peace are not just for resting, they allow us to prepare for times of trouble. King Asa recognized that this period of peace afforded the right time to build his defenses—the moment of attack would be too late.

It is also difficult to withstand spiritual attack unless adequate defenses are prepared beforehand. Decisions about how to face temptation must be made with a cool head long before the heat of battle.

Build your defenses *before* temptation strikes by scheduling times of rest, and using those times to recover from stress and to refresh your spirit. Remember to include prayer and Bible reading to boost your defenses.

BIBLE READING

¹When Abijah died, he was buried in the City of David. Then his son Asa became the next king. There was peace in the land for ten years, ²for Asa did what was pleasing and good in the sight of the LORD his God. ³He removed the pagan altars and the shrines. He smashed the sacred pillars and cut down the Asherah poles. ⁴He commanded the people of Judah to seek the LORD, the God of their ancestors, and to obey his law and his commands. ⁵Asa also removed the pagan shrines, as well as the incense altars from every one of Judah's towns. So Asa's kingdom enjoyed a period of peace. ⁶During those peaceful years, he was able to build up the fortified cities throughout Judah. No one tried to make war against him at this time, for the LORD was giving him rest from his enemies. ⁷Asa told the people of Judah, "Let us build towns and fortify them with walls, towers, gates, and bars. The land is ours because we sought the LORD our God, and he has given us rest from our enemies." So they went ahead with these projects and brought them to completion.   2 CHRONICLES 14:1-7

GAINST THE ODDS

PREVIEW

The odds are often against us in life. Finances, for example, are a continual struggle for many. Work always seems to exact much too high a price for the little reward it returns.

In this reading, the odds are against Jehoshaphat and his army. They're no match for the combined forces that are moving against them. But Jehoshaphat loves God and follows him. Although Jehoshaphat doesn't have military might, he is on God's side. Jehoshaphat keeps his trust in God throughout his military exploits, despite his allies' lack of faith. As you read this passage, look for the secret of Jehoshaphat's success.

Other lessons in this section include leading others in Bible reading and prayer; how *not* to take advice; and how to exercise authority.

PERSONAL APPLICATION

As the enemy bore down on the army of Judah, God spoke through the prophet Jahaziel: "Do not be afraid! Do not be discouraged . . . for the battle is not yours, but God's" (2 Chronicles 20:15).

We may not physically fight an enemy army, but every day we battle temptation, pressure, and "those mighty powers of darkness who rule this world" (Ephesians 6:12), who want us to fail or to stop doing good. Remember that we who are believers have God's Spirit in us. If we ask for God's help when we face struggles, God will fight for us. And God always wins.

How can you let God fight for you? (1) By realizing the battle is not yours, but God's; (2) by recognizing human limitations and allowing God's strength to work through your fears and weaknesses; (3) by making sure that you are pursuing God's interests and not just your own selfish desires; (4) by asking God for help in your daily battles; (5) by not forcing outcomes that are not yours to control; (6) by trusting that God is in control and not panicking; and (7) by doing your part and trusting God with the results (see 2 Samuel 10:12).

BIBLE READING

¹³As all the men of Judah stood before the LORD with their little ones, wives, and children, ¹⁴the Spirit of the LORD came upon one of the men standing there. His name was Jahaziel son of Zechariah, son of Benaiah, son of Jeiel, son of Mattaniah, a Levite who was a descendant of Asaph. ¹⁵He said, "Listen, King Jehoshaphat! Listen, all you people of Judah and Jerusalem! This is what the LORD says: Do not be afraid! Don't be discouraged by this mighty army, for the battle is not yours, but God's. ¹⁶Tomorrow, march out against them. You will find them coming up through the ascent of Ziz at the end of the valley that opens into the wilderness of Jeruel. ¹⁷But you will not even need to fight. Take your positions; then stand still and watch the Lord's victory. He is with you, O people of Judah and Jerusalem. Do not be afraid or discouraged. Go out there tomorrow, for the LORD is with you!"

¹⁸Then King Jehoshaphat bowed down with his face to the ground. And all the people of Judah and Jerusalem did the same, worshiping the LORD. ¹⁹Then the Levites from the clans of Kohath and Korah stood to praise the LORD, the God of Israel, with a very loud shout.   2 CHRONICLES 20:13-19

$\mathcal{P}$OTHOLES ON EASY STREET

PREVIEW

Some people believe that the reason people do bad things is because they don't have enough material goods. Give them what they need and they will be good people. This theory breaks down, though, when those who have everything do horrible things.

This passage tells the stories of Jehoram, Ahaziah, Athaliah, and Joash—a succession of kings and a queen. To call this family dysfunctional would be a gross understatement. All except Joash consistently did evil and even he had a lapse in his later years. Was their problem a lack of material prosperity? Did they go wrong because they just didn't have enough stuff? Far from it. Wealth doesn't do the trick. As you read, look for the lesson about prosperity.

You also will find these lessons: the trouble with marrying someone who hates God; testing the advice you receive; and a time for executions.

PERSONAL APPLICATION

Under Joash's rule, the Israelites repaired the temple and the nation prospered. But right after the death of his uncle (the priest Jehoiada), the nation again descended into the worship of false gods. Everything was going well in Judah, so why did they turn away from God (2 Chronicles 24:18)?

Having money may bring us some comforts, but it doesn't feed our spiritual needs. Wealth doesn't make us better people or insulate us from sin. Whatever our status, we must make decisions about whom to serve and worship every day. Serving God is something we must consciously choose.

Don't let good circumstances lure you into false security. If you're bankroll is always tight, don't think that having more will enhance your love for God. Be content with what you have, remembering that God owns all. He alone deserves our ultimate allegiance (see Deuteronomy 6:10-12; 8:11-14).

BIBLE READING

[17]But after Jehoiada's death, the leaders of Judah came and bowed before King Joash and persuaded the king to listen to their advice. [18]They decided to abandon the Temple of the LORD, the God of their ancestors, and they worshiped Asherah poles and idols instead! Then the anger of God burned against Judah and Jerusalem because of their sin. [19]The LORD sent prophets to bring them back to him, but the people would not listen.

[20]Then the Spirit of God came upon Zechariah son of Jehoiada the priest. He stood before the people and said, "This is what God says: Why do you disobey the Lord's commands so that you cannot prosper? You have abandoned the LORD, and now he has abandoned you!"

[21]Then the leaders plotted to kill Zechariah, and by order of King Joash himself, they stoned him to death in the courtyard of the Lord's Temple. [22]That was how King Joash repaid Jehoiada for his love and loyalty—by killing his son. Zechariah's last words as he died were, "May the LORD see what they are doing and hold them accountable!" 2 CHRONICLES 24:17-22

OUR ATTENTION, PLEASE

PREVIEW

Imagine this scenario and see if it has ever been your experience: Carla is trying to get the attention of her husband, Bob, who is across the room. "Bob, would you come here for a moment?" Carla waits. No response. "Bob?" Still no response. "*Bob?*" The plea is more insistent now. Still no response. Finally, "BOB!" "Huh?" he finally replies. He heard, but he didn't *hear.*

This parallels how God tries to get Ahaz's attention. This passage tells the story of Amaziah, Uzziah, Jotham, and Ahaz, all kings of Judah. Ahaz wins the award for Most Stubborn Rebel. In this passage, God uses hardship after hardship to shout to Ahaz, "Listen to me!" God has a message for Ahaz, but Ahaz is too distracted by his wild living to notice. Take a close look at Ahaz and learn from his mistakes.

You will also see that Amaziah has a problem with half-hearted faith but still makes some wise choices; Uzziah has great success, then spoils it; and Jotham becomes a model leader.

PERSONAL APPLICATION

As king of Judah, Ahaz had nothing but trouble. When his troubles hit, he was already in the midst of terrible sins; these problems were his wake up call—his opportunity to hear God. How did he respond? He refused to listen and committed even more evil (2 Chronicles 28:22).

No one knows why bad things happen to people. From the beginning of time, people have tried to invoke universal explanations. The truth is, we can't know exactly why tragedies occur. We cannot know why they happen to us. But when they do happen, we must remember to ask how God might be attempting to get our attention, to correct us.

When troubles hit, we need to respond to them as our teachers. Through hardship, God disciplines his children in love (see Hebrews 12:7). Rough times give us a chance to grow (see James 1:2-4). When you are facing difficulties and struggles, don't turn away from God— turn *to* him.

BIBLE READING

[16]About that time King Ahaz of Judah asked the king of Assyria for help against his enemies. [17]The armies of Edom had again invaded Judah and taken captives. [18]And the Philistines had raided towns located in the foothills of Judah and in the Negev. They had already captured Beth-shemesh, Aijalon, Gederoth, Soco with its villages, Timnah with its villages, and Gimzo with its villages, and the Philistines had occupied these towns. [19]The LORD was humbling Judah because of King Ahaz of Judah, for he had encouraged his people to sin and had been utterly unfaithful to the LORD. [20]So when King Tiglath-pileser of Assyria arrived, he oppressed King Ahaz instead of helping him. [21]Ahaz took valuable items from the LORD's Temple, the royal palace, and from the homes of his officials and gave them to the king of Assyria as tribute. But even this did not help him.

[22]And when trouble came to King Ahaz, he became even more unfaithful to the LORD. [23]He offered sacrifices to the gods of Damascus who had defeated him, for he said, "These gods helped the kings of Aram, so they will help me, too, if I sacrifice to them." But instead, they led to his ruin and the ruin of all Israel. [24]The king took the utensils from the Temple of God and broke them into pieces. He shut the doors of the LORD's Temple so that no one could worship there and then set up altars to pagan gods in every corner of Jerusalem. [25]He made pagan shrines in all the towns of Judah for offering sacrifices to other gods. In this way, he aroused the anger of the LORD, the God of his ancestors.

2 CHRONICLES 28:16-25

THIS IS A TEST

PREVIEW

Mistakes are always a two-edged sword. On the one hand, they hurt; on the other hand, they pack a lesson. If we get the point, it's something we'll likely never forget—which, in its own cruel way is a good thing. There's no teacher like experience.

Hezekiah, king of Judah, is a prime example of this. He's a good man, and he enjoys many successes. But that doesn't mean that Hezekiah is perfect, as he learns from his experience with some visitors from Babylon. Their visit is a test of Hezekiah's character. See how Hezekiah does on his test, and learn from his experience.

Hezekiah's life also tells us about restoring old Christian servants; making sacrifices; inviting others to follow Christ; getting rid of idols; and dealing with frightening situations.

PERSONAL APPLICATION

Envoys from Babylon came to visit the king of Judah, and he foolishly showed them his supply of gold, treasures, and weapons (see Isaiah 39:1-8). Hezekiah did not perceive Babylon as a threat. When the envoys came, Hezekiah had to decide whether to show off his treasures. He did, thinking that nothing bad would come of it. But the Babylonians would one day carry away all his treasures. His flirtation with pride led to a disaster for all Judah.

God presented the king with a choice to see what his heart was really like. God wanted to show Hezekiah his own shortcomings and the attitude of his heart (2 Chronicles 32:31).

Life brings many choices—each a test of character. Many of the circumstances and opportunities that you experience every day will test you, even if only in small ways. Consistently turn to God and do what pleases him.

BIBLE READING

²⁴About that time, Hezekiah became deathly ill. He prayed to the LORD, who healed him and gave him a miraculous sign. ²⁵But Hezekiah did not respond appropriately to the kindness shown him, and he became proud. So the Lord's anger came against him and against Judah and Jerusalem. ²⁶Then Hezekiah repented of his pride, and the people of Jerusalem humbled themselves. So the Lord's anger did not come against them during Hezekiah's lifetime.

²⁷Hezekiah was very wealthy and held in high esteem. He had to build special treasury buildings for his silver, gold, precious stones, and spices, and for his shields and other valuable items. ²⁸He also constructed many storehouses for his grain, new wine, and olive oil; and he made many stalls for his cattle and folds for his flocks of sheep and goats. ²⁹He built many towns and acquired vast flocks and herds, for God had given him great wealth. ³⁰He blocked up the upper spring of Gihon and brought the water down through a tunnel to the west side of the City of David. And so he succeeded in everything he did.

³¹However, when ambassadors arrived from Babylon to ask about the remarkable events that had taken place in the land, God withdrew from Hezekiah in order to test him and to see what was really in his heart.   2 CHRONICLES 32:24-31

ALL GROWN UP

PREVIEW

What did you have on your mind at the age of eight? Perhaps it was a long time ago, but think back if you can. What were your favorite subjects in school? What were your favorite activities? What did you want to be when you grew up?

Josiah didn't really have an opportunity to dream about what he wanted to be when he grew up. When Josiah was eight years old he became the king of Judah. Imagine the immense responsibility he had at such a young age. But his age wasn't a negative factor for the job. In fact, it may have been an asset. This story will make you rethink the potential that is packed in kids who love God.

As you read this passage, you will find other lessons in the lives of Judah's kings: exercising your second chances (Manasseh); not missing a cue (Amon); godly sorrow (Josiah); and the cost of overestimating one's own goodness (Josiah).

PERSONAL APPLICATION

Josiah became king when he was eight years old. In Josiah's day, boys were considered to be men at age twelve. By sixteen, Josiah understood the responsibility of his office (2 Chronicles 34:3). Even at this young age, Josiah showed greater wisdom than many of the older kings who had come before him, because he decided to seek the Lord God and his wisdom.

Some people use age as an excuse for not serving the Lord: "I'm too young," or "I'm too old," or "I've only been a Christian for a short time—I don't know enough." It is clear from this passage that God can use people of any age to make a difference for him. They just need to be willing and open.

Don't let your age make you feel disqualified from serving God. Learn from Josiah's example—that God can use you at any age if you will listen to him and obey his Word.

BIBLE READING

¹Josiah was eight years old when he became king, and he reigned in Jerusalem thirty-one years. ²He did what was pleasing in the Lord's sight and followed the example of his ancestor David. He did not turn aside from doing what was right.

³During the eighth year of his reign, while he was still young, Josiah began to seek the God of his ancestor David. Then in the twelfth year, he began to purify Judah and Jerusalem, destroying all the pagan shrines, the Asherah poles, and the carved idols and cast images. ⁴He saw to it that the altars for the images of Baal and their incense altars were torn down. He also made sure that the Asherah poles, the carved idols, and the cast images were smashed and scattered over the graves of those who had sacrificed to them. ⁵Then he burned the bones of the pagan priests on their own altars, and so he purified Judah and Jerusalem.

⁶He did the same thing in the towns of Manasseh, Ephraim, and Simeon, even as far as Naphtali. ⁷He destroyed the pagan altars and the Asherah poles, and he crushed the idols into dust. He cut down the incense altars throughout the land of Israel and then returned to Jerusalem.   2 CHRONICLES 34:1-7

*O*NE OF THOSE DAYS

PREVIEW

The people of Judah have "one of those days" when they are taken captive to Babylon. But don't feel sorry for them—God has warned his people for years that there would be consequences for their stubborn disobedience. Now they've used up their supply of warnings and the consequences are at hand. This is a sad story, but its lesson is helpful for us.

Also in this passage, you should be able to find lessons on God keeping his promises and God's people making big mistakes.

PERSONAL APPLICATION

The book of 2 Chronicles focuses on the rise and fall of the worship of God as symbolized by the Jerusalem temple. David planned the temple (1 Chronicles 22:5), Solomon built it (2 Chronicles 2:1), and King Nebuchadnezzar destroyed it (36:19).

The kings were gone, the temple lay in ruins, and many of the people had been taken to Babylon as captives. The nation had been stripped to its very foundation. Fortunately, there still existed a greater foundation—God himself. Forty-eight years after the temple's destruction, the year after Cyrus conquered Babylon, he announced his plans to rebuild God's temple (2 Chronicles 36:22-23). The situation seemed hopeless, at first, but God was there, working out his plan for his people all along.

At times our lives can seem devastated, conquered, and empty. After difficult defeats and struggles, every support can seem to have been stripped away. That's when we should remember that God is still with us and that he is working out his perfect plan for us.

When tough times come, when you have "one of those days," don't despair and give up. Instead, use those difficulties to push you closer to your loving heavenly Father. Trust in God and his promises to get you through the day, and remember that the bad times will one day pass.

BIBLE READING

¹⁷So the LORD brought the king of Babylon against them. The Babylonians killed Judah's young men, even chasing after them into the Temple. They had no pity on the people, killing both young and old, men and women, healthy and sick. God handed them all over to Nebuchadnezzar. ¹⁸The king also took home to Babylon all the utensils, large and small, used in the Temple of God, and the treasures from both the Lord's Temple and the royal palace. He also took with him all the royal princes. ¹⁹Then his army set fire to the Temple of God, broke down the walls of Jerusalem, burned all the palaces, and completely destroyed everything of value. ²⁰The few who survived were taken away to Babylon, and they became servants to the king and his sons until the kingdom of Persia came to power. ²¹So the message of the LORD spoken through Jeremiah was fulfilled. The land finally enjoyed its Sabbath rest, lying desolate for seventy years, just as the prophet had said.

²²In the first year of King Cyrus of Persia, the LORD fulfilled Jeremiah's prophecy by stirring the heart of Cyrus to put this proclamation into writing and to send it throughout his kingdom:

²³"This is what King Cyrus of Persia says: The LORD, the God of heaven, has given me all the kingdoms of the earth. He has appointed me to build him a Temple at Jerusalem in the land of Judah. All of you who are the Lord's people may return to Israel for this task. May the LORD your God be with you!"

2 CHRONICLES 36:17-23

$\mathcal{I}$ HATE WHEN I DO THAT

PREVIEW

A joke has been made out of the phrase, "I hate when I do that." That sentiment pokes fun at a truth about ourselves. The truth is that some-times we regret what we voluntarily do. What in your life makes you say, "I hate when I do that"?

Israel often hurt itself through poor choices and wrong actions. Despite their regrets, God always gave them another chance. In this reading, the first group of exiles returns to the land of Israel after having been in captivity for forty-eight years. They suddenly get the opportu-nity to return—and a second chance—as Cyrus offers them safe passage back to rebuild the temple. The heads of families along with the priests and Levites lead the way. This is more than a trip—it's a commitment to change. As you read, look for signs of God's love and forgiveness, and learn the lesson of the second chance.

In this passage, you will find these other lessons: hope and new beginnings; the importance of teamwork; God's protection; and giving.

PERSONAL APPLICATION

After forty-eight years of captivity, God's arrogant people had been humbled. When the people's attitudes and desires changed, God ended their punishment and gave them another opportunity to go home and try again.

Major changes occur on the inside when God works on our atti-tudes, beliefs, and desires. These inner changes lead to faithful actions. Paul wrote, "For God is working in you, giving you the desire to obey him and the power to do what pleases him" (Philippians 2:13). Doing God's will begins with one's desires.

Are you willing to be humble, to be open to God's opportunities, and to move at his direction? Ask God to give you the desire to follow him more closely. He's giving you another chance to change your mind. Change your desires and attitude to *want* to follow God.

BIBLE READING

⁵Then God stirred the hearts of the priests and Levites and the leaders of the tribes of Judah and Benjamin to return to Jerusalem to rebuild the Temple of the LORD. ⁶And all their neighbors assisted by giving them vessels of silver and gold, supplies for the journey, and livestock. They gave them many choice gifts in addition to all the freewill offerings.

⁷King Cyrus himself brought out the valuable items which King Nebuchadnezzar had taken from the Lord's Temple in Jerusalem and had placed in the temple of his own gods. ⁸Cyrus directed Mithredath, the treasurer of Persia, to count these items and present them to Sheshbazzar, the leader of the exiles returning to Judah.   EZRA 1:5-8

⁶⁴So a total of 42,360 people returned to Judah, ⁶⁵in addition to 7,337 servants and 200 singers, both men and women. ⁶⁶They took with them 736 horses, 245 mules, ⁶⁷435 camels, and 6,720 donkeys.

⁶⁸When they arrived at the Temple of the LORD in Jerusalem, some of the family leaders gave generously toward the rebuilding of God's Temple on its original site, ⁶⁹and each leader gave as much as he could. The total of their gifts came to 61,000 gold coins, 6,250 pounds of silver, and 100 robes for the priests.   EZRA 2:64-69

OME AT LAST!

PREVIEW

You turn the key, open the door, and enter the vacant house. "Ahh," you say with sincere pleasure, inhaling the stale and stuffy air, "Home at last!" You plop down on the couch and relax for the first time in two weeks. After an exhausting time away, it's good to be back home!

The Jews know what this feeling is like. They are glad to be home, glad to have returned from exile in Babylon to rebuild the temple in Jerusalem. There will be a lot to do, with planning, clearing the area, getting materials, and starting the work. But before they begin, they have some important business to take care of—"first things first" you might say. As you read, learn a lesson from the Israelites' priorities.

As the Israelites unpack, note also their lessons on avoiding partnerships with unbelievers; when (and how) to resist opposition; when (and how) to speak up for what is right; and God's sovereignty over even the most powerful people on earth.

PERSONAL APPLICATION

Almost immediately after arriving in their homeland, the returning exiles built an altar (Ezra 3:1-3). The people began worshiping God through sacrifices even before the temple foundations were laid. After many years in captivity, they had learned their lesson—God was their source of strength and success. Their parents and grandparents had been carried off by the Babylonians when they were relatively strong; this group was few, weak, and surrounded by enemies. They knew that they needed to rely on God's power.

Regardless of our good health and prosperity, God is our source of strength and help. We need to depend on him and make worshiping him our top priority. Make time for worship, even when you are very busy and tired. Submit to the Lord and depend on him to work through you.

BIBLE READING

¹Now in early autumn, when the Israelites had settled in their towns, all the people assembled together as one person in Jerusalem. ²Then Jeshua son of Jehozadak with his fellow priests and Zerubbabel son of Shealtiel with his family began to rebuild the altar of the God of Israel so they could sacrifice burnt offerings on it, as instructed in the law of Moses, the man of God. ³Even though the people were afraid of the local residents, they rebuilt the altar at its old site. Then they immediately began to sacrifice burnt offerings on the altar to the LORD. They did this each morning and evening.

⁴They celebrated the Festival of Shelters as prescribed in the law of Moses, sacrificing the burnt offerings specified for each day of the festival. ⁵They also offered the regular burnt offerings and the offerings required for the new moon celebrations and the other annual festivals to the LORD. Freewill offerings were also sacrificed to the LORD by the people. ⁶Fifteen days before the Festival of Shelters began, the priests had begun to sacrifice burnt offerings to the LORD. This was also before they had started to lay the foundation of the Lord's Temple.   EZRA 3:1-6

THANKYOUFORTHISFOOD, AMEN

PREVIEW

Family camping trips are supposed to be great fun, but too often a sense of dread accompanies them. It's all too easy to leave something crucial behind. One time it's the tent. Another time it's the food. Sound familiar?

The second group of exiles returns to Jerusalem from Babylonia, led by Ezra. But before they set out they have some important preparations to make, and Ezra makes sure they don't forget the most crucial ones. As you read, learn how to get prepared for any task God gives you.

In this passage you will find these other lessons: the qualities of an exemplary leader in action; acknowledging God's help and protection; and using your gifts and abilities for God's service.

PERSONAL APPLICATION

Ezra knew God's promises to protect his people, but he didn't take God for granted. He also knew that God's blessings come through prayer. So Ezra and the people humbled themselves by fasting and praying (Ezra 8:21-23). Fasting humbled the people because going without food was a reminder of their complete dependence on God. Fasting also gave them time to pray and think about God.

Too often, we pray glibly and superficially. We don't take time out from our busy schedules to commune with God seriously. Fasting is one way to free up the time to pray to God earnestly.

We need to take time to pray seriously. Not taking the time is an insult to God. When we approach him with our quick, unthoughtful prayers, we reduce him to a quick-service pharmacist with painkillers for every ailment. Serious prayer puts us in touch with God's will for our lives and can really change our hearts and minds.

Make time for prayer in which you *concentrate* on what you are saying and why you're saying it. That's the only way to be fully prepared for life. How much time do you spend in preparation?

BIBLE READING

²¹And there by the Ahava Canal, I gave orders for all of us to fast and humble ourselves before our God. We prayed that he would give us a safe journey and protect us, our children, and our goods as we traveled. ²²For I was ashamed to ask the king for soldiers and horsemen to accompany us and protect us from enemies along the way. After all, we had told the king, "Our God protects all those who worship him, but his fierce anger rages against those who abandon him." ²³So we fasted and earnestly prayed that our God would take care of us, and he heard our prayer.

³⁵Then the exiles who had returned from captivity sacrificed burnt offerings to the God of Israel. They presented twelve oxen for the people of Israel, as well as ninety-six rams and seventy-seven lambs. They also offered twelve goats as a sin offering. All this was given as a burnt offering to the LORD. ³⁶The king's decrees were delivered to his lieutenants and the governors of the province west of the Euphrates River, who then cooperated by supporting the people and the Temple of God.

EZRA 8:21-23, 35-36

OOPS!

PREVIEW

"I didn't know." If a driver says that when stopped for speeding, the police officer *may* let the speeder off, but he or she doesn't have to, because ignorance of the law is no excuse. If a child says it to Mom, she'll probably give the child another chance, but she'll also expect compliance from then on. It works best to learn the rules *before* the trouble comes, instead of the hard way.

Here, the Israelites are back in their homeland. Not knowing God's laws, some of the returned exiles carelessly end up breaking them. This causes Ezra much grief and shame before God, who has just brought his people back from being held in captivity and has given them a second chance.

As you read, notice Ezra's incredible humility before God, as well as the great sacrifice the Israelites make in order to repent for their sin.

Other lessons in this passage include avoiding certain kinds of partnerships and crying out for justice.

PERSONAL APPLICATION

Ezra pointed out a sin that the Israelites had been committing without really knowing it. They had intermarried with the pagan tribes around them, something God had forbidden (see Exodus 34:12-16; Deuteronomy 7:1-4). God knew that marrying into a family or clan meant accepting their gods. In order to reestablish the nation's relationship with God, Ezra pleaded for God's forgiveness (Ezra 9:5-15). Then the Israelites chose the painful course of repentance—ending their wrongful marriages.

In this reading, we should note the willingness we should have to sacrifice anything that causes sin in our lives. The Israelites sacrificed family relations in order to maintain a right relationship with God. What sacrifices, big or small, do you need to make in order to return to a right relationship with God and walk more closely with him?

True repentance does not end with words of confession—it must lead to corrected behavior and changed attitudes.

BIBLE READING

¹While Ezra prayed and made this confession, weeping and throwing himself to the ground in front of the Temple of God, a large crowd of people from Israel—men, women, and children—gathered and wept bitterly with him. ²Then Shecaniah son of Jehiel, a descendant of Elam, said to Ezra, "We confess that we have been unfaithful to our God, for we have married these pagan women of the land. But there is hope for Israel in spite of this. ³Let us now make a covenant with our God to divorce our pagan wives and to send them away with their children. We will follow the advice given by you and by the others who respect the commands of our God. We will obey the law of God. ⁴Take courage, for it is your duty to tell us how to proceed in setting things straight, and we will cooperate fully."

⁵So Ezra stood up and demanded that the leaders of the priests and the Levites and all the people of Israel swear that they would do as Shecaniah had said. And they all swore a solemn oath. ⁶Then Ezra left the front of the Temple of God and went to the room of Jehohanan son of Eliashib. He spent the night there, but he did not eat any food or drink. He was still in mourning because of the unfaithfulness of the returned exiles. ⁷Then a proclamation was made throughout Judah and Jerusalem that all the returned exiles should come to Jerusalem. ⁸Those who failed to come within three days would, if the leaders and elders so decided, forfeit all their property and be expelled from the assembly of the exiles.

⁹Within three days, all the people of Judah and Benjamin had gathered in Jerusalem. This took place on December 19, and all the people were sitting in the square before the Temple of God. They were trembling both because of the seriousness of the matter and because it was raining. ¹⁰Then Ezra the priest stood and said to them: "You have sinned, for you have married pagan women. Now we are even more deeply under condemnation than we were before. ¹¹Confess your sin to the LORD, the God of your ancestors, and do what he demands. Separate yourselves from the people of the land and from these pagan women."   EZRA 10:1-11

GIVE ME THE BAD NEWS FIRST

PREVIEW

Brenda got a phone call today and found out that her sister is financially strapped, has lost her job, and wrecked her car. Bad news aplenty, with no easy solutions in sight. What should Brenda do? get depressed? get a loan? get a stiff drink?

Though Nehemiah lives in Babylon, he's a Jew and he's concerned about his homeland. When he gets the reports of how the settlers are doing, it's all bad news. He's heard from home and everything's a wreck. But Nehemiah doesn't despair or distract himself—he takes action. In this passage, learn from Nehemiah's example about how to respond to bad news.

Nehemiah teaches us three other lessons: how to care for people; praying for success; and asking for help.

PERSONAL APPLICATION

Nehemiah was deeply grieved about the condition of Jerusalem, but he didn't just brood about it. After his initial grief, he prayed, pouring his heart out to God (Nehemiah 1:4-11), and looking for ways to improve the situation. Nehemiah put all his resources—his knowledge, experience, and organization into figuring out what should be done.

That's how we should confront bad news, too, responding with trust in God, belief in his sovereignty, and then constructive action.

When tragic or difficult news comes to you, don't wallow in self-pity or merely run and try to hide. First pray. Then seek ways to move beyond your grief to specific action that will help those who need it, including yourself.

BIBLE READING

¹Early the following spring, during the twentieth year of King Artaxerxes' reign, I was serving the king his wine. I had never appeared sad in his presence before this time. ²So the king asked me, "Why are you so sad? You aren't sick, are you? You look like a man with deep troubles."

Then I was badly frightened, ³but I replied, "Long live the king! Why shouldn't I be sad? For the city where my ancestors are buried is in ruins, and the gates have been burned down."

⁴The king asked, "Well, how can I help you?"

With a prayer to the God of heaven, ⁵I replied, "If it please Your Majesty and if you are pleased with me, your servant, send me to Judah to rebuild the city where my ancestors are buried."

⁶The king, with the queen sitting beside him, asked, "How long will you be gone? When will you return?" So the king agreed, and I set a date for my departure.

⁷I also said to the king, "If it please Your Majesty, give me letters to the governors of the province west of the Euphrates River, instructing them to let me travel safely through their territories on my way to Judah. ⁸And please send a letter to Asaph, the manager of the king's forest, instructing him to give me timber. I will need it to make beams for the gates of the Temple fortress, for the city walls, and for a house for myself." And the king granted these requests, because the gracious hand of God was on me.   NEHEMIAH 2:1-8

PLANNING AHEAD

PREVIEW

Commercial aircraft have four levels of backup in their navigational systems. If something goes wrong with the hydraulic lines that control the flaps, for example, a second set can take over. These planes also carry far more fuel than they need for every trip. This is just planning ahead. From planes to personal projects, such preparations mean the difference between risking failure and having great probability of success.

Nehemiah needs a workable plan to successfully accomplish the desire God has placed in his heart—to rebuild the walls of Jerusalem. Before Nehemiah can come up with a plan, however, he must do his homework. Nehemiah knows that he has his work cut out for him—the settlers' morale is low, and the neighboring kingdoms don't want the Jews to get ambitious. As you read this story, watch how Nehemiah designs his plan.

Nehemiah's project also has lessons about sharing dreams and about each believer doing his or her part in the body of Christ.

PERSONAL APPLICATION

Nehemiah arrived quietly in Jerusalem and spent several days carefully observing and assessing the damage to the walls. Nehemiah kept his mission a secret, surveying the walls by moonlight to prevent enemies from being alerted to his plans. Only after careful planning would he go public with his mission. A premature announcement could have caused rivalry among the Jews over the best way to begin. In this case, Nehemiah didn't need brainstorming sessions; he needed one plan that would bring quick action. Following this time of thoughtful consideration, he confidently presented his plan (Nehemiah 2:11-17).

Nehemiah demonstrated an excellent approach to problem solving. First, he got all the accurate information he needed to assess the situation. Then he presented a realistic strategy.

Before jumping into a project, follow Nehemiah's example and plan ahead. Check your information to make sure your ideas will work, and be realistic. Then you will be able to present your plan with confidence.

BIBLE READING

¹¹Three days after my arrival at Jerusalem, ¹²I slipped out during the night, taking only a few others with me. I had not told anyone about the plans God had put in my heart for Jerusalem. We took no pack animals with us, except the donkey that I myself was riding. ¹³I went out through the Valley Gate, past the Jackal's Well, and over to the Dung Gate to inspect the broken walls and burned gates. ¹⁴Then I went to the Fountain Gate and to the King's Pool, but my donkey couldn't get through the rubble. ¹⁵So I went up the Kidron Valley instead, inspecting the wall before I turned back and entered again at the Valley Gate.

¹⁶The city officials did not know I had been out there or what I was doing, for I had not yet said anything to anyone about my plans. I had not yet spoken to the religious and political leaders, the officials, or anyone else in the administration. ¹⁷But now I said to them, "You know full well the tragedy of our city. It lies in ruins, and its gates are burned. Let us rebuild the wall of Jerusalem and rid ourselves of this disgrace!" ¹⁸Then I told them about how the gracious hand of God had been on me, and about my conversation with the king.

They replied at once, "Good! Let's rebuild the wall!" So they began the good work. NEHEMIAH 2:11-18

ALL TOGETHER NOW

PREVIEW

A lot of work relationships form around competition. People show off skills and knowledge in subtle ways, jockeying for position and advantage. Yet smart people realize that teamwork has to thrive also. If individual assignments get tangled in a scramble to prove who's better than whom, sooner or later everyone will be helping close up shop. Teamwork is vital.

Nehemiah realized that teamwork was crucial to completing the wall. Without it, the Israelites would not only fail to complete the project, but could lose their lives as well. As Nehemiah continues leading the rebuilding of Jerusalem's city walls, he experiences opposition just as he had expected. He also faces poverty and other issues. It's too much for one man to handle alone, so he organizes the workers together to support each other as a team. As you read about Nehemiah, consider carefully his emphasis on teamwork, delegation, and supervision.

Other lessons in this section include how to tackle large tasks; how to loan money; what to do when someone attacks your character; and the importance of courage for leaders.

PERSONAL APPLICATION

Not only were the workers threatened by enemy attack, they were vulnerable because they were spread out along the wall. To solve this problem, Nehemiah devised a plan of defense that would unite and protect his people—half the men worked while the other half stood guard (Nehemiah 4:16).

Like Nehemiah's workers, Christians need to work together and look out for each other. We may not have to repair a wall to protect ourselves from an enemy army, but we do war against Satan and his forces (see Ephesians 6:12). Our battles may come in the form of persecution from a coworker or relative, or from adverse circumstances—such as losing a job, getting a divorce, or being estranged from a child. Don't cut yourself off from other Christians; instead join together for mutual benefit. You need fellow believers as much as they need you.

BIBLE READING

[12]The Jews who lived near the enemy came and told us again and again, "They will come from all directions and attack us!" [13]So I placed armed guards behind the lowest parts of the wall in the exposed areas. I stationed the people to stand guard by families, armed with swords, spears, and bows.

[14]Then as I looked over the situation, I called together the leaders and the people and said to them, "Don't be afraid of the enemy! Remember the Lord, who is great and glorious, and fight for your friends, your families, and your homes!"

[15]When our enemies heard that we knew of their plans and that God had frustrated them, we all returned to our work on the wall. [16]But from then on, only half my men worked while the other half stood guard with spears, shields, bows, and coats of mail. The officers stationed themselves behind the people of Judah [17]who were building the wall. The common laborers carried on their work with one hand supporting their load and one hand holding a weapon. [18]All the builders had a sword belted to their side. The trumpeter stayed with me to sound the alarm.

[19]Then I explained to the nobles and officials and all the people, "The work is very spread out, and we are widely separated from each other along the wall. [20]When you hear the blast of the trumpet, rush to wherever it is sounding. Then our God will fight for us!"

[21]We worked early and late, from sunrise to sunset. And half the men were always on guard. [22]I also told everyone living outside the walls to move into Jerusalem. That way they and their servants could go on guard duty at night as well as work during the day. [23]During this time, none of us—not I, nor my relatives, nor my servants, nor the guards who were with me—ever took off our clothes. We carried our weapons with us at all times, even when we went for water.   NEHEMIAH 4:12-23

OOKING BACK

PREVIEW

Think back to your childhood or adolescence. What is one lesson you have learned from that time? Get out a photo album if it'll help. What guiding principle did you pick up from those earlier years?

The Israelites seem to have forgotten the lessons learned from their past, so they ask Ezra to read the Scriptures to them. As the Levites explain the meaning of the passage, the Israelites weep. Nehemiah reminds the people, however, that this is not a time for weeping but for rejoicing. Let this passage prompt you to reflect on the mighty acts God has done for you and the profound lessons he has taught you over the years.

PERSONAL APPLICATION

Many prayers and speeches in the Bible include a long summary of Israel's history. The summary of God's work in Nehemiah 9:7-38 reminded the people of their great heritage and God's wonderful promises.

Like the Israelites, we, too, should remember our history. Reviewing the past serves two purposes: (1) it helps us to avoid repeating the mistakes of our past and (2) it shows us the pattern of our spiritual growth. This process, therefore, can strengthen our faith as we remember how God has forgiven us for our sins, and how he has been working in us and through us to make us more like Christ.

Take time to reflect on your personal history; then thank God for what he has done in your life. Learn from your past so that you can live for Christ in the present and become the person God wants you to be in the future.

BIBLE READING

¹On October 31 the people returned for another observance. This time they fasted and dressed in sackcloth and sprinkled dust on their heads. ²Those of Israelite descent separated themselves from all foreigners as they confessed their own sins and the sins of their ancestors. ³The Book of the Law of the LORD their God was read aloud to them for about three hours. Then for three more hours they took turns confessing their sins and worshiping the LORD their God.

³²"And now, our God, the great and mighty and awesome God, who keeps his covenant of unfailing love, do not let all the hardships we have suffered be as nothing to you. Great trouble has come upon us and upon our kings and princes and priests and prophets and ancestors from the days when the kings of Assyria first triumphed over us until now. ³³Every time you punished us you were being just. We have sinned greatly, and you gave us only what we deserved. ³⁴Our kings, princes, priests, and ancestors did not obey your law or listen to your commands and solemn warnings. ³⁵Even while they had their own kingdom, they did not serve you even though you showered your goodness on them. You gave them a large, fertile land, but they refused to turn from their wickedness.

³⁶"So now today we are slaves here in the land of plenty that you gave to our ancestors! We are slaves among all this abundance! ³⁷The lush produce of this land piles up in the hands of the kings whom you have set over us because of our sins. They have power over us and our cattle. We serve them at their pleasure, and we are in great misery.

³⁸"Yet in spite of all this, we are making a solemn promise and putting it in writing. On this sealed document are the names of our princes and Levites and priests."   NEHEMIAH 9:1-3, 32-38

*F*OLLOWING THE LEADER

PREVIEW

The word "leadership" usually evokes thoughts of people with titles and positions. But every person takes up the challenge of leadership from time to time. Have you ever led a group of kids in an activity? a group of adults in singing? a family devotion time? an out-of-town friend through the city? a child through the steps of learning a skill?

Although Nehemiah is a leader by title and position, he is also a leader by example. Nehemiah leads the Israelites in rebuilding the city walls and establishes policies for residents of the city. But he also helps renew the covenant and keeps the Israelites on track with God. Clearly, that is what good leaders should do.

Other lessons in this reading include: appropriate kinds of separation; keeping the Sabbath; and dealing with weaknesses.

PERSONAL APPLICATION

Nehemiah's life story provides many principles of effective leadership that are still valid today: (1) Have a clear purpose and keep evaluating it in light of God's will. (2) Be straightforward and honest. (3) Live above reproach. (4) Be a person of constant prayer, deriving power and wisdom from your contact with God.

We may think of leadership as glamorous, but it can often be lonely, thankless, and filled with pressures to compromise values and standards. Nehemiah was able to accomplish a huge task against incredible odds because he learned that there is no success without risk of failure, no reward without hard work, no opportunity without criticism, and no true leadership without trust in God. The book of Nehemiah is about rebuilding the wall of a great city, but it is also about spiritual renewal, rebuilding a people's dependence on God.

Whatever your leadership position or role, don't lose sight of doing what is most important—being a spiritual leader. Keep your focus on being God's person and doing what he wants.

BIBLE READING

[15]One Sabbath day I saw some men of Judah treading their winepresses. They were also bringing in bundles of grain and loading them on their donkeys. And on that day they were bringing their wine, grapes, figs, and all sorts of produce to Jerusalem to sell. So I rebuked them for selling their produce on the Sabbath. [16]There were also some men from Tyre bringing in fish and all kinds of merchandise. They were selling it on the Sabbath to the people of Judah—and in Jerusalem at that!

[17]So I confronted the leaders of Judah, "Why are you profaning the Sabbath in this evil way? [18]Wasn't it enough that your ancestors did this sort of thing, so that our God brought the present troubles upon us and our city? Now you are bringing even more wrath upon the people of Israel by permitting the Sabbath to be desecrated in this way!" [19]So I commanded that from then on the gates of the city should be shut as darkness fell every Friday evening, not to be opened until the Sabbath ended. I also sent some of my own servants to guard the gates so that no merchandise could be brought in on the Sabbath day. [20]The merchants and tradesmen with a variety of wares camped outside Jerusalem once or twice. [21]But I spoke sharply to them and said, "What are you doing out here, camping around the wall? If you do this again, I will arrest you!" And that was the last time they came on the Sabbath. [22]Then I commanded the Levites to purify themselves and to guard the gates in order to preserve the holiness of the Sabbath.

Remember this good deed also, O my God! Have compassion on me according to your great and unfailing love.

NEHEMIAH 13:15-22

TIMING IS EVERYTHING

PREVIEW

In baseball, whether you hit the ball out of the park or down the left field line depends a lot on timing—exactly when the bat hits the ball. Internal combustion engines won't even run if the timing is off. And just ask a baker if it matters when he or she takes the bread out of the oven. Timing is everything.

Esther knows this to be true. As her life changes for the better, knowing when to speak and what to say becomes a significant factor in preserving her life and the lives of her people. She learns that God placed her in her important position, and at just the right time, she acts.

As you read this exciting story, learn the lesson of God's perfect timing—and the importance of our well-timed obedience.

These chapters also present two other lessons: watching out for impulsive decisions and fulfilling God's purposes in the task at hand.

PERSONAL APPLICATION

Esther was a queen. We might imagine that this gave her every right to do as she pleased. In reality, she had virtually no rights and little access to the king. Under the circumstances, it was better for Esther not to reveal her Jewish identity immediately (Esther 2:10). She waited for a better time, a time when she could reveal the truth after the king had been prepared.

While boldness in stating our identity as God's people is our responsibility, at times a good strategy is to keep quiet until we have won the right to be heard. This is especially true when dealing with those in authority over us. We can always let them see the difference God makes in our lives, but we should make sure the timing is right before we speak.

Think of how your life displays your faith to your friends, neighbors, and coworkers. Next, consider when the right time would be to explain your faith to them. When God gives you the opportunity, carefully and lovingly share what you believe (see 1 Peter 3:15).

BIBLE READING

[10]Esther had not told anyone of her nationality and family background, for Mordecai had told her not to. [11]Every day Mordecai would take a walk near the courtyard of the harem to ask about Esther and to find out what was happening to her.

[12]Before each young woman was taken to the king's bed, she was given the prescribed twelve months of beauty treatments—six months with oil of myrrh, followed by six months with special perfumes and ointments. [13]When the time came for her to go in to the king, she was given her choice of whatever clothing or jewelry she wanted to enhance her beauty. [14]That evening she was taken to the king's private rooms, and the next morning she was brought to the second harem, where the king's wives lived. There she would be under the care of Shaashgaz, another of the king's eunuchs. She would live there for the rest of her life, never going to the king again unless he had especially enjoyed her and requested her by name.

[15]When it was Esther's turn to go to the king, she accepted the advice of Hegai, the eunuch in charge of the harem. She asked for nothing except what he suggested, and she was admired by everyone who saw her. [16]When Esther was taken to King Xerxes at the royal palace in early winter of the seventh year of his reign, [17]the king loved her more than any of the other young women. He was so delighted with her that he set the royal crown on her head and declared her queen instead of Vashti. [18]To celebrate the occasion, he gave a banquet in Esther's honor for all his princes and servants, giving generous gifts to everyone and declaring a public festival for the provinces.

[19]Even after all the young women had been transferred to the second harem and Mordecai had become a palace official, [20]Esther continued to keep her nationality and family background a secret. She was still following Mordecai's orders, just as she did when she was living in his home.   ESTHER 2:10-20

ISKY BUSINESS

PREVIEW

What is the risk in telling your deepest secret to a friend, starting a new job, or reconciling with an estranged relative? No matter how shy or bold a person is by nature, he or she must from time to time decide whether to take risks. It's inevitable. Some people find risk taking terrifying. Others think it's exhilarating. For every person the feeling has a lot to do with how successful other risks were. What's the feeling you get when you think of taking risks?

For Esther, risk taking is more terrifying than exhilarating. But in this reading, it is necessary for her survival, even though it may cost Esther her life. Learn from Esther about balancing risky living with doing God's will.

This passage also has other lessons on reverence, arrogance, and courage.

PERSONAL APPLICATION

Esther risked her life by coming before the king (Esther 4:11–5:2). Her courageous act gives us a model to follow when approaching a difficult or dangerous task. Like Esther, we should: (1) *Calculate the cost.* Esther realized her life was at stake. (2) *Set priorities.* Esther believed that the safety of the Jewish people was more important than her life. (3) *Prepare.* Esther gathered support, fasted, and prayed. (4) *Determine a course of action and move ahead boldly.* Esther didn't second-guess herself or allow her commitment to lessen.

Do you have to face a hostile audience, confront a friend on a delicate subject, make a crucial decision at work, or talk to your family about changes to be made? When you find yourself in a difficult situation that could cost you your job, a close relationship, your reputation, or even your future—follow Esther's example and take action with confidence. You don't have to be brash or brazen; just move ahead with what needs to be done, quietly confident in God's sovereign control of the outcome.

BIBLE READING

11"The whole world knows that anyone who appears before the king in his inner court without being invited is doomed to die unless the king holds out his gold scepter. And the king has not called for me to come to him in more than a month." 12So Hathach gave Esther's message to Mordecai.

13Mordecai sent back this reply to Esther: "Don't think for a moment that you will escape there in the palace when all other Jews are killed. 14If you keep quiet at a time like this, deliverance for the Jews will arise from some other place, but you and your relatives will die. What's more, who can say but that you have been elevated to the palace for just such a time as this?"

15Then Esther sent this reply to Mordecai: 16"Go and gather together all the Jews of Susa and fast for me. Do not eat or drink for three days, night or day. My maids and I will do the same. And then, though it is against the law, I will go in to see the king. If I must die, I am willing to die." 17So Mordecai went away and did as Esther told him.

5:1Three days later, Esther put on her royal robes and entered the inner court of the palace, just across from the king's hall. The king was sitting on his royal throne, facing the entrance. 2When he saw Queen Esther standing there in the inner court, he welcomed her, holding out the gold scepter to her. So Esther approached and touched its tip.   ESTHER 4:11—5:2

OOT IT OUT

PREVIEW

Plant an azalea bush and hope it doesn't die; pull a dandelion blossom and watch it grow back. That's part of the difference between garden plants and weeds—one requires your careful attention; the other defies it.

The same is true for what people plant in their hearts. As you read this passage, notice the difference between the plants Esther grows in her heart and the weeds Haman doesn't root out of his. Esther's courage and love stand out against the hatred and anger that spreads in Haman's wicked heart. He's not a little pot of dirt with a seed growing in him, he's a concrete slab with jagged, ugly, nameless weeds cracking the surface. These weeds will require more than a once-over with the garden shears.

This conclusion to Esther's story contains other lessons: trusting in God's sovereign control; seeing how sin catches up with us; rewards for obeying God; and using Christian holidays to remember God's acts of goodness.

PERSONAL APPLICATION

Hatred and bitterness are like weeds with long roots that grow in the heart and corrupt all of life. Haman is a perfect example of a person who let weeds grow in his heart. Haman was so consumed with hatred toward Mordecai that he could not even enjoy the honor of being invited to Esther's party (Esther 5:9).

Hebrews 12:15 warns us to "Watch out that no bitter root of unbelief rises up among you, for . . . many are corrupted by its poison." Ignoring bitterness, hiding it from others, or making superficial changes in behavior is not enough. If bitterness and unbelief aren't completely removed, they will grow back, making matters worse.

Don't let hatred and bitterness build up in your heart. Like Haman, you will find it corrupting you (Esther 6:13; 7:9-10). If the mere mention of someone's name provokes you to anger, confess to God your bitterness and sin.

BIBLE READING

³Then the king asked her, "What do you want, Queen Esther? What is your request? I will give it to you, even if it is half the kingdom!"

⁴And Esther replied, "If it please Your Majesty, let the king and Haman come today to a banquet I have prepared for the king."

⁵The king turned to his attendants and said, "Tell Haman to come quickly to a banquet, as Esther has requested." So the king and Haman went to Esther's banquet.

⁶And while they were drinking wine, the king said to Esther, "Now tell me what you really want. What is your request? I will give it to you, even if it is half the kingdom!"

⁷Esther replied, "This is my request and deepest wish. ⁸If Your Majesty is pleased with me and wants to grant my request, please come with Haman tomorrow to the banquet I will prepare for you. Then tomorrow I will explain what this is all about."

⁹What a happy man Haman was as he left the banquet! But when he saw Mordecai sitting at the gate, not standing up or trembling nervously before him, he was furious. ¹⁰However, he restrained himself and went on home. Then he gathered together his friends and Zeresh, his wife, ¹¹and boasted to them about his great wealth and his many children. He bragged about the honors the king had given him and how he had been promoted over all the other officials and leaders.

¹²Then Haman added, "And that's not all! Queen Esther invited only me and the king himself to the banquet she prepared for us. And she has invited me to dine with her and the king again tomorrow!" ¹³Then he added, "But all this is meaningless as long as I see Mordecai the Jew just sitting there at the palace gate."

¹⁴So Haman's wife, Zeresh, and all his friends suggested, "Set up a gallows that stands seventy-five feet tall, and in the morning ask the king to hang Mordecai on it. When this is done, you can go on your merry way to the banquet with the king." This pleased Haman immensely, and he ordered the gallows set up.

ESTHER 5:3-14

AIR-WEATHER FAITH

PREVIEW

Most of us have had fair-weather friends. Their friendship is a mirage. As long as you're rich and carefree, they love you, they stand by your side, and they laugh at your jokes. But as soon as you lose your job or popularity, those fair-weather friends disappear faster than your paycheck. The blows inflicted by such impostors do a lot of damage because they hit you when you're the most vulnerable.

In this reading, Satan thinks that Job's faith in God is that of a fair-weather friend. As long as life is good and things are going Job's way, of course his faith in God is secure. But the loss of loved ones here and a little disease there will make Job's faith extinct—at least that's what Satan thinks.

Also note in this passage who the real enemy is, what believers can expect from him, and how he attacks.

PERSONAL APPLICATION

Satan attacked Job's motives, saying that he was blameless and upright only because he had no reason to turn against God (Job 1:9). Everything was going well for Job. Satan wanted to prove that Job was worshiping God not out of love, but because God had given him so much.

Satan accurately analyzed why many people trust God. They are fair-weather believers, following God only when everything is going well. Adversity destroys such superficial faith. But adversity strengthens real faith by causing believers to dig their roots deeper into God in order to withstand the storms.

How deep does your faith go? Put the roots of your faith down deep into God when life's skies are sunny. Then when the storms come, you will be able to stand strong.

BIBLE READING

¹One day the angels came again to present themselves before the LORD, and Satan the Accuser came with them. ²"Where have you come from?" the LORD asked Satan.

And Satan answered the LORD, "I have been going back and forth across the earth, watching everything that's going on."

³Then the LORD asked Satan, "Have you noticed my servant Job? He is the finest man in all the earth—a man of complete integrity. He fears God and will have nothing to do with evil. And he has maintained his integrity, even though you persuaded me to harm him without cause."

⁴Satan replied to the LORD, "Skin for skin—he blesses you only because you bless him. A man will give up everything he has to save his life. ⁵But take away his health, and he will surely curse you to your face!"

⁶"All right, do with him as you please," the LORD said to Satan. "But spare his life." ⁷So Satan left the Lord's presence, and he struck Job with a terrible case of boils from head to foot.

JOB 2:1-7

Good Guys and Bad Guys

Preview

In any personal struggle or tragedy, more advice will come your way than you need or want. Some of it is helpful, but much of it is hurtful.

In this reading, Job receives the latter kind of advice—hurtful. In this first round of discussion between Job and his friends, the friends begin by gently explaining their belief that Job must have sinned to bring so much pain on himself. Job doesn't think so. Read and see who's right.

There are a lot of good points in this passage: despairing in suffering (Job); "messages from God" that aren't (Eliphaz); how to benefit from pain (Eliphaz); being slow to give advice to people who are upset (Job); a lasting source of security (Job); the effects of long-term suffering on our emotional state (Job); insensitivity (Zophar); and hope in life after death (Job).

Personal Application

Part of what Eliphaz said in Job 4:7-8 is true, and part is false. It is true that those who promote sin and trouble eventually will be punished; it is false that good and innocent people never suffer.

Because we live in a fallen world, those who love God and obey his commands are not necessarily immune to suffering. Although suffering is not a pleasant experience, we should try to have a joyful attitude when we go through it, knowing that it will be used by God to transform our character to be more like Christ (see James 1:2-4). In addition, we should look at suffering as a test of our faithfulness to Christ, and should strive to rely on his grace to pull us through these difficult times.

If you are struggling with a painful illness or sorrow, don't be quick to blame yourself for your suffering. Instead, rely on God and his goodness. Ask him to teach you and to lead you through it.

BIBLE READING

[3]"In the past you have encouraged many a troubled soul to trust in God; you have supported those who were weak. [4]Your words have strengthened the fallen; you steadied those who wavered. [5]But now when trouble strikes, you faint and are broken. [6]Does your reverence for God give you no confidence? Shouldn't you believe that God will care for those who are upright?

[7]"Stop and think! Does the innocent person perish? When has the upright person been destroyed? [8]My experience shows that those who plant trouble and cultivate evil will harvest the same. [9]They perish by a breath from God. They vanish in a blast of his anger. [10]Though they are fierce young lions, they will all be broken and destroyed. [11]The fierce lion will starve, and the cubs of the lioness will be scattered.

[12]"This truth was given me in secret, as though whispered in my ear. [13]It came in a vision at night as others slept. [14]Fear gripped me; I trembled and shook with terror. [15]A spirit swept past my face. Its wind sent shivers up my spine. [16]It stopped, but I couldn't see its shape. There was a form before my eyes, and a hushed voice said, [17]'Can a mortal be just and upright before God? Can a person be pure before the Creator?'"   JOB 4:3-17

WHAT ARE FRIENDS FOR?

PREVIEW

What do you most want from your friends? Think especially of your times of need, when you're emotionally down, defeated, confused, or vulnerable. What would you want your friends to do at times like that?

In the second round of discussion between Job and his friends, Job indirectly lists the ways in which his friends could comfort him. Unfortunately, they don't take the hint and, instead, go at him even harder. Some friends they are! As you read this passage, learn how *not* to relate to your friends in need.

Other lessons here include: finding real wisdom; being defensive (Bildad); and having confidence in God (Job).

PERSONAL APPLICATION

Job's friends were supposed to be comforting him in his grief. Instead they condemned him for causing his own suffering (Job 16:1–17:16). Job began his second reply to Eliphaz by calling him and his friends "miserable comforters" (16:2).

Job's words reveal several ways to become a better comforter to those in pain: (1) don't talk just for the sake of talking; (2) don't sermonize by giving pat answers; (3) don't accuse or criticize; (4) put yourself in the other person's place; and (5) offer help and encouragement.

The next time someone close to you is suffering, try Job's suggestions to comfort him or her, knowing that these suggestions were given by a person who needed great comfort. The best comforters are those who know something about personal suffering.

BIBLE READING

[1]Then Job spoke again:

[2]"I have heard all this before. What miserable comforters you are! [3]Won't you ever stop your flow of foolish words? What have I said that makes you speak so endlessly? [4]I could say the same things if you were in my place. I could spout off my criticisms against you and shake my head at you. [5]But that's not what I would do. I would speak in a way that helps you. I would try to take away your grief. [6]But as it is, my grief remains no matter how I defend myself. And it does not help if I refuse to speak."

[7]"O God, you have ground me down and devastated my family. [8]You have reduced me to skin and bones—as proof, they say, of my sins. [9]God hates me and tears angrily at my flesh. He gnashes his teeth at me and pierces me with his eyes. [10]People jeer and laugh at me. They slap my cheek in contempt. A mob gathers against me. [11]God has handed me over to sinners. He has tossed me into the hands of the wicked.

[12]"I was living quietly until he broke me apart. He took me by the neck and dashed me to pieces. Then he set me up as his target. [13]His archers surrounded me, and his arrows pierced me without mercy. The ground is wet with my blood. [14]Again and again he smashed me, charging at me like a warrior. [15]Here I sit in sackcloth. I have surrendered, and I sit in the dust. [16]My eyes are red with weeping; darkness covers my eyes. [17]Yet I am innocent, and my prayer is pure.   JOB 16:1-17

I'M INNOCENT, I TELL YOU

PREVIEW

Imagine that you've been framed for a crime. You feel frantic because no one believes your story. You're embarrassed because your name has been muddied. Despite your frustration and gloom, you decide not to give up and determine to fight harder.

In trying to explain why Job is suffering, his friends have falsely accused him of sinning. Job has denied that this is true, but the friends don't believe that Job is innocent—there is too much circumstantial evidence against him. Job isn't ready to give in yet, so he digs in his heels and defends his innocence.

Is Job innocent? Judge for yourself and learn from his defense.

See these other lessons as well: being careful in applying God's commands and moral standards to others (Eliphaz); showing compassion rather than giving advice (Job); and attacking others (Bildad).

PERSONAL APPLICATION

In the middle of all the accusations, Job declared that he was not a sinner and that his conscience was clear (Job 27:6). How could he make this claim? Job was not claiming to be perfect, neither was he belittling his need for God's redemption. He was simply saying that he had lived a righteous life before God (1:1). As a result, his conscience *was* clear.

Outward circumstances are not always an accurate indicator of a person's relationship with God. Some people who are blessed with health, power, or wealth are not righteous (see Matthew 5:45). Conversely, some people who are sick, poor, or powerless *are* righteous in God's eyes. Job's friends were wrong to assume that his suffering was a result of sin.

We must be careful not to make the same mistake that Job's friends made. We can't claim to have sinless lives, but we *can* claim forgiven lives. When we confess our sins to God he forgives us. Then we, too, can live with a clear conscience (see 1 John 1:9).

Be slow to judge others. And make it your goal to keep a clear conscience before God.

BIBLE READING

²"I make this vow by the living God, who has taken away my rights, by the Almighty who has embittered my soul. ³As long as I live, while I have breath from God, ⁴my lips will speak no evil, and my tongue will speak no lies. ⁵I will never concede that you are right; until I die, I will defend my innocence. ⁶I will maintain my innocence without wavering. My conscience is clear for as long as I live."   JOB 27:2-6

²⁰"I cry to you, O God, but you don't answer me. I stand before you, and you don't bother to look. ²¹You have become cruel toward me. You persecute me with your great power. ²²You throw me into the whirlwind and destroy me in the storm. ²³And I know that you are sending me to my death—the destination of all who live.

²⁴"Surely no one would turn against the needy when they cry for help. ²⁵Did I not weep for those in trouble? Was I not deeply grieved for the needy? ²⁶So I looked for good, but evil came instead. I waited for the light, but darkness fell. ²⁷My heart is troubled and restless. Days of affliction have come upon me. ²⁸I walk in gloom, without sunlight. I stand in the public square and cry for help. ²⁹But instead, I am considered a brother to jackals and a companion to ostriches. ³⁰My skin has turned dark, and my bones burn with fever. ³¹My harp plays sad music, and my flute accompanies those who weep.   JOB 30:20-31

WHY ASK WHY?

PREVIEW

A child will question the actions of the wisest, most loving parent. "Why must I brush my teeth?" "Why do I have to eat my vegetables?" Wise parents, whether they try to explain or not, insist that a child do what is best for them. They understand far more about the bigger picture than kids do.

Job has been asking *why* for a while now, and no one has been able to give him a satisfactory answer. But one person hasn't spoken up yet. That person is Elihu, the youngest "comforter" of the group. He has held his tongue until now because of his age, but he, too, is not satisfied with the answers given by Bildad, Eliphaz, and Zophar. Elihu rightly says that Job's friends have been wrong to accuse Job of sin, and that Job has been wrong to defend his goodness.

Look for other lessons in the way these men talk: the importance of speaking at the right time; applying truth; and giving advice to others.

PERSONAL APPLICATION

It's natural to want to know what's happening in our lives because being informed brings a sense of security.

Elihu claimed to have the answer for Job's biggest question, "Why doesn't God tell me what is happening?" Elihu told Job that God was trying to answer him, but he was not listening. Elihu misjudged both Job and God on this point. If God were to answer all our questions, we would not be adequately tested. What if God had said, "Job, Satan's going to test you and afflict you, but in the end you'll be healed and get everything back"? Job's greatest test was not the pain, but that he did not know *why* he was suffering.

Learn to trust in God who is good; not in the goodness of life.

BIBLE READING

⁵"Look up into the sky and see the clouds high above you. ⁶If you sin, what do you accomplish against him? Even if you sin again and again, what effect will it have on him? ⁷If you are good, is this some great gift to him? What could you possibly give him? ⁸No, your sins affect only people like yourself, and your good deeds affect only other people.

⁹"The oppressed cry out beneath the wrongs that are done to them. They groan beneath the power of the mighty. ¹⁰Yet they don't ask, 'Where is God my Creator, the one who gives songs in the night? ¹¹Where is the one who makes us wiser than the animals and birds?'

¹²"And if they do cry out and God does not answer, it is because of their pride. ¹³But it is wrong to say God doesn't listen, to say the Almighty isn't concerned. ¹⁴And it is even more false to say he doesn't see what is going on. He will bring about justice if you will only wait. ¹⁵But do you cry out against him because he does not respond in anger? ¹⁶Job, you have protested in vain. You have spoken like a fool."   JOB 35:5-16

UCH HIGHER WAYS

PREVIEW

Educators know that much of a person's ability to learn a particular skill depends on *readiness*—having developed the mental tools to learn. At the point of readiness, learning is easy, even effortless. Until then, the student simply isn't ready.

Job is not ready to understand the reasons for his suffering. Despite his well thought out arguments and reasonable appeals, he does not have the mental capacity to understand God's ways.

The attacks of Job's friends have only reinforced Job's belief that he never deserved to suffer in the first place. This belief has made him bitterly uncomfortable with his situation. He wants to know why God has treated him so badly without explaining his reasons or purpose. God finally speaks, saying (in effect), "Do I answer to you? You wouldn't understand even if I explained it to you. You need to trust me."

Other lessons are here for us relate to that idea—finding the answer in God and realizing that God's understanding is beyond our grasp.

PERSONAL APPLICATION

Out of a whirlwind, God spoke to Job (Job 38:1). He didn't answer any of Job's questions. Instead, God used Job's ignorance of the earth's natural order to reveal his ignorance of God's moral order. If Job did not understand the workings of God's physical creation, how could he possibly understand God's mind and character? There is no standard or criterion higher than God himself by which to judge. God is the standard. Our option is to submit to his authority and rest in his care.

BIBLE READING

[1]Then the LORD answered Job from the whirlwind:

[2]"Who is this that questions my wisdom with such ignorant words? [3]Brace yourself, because I have some questions for you, and you must answer them.

[4]"Where were you when I laid the foundations of the earth? Tell me, if you know so much. [5]Do you know how its dimensions were determined and who did the surveying? [6]What supports its foundations, and who laid its cornerstone [7]as the morning stars sang together and all the angels shouted for joy?

[8]"Who defined the boundaries of the sea as it burst from the womb, [9]and as I clothed it with clouds and thick darkness? [10]For I locked it behind barred gates, limiting its shores. [11]I said, 'Thus far and no farther will you come. Here your proud waves must stop!'

[12]"Have you ever commanded the morning to appear and caused the dawn to rise in the east? [13]Have you ever told the daylight to spread to the ends of the earth, to bring an end to the night's wickedness? [14]For the features of the earth take shape as the light approaches, and the dawn is robed in red. [15]The light disturbs the haunts of the wicked, and it stops the arm that is raised in violence.

[16]"Have you explored the springs from which the seas come? Have you walked about and explored their depths? [17]Do you know where the gates of death are located? Have you seen the gates of utter gloom? [18]Do you realize the extent of the earth? Tell me about it if you know!

[19]"Where does the light come from, and where does the darkness go? [20]Can you take it to its home? Do you know how to get there? [21]But of course you know all this! For you were born before it was all created, and you are so very experienced!

JOB 38:1-21

Running up the White Flag

PREVIEW

There are times when surrender makes more sense than the bravest fight. Consider three examples: fighting a war when your side has been decimated, campaigning for a candidate after he or she has lost the race, and arguing with a spouse when he or she is right and you're wrong. No honor comes from resisting at times like these.

In this reading, Job admits defeat and surrenders to God. This is not the end of Job, however, because God has plans for Job's future.

This concludes the story of Job. God has proven his point and Job's reply is an admission of defeat. It's the good kind of surrender. Don't feel sorry for Job—get in line, yourself.

Other lessons in this passage include: not judging others or interpreting their circumstances as a judgment on them; praying for our enemies; and the rewards of following God in trust.

PERSONAL APPLICATION

Throughout the book, Job's friends had asked him to admit his sin and ask for forgiveness. Eventually Job did indeed repent. Ironically, Job's repentance was not the kind called for by his friends. He did not ask for forgiveness for committing secret sins, but for questioning God's sovereignty and justice. Job repented of his attitude and acknowledged God's great power and perfect justice (Job 42:1-6).

We sin when we angrily ask, "If God is in control, how could he let this happen?" Because we are locked into time and are unable to see beyond today, we cannot know the reasons for everything that happens. Job openly and honestly faced God and admitted that he was the one who had been foolish.

Are you using what you can't understand as an excuse for your lack of trust? Admit to God that you don't have enough faith to trust him. True faith begins in such humility. Will you trust God with your unanswered questions?

BIBLE READING

¹Then Job replied to the LORD:

²"I know that you can do anything, and no one can stop you. ³You ask, 'Who is this that questions my wisdom with such ignorance?' It is I. And I was talking about things I did not understand, things far too wonderful for me.

⁴"You said, 'Listen and I will speak! I have some questions for you, and you must answer them.'

⁵"I had heard about you before, but now I have seen you with my own eyes. ⁶I take back everything I said, and I sit in dust and ashes to show my repentance."

⁷After the LORD had finished speaking to Job, he said to Eliphaz the Temanite: "I am angry with you and with your two friends, for you have not been right in what you said about me, as my servant Job was. ⁸Now take seven young bulls and seven rams and go to my servant Job and offer a burnt offering for yourselves. My servant Job will pray for you, and I will accept his prayer on your behalf. I will not treat you as you deserve, for you have not been right in what you said about me, as my servant Job was."

⁹So Eliphaz the Temanite, Bildad the Shuhite, and Zophar the Naamathite did as the LORD commanded them, and the LORD accepted Job's prayer.

¹⁰When Job prayed for his friends, the LORD restored his fortunes. In fact, the LORD gave him twice as much as before! ¹¹Then all his brothers, sisters, and former friends came and feasted with him in his home. And they consoled him and comforted him because of all the trials the LORD had brought against him. And each of them brought him a gift of money and a gold ring. JOB 42:1-11

leepless

PREVIEW

How well do you sleep when everything seems to be going wrong in your life? Do you lie awake all night worrying about the problems you'll face in the morning?

In this reading, David reveals his secret for sleeping through the night during an overwhelming crisis. David wrote Psalm 3 when he was on the run from his son, Absalom, who was bent on usurping his father's throne. Absalom orchestrated a slick revolt against David and pretty soon David was running for his life. Wouldn't that make *you* sleepless? But David found a cure. As you read Psalm 3, watch how David praises the aspects of God's character that give every believer cause to sleep well.

The other psalms in this section have other lessons if you're willing to pursue them: good reasons to live God's way (Psalm 1); God's ultimate rule (Psalm 2); and God's protection and peace (Psalm 4).

PERSONAL APPLICATION

Sleep does not come easily during a crisis. Most people toss and turn with the anxiety, thinking about the problem. David may have had sleepless nights when Absalom rebelled and gathered an army to kill him. But he slept peacefully, even during the rebellion (Psalm 3:5). What made the difference? He knew that the Lord was watching over him.

It is easier to sleep well when we trust God to control our circumstances. The next time you lie awake at night worrying about circumstances you cannot change, pour out your concerns to him until he brings the sleep you need. Ask him to intervene. And thank him that he is in control.

BIBLE READING

¹ O LORD, I have so many enemies;
    so many are against me.
² So many are saying,
    "God will never rescue him!"   *Interlude*

³ But you, O LORD, are a shield around me,
    my glory, and the one who lifts my head high.
⁴ I cried out to the LORD,
    and he answered me from his holy mountain. *Interlude*

⁵ I lay down and slept.
    I woke up in safety,
    for the LORD was watching over me.
⁶ I am not afraid of ten thousand enemies
    who surround me on every side.

⁷ Arise, O LORD!
    Rescue me, my God!
Slap all my enemies in the face!
    Shatter the teeth of the wicked!

⁸ Victory comes from you, O LORD.
    May your blessings rest on your people.   *Interlude*

PSALM 3:1-8

One Good Shove Deserves . . .

PREVIEW

Being falsely accused or slandered is inevitable, especially if you are living your life for God. But how should you respond to such an injustice? Should you defend yourself and fight back? Or should you turn the other cheek?

David knew how to respond to injustice. Psalm 7 reveals his response and solution for dealing with unjust people. David knows that restoring justice is God's responsibility, so he submits a request rather than taking matters into his own hands. Learn from David how to respond when you're angry about an injustice.

Other psalms in this section tell us that God defends us against slander (Psalm 5); God rescues us when we're in trouble (Psalm 6); and God the Creator cares for us (Psalm 8).

PERSONAL APPLICATION

David wrote Psalm 7 in response to the personal attacks of those who claimed that he was trying to kill Saul and seize the throne (see 1 Samuel 24:9-11). Instead of taking matters into his own hands and striking back, David entrusted himself to God and cried out to him for justice. David did not have the authority to enact justice himself, so he did not try.

That should be our response. Whenever we are slandered, we should pray, not slander back; whenever we are insulted, we should pray, not give a retort. God says, "I will take vengeance; I will repay those who deserve it" (see Romans 12:19; see also Deuteronomy 32:35; Hebrews 10:30).

The next time someone attacks you, ask God to take over your case, bring justice, and protect your reputation. Only he can deal justly with the offender.

BIBLE READING

¹ I come to you for protection, O LORD my God.
   Save me from my persecutors—rescue me!
² If you don't, they will maul me like a lion,
   tearing me to pieces with no one to rescue me.

³ O LORD my God, if I have done wrong
   or am guilty of injustice,
⁴ if I have betrayed a friend
   or plundered my enemy without cause,
⁵ then let my enemies capture me.
   Let them trample me into the ground.
   Let my honor be left in the dust.   *Interlude*

⁶ Arise, O LORD, in anger!
   Stand up against the fury of my enemies!
   Wake up, my God, and bring justice!
⁷ Gather the nations before you.
   Sit on your throne high above them.
⁸ The LORD passes judgment on the nations.
   Declare me righteous, O LORD,
   for I am innocent, O Most High!
⁹ End the wickedness of the ungodly,
   but help all those who obey you.
For you look deep within the mind and heart,
   O righteous God.   PSALM 7:1-9

To Tell the Truth

PREVIEW

As much as we favor honesty, falsehood can be terribly convenient. If you want to impress someone, a *slight* exaggeration of your various strengths and accomplishments may do the trick. Or if you want to get in the good graces of a person who has influence or status, flattery comes in handy. When you do something wrong, you know how natural it is to cover it up. Telling the truth can take conscious effort.

The words of Psalm 12 verify this fact. They also reveal that lying was just as much a problem in David's time as it is today. But in all the deceit, there is hope—God is in control and will deal justly with those who make a lifestyle out of lying. What a great lesson to learn!

Other psalms in this reading contain encouraging news about how God responds to our cries for help (Psalm 9); his awareness of injustice (Psalm 10); and his sovereignty over wicked people (Psalm 11).

PERSONAL APPLICATION

It seems as though each day we are bombarded with news stories about violence and perversity. This may lead us to think that lying and other forms of deceit are relatively harmless and less sinful. Psalm 12 makes it perfectly clear, however, that God does not overlook lies, flattery, or boasting. He hates all kinds of deceit and commands us not to use them (Exodus 20:16).

Deception comes from a desire to cover up what should not be hidden. In this, our tongue can be our greatest enemy. Though small, the tongue can do great damage (James 3:5).

Watch how you use your tongue. When you are tempted to deceive someone, remember that God hates lies. Strive to make your speech entirely truthful all the time for God's glory.

BIBLE READING

¹ Help, O LORD, for the godly are fast disappearing!
  The faithful have vanished from the earth!
² Neighbors lie to each other,
  speaking with flattering lips and insincere hearts.
³ May the LORD bring their flattery to an end
  and silence their proud tongues.
⁴ They say, "We will lie to our hearts' content.
  Our lips are our own—who can stop us?"

⁵ The LORD replies, "I have seen violence done to the helpless,
  and I have heard the groans of the poor.
 Now I will rise up to rescue them,
  as they have longed for me to do."
⁶ The LORD's promises are pure,
  like silver refined in a furnace,
  purified seven times over.

⁷ Therefore, LORD, we know you will protect the oppressed,
  preserving them forever from this lying generation,
⁸ even though the wicked strut about,
  and evil is praised throughout the land.   PSALM 12:1-8

ood Company

PREVIEW

With what kind of people do you hang out? How would you describe your friends? Are they a good influence on you? Or do you do things when you're with them that make you feel uncomfortable?

Psalm 16 shows us the people with whom we should keep company—and it's not the popular or influential crowd. In this psalm we see that David seeks out a certain kind of person—the kind we should get to know.

In other psalms, we find help with several dilemmas: what to do when God doesn't answer prayers of distress (Psalm 13); how to respond when people deny that God exists (Psalm 14); and how to live a life that no one can fault (Psalm 15).

PERSONAL APPLICATION

Some people try to impress their friends by name-dropping. If they have met a famous person, for example, they may casually mention this fact to others to enhance their status. Others spend time with certain people to bolster their image. But truly noble people don't do that. They don't try to become famous or gain recognition; they strive to live as God desires.

Beware of temptations to seek someone's company solely to enhance your status. And remember that although hanging out with the wrong crowd can be fun at first, if you desire to please God, the fun you have will soon turn to spiritual conflict. Instead, like David, seek the company of those who can build you up spiritually—those who are committed to God and have the right perspective on life (Psalm 16:3).

BIBLE READING

¹ Keep me safe, O God,
> for I have come to you for refuge.

² I said to the LORD, "You are my Master!
> All the good things I have are from you."

³ The godly people in the land
> are my true heroes!
> I take pleasure in them!

⁴ Those who chase after other gods will be filled with sorrow.
> I will not take part in their sacrifices
> or even speak the names of their gods.

⁵ LORD, you alone are my inheritance, my cup of blessing.
> You guard all that is mine.

⁶ The land you have given me is a pleasant land.
> What a wonderful inheritance!

⁷ I will bless the LORD who guides me;
> even at night my heart instructs me.

⁸ I know the LORD is always with me.
> I will not be shaken, for he is right beside me.

⁹ No wonder my heart is filled with joy,
> and my mouth shouts his praises!
> My body rests in safety.

¹⁰ For you will not leave my soul among the dead
> or allow your godly one to rot in the grave.

¹¹ You will show me the way of life,
> granting me the joy of your presence
> and the pleasures of living with you forever.

PSALM 16:1–11

 t's OK

PREVIEW

One night you get a call from the Christmas pageant chairperson at church. The chairperson wants you to help out this year. You know that you don't have time, but you feel too guilty to say no. After hanging up, you feel guilty for taking on a responsibility for which you really don't have time.

Psalm 19 deals with guilt in a constructive way. Here, David sees his guilt and talks to God about it. As you read this passage, look for the right way to deal with guilt.

Other psalms in this reading teach about crying to God for justice (Psalm 17); asking God for help and strength against evil (Psalm 18); and trusting in God for strength when facing challenges (Psalm 20).

PERSONAL APPLICATION

Guilt plagues most people. We worry that we may have committed a sin without knowing it, done something good but with selfish intentions, failed to put our best efforts into an important task, or brushed off a significant responsibility. Guilt isn't always bad, however—it can alert us to changes we need to make in our behavior or beliefs. But at the same time, we should be careful not to let our guilt cripple us or make us afraid to act.

We should follow David's example by asking God to "cleanse" us of our "hidden faults" and keep us from deliberately doing wrong. For when we confess our sins, we can take comfort in the fact that our fellowship with God is restored and our conscience cleared (see 1 John 1:9). We no longer have a reason to feel guilty.

Take care of your *real* guilt before God by confessing your sins to him. Then thank God that he has forgiven you.

BIBLE READING

⁷ The law of the LORD is perfect,
    reviving the soul.
The decrees of the LORD are trustworthy,
    making wise the simple.
⁸ The commandments of the LORD are right,
    bringing joy to the heart.
The commands of the LORD are clear,
    giving insight to life.
⁹ Reverence for the LORD is pure,
    lasting forever.
The laws of the LORD are true;
    each one is fair.
¹⁰ They are more desirable than gold,
    even the finest gold.
They are sweeter than honey,
    even honey dripping from the comb.
¹¹ They are a warning to those who hear them;
    there is great reward for those who obey them.

¹² How can I know all the sins lurking in my heart?
    Cleanse me from these hidden faults.
¹³ Keep me from deliberate sins!
    Don't let them control me.
Then I will be free of guilt
    and innocent of great sin.

¹⁴ May the words of my mouth and the thoughts of my heart
    be pleasing to you,
    O LORD, my rock and my redeemer.   PSALM 19:7-14

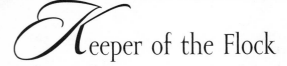eeper of the Flock

PREVIEW

Ask children about their favorite pets and you're likely to get a short list: dogs, cats, hamsters, fish, gerbils, and rabbits.

The parallels between our relationship to God and that of a child to his or her pet hold many lessons for us. Psalm 23, while not about pets in particular, portrays our relationship with God as that of sheep to their shepherd. Although being compared to sheep isn't necessarily flattering, God's love for us becomes more concrete and real as we see how he cares for us.

The other psalms in this reading contain prayers about experiencing victory in battle (Psalm 21); finding joy in suffering (Psalm 22); and being a good owner (Psalm 24).

PERSONAL APPLICATION

In portraying the Lord as a shepherd (Psalm 23:1), David wrote from his own experience because he had spent his early years caring for sheep (see 1 Samuel 16:10-11). Sheep depend completely on their shepherd—good shepherds make sure that their sheep get plenty of green pasture as well as shelter from the elements and wild animals. When David wrote, "The Lord is my shepherd," he showed us that God, like a shepherd, cares and provides for us much the way that human shepherds care and provide for their sheep.

In the New Testament, Jesus is called the good shepherd (John 10:11); the great Shepherd (Hebrews 13:20); and the head Shepherd (1 Peter 5:4). What a great truth that God cares for us like this!

Whenever you doubt God's love and care for you, reread Psalm 23 and remember how God, your Shepherd, cares for you.

BIBLE READING

[1] The LORD is my shepherd;
　　I have everything I need.
[2] He lets me rest in green meadows;
　　he leads me beside peaceful streams.
[3]　He renews my strength.
He guides me along right paths,
　　bringing honor to his name.

[4] Even when I walk
　　through the dark valley of death,
I will not be afraid,
　　for you are close beside me.
Your rod and your staff
　　protect and comfort me.

[5] You prepare a feast for me
　　in the presence of my enemies.
You welcome me as a guest,
　　anointing my head with oil.
　　My cup overflows with blessings.
[6] Surely your goodness and unfailing love will pursue me
　　all the days of my life,
and I will live in the house of the LORD
　　forever.　　　　　　　　　　PSALM 23:1-6

The Waiting Game

PREVIEW

Waiting can feel like torture when you're afraid. David wrote Psalm 27 at a time when he was terribly afraid, but he didn't panic. Instead, he called upon the Lord and pleaded his case before him. Then he waited patiently for the Lord to rescue him. Any scared person knows that fear can cause people to make hasty, unwise decisions, and cause them to act before they're ready. Fear can make people impatient and reckless. As you read this psalm, learn from David's example about taking your fears to God.

The three other psalms in this reading also have something to say about times of fear: when you're afraid of losing your honor (Psalm 25); your reputation (Psalm 26); or even your life (Psalm 28).

PERSONAL APPLICATION

David's men wanted him to kill Saul. David knew that it was not his job—the fulfillment of God's promise would come about in God's own timing. So David placed his trust in God and waited for the Lord, despite his fear (Psalm 27:14). As it turns out, David had to wait fourteen years before being crowned king.

Waiting for God takes effort. It may seem as though God has refused to answer our prayers or doesn't feel the urgency of our situation. But God knows much more than we do. Lamentations 3:24-26 urges us to hope in and wait for the Lord because often God uses waiting to refresh, renew, and teach us.

David trusted God to do what was right. Trust in God's timing and make use of your times of waiting by discovering what God may be trying to teach you.

BIBLE READING

¹ The LORD is my light and my salvation—
　　so why should I be afraid?
The LORD protects me from danger—
　　so why should I tremble?

² When evil people come to destroy me,
　　when my enemies and foes attack me,
　　they will stumble and fall.
³ Though a mighty army surrounds me,
　　my heart will know no fear.
Even if they attack me,
　　I remain confident.

⁴ The one thing I ask of the LORD—
　　the thing I seek most—
is to live in the house of the LORD all the days of my life,
　　delighting in the LORD's perfections
　　and meditating in his Temple.
⁵ For he will conceal me there when troubles come;
　　he will hide me in his sanctuary.
　　He will place me out of reach on a high rock.
⁶ Then I will hold my head high,
　　above my enemies who surround me.
At his Tabernacle I will offer sacrifices with shouts of joy,
　　singing and praising the LORD with music.

¹⁴ Wait patiently for the LORD.
　　Be brave and courageous.
　　Yes, wait patiently for the LORD.　　PSALM 27:1-6, 14

In Good Hands

PREVIEW

Thirty seconds of bungee jumping requires more trust than many people have in God over a lifetime. People entrust their lives to a total stranger and an unknown piece of equipment—all for a few seconds of excitement.

Unlike many people today, David knows where to place his trust—and it isn't in the hands of strangers. In Psalm 31, David unloads anguish over his circumstances—feeling alone, helpless, and threatened. His source of hope, however, is that he knows he's in good hands.

Trust is the theme of the psalms in this reading: trusting God to give us peace and strength through life's storms (Psalm 29); trusting ourselves to God (Psalm 30); and trusting God to free us from guilt (Psalm 32).

PERSONAL APPLICATION

David wrote many psalms about the attacks of his enemies and the utter ruin they made of his peace of mind. Psalm 31 is one of them. David was so plagued by opponents that he felt he was "dying from grief" (Psalm 31:10). Yet in the same prayer he added the words, "I entrust my spirit into your hand" (31:5), showing that he had complete trust in God.

Jesus used this phrase as he was dying on the cross—showing his absolute dependence on God the Father (see Luke 23:46). Stephen expressed a similar sentiment as he was being stoned to death (see Acts 7:59), confident that he was passing from God's earthly care to God's eternal care.

Having faith in God—really trusting him—risks nothing. That's why we can safely commit our possessions, our families, and our jobs to God.

BIBLE READING

¹ O LORD, I have come to you for protection;
  don't let me be put to shame.
  Rescue me, for you always do what is right.
² Bend down and listen to me;
  rescue me quickly.
  Be for me a great rock of safety,
  a fortress where my enemies cannot reach me.

³ You are my rock and my fortress.
  For the honor of your name, lead me out of this peril.
⁴ Pull me from the trap my enemies set for me,
  for I find protection in you alone.
⁵ I entrust my spirit into your hand.
  Rescue me, LORD, for you are a faithful God.

¹⁴ But I am trusting you, O LORD,
  saying, "You are my God!"
¹⁵ My future is in your hands.
  Rescue me from those who hunt me down relentlessly.

PSALM 31:1-5, 14-15

Everything We Need

PREVIEW

If you were to make a wish list, what would you include? Would you write down what you truly have a great need for, or just what you crave? Life, after all, isn't fair, and few people have enough money for all that they want.

Psalm 34 deals with needs and the wonderful way that God provides for them. Do you need something? Follow David's advice—his observation from his own experience is a truth more durable than any earthly goods.

There are many other things to praise God for in this group of psalms as well, such as the protection he gives us from death (Psalm 33) and unjust enemies (Psalm 35), and for his great goodness (Psalm 36).

PERSONAL APPLICATION

David said that "those who trust in the LORD will never lack any good thing" (Psalm 34:10). Can this be true? How can it be that God's people lack *nothing* good?

God knows what we truly need. Even though many Christians live in poverty and endure hardship, God gives them the spiritual nourishment they need in order to live for him. This is what David is saying here—if we have a relationship with God, we have all we need, despite our circumstances.

If you feel you don't have everything you need, ask yourself several questions: (1) Is this really a need? (2) Is this really good for me? (3) Is this the best time for me to have what I want? Even if you answer yes to all three questions, remember that God's thoughts are completely different from yours (Isaiah 55:8). He may want you to learn that you need *him* more than you think.

BIBLE READING

¹ I will praise the LORD at all times.
　　I will constantly speak his praises.
² I will boast only in the LORD;
　　let all who are discouraged take heart.
³ Come, let us tell of the LORD's greatness;
　　let us exalt his name together.

⁴ I prayed to the LORD, and he answered me,
　　freeing me from all my fears.
⁵ Those who look to him for help will be radiant with joy;
　　no shadow of shame will darken their faces.
⁶ I cried out to the LORD in my suffering, and he heard me.
　　He set me free from all my fears.
⁷ For the angel of the LORD guards all who fear him,
　　and he rescues them.

⁸ Taste and see that the LORD is good.
　　Oh, the joys of those who trust in him!
⁹ Let the LORD's people show him reverence,
　　for those who honor him will have all they need.
¹⁰ Even strong young lions sometimes go hungry,
　　but those who trust in the LORD will never lack any good
　　thing.　　　　　　　　　　　PSALM 34:1–10

elightful

PREVIEW

Sometimes it seems as if wicked people enjoy the most fulfilling lives. They live in luxury, get what they want, and commit awful deeds to maintain their lifestyle. It's very difficult not to look at these people and feel envious. Have you envied people who have little or no concern for God?

Psalm 37 lists a whole host of cures for envy. Focus your attention on verses 3 through 6, the cures that head up the list. Also keep a look out for other cures in this psalm—they're delightful!

As you read these psalms, note also the outcome of confessing sin (Psalm 38); the benefits of waiting for God's timing (Psalm 40); and how to pray when you feel sick or abandoned (Psalm 41).

PERSONAL APPLICATION

Taking delight in the Lord is the cure for envy. David urged us to do this and to commit to him everything we have and do (Psalm 37:3-6). But how does a person "take delight in the Lord" (37:4)? To *delight* means to enjoy, so to take delight in God means to enjoy his presence, his company, and his will. Our goal should be to enjoy God, to want what God wants, to seek his presence, to enjoy his company.

Review any goals you have for your life. Do they match what God wants for you? Make it your goal to take delight in God today. Change your desires and goals to match his.

BIBLE READING

¹ Don't worry about the wicked.

Don't envy those who do wrong.

² For like grass, they soon fade away.

Like springtime flowers, they soon wither.

³ Trust in the LORD and do good.

Then you will live safely in the land and prosper.

⁴ Take delight in the LORD,

and he will give you your heart's desires.

⁵ Commit everything you do to the LORD.

Trust him, and he will help you.

⁶ He will make your innocence as clear as the dawn,

and the justice of your cause will shine like the noonday
sun.

⁷ Be still in the presence of the LORD,

and wait patiently for him to act.

Don't worry about evil people who prosper

or fret about their wicked schemes.

⁸ Stop your anger!

Turn from your rage!

Do not envy others—

it only leads to harm.

⁹ For the wicked will be destroyed,

but those who trust in the LORD will possess the land.

PSALM 37:1-9

hirst Quencher

PREVIEW

A human being can go without food for about thirty to forty days, but can only go about three days without water. Extreme thirst will put you on a single-minded hunt for water. That makes *thirst* a good word for describing deep cravings, doesn't it?

In Psalm 42 we see a person thirsting for God, craving his presence, and still feeling alone or even abandoned by him. This person has longed for God's presence and found no ready source of relief. As you read this psalm, find, with the author, the answer to your own thirst.

Also, find hope in times of discouragement (Psalm 43); help when feeling weary and defeated (Psalm 44); and rejoicing in God's gift of marriage (Psalm 45).

PERSONAL APPLICATION

Do you ever feel alone in your faith? There come times in life when we thirst for God, weep for his help, or even endure ridicule for our faith while waiting for him to answer our prayers (Psalm 42:1-3). We want desperately to feel God's presence or to have some other tangible sign of his help and support. Times like these can lead to depression and discouragement for any Christian.

The writer of Psalm 42 discovered a remedy for these spiritually dry times. He remembered God's great blessings on his life. He realized that although God seemed silent, he was there and was worthy to be praised (42:4-5). He soaked in God's beautiful creation (42:6). He realized that he was never adrift from God's love (42:7-8). He faithfully expected God to act (42:11).

BIBLE READING

¹ As the deer pants for streams of water,
     so I long for you, O God.
² I thirst for God, the living God.
     When can I come and stand before him?
³ Day and night, I have only tears for food,
     while my enemies continually taunt me, saying,
     "Where is this God of yours?"

⁴ My heart is breaking
     as I remember how it used to be:
I walked among the crowds of worshipers,
     leading a great procession to the house of God,
singing for joy and giving thanks—
     it was the sound of a great celebration!

⁵ Why am I discouraged?
     Why so sad?
I will put my hope in God!
     I will praise him again—
     my Savior and ⁶my God!

  Now I am deeply discouraged,
     but I will remember your kindness—
from Mount Hermon, the source of the Jordan,
     from the land of Mount Mizar.
⁷ I hear the tumult of the raging seas
     as your waves and surging tides sweep over me.

⁸ Through each day the LORD pours his unfailing love
         upon me,
     and through each night I sing his songs,
     praying to God who gives me life.   PSALM 42:1-8

Moment of Silence

PREVIEW

In metropolitan areas you might find a sliver of quiet in the early morning hours; to get a taste of true silence, however, you have to go to more rural areas. Have you ever heard the difference? True silence contains no background noise at all. No one is driving by, shouting, or honking, and there is no hum and buzz of a thousand little noises in the distance. There are few places left on earth where you can truly experience silence.

Psalm 46 invites us to sample some silence. Read and consider it, even if you value the hustle and bustle of the big city. Silence allows us to meditate on God's goodness and the other lessons in this reading, such as his lordship over the whole world (Psalm 47) and his role as our guide and protector (Psalm 48).

PERSONAL APPLICATION

God is almighty and all-powerful. Psalm 46 says "God thunders, and the earth melts" (46:6). God has far greater power than even the most powerful forces of nature (46:2-3) or of humankind (46:6, 9). How fitting, then, for us to show him some respect—to stand quietly before him, reverently honoring him and his power and majesty (46:10).

With life's busyness and burdens weighing us down, why should we take the time to stand still? What is the benefit of being silent before God? Spending time in silence is an opportunity to forget about all of the worldly distractions that keep us from entering into God's presence. It's an opportunity to focus on God's goodness, mercy, might, and power.

Take time each day to experience silence, and use it to ponder the awesome greatness of God. Be still and silent before God so that you can exalt him. Let silence give you the opportunity to worship.

BIBLE READING

¹ God is our refuge and strength,
      always ready to help in times of trouble.
² So we will not fear, even if earthquakes come
      and the mountains crumble into the sea.
³ Let the oceans roar and foam.
      Let the mountains tremble as the waters surge!   *Interlude*

⁸ Come, see the glorious works of the LORD:
      See how he brings destruction upon the world
⁹ and causes wars to end throughout the earth.
      He breaks the bow and snaps the spear in two;
      he burns the shields with fire.

¹⁰ "Be silent, and know that I am God!
      I will be honored by every nation.
      I will be honored throughout the world."

¹¹ The LORD Almighty is here among us;
      the God of Israel is our fortress.   *Interlude*

PSALM 46:1-3, 8-11

aking Up

PREVIEW

Psalm 51 is the result of a tough—but right—decision. Here, David confesses his sins in order to restore his broken relationship with God. The other psalms in this reading also involve tough decisions about how we live and relate to God. The relationship we have with God can suffer ups and downs just as our human relationships can, and this involves confession and reconciliation.

Other lessons in this section of Scripture include being sincere (Psalm 50); having confidence that God will defeat all evil in his own time (Psalm 52); and admitting our need for God to save us from sin (Psalm 53).

PERSONAL APPLICATION

Has sin ever driven a wedge between you and God, making him seem distant? David's sins destroyed his ability to enjoy anything, even God's salvation (Psalm 51:3-17). David was confronted with his adultery with Bathsheba, could not deny it, and sought to repent. In his prayer he confessed his sin and cried, "Restore to me again the joy of your salvation" (51:12).

God wants us to be obedient to his Word so that we can have a close relationship with him. But when we disobey God and try to cover up our sin rather than confess it, we hurt our relationship with him, driving the wedge between us and God even further. Confess any sin that stands between you and God. You may still have to face the consequences, as David did, but God will give back the joy of your relationship with him.

BIBLE READING

[7] Purify me from my sins, and I will be clean;
  wash me, and I will be whiter than snow.
[8] Oh, give me back my joy again;
  you have broken me—
  now let me rejoice.
[9] Don't keep looking at my sins.
  Remove the stain of my guilt.
[10] Create in me a clean heart, O God.
  Renew a right spirit within me.
[11] Do not banish me from your presence,
  and don't take your Holy Spirit from me.
[12] Restore to me again the joy of your salvation,
  and make me willing to obey you.
[13] Then I will teach your ways to sinners,
  and they will return to you.

[16] You would not be pleased with sacrifices,
  or I would bring them.
 If I brought you a burnt offering,
  you would not accept it.
[17] The sacrifice you want is a broken spirit.
  A broken and repentant heart, O God,
  you will not despise. PSALM 51:7-13, 16-17

*W*hat Are You Afraid Of?

PREVIEW

Everyone is afraid of something:

> gangs
> disease
> the future
> a spouse
> the government
> failure
> speaking in public

Have you ever been stopped at a traffic light and seen one of those bumper stickers that reads "NO FEAR"? But the fact that the driver isn't running the red light reveals the truth.

Psalm 56 deals with fear. Although the author, David, was a mighty warrior, he was not immune to this emotion—especially when his enemies were out to get him. Fortunately, David found a cure for his fear and recorded it in this psalm.

Other psalms in this reading contain invaluable truths about God as well as important lessons on prayer.

PERSONAL APPLICATION

What could be more frightening than being surrounded by an enemy who is pressing in from all sides (Psalm 56:1-6)? David faced exactly that situation many times. As a man who had great trust in God, this is what he learned about dealing with fear: (1) remember that God is with you; (2) trust God for protection; (3) praise God for fulfilling his promises; and (4) use the resources that God has given you.

Our fear often comes from our overestimating our attackers and underestimating our own resources in God and the church. Whenever you are faced with persecution, insecurity, or poor odds, take the fear-fighting steps that David took and overcome your fear.

BIBLE READING

¹ O God, have mercy on me.

The enemy troops press in on me.

My foes attack me all day long.

² My slanderers hound me constantly,

and many are boldly attacking me.

³ But when I am afraid,

I put my trust in you.

⁴ O God, I praise your word.

I trust in God, so why should I be afraid?

What can mere mortals do to me?

⁵ They are always twisting what I say;

they spend their days plotting ways to harm me.

⁶ They come together to spy on me—

watching my every step, eager to kill me.

⁷ Don't let them get away with their wickedness;

in your anger, O God, throw them to the ground.

⁸ You keep track of all my sorrows.

You have collected all my tears in your bottle.

You have recorded each one in your book.

⁹ On the very day I call to you for help,

my enemies will retreat.

This I know: God is on my side.

¹⁰ O God, I praise your word.

Yes, LORD, I praise your word.

¹¹ I trust in God, so why should I be afraid?

What can mere mortals do to me?   PSALM 56:1-11

With Friends Like These . . .

PREVIEW

Betrayal from a close friend or relative often results in a significant turning point in life. Devastated and angry, we wonder how we could have ever trusted that person in the first place. What is worse, though, is that this one experience may affect our future relationships. Will we ever trust anyone again?

Few people know what it is like to be betrayed better than David. In Psalm 59, David prays to God for protection from those who have turned against him. Yes, he has been betrayed. This is his prayer—it's also his solution. We can learn from his example.

The other psalms in this reading provide prayers for healing and examples for scarred and beaten pilgrims who are looking for a reason believe. They speak of enjoying God's faithful love and help in times of trouble (Psalm 57), and leaving ultimate justice in God's hands (Psalm 58).

PERSONAL APPLICATION

David was hunted by those whose love had turned to jealousy, and this was driving them to try to murder him (Psalm 59:1-4). Trusted friends, and even one of David's sons, had turned against him. Despite the fact that their love for David had eroded, God's love for him was constant. David knew that he could count on God to deliver him from his enemies.

When people betray and hurt you, remember that God still loves you and that he will never betray you. So rest in his enduring love, even if you feel that he is allowing bad things to happen to you. When the situation passes, you will be able to see that God was with you, sustaining you through the whole ordeal.

BIBLE READING

¹ Rescue me from my enemies, O God.
    Protect me from those who have come to destroy me.
² Rescue me from these criminals;
    save me from these murderers.

³ They have set an ambush for me.
    Fierce enemies are out there waiting,
    though I have done them no wrong, O LORD.
⁴ Despite my innocence, they prepare to kill me.
    Rise up and help me! Look on my plight!
⁵ O LORD God Almighty, the God of Israel,
    rise up to punish hostile nations.
    Show no mercy to wicked traitors.   *Interlude*

⁶ They come at night,
    snarling like vicious dogs
    as they prowl the streets.
⁷ Listen to the filth that comes from their mouths,
    the piercing swords that fly from their lips.
    "Who can hurt us?" they sneer.

⁸ But LORD, you laugh at them.
    You scoff at all the hostile nations.
⁹ You are my strength; I wait for you to rescue me,
    for you, O God, are my place of safety.
¹⁰ In his unfailing love, my God will come and help me.
    He will let me look down in triumph on all my enemies.

PSALM 59:1-10

$\mathscr{P}$risoner of Resentment

PREVIEW

If you have ever harbored resentment toward a person who attacked your character, welcome to the club. We expect people to treat us with a certain amount of basic respect, and when they don't, it's quite natural to resent them.

Often attacked by his enemies, David had every excuse to resent others. Instead of doing that, however, he dealt with the situation in a more positive way. Read Psalm 62 and learn how to handle resentment.

Other themes in this section of Scripture include regaining control when chaos reigns (Psalm 60), and turning to God for security and help (Psalm 61).

PERSONAL APPLICATION

David was well acquainted with unjust personal attacks (Psalm 62:3-4), but he made a conscious effort not to harbor resentments or build up anger. Instead, he expressed his feelings to God and reaffirmed his faith. Through prayer, he released the tension of the emotional stress and handed it over to God. David was confident that the Lord would bring about justice, care for his life, and safeguard his reputation (62:2).

Choosing this attitude can change your entire outlook on life. You do not need to be held captive by resentment toward others when they hurt you. Instead, trust in God the Rock, and nothing will be able to shake you.

BIBLE READING

¹ I wait quietly before God,
    for my salvation comes from him.
² He alone is my rock and my salvation,
    my fortress where I will never be shaken.

³ So many enemies against one man—
    all of them trying to kill me.
To them I'm just a broken-down wall
    or a tottering fence.
⁴ They plan to topple me from my high position.
    They delight in telling lies about me.
They are friendly to my face,
    but they curse me in their hearts.   *Interlude*

⁵ I wait quietly before God,
    for my hope is in him.
⁶ He alone is my rock and my salvation,
    my fortress where I will not be shaken.
⁷ My salvation and my honor come from God alone.
    He is my refuge, a rock where no enemy can reach me.

⁸ O my people, trust in him at all times.
    Pour out your heart to him,
    for God is our refuge.   *Interlude*

PSALM 62:1-8

Complaints Department

PREVIEW

No one likes to listen to whining and complaining—no matter how legitimate the gripe. Negative talk is tiring and depressing. Where do you take your complaints? Do you torture your loved ones with a diatribe, yell at the mirror, scream at the television, write a letter, or just hold it in?

Psalm 64 talks about whining and griping and offers a solution. Read and learn that there *is* a legitimate place and time for complaints.

The other psalms in this reading encourage us to look to God for satisfaction (Psalm 63) and give thanks to God for all he provides (Psalm 65).

PERSONAL APPLICATION

Like many people today, David often complained about his circumstances and vented his feelings. *Unlike* most people, however, he took his complaints to God, as he did in Psalm 64:1-6.

Many people think it would be disrespectful to complain in prayer, supposing that God doesn't want to hear the complaints or that voicing negative thoughts directly to God is somehow unspiritual. David's model shows that in addition to our praise, confession, and requests, God wants to hear *everything*—even matters that we may not want to tell him. We cannot hide from God, so why should we try?

David expressed his complaints honestly to God, knowing that God would listen to him as a loving father listens to his children. The next time you feel like complaining, take it to God. He will listen to you.

BIBLE READING

¹ O God, listen to my complaint.
    Do not let my enemies' threats overwhelm me.
² Protect me from the plots of the wicked,
    from the scheming of those who do evil.
³ Sharp tongues are the swords they wield;
    bitter words are the arrows they aim.
⁴ They shoot from ambush at the innocent,
    attacking suddenly and fearlessly.
⁵ They encourage each other to do evil
    and plan how to set their traps.
    "Who will ever notice?" they ask.
⁶ As they plot their crimes, they say,
    "We have devised the perfect plan!"
    Yes, the human heart and mind are cunning.

⁷ But God himself will shoot them down.
    Suddenly, his arrows will pierce them.
⁸ Their own words will be turned against them,
        destroying them.
    All who see it happening will shake their heads in scorn.
⁹ Then everyone will stand in awe,
    proclaiming the mighty acts of God,
    realizing all the amazing things he does.

¹⁰ The godly will rejoice in the LORD
    and find shelter in him.
And those who do what is right
    will praise him.   PSALM 64:1-10

$\mathcal{T}$rue Confessions

PREVIEW

Do you remember when you were a kid and your mother would make you apologize when you didn't really feel like it? The real blow came when she insisted that you do it nicely. Even though you eventually said the words, in your heart true repentance was nowhere in sight.

Psalm 66 contains advice about saying you're sorry, even when you don't feel like it. In fact, this psalm shows us the good that can come from apologizing.

The psalms in this reading also show us different ways to pray: by example and by command. These life-changing prayers include a request for God's blessing (Psalm 67) and praise to God for his glory and power (Psalm 68).

PERSONAL APPLICATION

"If I had not confessed the sin in my heart, my Lord would not have listened" (Psalm 66:18). Confession of sin must be continual because we continually do wrong. But true confession requires us to listen to God and to want to stop sinning. David confessed his sin and prayed, "Keep me from deliberate sins" (see Psalm 19:13).

When we refuse to repent or when we harbor and cherish certain sins, we place a wall between us and God. We cannot remember every sin we have ever committed, but we can set our sights on doing right. True confession involves more than just saying words that describe the offense—it also involves taking a step toward change.

Tear down that wall between you and God. Be honest with him, admit your weakness, confess your sin, and share your feelings. Then he will listen to you!

BIBLE READING

⁸ Let the whole world bless our God
   and sing aloud his praises.
⁹ Our lives are in his hands,
   and he keeps our feet from stumbling.
¹⁰ You have tested us, O God;
   you have purified us like silver melted in a crucible.

¹⁶ Come and listen, all you who fear God,
   and I will tell you what he did for me.
¹⁷ For I cried out to him for help,
   praising him as I spoke.
¹⁸ If I had not confessed the sin in my heart,
   my Lord would not have listened.
¹⁹ But God did listen!
   He paid attention to my prayer.

²⁰ Praise God, who did not ignore my prayer
   and did not withdraw his unfailing love from me.

PSALM 66:8-10, 16-20

*U*nder Attack

PREVIEW

The rumor mill is in full swing, and you're the target. People are making statements about you that would pierce the toughest skin. Although nothing they're saying about you is true, the more you try to stop the rumors, the more guilty you look.

Psalm 69 talks about the damage rumors can cause and offers hope for those whose lives are left in the wake of hurtful rumors. People don't like it when others appear better than they are. If people who notice your faith don't necessarily like it, they may hate you for it. They may go to extremes to get you in trouble or to embarrass you. This psalm offers a prayer for times like that.

Other themes in this reading include asking for God's help in emergencies (Psalm 70); celebrating God's constant help (Psalm 71); and leading and ruling others (Psalm 72).

PERSONAL APPLICATION

Many believers feel tempted to turn from God, give up on life, or even go into hiding when they encounter the kind of persecution that David endured. Rather than turning away from God at times like these, we should run to him. He will strengthen us for the trial and rescue us from our enemies.

When you are persecuted for your faith in God, continue to pray to him no matter how you feel or how difficult it may be. God promises to hear your prayer and rescue you. Remember that God is your most faithful friend. Don't turn away from him, especially in your time of need.

BIBLE READING

⁴ Those who hate me without cause
   are more numerous than the hairs on my head.
These enemies who seek to destroy me
   are doing so without cause.
They attack me with lies,
   demanding that I give back what I didn't steal.

⁵ O God, you know how foolish I am;
   my sins cannot be hidden from you.
⁶ Don't let those who trust in you stumble because of me,
   O Sovereign LORD Almighty.
Don't let me cause them to be humiliated,
   O God of Israel.
⁷ For I am mocked and shamed for your sake;
   humiliation is written all over my face.
⁸ Even my own brothers pretend they don't know me;
   they treat me like a stranger.

¹² I am the favorite topic of town gossip,
   and all the drunkards sing about me.

¹³ But I keep right on praying to you, LORD,
   hoping this is the time you will show me favor.
In your unfailing love, O God,
   answer my prayer with your sure salvation.

PSALM 69:4–8, 12–13

hat, Me Worry?

PREVIEW

For many years it appeared as if Communists were succeeding in wiping out religion. When Soviet cosmonauts entered space, they boasted that they looked for God but found no trace of him. Ever since the days of Noah, skeptics have had such disbelief.

Psalm 74 is a plea for God to show himself to people who don't believe that he exists. If you have ever felt frustrated by God's silence in a day and age when people so brazenly say, "There is no God," you will find that this psalm has your answer.

The other themes in this reading include looking to future rewards (Psalm 73); getting help in times of need (Psalm 74); and relying on God to judge those who are wicked (Psalm 75).

PERSONAL APPLICATION

People who hate God have often thought that they could destroy God by wiping out his people. This attitude prevails today—many people try to eliminate religious holidays and traditions and erase God from subjects taught in our schools.

Christians should not become discouraged, because those attempts cannot succeed. We should strive to be more of an influence in our communities by truly caring for people the way Christ did and by living an exemplary life—with God's power and grace—before our neighbors.

What can you do to stand up for the truth? What changes should you make in your lifestyle to reflect Christ to your friends, coworkers, and neighbors?

BIBLE READING

⁹ We see no miraculous signs
  as evidence that you will save us.
 All the prophets are gone;
  no one can tell us when it will end.

¹² You, O God, are my king from ages past,
  bringing salvation to the earth.

¹⁸ See how these enemies scoff at you, LORD.
  A foolish nation has dishonored your name.
¹⁹ Don't let these wild beasts destroy your doves.
  Don't forget your afflicted people forever.

²⁰ Remember your covenant promises,
  for the land is full of darkness and violence!
²¹ Don't let the downtrodden be constantly disgraced!
  Instead, let these poor and needy ones give praise to your
  name.

²² Arise, O God, and defend your cause.
  Remember how these fools insult you all day long.
²³ Don't overlook these things your enemies have said.
  Their uproar of rebellion grows ever louder.

PSALM 74:9, 12, 18-23

Heirlooms

PREVIEW

How many photo albums do you have? Scrapbooks, curio boxes, and hope chests are valuable primarily because of the memories we attach to them. We all have special memories, and we cherish the things that help us remember.

Psalm 77 is about memories. The writer, Asaph, feels distraught, and he reaches into the past for comfort. What he finds there provides a valuable lesson.

The other themes in this section include asking God to punish evil-doers (Psalm 76); finding a source of courage (Psalm 77); and learning from history (Psalm 78).

PERSONAL APPLICATION

The story of the parting of the Red Sea (Psalm 77:16) was a memory that every Israelite would recall and cherish because it reminded them of God's power, protection, and love for them as a nation. Memories of God's miracles and faithfulness often sustained Israel through their difficulties (Psalm 77:11-12), reminding them that God was capable and trustworthy.

When encountering trials and tribulations, it is good to recall God's goodness and faithfulness. We can do this by reading favorite Bible verses, singing favorite songs, reviewing prayer journals, or discussing past blessings and miracles with a friend. Those remembrances can provide hope and strength for today.

Think of what you can do to help you remember how God has worked in your life. And if you are discouraged by your present circumstances, find a Christian friend to pray for you and to reminisce with you about God's blessings in the past.

BIBLE READING

⁷ Has the Lord rejected me forever?
  Will he never again show me favor?
⁸ Is his unfailing love gone forever?
  Have his promises permanently failed?
⁹ Has God forgotten to be kind?
  Has he slammed the door on his compassion?

Interlude

¹⁰ And I said, "This is my fate,
  that the blessings of the Most High have changed to
  hatred."
¹¹ I recall all you have done, O LORD;
  I remember your wonderful deeds of long ago.
¹² They are constantly in my thoughts.
  I cannot stop thinking about them.

¹³ O God, your ways are holy.
  Is there any god as mighty as you?
¹⁴ You are the God of miracles and wonders!
  You demonstrate your awesome power among the
  nations.
¹⁵ You have redeemed your people by your strength,
  the descendants of Jacob and of Joseph by your might.

Interlude

PSALM 77:7-15

It's Not Fair!

PREVIEW

Injustice. Unfairness. These are two ugly realities that everyone must face and deal with at some point in life. When will injustices in this world stop?

Psalm 79 is the prayer of a man with that question on his mind. It's the burning cry of a man who truly loves God, a man who really cares, a man who has been the victim. This psalm is a prayer for justice in Israel's time of distress, but it is still applicable to injustices committed today.

Other prayers in this passage include how to pray after experiencing defeat (Psalm 80) and celebrating God's goodness in view of our unfaithfulness (Psalm 81).

PERSONAL APPLICATION

Asaph (the author of Psalm 79) wanted to see the wrong that had been done made right. Like Asaph, we, too, want justice. However, the question remains: Can we expect to get it in this lifetime? We know for sure that, eventually, God will deal justly with everyone, but what about the present, the here and now?

We shouldn't expect to receive earthly justice in our lifetimes. This is not because God doesn't care, but because he often has a higher purpose in mind. So, we must endure injustice with patience and allow God to use it to strengthen us. In the meantime, we can bring our requests for justice to God. He won't ignore them.

Be ready to live in an unjust world—life *isn't* fair. And be prepared for criticism, jokes, and unkind remarks, because God does not always shield his people from the attacks of this world. Remember, however, that in the end the righteous will be vindicated. God will remember you!

BIBLE READING

⁵ O LORD, how long will you be angry with us? Forever?
　　How long will your jealousy burn like fire?
⁶ Pour out your wrath on the nations that refuse to
　　　recognize you—
　　on kingdoms that do not call upon your name.
⁷ For they have devoured your people Israel,
　　making the land a desolate wilderness.
⁸ Oh, do not hold us guilty for our former sins!
　　Let your tenderhearted mercies quickly meet our needs,
　　for we are brought low to the dust.
⁹ Help us, O God of our salvation!
　　Help us for the honor of your name.
　Oh, save us and forgive our sins
　　for the sake of your name.
¹⁰ Why should pagan nations be allowed to scoff,
　　asking, "Where is their God?"
　Show us your vengeance against the nations,
　　for they have spilled the blood of your servants.
¹¹ Listen to the moaning of the prisoners.
　　Demonstrate your great power by saving those
　　condemned to die.

¹² O Lord, take sevenfold vengeance on our neighbors
　　for the scorn they have hurled at you.
¹³ Then we your people, the sheep of your pasture,
　　will thank you forever and ever,
　　praising your greatness from generation to generation.
　　　　　　　　　　　　　　　　　PSALM 79:5-13

Libraries, Closets, and Other Quiet Spots

PREVIEW

Do you enjoy browsing in the library, going to see a friend, relaxing on the sofa, or walking through the woods? Sometimes the world becomes a pressure cooker, and we need to go to a place that refreshes us. Where is that place for you?

Psalm 84 talks of the place to go when we need refreshment.

Other psalms in this section of Scripture speak of ways to turn the tables and affect the world by defending the weak against unfair people (Psalm 82), and praying for people who hate or oppose God (Psalm 83).

PERSONAL APPLICATION

The writer of Psalm 84 had a deep desire to dwell in God's presence (84:1-4). In fact, he loved the Lord so much that he envied the sparrows because they could build nests near the altar (84:3). He recognized that those who seek God are richly rewarded (84:5-7). This was his cure for a meaningless and hectic existence.

We, like the psalmist, need to have a desire to know God intimately and a desire to dwell in his presence. Fortunately, we don't have to visit the temple to commune with God. Today, because of the death and resurrection of Christ, we can meet God anywhere, at any time. If we belong to him, his Holy Spirit lives within us, and his presence is always with us. We need only to go to God in prayer to enjoy being in his presence (see Hebrews 4:16).

When the busyness of this world catches up with you, get away and spend time alone with God. It will be well worth your time to do so.

BIBLE READING

¹ How lovely is your dwelling place,
   O LORD Almighty.
² I long, yes, I faint with longing
   to enter the courts of the LORD.
  With my whole being, body and soul,
   I will shout joyfully to the living God.
³ Even the sparrow finds a home there,
   and the swallow builds her nest
   and raises her young—
   at a place near your altar,
   O LORD Almighty, my King and my God!
⁴ How happy are those who can live in your house,
   always singing your praises.   *Interlude*

⁵ Happy are those who are strong in the LORD,
   who set their minds on a pilgrimage to Jerusalem.
⁶ When they walk through the Valley of Weeping,
   it will become a place of refreshing springs,
   where pools of blessing collect after the rains!
⁷ They will continue to grow stronger,
   and each of them will appear before God in Jerusalem.

⁸ O LORD God Almighty, hear my prayer.
   Listen, O God of Israel.   *Interlude*
                                                   PSALM 84:1-8

t's in Writing

PREVIEW

You can learn a lot about a person by the way he or she keeps or breaks promises. Each promise kept endears that person to you, proves the person's character to you, and builds trust between you. On the other hand, each promise broken disappoints you, makes you wonder about the person's character, and breaks down trust between you.

Psalm 89 celebrates some of the promises of the greatest promise keeper of all—God. The promises he keeps here have not only endeared him to the writer of this psalm but should also endear him to us.

Notice also the fulfilled promises in other psalms from this reading—promises of blessing, restoration, and answered prayer.

PERSONAL APPLICATION

God promised that he would preserve David's throne (Psalm 89:29). Even though Israel disobeyed God almost continually throughout its history, God promised to never fail his pledge to David (89:33). Through God's patient reminders and warnings, a small portion, or "remnant" of God's people always remained faithful to him. Centuries later, the Messiah arrived, the eternal King from David's line, just as God had promised.

We all have worries, some great, some small, and some just plain bothersome. Yet we can trust God to help us overcome our worries because he has taken care of our biggest worry—sin. God can be trusted to save us as he promised he would (see Hebrews 6:13-18).

God is completely reliable. Trust him in times of trouble. Relax in the security that God always keeps his promises.

BIBLE READING

¹ I will sing of the tender mercies of the LORD forever!
  Young and old will hear of your faithfulness.
² Your unfailing love will last forever.
  Your faithfulness is as enduring as the heavens.

³ The LORD said, "I have made a solemn agreement with
David, my chosen servant.
  I have sworn this oath to him:
⁴ 'I will establish your descendants as kings forever;
  they will sit on your throne from now until eternity.'"

                                                    Interlude

⁵ All heaven will praise your miracles, LORD;
  myriads of angels will praise you for your faithfulness.
⁶ For who in all of heaven can compare with the LORD?
  What mightiest angel is anything like the LORD?
⁷ The highest angelic powers stand in awe of God.
  He is far more awesome than those who surround his
  throne.
⁸ O LORD God Almighty!
  Where is there anyone as mighty as you, LORD?
  Faithfulness is your very character.   PSALM 89:1-8

ime Flies

PREVIEW

It's easy to pass the time when it's spent in an enjoyable activity. No wonder many of us reach old age wondering, *Where has the time gone?* Time passes quickly. In fact, the longer you live the faster the time seems to go.

Psalm 90 is Moses' reflection on the passing of time. What he has to say is pure wisdom and should stir us not only to appreciate the time we have but to live godly lives as well.

In this section we are also reminded to look to God for protection from danger (Psalm 91), and to be thankful every day (Psalm 92).

PERSONAL APPLICATION

Moses was well qualified to write the lines, "Teach us to make the most of our time, so that we may grow in wisdom" (Psalm 90:12). He had experienced life from all sides—from a wealthy, powerful existence in Egypt to a frugal, nomadic life in Midian. He knew, perhaps better than most people, how to put life's short amount of time to good use.

Unless we train ourselves to value time as a priceless treasure, we will never realize how short life really is. Then when we are older, with little time left, we will regret the time we wasted.

To make the most of your time on earth, avoid those activities that benefit no one. Spend less time watching TV. Learn to manage your time better and set goals for yourself. Ask yourself these questions: What do I want to see happen in my life before I die? What small step could I take toward that purpose today? Seek God's opinion on your goals. Then, if he doesn't direct otherwise, set out to accomplish them by his power and grace.

BIBLE READING

[1] Lord, through all the generations
    you have been our home!
[2] Before the mountains were created,
        before you made the earth and the world,
        you are God, without beginning or end.

[3] You turn people back to dust, saying,
        "Return to dust!"
[4] For you, a thousand years are as yesterday!
        They are like a few hours!
[5] You sweep people away like dreams that disappear
        or like grass that springs up in the morning.
[6] In the morning it blooms and flourishes,
        but by evening it is dry and withered.
[7] We wither beneath your anger;
        we are overwhelmed by your fury.
[8] You spread out our sins before you—
        our secret sins—and you see them all.
[9] We live our lives beneath your wrath.
        We end our lives with a groan.

[10] Seventy years are given to us!
        Some may even reach eighty.
    But even the best of these years are filled with pain and
            trouble;
        soon they disappear, and we are gone.

[16] Let us see your miracles again;
        let our children see your glory at work.
[17] And may the Lord our God show us his approval
        and make our efforts successful.
        Yes, make our efforts successful!   PSALM 90:1-10, 16-17

$\mathcal{M}$ore Bad News

PREVIEW

If you've ever been around a cynical person, you know how maddening such company can be. A cynical outlook on life has two problems: (1) Negative attitudes are rarely necessary and rarely appreciated. (2) A cynical outlook makes every situation *look* bleak, even when it is not. What cures the cynic?

Psalm 94 has the answer. You'll notice a lot of contemporary problems here, such as crime and corruption. That's because some things, namely, human wickedness, never change. But the psalmist did not forget to look on the bright side.

The other two psalms in this reading contain similar lessons, but from different angles: learning from God's creation (Psalm 93) and worshiping God (Psalm 95).

PERSONAL APPLICATION

Today we have technology's mixed blessing of finding out about events more quickly and in greater detail than ever before. So much of it, however, is negative news. When negative news fills our minds, it's hard not to be cynical.

In the first half of Psalm 94, it seems as if the psalmist could think of nothing but bad news. He saw evil people prospering and oppressing others (94:3-7), corrupt governments (94:20), and the condemnation of the innocent (94:21), much like what we see in our world today. But he had come to realize and take comfort in the fact that God would not allow evil to continue forever. By the end of the psalm, he expressed trust in God and a commitment to take responsibility for his life and to obey God.

The next time you feel overwhelmed by negative news, do what this psalm writer did: tell God how you feel, declare confidence in his wisdom and timing, and reaffirm your commitment to follow him.

BIBLE READING

⁸ Think again, you fools!
When will you finally catch on?
⁹ Is the one who made your ears deaf?
Is the one who formed your eyes blind?
¹⁰ He punishes the nations—won't he also punish you?
He knows everything—doesn't he also know what you are doing?
¹¹ The LORD knows people's thoughts,
that they are worthless!

¹² Happy are those whom you discipline, LORD,
and those whom you teach from your law.
¹³ You give them relief from troubled times
until a pit is dug for the wicked.
¹⁴ The LORD will not reject his people;
he will not abandon his own special possession.
¹⁵ Judgment will come again for the righteous,
and those who are upright will have a reward.

PSALM 94:8-15

ove and Hate

PREVIEW

What do you strongly dislike? If you included all the categories that question could cover—foods, locations, television shows, ideas, organizations, people—you would have a nearly endless list. So could anybody; much of what we do from day to day involves a feeling of love or hate.

Psalm 97 provides *the* criterion for selecting things not only to dislike but to really hate. That's right, *hate.* What God's people should hate should not surprise you, however. In fact, hatred toward this, as you will learn, is good.

Other psalms in this section focus on more positive themes: how to praise God (Psalm 96), and celebrating God's victories over evil (Psalm 98).

PERSONAL APPLICATION

"You who love the Lord, hate evil!" (Psalm 97:10). This means that those who sincerely desire to please God should realign their desires with God's desires. Their affections will begin to change; that is, they will begin to love what God loves and hate what God hates. As they grow in their love for the Lord, they will grow in their hatred for evil.

If you do not despise the actions of people who take advantage of others, if you admire people who only look out for themselves, or if you envy those who get ahead through cruelty, your desires are not God's desires. Learn to love God's ways and to hate evil in every form—not just the obvious sins, but also the ones that are easy to consider acceptable or to overlook.

BIBLE READING

¹ The LORD is king! Let the earth rejoice!
   Let the farthest islands be glad.
² Clouds and darkness surround him.
   Righteousness and justice are the foundation of his
   throne.
³ Fire goes forth before him
   and burns up all his foes.
⁴ His lightning flashes out across the world.
   The earth sees and trembles.
⁵ The mountains melt like wax before the LORD,
   before the Lord of all the earth.
⁶ The heavens declare his righteousness;
   every nation sees his glory.
⁷ Those who worship idols are disgraced—
   all who brag about their worthless gods—
   for every god must bow to him.
⁸ Jerusalem has heard and rejoiced,
   and all the cities of Judah are glad
   because of your justice, LORD!
⁹ For you, O LORD, are most high over all the earth;
   you are exalted far above all gods.

¹⁰ You who love the LORD, hate evil!
   He protects the lives of his godly people
   and rescues them from the power of the wicked.
¹¹ Light shines on the godly,
   and joy on those who do right.
¹² May all who are godly be happy in the LORD
   and praise his holy name!   PSALM 97:1-12

ind Your Manors

PREVIEW

It's a noble deed when kids stick up for siblings on the playground. That shouldn't surprise us, however, because family honor pulls family members together like nothing else does. But have you noticed how different it *usually* is between siblings? The politeness level quickly drops.

David knew all too well about how poorly family members treat each other. In Psalm 101, he wrote a prayer in which he asked God to help him act as he should at home. It's a prayer that every family member could benefit from reading.

Other prayers in this section concern trust in God's fairness and holiness (Psalm 99), and entering God's presence joyfully (Psalm 100).

PERSONAL APPLICATION

Living in close proximity to those with whom you have close relationships will always lead to conflict. Nowhere do we have more close relationships than at home. Thus, our homes can be difficult places in which to always be civil and kind. In most families, parents and children relax and remove their mask of good behavior, often treating each other with less respect and kindness than they show to friends, coworkers, or even strangers. David must have had this problem as he prayed to God for help (Psalm 101:2).

Like David, pray about your behavior and attitudes toward other family members. Pray that God will help you imitate Christ at home so that you will be able to genuinely love your family and show them kindness and respect.

BIBLE READING

1 I will sing of your love and justice.
    I will praise you, LORD, with songs.
2 I will be careful to live a blameless life—
    when will you come to my aid?
  I will lead a life of integrity
    in my own home.
3 I will refuse to look at
    anything vile and vulgar.
  I hate all crooked dealings;
    I will have nothing to do with them.
4 I will reject perverse ideas
    and stay away from every evil.
5 I will not tolerate people who slander their neighbors.
    I will not endure conceit and pride.

6 I will keep a protective eye on the godly,
    so they may dwell with me in safety.
  Only those who are above reproach
    will be allowed to serve me.
7 I will not allow deceivers to serve me,
    and liars will not be allowed to enter my presence.
8 My daily task will be to ferret out criminals
    and free the city of the LORD from their grip.

                                    PSALM 101:1-8

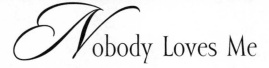obody Loves Me

PREVIEW

Some people live on the dark side of the moon. Phone them and they give you an earful about how the world is mistreating them. They can't think of anything for which to be thankful, and reminding them of their blessings only seems to irritate them.

Psalm 103 provides a great example. It's a count-your-blessings psalm, a simple reminder to be thankful.

The other two psalms in this reading also give us reasons to be thankful. Psalm 102 teaches us how to receive God's comfort when we're in distress. Psalm 104 helps us appreciate God through his creation and the way he cares for it.

PERSONAL APPLICATION

David's praise in Psalm 103 focused on God's glorious deeds (103:3-19). People often complain when they are tired, needy, and frustrated. But David's list gives us plenty for which to praise God: God forgives our sins, heals our diseases, redeems us from death, crowns us with love and compassion, satisfies our desires, and intervenes for people who suffer injustice (103:1-22).

The best part is that we receive all these blessings without deserving any of them. And God never shows partiality—giving good things to his favorites and leaving out the others.

No matter how difficult your circumstances are today, count your blessings—past, present, and future. Keep them in mind when you feel as though you have nothing for which to praise God. If that doesn't work, remind yourself of what God has done for you by reading David's list.

BIBLE READING

² Praise the LORD, I tell myself,
and never forget the good things he does for me.
³ He forgives all my sins
and heals all my diseases.
⁴ He ransoms me from death
and surrounds me with love and tender mercies.
⁵ He fills my life with good things.
My youth is renewed like the eagle's!
⁶ The LORD gives righteousness
and justice to all who are treated unfairly.
⁷ He revealed his character to Moses
and his deeds to the people of Israel.
⁸ The LORD is merciful and gracious;
he is slow to get angry and full of unfailing love.
⁹ He will not constantly accuse us,
nor remain angry forever.
¹⁰ He has not punished us for all our sins,
nor does he deal with us as we deserve.
¹¹ For his unfailing love toward those who fear him
is as great as the height of the heavens above the earth.
¹² He has removed our rebellious acts
as far away from us as the east is from the west.
¹³ The LORD is like a father to his children,
tender and compassionate to those who fear him.
¹⁴ For he understands how weak we are;
he knows we are only dust.   PSALM 103:2-14

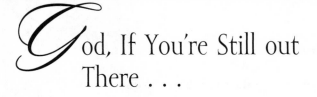

God, If You're Still out There . . .

PREVIEW

When I pray, it doesn't feel as if God is listening. When I read the Bible, it seems dull and lifeless. Have either of those concerns ever crossed your mind?

Consider the words of Psalm 105, which recall the many wonders God did for Israel—the miracles that helped them and the judgments on their enemies. David knows about spiritual dryness, and he knows that *remembering* can help a believer get through these times.

Also, if you make the mistake of not remembering God's goodness to you, Psalm 106 will teach you about learning from your mistakes.

PERSONAL APPLICATION

David knew that even God's people sometimes lose heart in their pursuit of God. Yet he also had discovered a remedy: remembering the way that God had helped his people in the past (Psalm 105:5).

God has always worked in the lives of his people, and he will continue to do so today. He is not far away but close by. That's why we should "Search for the Lord . . . and keep on searching" (105:4).

Whenever you feel far from God, remember his specific deeds in your life, as David did. Persist in seeking God. If you can't remember them, start writing them down, and read the Bible's reminders of God's past works. Then pray through your needs and thank God for his help.

BIBLE READING

¹ Give thanks to the LORD and proclaim his greatness.
    Let the whole world know what he has done.
² Sing to him; yes, sing his praises.
    Tell everyone about his miracles.
³ Exult in his holy name;
    O worshipers of the LORD, rejoice!
⁴ Search for the LORD and for his strength,
    and keep on searching.
⁵ Think of the wonderful works he has done,
    the miracles and the judgments he handed down,
⁶ O children of Abraham, God's servant,
    O descendants of Jacob, God's chosen one.
⁷ He is the LORD our God.
    His rule is seen throughout the land.
⁸ He always stands by his covenant—
    the commitment he made to a thousand generations.
⁹ This is the covenant he made with Abraham
    and the oath he swore to Isaac.
¹⁰ He confirmed it to Jacob as a decree,
    to the people of Israel as a never-ending treaty:
¹¹ "I will give you the land of Canaan
    as your special possession."   PSALM 105:1-11

God to the Rescue

PREVIEW

What has caused you to feel worried, anxious, or anguished lately? Don't feel awkward or uniquely rotten if you think of these easily; our adversary the devil sends a steady stream of troubles to distress us. He loves it when we worry about family members, money shortages, ill health, direction in life, conflicts with others, and consequences for mistakes.

Psalm 107 celebrates God's help for people in distress. Perhaps you can relate to some of the circumstances mentioned here.

Meanwhile, Psalm 108 urges us to rely on God's strength, and Psalm 109 teaches us how to pray for enemies and those who anger us.

PERSONAL APPLICATION

We don't know who wrote Psalm 107, but we can tell that the person was well acquainted with distress. The writer described four kinds of struggling people and how God helped them: people who were lost (107:4-9), prisoners who wanted to change (107:10-16), sick people (107:17-20), and storm-tossed sailors (107:23-30).

Everyone can identify with these kinds of people. At one time or another, we have all been lost, caught doing something wrong, sick, or afraid for our lives. But no matter how extreme the hardship, God never loses control of the situation and can help those who are in distress.

The next time you feel overwhelmed by worry, call on God to help you, and trust him to do what is right. You can bring him all your needs—he is able and willing to help.

BIBLE READING

[1] Give thanks to the LORD, for he is good!
    His faithful love endures forever.
[2] Has the LORD redeemed you? Then speak out!
    Tell others he has saved you from your enemies.
[3] For he has gathered the exiles from many lands,
    from east and west, from north and south.

[33] He changes rivers into deserts,
    and springs of water into dry land.
[34] He turns the fruitful land into salty wastelands,
    because of the wickedness of those who live there.
[35] But he also turns deserts into pools of water,
    the dry land into flowing springs.
[36] He brings the hungry to settle there
    and build their cities.
[37] They sow their fields, plant their vineyards,
    and harvest their bumper crops.

[42] The godly will see these things and be glad,
    while the wicked are stricken silent.
[43] Those who are wise will take all this to heart;
    they will see in our history the faithful love of the LORD.

PSALM 107:1-3, 33-37, 42-43

*S*mart Versus Wise

PREVIEW

Schools test children to measure intelligence, but they give no tests for wisdom. Moral choices fall outside the line of what schools can track, so you can be a brain (and a fool) and your foolishness will never show up on your report card. More to the point, if you want to be wise, you'll have to do an independent study. No one will make you stay after school if you don't.

So are you wise or foolish? Psalm 111 will help you assess your wisdom. If you don't measure up, this psalm will also get you going in the right direction.

Other sources of wisdom in this reading focus on getting to know the Messiah (Psalm 110), and reviewing the benefits of being faithful to God (Psalm 112).

PERSONAL APPLICATION

The only way to become truly wise begins with having reverence for God (Psalm 111:10, see also Proverbs 1:7). Too often we forget this and think that our own observations, a healthy dose of common sense, and a good college education will do the trick. But true wisdom doesn't come from any of these human sources. If we do not acknowledge God as the only source of wisdom, our foundation for making wise decisions will not be solid, and we will often make foolish choices that will lead to big mistakes.

Get into the habit of reading and studying God's Word to become familiar with God's principles and his timeless truths. Once you're familiar with the principles, review them again and again. Open your mind to what God says. He wants to fill you with wisdom.

BIBLE READING

¹ Praise the LORD!

> I will thank the LORD with all my heart
> > as I meet with his godly people.
> ² How amazing are the deeds of the LORD!
> > All who delight in him should ponder them.
> ³ Everything he does reveals his glory and majesty.
> > His righteousness never fails.
> ⁴ Who can forget the wonders he performs?
> > How gracious and merciful is our LORD!
> ⁵ He gives food to those who trust him;
> > he always remembers his covenant.
> ⁶ He has shown his great power to his people
> > by giving them the lands of other nations.
> ⁷ All he does is just and good,
> > and all his commandments are trustworthy.
> ⁸ They are forever true,
> > to be obeyed faithfully and with integrity.
> ⁹ He has paid a full ransom for his people.
> > He has guaranteed his covenant with them forever.
> > What a holy, awe-inspiring name he has!
> ¹⁰ Reverence for the LORD is the foundation of true wisdom.
> > The rewards of wisdom come to all who obey him.
>
> Praise his name forever!

PSALM 111:1–10

𝒥'd Like to Thank . . .

PREVIEW

Everyone is, to an extent, indebted to someone else for teaching them a valuable lesson or skill. Some acknowledge that person's contribution, while others take all the credit themselves for their achievements and success.

Psalm 115 deals with giving credit where it's due. The author of this psalm makes absolutely sure that God is given the glory for the success he sees around him. There are no false claims to fame here. As you read, learn the lesson about glorifying your Lord.

Other psalms here also give the glory to God. Psalm 113 praises God for his care for the poor, weak, and needy. Psalm 114 celebrates God's help in our lives.

PERSONAL APPLICATION

The writer of Psalm 115 asked that God's name, not the nation's, be glorified (115:1). Note the lack of false humility—this writer could do nothing but call attention to God's greatness and sincerely praise him.

It's natural to want to take credit for something we've accomplished. Instead, we should ask God to glorify *his* name, not ours. No one can fault us for leaving a good impression as a by-product of doing our duty; the problem comes when we try to get praise from others and withhold praise that belongs to God.

Before you pray, consider who will get the credit if God answers your prayer. Ask God to glorify *his* name through your achievements and success, not yours. Then when you do succeed, remember to give credit and thanks to God for his love and faithfulness.

BIBLE READING

[1] Not to us, O LORD, but to you goes all the glory
    for your unfailing love and faithfulness.
[2] Why let the nations say,
    "Where is their God?"
[3] For our God is in the heavens,
    and he does as he wishes.
[4] Their idols are merely things of silver and gold,
    shaped by human hands.
[5] They cannot talk, though they have mouths,
    or see, though they have eyes!
[6] They cannot hear with their ears,
    or smell with their noses,
[7] or feel with their hands,
    or walk with their feet,
    or utter sounds with their throats!
[8] And those who make them are just like them,
    as are all who trust in them.

[9] O Israel, trust the LORD!
    He is your helper; he is your shield.
[10] O priests of Aaron, trust the LORD!
    He is your helper; he is your shield.
[11] All you who fear the LORD, trust the LORD!
    He is your helper; he is your shield.   PSALM 115:1-11

Death in the Family

PREVIEW

Everyone has a perspective on death. Some welcome its coming. Others fear death and try to prolong their time on earth as long as possible. But what should Christians think? Should we welcome it or fear it?

The author of Psalm 116 was near death and feared for his life. But he didn't just worry about it—he cried out to God, "Save me!" God did, and the psalm writer praised him. This psalm speaks a lot about what he has learned. Read it and you can learn, too.

This reading gives other reasons for praising God: his unlimited love for us (Psalm 117), and the security his eternal love provides for us when our circumstances keep changing (Psalm 118).

PERSONAL APPLICATION

God stays close to us even when we face death (Psalm 116:15). The death of a person matters to God; he does not take it lightly or count it cheaply. When someone we love nears death, we may become angry or feel abandoned. But God considers every believer precious, and he carefully chooses the time when they will be called into his presence.

Let this truth guide you when a loved one has a grave illness or a life-threatening injury; let it provide comfort when a loved one has died. God sees and cares for each and every life. No one takes death more seriously than God.

BIBLE READING

¹ I love the LORD because he hears
and answers my prayers.
² Because he bends down and listens,
I will pray as long as I have breath!
³ Death had its hands around my throat;
the terrors of the grave overtook me.
I saw only trouble and sorrow.
⁴ Then I called on the name of the LORD:
"Please, LORD, save me!"
⁵ How kind the LORD is! How good he is!
So merciful, this God of ours!
⁶ The LORD protects those of childlike faith;
I was facing death, and then he saved me.
⁷ Now I can rest again,
for the LORD has been so good to me.
⁸ He has saved me from death,
my eyes from tears,
my feet from stumbling.
⁹ And so I walk in the LORD's presence
as I live here on earth!
¹⁰ I believed in you, so I prayed,
"I am deeply troubled, LORD."
¹¹ In my anxiety I cried out to you,
"These people are all liars!"
¹² What can I offer the LORD
for all he has done for me?
¹³ I will lift up a cup symbolizing his salvation;
I will praise the LORD's name for saving me.
¹⁴ I will keep my promises to the LORD
in the presence of all his people.   PSALM 116:1-14

Better Than Money

PREVIEW

State lotteries have thrived in this country. Each week, millions of dollars are promised to a handful of winners. For a chance to be set for life financially, just buy a ticket.

Psalm 119, the longest chapter in the Bible, discusses something that has much more value than money: God's law. Almost every verse mentions the virtues of knowing, learning, loving, keeping, and telling others about God's law. In a word: God's law is *valuable!* And where does this leave the yardstick of all worldly value? Read on for some perspective.

Other lessons in this psalm include appreciating the value of God's Word; appreciating God's rules; and asking God for insight into his Word.

PERSONAL APPLICATION

In today's world, where advertisements continually entice us to buy things, thinking selfishly comes almost automatically. We can easily imagine that contentment and happiness lie just beyond the next income level. Making the lust for money even stronger is the fact that in our society money represents power, influence, and success.

Certainly, money can buy comforts and offer some security, but it offers nothing that will last or that can ultimately satisfy us. Besides, God determines what we have (see Proverbs 22:2). The Bible, God's Word, offers far more than money. In Scripture we find direction, guidance, and the meaning to life.

What means more to you? Knowing God or being rich? Make the psalm writer's prayer your own—that God will give you a love for his statutes and not for making money.

BIBLE READING

³³ Teach me, O LORD,
to follow every one of your principles.

³⁴ Give me understanding and I will obey your law;
I will put it into practice with all my heart.

³⁵ Make me walk along the path of your commands,
for that is where my happiness is found.

³⁶ Give me an eagerness for your decrees;
do not inflict me with love for money!

³⁷ Turn my eyes from worthless things,
and give me life through your word.

³⁸ Reassure me of your promise,
which is for those who honor you.

³⁹ Help me abandon my shameful ways;
your laws are all I want in life.

⁴⁰ I long to obey your commandments!
Renew my life with your goodness.

⁴¹ LORD, give to me your unfailing love,
the salvation that you promised me.

⁴² Then I will have an answer for those who taunt me,
for I trust in your word.

⁴³ Do not snatch your word of truth from me,
for my only hope is in your laws.

⁴⁴ I will keep on obeying your law
forever and forever.

⁴⁵ I will walk in freedom,
for I have devoted myself to your commandments.

⁴⁶ I will speak to kings about your decrees,
and I will not be ashamed.

⁴⁷ How I delight in your commands!
How I love them!

⁴⁸ I honor and love your commands.
I meditate on your principles.   PSALM 119:33-48

*P*eacemaking

PREVIEW

Psalm 120 was written by a man who had some thoughts on fighting. He had seen a lot of action and wanted a little peace. But chances are he didn't get any—at least not from his adversaries. As you read this psalm, learn the value of being a peacemaker.

The other psalms in this reading cover many different topics: knowing where your help comes from (Psalm 121); entering God's presence (Psalm 122); looking to God for mercy (Psalm 123); and celebrating God's protection when you are attacked by others (Psalm 124).

PERSONAL APPLICATION

The psalm writer wrote, "I am for peace; but . . . they are for war" (Psalm 120:7). Many people feel that way and would rather fight for what they believe in than back down or compromise for the sake of peace. For those people, the glory of battle lies in winning. But when someone wins like that, somebody else loses.

In contrast, the glory of peacemaking lies in the fact that it can produce two winners. Peacemaking is God's way (see Matthew 5:9), so, we, too, should strive to be peacemakers by carefully and prayerfully trying to resolve conflicts without force. But at the same time, we should keep in mind that peace at all costs is not peace. Therefore, we should not sacrifice God's principles to achieve a lesser peace.

The next time you are involved in a disagreement, look for things on which you both can agree. Work from there toward a solution that is mutually beneficial and pleasing to God. Be a peacemaker.

BIBLE READING

¹ I took my troubles to the LORD;
   I cried out to him, and he answered my prayer.
² Rescue me, O LORD, from liars
   and from all deceitful people.
³ O deceptive tongue, what will God do to you?
   How will he increase your punishment?
⁴ You will be pierced with sharp arrows
   and burned with glowing coals.

⁵ How I suffer among these scoundrels of Meshech!
   It pains me to live with these people from Kedar!
⁶ I am tired of living here
   among people who hate peace.
⁷ As for me, I am for peace;
   but when I speak, they are for war!   PSALM 120:1-7

 ug Rats

PREVIEW

Does our society today think highly of children? It's hard to tell. Never have the laws against child abuse been tougher. Never have children had so many enjoyable opportunities geared just for them. But never have more abortions been performed, and never have so many children spent their early years in day care.

If ever we needed a "family psalm," it's now! And God has given it to us in Psalm 127. Among this psalm's pearls you will find a blanket statement about children, leaving little doubt as to what God thinks of them. As you read, consider whether this requires an adjustment of *your* attitude.

Other psalms in this reading give a plan for overcoming insecurity (Psalm 125); for celebrating God's great works on our behalf (Psalm 126); for letting God rule in the home (Psalm 128); and for looking to God when others oppose us (Psalm 129).

PERSONAL APPLICATION

God values children highly (Psalm 127:3-5). When God grants children to a couple, he grants them a blessing—bringing good to them, rewarding them. Therefore, we should value children and treat them as precious gifts.

Children are not annoying distractions, but an opportunity to shape the future. Too often we treat children like burdens rather than blessings.

If you have children, consider what you can do today to show them how much you love and care for them. If you don't have children of your own, consider how you can affirm and help the children at your church and in your neighborhood and extended family. Begin today to cultivate care and value for children.

BIBLE READING

¹ Unless the LORD builds a house,
    the work of the builders is useless.
  Unless the LORD protects a city,
    guarding it with sentries will do no good.
² It is useless for you to work so hard
    from early morning until late at night,
  anxiously working for food to eat;
    for God gives rest to his loved ones.

³ Children are a gift from the LORD;
    they are a reward from him.
⁴ Children born to a young man
    are like sharp arrows in a warrior's hands.
⁵ How happy is the man whose quiver is full of them!
    He will not be put to shame when he confronts his
    accusers at the city gates.   PSALM 127:1-5

n Harmony

PREVIEW

We don't have to look far to find examples of unity and its benefits. Any choir, sports team, play, or family will work far better if there's unity among its members. What area of your life depends on unity?

When we have to work with others, sometimes it helps to be reminded of the value of unity. Psalm 133 is just such a reminder—check it out.

Other psalms in this reading will remind you of God's forgiveness (Psalm 130); of where to find contentment (Psalm 131); of the source of public honor (Psalm 132); and of finding joy in God's blessings (Psalm 134).

PERSONAL APPLICATION

David described unity as pleasant and precious (Psalm 133:1-3). Unfortunately, unity does not come without effort—in fact, it costs a great deal. We naturally disagree and divide ranks, usually over issues that matter, but just as often over unimportant ones, too. It takes work to overcome this nature. Yet unity is important enough to work at making this change for several reasons: (1) It makes God's people a positive example and helps draw others to him. (2) It helps us cooperate as God meant us to, giving us a foretaste of heaven. (3) It renews and revitalizes ministry because there is less tension to sap our energy.

Living in unity does not mean that God's people have to agree on everything. But we must agree on the issue that matters most—our ultimate purpose in life—loving God and one another.

BIBLE READING

[1] How wonderful it is, how pleasant,
    when brothers live together in harmony!
[2] For harmony is as precious as the fragrant anointing oil
    that was poured over Aaron's head,
    that ran down his beard
    and onto the border of his robe.
[3] Harmony is as refreshing as the dew from Mount Hermon
    that falls on the mountains of Zion.
And the LORD has pronounced his blessing,
    even life forevermore.   PSALM 133:1-3

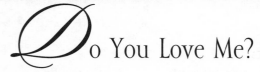o You Love Me?

PREVIEW

If you want to reassure someone of your love, whether a child, spouse, or friend, you have several methods available. You could give a gift, give a hug, spend some time with that person, or say "I love you." Many people say those words so easily, but the proof—their actions—isn't always there.

Psalm 136 recites many ways in which God has shown his love to his people. Read this extensive list and praise your loving heavenly Father.

This reading also teaches how to praise God (Psalm 135), and how to pray during times of sadness (Psalm 137).

PERSONAL APPLICATION

Psalm 136 repeats the phrase "His faithful love endures forever" twenty-six times, once in every verse. This psalm may have been a responsive reading, with the congregation saying these words in unison after phrases spoken by a leader.

The repetition makes the importance of this message obvious: God loves us, and that love doesn't die, stop, wear out, fade, or lessen. It lives on, continues, keeps going, lasts. God has done more for us than we could ever deserve: He created us, gave us life to enjoy, and, through Christ, freed us from sin. But he didn't stop with the deeds; he went on to write it down—to say the words.

You never have to worry that God will run out of love for you. If you ever do, just reread Psalm 136.

BIBLE READING

¹ Give thanks to the LORD, for he is good!
> *His faithful love endures forever*

² Give thanks to the God of gods.
> *His faithful love endures forever*

³ Give thanks to the Lord of lords.
> *His faithful love endures forever*

⁴ Give thanks to him who alone does mighty miracles.
> *His faithful love endures forever*

⁵ Give thanks to him who made the heavens so skillfully.
> *His faithful love endures forever*

⁶ Give thanks to him who placed the earth on the water.
> *His faithful love endures forever*

⁷ Give thanks to him who made the heavenly lights—
> *His faithful love endures forever*

⁸ the sun to rule the day,
> *His faithful love endures forever*

⁹ and the moon and stars to rule the night.
> *His faithful love endures forever*

²³ He remembered our utter weakness.
> *His faithful love endures forever*

²⁴ He saved us from our enemies.
> *His faithful love endures forever*

²⁵ He gives food to every living thing.
> *His faithful love endures forever*

²⁶ Give thanks to the God of heaven.
> *His faithful love endures forever*

PSALM 136:1-9, 23-26

Amazing Knowledge and Love

PREVIEW

A really close friend can help you identify and overcome weaknesses, identify and use your strengths, and make other important changes. The help you get from someone who knows you well—yet still accepts you—can make more difference than a hundred self-help books.

Psalm 139 is a celebration, from first verse to last, of a close friend—God. He knows us better than our closest confidant, even better than we know ourselves. As you read this psalm, celebrate with the writer God's great knowledge and love.

One psalm in this reading celebrates God's love in answering our prayers (Psalm 138), while the other one teaches how to survive slander and threats (Psalm 140).

PERSONAL APPLICATION

God knows everything about us, even down to the number of hairs on our heads (see Matthew 10:30). He knows what we do as well as what we are. He even knows what we think about (Psalm 139:1-5). Should we expect anything less from our Creator (139:13-14)?

Sometimes we don't let people get to know us because we are afraid they will discover something about us that they won't like. Or we try to pull back from them because we fear that they've already found something distasteful and will reject us. That cannot happen with God. He knows us completely and still he accepts and loves us.

When you fear (or actually face) rejection from others—whether coworkers, neighbors, friends, or even family members—remember that God made you and has already accepted you, exactly as you are.

BIBLE READING

¹ O LORD, you have examined my heart
and know everything about me.
² You know when I sit down or stand up.
You know my every thought when far away.
³ You chart the path ahead of me
and tell me where to stop and rest.
Every moment you know where I am.
⁴ You know what I am going to say
even before I say it, LORD.
⁵ You both precede and follow me.
You place your hand of blessing on my head.
⁶ Such knowledge is too wonderful for me,
too great for me to know!

⁷ I can never escape from your spirit!
I can never get away from your presence!
⁸ If I go up to heaven, you are there;
if I go down to the place of the dead, you are there.
⁹ If I ride the wings of the morning,
if I dwell by the farthest oceans,
¹⁰ even there your hand will guide me,
and your strength will support me.

¹⁷ How precious are your thoughts about me, O God!
They are innumerable!
¹⁸ I can't even count them;
they outnumber the grains of sand!
And when I wake up in the morning,
you are still with me!   PSALM 139:1-10, 17-18

*C*ritical Masses

PREVIEW

When was the last time someone criticized you? How did you respond? How do you *wish* you had responded? What leftover conflicts has it created? Most people find criticism difficult to take, even when it's given by someone who knows what he or she is talking about.

As he does in many of his psalms, in Psalm 141 David talks to God about his many enemies. As you read, you will see that David knows he can dismiss his enemies' accusations, taunts, and lies. There is one type of criticism, however, that he cannot discount.

David provides other lessons on prayer in this reading as well: how to pray whenever you are overwhelmed or desperate (Psalm 142); how to pray whenever you feel hopeless or depressed (Psalm 143); and how to pray when you are hemmed in or outnumbered by unbelievers (Psalm 144).

PERSONAL APPLICATION

David said that being corrected by a righteous person would be doing him a favor (Psalm 141:5). He knew that though no one really likes to hear criticism, everyone can benefit from the kind that makes good points, but only if the criticism is taken with humility. According to David we should take these three steps to accept well-given and well-placed criticism: (1) don't refuse it, (2) consider it a kindness, and (3) keep quiet (don't fight back).

The next time critics target you, put these suggestions into practice. They'll help you control how you react, making your response productive rather than destructive, no matter what the motives behind the critique.

BIBLE READING

[1] O LORD, I am calling to you. Please hurry!
     Listen when I cry to you for help!
[2] Accept my prayer as incense offered to you,
     and my upraised hands as an evening offering.

[3] Take control of what I say, O LORD,
     and keep my lips sealed.
[4] Don't let me lust for evil things;
     don't let me participate in acts of wickedness.
Don't let me share in the delicacies
     of those who do evil.

[5] Let the godly strike me!
     It will be a kindness!
If they reprove me, it is soothing medicine.
     Don't let me refuse it.

 But I am in constant prayer
     against the wicked and their deeds.
[6] When their leaders are thrown down from a cliff,
     they will listen to my words and find them pleasing.
[7] Even as a farmer breaks up the soil and brings up rocks,
     so the bones of the wicked will be scattered without a
     decent burial.

[8] I look to you for help, O Sovereign LORD.
     You are my refuge; don't let them kill me.
[9] Keep me out of the traps they have set for me,
     out of the snares of those who do evil.
[10] Let the wicked fall into their own snares,
     but let me escape.   PSALM 141:1-10

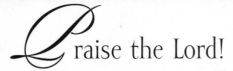

raise the Lord!

PREVIEW

What do you think when someone says, "Praise the Lord"? Does it strike you as strange, appropriate, logical, or weird? Does it make you uncomfortable? Or does it make you feel at ease?

David, the author of Psalm 145, didn't feel shy about expressing his love for God. In 2 Samuel 6:14, he danced for joy before the Lord, and here he says boldly, "Praise the Lord!" As you read, see what you can learn about praise.

Other psalms in this section give advice for people in need (Psalm 146); tell how to please God (Psalm 147); and list many reasons and ways to praise and worship God (Psalm 148-150).

PERSONAL APPLICATION

Sometimes life goes on with such an even rhythm that we may wonder why we should praise God. In Psalm 145, David gives us many good reasons: God is great (v. 3). God does mighty, wonderful deeds (vv. 4-6). God is righteous (v. 7). God is gracious, compassionate, patient, and loving (vv. 8-9). God rules over an everlasting kingdom (v. 13). God lifts us up when we are down (v. 14). God meets all our daily needs (vv. 15-16). God is righteous and loving in all he does (v. 17). God stays near to those who call on him (v. 18). God hears our cries and saves us (vv. 19-20).

If you are looking for a reason to praise God, start here. He is ready to listen.

BIBLE READING

[1] I will praise you, my God and King,
    and bless your name forever and ever.
[2] I will bless you every day,
    and I will praise you forever.
[3] Great is the LORD! He is most worthy of praise!
    His greatness is beyond discovery!

[4] Let each generation tell its children
    of your mighty acts.
[5] I will meditate on your majestic, glorious splendor
    and your wonderful miracles.
[6] Your awe-inspiring deeds will be on every tongue;
    I will proclaim your greatness.
[7] Everyone will share the story of your wonderful goodness;
    they will sing with joy of your righteousness.

[17] The LORD is righteous in everything he does;
    he is filled with kindness.
[18] The LORD is close to all who call on him,
    yes, to all who call on him sincerely.
[19] He fulfills the desires of those who fear him;
    he hears their cries for help and rescues them.
[20] The LORD protects all those who love him,
    but he destroys the wicked.

[21] I will praise the LORD,
    and everyone on earth will bless his holy name
    forever and forever.   PSALM 145:1-7, 17-21

now-It-Alls

PREVIEW

You can spot the compulsive know-it-all by the way he or she dodges all possibility of admitting wrong. This person will use his or her knowledge to impress others, using words that people won't understand just to have the satisfaction of seeing them concede his or her superior knowledge. People like this are the ones that everyone tries to avoid at social gatherings.

This first chapter of Proverbs begins, appropriately, with a brief discourse on know-it-alls. The truth presented here is one that you've probably thought about before, but never really expressed in words.

Other lessons in this chapter highlight the difference between knowledge and wisdom; dangers in what you hear; and how to get God's advice.

PERSONAL APPLICATION

Know-it-alls may have a great deal of knowledge, but they usually have little wisdom. Solomon called this kind of person a fool (Proverbs 1:7-9).

Much of what we know has no connection to how wise we are; for example, a brilliant surgeon can live a foolish life. Truly wise people know their knowledge is not complete and go to God for wisdom and more knowledge. All that we know has been granted to us by God as a gift for use in serving others and him. Therefore, we should use our knowledge with humility.

Don't act like a know-it-all, even if you have a lot of knowledge. Remember that all knowledge and wisdom come from God. Give him the glory!

BIBLE READING

²The purpose of these proverbs is to teach people wisdom and discipline, and to help them understand wise sayings. ³Through these proverbs, people will receive instruction in discipline, good conduct, and doing what is right, just, and fair. ⁴These proverbs will make the simpleminded clever. They will give knowledge and purpose to young people.

⁵Let those who are wise listen to these proverbs and become even wiser. And let those who understand receive guidance ⁶by exploring the depth of meaning in these proverbs, parables, wise sayings, and riddles.

⁷Fear of the LORD is the beginning of knowledge. Only fools despise wisdom and discipline.

²⁰Wisdom shouts in the streets. She cries out in the public square. ²¹She calls out to the crowds along the main street, and to those in front of city hall. ²²"You simpletons!" she cries. "How long will you go on being simpleminded? How long will you mockers relish your mocking? How long will you fools fight the facts? ²³Come here and listen to me! I'll pour out the spirit of wisdom upon you and make you wise.

²⁴"I called you so often, but you didn't come. I reached out to you, but you paid no attention. ²⁵You ignored my advice and rejected the correction I offered. ²⁶So I will laugh when you are in trouble! I will mock you when disaster overtakes you—²⁷when calamity overcomes you like a storm, when you are engulfed by trouble, and when anguish and distress overwhelm you."

PROVERBS 1:2-7, 20-27

rowing Wise

PREVIEW

Modern technology presents new moral dilemmas almost daily: the abortion pill, pornography on the internet, movies and TV, life-support systems, and many others. When these technologies are created, they are often in widespread use before anyone even has the chance to ask, *Is this wrong?* The quest for broader insight (wisdom) will speak to these specific dilemmas, even when there are no Bible verses that speak directly to the problem at hand.

This chapter contains some advice about becoming wise. It takes more than an afternoon at a good seminar, and *much* more than an aptitude for common sense. Read Proverbs 2 to discover some of the sources of wisdom and to learn how long the process of getting it can take.

Other lessons to get out of this chapter include how and where to get wisdom and ways in which wisdom can save you.

PERSONAL APPLICATION

Some people naturally have more insight than discretion; others have more knowledge than common sense. But no one is born wise. Growing wise doesn't happen quickly—it happens only through a consistent effort and only through God's Word. Wisdom comes through reading the Bible on a regular basis, accepting it, and putting its principles into practice.

Seek wisdom daily. Study and apply God's Word. Ask God to make your searches fruitful—you will be amazed at what you will learn and how your life will change.

BIBLE READING

[1]My child, listen to me and treasure my instructions. [2]Tune your ears to wisdom, and concentrate on understanding. [3]Cry out for insight and understanding. [4]Search for them as you would for lost money or hidden treasure. [5]Then you will understand what it means to fear the LORD, and you will gain knowledge of God. [6]For the LORD grants wisdom! From his mouth come knowledge and understanding. [7]He grants a treasure of good sense to the godly. He is their shield, protecting those who walk with integrity. [8]He guards the paths of justice and protects those who are faithful to him.

[9]Then you will understand what is right, just, and fair, and you will know how to find the right course of action every time. [10]For wisdom will enter your heart, and knowledge will fill you with joy. [11]Wise planning will watch over you. Understanding will keep you safe.

[12]Wisdom will save you from evil people, from those whose speech is corrupt. [13]These people turn from right ways to walk down dark and evil paths. [14]They rejoice in doing wrong, and they enjoy evil as it turns things upside down. [15]What they do is crooked, and their ways are wrong.   PROVERBS 2:1-15

eftovers Again!

PREVIEW

Some people absolutely love leftovers for dinner. Other people just plain dislike them, preferring a freshly made meal every night.

Although leftovers from meals are good, other kinds of "leftovers" can cause problems. For instance, giving your spouse a little time at the end of a day rather than investing your free time with him or her is not a good idea. The same applies to our relationships with God. As you read this chapter, hear the challenge to give God your *best part*, not your leftovers.

This chapter also has lessons on how to live a long and prosperous life; how to make good choices; the benefits of wisdom; and how to treat one's neighbor.

PERSONAL APPLICATION

God wants us to honor him with the "best part" of what we earn (Proverbs 3:9-10). The "best part" refers to the practice of giving to God the first and best portion of the harvest (see Deuteronomy 26:9-11).

For Christians today, this means writing the first check from their income to their local church or other Christian ministry. Unfortunately, many Christians give God what is left after they pay the bills and buy groceries. Then if they can afford to donate anything, they do so. But it is better to give God the *first* part of our income. This demonstrates that God, not possessions, has top place in our lives and that our resources belong to him—we are only managers of what he has given us. Giving to God first helps us conquer greed, helps us properly manage God's resources, demonstrates our faith in God to provide for our needs, and prepares us to receive his special blessings.

BIBLE READING

[1]My child, never forget the things I have taught you. Store my commands in your heart, [2]for they will give you a long and satisfying life. [3]Never let loyalty and kindness get away from you! Wear them like a necklace; write them deep within your heart. [4]Then you will find favor with both God and people, and you will gain a good reputation.

[5]Trust in the LORD with all your heart; do not depend on your own understanding. [6]Seek his will in all you do, and he will direct your paths.

[7]Don't be impressed with your own wisdom. Instead, fear the LORD and turn your back on evil. [8]Then you will gain renewed health and vitality.

[9]Honor the LORD with your wealth and with the best part of everything your land produces. [10]Then he will fill your barns with grain, and your vats will overflow with the finest wine.

PROVERBS 3:1-10

 o Detours

PREVIEW

The process of fending off temptation always involves a conversation with our feelings. *You really don't* need *this, you know. You just* want *it.* But desires tug at the heart. If there were no enjoyment to be had, where would the struggle be?

Proverbs 4 has some instructions about affection—those feelings of love and desire. It's about disciplining that part of the person that feels and desires the wrong pleasures (or the right ones at the wrong time). This is a difficult struggle—no one wants to go through life never doing what he or she enjoys. Read and learn.

Other areas of life covered in this chapter include lessons from parents; a goal that everyone should have; and the benefits of following wise advice and consequences of ignoring it.

PERSONAL APPLICATION

Our affections can give us both pain and pleasure. On one hand, we can desire and enjoy good—such as wanting to help someone solve a problem or enjoying sexual pleasure in marriage. On the other hand, we can desire and enjoy what we shouldn't—such as being lazy or enjoying sex outside of marriage. Our affections define what we enjoy, but what we enjoy isn't always what we should do. Proverbs 4:23-27 tells us to guard these affections above all else, making sure we concentrate on those desires that will keep us on the right path.

Many people have the idea that God is against pleasure, but they are mistaken. He's only against letting pleasure rule our lives. Living in obedience to God begins with knowing the difference between our wants and our needs—and then making the right choice regardless of the pleasure involved.

BIBLE READING

[10]My child, listen to me and do as I say, and you will have a long, good life. [11]I will teach you wisdom's ways and lead you in straight paths. [12]If you live a life guided by wisdom, you won't limp or stumble as you run. [13]Carry out my instructions; don't forsake them. Guard them, for they will lead you to a fulfilled life.

[14]Do not do as the wicked do or follow the path of evildoers. [15]Avoid their haunts. Turn away and go somewhere else, [16]for evil people cannot sleep until they have done their evil deed for the day. They cannot rest unless they have caused someone to stumble. [17]They eat wickedness and drink violence!

[18]The way of the righteous is like the first gleam of dawn, which shines ever brighter until the full light of day. [19]But the way of the wicked is like complete darkness. Those who follow it have no idea what they are stumbling over.

[20]Pay attention, my child, to what I say. Listen carefully. [21]Don't lose sight of my words. Let them penetrate deep within your heart, [22]for they bring life and radiant health to anyone who discovers their meaning.

[23]Above all else, guard your heart, for it affects everything you do.

[24]Avoid all perverse talk; stay far from corrupt speech.

[25]Look straight ahead, and fix your eyes on what lies before you. [26]Mark out a straight path for your feet; then stick to the path and stay safe. [27]Don't get sidetracked; keep your feet from following evil.   PROVERBS 4:10-27

Happily Married

PREVIEW

In America, 95 percent of all adults eventually marry. In a country where arranged marriages hardly ever happen, these couples marry because they *want* to. No one forces them to get married; there are no penalties for staying single. But there is one problem for many of those couples who marry—individuals can still change their minds. Some will no longer want to stay with their spouse, or might desire another companion.

Proverbs 5 gives advice on how to have a happy marriage, as well as good reasons why we should avoid infidelity. This chapter prohibits sex outside of marriage, but it encourages enjoyment of sexual pleasure within marriage. This reading also includes lessons on the consequences of adultery.

PERSONAL APPLICATION

"Drink water from your own well" (Proverbs 5:15). In desert lands, water is incredibly precious, and a family's very survival depends on a well or cistern. In Old Testament times, it was considered a crime to steal water from someone else's well. In the sexual context of this passage, the message is clear: don't take what doesn't belong to you, especially someone else's husband or wife.

To a thirsty person in a hot, dry land, water satisfies like nothing else. If you're thirsty, you should go to your well and drink. God wants married couples to look only to each other for lifelong satisfaction and companionship. That is his provision. That is his desire. Enjoy.

BIBLE READING

[1]My son, pay attention to my wisdom; listen carefully to my wise counsel. [2]Then you will learn to be discreet and will store up knowledge.

[3]The lips of an immoral woman are as sweet as honey, and her mouth is smoother than oil. [4]But the result is as bitter as poison, sharp as a double-edged sword. [5]Her feet go down to death; her steps lead straight to the grave. [6]For she does not care about the path to life. She staggers down a crooked trail and doesn't even realize where it leads.

[15]Drink water from your own well—share your love only with your wife. [16]Why spill the water of your springs in public, having sex with just anyone? [17]You should reserve it for yourselves. Don't share it with strangers.

[18]Let your wife be a fountain of blessing for you. Rejoice in the wife of your youth. [19]She is a loving doe, a graceful deer. Let her breasts satisfy you always. May you always be captivated by her love. [20]Why be captivated, my son, with an immoral woman, or embrace the breasts of an adulterous woman?

[21]For the LORD sees clearly what a man does, examining every path he takes. [22]An evil man is held captive by his own sins; they are ropes that catch and hold him. [23]He will die for lack of self-control; he will be lost because of his incredible folly.

PROVERBS 5:1-6, 15-23

leeping In

PREVIEW

If there were a television show called "Important Inventions That Everyone Takes for Granted," the series would no doubt feature a profile of the snooze button. This workhorse feature of the alarm clock gives many people those few, crucial, extra minutes of rest. Its value far outweighs its price! For those who love to sleep, the snooze button lets them make the transition to wakefulness a little more slowly.

Proverbs 6 contains some advice on sleeping in and its close cousin, laziness. Don't sleep through this lesson.

Other proverbs in this chapter deal with the hazards of too much generosity; and the consequences of scheming, displeasing God, and moral compromise.

PERSONAL APPLICATION

Some days, a little extra sleep seems like a necessity—and to some people it actually is. But Proverbs warns us against sleeping in too much (Proverbs 6:10-11). Of course, God isn't saying that people should never rest. He commanded the Jews to observe the Sabbath, a weekly day of rest and restoration. But he also knows that human beings find it easier to sleep in than to get up and work.

Take responsibility for getting up and starting your day. Don't wait for someone else to do it for you. Get a good night's rest, but when the alarm goes off, be sure to get up and get to work.

BIBLE READING

[1]My child, if you co-sign a loan for a friend or guarantee the debt of someone you hardly know—[2]if you have trapped yourself by your agreement and are caught by what you said—[3]quick, get out of it if you possibly can! You have placed yourself at your friend's mercy. Now swallow your pride; go and beg to have your name erased. [4]Don't put it off. Do it now! Don't rest until you do. [5]Save yourself like a deer escaping from a hunter, like a bird fleeing from a net.

[6]Take a lesson from the ants, you lazybones. Learn from their ways and be wise! [7]Even though they have no prince, governor, or ruler to make them work, [8]they labor hard all summer, gathering food for the winter. [9]But you, lazybones, how long will you sleep? When will you wake up? I want you to learn this lesson: [10]A little extra sleep, a little more slumber, a little folding of the hands to rest—[11]and poverty will pounce on you like a bandit; scarcity will attack you like an armed robber.

[12]Here is a description of worthless and wicked people: They are constant liars, [13]signaling their true intentions to their friends by making signs with their eyes and feet and fingers. [14]Their perverted hearts plot evil. They stir up trouble constantly. [15]But they will be destroyed suddenly, broken beyond all hope of healing. PROVERBS 6:1-15

emptation-Proof

PREVIEW

One of the best ways to survive a walk through a minefield is to avoid it altogether. Don't go there, and you won't get blown up. But the idea behind a minefield is the element of surprise—you don't know where the mines are because they're hidden. Therefore, the most realistic defense against getting blown up is to have a healthy suspicion of where the mines might be laid. Heads up and don't be naive, we might say.

Proverbs 7 is a map to help you navigate your way through your own minefields—those areas of life in which you are susceptible to temptation. Self-defense comes in many forms, and this one should be a part of everyone's arsenal.

The other lessons in this chapter relate to sexual purity.

PERSONAL APPLICATION

This chapter of Proverbs contains a dark description of a young woman seducing a young man into sexual compromise (Proverbs 7:6-23). The underlying principle applies to young women as well: Don't be naive. The person who has no purpose in life is simpleminded (7:7). Without aim or direction, an empty life is unstable and vulnerable to many temptations. Even though the young man in this passage doesn't know where he is going, the adulteress knows where she wants him. She preys on his naiveté: she dresses seductively (7:10); she boldly kisses him (7:13); she invites him over to her place (7:16-18); she cunningly answers his every objection (7:19-20); she persuades him with smooth talk (7:21). When she's done, he succumbs, as though he were a trapped animal (7:23).

The best way to avoid being entrapped by temptation is to have your eyes wide open about such schemes. Don't be naive—know your weaknesses, and run away.

BIBLE READING

[6]I was looking out the window of my house one day [7]and saw a simpleminded young man who lacked common sense. [8]He was crossing the street near the house of an immoral woman. He was strolling down the path by her house [9]at twilight, as the day was fading, as the dark of night set in. [10]The woman approached him, dressed seductively and sly of heart. [11]She was the brash, rebellious type who never stays at home. [12]She is often seen in the streets and markets, soliciting at every corner.

[13]She threw her arms around him and kissed him, and with a brazen look she said, [14]"I've offered my sacrifices and just finished my vows. [15]It's you I was looking for! I came out to find you, and here you are! [16]My bed is spread with colored sheets of finest linen imported from Egypt. [17]I've perfumed my bed with myrrh, aloes, and cinnamon. [18]Come, let's drink our fill of love until morning. Let's enjoy each other's caresses, [19]for my husband is not home. He's away on a long trip. [20]He has taken a wallet full of money with him, and he won't return until later in the month."

[21]So she seduced him with her pretty speech. With her flattery she enticed him. [22]He followed her at once, like an ox going to the slaughter or like a trapped stag, [23]awaiting the arrow that would pierce its heart. He was like a bird flying into a snare, little knowing it would cost him his life.

[24]Listen to me, my sons, and pay attention to my words. [25]Don't let your hearts stray away toward her. Don't wander down her wayward path. [26]For she has been the ruin of many; numerous men have been her victims. [27]Her house is the road to the grave. Her bedroom is the den of death.   PROVERBS 7:6-27

o Swirls Allowed

PREVIEW

Ice cream can sometimes be bought in a "swirl"—a mix of two flavors, usually chocolate and vanilla. It's for those who can't decide on one or the other, or who like both equally well, or who like the mix itself. But what is good in ice cream is bad in moral habits.

Proverbs 8 is a call to make right choices—to hate evil. There is no mixing of good and evil here.

Other proverbs in this chapter teach us why wisdom is more valuable than gold and even priceless.

PERSONAL APPLICATION

"All who fear the Lord will hate evil. That is why I hate pride, arrogance, corruption, and perverted speech" (Proverbs 8:13). Most of us have a mix of love and hate for evil. We know we should hate lying and hypocrisy, yet there are times when they come in handy. We know we should love sexual purity and honesty, yet there are times when our minds turn to impure thoughts, and deceit seems less painful than being honest.

Respect for God clears away the inconsistencies. Think about the place God deserves to have in your life, and fear the consequences of not giving him proper place. When you make the decision to love God wholeheartedly, love for sin will not be able to coexist in your life.

BIBLE READING

[1]Listen as wisdom calls out! Hear as understanding raises her voice! [2]She stands on the hilltop and at the crossroads. [3]At the entrance to the city, at the city gates, she cries aloud, [4]"I call to you, to all of you! I am raising my voice to all people. [5]How naive you are! Let me give you common sense. O foolish ones, let me give you understanding. [6]Listen to me! For I have excellent things to tell you. Everything I say is right, [7]for I speak the truth and hate every kind of deception. [8]My advice is wholesome and good. There is nothing crooked or twisted in it. [9]My words are plain to anyone with understanding, clear to those who want to learn.

[10]"Choose my instruction rather than silver, and knowledge over pure gold. [11]For wisdom is far more valuable than rubies. Nothing you desire can be compared with it.

[12]"I, Wisdom, live together with good judgment. I know where to discover knowledge and discernment. [13]All who fear the LORD will hate evil. That is why I hate pride, arrogance, corruption, and perverted speech. [14]Good advice and success belong to me. Insight and strength are mine. [15]Because of me, kings reign, and rulers make just laws. [16]Rulers lead with my help, and nobles make righteous judgments." PROVERBS 8:1-16

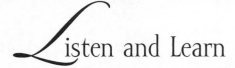isten and Learn

PREVIEW

Columnists tell what's right and wrong with society. Theater critics explain who performed well and who faltered. Literary critics pronounce what's worth reading and what's not. Others, such as friends, neighbors, coworkers, and fellow drivers, give personal criticism in the many areas of life.

Proverbs 9 includes several principles regarding how to respond—or not respond—to criticism. As you read, be sure to notice the difference between being a wise person and a "mocker."

Other lessons here include how to tell the difference between wisdom and foolishness, and good reasons for avoiding prostitutes.

PERSONAL APPLICATION

Are you a wise person or a "mocker"? You can tell by the way you respond to criticism (Proverbs 9:7-10). For instance, how do you normally respond to these situations? A relative rebukes you for something relatively insignificant that you did a while back; a coworker questions your judgment on a project; your spouse critiques your attire; your kids demand that you spend more time with them. Do you toss back a quick put-down or clever retort? Or do you listen to what is being said? A wise person learns from rebukes and criticism (9:8-9).

Instead of dismissing every critique of your behavior, try to see each from the critic's perspective. Search their words for ways you can improve yourself. Look for lessons in what they have to say and do not mock them. It bears repeating: How you respond to criticism tells a lot about you. A wise person accepts it and tries to learn from it. A fool throws it back. Don't be a fool.

BIBLE READING

¹Wisdom has built her spacious house with seven pillars. ²She has prepared a great banquet, mixed the wines, and set the table. ³She has sent her servants to invite everyone to come. She calls out from the heights overlooking the city. ⁴"Come home with me," she urges the simple. To those without good judgment, she says, ⁵"Come, eat my food, and drink the wine I have mixed. ⁶Leave your foolish ways behind, and begin to live; learn how to be wise."

⁷Anyone who rebukes a mocker will get a smart retort. Anyone who rebukes the wicked will get hurt. ⁸So don't bother rebuking mockers; they will only hate you. But the wise, when rebuked, will love you all the more. ⁹Teach the wise, and they will be wiser. Teach the righteous, and they will learn more.

¹⁰Fear of the LORD is the beginning of wisdom. Knowledge of the Holy One results in understanding.

¹¹Wisdom will multiply your days and add years to your life. ¹²If you become wise, you will be the one to benefit. If you scorn wisdom, you will be the one to suffer.   PROVERBS 9:1-12

empered

Preview

Are there certain people, who, even just the mention of their name can set you off in three seconds flat? Although you don't particularly care for the way you respond, you can't forget how badly that person treated you. Normally you're not a hateful person, but your feelings for so-and-so cross the line of hatred.

Proverbs 10 urges us to deal with this ugly emotion head-on. That's easy to say but not so easy to do. The principles in this reading, however, will help you out.

Other lessons in this chapter will teach you how to avoid sorrow; how to keep your foot out of your mouth; and how to avoid aggravating your employer.

Personal Application

Many people spend their whole lives hating certain people. They cannot let go of wrongs done to them, or forgive offenses from the distant past. Their statements about these people become laced with unkind words and slander. Harboring hatred destroys the person doing the hating and causes nothing but conflict with others (Proverbs 10:12). "To hide hatred is to be a liar; to slander is to be a fool" (10:18). In contrast, those who love bring forgiveness and healing because "love covers all offenses" (10:12). Love forgives and forgets.

Beware of hatred. If you try to conceal your hatred, you only lie about your true feelings. If you slander the other person, you become a fool. The only way out is to admit your hateful feelings to God, ask him to change your heart, and forgive the other person. Let God's love go beyond the other person's offense and help you to actually forgive the offender (10:12). Ask God to help you love instead of hate.

BIBLE READING

[7]We all have happy memories of the godly, but the name of a wicked person rots away.

[8]The wise are glad to be instructed, but babbling fools fall flat on their faces.

[9]People with integrity have firm footing, but those who follow crooked paths will slip and fall.

[10]People who wink at wrong cause trouble, but a bold reproof promotes peace.

[11]The words of the godly lead to life; evil people cover up their harmful intentions.

[12]Hatred stirs up quarrels, but love covers all offenses.

[13]Wise words come from the lips of people with understanding, but fools will be punished with a rod.

[14]Wise people treasure knowledge, but the babbling of a fool invites trouble.

[15]The wealth of the rich is their fortress; the poverty of the poor is their calamity.

[16]The earnings of the godly enhance their lives, but evil people squander their money on sin.

[17]People who accept correction are on the pathway to life, but those who ignore it will lead others astray.

[18]To hide hatred is to be a liar; to slander is to be a fool.

PROVERBS 10:7-18

Sticks, Stones, and Other Power Tools

PREVIEW

The power of words is amazing. Say a word and you can make a roomful of people laugh; say another and you can make them cry. An entire nation's morale can change with the words of its leaders. You could even completely destroy a person's reputation with a thoughtless word or two. It has been said that the pen is mightier than the sword—and for good reason.

Proverbs 11 contains some thoughts on the destructiveness of words and stands as a good reminder for us to watch what we say.

This chapter also has thoughts on wealth; abuse of power; leadership; and generosity.

PERSONAL APPLICATION

Like power tools, words have the potential to do great good or enormous damage, depending on how we use them. We can either use words to damage a relationship or make it better (Proverbs 11:9, 11-13). Unfortunately, most people use words to destroy more often than to build up.

Each bit of gossip and each word of slander we speak not only hurts those around us, but it also wastes an opportunity to help. Every day brings many opportunities to use words negatively or positively. Sadly, it takes less effort to gossip than to praise; less skill to cut with sarcasm than to repair with thanks. So, most people hear far more destructive comments than constructive ones.

Remember that every person with whom you interact today will be either better or worse off as a consequence of your words. Your words could make the difference. Think before you talk!

BIBLE READING

²Pride leads to disgrace, but with humility comes wisdom.

³Good people are guided by their honesty; treacherous people are destroyed by their dishonesty.

⁴Riches won't help on the day of judgment, but right living is a safeguard against death.

⁵The godly are directed by their honesty; the wicked fall beneath their load of sin.

⁶The godliness of good people rescues them; the ambition of treacherous people traps them.

⁷When the wicked die, their hopes all perish, for they rely on their own feeble strength.

⁸God rescues the godly from danger, but he lets the wicked fall into trouble.

⁹Evil words destroy one's friends; wise discernment rescues the godly.

¹⁰The whole city celebrates when the godly succeed; they shout for joy when the godless die.

¹¹Upright citizens bless a city and make it prosper, but the talk of the wicked tears it apart.

¹²It is foolish to belittle a neighbor; a person with good sense remains silent.

¹³A gossip goes around revealing secrets, but those who are trustworthy can keep a confidence.

¹⁴Without wise leadership, a nation falls; with many counselors, there is safety. PROVERBS 11:2-14

eal Success

PREVIEW

Cheating, cutting in line, fudging the numbers, covering up your mistakes, and working so many hours that you neglect your family responsibilities—these are the techniques people use to get ahead. This is the "American way." Is it yours?

When it comes to achieving success, there is a tremendous contrast between the techniques used by the wicked and those used by the righteous. There's also a big difference between whom the wicked and the righteous worship. In the end, only one will really be successful. As you read, look for the proverbs that teach how to attain real success.

You will also find these topics in Proverbs 12: a smart step that everyone can take; tips for responding to insults; how to use words; and laziness.

PERSONAL APPLICATION

"Wickedness never brings stability; only the godly have deep roots" (Proverbs 12:3). This proverb refers to success. Everyone knows people who have cheated to pass a test or to get a larger tax refund. While they may get away with it and enjoy a good grade or a bigger refund, don't be tempted to view them as successful or desire to emulate them. Real success comes only to those who do what is right (12:3). Although the efforts of the righteous may not always be successful from the world's point of view, their efforts will have lasting worth. The apparent successes of the wicked will not last.

The choices that will set you on the path to real success—obedience to God and doing his will—have everlasting consequences. If you are not a success by God's standards, you have not achieved success at all.

Determine to be firmly rooted in living God's way. Don't sell your character to achieve worldly success.

BIBLE READING

¹To learn, you must love discipline; it is stupid to hate correction.

²The LORD approves of those who are good, but he condemns those who plan wickedness.

³Wickedness never brings stability; only the godly have deep roots.

⁴A worthy wife is her husband's joy and crown; a shameful wife saps his strength.

⁵The plans of the godly are just; the advice of the wicked is treacherous.

⁶The words of the wicked are like a murderous ambush, but the words of the godly save lives.

⁷The wicked perish and are gone, but the children of the godly stand firm.

⁸Everyone admires a person with good sense, but a warped mind is despised.

⁹It is better to be a nobody with a servant than to be self-important but have no food.

¹⁰The godly are concerned for the welfare of their animals, but even the kindness of the wicked is cruel.

¹¹Hard work means prosperity; only fools idle away their time.

¹²Thieves are jealous of each other's loot, while the godly bear their own fruit.

¹³The wicked are trapped by their own words, but the godly escape such trouble.   PROVERBS 12:1-13

$\mathscr{S}$hoot Straight with Me

PREVIEW

What kind of advice do you get from your friends? Are you satisfied with it? Do you sometimes sense that some of your problems baffle your friends, leaving them unable to offer wise and insightful counsel? You may even wonder where you would turn if you ever needed counseling for a true problem.

Proverbs 13 contains many helpful words of advice about choosing friends and how to benefit from the people who walk the same path. You're right if you've been thinking you need some wise friends, friends who can guide you along the way. Here's how to get them.

There's much more here on several other subjects, including: ways to benefit from your words; the benefits of being poor and the hazards of having wealth; a warning about pride; and the importance of disciplining children.

PERSONAL APPLICATION

When seeking friends, most people look for those who make them feel good about themselves. But that's not the most important ingredient in friendship. In fact, people who make us feel good about ourselves may not be the best influence on us, and they may not have our best interests at heart.

Our friends help determine the direction that our lives take. If our friends are wise, we will be too. If they are fools, so will we be (Proverbs 13:20). Thus, we need to choose our friends very carefully. We should seek out friends who can advise us, set an example for us, and help us stay on the right track. Some of them should be older, and the best ones should be wiser.

Seek out wise people who have experienced life—and have succeeded. Seek out friends who are not afraid to tell you the truth, who will move you in God's direction.

BIBLE READING

¹³People who despise advice will find themselves in trouble; those who respect it will succeed.

¹⁴The advice of the wise is like a life-giving fountain; those who accept it avoid the snares of death.

¹⁵A person with good sense is respected; a treacherous person walks a rocky road.

¹⁶Wise people think before they act; fools don't and even brag about it!

¹⁷An unreliable messenger stumbles into trouble, but a reliable messenger brings healing.

¹⁸If you ignore criticism, you will end in poverty and disgrace; if you accept criticism, you will be honored.

¹⁹It is pleasant to see dreams come true, but fools will not turn from evil to attain them.

²⁰Whoever walks with the wise will become wise; whoever walks with fools will suffer harm.

²¹Trouble chases sinners, while blessings chase the righteous!

²²Good people leave an inheritance to their grandchildren, but the sinner's wealth passes to the godly.

²³A poor person's farm may produce much food, but injustice sweeps it all away.

²⁴If you refuse to discipline your children, it proves you don't love them; if you love your children, you will be prompt to discipline them.

²⁵The godly eat to their hearts' content, but the belly of the wicked goes hungry.   PROVERBS 13:13-25

# *G*ood Will

PREVIEW

"Hackers," or people who write destructive computer viruses, don't feel at fault when their viruses destroy people's data. *If I can hack my way into your computer,* many of them reason, *it's your own fault for not better protecting yourself.* What's wrong with that way of thinking?

Proverbs 14 contains the answer for those who can accept it. It's also the answer to Cain's infamous question, "Am I my brother's keeper?" (see Genesis 4:9).

Other proverbs in this chapter touch on many areas of relationships: advice for women; a way to avoid some unnecessary trouble; certain people to avoid; where to find help; reasons for controlling one's temper; and treatment of the poor.

PERSONAL APPLICATION

People who love God care about what happens to others and try to do what will be helpful to them, not hurtful. They practice good will toward others (Proverbs 14:9, 21). They (1) think the best of others, (2) assume that others have good motives and intend to do what is right, (3) look out for others, and (4) make amends whenever they wrong someone.

In everything you do that affects others, ask yourself, *Does this show good will?* And in each interaction with another person, whether a phone call, gesture, E-mail, or face-to-face conversation, ask, *How can I help this person?*

BIBLE READING

[9]Fools make fun of guilt, but the godly acknowledge it and seek reconciliation.

[10]Each heart knows its own bitterness, and no one else can fully share its joy.

[11]The house of the wicked will perish, but the tent of the godly will flourish.

[12]There is a path before each person that seems right, but it ends in death.

[13]Laughter can conceal a heavy heart; when the laughter ends, the grief remains.

[14]Backsliders get what they deserve; good people receive their reward.

[15]Only simpletons believe everything they are told! The prudent carefully consider their steps.

[16]The wise are cautious and avoid danger; fools plunge ahead with great confidence.

[17]Those who are short-tempered do foolish things, and schemers are hated.

[18]The simpleton is clothed with folly, but the wise person is crowned with knowledge.

[19]Evil people will bow before good people; the wicked will bow at the gates of the godly.

[20]The poor are despised even by their neighbors, while the rich have many "friends."

[21]It is sin to despise one's neighbors; blessed are those who help the poor.

[22]If you plot evil, you will be lost; but if you plan good, you will be granted unfailing love and faithfulness.

PROVERBS 14:9-22

Attitude Adjustment

PREVIEW

A construction crew has been tearing up your route to work lately. It looks—as usual—as though they have chosen to do more than they can manage. Lanes and road shoulders are torn up, heavy equipment is scattered throughout the construction zone, and mud and debris are everywhere. As you pass through this mess, what do you see? Do you see a colossal inconvenience, or do you see a new era of smooth rides to work? Which would you rather do—curse the potholes or bless the highway department for filling them in?

Several verses in Proverbs 15 discuss attitudes—both cheerful and gloomy. They offer common sense on human emotions that you won't find in a modern-day psychology book.

You will find these other lessons in this reading: how to defuse erupting fights; what God loves; what your reading material says about you; the value of love; one way to protect your family; and one way to attract honor.

PERSONAL APPLICATION

Our attitudes color every experience we have (Proverbs 15:4, 13, 15, 30). The way we interpret and respond to our experiences is entirely up to us. We can choose to respond cheerfully, or we can choose to respond grumpily. The secret to responding optimistically and having a good day is to have a cheerful heart (15:15). We can have this positive attitude despite wretched circumstances if we focus our attention on God—his character, his sovereignty, and his goodness to us.

As you face the struggles of daily living, look at your attitudes and examine what you choose to dwell on. If you have a bad attitude, shift your focus from your circumstances to God. It will make all the difference.

BIBLE READING

⁴Gentle words bring life and health; a deceitful tongue crushes the spirit.

⁵Only a fool despises a parent's discipline; whoever learns from correction is wise.

⁶There is treasure in the house of the godly, but the earnings of the wicked bring trouble.

⁷Only the wise can give good advice; fools cannot do so.

⁸The LORD hates the sacrifice of the wicked, but he delights in the prayers of the upright.

⁹The LORD despises the way of the wicked, but he loves those who pursue godliness.

¹⁰Whoever abandons the right path will be severely punished; whoever hates correction will die.

¹¹Even the depths of Death and Destruction are known by the LORD. How much more does he know the human heart!

¹²Mockers don't love those who rebuke them, so they stay away from the wise.

¹³A glad heart makes a happy face; a broken heart crushes the spirit.

¹⁴A wise person is hungry for truth, while the fool feeds on trash.

¹⁵For the poor, every day brings trouble; for the happy heart, life is a continual feast. PROVERBS 15:4-15

ommit It

PREVIEW

Many people fear getting married. Marriage changes everything—for the rest of your life. No one should blame a bride or groom for being nervous. Uncertainty over the future is the most nerve-racking kind of all. How do they know this will work? So many marriages don't last. Will theirs?

Predicting the future has many hazards. A better approach would be to consider the advice in Proverbs 16 about committing your way (or future) to God.

In this chapter you will also learn about making plans; dealing with pride; being fair in business; using pleasant words; and strengthening the bond between friends.

PERSONAL APPLICATION

Proverbs 16:3 says, "Commit your work to the Lord, and then your plans will succeed." What does this mean? To "commit your work to the Lord" means to dedicate everything you do to God's purposes through prayer—turning it over to him. It also means doing your best for God's glory and depending on him for the results.

What work should you commit to God? Any plan, task, or endeavor that you want to succeed: buying a car, starting school, initiating a new church program, getting engaged or married, going on vacation, changing jobs, entering retirement—these all qualify.

Think of a specific effort in which you are involved right now—how might you commit it to the Lord?

BIBLE READING

[1]We can gather our thoughts, but the LORD gives the right answer.

[2]People may be pure in their own eyes, but the LORD examines their motives.

[3]Commit your work to the LORD, and then your plans will succeed.

[4]The LORD has made everything for his own purposes, even the wicked for punishment.

[5]The LORD despises pride; be assured that the proud will be punished.

[6]Unfailing love and faithfulness cover sin; evil is avoided by fear of the LORD.

[7]When the ways of people please the LORD, he makes even their enemies live at peace with them.

[8]It is better to be poor and godly than rich and dishonest.

[9]We can make our plans, but the LORD determines our steps.

PROVERBS 16:1-9

eal Losers

PREVIEW

It's not surprising to see a winning team celebrate a victory. That's what victors are entitled to do. Some fans, however, dislike winning teams that take the celebration too far. They know that there's a place for respecting the loser, even if the gap between winner and loser is quite wide. They also hope that someday the roles will be reversed.

In an indirect way, Proverbs 17 talks about winners and losers. More to the point, it's about people who mock those less fortunate than they—the losers, you might say. As you read this chapter, be prepared to put away that "We're Number One!" chant.

Also in this chapter you will find one reason for suffering; one reward in getting old; one hazard in associating with a fool; one rule to being a best friend; one use for a positive attitude; and one more reason to hold your tongue.

PERSONAL APPLICATION

Making fun of those less fortunate than others is an old tradition for humankind. The vulnerable can count on being ridiculed and exploited—especially the poor, but also children and senior citizens.

Those who take advantage of the vulnerable do so because it makes them feel stronger or more successful than the less fortunate. But mocking the poor mocks the God who made them (Proverbs 17:5), and we might reasonably extend that to the weak and downtrodden as well.

The next time you catch yourself putting others down, stop and think about who created them.

BIBLE READING

¹A dry crust eaten in peace is better than a great feast with strife.

²A wise slave will rule over the master's shameful sons and will share their inheritance.

³Fire tests the purity of silver and gold, but the LORD tests the heart.

⁴Wrongdoers listen to wicked talk; liars pay attention to destructive words.

⁵Those who mock the poor insult their Maker; those who rejoice at the misfortune of others will be punished.

⁶Grandchildren are the crowning glory of the aged; parents are the pride of their children.

⁷Eloquent speech is not fitting for a fool; even less are lies fitting for a ruler.

⁸A bribe seems to work like magic for those who give it; they succeed in all they do.

⁹Disregarding another person's faults preserves love; telling about them separates close friends.

¹⁰A single rebuke does more for a person of understanding than a hundred lashes on the back of a fool.   PROVERBS 17:1-10

est Friends

PREVIEW

When you were a little kid, best friends really meant *best friends*. You played together every day. You invited each other over all the time. You stuck up for each other when the neighborhood bully showed up. You shared secrets, passwords, and favorite things. It was all about one thing: loyalty.

Proverbs 18 covers friends—the loyal ones, the kind you can't do without. As you read, you will find a challenge to live up to the standard of an ideal friend. You will also find a warning to avoid those who pretend to be friends but aren't.

Other verses here deal with sharing your opinion; a popular myth about wealth; and getting both sides of the story.

PERSONAL APPLICATION

Today, more than ever, friendlessness plagues many people. With all the advances in technology, people, for the most part, are no longer dependent upon one another. It's no wonder, then, why some people feel cut off and alienated from others, even those they consider "friends."

God, however, made us to be social beings, in need of close, meaningful relationships. Each one of us needs a friend who will listen, care, stick close, and offer help whenever we need it—in good times and bad. One such friend means more than dozens of superficial acquaintances (Proverbs 18:24).

If you're lonely and in need of a good friend, take the first step to developing great friendships: seek to become a true and loyal friend to someone else. Ask God to reveal this person to you. Then take on the challenge of being a true friend by caring, listening, helping, and affirming. Your friends need your friendship as much as you need theirs.

BIBLE READING

[14]The human spirit can endure a sick body, but who can bear it if the spirit is crushed?

[15]Intelligent people are always open to new ideas. In fact, they look for them.

[16]Giving a gift works wonders; it may bring you before important people!

[17]Any story sounds true until someone sets the record straight.

[18]Casting lots can end arguments and settle disputes between powerful opponents.

[19]It's harder to make amends with an offended friend than to capture a fortified city. Arguments separate friends like a gate locked with iron bars.

[20]Words satisfy the soul as food satisfies the stomach; the right words on a person's lips bring satisfaction.

[21]Those who love to talk will experience the consequences, for the tongue can kill or nourish life.

[22]The man who finds a wife finds a treasure and receives favor from the LORD.

[23]The poor plead for mercy; the rich answer with insults.

[24]There are "friends" who destroy each other, but a real friend sticks closer than a brother.   PROVERBS 18:14-24

$\mathscr{N}$othing but the Truth

PREVIEW

Some things have been disappearing from the office lately—small but expensive items. Talk turns to speculation on who could be doing it. Circumstantial evidence points to one person in particular, but no one is willing to believe that he could be guilty. He just isn't the kind of person who would do that—he's too honest.

Proverbs 19 addresses the subject of dishonesty. The consequences of dishonesty are not pleasant. As you read, you'll see what I mean . . . honest!

In addition, this chapter contains five don'ts and one do: don't be hasty; don't lie; don't be quarrelsome; don't be lazy; don't be stingy; but do listen to advice.

PERSONAL APPLICATION

"A false witness will not go unpunished"—those words appear twice in this chapter (Proverbs 19:5, 9). Other verses make similar statements about the practical value of truth and the foolishness of deceiving others (19:1, 28).

Honesty is God's policy. Having a reputation for speaking the truth is better than lying and living well. Unfortunately, however, most people don't believe this, so in order to get ahead they cut moral corners when it comes to telling the truth.

Don't buy the world's line that lying is OK. Remember, being honest will keep you out of trouble with God, and it may also build your reputation. Be known as a person who tells the truth.

BIBLE READING

¹It is better to be poor and honest than to be a fool and dishonest.

²Zeal without knowledge is not good; a person who moves too quickly may go the wrong way.

³People ruin their lives by their own foolishness and then are angry at the LORD.

⁴Wealth makes many "friends"; poverty drives them away.

⁵A false witness will not go unpunished, nor will a liar escape.

⁶Many beg favors from a prince; everyone is the friend of a person who gives gifts!

⁷If the relatives of the poor despise them, how much more will their friends avoid them. The poor call after them, but they are gone.

⁸To acquire wisdom is to love oneself; people who cherish understanding will prosper.

⁹A false witness will not go unpunished, and a liar will be destroyed.

¹⁰It isn't right for a fool to live in luxury or for a slave to rule over princes!

¹¹People with good sense restrain their anger; they earn esteem by overlooking wrongs.   PROVERBS 19:1-11

To Putter or Not to Putter, That Is the Question

PREVIEW

Everyone has wasted time. Perhaps you've watched a mindless television program when the lawn needed mowing. Maybe you've played games on your computer at work when you really needed to finish a report. Or perhaps you've put off doing a necessary but unpleasant task by immersing yourself in a magazine or newspaper. There are countless other ways to kill time. What is your favorite time-wasting activity?

Proverbs 20 says that there's a problem with wasting time, with putting off responsibilities in favor of puttering around. In some cases the consequences of wasting time can be serious. As you read, you will discover good reasons for being responsible.

Note also the other consequences here for getting drunk, sleeping in too much, and cursing one's parents. This chapter doesn't just dwell on consequences, though. It shows the many blessings for children of an honest parent; for those who have good sense; and for a leader who is fair, honest, and kind.

PERSONAL APPLICATION

"If you are too lazy to plow in the right season, you will have no food at the harvest" (Proverbs 20:4). You've probably heard similar warnings: "If you don't study, you'll fail the test," or "If you don't save, you won't have money when you need it." Although God will provide for our needs, he wants us to take responsibility for ourselves and use wisely what he has given us. Refusing to take responsibility for ourselves today can mean suffering the consequences of our irresponsibility tomorrow. And we cannot expect God to come to our rescue whenever we foolishly do not plan ahead.

What's on your must-do list? Let nothing hold you back from fulfilling your responsibilities and promises.

BIBLE READING

¹Wine produces mockers; liquor leads to brawls. Whoever is led astray by drink cannot be wise.

²The king's fury is like a lion's roar; to rouse his anger is to risk your life.

³Avoiding a fight is a mark of honor; only fools insist on quarreling.

⁴If you are too lazy to plow in the right season, you will have no food at the harvest.

⁵Though good advice lies deep within a person's heart, the wise will draw it out.

⁶Many will say they are loyal friends, but who can find one who is really faithful?

⁷The godly walk with integrity; blessed are their children after them.

⁸When a king judges, he carefully weighs all the evidence, distinguishing the bad from the good.

⁹Who can say, "I have cleansed my heart; I am pure and free from sin"?

¹⁰The LORD despises double standards of every kind.

¹¹Even children are known by the way they act, whether their conduct is pure and right.   PROVERBS 20:1-11

True/False Test

PREVIEW

Do you know someone who seems to have an answer for every critic? In conversation you may have come to realize that this person can rationalize their every action. In fact, this person seems to have good reasons for all the wrong choices that he or she has ever made!

Yesterday's reading, Proverbs 20, urged us to be honest with others. This reading, Proverbs 21, urges us to bring the lesson home and be honest with ourselves. Call it a true/false test for motives.

Other topics in this chapter challenge us to be honest with ourselves in the areas of business, pleasure, pride, and savings.

PERSONAL APPLICATION

"People may think they are doing what is right, but the Lord examines the heart" (Proverbs 21:2). It's amazing how readily we can justify whatever we set out to do. Every action seems right, so with a little thought, we can find an excuse for doing almost anything. The truth can often hurt, so we tend to deceive ourselves about why we're really doing what we're doing. But God always looks behind our excuses to our motives. We can't hide the truth from him; so, we should be honest about why we're really doing something.

To cure this tendency to deceive ourselves and rationalize, we must examine our excuses carefully to make sure they aren't covering up sinful actions, poor choices, or wrong motives. A test to use to cut through an excuse is to ask, *Would God be pleased with my real reasons for doing this?* If the answer is no, then we shouldn't do it.

God wants you to be honest, to admit when you've done wrong, and to do what is right. He also wants you to do good deeds for the right reasons. If you do, you will find life!

BIBLE READING

[1]The king's heart is like a stream of water directed by the LORD; he turns it wherever he pleases.

[2]People may think they are doing what is right, but the LORD examines the heart.

[3]The LORD is more pleased when we do what is just and right than when we give him sacrifices.

[4]Haughty eyes, a proud heart, and evil actions are all sin.

[5]Good planning and hard work lead to prosperity, but hasty shortcuts lead to poverty.

[6]Wealth created by lying is a vanishing mist and a deadly trap.

[7]Because the wicked refuse to do what is just, their violence boomerangs and destroys them.

[8]The guilty walk a crooked path; the innocent travel a straight road.

[9]It is better to live alone in the corner of an attic than with a contentious wife in a lovely home.

[10]Evil people love to harm others; their neighbors get no mercy from them.

[11]A simpleton can learn only by seeing mockers punished; a wise person learns from instruction.

[12]The Righteous One knows what is going on in the homes of the wicked; he will bring the wicked to disaster.

PROVERBS 21:1-12

Of Bullies and Tyrants

PREVIEW

With few exceptions, bullies use fear and intimidation only against people who are weaker than they are. They don't threaten those who are bigger and stronger because they don't want to lose. Their reign of terror depends on scaring people. That's why they'll hurt people just to make a point.

In Proverbs 22 you will find warnings for leaders who rule by fear and intimidation, just like bullies. Take heed.

You will also find thoughts on pursuing a good reputation; responding to dangers and hazards; rearing children; being rewarded for doing good; avoiding the sure road to poverty; and learning a skill.

PERSONAL APPLICATION

God hates it when people use fear and intimidation to control others. Although he has given leaders the freedom to lead as they see fit, he doesn't stand back and ignore their abuse of power and influence. When abuse of power occurs, God will sometimes intervene directly and destroy the tyrant, but more often he uses other rulers or even the oppressed people to remove the tyrant from power (Proverbs 22:8, 22-23).

If you must live or work under an abusive leader, take these verses as a message of hope: God has not forgotten you and does not overlook your leader's abuses. If you lead or have any authority at all— either at church, work, or home—remember what happens to tyrants.

Leadership through kindness works better and lasts longer than leadership by force. Fear and intimidation are the human way, not God's way. Jesus never led by fear and intimidation and neither should we.

BIBLE READING

[17]Listen to the words of the wise; apply your heart to my instruction. [18]For it is good to keep these sayings deep within yourself, always ready on your lips. [19]I am teaching you today—yes, you—so you will trust in the LORD. [20]I have written thirty sayings for you, filled with advice and knowledge. [21]In this way, you may know the truth and bring an accurate report to those who sent you.

[22]Do not rob the poor because they are poor or exploit the needy in court. [23]For the LORD is their defender. He will injure anyone who injures them.

[24]Keep away from angry, short-tempered people, [25]or you will learn to be like them and endanger your soul.

[26]Do not co-sign another person's note or put up a guarantee for someone else's loan. [27]If you can't pay it, even your bed will be snatched from under you.

[28]Do not steal your neighbor's property by moving the ancient boundary markers set up by your ancestors.

[29]Do you see any truly competent workers? They will serve kings rather than ordinary people.   PROVERBS 22:17-29

*F*ood, Glorious Food!

PREVIEW

"You're not overweight!" friends tell Juan. "Diet any more and you're going to blow away!" Ruth tells Nancy. "I only drink at weddings and other celebrations," explains Jolene. "I don't have a drinking problem—I can quit any time I want," Mike insists. Eating and drinking—sources of pleasure and sources of grief.

Does the Bible talk about food and drink? You better believe it. Here in Proverbs 23 are some of the choicest morsels. Dig in.

Other verses in this chapter say more to modern living than the advice columns of most major newspapers. They address: accepting bribes; the wrong reason to work hard; what to think of party animals; what to do with your parents when they are old; and the truth about alcohol.

PERSONAL APPLICATION

Gluttony and drunkenness make poor friends. They not only make us overweight (and possibly alcoholic), they can also weaken our character and drain our pockets (Proverbs 23:19-21).

Not everyone struggles with overeating or alcoholism, but those who do certainly never planned on it. If you do have these struggles, there are some steps that you can take to overcome them: (1) realize you have a problem; (2) ask God to grant you the strength to resist the temptation; (3) seek professional help if necessary; and (4) avoid the source of your temptation.

Work at getting control of your appetites—God desires that you live a life of freedom!

BIBLE READING

[1]When dining with a ruler, pay attention to what is put before you. [2]If you are a big eater, put a knife to your throat, [3]and don't desire all the delicacies—deception may be involved.

[4]Don't weary yourself trying to get rich. Why waste your time? [5]For riches can disappear as though they had the wings of a bird!

[6]Don't eat with people who are stingy; don't desire their delicacies. [7]"Eat and drink," they say, but they don't mean it. They are always thinking about how much it costs. [8]You will vomit up the delicious food they serve, and you will have to take back your words of appreciation for their "kindness."

[15]My child, how I will rejoice if you become wise. [16]Yes, my heart will thrill when you speak what is right and just.

[17]Don't envy sinners, but always continue to fear the LORD. [18]For surely you have a future ahead of you; your hope will not be disappointed.

[19]My child, listen and be wise. Keep your heart on the right course. [20]Do not carouse with drunkards and gluttons, [21]for they are on their way to poverty. Too much sleep clothes a person with rags.   PROVERBS 23:1-8, 15-21

Brave Warrior, Go to the Dentist

PREVIEW

Many people are terrified of going to the dentist. The mere thought of the needle and the drill gives them the shivers. They long to overcome this fear, because they know what awaits them if they don't go to the dentist regularly—dentures.

Proverbs 24 talks about adversity and what our responses to it reveal about us. The wisdom here is a prescription for the fear of pain. If you suffer from this fear, don't forget to take your medicine regularly.

Other prescriptions in this chapter should be taken if you envy others; are struggling through tough times; associate with radicals; worry about the future; or struggle with laziness.

PERSONAL APPLICATION

Adversity does us a favor—it gives us opportunity to see what we're made of (Proverbs 24:10). If we whine and whimper at every threat of illness, inconvenience, or irritation, we may have a character problem. People who love and obey God don't cave in easily because God sustains them (Proverbs 24:16; see also Nehemiah 9:21; Jeremiah 15:15-16).

How do you respond when you're not feeling well, when it rains, or when you have a bad day? Do you whine and complain? Don't grumble about your problems. Realize that the adversity you face today is training you to be strong for more difficult situations in the future.

BIBLE READING

³A house is built by wisdom and becomes strong through good sense. ⁴Through knowledge its rooms are filled with all sorts of precious riches and valuables.

⁵A wise man is mightier than a strong man, and a man of knowledge is more powerful than a strong man. ⁶So don't go to war without wise guidance; victory depends on having many counselors.

⁷Wisdom is too much for a fool. When the leaders gather, the fool has nothing to say.

⁸A person who plans evil will get a reputation as a trouble-maker. ⁹The schemes of a fool are sinful; everyone despises a mocker.

¹⁰If you fail under pressure, your strength is not very great.

¹¹Rescue those who are unjustly sentenced to death; don't stand back and let them die. ¹²Don't try to avoid responsibility by saying you didn't know about it. For God knows all hearts, and he sees you. He keeps watch over your soul, and he knows you knew! And he will judge all people according to what they have done.

¹³My child, eat honey, for it is good, and the honeycomb is sweet to the taste. ¹⁴In the same way, wisdom is sweet to your soul. If you find it, you will have a bright future, and your hopes will not be cut short.

¹⁵Do not lie in wait like an outlaw at the home of the godly. And don't raid the house where the godly live. ¹⁶They may trip seven times, but each time they will rise again. But one calamity is enough to lay the wicked low.　　　　PROVERBS 24:3-16

houlder Pads

PREVIEW

One day a friend reveals a major problem. You're uncomfortable with this disclosure and your friend's ensuing tears. "Buck up!" you say. "Tough times never last, but tough people do! It's just so much water under the bridge! Cheer up! You'll feel better soon!"

Proverbs 25 contains a critique of the classic stoic approach to counseling, and the review is not good.

In this chapter you will also find these lessons: not exalting yourself; appropriate rebukes; how to ensure your plans will fail; and the value of self-control.

PERSONAL APPLICATION

Proverbs 25:20 urges us to avoid being light and cheery around those who are grieving and sad. In fact, to say "Cheer up!" and discount the feelings of a hurting or distraught friend can have the opposite effect.

Whenever you encounter people who are sad or hurting, don't deny or minimize their pain, or belittle them for feeling the way they do. Instead, respect their feelings. Parents, do this for your children. Married person, do this for your spouse. Do this for your friends. Do this for anyone who confides in you. Listen with compassion and offer support. Give them a shoulder to lean on.

BIBLE READING

[11]Timely advice is as lovely as golden apples in a silver basket.

[12]Valid criticism is as treasured by the one who heeds it as jewelry made from finest gold.

[13]Faithful messengers are as refreshing as snow in the heat of summer. They revive the spirit of their employer.

[14]A person who doesn't give a promised gift is like clouds and wind that don't bring rain.

[15]Patience can persuade a prince, and soft speech can crush strong opposition.

[16]Do you like honey? Don't eat too much of it, or it will make you sick!

[17]Don't visit your neighbors too often, or you will wear out your welcome.

[18]Telling lies about others is as harmful as hitting them with an ax, wounding them with a sword, or shooting them with a sharp arrow.

[19]Putting confidence in an unreliable person is like chewing with a toothache or walking on a broken foot.

[20]Singing cheerful songs to a person whose heart is heavy is as bad as stealing someone's jacket in cold weather or rubbing salt in a wound.

[21]If your enemies are hungry, give them food to eat. If they are thirsty, give them water to drink. [22]You will heap burning coals on their heads, and the LORD will reward you.

PROVERBS 25:11-22

um Equipment

PREVIEW

Lazy people never seem to begin their responsibilities. Those they do start they never seem to finish. They let things wait until the last minute. They would rather listen to the radio or watch television than do their job. You know the type—maybe you've had to pick up the resulting slack.

Read through Proverbs 26 and look for verses on laziness. See what areas of your life could benefit from a hardworking perspective.

Two other major themes deserve attention: (1) fools (what they're like and what they deserve), and (2) gossip (its power and its harmfulness).

PERSONAL APPLICATION

The person who doesn't want to work can find an excuse for avoiding every form of physical exertion (Proverbs 26:13-16). But laziness does more than just leave work undone. The less you do, the less you want to do—and the worse the cycle becomes. Unless you live and work entirely alone, others will have to do the work that you neglect.

If you struggle with the temptation to be lazy in any area of your life, apply these three steps: (1) Identify the responsibilities that you avoid and always do them first. (2) Identify the leisure pursuits that you overpursue and do them last. (3) Each time you feel the temptation to be lazy, take one small step toward doing what you need to do. Then take another.

If temptations to laziness plague you constantly, set simple, realistic goals for yourself. Figure out the steps needed to reach each goal and follow those steps one at a time. All along the way, ask God for strength and persistence.

BIBLE READING

[10]An employer who hires a fool or a bystander is like an archer who shoots recklessly.

[11]As a dog returns to its vomit, so a fool repeats his folly.

[12]There is more hope for fools than for people who think they are wise.

[13]The lazy person is full of excuses, saying, "I can't go outside because there might be a lion on the road! Yes, I'm sure there's a lion out there!"

[14]As a door turns back and forth on its hinges, so the lazy person turns over in bed.

[15]Some people are so lazy that they won't lift a finger to feed themselves.

[16]Lazy people consider themselves smarter than seven wise counselors.

[17]Yanking a dog's ears is as foolish as interfering in someone else's argument. PROVERBS 26:10-17

ag, Nag, Nag

PREVIEW

"When are you going to fix the sink? Will you *please* fix the sink? I'm tired of waiting for you to fix the sink." That's a great conversation, isn't it?

Proverbs 27 takes aim at nagging. What alternatives are there to this persistent complaining? Words of love, for starters.

As you read about nagging, note the other lessons in this chapter on not boasting about tomorrow; not withholding a rebuke; and not making promises for others.

PERSONAL APPLICATION

Nagging, a persistent attempt to make another person do something, has been called a mild form of domestic torture. Unfortunately, this steady stream of unwanted advice abuses the person our advice is meant to help. People also nag to make others do things, but that isn't right, either (Proverbs 27:15-16). Besides, constantly pushing someone will only make them less willing to sympathize with your agenda.

The next time you're tempted to nag, try to imagine *why* the person might not be acting on your advice or wishes. You may discover that those reasons may be as legitimate as your own. In addition, you may want to examine your motives: are you more concerned about your-self—getting your way—than about the other person? If you truly care about other people, try using a more effective way to communicate your concerns. For example, ask the person to do something in an open-ended way, leaving the person some options for accomplishing the task. You could even offer to help.

BIBLE READING

⁵An open rebuke is better than hidden love!

⁶Wounds from a friend are better than many kisses from an enemy.

⁷Honey seems tasteless to a person who is full, but even bitter food tastes sweet to the hungry.

⁸A person who strays from home is like a bird that strays from its nest.

⁹The heartfelt counsel of a friend is as sweet as perfume and incense.

¹⁰Never abandon a friend—either yours or your father's. Then in your time of need, you won't have to ask your relatives for assistance. It is better to go to a neighbor than to a relative who lives far away.

¹¹My child, how happy I will be if you turn out to be wise! Then I will be able to answer my critics.

¹²A prudent person foresees the danger ahead and takes precautions. The simpleton goes blindly on and suffers the consequences.

¹³Be sure to get collateral from anyone who guarantees the debt of a stranger. Get a deposit if someone guarantees the debt of an adulterous woman.

¹⁴If you shout a pleasant greeting to your neighbor too early in the morning, it will be counted as a curse!

¹⁵A nagging wife is as annoying as the constant dripping on a rainy day. ¹⁶Trying to stop her complaints is like trying to stop the wind or hold something with greased hands.

PROVERBS 27:5-16

Right about Wrong

PREVIEW

You can't tell whether your friend is serious or not at first, but then his face convinces you. He's just confessed a bitterness he's had against you and asked for your forgiveness. At first you're surprised, not because you didn't think he would have this problem, but because you never expected him to be so honest. Mostly you admire him for taking the risk of being vulnerable.

Since admitting that we're wrong comes at great expense, Proverbs 28 goes over some of the benefits, to help us move in that direction. If you're not used to doing this, take it slow. But there's a lot to gain by confessing your mistakes. Swallow hard and give it a try.

Other thoughts in this chapter include keeping the law; avoiding quick riches; and working hard.

PERSONAL APPLICATION

"People who cover over their sins will not prosper. But if they confess and forsake them, they will receive mercy" (Proverbs 28:13). Despite this wisdom, something in each of us strongly resists admitting our mistakes and sins. That may be why we admire people who openly and graciously do exactly that. These people have a strong self-image. They do not always have to be right to feel good about themselves.

It may be painful to admit our mistakes and sins, but this is the path we must take if we want to truly correct our behavior and to seek others' forgiveness.

Be willing to admit when you're wrong and to seek forgiveness from others. Being open and honest is the first step to experiencing peace and joy in your relationship with Christ and with others. To be successful in life—admit your mistakes.

BIBLE READING

¹The wicked run away when no one is chasing them, but the godly are as bold as lions.

²When there is moral rot within a nation, its government topples easily. But with wise and knowledgeable leaders, there is stability.

³A poor person who oppresses the poor is like a pounding rain that destroys the crops.

⁴To reject the law is to praise the wicked; to obey the law is to fight them.

⁵Evil people don't understand justice, but those who follow the LORD understand completely.

⁶It is better to be poor and honest than rich and crooked.

⁷Young people who obey the law are wise; those who seek out worthless companions bring shame to their parents.

⁸A person who makes money by charging interest will lose it. It will end up in the hands of someone who is kind to the poor.

⁹The prayers of a person who ignores the law are despised.

¹⁰Those who lead the upright into sin will fall into their own trap, but the honest will inherit good things.

¹¹Rich people picture themselves as wise, but their real poverty is evident to the poor.

¹²When the godly succeed, everyone is glad. When the wicked take charge, people go into hiding.

¹³People who cover over their sins will not prosper. But if they confess and forsake them, they will receive mercy.

¹⁴Blessed are those who have a tender conscience, but the stubborn are headed for serious trouble.   PROVERBS 28:1-14

ow Flattering!

PREVIEW

"You're the best!" "You're so beautiful!" "I couldn't possibly do that as fast as you!" Do you notice anything suspicious, here?

Proverbs 29 discusses flattery, as well as how to appropriately respond to other people's anger, how to vent your frustration, and how to get justice.

PERSONAL APPLICATION

"To flatter people is to lay a trap for their feet" (Proverbs 29:5). That states it clearly. Everyone wants to be liked, so we tend to encourage and excuse flattery. In fact, many people do not even consider flattery wrong, but use it as a handy tool for advancing themselves and their agendas. But each use of flattery, as the Scriptures say, sets a trap and endangers those who get caught in it.

Avoid using flattery to manipulate people. Instead, be sincere when you praise others for their achievements, appearance, or character. At the same time, don't believe everything you hear about yourself. Honestly evaluate your abilities, appearance, and personality. Know your strengths and weaknesses so you will know when others are flattering you. Learn to distinguish between truth and flattery, and learn to accept compliments graciously.

BIBLE READING

¹Whoever stubbornly refuses to accept criticism will suddenly be broken beyond repair.

²When the godly are in authority, the people rejoice. But when the wicked are in power, they groan.

³The man who loves wisdom brings joy to his father, but if he hangs around with prostitutes, his wealth is wasted.

⁴A just king gives stability to his nation, but one who demands bribes destroys it.

⁵To flatter people is to lay a trap for their feet.

⁶Evil people are trapped by sin, but the righteous escape, shouting for joy.

⁷The godly know the rights of the poor; the wicked don't care to know.

⁸Mockers can get a whole town agitated, but those who are wise will calm anger.

⁹If a wise person takes a fool to court, there will be ranting and ridicule but no satisfaction.

¹⁰The bloodthirsty hate the honest, but the upright seek out the honest.

¹¹A fool gives full vent to anger, but a wise person quietly holds it back.

¹²If a ruler honors liars, all his advisers will be wicked.

PROVERBS 29:1-12

*R*ags Versus Riches

PREVIEW

Winning the lottery or getting some other financial windfall plays itself out in the imaginations of almost everyone. We imagine how our lives would be different, better, easier. Sure, there might be higher taxes, strained relationships, and uncontrollable spending habits, but that would be better than poverty, right?

Proverbs 30 contains some profound thoughts about riches, as well as thoughts on God's character; false accusations; mockers; and pride.

PERSONAL APPLICATION

Agur, the writer of these proverbs, prayed, "Give me neither poverty nor riches!" (Proverbs 30:8). Some people imagine that money can solve all their problems. Others believe that it will solve none of them. Both miss the point—it is the *love* of money that is at the root of evil (see I Timothy 6:10). Having too much money can give us the false impression that we don't need God. Like the apostle Paul, we should learn to live whether we have little or plenty (see Philippians 4:12), but our lives are likely to be more effective for God if, like the psalmist, we have "neither poverty nor riches."

Make Agur's prayer your prayer. Ask God to keep you from desiring material wealth, knowing that it isn't eternal and will one day be gone. At the same time, pray that God will strengthen your trust in him to provide for your needs.

BIBLE READING

¹The message of Agur son of Jakeh. An oracle.

I am weary, O God; I am weary and worn out, O God. ²I am too ignorant to be human, and I lack common sense. ³I have not mastered human wisdom, nor do I know the Holy One.

⁴Who but God goes up to heaven and comes back down? Who holds the wind in his fists? Who wraps up the oceans in his cloak? Who has created the whole wide world? What is his name—and his son's name? Tell me if you know!

⁵Every word of God proves true. He defends all who come to him for protection. ⁶Do not add to his words, or he may rebuke you, and you will be found a liar. ⁷O God, I beg two favors from you before I die. ⁸First, help me never to tell a lie. Second, give me neither poverty nor riches! Give me just enough to satisfy my needs. ⁹For if I grow rich, I may deny you and say, "Who is the LORD?" And if I am too poor, I may steal and thus insult God's holy name.

¹⁰Never slander a person to his employer. If you do, the person will curse you, and you will pay for it.

¹¹Some people curse their father and do not thank their mother. ¹²They feel pure, but they are filthy and unwashed. ¹³They are proud beyond description and disdainful. ¹⁴They devour the poor with teeth as sharp as swords or knives. They destroy the needy from the face of the earth.   PROVERBS 30:1-14

A Good Woman Is . . .

PREVIEW

Many women today have come to a difficult crossroads. Some "career women" regret not devoting more time to their kids; some "stay-at-home moms" regret not having a career.

A wise woman will give serious thought to Proverbs 31. Contrary to popular belief, this passage does not describe an ideal too lofty to attain—no, the chief characteristic of the truly noble woman is *balance*. That's what happens when each of us takes our cues from God and God alone—it's the message of the entire book of Proverbs, isn't it?

Proverbs 31 doesn't discuss only female roles; other topics include drinking; leading; fulfilling responsibilities; and working.

PERSONAL APPLICATION

Proverbs ends with a positive description of a godly woman—a woman of strong character, great wisdom, many skills, and compassion.

Some people have the mistaken idea that the ideal woman in the Bible is passive, submissive, and domestic. Not so! This woman takes her roles as a wife and mother quite proactively. She does not delegate her responsibilities to someone else. She manufactures, imports, manages, invests, farms, sews, buys, sells, and shares. Her strength and dignity do not come from amazing achievements, but from reverence for God. Her attractiveness comes from her strength of character. And that's the point.

Whoever you are, you can learn this lesson: A godly person is one who strives to be a person of character, integrity, devotion, and balance.

BIBLE READING

[10]Who can find a virtuous and capable wife? She is worth more than precious rubies. [11]Her husband can trust her, and she will greatly enrich his life. [12]She will not hinder him but help him all her life.

[13]She finds wool and flax and busily spins it. [14]She is like a merchant's ship; she brings her food from afar. [15]She gets up before dawn to prepare breakfast for her household and plan the day's work for her servant girls. [16]She goes out to inspect a field and buys it; with her earnings she plants a vineyard.

[17]She is energetic and strong, a hard worker. [18]She watches for bargains; her lights burn late into the night. [19]Her hands are busy spinning thread, her fingers twisting fiber.

[20]She extends a helping hand to the poor and opens her arms to the needy.

[21]She has no fear of winter for her household because all of them have warm clothes. [22]She quilts her own bedspreads. She dresses like royalty in gowns of finest cloth.

[23]Her husband is well known, for he sits in the council meeting with the other civic leaders.

[24]She makes belted linen garments and sashes to sell to the merchants.

[25]She is clothed with strength and dignity, and she laughs with no fear of the future. [26]When she speaks, her words are wise, and kindness is the rule when she gives instructions. [27]She carefully watches all that goes on in her household and does not have to bear the consequences of laziness.

[28]Her children stand and bless her. Her husband praises her: [29]"There are many virtuous and capable women in the world, but you surpass them all!"

[30]Charm is deceptive, and beauty does not last; but a woman who fears the LORD will be greatly praised. [31]Reward her for all she has done. Let her deeds publicly declare her praise.

PROVERBS 31:10-31

 appy Campers

PREVIEW

At one time or another, everyone thinks *If only*. The thought usually ends with a dream of some fantastic ideal—a different job, a new house, a hot car, or more money. The fountain of happiness always lies just beyond our grasp. If only . . .

Solomon begins the book of Ecclesiastes by reflecting on his past and noting how he has changed. You can detect some "if only" thoughts in his observations. Like each of us, Solomon wanted to be happy—this is what he found.

PERSONAL APPLICATION

Would you be happier if you had more money, fame, or power? Solomon wasn't (Ecclesiastes 1:1-2, 12-15; 2:1-11). The world tells us to demand happiness, to do all we can to attain it, and to make personal satisfaction our chief goal. The world holds out many promises, all of which require dependence on some thing or experience that won't last. Solomon had attained everything the world thought he needed to guarantee happiness and fulfillment, but reflecting back on his life, he discovered that his wealth, power, position, wives, and accomplishments had not made him happy or brought meaning to his life.

In contrast to the world's view, the Bible says that true and lasting happiness comes from pleasing God. (Eventually Solomon found this to be true.) Real happiness can only be received through a right relationship with God.

BIBLE READING

¹These are the words of the Teacher, King David's son, who ruled in Jerusalem.

²"Everything is meaningless," says the Teacher, "utterly meaningless!"

³What do people get for all their hard work? ⁴Generations come and go, but nothing really changes. ⁵The sun rises and sets and hurries around to rise again. ⁶The wind blows south and north, here and there, twisting back and forth, getting nowhere. ⁷The rivers run into the sea, but the sea is never full. Then the water returns again to the rivers and flows again to the sea. ⁸Everything is so weary and tiresome! No matter how much we see, we are never satisfied. No matter how much we hear, we are not content.

⁹History merely repeats itself. It has all been done before. Nothing under the sun is truly new. ¹⁰What can you point to that is new? How do you know it didn't already exist long ago? ¹¹We don't remember what happened in those former times. And in future generations, no one will remember what we are doing now.

¹²I, the Teacher, was king of Israel, and I lived in Jerusalem. ¹³I devoted myself to search for understanding and to explore by wisdom everything being done in the world. I soon discovered that God has dealt a tragic existence to the human race. ¹⁴Everything under the sun is meaningless, like chasing the wind. ¹⁵What is wrong cannot be righted. What is missing cannot be recovered.

ECCLESIASTES 1:1-15

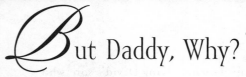

But Daddy, Why?

PREVIEW

Children who have reached the "Why?" stage remind us that they live in a smaller, simpler world than adults do. Often, the questions and truths that intrigue the young are beyond their comprehension.

Solomon lists several disappointments he has observed in the world and asks why they have to exist. Unable to grasp the answers, he has to come to a sort of compromise. Let him lead you to the "grown-up" who can explain.

This reading also comments further on three areas of life that touch us all: death, work, and friendship.

PERSONAL APPLICATION

In Ecclesiastes 3:16–4:12, Solomon reflects on six apparent contradictions in the world. First, wickedness rules where justice should (3:16). Second, people created in God's image die just as the animals do (3:18-21). Third, no one comforts oppressed people (4:1). Fourth, many people work because they envy what others have, not because they love their work (4:4). Fifth, people are lonely (4:7-12). Sixth, fame doesn't last (4:13-16).

Many questions in life cannot be answered to our satisfaction because we lack the ability to understand the answers, not because the answers don't exist. Although we cannot understand the answers today, one day we will. In the meantime, we should trust life's apparent contradictions to God and not lose faith in him when we don't understand something.

BIBLE READING

[9]What do people really get for all their hard work? [10]I have thought about this in connection with the various kinds of work God has given people to do. [11]God has made everything beautiful for its own time. He has planted eternity in the human heart, but even so, people cannot see the whole scope of God's work from beginning to end. [12]So I concluded that there is nothing better for people than to be happy and to enjoy themselves as long as they can. [13]And people should eat and drink and enjoy the fruits of their labor, for these are gifts from God.

[14]And I know that whatever God does is final. Nothing can be added to it or taken from it. God's purpose in this is that people should fear him. [15]Whatever exists today and whatever will exist in the future has already existed in the past. For God calls each event back in its turn.

[16]I also noticed that throughout the world there is evil in the courtroom. Yes, even the courts of law are corrupt! [17]I said to myself, "In due season God will judge everyone, both good and bad, for all their deeds."

[18]Then I realized that God allows people to continue in their sinful ways so he can test them. That way, they can see for themselves they are no better than animals. [19]For humans and animals both breathe the same air, and both die. So people have no real advantage over the animals. How meaningless! [20]Both go to the same place—the dust from which they came and to which they must return. [21]For who can prove that the human spirit goes upward and the spirit of animals goes downward into the earth? [22]So I saw that there is nothing better for people than to be happy in their work. That is why they are here! No one will bring them back from death to enjoy life in the future.

ECCLESIASTES 3:9-22

Holier Than Thou

PREVIEW

Sam is repulsed by his neighbor Doug, an outspoken Christian. Doug is always calling attention to his good deeds and overly stating his revulsion toward immorality and decadence. Most of the neighbors call him obnoxious. The kinder ones say he's just trying too hard.

This reading exposes some "negative" aspects of goodness and wisdom. Can you have too much of a good thing? Apparently so.

There is additional insight on meaningless activities; on work and earning money; and on fame, death, sorrow, and happiness. You will also find some sober advice on how to enjoy life, even when everything seems meaningless.

PERSONAL APPLICATION

"Don't be too good or too wise!" (Ecclesiastes 7:16). That's a warning against religious conceit—taking pride in your goodness or righteousness. How can a person be too righteous or too wise? Some people invent grand schemes for appearing righteous and accomplish nothing in the process. They sit atop poles, deny themselves food, give up pleasurable things, and pursue other drastic steps that do little more than ruin their health. "Why destroy yourself?" Solomon asks.

Don't lose sight of true goodness—honoring God—in favor of a nearly suicidal effort to make yourself artificially perfect. Do whatever God asks of you, and leave it at that.

BIBLE READING

[5]It is better to be criticized by a wise person than to be praised by a fool! [6]Indeed, a fool's laughter is quickly gone, like thorns crackling in a fire. This also is meaningless.

[7]Extortion turns wise people into fools, and bribes corrupt the heart.

[8]Finishing is better than starting. Patience is better than pride.

[9]Don't be quick-tempered, for anger is the friend of fools.

[10]Don't long for "the good old days," for you don't know whether they were any better than today.

[11]Being wise is as good as being rich; in fact, it is better. [12]Wisdom or money can get you almost anything, but it's important to know that only wisdom can save your life.

[13]Notice the way God does things; then fall into line. Don't fight the ways of God, for who can straighten out what he has made crooked?

[14]Enjoy prosperity while you can. But when hard times strike, realize that both come from God. That way you will realize that nothing is certain in this life.

[15]In this meaningless life, I have seen everything, including the fact that some good people die young and some wicked people live on and on. [16]So don't be too good or too wise! Why destroy yourself? [17]On the other hand, don't be too wicked either—don't be a fool! Why should you die before your time? [18]So try to walk a middle course—but those who fear God will succeed either way.

ECCLESIASTES 7:5-18

What's the Point?

PREVIEW

Many years ago the phenomenon of a *midlife crisis* was given its name. Many people approaching the second half of their adult lives want to ensure that all they've ever worked for, lived for, and hoped for hasn't just been one big mistake.

The entire book of Ecclesiastes addresses the meaning of life, but this passage in particular punctuates his point. Solomon's summary makes it difficult to miss. Read on for help with that age-old set of questions that demand an answer somewhere around the halftime of your life.

In this passage you will also find specific lessons on death, wisdom, investing, and growing old.

PERSONAL APPLICATION

Solomon concludes this book by giving advice on how to live a full life. Solomon's final conclusion is that "the duty of every person" is to fear and obey God (Ecclesiastes 12:13). Solomon gave this advice because he knew that one day we will have to stand before God and be judged for how we have lived (12:14). We will not be able to use excuses to justify our failures and sins. So we need to learn how God wants us to live and then to do it. When we do this, we then complete our search for meaning.

Don't let the excitement of being young cause you to forget about your Creator. And don't spend your life trying to substitute your own rules for the ones God has given you—as if living your own way will somehow be easier, or as if God won't notice. Keep your values and priorities in line—keep God in first place in your life.

BIBLE READING

[1]Don't let the excitement of youth cause you to forget your Creator. Honor him in your youth before you grow old and no longer enjoy living.

[6]Yes, remember your Creator now while you are young, before the silver cord of life snaps and the golden bowl is broken. Don't wait until the water jar is smashed at the spring and the pulley is broken at the well. [7]For then the dust will return to the earth, and the spirit will return to God who gave it.

[8]"All is meaningless," says the Teacher, "utterly meaningless."

[9]Because the Teacher was wise, he taught the people everything he knew. He collected proverbs and classified them. [10]Indeed, the Teacher taught the plain truth, and he did so in an interesting way.

[11]A wise teacher's words spur students to action and emphasize important truths. The collected sayings of the wise are like guidance from a shepherd.

[12]But, my child, be warned: There is no end of opinions ready to be expressed. Studying them can go on forever and become very exhausting!

[13]Here is my final conclusion: Fear God and obey his commands, for this is the duty of every person. [14]God will judge us for everything we do, including every secret thing, whether good or bad.   ECCLESIASTES 12:1, 6–14

$\mathscr{P}$ermanently in Love

PREVIEW

The Song of Songs is a beautiful story of love between a husband and a wife. Also, in a day when marriages are falling apart all around us, this is an encouraging book to read. Marriage can last and still be passionate.

If you want to look for more specific treasures, dig for facets of this two-sided gem: what to say to your spouse and what to do for your spouse. If you are unmarried, look for ways to support your married friends and encourage them to make their marriages work. They need cheerleaders.

PERSONAL APPLICATION

As surely as time itself passes, the growth of familiarity in a marriage will cause the relationship to lose its initial sparkle. Glances and touches will no longer produce the same emotional responses. Conflicts and pressures will creep in, causing the man to lose his tenderness and the woman to lose her zeal for flirting. The world doesn't help, either; in fact, external stress often works against the marriage relationship. But spouses can learn to be shelters for each other, and they can learn to make marriage fun.

When intimacy and passion decline, remember that they can be renewed. Take time to remember those first thrills, the excitement of sex, your spouse's strengths, and the commitment you made in your wedding vows (Song of Songs 5:2-8). Be affectionate to each other every day and watch the excitement return to your relationship!

BIBLE READING

Young Man: [8]"Come with me from Lebanon, my bride. Come down from the top of Mount Amana, from Mount Senir and Mount Hermon, where lions have their dens and panthers prowl. [9]You have ravished my heart, my treasure, my bride. I am overcome by one glance of your eyes, by a single bead of your necklace. [10]How sweet is your love, my treasure, my bride! How much better it is than wine! Your perfume is more fragrant than the richest of spices. [11]Your lips, my bride, are as sweet as honey. Yes, honey and cream are under your tongue. The scent of your clothing is like that of the mountains and the cedars of Lebanon.

[12]"You are like a private garden, my treasure, my bride! You are like a spring that no one else can drink from, a fountain of my own. [13]You are like a lovely orchard bearing precious fruit, with the rarest of perfumes: [14]nard and saffron, calamus and cinnamon, myrrh and aloes, perfume from every incense tree, and every other lovely spice. [15]You are a garden fountain, a well of living water, as refreshing as the streams from the Lebanon mountains."

Young Woman: [16]"Awake, north wind! Come, south wind! Blow on my garden and waft its lovely perfume to my lover. Let him come into his garden and eat its choicest fruits."

[5:1]*Young Man:* "I am here in my garden, my treasure, my bride! I gather my myrrh with my spices and eat my honeycomb with my honey. I drink my wine with my milk."

Young Women of Jerusalem: "Oh, lover and beloved, eat and drink! Yes, drink deeply of this love!"

SONG OF SONGS 4:8–5:1

ashion Statement

PREVIEW

Although the latest style is supposedly always new, fashion and the fashion conscious have been around for a long time. The Judean women of Isaiah's time were no different than many women today—they were slaves to fashion. So much so that they angered God, who sent Isaiah to straighten them out.

The women of Judah aren't the only ones who need to set their priorities straight in this reading. Isaiah has a lot to say to the Judeans and to us about the importance we place (or don't place) on what God wants. As you read, notice the loving proposal God makes to his people; the good reasons to respect God; some bad mistakes to avoid; and how Isaiah became God's servant.

PERSONAL APPLICATION

Isaiah's prophecies were not condemning the women for buying nice clothing, jewelry, and makeup. Rather he was condemning their prideful attitudes and self-centered concerns. Looking good is not wrong in and of itself. But when we become engrossed in our appearance while we neglect God's commands and others' needs, we've gone too far.

Strive for a balance between maintaining a well-groomed appearance and keeping your priorities and responsibilities straight. Remember that God is more concerned with your character than your looks (see 1 Samuel 16:7; Matthew 23:25-28). Use what you have to help others, not impress them.

BIBLE READING

[14]The leaders and the princes will be the first to feel the Lord's judgment. "You have ruined Israel, which is my vineyard. You have taken advantage of the poor, filling your barns with grain extorted from helpless people. [15]How dare you grind my people into the dust like that!" demands the Lord, the LORD Almighty.

[16]Next the LORD will judge the women of Jerusalem, who walk around with their noses in the air, with tinkling ornaments on their ankles. Their eyes rove among the crowds, flirting with the men. [17]The Lord will send a plague of scabs to ornament their heads. Yes, the LORD will make them bald for all to see!

[18]The Lord will strip away their artful beauty—their ornaments, headbands, and crescent necklaces; [19]their earrings, bracelets, and veils of shimmering gauze. [20]Gone will be their scarves, ankle chains, sashes, perfumes, and charms; [21]their rings, jewels, [22]party clothes, gowns, capes, and purses; [23]their mirrors, linen garments, head ornaments, and shawls. [24]Instead of smelling of sweet perfume, they will stink. They will wear ropes for sashes, and their well-set hair will fall out. They will wear rough sackcloth instead of rich robes. Their beauty will be gone. Only shame will be left to them.

[25]The men of the city will die in battle. [26]The gates of Jerusalem will weep and mourn. The city will be like a ravaged woman, huddled on the ground. ISAIAH 3:14-26

Looking for a Fall Guy

PREVIEW

Blame shifting kicks into high gear whenever someone has been caught. You can almost guarantee that the guilty person will try to blame somebody else (or some overpowering circumstance) for the offense.

Sadly, some believers do this, too, without even thinking about it. But this is nothing new for God's people. The Judeans, Isaiah predicted, would start pointing fingers as soon as the consequences of their sin came upon them. As you read, notice who gets blamed here.

This reading is an interesting mixture of hope and despair. Note the famous prophecies about Christ (Isaiah 7, 9, 11); the harsh words about conceit and favoring the strong (Isaiah 9–10); and the kind words for those who remain faithful to God (Isaiah 10, 12).

PERSONAL APPLICATION

The people of Israel listened to false prophets instead of to Isaiah, and as a result they were "led away as captives, weary and hungry" (Isaiah 8:21). They blamed God for their troubles. After rejecting God's plan for them, the people tried to indict God for rejecting them!

Unfortunately, that's how we often behave. We blame God for problems that we have brought on ourselves instead of admitting that we deserve what has happened and making the appropriate changes.

How do you respond to the unpleasant results of your choices? Be honest with yourself and God—admit your sins, ask forgiveness, and, if necessary, make restitution.

BIBLE READING

[11]"The LORD has said to me in the strongest terms: "Do not think like everyone else does. [12]Do not be afraid that some plan conceived behind closed doors will be the end of you. [13]Do not fear anything except the LORD Almighty. He alone is the Holy One. If you fear him, you need fear nothing else. [14]He will keep you safe. But to Israel and Judah he will be a stone that causes people to stumble and a rock that makes them fall. And for the people of Jerusalem he will be a trap that entangles them. [15]Many of them will stumble and fall, never to rise again. Many will be captured."

[16]I will write down all these things as a testimony of what the LORD will do. I will entrust it to my disciples, who will pass it down to future generations. [17]I will wait for the LORD to help us, though he has turned away from the people of Israel. My only hope is in him. [18]I and the children the LORD has given me have names that reveal the plans the LORD Almighty has for his people. [19]So why are you trying to find out the future by consulting mediums and psychics? Do not listen to their whisperings and mutterings. Can the living find out the future from the dead? Why not ask your God?

[20]"Check their predictions against my testimony," says the LORD. "If their predictions are different from mine, it is because there is no light or truth in them. [21]My people will be led away as captives, weary and hungry. And because they are hungry, they will rage and shake their fists at heaven and curse their king and their God. [22]Wherever they look, there will be trouble and anguish and dark despair. They will be thrown out into the darkness."   ISAIAH 8:11-22

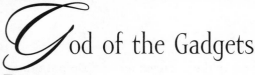 God of the Gadgets

Preview

The world stood up and took notice when the Apollo astronauts first landed on the moon. This was a truly great accomplishment because it had never been done before. But it also fed the belief that science would rescue us from all our ills.

A similar belief existed among the people of Damascus. They made idols and placed their trust in them. Because they turned their backs on God, God gave them some bad news.

If you ever wondered whether God holds *groups* of people accountable, this reading should answer your question.

Personal Application

The people of Damascus looked to their idols and to their own strength for all the answers (Isaiah 17:8-11). They believed in gods they could see and control, not in an invisible God. God's message to them through Isaiah was that their cities would be completely destroyed (17:1-3). The people of Damascus had turned from the God who could save them and toward themselves, as represented by their man-made gods. They forgot God's place in the grand scheme of things.

Often we depend on our own knowledge and technologies (faster computers, more efficient energy sources, and more effective medical treatments) to save us from all our ills. But placing our trust in human technologies rather than in God is wrong—it's idolatry. This is not to say that good technologies don't have their place—they do—but not as gods. Appreciate progress, but never bow down to it.

BIBLE READING

¹"Look, Damascus will disappear! It will become a heap of ruins. ²The cities of Aroer will be deserted. Sheep will graze in the streets and lie down unafraid. There will be no one to chase them away. ³The fortified cities of Israel will also be destroyed, and the power of Damascus will end. The few left in Aram will share the fate of Israel's departed glory," says the LORD Almighty.

⁴"In that day the glory of Israel will be very dim, for poverty will stalk the land. ⁵Israel will be abandoned like the grainfields in the valley of Rephaim after the harvest. ⁶Only a few of its people will be left, like the stray olives left on the tree after the harvest. Only two or three remain in the highest branches, four or five out on the tips of the limbs. Yes, Israel will be stripped bare of people," says the LORD, the God of Israel.

⁷Then at last the people will think of their Creator and have respect for the Holy One of Israel. ⁸They will no longer ask their idols for help or worship what their own hands have made. They will never again bow down to their Asherah poles or burn incense on the altars they built.

¹²Look! The armies rush forward like waves thundering toward the shore. ¹³But though they roar like breakers on a beach, God will silence them. They will flee like chaff scattered by the wind or like dust whirling before a storm. ¹⁴In the evening Israel waits in terror, but by dawn its enemies are dead. This is the just reward of those who plunder and destroy the people of God.

ISAIAH 17:1-7, 12-14

oo Hoo

PREVIEW

Do you cry at movies? Some people do. Eyes and noses just drip, flow, and gush uncontrollably. People cry when overcome with great emotion—at the movies and in real life.

In this reading, Isaiah weeps because God's people are destroying themselves. He warns them repeatedly. But they just aren't listening. What's a prophet to do? What would you do?

This reading also contains the second half of the list of prophecies against Judah's neighbors (Egypt, Ethiopia, Babylon, Edom, Arabia, and Tyre). If you thought God was singling out Judah for punishment, think again.

PERSONAL APPLICATION

Isaiah delivered God's messages to God's people, but that didn't mean that Isaiah was just a courier. As a fellow Judean, Isaiah cared deeply for his and God's people. Isaiah knew that because the Judeans did not heed God's warnings, they would experience his judgment. This saddened Isaiah and he wept for them (Isaiah 22:4).

Sometimes family and friends ignore our attempts to help, so they suffer the very grief we wanted to spare them. At these times we grieve because of our concern.

Have you pulled back from getting close to someone because of a fear of getting hurt? It can be tempting to insulate yourself from hurt by avoiding all close relationships. But God wants you, like Isaiah, to love others. To love someone carries with it the risk of getting hurt by that person's choices. But be willing to take that risk, and trust God for the outcome.

BIBLE READING

¹What is happening? Why is everyone running to the rooftops?
²The whole city is in a terrible uproar. What do I see in this
reveling city? Bodies are lying everywhere, killed by famine and
disease. ³All your leaders flee. They surrender without resistance.
The people try to slip away, but they are captured, too. ⁴Leave me
alone to weep; do not try to comfort me. Let me cry for my
people as I watch them being destroyed.

⁵Oh, what a day of crushing trouble! What a day of confusion
and terror the Lord, the LORD Almighty, has brought upon the
Valley of Vision! The walls of Jerusalem have been broken, and
cries of death echo from the mountainsides. ⁶Elamites are the
archers; Arameans drive the chariots. The men of Kir hold up
the shields. ⁷They fill your beautiful valleys and crowd against
your gates. ⁸Judah's defenses have been stripped away. You run to
the armory for your weapons. ⁹You inspect the walls of Jerusalem
to see what needs to be repaired. You store up water in the lower
pool. ¹⁰You check the houses and tear some down to get stone to
fix the walls. ¹¹Between the city walls, you build a reservoir for
water from the old pool. But all your feverish plans are to no
avail because you never ask God for help. He is the one who
planned this long ago.

¹²The Lord, the LORD Almighty, called you to weep and
mourn. He told you to shave your heads in sorrow for your sins
and to wear clothes of sackcloth to show your remorse. ¹³But
instead, you dance and play; you slaughter sacrificial animals,
feast on meat, and drink wine. "Let's eat, drink, and be merry,"
you say. "What's the difference, for tomorrow we die." ¹⁴The
LORD Almighty has revealed to me that this sin will never be
forgiven you until the day you die. That is the judgment of the
Lord, the LORD Almighty.   ISAIAH 22:1-14

eft Out

PREVIEW

In George Orwell's classic novel *Animal Farm,* all the animals enjoy equal rights until it becomes apparent that some animals consider themselves "more equal" than others.

God doesn't judge superficially—he judges people by their character and not by their appearance. In this reading, Isaiah celebrates God's impartiality. God's only requirement is that we love and serve him.

PERSONAL APPLICATION

Isaiah praised God for his greatness and described God's wonderful acts. Isaiah specifically praised God for making salvation available to all who would turn from their sin. God welcomes "everyone around the world" (Isaiah 25:6). God's banquet has an international guest list. This means that men and women of every color, race, language, and custom who love God will dwell together in heaven. There will be no segregation there.

Be willing to share your life with people who differ from you. Don't discriminate against them just because they are a different sex or different color, have different customs or speak a different language. Remember, if they also trust in Christ, they are your brothers and sisters and will sit with you at God's banquet table. Include others—it's a very God-like action to take.

BIBLE READING

¹O LORD, I will honor and praise your name, for you are my God. You do such wonderful things! You planned them long ago, and now you have accomplished them. ²You turn mighty cities into heaps of ruins. Cities with strong walls are turned to rubble. Beautiful palaces in distant lands disappear and will never be rebuilt. ³Therefore, strong nations will declare your glory; ruthless nations will revere you.

⁴But to the poor, O LORD, you are a refuge from the storm. To the needy in distress, you are a shelter from the rain and the heat. For the oppressive acts of ruthless people are like a storm beating against a wall, ⁵or like the relentless heat of the desert. But you silence the roar of foreign nations. You cool the land with the shade of a cloud. So the boastful songs of ruthless people are stilled.

⁶In Jerusalem, the LORD Almighty will spread a wonderful feast for everyone around the world. It will be a delicious feast of good food, with clear, well-aged wine and choice beef. ⁷In that day he will remove the cloud of gloom, the shadow of death that hangs over the earth. ⁸He will swallow up death forever! The Sovereign LORD will wipe away all tears. He will remove forever all insults and mockery against his land and people. The LORD has spoken!

⁹In that day the people will proclaim, "This is our God. We trusted in him, and he saved us. This is the LORD, in whom we trusted. Let us rejoice in the salvation he brings!" ¹⁰For the Lord's good hand will rest on Jerusalem.   ISAIAH 25:1-10

$\mathcal{S}$ensitivity Training

PREVIEW

Many descriptions of the 1980s and 1990s include a reference to male sensitivity—or lack of it. Because of women's liberation and concern over stereotypes, men have been encouraged to be more sensitive, to allow more feelings to show, and to have more concern for others in general. Some men squawked, others cheered.

This passage contains a lesson on sensitivity. As you read, you will see that power and sensitivity can live together.

Also in this reading, Isaiah pronounces a series of woes on those who resist being taught, who live double lives, and who go their own way instead of God's way.

PERSONAL APPLICATION

The farmer uses special tools to plant and harvest tender herbs so he will not destroy them. He takes into account how fragile they are. In the same way God takes all our individual circumstances and weaknesses into account (Isaiah 28:23-29). He deals with each of us sensitively.

We should follow his example whenever we deal with others, because different people require different treatment. Sensitivity is required.

Be sensitive to the unique personalities and needs of those around you, being careful not to overpower the weak or to coddle the strong. Be aware of the special treatment that each person may need and the special circumstances in each one's life, then relate and lead accordingly.

BIBLE READING

[17]"I will take the measuring line of justice and the plumb line of righteousness to check the foundation wall you have built. Your refuge looks strong, but since it is made of lies, a hailstorm will knock it down. Since it is made of deception, the enemy will come like a flood to sweep it away. [18]I will cancel the bargain you made to avoid death, and I will overturn your deal to dodge the grave. When the terrible enemy floods in, you will be trampled into the ground. [19]Again and again that flood will come, morning after morning, day and night, until you are carried away."

[23]Listen to me; listen as I plead! [24]Does a farmer always plow and never sow? Is he forever cultivating the soil and never planting it? [25]Does he not finally plant his seeds for dill, cumin, wheat, barley, and spelt, each in its own section of his land? [26]The farmer knows just what to do, for God has given him understanding. [27]He doesn't thresh all his crops the same way. A heavy sledge is never used on dill; rather, it is beaten with a light stick. A threshing wheel is never rolled on cumin; instead, it is beaten softly with a flail. [28]Bread grain is easily crushed, so he doesn't keep on pounding it. He threshes it under the wheels of a cart, but he doesn't pulverize it. [29]The LORD Almighty is a wonderful teacher, and he gives the farmer great wisdom.

ISAIAH 28:17-19, 23-29

romise Keepers

PREVIEW

Have you ever been hurt by a broken promise? Some people have been fortunate enough to escape the scars from broken promises, but others will forever feel the effects. They'll carry a memory, a regret, or a grudge.

The prophecies in this reading deal with promise-breakers and their victims. For the promise-breaking Assyrians, Isaiah brings a message of condemnation. For the Assyrians' victims, the Israelites, Isaiah brings a message of hope, comfort, and peace. For us, it's good to know God cares about promises—kept and broken. Read this passage for a message of hope.

Also in this reading you will find that God is out to take back what belongs to him.

PERSONAL APPLICATION

The rulers of Assyria came under God's judgment because they broke their promises while demanding that others keep theirs (Isaiah 33:1). They observed a selfish double standard that protected them and exploited others.

Like the Assyrian rulers, we find it easy to expect a lot out of others while requiring less of ourselves. But God takes promises very seriously and he wants us to be fair. Broken promises shatter trust and destroy relationships.

Determine to keep your promises. Negotiate in good faith. Demand the same faithfulness of yourself that you ask of everyone else.

BIBLE READING

[1]Destruction is certain for you Assyrians, who have destroyed everything around you but have never felt destruction yourselves. You expect others to respect their promises to you, while you betray your promises to them. Now you, too, will be betrayed and destroyed!

[2]But LORD, be merciful to us, for we have waited for you. Be our strength each day and our salvation in times of trouble. [3]The enemy runs at the sound of your voice. When you stand up, the nations flee! [4]Just as locusts strip the fields and vines, so Jerusalem will strip the fallen army of Assyria!

[5]Though the LORD is very great and lives in heaven, he will make Jerusalem his home of justice and righteousness. [6]In that day he will be your sure foundation, providing a rich store of salvation, wisdom, and knowledge. The fear of the LORD is the key to this treasure.

[10]The LORD says: "I will stand up and show my power and might. [11]You Assyrians will gain nothing by all your efforts. Your own breath will turn to fire and kill you. [12]Your people will be burned up completely, like thorns cut down and tossed in a fire. [13]Listen to what I have done, you nations far away! And you that are near, acknowledge my might!"

[14]The sinners in Jerusalem shake with fear. "Which one of us," they cry, "can live here in the presence of this all-consuming fire?" [15]The ones who can live here are those who are honest and fair, who reject making a profit by fraud, who stay far away from bribes, who refuse to listen to those who plot murder, who shut their eyes to all enticement to do wrong. [16]These are the ones who will dwell on high. The rocks of the mountains will be their fortress of safety. Food will be supplied to them, and they will have water in abundance.   ISAIAH 33:1-6, 10-16

$\mathcal{S}$mooth Operator

PREVIEW

How do you know if someone is lying to you? Often you can't tell—that's the trouble. You can't spot deceivers just by their appearance.

Hezekiah, a good king, has to deal with a smooth-talking deceiver here, the field commander of Assyria. According to the commander, Hezekiah has failed. "You're an incompetent leader and a disgrace to God," he basically says. Read this passage to see whether Hezekiah will believe the commander or God.

Even if you're not a leader, there are many lessons here on dealing with threats; praying; depending on God; coping with illness; and keeping a level head when your fortunes shift for the better.

PERSONAL APPLICATION

The field commander from Assyria tried to talk Hezekiah out of resisting. He claimed that Hezekiah had insulted God by tearing down pagan altars and making the people worship only in Jerusalem (Isaiah 36:7). But Hezekiah knew better. His reform had sought to eliminate the worship of false gods, so that the people would worship only the true God, as they should. Either the Assyrian commander didn't know about the true God, or he wanted to trick the people into thinking they had angered a more powerful god than the Lord. But Hezekiah knew God and his Word well enough not to believe the lies. The field commander's plan failed.

Like Hezekiah, don't be naive. Study God's Word carefully and regularly. When you know what God says, you will not fall for lies.

BIBLE READING

⁹Soon afterward King Sennacherib received word that King Tirhakah of Ethiopia was leading an army to fight against him. Before leaving to meet the attack, he sent this message back to Hezekiah in Jerusalem:

¹⁰"This message is for King Hezekiah of Judah. Don't let this God you trust deceive you with promises that Jerusalem will not be captured by the king of Assyria. ¹¹You know perfectly well what the kings of Assyria have done wherever they have gone. They have crushed everyone who stood in their way! Why should you be any different? ¹²Have the gods of other nations rescued them—such nations as Gozan, Haran, Rezeph, and the people of Eden who were in Tel-assar? The former kings of Assyria destroyed them all! ¹³What happened to the king of Hamath and the king of Arpad? What happened to the kings of Sepharvaim, Hena, and Ivvah?"

¹⁴After Hezekiah received the letter and read it, he went up to the LORD's Temple and spread it out before the LORD. ¹⁵And Hezekiah prayed this prayer before the LORD: ¹⁶"O LORD Almighty, God of Israel, you are enthroned between the mighty cherubim! You alone are God of all the kingdoms of the earth. You alone created the heavens and the earth. ¹⁷Listen to me, O LORD, and hear! Open your eyes, O LORD, and see! Listen to Sennacherib's words of defiance against the living God."

ISAIAH 37:9-17

ll Tuckered Out

PREVIEW

Hectic work schedules, bad nutrition, poor health, small children, or just plain old age can make people weary. What makes you feel tired or weak?

In Isaiah 40:1—48:22 you will read about a tired people—Israel and Judah exiled in Babylon. They've been away from home for a long time. Isaiah brings them strong, energizing words.

The other sections in this passage all relate to Israel's release from captivity—a happy, joyous time. Here are words of encouragement and hope from this servant of the Lord.

PERSONAL APPLICATION

Isaiah had words of encouragement for God's people: Their punishment wouldn't last forever, deliverance would come, and God would restore them. God didn't want them to despair, so he reassured them of his power (Isaiah 40:12-31).

Just as Israel and Judah's punishment overwhelmed them, so the pace of life overwhelms every person at times, even those who are strong (40:30). This may be because of our overzealous desire to do more than we should. Or it may be that we just don't trust in God and his power to help us move the mountain of work set before us. But God and his power should be our source of strength, especially when we feel overwhelmed.

Whenever you feel tired and weary, take time to rest—show your confidence in God's control over the events in your life. Let him renew your strength. Then wait for his timing before reentering the marathon called life, or you may not be able to finish the race at all. God will help you finish in good time.

BIBLE READING

¹"Comfort, comfort my people," says your God. ²"Speak tenderly to Jerusalem. Tell her that her sad days are gone and that her sins are pardoned. Yes, the LORD has punished her in full for all her sins."

³Listen! I hear the voice of someone shouting, "Make a highway for the LORD through the wilderness. Make a straight, smooth road through the desert for our God. ⁴Fill the valleys and level the hills. Straighten out the curves and smooth off the rough spots. ⁵Then the glory of the LORD will be revealed, and all people will see it together. The LORD has spoken!"

⁹Messenger of good news, shout to Zion from the mountaintops! Shout louder to Jerusalem—do not be afraid. Tell the towns of Judah, "Your God is coming!" ¹⁰Yes, the Sovereign LORD is coming in all his glorious power. He will rule with awesome strength. See, he brings his reward with him as he comes. ¹¹He will feed his flock like a shepherd. He will carry the lambs in his arms, holding them close to his heart. He will gently lead the mother sheep with their young.

²⁷O Israel, how can you say the LORD does not see your troubles? How can you say God refuses to hear your case? ²⁸Have you never heard or understood? Don't you know that the LORD is the everlasting God, the Creator of all the earth? He never grows faint or weary. No one can measure the depths of his understanding. ²⁹He gives power to those who are tired and worn out; he offers strength to the weak. ³⁰Even youths will become exhausted, and young men will give up. ³¹But those who wait on the LORD will find new strength. They will fly high on wings like eagles. They will run and not grow weary. They will walk and not faint.   ISAIAH 40:1-5, 9-11, 27-31

igots

PREVIEW

If you are discouraged about your faith and are thinking about giving up on God, wait! Isaiah has something to say to you. And it's all good news! In this set of prophecies, Isaiah has many encouraging words for those who keep God's laws.

Other messages of good news in this passage concern Israel's homecoming from captivity and reasons not to fear other people.

PERSONAL APPLICATION

Not everyone in Israel thumbed their nose at God. Some, a small minority, often called a "remnant" in the Bible, loved God and obeyed his laws. As often happens to minorities, they drew insults and slander from others for being different. In this case, they were abused for loving and obeying God. But Isaiah had prophecies for them, too (Isaiah 51:7). These prophecies gave them hope for when they faced others' reproach or insults because of their God-honoring lifestyle.

We need not fear when people insult us for our moral choices, because God is with us and he will help us prevail.

If people make fun of you or dislike you because you go to church and stay faithful to your spouse, remember that they are not against you personally but against God. God will deal with them; you should concentrate on loving and obeying him. When you do, God will bless you for it!

BIBLE READING

[1]"Listen to me, all who hope for deliverance—all who seek the LORD! Consider the quarry from which you were mined, the rock from which you were cut! [2]Yes, think about your ancestors Abraham and Sarah, from whom you came. Abraham was alone when I called him. But when I blessed him, he became a great nation."

[3]The LORD will comfort Israel again and make her deserts blossom. Her barren wilderness will become as beautiful as Eden—the garden of the LORD. Joy and gladness will be found there. Lovely songs of thanksgiving will fill the air.

[4]"Listen to me, my people. Hear me, Israel, for my law will be proclaimed, and my justice will become a light to the nations. [5]My mercy and justice are coming soon. Your salvation is on the way. I will rule the nations. They will wait for me and long for my power. [6]Look up to the skies above, and gaze down on the earth beneath. For the skies will disappear like smoke, and the earth will wear out like a piece of clothing. The people of the earth will die like flies, but my salvation lasts forever. My righteous rule will never end!

[7]"Listen to me, you who know right from wrong and cherish my law in your hearts. Do not be afraid of people's scorn or their slanderous talk. [8]For the moth will destroy them as it destroys clothing. The worm will eat away at them as it eats wool. But my righteousness will last forever. My salvation will continue from generation to generation."

[11]Those who have been ransomed by the LORD will return to Jerusalem, singing songs of everlasting joy. Sorrow and mourning will disappear, and they will be overcome with joy and gladness.   ISAIAH 51:1-8, 11

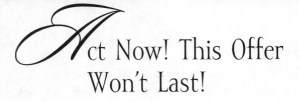

ct Now! This Offer Won't Last!

PREVIEW

Making big decisions usually takes a while. A person doesn't typically get married, buy a house, or have a child on a whim. On the other hand, some decisions *can't* wait. The opportunity is here today—it may be gone tomorrow.

This reading contains an offer from God to take advantage of *now*. So put it at the top of your list of things to do, and don't delay. This is one offer that definitely doesn't get any better and won't be around forever.

Other offers not to miss in this reading include Christ's payment for sin and a free reminder that God's ways are higher than ours.

PERSONAL APPLICATION

Isaiah told his people to call on the Lord while he is near (Isaiah 55:6-7). He wanted them to respond to God while they still had the chance, and not delay.

God doesn't make occasional appearances and then leave us, but he also doesn't wait forever while we "think about" whether or not we'll respond to him. Deliberately putting off the decision to accept Christ as Savior tests God's patience.

Don't test God's patience or wait until you're "ready" to call on him. Turning to him later in life may be far more difficult than it is now. Or worse, you may die or Christ may return to judge the earth before you decide to follow him. Therefore, seek God now, while you can, before it is too late. Someday it will be.

BIBLE READING

[1]"Is anyone thirsty? Come and drink—even if you have no money! Come, take your choice of wine or milk—it's all free! [2]Why spend your money on food that does not give you strength? Why pay for food that does you no good? Listen, and I will tell you where to get food that is good for the soul!

[3]"Come to me with your ears wide open. Listen, for the life of your soul is at stake. I am ready to make an everlasting covenant with you. I will give you all the mercies and unfailing love that I promised to David. [4]He displayed my power by being my witness and a leader among the nations. [5]You also will command the nations, and they will come running to obey, because I, the LORD your God, the Holy One of Israel, have made you glorious."

[6]Seek the LORD while you can find him. Call on him now while he is near. [7]Let the people turn from their wicked deeds. Let them banish from their minds the very thought of doing wrong! Let them turn to the LORD that he may have mercy on them. Yes, turn to our God, for he will abundantly pardon.

[8]"My thoughts are completely different from yours," says the LORD. "And my ways are far beyond anything you could imagine. [9]For just as the heavens are higher than the earth, so are my ways higher than your ways and my thoughts higher than your thoughts."   ISAIAH 55:1-9

etting Religion

PREVIEW

It's easy to act like a religious person—to go to church, go along with what happens there, and go about your business. Many people go to church—anyone can do it, with or without sincerity.

The people of Israel were definitely religious. This portion of Isaiah's message supports that fact. But their piety doesn't please the Lord, and he lets them know it. He says, "What good is your religion if it doesn't affect the way you live?"

Two other messages come through loud and clear in this reading: God *loves* it when we love; God *hates* it when we sin.

PERSONAL APPLICATION

To the people of Isaiah's day, worshiping God consisted entirely of religious ritual—going to the temple every day, fasting, and listening to Scripture readings. They thought nothing of the fact that they oppressed the poor and denied help to the weak (Isaiah 58:1-12). In fact, they loved their worship practices, even as they refused to love hurting people.

Religious people who miss the point of a living, vital relationship with God forget that God cares about people, not performances. God does not want us merely to act pious—he wants our behavior to reflect our relationship with him. More important to God even than correct worship, liturgy, and doctrine is genuine compassion for people who are poor, helpless, homeless, or oppressed.

To God, true worship is simply this: doing deeds of love and kindness for others, especially those who need help or are defenseless. Set aside empty religious rituals and practice true worship. This is what really pleases God. Who needs a touch of God's love through you? Reach out to that person *today*.

BIBLE READING

⁴"What good is fasting when you keep on fighting and quarreling? This kind of fasting will never get you anywhere with me. ⁵You humble yourselves by going through the motions of penance, bowing your heads like a blade of grass in the wind. You dress in sackcloth and cover yourselves with ashes. Is this what you call fasting? Do you really think this will please the LORD?

⁶"No, the kind of fasting I want calls you to free those who are wrongly imprisoned and to stop oppressing those who work for you. Treat them fairly and give them what they earn. ⁷I want you to share your food with the hungry and to welcome poor wanderers into your homes. Give clothes to those who need them, and do not hide from relatives who need your help.

⁸"If you do these things, your salvation will come like the dawn. Yes, your healing will come quickly. Your godliness will lead you forward, and the glory of the LORD will protect you from behind. ⁹Then when you call, the LORD will answer. 'Yes, I am here,' he will quickly reply.

"Stop oppressing the helpless and stop making false accusations and spreading vicious rumors! ¹⁰Feed the hungry and help those in trouble. Then your light will shine out from the darkness, and the darkness around you will be as bright as day. ¹¹The LORD will guide you continually, watering your life when you are dry and keeping you healthy, too. You will be like a well-watered garden, like an ever-flowing spring. ¹²Your children will rebuild the deserted ruins of your cities. Then you will be known as the people who rebuild their walls and cities."   ISAIAH 58:4-12

Caring Enough to Pray

PREVIEW

Hardly anything happens to shoreline rocks each time a wave rolls in. The water is no match for the stone. Indeed, if you were to come back day after day to watch, you would see *no change:* waves pound, rocks win. Yet the waves are making an impact, and over a very long time, you would be able to see the cumulative effect. The rocks will wear down.

Like a relentless surf, Isaiah has spoken to his people time and time again. He has warned them about their need to change, and they, rock-like, have not responded—so far. Isaiah has no guarantee that they will *ever* respond in his lifetime. He certainly hasn't seen any change. So he faithfully gets on his knees. As you read this passage, learn from Isaiah's example.

PERSONAL APPLICATION

When we warn or counsel others, sometimes they don't listen. Sometimes we can see their painful consequences, but they refuse to see the danger. After we've offered our warnings, our advice, and our pleas, we still have one potent option—prayer. That's why Jesus taught his followers to pray, "May your kingdom come soon. May your will be done here on earth, just as it is in heaven" (Matthew 6:10).

You cannot control others who are about to make a foolish choice or when they're toying with a temptation that could bring painful consequences, but you can pray for them. Keep praying persistently for the people you love.

BIBLE READING

¹Because I love Zion, because my heart yearns for Jerusalem, I cannot remain silent. I will not stop praying for her until her righteousness shines like the dawn, and her salvation blazes like a burning torch.

⁶O Jerusalem, I have posted watchmen on your walls; they will pray to the LORD day and night for the fulfillment of his promises. Take no rest, all you who pray. ⁷Give the LORD no rest until he makes Jerusalem the object of praise throughout the earth. ⁸The LORD has sworn to Jerusalem by his own strength: "I will never again hand you over to your enemies. Never again will foreign warriors come and take away your grain and wine. ⁹You raised it, and you will keep it, praising the LORD. Within the courtyards of the Temple, you yourselves will drink the wine that you have pressed."

¹⁰Go out! Prepare the highway for my people to return! Smooth out the road; pull out the boulders; raise a flag for all the nations to see. ¹¹The LORD has sent this message to every land: "Tell the people of Israel, 'Look, your Savior is coming. See, he brings his reward with him as he comes.'" ¹²They will be called the Holy People and the People Redeemed by the LORD. And Jerusalem will be known as the Desirable Place and the City No Longer Forsaken.   ISAIAH 62:1, 6-12

ever Too Young

PREVIEW

Youth is hampered in many ways: too little experience; not enough maturity; insufficient skills. If only we could have both the energy and the wisdom at the same time.

Welcome to the opening chapters of Jeremiah, the prophecies of a man who considers himself too young to serve God. True, Jeremiah is young. But you will see that when it comes to serving God, a person's age doesn't matter—it's the heart that counts.

Besides reading Jeremiah's call to service, in this passage you will learn that Judah has come under God's judgment because they have forsaken God and have been unfaithful to him.

PERSONAL APPLICATION

It's not unusual for people to struggle with new challenges because they feel too young or because they don't have enough ability, training, or experience. Jeremiah thought he was too young and inexperienced to be God's spokesman to the world. But God told him not to worry and to go ahead with his assignment (Jeremiah 1:6-8).

We must not allow our feelings of inadequacy to keep us from doing what God has called us to do. Instead, we should trust him to always be with us and to give us wisdom and guidance for the task.

When you find yourself avoiding something you know you should do, be careful not to use inadequacy as an excuse. Ask God for the courage to take on the job; then trust him wholeheartedly for the strength to complete it. Whether or not you succeed is God's concern. Leave your feelings of inadequacy with him so you can concentrate on doing his will. He will provide everything you need to do it.

BIBLE READING

⁴The LORD gave me a message. He said, ⁵"I knew you before I formed you in your mother's womb. Before you were born I set you apart and appointed you as my spokesman to the world."

⁶"O Sovereign LORD," I said, "I can't speak for you! I'm too young!"

⁷"Don't say that," the LORD replied, "for you must go wherever I send you and say whatever I tell you. ⁸And don't be afraid of the people, for I will be with you and take care of you. I, the LORD, have spoken!"

⁹Then the LORD touched my mouth and said, "See, I have put my words in your mouth! ¹⁰Today I appoint you to stand up against nations and kingdoms. You are to uproot some and tear them down, to destroy and overthrow them. You are to build others up and plant them."

¹¹Then the LORD said to me, "Look, Jeremiah! What do you see?"

And I replied, "I see a branch from an almond tree."

¹²And the LORD said, "That's right, and it means that I am watching, and I will surely carry out my threats of punishment."

¹³Then the LORD spoke to me again and asked, "What do you see now?"

And I replied, "I see a pot of boiling water, tipping from the north."

¹⁴"Yes," the LORD said, "for terror from the north will boil out on the people of this land. . . . ¹⁶I will pronounce judgment on my people for all their evil—for deserting me and worshiping other gods. Yes, they worship idols that they themselves have made!"   JEREMIAH 1:4-16

ucky Charms

PREVIEW

Many people believe that lucky charms will protect or help them. Some people carry a rabbit's foot or wear a lucky hat, shirt, or tie. Many Christians have one of these charms, and many others have their own variations—a cross necklace, an angel pin, or maybe a way of praying that they think has special significance.

When it comes to lucky charms, the people of Judah were no different from people today. In this passage, Jeremiah exposes their misplaced dependence on one religious artifact. Unlike people's lucky charms today, however, Judah's charm wasn't small enough to wear or carry. In this passage you will find proof that objects don't bring luck to anyone.

PERSONAL APPLICATION

The people who lived in Jerusalem depended on the ultimate good-luck charm: the temple. They thought that as long as the temple stood in Jerusalem they would have God's favor and be protected from harm (Jeremiah 7:4, 10). Meanwhile, they lived sinful lives, oppressing aliens, widows, and orphans, and worshiping false gods (7:5-7). They had misplaced their faith—instead of trusting in God, they were trusting in the temple.

True faith never involves superstitious belief in the power of an object. God wants us to respond personally to him and his will. Attending church, taking Communion, teaching Sunday school, singing in the choir, wearing a cross—these exercises grow out of our love for God; they don't gain us his favor or protection.

BIBLE READING

¹The LORD gave another message to Jeremiah. He said, ²"Go to the entrance of the Lord's Temple, and give this message to the people: 'O Judah, listen to this message from the LORD! Listen to it, all of you who worship here! ³The LORD Almighty, the God of Israel, says: Even now, if you quit your evil ways, I will let you stay in your own land. ⁴But do not be fooled by those who repeatedly promise your safety because the Temple of the LORD is here. ⁵I will be merciful only if you stop your wicked thoughts and deeds and are fair to others; ⁶and if you stop exploiting foreigners, orphans, and widows; and if you stop your murdering; and if you stop worshiping idols as you now do to your own harm. ⁷Then I will let you stay in this land that I gave to your ancestors to keep forever.

⁸" 'Do you think that because the Temple is here you will never suffer? Don't fool yourselves! ⁹Do you really think you can steal, murder, commit adultery, lie, and worship Baal and all those other new gods of yours, ¹⁰and then come here and stand before me in my Temple and chant, "We are safe!"—only to go right back to all those evils again? ¹¹Do you think this Temple, which honors my name, is a den of thieves? I see all the evil going on there, says the LORD.'"   JEREMIAH 7:1-11

Run out of Town

PREVIEW

People like or dislike meteorologists depending on how accurately they predict the weather. But what is worse is that some people dislike meteorologists just for predicting bad weather, despite how accurate they may be. It's not their fault that it's raining—shouldn't we cut them some slack? At least they warned us about the bad weather, right?

Jeremiah gets about as much respect as a forecaster who predicts bad weather all the time. Even the folks he grew up with don't want him around. In fact, they want him *dead*. But unlike a meteorologist, Jeremiah can't leave this job or area because God has placed Jeremiah just where he wants him, so Jeremiah must continue to give the people the bad reports.

PERSONAL APPLICATION

People today sometimes oppose believers who share God's message for the same reasons that motivated the people of Anathoth to plot Jeremiah's death. Certainly it would be tempting to remain silent or to change the message in the face of such opposition. Instead, we must be faithful to our calling, faithful to our Lord.

If you speak to others about God, you don't need to be obnoxious, pushy, or abrasive. Like Jeremiah, speak respectfully, time what you say properly, and make sure that you're representing God and not your own biases. But also like Jeremiah, keep speaking, and pray that the plans of your opponents will fail (Jeremiah 11:20). Let God be your protection.

BIBLE READING

[18]Then the LORD told me about the plots my enemies were making against me. [19]I had been as unaware as a lamb on the way to its slaughter. I had no idea that they were planning to kill me! "Let's destroy this man and all his words," they said. "Let's kill him, so his name will be forgotten forever."

[20]O LORD Almighty, you are just, and you examine the deepest thoughts of hearts and minds. Let me see your vengeance against them, for I have committed my cause to you.

[21]The men of Anathoth wanted me dead. They said they would kill me if I did not stop speaking in the LORD's name. [22]So this is what the LORD Almighty says about them: "I will punish them! Their young men will die in battle, and their little boys and girls will starve. [23]Not one of these plotters from Anathoth will survive, for I will bring disaster upon them when their time of punishment comes."

[12:1]LORD, you always give me justice when I bring a case before you. Now let me bring you this complaint: Why are the wicked so prosperous? Why are evil people so happy? [2]You have planted them, and they have taken root and prospered. Your name is on their lips, but in their hearts they give you no credit at all.

[5]Then the LORD replied to me, "If racing against mere men makes you tired, how will you race against horses? If you stumble and fall on open ground, what will you do in the thickets near the Jordan? [6]Even your own brothers, members of your own family, have turned on you. They have plotted, raising a cry against you. Do not trust them, no matter how pleasantly they speak." JEREMIAH 11:18-23; 12:2, 5-6

lay Pots

PREVIEW

Cute, furry creatures talk, sing, and dance across the screen and entertain children. Mom and Dad know, however, that the entertainers are just puppets, controlled by puppeteers offstage and off camera. Have you ever wondered whether you are just a puppet in God's hand? He is, after all, *sovereign*. Doesn't that mean he controls your every move?

This passage answers that question directly. In one prophecy delivered by Jeremiah, he compares people to living clay in the hands of God.

Jeremiah's other prophecies tell of impending doom, but also how the people can avoid it. Jeremiah gets a rude reception anyway. (Aren't you glad you're not a prophet?)

PERSONAL APPLICATION

Because the people of Judah did not repent of their sins and return to the Lord, they were like a jar that didn't turn out as the potter had intended (Jeremiah 18:4-6). Defective jars are not useful. And even as a potter takes a defective jar and kneads it back into a lump of clay, so also was the Lord planning to destroy Judah and reshape it.

Choosing to live in sin makes our lives less moldable and more defective to God. He wants us to be useful to him—he wants to shape us into a beautiful creation. But he will only do so if we allow ourselves to be moldable.

The shape your life takes is a cooperative effort between you and God. Do not become hard and unreceptive to his molding, but be soft and receptive to his hand on you. As you yield to God, he will shape you into a valuable vessel. Submit to him, the divine, loving Potter.

BIBLE READING

¹The LORD gave another message to Jeremiah. He said, ²"Go down to the shop where clay pots and jars are made. I will speak to you while you are there." ³So I did as he told me and found the potter working at his wheel. ⁴But the jar he was making did not turn out as he had hoped, so the potter squashed the jar into a lump of clay and started again.

⁵Then the LORD gave me this message: ⁶"O Israel, can I not do to you as this potter has done to his clay? As the clay is in the potter's hand, so are you in my hand. ⁷If I announce that a certain nation or kingdom is to be uprooted, torn down, and destroyed, ⁸but then that nation renounces its evil ways, I will not destroy it as I had planned. ⁹And if I announce that I will build up and plant a certain nation or kingdom, making it strong and great, ¹⁰but then that nation turns to evil and refuses to obey me, I will not bless that nation as I had said I would.

¹¹"Therefore, Jeremiah, go and warn all Judah and Jerusalem. Say to them, 'This is what the LORD says: I am planning disaster against you instead of good. So turn from your evil ways, each of you, and do what is right.'"

¹²But they replied, "Don't waste your breath. We will continue to live as we want to, following our own evil desires."

JEREMIAH 18:1-12

When the Truth Hurts

PREVIEW

Some people just don't want to hear bad news. They don't watch the news on television because it gets them too depressed. The news stations keep broadcasting the negative stories, insisting that they are exactly what keep viewers tuned in. News directors say that if they air only good news, the viewers lose interest and switch to stations that feature murders, fires, and political scandals. So the question remains: Do we want to hear bad news or don't we?

From Jeremiah's experience, he'd probably tell you that people don't want to hear bad news at all. As he shares God's newsflashes with the people in this passage, they denounce him and God for the bad news. But the really bad news isn't coming from God or Jeremiah.

PERSONAL APPLICATION

You can ignore some criticism. "Where'd you get that awful tie?" for example. But sometimes the issue hits close to home and won't let you escape so easily: "You shouldn't use bad language or read those dirty magazines." It's the inescapable criticism that gave Jeremiah's listeners fits. When people deliver bad news that carries the weight of Scripture, we simply don't have the option to turn our backs on their words.

Have you ever rejected a message or made fun of it because it would require you to change your ways? Before dismissing someone who says something negative about you, consider what he or she has to say. The message this person brings may contain some invaluable truth that will help to change your life for the better.

BIBLE READING

[9]My heart is broken because of the false prophets, and I tremble uncontrollably. I stagger like a drunkard, like someone overcome by wine, because of the holy words the LORD has spoken against them. [10]For the land is full of adultery, and it lies under a curse. The land itself is in mourning—its pastures are dried up. For the prophets do evil and abuse their power.

[13]"I saw that the prophets of Samaria were terribly evil, for they prophesied by Baal and led my people of Israel into sin. [14]But now I see that the prophets of Jerusalem are even worse! They commit adultery, and they love dishonesty. They encourage those who are doing evil instead of turning them away from their sins. These prophets are as wicked as the people of Sodom and Gomorrah once were."

[15]Therefore, this is what the LORD Almighty says concerning the prophets: "I will feed them with bitterness and give them poison to drink. For it is because of Jerusalem's prophets that wickedness fills this land. [16]This is my warning to my people," says the LORD Almighty. "Do not listen to these prophets when they prophesy to you, filling you with futile hopes. They are making up everything they say. They do not speak for the LORD! [17]They keep saying to these rebels who despise my word, 'Don't worry! The LORD says you will have peace!' And to those who stubbornly follow their own evil desires, they say, 'No harm will come your way!'

[18]"But can you name even one of these prophets who knows the LORD well enough to hear what he is saying? Has even one of them cared enough to listen? [19]Look! The Lord's anger bursts out like a storm, a whirlwind that swirls down on the heads of the wicked."   JEREMIAH 23:9-10, 13-19

letter from Home

Preview

When you're away at college, at boot camp, or almost anywhere else, there's nothing quite like a letter from home. You know that the familiar handwriting means the message inside is just for you

Jeremiah's friends, neighbors, and other fellow citizens were a long way from home. Conquered by invaders, they lived in exile, in Babylon. In this set of prophecies, Jeremiah deals with lonely, grief-stricken people. They want only to go back home to Jerusalem. Jeremiah knows, however, that they will be in Babylon for a long time, so he sends them a letter to help them get on with their lives. Look for a lesson about making the most of a bad situation.

Personal Application

We should not let our lives grind to a halt during troubled times. In an unpleasant or distressing situation, we must accept what we cannot change, adjust whatever we can, and get on with our responsibilities. Some circumstances are unavoidable. Perhaps they aren't going to change anytime soon, or there is no end in sight. God places us in these circumstances for good reasons, either to discipline us or to teach us a lesson.

When you enter times of trouble or sudden change, or when you realize that your difficult circumstances aren't going to change, pray often. Don't give in to fear or give up in discouragement; instead, do what you can to fulfill your responsibilities.

BIBLE READING

[4]The LORD Almighty, the God of Israel, sends this message to all the captives he has exiled to Babylon from Jerusalem: [5]"Build homes, and plan to stay. Plant gardens, and eat the food you produce. [6]Marry, and have children. Then find spouses for them, and have many grandchildren. Multiply! Do not dwindle away! [7]And work for the peace and prosperity of Babylon. Pray to the LORD for that city where you are held captive, for if Babylon has peace, so will you."

[11]"For I know the plans I have for you," says the LORD. "They are plans for good and not for disaster, to give you a future and a hope. [12]In those days when you pray, I will listen. [13]If you look for me in earnest, you will find me when you seek me. [14]I will be found by you," says the LORD. "I will end your captivity and restore your fortunes. I will gather you out of the nations where I sent you and bring you home again to your own land."

[15]You may claim that the LORD has raised up prophets for you in Babylon. [16]But this is what the LORD says about the king who sits on David's throne and all those still living here in Jerusalem—your relatives who were not exiled to Babylon. [17]This is what the LORD Almighty says: "I will send war, famine, and disease upon them and make them like rotting figs—too bad to eat. [18]Yes, I will pursue them with war, famine, and disease, and I will scatter them around the world. In every nation where I send them, I will make them an object of damnation, horror, contempt, and mockery. [19]For they refuse to listen to me, though I have spoken to them repeatedly through my prophets. And you who are in exile have not listened either," says the LORD.

JEREMIAH 29:4-7, 11-19

hat's Reassuring!

PREVIEW

When friends fight, as they sometimes do, it's as if they've blown a circuit. To reset the breaker, so to speak, they apologize and make amends. The same is true in our relationship with God—only we do all the breaking.

This reading is about God resetting the breaker with the people of Judah. Though they will be spending some time in Babylon as a punishment for their sins, God reassures them that this won't last forever. As proof of this promise, Jeremiah buys a field back home in Judah.

PERSONAL APPLICATION

People who don't know God typically make one of two false assumptions about him. First, some suppose that God loves them so much that he doesn't care about their sinful behavior. These people also don't believe in hell or that God would punish anybody. Second, others assume God is an angry tyrant. People caught in this falsehood imagine that God cannot possibly love them because they are too sinful. They don't believe in heaven (at least for them) or that God could accept anybody (as bad as they).

Jeremiah's prophecies in this reading address this second assumption. Though God doesn't like it when we sin, he loves us enough to reach out and draw us to him (Jeremiah 31:3). He is eager for us to repent of our sins and turn to him for salvation. He doesn't hold grudges or fume over our every past offense. Rather he forgives us and forgets each sin when we repent.

BIBLE READING

[3]Long ago the LORD said to Israel: "I have loved you, my people, with an everlasting love. With unfailing love I have drawn you to myself. [4]I will rebuild you, my virgin Israel. You will again be happy and dance merrily with tambourines. [5]Again you will plant your vineyards on the mountains of Samaria and eat from your own gardens there. [6]The day will come when watchmen will shout from the hill country of Ephraim, 'Come, let us go up to Jerusalem to worship the LORD our God.'"

[10]"Listen to this message from the LORD, you nations of the world; proclaim it in distant coastlands: The LORD, who scattered his people, will gather them together and watch over them as a shepherd does his flock. [11]For the LORD has redeemed Israel from those too strong for them. [12]They will come home and sing songs of joy on the heights of Jerusalem. They will be radiant because of the many gifts the LORD has given them—the good crops of wheat, wine, and oil, and the healthy flocks and herds. Their life will be like a watered garden, and all their sorrows will be gone. [13]The young women will dance for joy, and the men— old and young—will join in the celebration. I will turn their mourning into joy. I will comfort them and exchange their sorrow for rejoicing. [14]I will supply the priests with an abundance of offerings. I will satisfy my people with my bounty. I, the LORD, have spoken!"   JEREMIAH 31:3-6, 10-14

radition!

PREVIEW

Every family has a special link to the past. Some remember their ethnic roots and can tell you about their proud heritage. Others have favorite stories of the struggles that their grandparents or great-grandparents endured. Still others remember the heroic acts, faith, wisdom, or accomplishments of an ancestor who made a mark and left a story (if not a photo), making the relatives who live today somehow special.

This passage contains Jeremiah's last-minute prophecies and what happened to him and to the nation around the time he was giving them. It's Judah's last hour—Jerusalem is under siege by the Babylonians (as Jeremiah predicted) and is about to fall. In case anyone doesn't understand *why*, Jeremiah provides a vivid illustration through the Recabite family and their cherished past.

PERSONAL APPLICATION

As Christians, we have a long and glorious family tradition of seeking God and living for him. Although we should not emulate our spiritual ancestors merely out of tradition, we can and should learn from their example. We should seek God with all our heart and obey his Word in every aspect of life, even if it means dying for Jesus Christ.

Take some time to reflect on your personal spiritual heritage. Thank God for godly parents, grandparents, and other relatives who have kept your family on the right path. If you have no such memories or heritage, determine that it will begin with you and your family. Make spiritual memories that your children and grandchildren will reflect upon to gain strength and inspiration.

BIBLE READING

⁵I set cups and jugs of wine before them and invited them to have a drink, ⁶but they refused. "No," they said. "We don't drink wine, because Jehonadab son of Recab, our ancestor, gave us this command: 'You and your descendants must never drink wine. ⁷And do not build houses or plant crops or vineyards, but always live in tents. If you follow these commands, you will live long, good lives in the land.' ⁸So we have obeyed him in all these things. We have never had a drink of wine since then, nor have our wives, our sons, or our daughters. ⁹We haven't built houses or owned vineyards or farms or planted crops. ¹⁰We have lived in tents and have fully obeyed all the commands of Jehonadab, our ancestor. . . ."

¹²Then the LORD gave this message to Jeremiah: ¹³"The LORD Almighty, the God of Israel, says: Go and say to the people in Judah and Jerusalem, 'Come and learn a lesson about how to obey me. ¹⁴The Recabites do not drink wine because their ancestor Jehonadab told them not to. But I have spoken to you again and again, and you refuse to listen or obey. ¹⁵I have sent you prophet after prophet to tell you to turn from your wicked ways and to stop worshiping other gods, so that you might live in peace here in the land I gave to you and your ancestors. But you would not listen to me or obey. ¹⁶The families of Recab have obeyed their ancestor completely, but you have refused to listen to me. . . .'"

¹⁸Then Jeremiah turned to the Recabites and said, "This is what the LORD Almighty, the God of Israel, says: You have obeyed your ancestor Jehonadab in every respect, following all his instructions. ¹⁹Because of this, Jehonadab son of Recab will always have descendants who serve me. I, the LORD Almighty, the God of Israel, have spoken!"   JEREMIAH 35:5-19

 # Planning Ahead

PREVIEW

Running errands, going on vacation, working on projects—all of these activities require planning. Planning makes things easier to accomplish. But sometimes even plans aren't enough to achieve success.

Enter the forward-thinking Johanan, who has some plans. Like any good Israelite, he wants God to bless his plans and asks Jeremiah to pray for him. But something rotten shows itself as soon as God reveals the truth about Johanan's true motives. As you read, look for the lesson about truly seeking and doing God's will.

PERSONAL APPLICATION

Johanan and his tiny band came to Jeremiah and asked him to pray for God's approval of their plan (Jeremiah 42:1–43:3). But they didn't really care what God wanted; they wanted approval of their wicked plans.

This is a common problem—seeking God's approval of our desires rather than asking him to shape our desires. We should not make plans unless we are willing to have God shape and change them, and it is not good to place conditions on our willingness to accept God's answer. Whenever we seek God's blessing, we should say, "*Your* will be done" (Matthew 6:10).

What plans are you making these days? How do they match up with what God wants? Talk to God; yield your goals and your plans to him and he'll bless your decisions.

BIBLE READING

[1]Then all the army officers, including Johanan son of Kareah and Jezaniah son of Hoshaiah, and all the people, from the least to the greatest, approached [2]Jeremiah the prophet. They said, "Please pray to the LORD your God for us. As you know, we are only a tiny remnant compared to what we were before. [3]Beg the LORD your God to show us what to do and where to go. . . . [5]May the LORD your God be a faithful witness against us if we refuse to obey whatever he tells us to do! [6]Whether we like it or not, we will obey the LORD our God to whom we send you with our plea. For if we obey him, everything will turn out well for us."

[19]"Listen, you remnant of Judah. The LORD has told you: 'Do not go to Egypt!' Don't forget this warning I have given you today. [20]For you were deceitful when you sent me to pray to the LORD your God for you, saying, 'Just tell us what the LORD our God says, and we will do it!' [21]And today I have told you exactly what he said, but you will not obey the LORD your God any better now than you have in the past. [22]So you can be sure that you will die from war, famine, and disease in Egypt, where you insist on going."

[43:1]When Jeremiah had finished giving this message from the LORD their God to all the people, [2]Azariah son of Hoshaiah and Johanan son of Kareah and all the other proud men said to Jeremiah, "You lie! The LORD our God hasn't forbidden us to go to Egypt! [3]Baruch son of Neriah has convinced you to say this, so we will stay here and be killed by the Babylonians or be carried off into exile."   JEREMIAH 42:1-6, 19-22; 43:1-3

oul Disease

PREVIEW

Vaccinations have given the world a prevention for several deadly diseases, most notably, polio, smallpox, whooping cough, mumps, and diphtheria. Also, common antibiotics have all but eliminated the threat from bacterial diseases such as bubonic plague and strep throat. Death has fewer weapons in its arsenal, it appears, so scientists are going after the rest of them, including the biggest ones: cancer and AIDS. Though cures for these have proven much more difficult to discover, hope runs high. Medical scientists have succeeded before, surely they'll do it again. After all, medical science can do anything, right?

Not all diseases focus their attack on the body—some target the soul. Pride, for instance, is one of these diseases, and the final section of Jeremiah's prophecies concerns Babylon, a country infected with pride. Will we ever understand how much damage this sin can cause? Or will we always see it as a natural right? As you read this section, check your life for pride.

PERSONAL APPLICATION

Pride, or arrogance, was Babylon's characteristic sin (Jeremiah 50:32). At best, pride is an oversight—a failure to recognize our total dependence on God for everything (life, health, and every skill). At worst, pride is spitting in the face of the one who created us.

We depend on God for our very lives. Only a humble acknowledgment of this makes any sense at all. That is why God resists the proud (see James 4:6). Because of sin, we naturally want to hold on to our pride, but there are steps we can take to overcome it by God's power and grace.

BIBLE READING

[25]"The LORD has opened his armory and brought out weapons to vent his fury against his enemies. The terror that falls upon the Babylonians will be the work of the Sovereign LORD Almighty. [26]Yes, come against her from distant lands. Break open her granaries. Crush her walls and houses into heaps of rubble. Destroy her completely, and leave nothing! [27]Even destroy her cattle—it will be terrible for them, too! Slaughter them all! For the time has come for Babylon to be devastated. [28]Listen to the people who have escaped from Babylon, as they declare in Jerusalem how the LORD our God has taken vengeance against those who destroyed his Temple.

[29]"Send out a call for archers to come to Babylon. Surround the city so none can escape. Do to her as she has done to others, for she has defied the LORD, the Holy One of Israel. [30]Her young men will fall in the streets and die. Her warriors will all be killed," says the LORD.

[31]"See, I am your enemy, O proud people," says the Lord, the LORD Almighty. "Your day of reckoning has arrived. [32]O land of pride, you will stumble and fall, and no one will raise you up. For I will light a fire in the cities of Babylon that will burn everything around them."

[33]And now the LORD Almighty says this: "The people of Israel and Judah have been wronged. Their captors hold them and refuse to let them go. [34]But the one who redeems them is strong. His name is the LORD Almighty. He will defend them and give them rest again in Israel. But the people of Babylon—there will be no rest for them!"   JEREMIAH 50:25-34

oly Places

PREVIEW

People go to a particular church for many different reasons. For some it's the architecture of the building. For some, it's the pastor's sermons. For others, it's Sunday School and church programs. In theory, everyone goes to worship God.

It seems as though the people of Jerusalem also went to church—in their case the temple—for reasons other than to worship God. In Lamentations, Jeremiah reveals why God has "rejected his own altar" (Lamentations 2:7). It has everything to do with the people's worship practices, and what Jeremiah compares their worship to is startling. As you read, take an honest appraisal of your motives for attending church.

PERSONAL APPLICATION

When we go to church and worship God, we should examine our motives for doing so. If we're there for any reason other than worshiping him, then we need to reorder our priorities for attending church. In addition, we can practice three steps to help us focus our attention on praising and worshiping God. First, we can meditate on God as we participate in the service each Sunday. Second, we can try to ignore the distractions that occur during the service. Third, we can let the service create in us a sense of wonder at God's greatness and great deeds.

When you attend church, enjoy the fellowship and company of other believers, but also go to worship God with a sincere heart. The sincerity of our worship matters more to God than where or how we worship.

BIBLE READING

¹The Lord in his anger has cast a dark shadow over Jerusalem. The fairest of Israel's cities lies in the dust, thrown down from the heights of heaven. In his day of awesome fury, the Lord has shown no mercy even to his Temple.

²Without mercy the Lord has destroyed every home in Israel. In his anger he has broken down the fortress walls of Jerusalem. He has brought to dust the kingdom and all its rulers.

⁷The Lord has rejected his own altar; he despises his own sanctuary. He has given Jerusalem's palaces to her enemies. They shout in the LORD's Temple as though it were a day of celebration.

⁸The LORD was determined to destroy the walls of Jerusalem. He made careful plans for their destruction, then he went ahead and did it. Therefore, the ramparts and walls have fallen down before him.

⁹Jerusalem's gates have sunk into the ground. All their locks and bars are destroyed, for he has smashed them. Her kings and princes have been exiled to distant lands; the law is no more. Her prophets receive no more visions from the LORD.

¹⁰The leaders of Jerusalem sit on the ground in silence, clothed in sackcloth. They throw dust on their heads in sorrow and despair. The young women of Jerusalem hang their heads in shame.

¹¹I have cried until the tears no longer come. My heart is broken, my spirit poured out, as I see what has happened to my people. Little children and tiny babies are fainting and dying in the streets.   LAMENTATIONS 2:1-2, 7-11

*Wh*y Bother?

PREVIEW

Suppose you have a friend, relative, or neighbor who has made a lot of foolish mistakes in the past. He or she has paid a heavy price for these mistakes, but for some reason the lesson just hasn't sunk in yet. Now this person is on the verge of making another big mistake. Should you warn him or her?

Ezekiel is in this kind of position. Despite repeated warnings of punishment from several prophets, the Jews refused to listen and kept on sinning. As a result, God let the Babylonians destroy Israel and take the Jews into captivity. Apparently the Israelites didn't learn their lesson, however, and they continued to sin in Babylon. So God appointed Ezekiel to bring his message to the Jews there. God also told Ezekiel if he didn't give the Jews his message, he, too, would pay for their sins.

As you read this section of Ezekiel, note the prophet's faithfulness in carrying out his responsibilities. Also look for the many symbols of God in Ezekiel's call to prophesy. Let these symbols lead you in worship.

PERSONAL APPLICATION

Ezekiel was bitter and angry at God's people (Ezekiel 3:14-15), and understandably so. Ezekiel had no guarantee that they would listen to him either (3:11). Still Ezekiel delivered the messages God gave him and sacrificed his own comforts to communicate God's warnings.

You may feel like Ezekiel when Christian brothers or sisters scorn God's Word. But don't be discouraged. If Christian friends have strayed from God, speak up, even if they aren't listening, and even if it seems unlikely that they will take your advice.

BIBLE READING

[1]"Stand up, son of man," said the voice. "I want to speak with you." [2]The Spirit came into me as he spoke and set me on my feet. I listened carefully to his words. [3]"Son of man," he said, "I am sending you to the nation of Israel, a nation that is rebelling against me. Their ancestors have rebelled against me from the beginning, and they are still in revolt to this very day. [4]They are a hard-hearted and stubborn people. But I am sending you to say to them, 'This is what the Sovereign LORD says!' [5]And whether they listen or not—for remember, they are rebels—at least they will know they have had a prophet among them.

[6]"Son of man, do not fear them. Don't be afraid even though their threats are sharp as thorns and barbed like briers, and they sting like scorpions. Do not be dismayed by their dark scowls. For remember, they are rebels! [7]You must give them my messages whether they listen or not. But they won't listen, for they are completely rebellious! [8]Son of man, listen to what I say to you. Do not join them in being a rebel. Open your mouth, and eat what I give you."

[9]Then I looked and saw a hand reaching out to me, and it held a scroll. [10]He unrolled it, and I saw that both sides were covered with funeral songs, other words of sorrow, and pronouncements of doom.

[3:1]The voice said to me, "Son of man, eat what I am giving you—eat this scroll! Then go and give its message to the people of Israel." [2]So I opened my mouth, and he fed me the scroll. [3]"Eat it all," he said. And when I ate it, it tasted as sweet as honey.

[4]Then he said, "Son of man, go to the people of Israel with my messages."   EZEKIEL 2:1–3:4

One Nation under God

PREVIEW

When discussing with people about what makes America great, you may eventually come to the topic of religious freedom. In America, whatever people want to believe, they can believe. Whatever god they want, they can have. It is a nation of options.

The Jews had many gods, but they weren't supposed to. The Lord was their God, and they were not to worship anything or anyone else. That's why many of Ezekiel's prophecies in this reading foretell terrible punishments to come.

From the sidelines, also watch the prophet because he is a good example to us all. He goes to great lengths to get God's message across (whatever God asks, he does!). And see what happens when a man is exposed to God's glory.

PERSONAL APPLICATION

The people to whom Ezekiel had prophesied had abandoned God in many ways. They had worshiped man-made idols. They had disobeyed God's laws. They had ignored the words of several prophets. Even in exile they still had stubborn hearts. Many of the tragic events that Ezekiel foretold and spoke about had one aim: to impress upon God's people (and, incidentally, the rest of the world) that the Lord is the only true and living God.

It is easy to forget that the Lord alone is God, the supreme authority and the only source of eternal life. Sometimes God uses the difficulties of life to remind people of his authority. When trials happen, we should not ask, "Oh, how could God let this happen?" Rather, we should ask, "Have we forgotten the Lord? Have we replaced God with something else? Have we brought this on ourselves?" Have no other god but the Lord.

BIBLE READING

[3]"Give the mountains of Israel this message from the Sovereign LORD. This is what the Sovereign LORD says to the mountains and hills and to the ravines and valleys: I am about to bring war upon you, and I will destroy your pagan shrines. [4]All your altars will be demolished, and your incense altars will be smashed. I will kill your people in front of your idols. [5]I will lay your corpses in front of your idols and scatter your bones around your altars. [6]Wherever you live there will be desolation. I will destroy your pagan shrines, your altars, your idols, your incense altars, and all the other religious objects you have made. [7]Then when the place is littered with corpses, you will know that I am the LORD.

[8]"But I will let a few of my people escape destruction, and they will be scattered among the nations of the world. [9]Then when they are exiled among the nations, they will remember me. They will recognize how grieved I am by their unfaithful hearts and lustful eyes that long for other gods. Then at last they will hate themselves for all their wickedness. [10]They will know that I alone am the LORD and that I was serious when I predicted that all this would happen to them.

[11]"This is what the Sovereign LORD says: Clap your hands in horror, and stamp your feet. Cry out, 'Alas!' because of all the evil that the people of Israel have done. Now they are going to die from war and famine and disease. [12]Disease will strike down those who are far away in exile. War will destroy those who are nearby. And anyone who survives will be killed by famine. So at last I will spend my fury on them. . . . [14]Then they will know that I am the LORD."

EZEKIEL 6:3-14

Bad Rep

PREVIEW

People who speak for someone else have a responsibility to represent their clients or constituents accurately and adamantly.

It's no wonder that God was upset with a group of false prophets. These people claimed to represent God, but the messages they gave to the Jews didn't even come close to representing God's views. So God sent his appointed representative, Ezekiel, to speak out against them. What God had to say wasn't comforting news for those who misrepresented him. Check it out.

Also, note the change that lies ahead for God's people as reported by the true prophet, Ezekiel, because of their choices. It can really make you stop and think.

PERSONAL APPLICATION

Anyone can say, "I speak for God." But who can actually represent him? The desire to draw attention to ourselves, to be liked, and to be seen as an authority can entrap us. This same desire entrapped the false prophets in a quest to gain admirers rather than God's approval.

Be careful how you represent God's viewpoint to others. Make sure your message does indeed come from God's Word and not just from your own opinions or biases. And don't look to approval from others as proof that you are right. Many people will willingly believe a falsehood if it suits them. Watch carefully what you believe and be careful in how you represent it to others.

BIBLE READING

[4]"O people of Israel, these prophets of yours are like jackals digging around in the ruins. [5]They have done nothing to strengthen the breaks in the walls around the nation. They have not helped it to stand firm in battle on the day of the LORD. [6]Instead, they have lied and said, 'My message is from the LORD,' even though the LORD never sent them. And yet they expect him to fulfill their prophecies! [7]Can your visions be anything but false if you claim, 'This message is from the LORD,' when I have not even spoken to you?

[8]"Therefore, this is what the Sovereign LORD says: Because what you say is false and your visions are a lie, I will stand against you, says the Sovereign LORD. [9]I will raise my fist against all the lying prophets, and they will be banished from the community of Israel. I will blot their names from Israel's record books, and they will never again see their own land. Then you will know that I am the Sovereign LORD!

[10]"These evil prophets deceive my people by saying, 'All is peaceful!' when there is no peace at all! It's as if the people have built a flimsy wall, and these prophets are trying to hold it together by covering it with whitewash! [11]Tell these whitewashers that their wall will soon fall down. A heavy rainstorm will undermine it; great hailstones and mighty winds will knock it down. [12]And when the wall falls, the people will cry out, 'Where is the whitewash you applied?'

[13]"Therefore, this is what the Sovereign LORD says: I will sweep away your whitewashed wall with a storm of indignation, with a great flood of anger, and with hailstones of fury. [14]I will break down your wall right to the foundation, and when it falls, it will crush you. Then you will know that I am the LORD!"

EZEKIEL 13:4-14

Child Abuse

PREVIEW

Some of the Jewish children of Ezekiel's time were physically abused by their parents. They did not even have a chance to grow up. In this reading, Ezekiel confronts the Jews about one of their most heinous practices—child sacrifice. What may be even more shocking than this, however, is what the Jews did after sacrificing their children.

Also in this reading, you can see God's people trying to deflect their responsibility for their sin. They say it's unfair, that they're not guilty, that they don't deserve it. But Ezekiel won't accept these excuses.

PERSONAL APPLICATION

Today children aren't often killed in religious rituals, but they are some-times sacrificed in other ways. Some are abused by adults who take out their anger on them or, worse, derive sexual pleasure from them. Some children are neglected by parents who are too busy to spend time with them. Other parents selfishly indulge their appetites and don't provide for their children's needs. All of these atrocities are modern-day examples of child sacrifice. Children have no power to stop those who treat them with contempt. We should not abuse or neglect children in any way. Rather, we should treat them as the precious gifts from God that they are.

BIBLE READING

[36]The LORD said to me, "Son of man, you must accuse Oholah and Oholibah of all their awful deeds. [37]They have committed both adultery and murder—adultery by worshiping idols and murder by burning their children as sacrifices on their altars. [38]Then after doing these terrible things, they defiled my Temple and violated my Sabbath day! [39]On the very day that they murdered their children in front of their idols, they boldly came into my Temple to worship! They came in and defiled my house!

[46]"Now this is what the Sovereign LORD says: Bring an army against them and hand them over to be terrorized and plundered. [47]For their enemies will stone them and kill them with swords. They will butcher their sons and daughters and burn their homes. [48]In this way, I will put an end to lewdness and idolatry in the land, and my judgment will be a warning to others not to follow their wicked example. [49]You will be fully repaid for all your prostitution—your worship of idols. Yes, you will suffer the full penalty! Then you will know that I am the Sovereign LORD."

EZEKIEL 23:36-39, 46-49

Credit Limit

PREVIEW

Bob is proud. He has built his business from the ground up. He has worked long hours, pushed through lean times, hired many employees, and let a few go. Now he's selling what he so skillfully built, and the proceeds will set him up for an early retirement. He has what you might call "bragging rights."

In this set of prophecies, we learn a negative lesson on pride as demonstrated by Egypt. They've got a jewel in the Nile, and they know it. But along with this source of pride comes a caution.

You will find other cautions here—especially judgments against Ammon, Moab, Edom, Philistia, Tyre, and Egypt (all nations that bordered Israel). These show that *everybody* has to answer to God, even those who don't acknowledge him.

PERSONAL APPLICATION

The Egyptian people took great pride in the Nile River. This unstoppable source of fresh water cut through the desert and turned barren land into fertile soil, making life in Egypt possible. It was a reliable source of all the food they could ever need. All they had to do was work the land year after year, and it would yield abundant amounts of grain and vegetables. Rather than thanking God for this great provision, however, the Egyptians proudly boasted, "The Nile River is mine; I made it" (Ezekiel 29:9-10).

God's provisions come to us in many forms: a home, a job, a church, a business, a family, a reputation. Each gives us opportunity to say, "Thank you, Lord." Each also tempts us to boast, especially if we have invested a great deal of time and energy in the good we enjoy.

BIBLE READING

⁶"All the people of Egypt will discover that I am the LORD, for you collapsed like a reed when Israel looked to you for help. ⁷Israel leaned on you, but like a cracked staff, you splintered and stabbed her in the armpit. When she put her weight on you, you gave way, and her back was thrown out of joint. ⁸So now the Sovereign LORD says: I will bring an army against you, O Egypt, and destroy both people and animals. ⁹The land of Egypt will become a desolate wasteland, and the Egyptians will know that I am the LORD.

"Because you said, 'The Nile River is mine; I made it,' ¹⁰I am now the enemy of both you and your river. I will utterly destroy the land of Egypt, from Migdol to Aswan, as far south as the border of Ethiopia. ¹¹For forty years not a soul will pass that way, neither people nor animals. It will be completely uninhabited. ¹²I will make Egypt desolate, and it will be surrounded by other desolate nations. Its cities will be empty and desolate for forty years, surrounded by other desolate cities. I will scatter the Egyptians to distant lands.

¹³"But the Sovereign LORD also says: At the end of the forty years I will bring the Egyptians home again from the nations to which they have been scattered. ¹⁴I will restore the prosperity of Egypt and bring its people back to the land of Pathros in southern Egypt from which they came. But Egypt will remain an unimportant, minor kingdom. ¹⁵It will be the lowliest of all the nations, never again great enough to rise above its neighbors.

¹⁶"Then Israel will no longer be tempted to trust in Egypt for help. Egypt's shattered condition will remind Israel of how sinful she was to trust Egypt in earlier days. Then Israel will know that I alone am the Sovereign LORD."   EZEKIEL 29:6-16

*G*od Loves Me

PREVIEW

Suppose you really blow it. You feel quite certain that God could never forgive you, or use you, or care whether you get up the next morning. Where do you go from here?

This portion of Ezekiel has the answer. As you read, notice the Jews' change in attitude toward God. Once they were hardened—now they're repentant. The tone of Ezekiel's prophecies changes to match. The people begin to listen, and God responds. Here is the turning point: God's enemies will be wiped out and good times will return. Restoration and new life lie ahead.

PERSONAL APPLICATION

Thirty-two chapters of Ezekiel record how Judah, and many of the surrounding nations, would be punished for their sins. At first none of the people listened to these divine rebukes. Finally God's people admitted their guilt and set aside their stubborn rebellion. But then they felt overwhelmed by their sorrow: "Our sins are heavy upon us; we are wasting away!" (Ezekiel 33:10). God responded by saying that he would not punish those who repented (33:10-12).

God doesn't enjoy punishing people, nor does he abandon us when we stray from him. In every warning he calls us back. He prefers that we turn from our sins, seek his forgiveness, and begin to follow him again. No matter how far we've gone astray, we can always come back to God, because he *wants* us back.

When you sin, don't resign yourself to a pitiless fate of isolation from God. Simply confess your sins and acknowledge his right to guide you. Don't let past disobedience ever keep you from returning to God.

BIBLE READING

¹Once again a message came to me from the LORD: ²"Son of man, give your people this message: When I bring an army against a country, the people of that land choose a watchman. ³When the watchman sees the enemy coming, he blows the alarm to warn the people. ⁴Then if those who hear the alarm refuse to take action— well, it is their own fault if they die. ⁵They heard the warning but wouldn't listen, so the responsibility is theirs. If they had listened to the warning, they could have saved their lives. ⁶But if the watchman sees the enemy coming and doesn't sound the alarm to warn the people, he is responsible for their deaths. They will die in their sins, but I will hold the watchman accountable.

⁷"Now, son of man, I am making you a watchman for the people of Israel. Therefore, listen to what I say and warn them for me. ⁸If I announce that some wicked people are sure to die and you fail to warn them about changing their ways, then they will die in their sins, but I will hold you responsible for their deaths. ⁹But if you warn them to repent and they don't repent, they will die in their sins, but you will not be held responsible.

¹⁰"Son of man, give the people of Israel this message: You are saying, 'Our sins are heavy upon us; we are wasting away! How can we survive?' ¹¹As surely as I live, says the Sovereign LORD, I take no pleasure in the death of wicked people. I only want them to turn from their wicked ways so they can live. Turn! Turn from your wickedness, O people of Israel! Why should you die?

¹²"Son of man, give your people this message: The good works of righteous people will not save them if they turn to sin, nor will the sins of evil people destroy them if they repent and turn from their sins."   EZEKIEL 33:1-12

n-tic-i-pa-tion

PREVIEW

Surely no holiday generates more anticipation than Christmas—the waiting, the countdown of days till that bright morning when the ripping of wrapping paper becomes welcome chaos. Countless children have counted the days. Countless more have slept poorly—or not at all—the night before. The anticipation is just too much.

That's the point of this prophetic passage: anticipation. Ezekiel's vision contains such hope for the future, that it can get you a little worked up. Don't speed-read through this and miss the splendor.

PERSONAL APPLICATION

King Nebuchadnezzar's invading armies had completely destroyed the temple. But one day that terrible event would only be a distant memory. In one of Ezekiel's visions, he saw a new temple of great beauty and splendor, where worship flourished. Ezekiel wrote down a very detailed description of that temple and the worship that would take place there among God's people (Ezekiel 40:1–46:24). To a group of exiles in Babylon, with the memory of their devastated homeland still fresh in their minds, this vision came as a great encouragement. Ezekiel's vision meant that God had not abandoned his people, and that one day the Lord and his great blessings would once again become the focal point of Israel's life.

Don't let the details of this blueprint obscure the point of Ezekiel's vision. Eventually God's people will enjoy eternal life with him, and it will be indescribably wonderful. Our present troubles will end before long, and the life that awaits us will make all our service and obedience to God worthwhile.

BIBLE READING

[1]After this, the man brought me back around to the east gateway.
[2]Suddenly, the glory of the God of Israel appeared from the east.
The sound of his coming was like the roar of rushing waters, and
the whole landscape shone with his glory. [3]This vision was just
like the others I had seen, first by the Kebar River and then when
he came to destroy Jerusalem. And I fell down before him with
my face in the dust. [4]And the glory of the LORD came into the
Temple through the east gateway.

[5]Then the Spirit took me up and brought me into the inner
courtyard, and the glory of the LORD filled the Temple. [6]And I
heard someone speaking to me from within the Temple. (The
man who had been measuring was still standing beside me.) [7]And
the LORD said to me, "Son of man, this is the place of my throne
and the place where I will rest my feet. I will remain here forever,
living among the people of Israel. They and their kings will not
defile my holy name any longer by their adulterous worship of
other gods or by raising monuments in honor of their dead
kings. [8]They put their idol altars right next to mine with only a
wall between them and me. They defiled my holy name by such
wickedness, so I consumed them in my anger. [9]Now let them put
away their idols and the sacred pillars erected to honor their
kings, and I will live among them forever.

[10]"Son of man, describe to the people of Israel the Temple I
have shown you. Tell them its appearance and its plan so they will
be ashamed of all their sins. [11]And if they are ashamed of what
they have done, describe to them all the specifications of its
construction—including its entrances and doors—and everything
else about it. Write down all these specifications and directions as
they watch so they will be sure to remember them. [12]And this is
the basic law of the Temple: absolute holiness! The entire top of
the hill where the Temple is built is holy. Yes, this is the primary
law of the Temple."   EZEKIEL 43:1-12

$\mathcal{R}$eal Men Don't . . .

PREVIEW

Sometimes having a job means having to make some big ethical choices. For instance, your employer may ask you to do something that is wrong and then tell you that it's not optional. You have to decide whether you're going to go through with it.

This situation is similar to the one in which Shadrach, Meshach, and Abednego find themselves. They each have an important job in the Babylonian government, and they too have a big decision to make. But the consequence they face for upsetting their boss is serious—a decision to do what is right here means death. As you read, determine whether their actions are foolish or courageous.

PERSONAL APPLICATION

Shadrach, Meshach, and Abednego had been ordered to bow down and worship a statue, but they refused. To worship the image would violate God's command in Exodus 20:3, "Do not worship any other gods besides me." When threatened with execution, they still refused. Then they were given one more chance (Daniel 3:15). At that point they could have used any number of excuses for bowing to the image to save their lives ("It's just one time"; "We had no choice"; "It's just a Babylonian custom"; "It isn't so bad"; "We're not hurting anybody"; "We can always say we did it against our will"). But instead of making excuses, Shadrach, Meshach, and Abednego simply obeyed God. The outcome of their courageous decision lay with God, so that is where they left it.

Don't make excuses for wrong choices. Like these young men, have the courage to do what's right. Know that God is pleased with your obedience and trust him to work out the best for the situation.

BIBLE READING

[8]But some of the astrologers went to the king and informed on the Jews. [9]They said to King Nebuchadnezzar, "Long live the king! [10]You issued a decree requiring all the people to bow down and worship the gold statue when they hear the sound of the musical instruments. [11]That decree also states that those who refuse to obey must be thrown into a blazing furnace. [12]But there are some Jews—Shadrach, Meshach, and Abednego—whom you have put in charge of the province of Babylon. They have defied Your Majesty by refusing to serve your gods or to worship the gold statue you have set up."

[13]Then Nebuchadnezzar flew into a rage and ordered Shadrach, Meshach, and Abednego to be brought before him. When they were brought in, [14]Nebuchadnezzar said to them, "Is it true, Shadrach, Meshach, and Abednego, that you refuse to serve my gods or to worship the gold statue I have set up? [15]I will give you one more chance. If you bow down and worship the statue I have made when you hear the sound of the musical instruments, all will be well. But if you refuse, you will be thrown immediately into the blazing furnace. What god will be able to rescue you from my power then?"

[16]Shadrach, Meshach, and Abednego replied, "O Nebuchadnezzar, we do not need to defend ourselves before you. [17]If we are thrown into the blazing furnace, the God whom we serve is able to save us. He will rescue us from your power, Your Majesty. [18]But even if he doesn't, Your Majesty can be sure that we will never serve your gods or worship the gold statue you have set up."

DANIEL 3:8-18

$\mathcal{D}$on't Get Even, Get over It

PREVIEW

Revenge is a natural response. Anyone can do it, and everyone does. Tell others about a time when you responded that way, and they will be able to sympathize with you. It's understandable and logical. It's even intuitive. For many it's a way of life. For a few it's not even an option.

Daniel was one of the few, the humble, the forgiving. In this reading, he learns of the tragic future awaiting King Nebuchadnezzar, a man who has offended Daniel beyond the limits of reason. As you read, notice especially Daniel's attitude toward the king. Daniel sets an example to follow.

PERSONAL APPLICATION

Daniel served King Nebuchadnezzar of Babylon—a mixed blessing. Nebuchadnezzar had destroyed Daniel's home, killed many of Daniel's people, and leveled the temple of Daniel's God. Daniel, the servant of God, was forced to serve an enemy king. Yet as soon as Daniel understood Nebuchadnezzar's dream—foretelling a horrible future for this rogue—he was "aghast" and wondered how to break the news. He even told the king he wished that the dream's foreshadowed judgments would happen to the king's enemies and not to Nebuchadnezzar (Daniel 4:19)! How could Daniel so deeply grieve the fate of an enemy? He had forgiven the king.

You do not have to like or endorse hurtful actions. Perhaps you will even need to put a stop to them. But you *can* forgive the offender. God may even use you in an extraordinary way in that person's life, much as he used Daniel in Nebuchadnezzar's. The next time someone hurts or mistreats you, ask God to help you forgive him or her, and lay aside any plans you may have to get even.

BIBLE READING

[19]"[Daniel] replied, 'Oh, how I wish the events foreshadowed in this dream would happen to your enemies, my lord, and not to you! [20]You saw a tree growing very tall and strong, reaching high into the heavens for all the world to see. [21]It had fresh green leaves, and it was loaded with fruit for all to eat. Wild animals lived in its shade, and birds nested in its branches. [22]That tree, Your Majesty, is you. For you have grown strong and great; your greatness reaches up to heaven, and your rule to the ends of the earth.

[23]"'Then you saw a messenger, a holy one, coming down from heaven and saying, "Cut down the tree and destroy it. But leave the stump and the roots in the ground, bound with a band of iron and bronze and surrounded by tender grass. Let him be drenched with the dew of heaven. Let him eat grass with the animals of the field for seven periods of time."

[24]"'This is what the dream means, Your Majesty, and what the Most High has declared will happen to you. [25]You will be driven from human society, and you will live in the fields with the wild animals. You will eat grass like a cow, and you will be drenched with the dew of heaven. Seven periods of time will pass while you live this way, until you learn that the Most High rules over the kingdoms of the world and gives them to anyone he chooses. [26]But the stump and the roots were left in the ground. This means that you will receive your kingdom back again when you have learned that heaven rules.

[27]"'O King Nebuchadnezzar, please listen to me. Stop sinning and do what is right. Break from your wicked past by being merciful to the poor. Perhaps then you will continue to prosper.'

[28]"But all these things did happen to King Nebuchadnezzar."

DANIEL 4:19–28

 rayer 101

PREVIEW

The word "confession" holds very different meanings for different people. Some think of it as an out-of-date religious custom. Others have good memories of relieving a guilty conscience in the privacy of a confessional. Still others think of the humiliation of secret sins being publicly revealed in a courtroom. What connotations does the word *confession* hold for you?

Confession has an important place in this set of prophecies. All of Daniel 7:1–12:13 concerns the future, and a lot of it does not bode well for God's people. As Daniel learns the bad news, he prays . . . and confesses.

PERSONAL APPLICATION

Daniel loved God and wanted to do God's will, yet the prayer he recorded in Daniel 9 included his confession of sin (Daniel 9:3-19). We have no record of any of Daniel's mistakes or sins. The book of Daniel always portrays him as an exceptional man of God. But even Daniel had offended God (see Romans 3:23-24), and he shared in the guilt of his people's rebellion. So in Daniel's prayers he took responsibility for the sins that he and his people had committed. He didn't gloss over them, excuse them, minimize them, or deny them. He admitted his guilt and placed it in God's merciful hands.

That's the pattern of confession that every believer should follow. Whenever we pray, we should openly admit our sins. We should not deny the faults we have and the sins we commit.

Like Daniel, be honest with God. Confess your sins to him and feel clean, relieved, prepared to serve him—forgiven.

BIBLE READING

[4]I prayed to the LORD my God and confessed: "O Lord, you are a great and awesome God! You always fulfill your promises of unfailing love to those who love you and keep your commands. [5]But we have sinned and done wrong. We have rebelled against you and scorned your commands and regulations. [6]We have refused to listen to your servants the prophets, who spoke your messages to our kings and princes and ancestors and to all the people of the land.

[7]"Lord, you are in the right; but our faces are covered with shame, just as you see us now. This is true of us all, including the people of Judah and Jerusalem and all Israel, scattered near and far, wherever you have driven us because of our disloyalty to you. [8]O LORD, we and our kings, princes, and ancestors are covered with shame because we have sinned against you. [9]But the Lord our God is merciful and forgiving, even though we have rebelled against him. [10]We have not obeyed the LORD our God, for we have not followed the laws he gave us through his servants the prophets. [11]All Israel has disobeyed your law and turned away, refusing to listen to your voice.

[19]"O Lord, hear. O Lord, forgive. O Lord, listen and act! For your own sake, O my God, do not delay, for your people and your city bear your name."   DANIEL 9:4-11, 19

 ruly Devoted

PREVIEW

You can tell how devoted fans are to a team by the way they act when the team isn't winning. You can also tell how devoted a dating couple is by how they act when they're separated by distance. And you can tell how devoted a spouse is by how he or she acts when the partner develops a severe disability.

In this reading, Hosea pays a huge price to maintain his relationship with God. Some people may think this is too high a price to pay, but not Hosea. He is devoted to God, and he obeys God regardless of the cost. As you read Hosea's story, consider whether you would be willing to go that far for God.

PERSONAL APPLICATION

God often required extraordinary obedience from his prophets. For Hosea that meant marrying a woman who would be unfaithful to him (Hosea 1:2-3). But God had good reasons for commanding Hosea to do this. Through this marriage God would illustrate the way Israel had been unfaithful to him despite the fact that he remained faithful to them.

Sometimes God's commands make no sense to us at all, and the obligation to obey them seems really unattractive. But those who devote themselves to God, like Hosea, obey his teachings and commands without hesitation.

Always obey God, even if you don't understand his purposes. He has given us his commands for our own good, and he will reward us with more than we deserve for obeying him. What has God told you to do that you have put off? Obey him in response to his love for you.

BIBLE READING

[2]When the LORD first began speaking to Israel through Hosea, he said to him, "Go and marry a prostitute, so some of her children will be born to you from other men. This will illustrate the way my people have been untrue to me, openly committing adultery against the LORD by worshiping other gods."

[3]So Hosea married Gomer, the daughter of Diblaim, and she became pregnant and gave Hosea a son. [4]And the LORD said, "Name the child Jezreel, for I am about to punish King Jehu's dynasty to avenge the murders he committed at Jezreel. [5]In fact, I will put an end to Israel's independence by breaking its military power in the Jezreel Valley."

[6]Soon Gomer became pregnant again and gave birth to a daughter. And the LORD said to Hosea, "Name your daughter Lo-ruhamah—'Not loved'—for I will no longer show love to the people of Israel or forgive them. [7]But I, the LORD their God, will show love to the people of Judah. I will personally free them from their enemies without any help from weapons or armies."

[8]After Gomer had weaned Lo-ruhamah, she again became pregnant and gave birth to a second son. [9]And the LORD said, "Name him Lo-ammi—'Not my people'—for Israel is not my people, and I am not their God. [10]Yet the time will come when Israel will prosper and become a great nation. In that day its people will be like the sands of the seashore—too many to count! Then, at the place where they were told, 'You are not my people,' it will be said, 'You are children of the living God.' [11]Then the people of Judah and Israel will unite under one leader, and they will return from exile together. What a day that will be—the day of Jezreel —when God will again plant his people in his land." HOSEA 1:2-11

Not Going Down with the Ship

PREVIEW

Steve Johnson is captain of the USS Maxum, a small but capable boat that can hold up to twelve passengers and crew. As captain, Steve has many responsibilities, but foremost is the safety of those on board. It's his job to make sure the boat is safe to operate and that everyone on board always gets to shore safely, no matter what. The people on board are his responsibility—that's what it means to be captain.

The leaders of Israel also have a responsibility for others. But they have been irresponsible—they've neglected their duty to teach and guide the people in God's ways. When Hosea confronts them about this, they try to shift the blame to someone else. Like bad ship captains, they have sunk the ship and stolen all the lifeboats. As you read this section of Scripture, look for the lessons on leadership.

PERSONAL APPLICATION

The priests had dropped their responsibility to correctly lead. Instead of instructing the nation in religion and morality, they had led the way toward idolatry and immorality. Yet they didn't want to face the consequences. When their sins came under scrutiny, they tried to divert attention from themselves to the people. They tried to justify their own irresponsible actions by pointing to the sins of others. But the sins of others didn't exonerate them.

All of us share a mandate to lead others—by setting an example if not by holding a position or responsibility (see 1 Timothy 4:12). The fact that some people won't follow doesn't excuse us from leading the way.

Take responsibility for the people who follow you. Teach them, guide them, and lead them in God's way.

BIBLE READING

¹Hear the word of the LORD, O people of Israel! The LORD has filed a lawsuit against you, saying: "There is no faithfulness, no kindness, no knowledge of God in your land. ²You curse and lie and kill and steal and commit adultery. There is violence everywhere, with one murder after another. ³That is why your land is not producing. It is filled with sadness, and all living things are becoming sick and dying. Even the animals, birds, and fish have begun to disappear.

⁴"Don't point your finger at someone else and try to pass the blame! Look, you priests, my complaint is with you! ⁵As a sentence for your crimes, you will stumble in broad daylight, just as you might at night, and so will your false prophets. And I will destroy your mother, Israel. ⁶My people are being destroyed because they don't know me. It is all your fault, you priests, for you yourselves refuse to know me. Now I refuse to recognize you as my priests. Since you have forgotten the laws of your God, I will forget to bless your children. ⁷The more priests there are, the more they sin against me. They have exchanged the glory of God for the disgrace of idols.

⁸"The priests get fed when the people sin and bring their sin offerings to them. So the priests are glad when the people sin! ⁹'Like priests, like people'—since the priests are wicked, the people are wicked, too. So now I will punish both priests and people for all their wicked deeds. ¹⁰They will eat and still be hungry. Though they do a big business as prostitutes, they will have no children, for they have deserted the LORD to worship other gods."   HOSEA 4:1-10

Honey, This Applies to You!

PREVIEW

When sitting in church, married people can often think of a thousand ways that their spouse should put the sermon they're hearing to good use. *More patience, less judging—yes, that's what he (or she) needs. If only my spouse would listen.*

In this reading, Hosea is talking directly to the Israelites. They have a tendency of finding fault with others far away. They need to take a good look in the mirror before pointing fingers.

That's not all Israel needs to do, however. There are more good lessons in this passage for them to hear, if they're willing: lessons such as how a person reaps what he or she sows; the cost of serving false gods; and prosperity not being an indicator of God's approval.

PERSONAL APPLICATION

God said, "Even though I gave them all my laws, they act as if those laws don't apply to them." (Hosea 8:12). The Israelites needed to look at how the laws applied to them, not to others. Anyone can listen to a sermon and think of other people who need to hear it. Everyone, at least occasionally, reads the Bible, comes upon a great truth, and thinks, "If only so and so would do what this passage teaches!" When we do that, we miss the point. God has given the message to *us,* and that's where the response must begin. Maybe the person we have in mind does need to change, but even then the best way to change him or her involves setting a good example ourselves.

Whenever you encounter a rule to live by, apply it to yourself first. Then pray for others who you think could also benefit from it.

BIBLE READING

[1]"Sound the alarm! The enemy descends like an eagle on the people of the LORD, for they have broken my covenant and revolted against my law. [2]Now Israel pleads with me, 'Help us, for you are our God!' [3]But it is too late! The people of Israel have rejected what is good, and now their enemies will chase after them. [4]The people have appointed kings and princes, but not with my consent. By making idols for themselves from their silver and gold, they have brought about their own destruction.

[5]"O Samaria, I reject this calf—this idol you have made. My fury burns against you. How long will you be incapable of innocence? [6]This calf you worship was crafted by your own hands! It is not God! Therefore, it must be smashed to bits.

[7]"They have planted the wind and will harvest the whirlwind. The stalks of wheat wither, producing no grain. And if there is any grain, foreigners will eat it. [8]The people of Israel have been swallowed up; they lie among the nations like an old pot that no one wants. [9]Like a wild donkey looking for a mate, they have gone up to Assyria. The people of Israel have sold themselves to many lovers. [10]But though they have sold themselves to many lands, I will now gather them together. Then they will writhe under the burden of the great king!

[11]"Israel has built many altars to take away sin, but these very altars became places for sinning! [12]Even though I gave them all my laws, they act as if those laws don't apply to them. [13]The people of Israel love their rituals of sacrifice, but to me their sacrifices are all meaningless! I will call my people to account for their sins, and I will punish them. They will go back down to Egypt.

[14]"Israel has built great palaces, and Judah has fortified its cities. But they have both forgotten their Maker. Therefore, I will send down fire on their palaces and burn their fortresses."

HOSEA 8:1-14

Love Versus Justice

PREVIEW

The issue of reducing crime presents many dilemmas. Some believe that spending more money on social programs will help reduce the number of people who turn to crime as an alternative lifestyle. Others believe building more prisons and increasing the length of prison sentences will deter people from committing crimes. Each view has good and bad points. But neither is balanced. One involves love or caring without justice—the other uses justice without love or caring.

Hosea brings a simple message to God's people in this passage regarding the love-and-justice tug-of-war. As you read, look for God's desire that his people concern themselves with both love and justice.

PERSONAL APPLICATION

Hosea's people neither looked out for others nor transacted business honestly or fairly. God's prescription for their sins involved making a simple, two-sided adjustment: living by love and living by justice (Hosea 12:6).

Love and justice lie at the very foundation of God's character. If we are to live rightly at all, we must begin there. Some people love others so much that they excuse all wrongdoing. Others insist so vigorously on being just that they ignore the effects of their actions on people. But love without justice, because it aims at a low standard, leaves people in their sins. Justice without love, because it aims at an impossibly high standard, drives people away from God. We need to live by both principles, in imitation of God's character.

Consider your relationships at work, in the community, at church, and in your home. How should you act in order to be more loving? What should you change to be more just?

BIBLE READING

¹The people of Israel feed on the wind; they chase after the east wind all day long. They multiply lies and violence; they make alliances with Assyria and cut deals with the Egyptians.

²Now the LORD is bringing a lawsuit against Judah. He is about to punish Jacob for all his deceitful ways. ³Before Jacob was born, he struggled with his brother; when he became a man, he even fought with God. ⁴Yes, he wrestled with the angel and won. He wept and pleaded for a blessing from him. There at Bethel he met God face to face, and God spoke to him —⁵the LORD God Almighty, the LORD is his name! ⁶So now, come back to your God! Act on the principles of love and justice, and always live in confident dependence on your God.

⁷But no, the people are like crafty merchants selling from dishonest scales—they love to cheat. ⁸Israel boasts, "I am rich, and I've gotten it all by myself! No one can say I got it by cheating! My record is spotless!"

⁹"I am the LORD your God, who rescued you from your slavery in Egypt. And I will make you live in tents again, as you do each year when you celebrate the Festival of Shelters. ¹⁰I sent my prophets to warn you with many visions and parables."

¹¹But Gilead is filled with sinners who worship idols. And in Gilgal, too, they sacrifice bulls; their altars are lined up like the heaps of stone along the edges of a plowed field. ¹²Jacob fled to the land of Aram and earned a wife by tending sheep. ¹³Then the LORD led Jacob's descendants, the Israelites, out of Egypt by a prophet, who guided and protected them. ¹⁴But the people of Israel have bitterly provoked the LORD, so their Lord will now sentence them to death in payment for their sins.

HOSEA 12:1-14

The Bright Side of Dark

PREVIEW

If you could convey one message to the next generation, what would it be? What piece of invaluable advice would you pass on to them? Would it be financial, political, spiritual, or something else?

In this passage, the prophet Joel urges parents to pass on to their children the stories he is about to tell them—to open up the details of their past, to tell what has happened to them, to reveal the hidden details that kids would never know. They're not pleasant stories, but they contain a valuable lesson: Obey God or endure the consequences.

PERSONAL APPLICATION

God urged the parents of Judah to tell their children all about the terrible events that Joel was about to describe. God wanted them to pass along the important lessons they learned through these horrible events (Joel 1:3).

Is there any point in telling others about the downturns you've had because of bad choices? After all, some people think they have nothing to offer. They think that their mistakes have canceled out all successes, leaving them nothing to share. But they are wrong. God can use people's wounds to heal others. The apostle Paul, for example, wrote, "All these events happened to them as examples for us. They were written down to warn us" (see 1 Corinthians 10:11).

Give younger people your own testimony of God's truth—disobeying God can bring pain and consequences—and you do them a world of good. Telling these stories can help others avoid your mistakes and duplicate your successes. God can use your wounds to heal others. God's rebukes and lessons to you can help teach others, especially if the lessons were painful or difficult to learn.

BIBLE READING

¹The LORD gave this message to Joel son of Pethuel.

²Hear this, you leaders of the people! Everyone listen! In all your history, has anything like this ever happened before? ³Tell your children about it in the years to come. Pass the awful story down from generation to generation. ⁴After the cutting locusts finished eating the crops, the swarming locusts took what was left! After them came the hopping locusts, and then the stripping locusts, too!

⁵Wake up, you drunkards, and weep! All the grapes are ruined, and all your new wine is gone! ⁶A vast army of locusts has invaded my land. It is a terrible army, too numerous to count! Its teeth are as sharp as the teeth of lions! ⁷They have destroyed my grapevines and fig trees, stripping their bark and leaving the branches white and bare.

⁸Weep with sorrow, as a virgin weeps when her fiancé has died. ⁹There is no grain or wine to offer at the Temple of the LORD. The priests are mourning because there are no offerings. Listen to the weeping of these ministers of the LORD! ¹⁰The fields are ruined and empty of crops. The grain, the wine, and the olive oil are gone.

¹¹Despair, all you farmers! Wail, all you vine growers! Weep, because the wheat and barley—yes, all the field crops—are ruined. ¹²The grapevines and the fig trees have all withered. The pomegranate trees, palm trees, and apple trees—yes, all the fruit trees—have dried up. All joy has dried up with them. JOEL 1:1-12

udgment Day

PREVIEW

He stands on the street corner every day, trumpeting a message of warning and doom. "The world is going to end soon," he says. "You'd better repent now while there's still time."

In this reading, Joel sounds like a doomsaying street preacher. But not all of his news is bad. For those who love the Lord, Joel's message is filled with hope. The Lord will be gentle with his people. For his enemies, however . . . it's not too late to repent!

PERSONAL APPLICATION

Joel's messages included many references to the "Day of the Lord," a final day of judgment that still lay in the future. On that final judgment day, every person who has ever lived—dead, living, and yet to be born—will face God (Joel 3:2, 12, 14).

Today many people don't believe in a final day of judgment. Some even mock the idea, pointing to the many doomsayers who have come and gone with their warnings unfulfilled. But we don't disbelieve in medical science because some doctors are quacks. Likewise, we shouldn't disbelieve the Bible's prophecies because of false prophets in the present day.

God has told us that we will be held accountable for our actions, and we will. We need to acknowledge and prepare for that time.

To be prepared for the Judgment Day, live according to God's Word, and tell others of his love for them. Let the coming Day of the Lord motivate you to action.

BIBLE READING

[12]"Let the nations be called to arms. Let them march to the valley of Jehoshaphat. There I, the LORD, will sit to pronounce judgment on them all. [13]Now let the sickle do its work, for the harvest is ripe. Come, tread the winepress because it is full. The storage vats are overflowing with the wickedness of these people."

[14]Thousands upon thousands are waiting in the valley of decision. It is there that the day of the LORD will soon arrive. [15]The sun and moon will grow dark, and the stars will no longer shine. [16]The Lord's voice will roar from Zion and thunder from Jerusalem, and the earth and heavens will begin to shake. But to his people of Israel, the LORD will be a welcoming refuge and a strong fortress.

[17]"Then you will know that I, the LORD your God, live in Zion, my holy mountain. Jerusalem will be holy forever, and foreign armies will never conquer her again. [18]In that day the mountains will drip with sweet wine, and the hills will flow with milk. Water will fill the dry streambeds of Judah, and a fountain will burst forth from the Lord's Temple, watering the arid valley of acacias. [19]Egypt will become a wasteland and Edom a wilderness, because they attacked Judah and killed her innocent people.

[20]"But Judah will remain forever, and Jerusalem will endure through all future generations. [21]I will pardon my people's crimes, which I have not yet pardoned; and I, the LORD, will make my home in Jerusalem with my people."   JOEL 3:12-21

Touchdown

Preview

If you follow football, you know that the game has seen a lot of changes over the past decade. Of all the changes though, the worst one has to be the new attitudes of many who play. These players often act cocky, intimidating, and unsportsmanlike.

In this set of prophecies, Amos takes aim at cockiness and unfettered bravado. Arrogant warriors, beware. God is not impressed.

Amos's other prophecies in this reading contain clues that God doesn't always respect what we do. Note, for example, what God can do with a mere shepherd and fig grower. Second, mark God's words toward some upper class types who exploit the poor while giving extra tithes and sacrifices. It's kind of sobering.

Personal Application

Television and movies bombard us with heroes (and heroines) who defy death and all foes with a huge arsenal of skill, tools, intelligence, luck, and bravado. Because of their incredible fortune, they appear to fear nothing. Many people try to model their lives after these fake images, even though their heroes don't exist in real life. They try to be like these cellophane gods: tough, indestructible, and fearless. But God is not impressed with skill or bravado. He says that even the best, most skilled, and toughest people will be terrified when his judgment comes (Amos 2:16). And it *will* come.

Don't be swayed by the self-assured rhetoric of those who think they can make it through life without God. Don't let them lead you to conceit—don't trust in your own brain power, skill, or bravado. God fears no one, and one day all people will fear him.

BIBLE READING

⁴This is what the LORD says: "The people of Judah have sinned again and again, and I will not forget it. I will not let them go unpunished any longer! They have rejected the laws of the LORD, refusing to obey him. They have been led astray by the same lies that deceived their ancestors. ⁵So I will send down fire on Judah, and all the fortresses of Jerusalem will be destroyed."

⁶This is what the LORD says: "The people of Israel have sinned again and again, and I will not forget it. I will not let them go unpunished any longer! They have perverted justice by selling honest people for silver and poor people for a pair of sandals. ⁷They trample helpless people in the dust and deny justice to those who are oppressed. Both father and son sleep with the same woman, corrupting my holy name. ⁸At their religious festivals, they lounge around in clothing stolen from their debtors. In the house of their god, they present offerings of wine purchased with stolen money.

⁹"Yet think of all I did for my people! I destroyed the Amorites before my people arrived in the land. The Amorites were as tall as cedar trees and strong as oaks, but I destroyed their fruit and dug out their roots. ¹⁰It was I who rescued you from Egypt and led you through the desert for forty years so you could possess the land of the Amorites. ¹¹I chose some of your sons to be prophets and others to be Nazirites. Can you deny this, my people of Israel?" asks the LORD. ¹²"But you caused the Nazirites to sin by making them drink your wine, and you said to my prophets, 'Shut up!'

¹³"So I will make you groan as a wagon groans when it is loaded down with grain. ¹⁴Your fastest runners will not get away. The strongest among you will become weak. Even the mightiest warriors will be unable to save themselves. ¹⁵The archers will fail to stand their ground. The swiftest soldiers won't be fast enough to escape. Even warriors on horses won't be able to outrun the danger. ¹⁶On that day, the most courageous of your fighting men will drop their weapons and run for their lives. I, the LORD, have spoken!"

AMOS 2:4–16

 oor Talk

PREVIEW

How many times have you heard this scenario: Someone who is falsely accused can't afford a good lawyer and ends up being convicted. Or someone who is guilty but has money hires a good lawyer and goes free. For the poor, justice never seems to be affordable.

In this reading, you will find Amos accusing God's people of denying justice to the poor. "Stop cheating the poor and start helping them," Amos says.

You will also see that this isn't the only sin on Israel's record. The rap sheet God has on them is a mile long.

PERSONAL APPLICATION

Amos prophesied against the people of Israel for neglecting and abusing powerless people (Amos 5:12). They favored the rich, took bribes, and exploited the poor.

Today we have our own excuses for not helping the poor or speaking out against those who exploit them ("They don't deserve help"; "I don't know any poor people"; "I've got to look out for myself"; "Any money I give will just be wasted or stolen"; "No one will listen to me—I'm not important"; "The little bit I could give wouldn't make any difference"). We still have a responsibility, however, to care for the poor just as much as the people of Israel did. To neglect them is sin.

What programs to help the needy does your church sponsor? With what poverty-fighting community groups could you work? In what mercy ministry can you serve? As an individual, you may think that you can't accomplish much, but with the love of God in your heart you can. And when you join with others who care, the difference you can make will be even more apparent.

BIBLE READING

[6]Come back to the LORD and live! If you don't, he will roar through Israel like a fire, devouring you completely. Your gods in Bethel certainly won't be able to quench the flames! [7]You wicked people! You twist justice, making it a bitter pill for the poor and oppressed. Righteousness and fair play are meaningless fictions to you.

[8]It is the LORD who created the stars, the Pleiades and Orion. It is he who turns darkness into morning and day into night. It is he who draws up water from the oceans and pours it down as rain on the land. The LORD is his name! [9]With blinding speed and power he destroys the strong, crushing all their defenses.

[10]How you hate honest judges! How you despise people who tell the truth! [11]You trample the poor and steal what little they have through taxes and unfair rent. Therefore, you will never live in the beautiful stone houses you are building. You will never drink wine from the lush vineyards you are planting. [12]For I know the vast number of your sins and rebellions. You oppress good people by taking bribes and deprive the poor of justice in the courts. [13]So those who are wise will keep quiet, for it is an evil time.

[14]Do what is good and run from evil—that you may live! Then the LORD God Almighty will truly be your helper, just as you have claimed he is. [15]Hate evil and love what is good; remodel your courts into true halls of justice. Perhaps even yet the LORD God Almighty will have mercy on his people who remain.

[16]Therefore, this is what the Lord, the LORD God Almighty, says: "There will be crying in all the public squares and in every street. Call for the farmers to weep with you, and summon professional mourners to wail and lament. [17]There will be wailing in every vineyard, for I will pass through and destroy them all. I, the LORD, have spoken!"   AMOS 5:6-17

You Don't Know What You've Got Till It's Gone

PREVIEW

It's funny how we appreciate some things only after they're gone. The kids grow up and move away, and suddenly the house is much too quiet. Or the job we once called boring now looks like the best one we ever had. Whether we took it for granted or not, something good has come and gone, and how we miss it now!

As Amos continues prophesying against Israel and Judah, his words reveal one precious commodity that they are about to lose: God's Word. Up to this point they haven't seen its value. They've taken it for granted and left it unused. It will soon be gone and someday they will miss it—the day when they need it most.

That's why Amos sees visions of judgment, from which no one can escape. Fortunately for those who listen, the visions also include promise of restoration (a constant theme from our God, who disciplines those he loves). As you read this passage, consider how much you really value God's Word.

PERSONAL APPLICATION

The people to whom Amos preached wanted nothing to do with God's Word. Though they had the law of Moses, they ignored it. When God graciously sent prophets like Amos to warn the Israelites to pay attention to his Word, they ignored that, too. They didn't want to hear what God had to say. It is no wonder, then, that the day would come when all this apathy toward Scripture would come back to haunt them. They would crave the opportunity to hear his Word and not be able to find it anywhere—taken for granted and taken away (Amos 8:11-13).

Amos's message speaks to us as well. We disregard the Bible to our own peril. If we set it aside, the day may come when we will need it and it will be gone. How we treat the Bible each day makes a huge difference.

BIBLE READING

[4]Listen to this, you who rob the poor and trample the needy! [5]You can't wait for the Sabbath day to be over and the religious festivals to end so you can get back to cheating the helpless. You measure out your grain in false measures and weigh it out on dishonest scales. [6]And you mix the wheat you sell with chaff swept from the floor! Then you enslave poor people for a debt of one piece of silver or a pair of sandals.

[7]Now the LORD has sworn this oath by his own name, the Pride of Israel: "I will never forget the wicked things you have done! [8]The earth will tremble for your deeds, and everyone will mourn. The land will rise up like the Nile River at floodtime, toss about, and sink again. [9]At that time," says the Sovereign LORD, "I will make the sun go down at noon and darken the earth while it is still day. [10]I will turn your celebrations into times of mourning, and your songs of joy will be turned to weeping. You will wear funeral clothes and shave your heads as signs of sorrow, as if your only son had died. How very bitter that day will be!

[11]"The time is surely coming," says the Sovereign LORD, "when I will send a famine on the land—not a famine of bread or water but of hearing the words of the LORD. [12]People will stagger everywhere from sea to sea, searching for the word of the LORD, running here and going there, but they will not find it. [13]Beautiful girls and fine young men will grow faint and weary, thirsting for the Lord's word. [14]And those who worship and swear by the idols of Samaria, Dan, and Beersheba will fall down, never to rise again."

AMOS 8:4-14

Investing in Securities

PREVIEW

Everyone gets a sense of security from something or someone. For young children, security may be found in a blanket or the arms of a parent. For adults it may be in a career, a big salary, or a relationship with a spouse.

Obadiah's little book is about securities—false securities to be exact. Edom, one of Israel's neighbors, has developed a false sense of security in the safety of their homeland (the cliffs, crags, and caves of Petra in modern-day Jordan). Their sense of security may have even led them to commit hateful acts against Israel. As you read, you will see that despite Edom's strategic location, they are not invulnerable. God will make sure of that.

PERSONAL APPLICATION

The Edomites felt secure and were proud of their self-sufficiency. They lived in homes protected by high, inaccessible cliffs. Looking around, they analyzed their situation and thought: "Who can ever reach us way up here?" (Obadiah 1:3). God didn't appreciate their pride, however, and he wasn't happy with the way they were treating Israel (their relatives through Esau). Therefore, God sent Obadiah to the Edomites with a message of impending doom: The security they found in the cliffs would be their downfall, literally, as their friends and allies would turn against them and take their land.

Placing one's security in something other than God, such as a job, a family, a retirement plan, a relationship, or intellect is foolish—they can disappear in a moment. Only God is strong, sure, lasting, and trustworthy. Only he can supply true security.

Don't be like the Edomites. Don't rely only on yourself and your position. Recognize your vulnerability, ask God for help, and find your security in him.

BIBLE READING

²The LORD says, "I will cut you down to size among the nations, Edom; you will be small and despised. ³You are proud because you live in a rock fortress and make your home high in the mountains. 'Who can ever reach us way up here?' you ask boastfully. Don't fool yourselves! ⁴Though you soar as high as eagles and build your nest among the stars, I will bring you crashing down. I, the LORD, have spoken!

⁷"All your allies will turn against you. They will help to chase you from your land. They will promise you peace, while plotting your destruction. Your trusted friends will set traps for you, and you won't even know about it. ⁸At that time not a single wise person will be left in the whole land of Edom!" says the LORD. "For on the mountains of Edom I will destroy everyone who has wisdom and understanding. ⁹The mightiest warriors of Teman will be terrified, and everyone on the mountains of Edom will be cut down in the slaughter.

¹⁰"And why? Because of the violence you did to your close relatives in Israel. Now you will be destroyed completely and filled with shame forever. ¹¹For you deserted your relatives in Israel during their time of greatest need. You stood aloof, refusing to lift a finger to help when foreign invaders carried off their wealth and cast lots to divide up Jerusalem. You acted as though you were one of Israel's enemies.

¹²"You shouldn't have done this! You shouldn't have gloated when they exiled your relatives to distant lands. You shouldn't have rejoiced because they were suffering such misfortune. You shouldn't have crowed over them as they suffered these disasters. ¹³You shouldn't have plundered the land of Israel when they were suffering such calamity. You shouldn't have gloated over the destruction of your relatives, looting their homes and making yourselves rich at their expense."   OBADIAH 1:1-4, 7-13

Getting Away from It All

PREVIEW

People have strong feelings about cities. Some feel loyal to a particular city because that's their hometown, they have fond memories of a recent visit, or their favorite sports team resides there. Others absolutely detest certain cities because of a sports team rivalry, a bad experience during a recent visit, or a misunderstanding of the people who live there.

Jonah, one of God's prophets, has strong feelings toward a certain Assyrian city called Nineveh, and for good reason. The Assyrians were Israel's bitter enemies, and Ninevah stood as the symbol of evil. So when Jonah gets a call from God to go to Ninevah to warn them about God's judgment, he takes off running—in the opposite direction. But his travel plans end up taking a detour. In this passage, find a lesson about obeying God, no matter what.

PERSONAL APPLICATION

Every change for the better begins by giving up the attempt to flee and surrendering to God's will. We sometimes pull the same stunts as Jonah. Like him, we cannot get away with them forever. Sooner or later God will call us back.

From what responsibilities have you tried to run away? Has God been urging you to reconcile with an enemy, to reach out to someone obnoxious and uncaring, or to help a person who has wronged you in the past? In what ways have you tried to run from God? Stop running and surrender to the Lord. Go his direction; do his appointed task.

BIBLE READING

¹The LORD gave this message to Jonah son of Amittai: ²"Get up and go to the great city of Nineveh! Announce my judgment against it because I have seen how wicked its people are."

³But Jonah got up and went in the opposite direction in order to get away from the LORD. He went down to the seacoast, to the port of Joppa, where he found a ship leaving for Tarshish. He bought a ticket and went on board, hoping that by going away to the west he could escape from the LORD.

⁴But as the ship was sailing along, suddenly the LORD flung a powerful wind over the sea, causing a violent storm that threatened to send them to the bottom. ⁵Fearing for their lives, the desperate sailors shouted to their gods for help and threw the cargo overboard to lighten the ship. And all this time Jonah was sound asleep down in the hold. ⁶So the captain went down after him. "How can you sleep at a time like this?" he shouted. "Get up and pray to your god! Maybe he will have mercy on us and spare our lives."

¹²"Throw me into the sea," Jonah said, "and it will become calm again. For I know that this terrible storm is all my fault."

¹³Instead, the sailors tried even harder to row the boat ashore. But the stormy sea was too violent for them, and they couldn't make it. ¹⁴Then they cried out to the LORD, Jonah's God. "O LORD," they pleaded, "don't make us die for this man's sin. And don't hold us responsible for his death, because it isn't our fault. O LORD, you have sent this storm upon him for your own good reasons."

¹⁵Then the sailors picked Jonah up and threw him into the raging sea, and the storm stopped at once! ¹⁶The sailors were awestruck by the Lord's great power, and they offered him a sacrifice and vowed to serve him.   JONAH 1:1-6, 12-16

*I*t's a Mad, Mad World

PREVIEW

If you want an example of anger, look no further than Jonah. He finally gets around to doing what God wants him to do, preaching to the people of Ninevah. Jonah would rather *not* be doing this, however; so when it goes well, he'd just as soon call it a loss. God would rather teach him a lesson about his anger.

In this reading, you will see an amazing picture of God's mercy. You will also find the lessons that it's never too late for repentance and that sometimes believers have bad reasons for being angry.

PERSONAL APPLICATION

Sometimes we wish only that terrible suffering or judgment would come upon evil people. Even David expressed those very wishes in many of the psalms that he wrote (see Psalms 3, 7, 28, 35, 54, 55, 58, 109, 140, 141, 143). But God is more merciful than we can imagine, and he feels compassion for the sinners that we want him to punish. Because of his great mercy, God devises plans to bring sinners to himself. David realized this. And although David hated wicked people, he also prayed for God's glory and that all people would come to know the Lord.

What is your attitude toward those who are especially wicked? Do you want them destroyed? Or do you wish that they could experience God's mercy and forgiveness? Pray for people who need to know God. Hate their evil deeds, but do what you can to persuade them to follow Christ. In addition, keep in mind that in many ways you too were once like the wicked and that God has been more merciful to you than you may ever realize.

BIBLE READING

¹This change of plans upset Jonah, and he became very angry. ²So
he complained to the LORD about it: "Didn't I say before I left
home that you would do this, LORD? That is why I ran away to
Tarshish! I knew that you were a gracious and compassionate
God, slow to get angry and filled with unfailing love. I knew how
easily you could cancel your plans for destroying these people.
³Just kill me now, LORD! I'd rather be dead than alive because
nothing I predicted is going to happen."

⁴The LORD replied, "Is it right for you to be angry about
this?"

⁵Then Jonah went out to the east side of the city and made a
shelter to sit under as he waited to see if anything would happen
to the city. ⁶And the LORD God arranged for a leafy plant to grow
there, and soon it spread its broad leaves over Jonah's head,
shading him from the sun. This eased some of his discomfort,
and Jonah was very grateful for the plant.

⁷But God also prepared a worm! The next morning at dawn
the worm ate through the stem of the plant, so that it soon died
and withered away. ⁸And as the sun grew hot, God sent a scorch-
ing east wind to blow on Jonah. The sun beat down on his head
until he grew faint and wished to die. "Death is certainly better
than this!" he exclaimed.

⁹Then God said to Jonah, "Is it right for you to be angry
because the plant died?"

"Yes," Jonah retorted, "even angry enough to die!"

¹⁰Then the LORD said, "You feel sorry about the plant, though
you did nothing to put it there. And a plant is only, at best, short
lived. ¹¹But Nineveh has more than 120,000 people living in
spiritual darkness, not to mention all the animals. Shouldn't I
feel sorry for such a great city?"   JONAH 4:1-11

$\mathcal{D}$irty Rotten Scoundrels

PREVIEW

When was the last time you lay awake at night eagerly awaiting the next day? Perhaps it was an upcoming fishing trip that you and Dad had been planning for weeks. Or maybe it was Christmas Eve, and you just couldn't get your mind off the presents, lights, excitement, cookies, and music.

Micah's prophecies comment on the thoughts for the next day that kept Israelites up at night. But their anticipation involves trips and activities far different than fishing and holiday decorating—theirs were plans for fraud, threats, and violence. That's why Micah's prophecies include visions of judgment for both Israel and Judah and messages directed to the kings who could have stopped it.

PERSONAL APPLICATION

Today, many people fall prey to the ambitions of the powerful. Some lose their houses, jobs, life savings, and even their lives. Some of these wrongs are protected by the law. But just because the law allows us to do something doesn't mean that we should do it. Taking away people's possessions "by fraud and violence" invites God's judgment.

Never use position or power to take what you want by force. Instead, be content with what God has blessed you with, and rely on him to provide for your needs and fulfill your heart's desire.

BIBLE READING

¹How terrible it will be for you who lie awake at night, thinking up evil plans. You rise at dawn and hurry to carry out any of the wicked schemes you have power to accomplish. ²When you want a certain piece of land, you find a way to seize it. When you want someone's house, you take it by fraud and violence. No one's family or inheritance is safe with you around!

³But this is what the LORD says: "I will reward your evil with evil; you won't be able to escape! After I am through with you, none of you will ever again walk proudly in the streets."

⁴In that day your enemies will make fun of you by singing this song of despair about your experience:

"We are finished,
    completely ruined!
God has confiscated our land,
    taking it from us.
He has given our fields
    to those who betrayed us."

¹²"Someday, O Israel, I will gather the few of you who are left. I will bring you together again like sheep in a fold, like a flock in its pasture. Yes, your land will again be filled with noisy crowds! ¹³Your leader will break out and lead you out of exile. He will bring you through the gates of your cities of captivity, back to your own land. Your king will lead you; the LORD himself will guide you."   MICAH 2:1-4, 12-13

t Your Service

PREVIEW

Many people regard teaching as an underpaid profession. "Teach because you love it," they say, "don't do it for the money. The hours are long and the hassles are plenty." The same could be said for related professions, such as preaching and social work.

Ironically, this set of prophecies contains a harsh message for some preachers and teachers who have found a way around their profession's classic compensation problem. But their cure is worse than the disease, and God says it's *not* all right.

Micah's words also contain one promise that is still to be fulfilled, and another that already has been, and is still being, celebrated.

PERSONAL APPLICATION

Some of Micah's sternest words condemned religious leaders who accepted bribes or who ministered only if they were compensated well for their work (Micah 3:11). The priests and prophets of Israel had come to love money more than their jobs—a serious problem of inverted values.

When Christians preach or teach for personal rewards, the point of their ministry evaporates. "Ministering" means "serving."

Whenever you serve or minister to others, do it cheerfully and willingly—for Christ—even if no one pays or rewards you for it. And encourage other Christian workers to do the same by never using your giving to impose your preferences on them.

BIBLE READING

¹Listen, you leaders of Israel! You are supposed to know right from wrong, ²but you are the very ones who hate good and love evil. You skin my people alive and tear the flesh off their bones. ³You eat my people's flesh, cut away their skin, and break their bones. You chop them up like meat for the cooking pot. ⁴Then you beg the LORD for help in times of trouble! Do you really expect him to listen? After all the evil you have done, he won't even look at you!

⁵This is what the LORD says to you false prophets: "You are leading my people astray! You promise peace for those who give you food, but you declare war on anyone who refuses to pay you. ⁶Now the night will close around you, cutting off all your visions. Darkness will cover you, making it impossible for you to predict the future. The sun will set for you prophets, and your day will come to an end. ⁷Then you seers will cover your faces in shame, and you diviners will be disgraced. And you will admit that your messages were not from God."

⁸But as for me, I am filled with power and the Spirit of the LORD. I am filled with justice and might, fearlessly pointing out Israel's sin and rebellion. ⁹Listen to me, you leaders of Israel! You hate justice and twist all that is right. ¹⁰You are building Jerusalem on a foundation of murder and corruption. ¹¹You rulers govern for the bribes you can get; you priests teach God's laws only for a price; you prophets won't prophesy unless you are paid. Yet all of you claim you are depending on the LORD. "No harm can come to us," you say, "for the LORD is here among us."

¹²So because of you, Mount Zion will be plowed like an open field; Jerusalem will be reduced to rubble! A great forest will grow on the hilltop, where the Temple now stands.

MICAH 3:1-12

o Deals

PREVIEW

The only thing worse than giving the sales pitch for a defective piece of merchandise is falling for it. Has that ever happened to you? At first you say no, but the insistent salesperson keeps at you until you cave in. Suddenly you feel like part of the problem. "Never again," you vow.

In this reading of Micah's prophecies you will see that the people of Israel tried to sell God on a bad idea. They thought that he could be bought or bribed into changing his mind about their sins. But a holy God won't exchange sacrifices for permission to sin. "No deal," God says.

PERSONAL APPLICATION

Israel had forgotten how kind God had been to them. As a result, they were ungrateful and unresponsive to him and became cheaters, liars, and blackmailers. When Micah explained that they would suffer God's judgment for their sins, they tried to make a deal with God. "What's your price?" they asked him. "What do you want us to give you to leave us alone? Do you want more sacrifices?" Basically, the people wanted to continue sinning, appeasing God with some sort of penance or payment. But Micah told the Israelites that God wasn't interested in their offer and that he wanted them "to do what is right, to love mercy, and to walk humbly with [their] God" (Micah 6: 8).

God cannot be bought, and we should not attempt to purchase the right to sin with confessions, penances, or sacrifices. We cannot "balance out" our bad deeds with good ones. Pleasing God means giving up all our sins, even the ones we love dearly, and living by God's standards of righteousness, as we depend on his help and presence at every step.

When you give to God, do it out of love and obedience, not out of a desire to buy him off.

BIBLE READING

¹Listen to what the LORD is saying: "Stand up and state your case against me. Let the mountains and hills be called to witness your complaints.

²"And now, O mountains, listen to the LORD's complaint! He has a case against his people Israel! He will prosecute them to the full extent of the law. ³O my people, what have I done to make you turn from me? Tell me why your patience is exhausted! Answer me! ⁴For I brought you out of Egypt and redeemed you from your slavery. I sent Moses, Aaron, and Miriam to help you.

⁵"Don't you remember, my people, how King Balak of Moab tried to have you cursed and how Balaam son of Beor blessed you instead? And remember your journey from Acacia to Gilgal, when I, the LORD, did everything I could to teach you about my faithfulness."

⁶What can we bring to the LORD to make up for what we've done? Should we bow before God with offerings of yearling calves? ⁷Should we offer him thousands of rams and tens of thousands of rivers of olive oil? Would that please the LORD? Should we sacrifice our firstborn children to pay for the sins of our souls? Would that make him glad?

⁸No, O people, the LORD has already told you what is good, and this is what he requires: to do what is right, to love mercy, and to walk humbly with your God.   MICAH 6:1-8

How Charming

PREVIEW

Smooth talkers. Eve fell prey to one in the garden. Consumers fall prey to one when they enter a showroom and are enticed into making an unnecessary purchase. It seems that sooner or later everybody falls prey to one—a smooth talker who comes along and persuades us to do something foolish. It's hard not to admire these tempters, because they're so successful at what they do. They often dress, talk, and look like real winners.

Smooth talkers—or charmers—are the topic of Nahum. In his book by the same name, Nahum prophesies against the people of Nineveh for their deceptive practices. He tells them that their wicked deeds have been seen by God and will cost them dearly. As you read, learn the lesson that doom is certain for those who oppose God.

PERSONAL APPLICATION

Nothing deceives quite like charm. Politicians know this. That's why they pour it on around election time. Unfortunately, they're not the only ones who know how to use charm to get what they want. Con artists use it to swindle people out of their life savings, other properties, and even their virginity or sexual purity. Charm bewitches us today just as much as it did in Nahum's day.

To escape the influence of evil charm, we need to be wise and have a healthy suspicion of people—and offers—who seem too good to be true.

Look closely at any company, salesperson, movement, or even ministry before you trust them. Make sure that people and institutions deal truthfully with you. And never forget to ask God for discernment when dealing with individuals or organizations with whom you're unfamiliar. Seek the counsel of wise and experienced Christians. God knows people's true motives, and you can trust his advice.

BIBLE READING

[11]"And you, Nineveh, will also stagger like a drunkard. You will hide for fear of the attacking enemy. [12]All your fortresses will fall. They will be devoured like the ripe figs that fall into the mouths of those who shake the trees. [13]Your troops will be as weak and helpless as women. The gates of your land will be opened wide to the enemy and set on fire and burned.

[14]Get ready for the siege! Store up water! Strengthen the defenses! Make bricks to repair the walls! Go into the pits to trample clay, and pack it into molds! [15]But in the middle of your preparations, the fire will devour you; the sword will cut you down. The enemy will consume you like locusts, devouring everything they see. There will be no escape, even if you multiply like grasshoppers. [16]Merchants, as numerous as the stars, have filled your city with vast wealth. But like a swarm of locusts, they strip the land and then fly away. [17]Your princes and officials are also like locusts, crowding together in the hedges to survive the cold. But like locusts that fly away when the sun comes up to warm the earth, all of them will fly away and disappear.

[18]O Assyrian king, your princes lie dead in the dust. Your people are scattered across the mountains. There is no longer a shepherd to gather them together. [19]There is no healing for your wound; your injury is fatal. All who hear of your destruction will clap their hands for joy. Where can anyone be found who has not suffered from your cruelty?　　　　　NAHUM 3:11-19

# Is It Time Yet?

PREVIEW

To enjoy some good things we must wait. For instance, farmers must wait until the crop is ripe before harvesting it. Expectant parents must wait the full nine months for their child to develop before they can enjoy a relationship with him or her. And employees must wait for the coffeemaker to finish brewing before they can enjoy that first cup at the office.

Justice is no different. In this reading Habakkuk struggles with waiting for God to deal justly with the wicked. But through his struggle he learns two important lessons: patience and trust. He also encounters God and is blessed by his presence. By the end of this book, Habakkuk's outlook on life is remarkably different, and he no longer asks God if the time for justice has come yet.

PERSONAL APPLICATION

Habakkuk was disturbed that evil and injustice seemed to have the upper hand among his people (Habakkuk 1:3). Habakkuk questioned God about the situation and pleaded with him to do something. God promised that he would. God assured him that all would be put right. "Wait patiently," he said (2:3).

Like Habakkuk, we often feel angry and discouraged by what we see going on in the world. But we need to remember that God hates sin even more than we do. Certainly God will punish those who deserve it. If we preoccupy ourselves with the evil we see, however, and keep staring at headlines that mention rape and murder and watch the news programs that expose the latest scam, then we will continue to be frustrated and angry. But if we refuse to dwell on the evil in this world and trust God to deal justly with the wicked, then we will be able to wait for him to bring about justice.

BIBLE READING

²How long, O LORD, must I call for help? But you do not listen! "Violence!" I cry, but you do not come to save. ³Must I forever see this sin and misery all around me? Wherever I look, I see destruction and violence. I am surrounded by people who love to argue and fight. ⁴The law has become paralyzed and useless, and there is no justice given in the courts. The wicked far outnumber the righteous, and justice is perverted with bribes and trickery.

⁵The LORD replied, "Look at the nations and be amazed! Watch and be astounded at what I will do! For I am doing something in your own day, something you wouldn't believe even if someone told you about it. ⁶I am raising up the Babylonians to be a new power on the world scene. They are a cruel and violent nation who will march across the world and conquer it. ⁷They are notorious for their cruelty. They do as they like, and no one can stop them. ⁸Their horses are swifter than leopards. They are a fierce people, more fierce than wolves at dusk. Their horsemen race forward from distant places. Like eagles they swoop down to pounce on their prey.

⁹"On they come, all of them bent on violence. Their hordes advance like a wind from the desert, sweeping captives ahead of them like sand. ¹⁰They scoff at kings and princes and scorn all their defenses. They simply pile ramps of earth against their walls and capture them! ¹¹They sweep past like the wind and are gone. But they are deeply guilty, for their own strength is their god."

HABAKKUK 1:2-11

oney Doesn't Talk

PREVIEW

In Zephaniah's time some of the people of Judah were financially secure. However, Zephaniah had a message from the Lord for them on investing. Apparently, some of them had received a bad investment tip and were at risk of losing it all. As you read this passage, learn the lesson that some things cannot be bought at any price.

PERSONAL APPLICATION

Israel had silver and gold, but no holiness. God said that their riches would not help them when it came time to account for their sins (Zephaniah 1:18).

In this life, we often rely on money for a sense of security and power. When we are poor, we feel weak. When we are rich, we feel strong. But wealth doesn't make us right with God. Nor can it buy our salvation or influence God's will. At the final judgment our riches will be worthless.

If you're already rich, ask God to help you maintain a humble attitude, use what you have for his glory, and live righteously. If you're middle class or poor, rather than working to accumulate wealth, work at cultivating holiness. It's the one thing you *can* take with you when you die.

BIBLE READING

⁷Stand in silence in the presence of the Sovereign LORD, for the awesome day of the Lord's judgment has come. The LORD has prepared his people for a great slaughter and has chosen their executioners. ⁸"On that day of judgment," says the LORD, "I will punish the leaders and princes of Judah and all those following pagan customs. ⁹Yes, I will punish those who participate in pagan worship ceremonies, and those who steal and kill to fill their masters' homes with loot.

¹²"I will search with lanterns in Jerusalem's darkest corners to find and punish those who sit contented in their sins, indifferent to the LORD, thinking he will do nothing at all to them. ¹³They are the very ones whose property will be plundered by the enemy, whose homes will be ransacked. They will never have a chance to live in the new homes they have built. They will never drink wine from the vineyards they have planted."

¹⁸Your silver and gold will be of no use to you on that day of the Lord's anger. For the whole land will be devoured by the fire of his jealousy. He will make a terrifying end of all the people on earth.

²·¹Gather together and pray, you shameless nation. ²Gather while there is still time, before judgment begins and your opportunity is blown away like chaff. Act now, before the fierce fury of the LORD falls and the terrible day of the Lord's anger begins. ³Beg the LORD to save you—all you who are humble, all you who uphold justice. Walk humbly and do what is right. Perhaps even yet the LORD will protect you from his anger on that day of destruction.   ZEPHANIAH 1:7-9, 12-13, 18; 2:1-3

*H*ome Improvement

PREVIEW

Jake has a long list of unfinished projects. There's a hole in the stairwell wall still waiting for a patch, a bare window in the bedroom still awaiting curtains, and a tight pair of pants still waiting for his diet to get under way. But these things will have to wait. He's got more important things to do than patch walls, put up curtains, and improve his eating habits. These unfinished projects will have to wait.

That's what the people of Judah are saying about the temple, which is badly in need of repair. It is their highest priority, but they've got their minds on their own home improvements. In this reading, Haggai prophesies to them about reprioritizing the items on their to-do list.

PERSONAL APPLICATION

The focal point of Judah's relationship with God, the temple, lay in ruins. Instead of rebuilding it, the people had put their energies into beautifying their own homes. But the harder the people worked for themselves, the less they had. The harvests kept getting smaller. Their income never quite covered their expenses. Because of a coming drought, they would not even be able to meet their most basic needs. All of this resulted from one cause—neglecting their spiritual priorities (Haggai 1:2-6, 9-11).

If you never have enough, it may be because of a misplaced value. Guard your spiritual priorities. As you parcel out your time, money, and energy, don't forget the importance of activities and pursuits that matter to God. He will provide for you if you put him first.

BIBLE READING

[1]On August 29 of the second year of King Darius's reign, the LORD gave a message through the prophet Haggai to Zerubbabel son of Shealtiel, governor of Judah, and to Jeshua son of Jehozadak, the high priest. [2]"This is what the LORD Almighty says: The people are saying, 'The time has not yet come to rebuild the Lord's house—the Temple.'"

[3]So the LORD sent this message through the prophet Haggai: [4]"Why are you living in luxurious houses while my house lies in ruins? [5]This is what the LORD Almighty says: Consider how things are going for you! [6]You have planted much but harvested little. You have food to eat, but not enough to fill you up. You have wine to drink, but not enough to satisfy your thirst. You have clothing to wear, but not enough to keep you warm. Your wages disappear as though you were putting them in pockets filled with holes!

[7]"This is what the LORD Almighty says: Consider how things are going for you! [8]Now go up into the hills, bring down timber, and rebuild my house. Then I will take pleasure in it and be honored, says the LORD. [9]You hoped for rich harvests, but they were poor. And when you brought your harvest home, I blew it away. Why? Because my house lies in ruins, says the LORD Almighty, while you are all busy building your own fine houses. [10]That is why the heavens have withheld the dew and the earth has withheld its crops. [11]I have called for a drought on your fields and hills—a drought to wither the grain and grapes and olives and all your other crops, a drought to starve both you and your cattle and to ruin everything you have worked so hard to get."

HAGGAI 1:1-11

$\mathcal{S}$queaky-Clean

PREVIEW

Everyone who has ever done laundry knows how stubborn some dirt can be. You treat it, soak it, scrub it, and rewash it, but nothing you do takes out the stain.

Dirt comes in more forms than just the physical. We say that we have dirt in our past and try to avoid airing our "dirty laundry." Like stained clothes, dirt in lives is hard to get out. That's why, for this set of prophecies, God shows Zechariah a vision of Jeshua, the high priest, in dirty clothes. As you read, pay close attention to this vivid illustration of God's work of mercy in our lives.

PERSONAL APPLICATION

In Zechariah's vision Satan made many accusations against Jeshua (Israel) (Zechariah 3:2-4). Jeshua could not deny them, either, because they were true. But God rejected the accusations and declared mercy on Jeshua. By having Jeshua's filthy clothes removed and replaced by fine new ones, God graphically portrayed how people receive his mercy. There is nothing they can do to earn it. God grants mercy and forgiveness out of his tremendous love for his people. He removes the filthy clothes (sins) and then provides new, clean, rich garments (his righteousness and holiness). (See also 2 Corinthians 5:21, Ephesians 4:24, and Revelation 19:8.)

Whenever you feel dirty and unworthy, go to God for cleansing. He can remove the stain of your sin and guilt, and replace it with a clean conscience and pure heart.

BIBLE READING

¹Then the angel showed me Jeshua the high priest standing before the angel of the LORD. Satan was there at the angel's right hand, accusing Jeshua of many things. ²And the LORD said to Satan, "I, the LORD, reject your accusations, Satan. Yes, the LORD, who has chosen Jerusalem, rebukes you. This man is like a burning stick that has been snatched from a fire."

³Jeshua's clothing was filthy as he stood there before the angel. ⁴So the angel said to the others standing there, "Take off his filthy clothes." And turning to Jeshua he said, "See, I have taken away your sins, and now I am giving you these fine new clothes."

⁵Then I said, "Please, could he also have a clean turban on his head?" So they put a clean priestly turban on his head and dressed him in new clothes while the angel of the LORD stood by.

⁶Then the angel of the LORD spoke very solemnly to Jeshua and said, ⁷"This is what the LORD Almighty says: If you follow my ways and obey my requirements, then you will be given authority over my Temple and its courtyards. I will let you walk in and out of my presence along with these others standing here. ⁸Listen to me, O Jeshua the high priest, and all you other priests. You are symbols of the good things to come. Soon I am going to bring my servant, the Branch. ⁹Now look at the jewel I have set before Jeshua, a single stone with seven facets. I will engrave an inscription on it, says the LORD Almighty, and I will remove the sins of this land in a single day. ¹⁰And on that day, says the LORD Almighty, each of you will invite your neighbor into your home to share your peace and prosperity."   ZECHARIAH 3:1-10

 e Prepared

PREVIEW

What would you do if you went to work and your boss announced to you: "Clean out your desk. This is your last day." Would you be ready? Would your family be ready? Would you know what to do?

"Be prepared" is the theme of this passage. This portion of Zechariah contains many prophecies about the Messiah, some of which were fulfilled when Jesus Christ came and paid the penalty for sin. But God's people still await the fulfillment of the remaining prophecies—when Jesus comes back to take them to heaven with him. As you read, hear Zechariah's strong message: "Be ready."

PERSONAL APPLICATION

Zechariah predicted the Triumphal Entry of Jesus riding into Jerusalem (see Matthew 21:1-11) more than five hundred years before it happened (Zechariah 9:9). Other portions of Zechariah's prophesies about Christ, such as the coming day of the Lord (Zechariah 14:1-9), have not yet been fulfilled. Jesus told his disciples that he would return (see Matthew 25:31). Meanwhile, he wants his followers to "watch" for his coming (a command often paired with prophecies about his return, as here in Zechariah 14:1).

We often make two mistakes with regard to the return of Christ: (1) we ignore it, or (2) we presume to know the date. We don't know when Christ will return, so we shouldn't pretend that we do. But we do know that he will come back, and God wants us to be ready at all times.

If Christ were to come back today, would you be ready? If not, you can get ready by living according to God's Word consistently. Spread the Good News of Jesus Christ, live a morally pure life, and spend time with God on a regular basis. Be prepared by living each day in anticipation of his return.

BIBLE READING

¹Watch, for the day of the LORD is coming when your possessions will be plundered right in front of you! ²On that day I will gather all the nations to fight against Jerusalem. The city will be taken, the houses plundered, and the women raped. Half the population will be taken away into captivity, and half will be left among the ruins of the city.

³Then the LORD will go out to fight against those nations, as he has fought in times past. ⁴On that day his feet will stand on the Mount of Olives, which faces Jerusalem on the east. And the Mount of Olives will split apart, making a wide valley running from east to west, for half the mountain will move toward the north and half toward the south. ⁵You will flee through this valley, for it will reach across to Azal. Yes, you will flee as you did from the earthquake in the days of King Uzziah of Judah. Then the LORD my God will come, and all his holy ones with him.

⁶On that day the sources of light will no longer shine, ⁷yet there will be continuous day! Only the LORD knows how this could happen! There will be no normal day and night, for at evening time it will still be light. ⁸On that day life-giving waters will flow out from Jerusalem, half toward the Dead Sea and half toward the Mediterranean, flowing continuously both in summer and in winter.

⁹And the LORD will be king over all the earth. On that day there will be one LORD—his name alone will be worshiped. ¹⁰All the land from Geba, north of Judah, to Rimmon, south of Jerusalem, will become one vast plain. But Jerusalem will be raised up in its original place and will be inhabited all the way from the Benjamin Gate over to the site of the old gate, then to the Corner Gate, and from the Tower of Hananel to the king's winepresses. ¹¹And Jerusalem will be filled, safe at last, never again to be cursed and destroyed. ZECHARIAH 14:1-11

Working Class

PREVIEW

Imagine that all the money you have ever given to the Lord in tithes has been kept in a trust fund earning 10 percent a year. Before long, you will get it all back. Would you be rich? Or would you be no better off?

Malachi's audience have that sort of question to think about. They've been skimping on their tithes for some time now, and it's affecting their bottom line.

PERSONAL APPLICATION

Malachi urged the people to stop holding back their tithes, to stop keeping from God what he deserved (Malachi 3:8-12). The tithing system had begun during the time of Moses (see Leviticus 27:30-34; Deuteronomy 14:22). It was set up by God to provide an income for the Levites who ministered in the tabernacle and later the temple of the Lord (see Numbers 18:20-21). During Malachi's day, the people did not give. They had forgotten that everything they had was from God; as a result, they stopped tithing. Because of this, the Levites were forced to earn a living and neglect their God-given responsibilities to care for the temple and the service of worship.

We too can fall into this trap when we forget that God is our real provider—everything we have comes from him. When we stop giving God a portion of what he has given us, we essentially steal from him.

Be faithful in giving back a percentage of your income to God because there is still a practical reason for tithing: Your pastor and other church staff depend on it. In addition, you won't be disappointed with the interest rates God pays on your faithfulness to him.

BIBLE READING

[1]"Look! I am sending my messenger, and he will prepare the way before me. Then the Lord you are seeking will suddenly come to his Temple. The messenger of the covenant, whom you look for so eagerly, is surely coming," says the LORD Almighty. [2]"But who will be able to endure it when he comes? Who will be able to stand and face him when he appears? For he will be like a blazing fire that refines metal or like a strong soap that whitens clothes. [3]He will sit and judge like a refiner of silver, watching closely as the dross is burned away.

[6]"I am the LORD, and I do not change. That is why you descendants of Jacob are not already completely destroyed. [7]Ever since the days of your ancestors, you have scorned my laws and failed to obey them. Now return to me, and I will return to you," says the LORD Almighty.

"But you ask, 'How can we return when we have never gone away?'

[8]"Should people cheat God? Yet you have cheated me!

"But you ask, 'What do you mean? When did we ever cheat you?'

"You have cheated me of the tithes and offerings due to me. [9]You are under a curse, for your whole nation has been cheating me. [10]Bring all the tithes into the storehouse so there will be enough food in my Temple. If you do," says the LORD Almighty, "I will open the windows of heaven for you. I will pour out a blessing so great you won't have enough room to take it in! Try it! Let me prove it to you! [11]Your crops will be abundant, for I will guard them from insects and disease. Your grapes will not shrivel before they are ripe," says the LORD Almighty. [12]"Then all nations will call you blessed, for your land will be such a delight," says the LORD Almighty.   MALACHI 3:1-3, 6-12

Wise Guys

PREVIEW

Most people long to be smarter. To increase their IQ, some try the latest "brain foods," while others take up brain-stimulating hobbies. Intelligence is a priceless commodity. The smarter people are, the more money they can make, the more respect they will receive, and the more influence they will have.

Although it's good to be smart, intelligence isn't everything. In fact, three men in this reading have something more important—wisdom. Wisdom may seem to be more difficult to gain than intelligence, but these men show how easy it is to start down the road in that direction. As you read, follow the example of these men.

PERSONAL APPLICATION

Three astrologers from the east traveled a great distance to a foreign land to find Jesus. They said they wanted to worship him, but that was only half true. As soon as they found Jesus, they also honored him as king by giving gifts. Then they left (Matthew 2:1-12). Though their encounter with Jesus probably lasted only a day, the wisdom they displayed in worshiping him has been recorded for eternity.

Today, many people demonstrate foolishness in their attitudes and actions toward Jesus. Some treat him as a quaint and harmless idealist, too human to be worshiped. Others expect him to accommodate them. Some even treat Jesus with contempt and irreverence. Yet those who are wise recognize Jesus for who he is and feel a personal responsibility to bow down to and serve him.

Honor Jesus in your attitude and actions. Give your life to him because he gave his for you, and don't forget to give him the praise and worship he deserves. In doing this, you will be truly wise.

BIBLE READING

¹Jesus was born in the town of Bethlehem in Judea, during the reign of King Herod. About that time some wise men from eastern lands arrived in Jerusalem, asking, ²"Where is the newborn king of the Jews? We have seen his star as it arose, and we have come to worship him."

³Herod was deeply disturbed by their question, as was all of Jerusalem. ⁴He called a meeting of the leading priests and teachers of religious law. "Where did the prophets say the Messiah would be born?" he asked them.

⁵"In Bethlehem," they said, "for this is what the prophet wrote:

⁶ 'O Bethlehem of Judah,
    you are not just a lowly village in Judah,
  for a ruler will come from you
    who will be the shepherd for my people Israel.'"

⁷Then Herod sent a private message to the wise men, asking them to come see him. At this meeting he learned the exact time when they first saw the star. ⁸Then he told them, "Go to Bethlehem and search carefully for the child. And when you find him, come back and tell me so that I can go and worship him, too!"

⁹After this interview the wise men went their way. Once again the star appeared to them, guiding them to Bethlehem. It went ahead of them and stopped over the place where the child was. ¹⁰When they saw the star, they were filled with joy! ¹¹They entered the house where the child and his mother, Mary, were, and they fell down before him and worshiped him. Then they opened their treasure chests and gave him gifts of gold, frankincense, and myrrh. ¹²But when it was time to leave, they went home another way, because God had warned them in a dream not to return to Herod.   MATTHEW 2:1-12

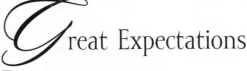

Great Expectations

PREVIEW

Have you ever had a teacher who expected a lot out of you? What about a parent or relative who assumed that you would act responsibly and morally? People who believe in you usually expect a lot of you— your conduct and your work. Although it may be frustrating to have someone hold you to such high standards—not to mention trying to live up to them—it can be very beneficial.

Similar to this teacher, parent, or relative, Jesus wanted, and expected, the best for his followers, and he set high standards for them to live by. This passage, known as the Sermon on the Mount, spells out some of those standards. Jesus set them up to help you.

PERSONAL APPLICATION

Jesus' standards required a new way of holiness that neither the crowds nor the religious authorities could grasp. They couldn't understand because his standards turned theirs and their world's way of thinking upside down. Consider some of Jesus' teachings: True happiness involves humility, mourning, longing, purity, and persecution (Matthew 5:3-11); anger can place you in danger of judgment (5:22); do not even *look* at others lustfully (5:28); never take revenge (5:39); and love your enemies (5:44). Jesus' listeners that day also didn't realize that to live by his standards required God's power, faith in Christ, and change brought by the Holy Spirit.

Although Jesus' standards are steep, they are his formula for happiness and success. Christians should strive to live up to them only with the help of the Holy Spirit. When we get discouraged by trying to live up to such high standards, we should remember that living by them will bring rewards—though not the kind most people seek, and not necessarily in this life (5:12).

BIBLE READING

[1]One day as the crowds were gathering, Jesus went up the mountainside with his disciples and sat down to teach them.

[2]This is what he taught them:

[3] "God blesses those who realize their need for him,
   for the Kingdom of Heaven is given to them.
[4] God blesses those who mourn,
   for they will be comforted.
[5] God blesses those who are gentle and lowly,
   for the whole earth will belong to them.
[6] God blesses those who are hungry and thirsty for justice,
   for they will receive it in full.
[7] God blesses those who are merciful,
   for they will be shown mercy.
[8] God blesses those whose hearts are pure,
   for they will see God.
[9] God blesses those who work for peace,
   for they will be called the children of God.
[10] God blesses those who are persecuted because they live for God,
   for the Kingdom of Heaven is theirs.

[11]"God blesses you when you are mocked and persecuted and lied about because you are my followers. [12]Be happy about it! Be very glad! For a great reward awaits you in heaven. And remember, the ancient prophets were persecuted, too."

MATTHEW 5:1-12

Rewiring the Panic Button

PREVIEW

"I'm not worried," we say nervously, "just quite concerned."

Life is full of concerns—fleeting, chronic, financial, relational, mild, or severe. These worries can drive us crazy just thinking about them. They can also cause us to question our faith in God. Does God care about our concerns? Is he doing anything to help us out?

In this passage, Jesus points out the lessons in trust that we can learn from nature, assuring us of the futility of worry and of the certainty of God's care. As you read, strengthen your dependence on God's gracious care, and watch your worries melt away.

PERSONAL APPLICATION

Jesus knew that his disciples naturally worried about having enough of life's necessities, so he reassured them that God would provide for their needs. He pointed out that God provides for the animal kingdom, so he also would provide for them—they mattered much more than the animals (Matthew 6:25-34).

Worrying about our needs accomplishes nothing and ignores the fact that God works to meet those needs. Jesus didn't tell his disciples to be lazy or not to work, just to trust God and not to worry.

Do what you can about the concerns you have, but also realize that God, who loves and cares for you, has made provision for them as well. He will not let your needs overwhelm you. Whenever worries plague you, follow these three steps: (1) tell God about your concerns, asking him to provide for your needs; (2) do what you humanly can to work on your concerns; and (3) trust in God's goodness—remember that he cares for you more than even you care for yourself and will provide all you need at the right time.

BIBLE READING

[19]"Don't store up treasures here on earth, where they can be eaten by moths and get rusty, and where thieves break in and steal. [20]Store your treasures in heaven, where they will never become moth-eaten or rusty and where they will be safe from thieves. [21]Wherever your treasure is, there your heart and thoughts will also be.

[24]"No one can serve two masters. For you will hate one and love the other, or be devoted to one and despise the other. You cannot serve both God and money.

[25]"So I tell you, don't worry about everyday life—whether you have enough food, drink, and clothes. Doesn't life consist of more than food and clothing? [26]Look at the birds. They don't need to plant or harvest or put food in barns because your heavenly Father feeds them. And you are far more valuable to him than they are. [27]Can all your worries add a single moment to your life? Of course not.

[28]"And why worry about your clothes? Look at the lilies and how they grow. They don't work or make their clothing, [29]yet Solomon in all his glory was not dressed as beautifully as they are. [30]And if God cares so wonderfully for flowers that are here today and gone tomorrow, won't he more surely care for you? You have so little faith!

[31]"So don't worry about having enough food or drink or clothing. [32]Why be like the pagans who are so deeply concerned about these things? Your heavenly Father already knows all your needs, [33]and he will give you all you need from day to day if you live for him and make the Kingdom of God your primary concern.

[34]"So don't worry about tomorrow, for tomorrow will bring its own worries. Today's trouble is enough for today."

MATTHEW 6:19-21, 24-34

Chairman of the Board and Speck

PREVIEW

I pay attention to details; *she's* way too picky. *I* am a person of conviction; *he* is just plain stubborn. In these and a host of other ways, we justify our own behavior while condemning the same actions in others.

In this reading, Jesus' sermon continues with a rebuke for those who spend more time pointing out others' moral shortcomings than correcting their own. Using the vivid imagery of boards and specks in the eye, Jesus explains how to fix the problem.

Other solutions can also be found in this passage. As you read, look for lessons on asking and faith building, as well as directions to heaven.

PERSONAL APPLICATION

Jesus told his disciples to be careful how they criticized others (Matthew 7:1-2). He said that to criticize and judge is like trying to extract a splinter from someone else's eye when you've got a piece of lumber in your own (7:3-6). If you want to help your friend get the splinter out, fine, but first get the board out of yours.

We tend to judge others much more harshly than we judge ourselves. Therefore, we need to be careful how severely we speak to others when we spot their defects.

If you find fault with someone else, first stop and ask whether or not you have the same problem. Don't deny or cover up your own faults. Don't be self-righteous in condemning others. Be as sensitive in dealing with others' faults as you would wish them to be with you.

BIBLE READING

[1]"Stop judging others, and you will not be judged. [2]For others will treat you as you treat them. Whatever measure you use in judging others, it will be used to measure how you are judged. [3]And why worry about a speck in your friend's eye when you have a log in your own? [4]How can you think of saying, 'Let me help you get rid of that speck in your eye,' when you can't see past the log in your own eye? [5]Hypocrite! First get rid of the log from your own eye; then perhaps you will see well enough to deal with the speck in your friend's eye.

[6]"Don't give what is holy to unholy people. Don't give pearls to swine! They will trample the pearls, then turn and attack you.

[7]"Keep on asking, and you will be given what you ask for. Keep on looking, and you will find. Keep on knocking, and the door will be opened. [8]For everyone who asks, receives. Everyone who seeks, finds. And the door is opened to everyone who knocks. [9]You parents—if your children ask for a loaf of bread, do you give them a stone instead? [10]Or if they ask for a fish, do you give them a snake? Of course not! [11]If you sinful people know how to give good gifts to your children, how much more will your heavenly Father give good gifts to those who ask him.

[12]"Do for others what you would like them to do for you. This is a summary of all that is taught in the law and the prophets.

[13]"You can enter God's Kingdom only through the narrow gate. The highway to hell is broad, and its gate is wide for the many who choose the easy way. [14]But the gateway to life is small, and the road is narrow, and only a few ever find it."

MATTHEW 7:1-14

ad Company

PREVIEW

From the early grades in school, we worry that certain friendships might cause us embarrassment. "What will people think if I'm seen with *them?*" we fret. Often we'll do just about anything to associate with people who might elevate our public image, and avoid those who drag it down.

Jesus didn't worry about his social status. In fact, he risks social disgrace in this reading by going to Matthew's house for dinner. But in doing so, Jesus helps another, regardless of his status. In this reading, we also learn that when it comes to a person's receptivity to spiritual matters, appearances can be deceiving. As you read, consider how you can focus on others and not just yourself.

PERSONAL APPLICATION

Some of the Pharisees tried hard to find fault with Jesus. Often their attacks involved some sort of interview over fine points of doctrine, but they also went after his actions. On this occasion, they noticed what looked like a perfect opportunity to trap Jesus in a political blunder— associating with criminals (Matthew 9:11-12). Jesus shocked them, first of all, by not caring about his image and second, by faulting *them* for doing so.

In the public eye, everyone notices whose company we keep. But this shouldn't matter, provided that we are influencing others for good and aren't being influenced by them for evil.

If you are overly concerned with whom you're seen, pray for the courage to follow Jesus' example by loving and helping the social outcasts. Your reputation may suffer on earth, but it won't suffer in heaven.

BIBLE READING

¹Jesus climbed into a boat and went back across the lake to his own town. ²Some people brought to him a paralyzed man on a mat. Seeing their faith, Jesus said to the paralyzed man, "Take heart, son! Your sins are forgiven."

³"Blasphemy! This man talks like he is God!" some of the teachers of religious law said among themselves.

⁴Jesus knew what they were thinking, so he asked them, "Why are you thinking such evil thoughts? ⁵Is it easier to say, 'Your sins are forgiven' or 'Get up and walk'? ⁶I will prove that I, the Son of Man, have the authority on earth to forgive sins." Then Jesus turned to the paralyzed man and said, "Stand up, take your mat, and go on home, because you are healed!"

⁷And the man jumped up and went home! ⁸Fear swept through the crowd as they saw this happen right before their eyes. They praised God for sending a man with such great authority.

⁹As Jesus was going down the road, he saw Matthew sitting at his tax-collection booth. "Come, be my disciple," Jesus said to him. So Matthew got up and followed him.

¹⁰That night Matthew invited Jesus and his disciples to be his dinner guests, along with his fellow tax collectors and many other notorious sinners. ¹¹The Pharisees were indignant. "Why does your teacher eat with such scum?" they asked his disciples.

¹²When he heard this, Jesus replied, "Healthy people don't need a doctor—sick people do." ¹³Then he added, "Now go and learn the meaning of this Scripture: 'I want you to be merciful; I don't want your sacrifices.' For I have come to call sinners, not those who think they are already good enough."

MATTHEW 9:1-13

Second-Guessers Anonymous

PREVIEW

Some people can second-guess themselves into a state of paralysis. "I don't know if I'm doing the right thing," they may say. Here's another favorite: "I just want to do what is right." They may pray for "peace" and do what gives them that peaceful feeling: "I know what I'm doing sounds crazy, but I just really have a sense of peace about it." If peace escapes them, they may look to others for reassurance that they are on the right track.

Although John the Baptist was not a double-minded man, this passage reports how he began to second-guess his original conclusions about Jesus. As you read, notice especially Jesus' reaction to John's doubts—it will teach you a bit about dealing with your own uncertainties.

PERSONAL APPLICATION

John's God-given mission had been to prepare people for the Messiah's coming. Now that he was in prison, his ministry wasn't going very well. Had he been wrong about Jesus? John wanted to be sure, so he sent some of his followers to talk with Jesus. Jesus told John's disciples to report to John what they saw and heard—the blind see, the deaf hear, the dead are raised to life. Jesus gave John the reassurance he sought (Matthew 11:2-6).

John did not come to his conclusion about who Jesus was based on his impressions or feelings. Instead, he went to the source, Jesus, to get the facts on which he would base his decision. We should take the same approach when dealing with our uncertainties.

When in doubt, check with the source of truth. Rather than relying on a feeling or conviction, search God's Word for reassurance that Jesus is the Messiah, the Son of God. If you study what Jesus said and did, your faith will be renewed and strengthened.

BIBLE READING

²John the Baptist, who was now in prison, heard about all the things the Messiah was doing. So he sent his disciples to ask Jesus, ³"Are you really the Messiah we've been waiting for, or should we keep looking for someone else?"

⁴Jesus told them, "Go back to John and tell him about what you have heard and seen—⁵the blind see, the lame walk, the lepers are cured, the deaf hear, the dead are raised to life, and the Good News is being preached to the poor. ⁶And tell him: 'God blesses those who are not offended by me.'"

⁷When John's disciples had gone, Jesus began talking about him to the crowds. "Who is this man in the wilderness that you went out to see? Did you find him weak as a reed, moved by every breath of wind? ⁸Or were you expecting to see a man dressed in expensive clothes? Those who dress like that live in palaces, not out in the wilderness. ⁹Were you looking for a prophet? Yes, and he is more than a prophet. ¹⁰John is the man to whom the Scriptures refer when they say,

> 'Look, I am sending my messenger before you,
>   and he will prepare your way before you.'

¹¹"I assure you, of all who have ever lived, none is greater than John the Baptist. Yet even the most insignificant person in the Kingdom of Heaven is greater than he is! ¹²And from the time John the Baptist began preaching and baptizing until now, the Kingdom of Heaven has been forcefully advancing, and violent people attack it. ¹³For before John came, all the teachings of the Scriptures looked forward to this present time. ¹⁴And if you are willing to accept what I say, he is Elijah, the one the prophets said would come. ¹⁵Anyone who is willing to hear should listen and understand!"   MATTHEW 11:2-15

Look Out

PREVIEW

Look is one of the first words that many children learn to read. The command form of look—as in, "Look out!" is really important. Often in life we need to use or to heed this word.

Although it is usually good to *look out*, doing so can cause problems in the area of faith. In this passage Jesus' most impulsive disciple literally steps out in faith. Unfortunately, he looks *out* and gets into deep trouble. As you read, note the importance of keeping your eyes on Christ and not on your circumstances.

Also in this passage you will see the action heating up as Herod kills John, Jesus feeds a huge crowd of people with a single entree, and more and more people are healed.

PERSONAL APPLICATION

When the disciples saw Jesus walking on the water, they could hardly believe their eyes. Peter asked Jesus to summon him to walk on the water (Matthew 14:28). That was quite a step of faith for Peter to take. When Jesus invited him to walk, Peter stepped out of the boat and began to walk on the water's surface. But as soon as he looked away from Jesus and looked around at the windswept waves and murky depths, he started to sink.

As Peter's example proves, a person's faith doesn't stay constant. It increases or decreases depending on where that person chooses to focus his or her attention. Those who focus on their problems are likely to find their faith decreasing. But those who focus their attention on Jesus are likely to find their faith increasing.

Maintain and increase your faith by keeping your attention focused on Jesus. Remind yourself of his presence, power, care, and willingness to help, and keep your eyes off your inadequacies and circumstances.

BIBLE READING

²²Immediately after this, Jesus made his disciples get back into the boat and cross to the other side of the lake while he sent the people home. ²³Afterward he went up into the hills by himself to pray. Night fell while he was there alone. ²⁴Meanwhile, the disciples were in trouble far away from land, for a strong wind had risen, and they were fighting heavy waves.

²⁵About three o'clock in the morning Jesus came to them, walking on the water. ²⁶When the disciples saw him, they screamed in terror, thinking he was a ghost. ²⁷But Jesus spoke to them at once. "It's all right," he said. "I am here! Don't be afraid."

²⁸Then Peter called to him, "Lord, if it's really you, tell me to come to you by walking on water."

²⁹"All right, come," Jesus said.

So Peter went over the side of the boat and walked on the water toward Jesus. ³⁰But when he looked around at the high waves, he was terrified and began to sink. "Save me, Lord!" he shouted.

³¹Instantly Jesus reached out his hand and grabbed him. "You don't have much faith," Jesus said. "Why did you doubt me?" ³²And when they climbed back into the boat, the wind stopped.

³³Then the disciples worshiped him. "You really are the Son of God!" they exclaimed.

³⁴After they had crossed the lake, they landed at Gennesaret. ³⁵The news of their arrival spread quickly throughout the whole surrounding area, and soon people were bringing all their sick to be healed. ³⁶The sick begged him to let them touch even the fringe of his robe, and all who touched it were healed.

MATTHEW 14:22-36

roof Positive

PREVIEW

Many people set standards of behavior for God as a condition for their faith. "If God would just solve this one problem for me, I'd have no trouble believing." Usually it involves some kind of miraculous appearance or deed.

Many people have set such conditions for God, but few have tried harder than the Pharisees and Sadducees. We see how they make their demands for a miracle quite plain to Jesus. But Jesus, just as plainly, declines and leaves them in the dust of their doubt.

Believers and nonbelievers become harder to label in this passage. As the disciples pledge their belief in Jesus, they can't cope with his predictions of his death, and they even squabble over who will be the greatest in his kingdom. As you read, ask yourself, "What kind of proof would convince me of Christ's divinity?"

PERSONAL APPLICATION

Miracles never convince skeptical people. They have already committed themselves to disbelief. One more miracle would only compel them to explain it away. Today, many people demand proof of God's existence or power, but their demands mask the real issue—that they have already chosen not to believe in God. Until we believe that God *can* do miracles, we won't even entertain the possibility that something we saw *was* a miracle.

If you doubt Christ because you haven't "seen a miracle," ask whether a bona fide miracle would really convince you or just entrench your skepticism. Jesus said, "Blessed are those who haven't seen me and believe anyway" (John 20:29). Seeing God's work in your life begins when you simply step forward in faith and believe in Jesus as God's Son and as the only way of salvation.

BIBLE READING

¹One day the Pharisees and Sadducees came to test Jesus' claims by asking him to show them a miraculous sign from heaven.

²He replied, "You know the saying, 'Red sky at night means fair weather tomorrow, ³red sky in the morning means foul weather all day.' You are good at reading the weather signs in the sky, but you can't read the obvious signs of the times! ⁴Only an evil, faithless generation would ask for a miraculous sign, but the only sign I will give them is the sign of the prophet Jonah." Then Jesus left them and went away.

⁵Later, after they crossed to the other side of the lake, the disciples discovered they had forgotten to bring any food. ⁶"Watch out!" Jesus warned them. "Beware of the yeast of the Pharisees and Sadducees."

⁷They decided he was saying this because they hadn't brought any bread. ⁸Jesus knew what they were thinking, so he said, "You have so little faith! Why are you worried about having no food? ⁹Won't you ever understand? Don't you remember the five thousand I fed with five loaves, and the baskets of food that were left over? ¹⁰Don't you remember the four thousand I fed with seven loaves, with baskets of food left over? ¹¹How could you even think I was talking about food? So again I say, 'Beware of the yeast of the Pharisees and Sadducees.'"

¹²Then at last they understood that he wasn't speaking about yeast or bread but about the false teaching of the Pharisees and Sadducees. MATTHEW 16:1-12

Worth the Wait

PREVIEW

Anger, fatigue, frustration, insults, setbacks—some people will endure all this and more for the promise of an eventual reward. Without some future payoff, however, you would be hard-pressed to find one person who would be willing to endure a great deal of difficulty.

Reward is one of Peter's concerns in this reading. After Jesus makes a startling revelation about wealthy people and salvation, Peter begins to worry about his chances of being saved. In addition, he begins to wonder if leaving everything behind to follow Jesus is worth it. But Jesus knew that the cost of being one of his followers was great, and he didn't expect those who followed him to leave everything for nothing. He did, however, expect them to trust him and learn the truth about who is doing the saving and why. As you read, check your level of commitment to the Lord.

PERSONAL APPLICATION

God's rewards don't appeal to those, like the rich young man, who desire instant gratification. If God gave out immediate and material rewards for obedience, some people would obey him for the wrong reasons. And God doesn't want people to obey him just for the potential rewards. He prefers that people obey him out of love and gratitude. That's why the rewards he offers for obedience and service to him appeal to those who long for something more than material prosperity, who long for such things as truth, justice, mercy, and peace.

Don't look for the immediate rewards of money, comfort, and status when serving God. Instead, be willing to wait for the greater reward of spending eternity in his presence. But most of all, serve God out of gratitude for what he has done for you and out of love for who he is, not for the rewards that he will give you.

BIBLE READING

[16]"Teacher, what good things must I do to have eternal life?"

[17]"Why ask me about what is good?" Jesus replied. "Only God is good. But to answer your question, you can receive eternal life if you keep the commandments."

[18]"Which ones?" the man asked.

And Jesus replied: " 'Do not murder. Do not commit adultery. Do not steal. Do not testify falsely. [19]Honor your father and mother. Love your neighbor as yourself.'"

[20]"I've obeyed all these commandments," the young man replied. "What else must I do?"

[21]Jesus told him, "If you want to be perfect, go and sell all you have and give the money to the poor, and you will have treasure in heaven. Then come, follow me." [22]But when the young man heard this, he went sadly away because he had many possessions.

[23]Then Jesus said to his disciples, "I tell you the truth, it is very hard for a rich person to get into the Kingdom of Heaven. [24]I say it again—it is easier for a camel to go through the eye of a needle than for a rich person to enter the Kingdom of God!"

[25]The disciples were astounded. "Then who in the world can be saved?" they asked.

[26]Jesus looked at them intently and said, "Humanly speaking, it is impossible. But with God everything is possible."

[27]Then Peter said to him, "We've given up everything to follow you. What will we get out of it?"

[28]And Jesus replied, "I assure you that when I, the Son of Man, sit upon my glorious throne in the Kingdom, you who have been my followers will also sit on twelve thrones, judging the twelve tribes of Israel. [29]And everyone who has given up houses or brothers or sisters or father or mother or children or property, for my sake, will receive a hundred times as much in return and will have eternal life."   MATTHEW 19:16-29

retenders

PREVIEW

Have you ever met someone who looked like they stepped out of a glamour magazine, yet whose attitude and character were as ugly as sin? It's amazing how a person's outward appearance can be so different from his or her character.

Today's reading includes strong words for such people—those who are so concerned with how they appear to others that they neglect to take care of their character. Jesus directs his words at some of the Pharisees and Sadducees, but we can tell they are for anyone who focuses on life's minor issues instead of being concerned about what really matters to God. As you read, determine to focus on what's on the inside, instead of merely working on your outward appearances.

The passage also includes Jesus' entry into Jerusalem (which begins the final week of his life); more parables about the kingdom of God; and more vivid criticism of the scribes and Pharisees.

PERSONAL APPLICATION

Jesus condemned some of the Pharisees and religious leaders for hiding their corruption and greed behind a veneer of good behavior (Matthew 23:25-28). They kept a long list of rules by which they defined obedience to the Law. But they also harbored attitudes and behaviors that dishonored the God who had given them the Law, including greed, conceit, injustice toward others, pretense, and pride. That's the heart of hypocrisy—pretending to be what you're not.

Appearing to be a Christian isn't the same as being one. What's inside your heart? Are you hiding behind a mask? Are you pretending to be a Christian? Are you covering up sins? Work on your inner attitudes and motivations and not on your image. Don't be like the Pharisees. Don't be a hypocrite.

BIBLE READING

[25]"How terrible it will be for you teachers of religious law and you Pharisees. Hypocrites! You are so careful to clean the outside of the cup and the dish, but inside you are filthy—full of greed and self-indulgence! [26]Blind Pharisees! First wash the inside of the cup, and then the outside will become clean, too.

[27]"How terrible it will be for you teachers of religious law and you Pharisees. Hypocrites! You are like whitewashed tombs— beautiful on the outside but filled on the inside with dead people's bones and all sorts of impurity. [28]You try to look like upright people outwardly, but inside your hearts are filled with hypocrisy and lawlessness.

[29]"How terrible it will be for you teachers of religious law and you Pharisees. Hypocrites! For you build tombs for the prophets your ancestors killed and decorate the graves of the godly people your ancestors destroyed. [30]Then you say, 'We never would have joined them in killing the prophets.'

[31]"In saying that, you are accusing yourselves of being the descendants of those who murdered the prophets. [32]Go ahead. Finish what they started. [33]Snakes! Sons of vipers! How will you escape the judgment of hell? [34]I will send you prophets and wise men and teachers of religious law. You will kill some by crucifixion and whip others in your synagogues, chasing them from city to city. [35]As a result, you will become guilty of murdering all the godly people from righteous Abel to Zechariah son of Barachiah, whom you murdered in the Temple between the altar and the sanctuary. [36]I assure you, all the accumulated judgment of the centuries will break upon the heads of this very generation."

MATTHEW 23:25-36

Use It or Lose It

PREVIEW

"What a shame," people say. "She had so much potential, but she has really wasted her talent." We hear it said of athletes, young scholars, artists, and other talented people.

Jesus has more than head shaking for those who do nothing with their God-given talents. Here he uses a story about investing to convince his listeners that when God gives us an asset, he expects us to invest it. As you read, consider how you are investing the resources that God has entrusted to your care.

In addition to this story, Jesus' teaching here includes predictions about the future and warnings about God's judgment.

PERSONAL APPLICATION

In the parable of the loaned money, Jesus gave his disciples a picture of our own service to God. The master entrusted three of his servants with money to invest; in a similar way, God entrusts us with skills, money, time, and other resources. The master gave each servant only as much money as he felt the servant could handle; God gives us only what we can handle. The master rewarded those who invested his money; God rewards us when we employ his gifts in his service. And the master punished the servant who hid his money instead of investing it; God takes away what we refuse to use.

God has given each person many talents and other resources to use for his service. What has God given you to glorify him? Invest those gifts by serving him and the people he loves. He will ensure a good return.

BIBLE READING

¹⁴"Again, the Kingdom of Heaven can be illustrated by the story of a man going on a trip. He called together his servants and gave them money to invest for him while he was gone. ¹⁵He gave five bags of gold to one, two bags of gold to another, and one bag of gold to the last—dividing it in proportion to their abilities—and then left on his trip. ¹⁶The servant who received the five bags of gold began immediately to invest the money and soon doubled it. ¹⁷The servant with two bags of gold also went right to work and doubled the money. ¹⁸But the servant who received the one bag of gold dug a hole in the ground and hid the master's money for safekeeping.

¹⁹"After a long time their master returned from his trip and called them to give an account of how they had used his money. ²⁰The servant to whom he had entrusted the five bags of gold said, 'Sir, you gave me five bags of gold to invest, and I have doubled the amount.' ²¹The master was full of praise. 'Well done, my good and faithful servant. You have been faithful in handling this small amount, so now I will give you many more responsibilities. Let's celebrate together!'

²²"Next came the servant who had received the two bags of gold. . . .

²⁴"Then the servant with the one bag of gold came and said, 'Sir, I know you are a hard man, harvesting crops you didn't plant and gathering crops you didn't cultivate. ²⁵I was afraid I would lose your money, so I hid it in the earth and here it is.'

²⁶"But the master replied, 'You wicked and lazy servant! You think I'm a hard man, do you, harvesting crops I didn't plant and gathering crops I didn't cultivate? ²⁷Well, you should at least have put my money into the bank so I could have some interest. ²⁸Take the money from this servant and give it to the one with the ten bags of gold. ²⁹To those who use well what they are given, even more will be given, and they will have an abundance. But from those who are unfaithful, even what little they have will be taken away.'"

MATTHEW 25:14-29

Famous Last Words

PREVIEW

The last words of many famous people have been recorded and pondered. Final statements from the lips of the dying become a rich source for everything from term paper quotations to attention grabbers in sermons.

This last passage of Matthew contains Jesus' famous last words. But unlike the somber, reflective words of a dying man, Christ's words have a triumphant ring to them. That's because he has overcome death and has faithfully completed the task given to him by his Father. As Jesus prepares to return to his Father, he gives his disciples their final mission. As you read, listen carefully to Jesus' commission to his disciples (and you)—to reach the world for him.

PERSONAL APPLICATION

Just before leaving the earth, Jesus gave his disciples some final instructions: "Go and make disciples" (Matthew 28:18-20).

Although Jesus gave this command to the disciples present at his ascension into heaven, it still applies to all believers today. Every disciple needs to make other disciples, to tell others about Jesus and his invitation to receive him as Savior and Lord. Some imagine that the job of sharing the good news about Christ falls mainly to full-time evangelists, but that's not what Jesus said on that mountain. Any method of communicating the gospel, any means of helping people feel or recognize their need for Christ, any help to others taking steps of faith makes disciples. Jesus didn't limit the spreading of the Good News to formal presentations in front of crowds. All believers can communicate the news about Christ, and we all have gifts that we can use to tell his story in a significant way.

BIBLE READING

[1]Early on Sunday morning, as the new day was dawning, Mary Magdalene and the other Mary went out to see the tomb. [2]Suddenly there was a great earthquake, because an angel of the Lord came down from heaven and rolled aside the stone and sat on it. [3]His face shone like lightning, and his clothing was as white as snow. [4]The guards shook with fear when they saw him, and they fell into a dead faint.

[5]Then the angel spoke to the women. "Don't be afraid!" he said. "I know you are looking for Jesus, who was crucified. [6]He isn't here! He has been raised from the dead, just as he said would happen. Come, see where his body was lying. [7]And now, go quickly and tell his disciples he has been raised from the dead, and he is going ahead of you to Galilee. You will see him there. Remember, I have told you."

[8]The women ran quickly from the tomb. They were very frightened but also filled with great joy, and they rushed to find the disciples to give them the angel's message.

[16]Then the eleven disciples left for Galilee, going to the mountain where Jesus had told them to go. [17]When they saw him, they worshiped him—but some of them still doubted!

[18]Jesus came and told his disciples, "I have been given complete authority in heaven and on earth. [19]Therefore, go and make disciples of all the nations, baptizing them in the name of the Father and the Son and the Holy Spirit. [20]Teach these new disciples to obey all the commands I have given you. And be sure of this: I am with you always, even to the end of the age."

MATTHEW 28:1-8, 16-20

The Untouchables

PREVIEW

When making a new acquaintance, you probably greet the person warmly, perhaps even with a friendly handshake, especially if the emotional connections or mutual friendships are right. But what if you learned that the person had AIDS? Would you feel shocked and fearful? Would you involuntarily pull your hand back into your pocket?

The disease of leprosy received that kind of negative reaction in Jesus' day. As with AIDS today, leprosy was seen as a death sentence, wreaking horrible physical devastation on the infected person. Lepers were unclean outcasts—no one came near them.

Despite the social and physical consequences, Jesus, filled with compassion, reached out and touched a leper (Mark 1:41). The empathy and love demonstrated by our Lord challenges us to reach today's outcasts.

PERSONAL APPLICATION

Understand this in context. People greatly feared lepers. Many kinds of leprosy had no cure—once a leper, always a leper. And the disease's side effects meant disfigurement and paralysis. In addition, the law in Leviticus 13 and 14 said that people with leprosy were unclean and were barred from all religious and social activities. Lepers had no status; they lived as total outcasts. Some people even threw rocks at lepers to keep them away.

Certainly you know people who wear the stigma of a disease (such as AIDS), a disability (such as cerebral palsy), or some other condition. The natural response of revulsion or disgust will only prevent you from reaching out to those people in any meaningful way. God's love compels his people to be friendly, accepting, and kind (and to help them, if possible). Reach out and touch an "untouchable."

BIBLE READING

[35]The next morning Jesus awoke long before daybreak and went out alone into the wilderness to pray. [36]Later Simon and the others went out to find him. [37]They said, "Everyone is asking for you."

[38]But he replied, "We must go on to other towns as well, and I will preach to them, too, because that is why I came." [39]So he traveled throughout the region of Galilee, preaching in the synagogues and expelling demons from many people.

[40]A man with leprosy came and knelt in front of Jesus, begging to be healed. "If you want to, you can make me well again," he said.

[41]Moved with pity, Jesus touched him. "I want to," he said. "Be healed!" [42]Instantly the leprosy disappeared—the man was healed. [43]Then Jesus sent him on his way and told him sternly, [44]"Go right over to the priest and let him examine you. Don't talk to anyone along the way. Take along the offering required in the law of Moses for those who have been healed of leprosy, so everyone will have proof of your healing."

[45]But as the man went on his way, he spread the news, telling everyone what had happened to him. As a result, such crowds soon surrounded Jesus that he couldn't enter a town anywhere publicly. He had to stay out in the secluded places, and people from everywhere came to him there. MARK 1:35-45

eed Planting

PREVIEW

If you've ever tried to garden, you know that each plant, each vegetable or flower, is a unique living thing. Each grows differently. And one growing season can differ greatly from the next. But you're always hoping for the best *every* season.

Jesus knew that parables from the land would find receptivity from an audience who understood gardening and farming. We, too, can learn how faith can grow and thrive, or shrivel and die. We can see that there is more than one possible response to God (soil), more than one way that the seeds of faith can fare. As you read, consider what kind of soil you are. That is, how receptive are you to God's seeds?

PERSONAL APPLICATION

As the parable illustrates, not everyone who hears the Word of God receives it. Some forget what they hear almost immediately. Others receive it with joy but fall away when persecution comes. Some receive the Word but then let the attractions and wealth of this world crowd out God's Word from their lives. A few, however, receive God's Word and take it to heart, producing a good crop of righteousness.

When you hear or read God's Word, do you harden your heart and refuse to believe what you've just heard or read? Or are you easily distracted by the cares of this world from paying attention to God's message? If you struggle with one of these attitudes, here are some steps you can take to receive God's Word with joy: (1) Whenever you read the Bible or hear a sermon, do not close your heart to the message. (2) Watch out for the world's distractions that try to turn you off to God's Word. (3) Realize that although parts of God's message will bring joy, other parts may bring sorrow, especially when you examine your life in light of his Word.

BIBLE READING

[1]Once again Jesus began teaching by the lakeshore. There was such a large crowd along the shore that he got into a boat and sat down and spoke from there. [2]He began to teach the people by telling many stories such as this one:

[3]"Listen! A farmer went out to plant some seed. [4]As he scattered it across his field, some seed fell on a footpath, and the birds came and ate it. [5]Other seed fell on shallow soil with underlying rock. The plant sprang up quickly, [6]but it soon wilted beneath the hot sun and died because the roots had no nourishment in the shallow soil. [7]Other seed fell among thorns that shot up and choked out the tender blades so that it produced no grain. [8]Still other seed fell on fertile soil and produced a crop that was thirty, sixty, and even a hundred times as much as had been planted." Then he said, [9]"Anyone who is willing to hear should listen and understand!"

[14]"The farmer I talked about is the one who brings God's message to others. [15]The seed that fell on the hard path represents those who hear the message, but then Satan comes at once and takes it away from them. [16]The rocky soil represents those who hear the message and receive it with joy. [17]But like young plants in such soil, their roots don't go very deep. At first they get along fine, but they wilt as soon as they have problems or are persecuted because they believe the word. [18]The thorny ground represents those who hear and accept the Good News, [19]but all too quickly the message is crowded out by the cares of this life, the lure of wealth, and the desire for nice things, so no crop is produced. [20]But the good soil represents those who hear and accept God's message and produce a huge harvest—thirty, sixty, or even a hundred times as much as had been planted."

MARK 4:1-9, 14-20

Perspective

PREVIEW

When you join a club or organization, you do so because you know something of its philosophy, goals, and activities. When decisions are made and events planned that seem contrary to your knowledge of the club's purpose, you wonder what is going on. You may even speak up and question the club's integrity.

Peter thought he had signed up with the Triumphant King Club, but here he receives a rude awakening. Jesus sets Peter straight, gives him the proper picture, and puts him back on the path of service. As you read, consider what really is involved in becoming a follower of the King.

In this passage Jesus also heals the sick and blind, feeds the hungry, teaches the disciples, corrects the misapprehensions of others, and predicts his death for the first time.

PERSONAL APPLICATION

When Jesus talked about the rejection, suffering, and death that he would soon face, Peter took him aside and told him to stop. In modern words Peter was saying, "Quit that negative talk!" Jesus' response left no doubt where Peter had steered wrong: "You are seeing things merely from a human point of view, not from God's" (Mark 8:33).

Perspective makes all the difference. Peter misjudged Jesus' statement because of his poor perspective. We need to look on our circumstances from God's point of view. This requires that we become familiar with God's priorities and values and see the big picture. This only comes by reading and studying the Scriptures.

The next time God's ways seem silly or out of line with "enlightened thinking," stop and ask God to help you see it all from his angle.

BIBLE READING

²⁷Jesus and his disciples left Galilee and went up to the villages of Caesarea Philippi. As they were walking along, he asked them, "Who do people say I am?"

²⁸"Well," they replied, "some say John the Baptist, some say Elijah, and others say you are one of the other prophets."

²⁹Then Jesus asked, "Who do you say I am?"

Peter replied, "You are the Messiah." ³⁰But Jesus warned them not to tell anyone about him.

³¹Then Jesus began to tell them that he, the Son of Man, would suffer many terrible things and be rejected by the leaders, the leading priests, and the teachers of religious law. He would be killed, and three days later he would rise again. ³²As he talked about this openly with his disciples, Peter took him aside and told him he shouldn't say things like that.

³³Jesus turned and looked at his disciples and then said to Peter very sternly, "Get away from me, Satan! You are seeing things merely from a human point of view, not from God's."

³⁴Then he called his disciples and the crowds to come over and listen. "If any of you wants to be my follower," he told them, "you must put aside your selfish ambition, shoulder your cross, and follow me. ³⁵If you try to keep your life for yourself, you will lose it. But if you give up your life for my sake and for the sake of the Good News, you will find true life. ³⁶And how do you benefit if you gain the whole world but lose your own soul in the process? ³⁷Is anything worth more than your soul? ³⁸If a person is ashamed of me and my message in these adulterous and sinful days, I, the Son of Man, will be ashamed of that person when I return in the glory of my Father with the holy angels."

MARK 8:27-38

*D*oors, Walls, and Fences

PREVIEW

Everyone lives with physical barriers—the doors, walls, and fences that keep valuables in and intruders out. These barriers have counterparts in the moral and spiritual arena—beliefs, attitudes, and actions that define and limit a person's choices. Think, for example, of the fences put up by prejudice, the doors shut by negative self-worth, and the walls built with pride or rebellion.

The young man in today's passage wasn't even aware of the barrier that he had put around his heart. Jesus knocked on the barrier, but the young man was unwilling even to make an opening, much less tear it down. This caused a problem. From the text we can see that all of the young man's good intentions and law-abiding behavior didn't count as much with Jesus as did removing that barrier around his heart.

PERSONAL APPLICATION

When Jesus told the rich young man to sell all he had, the man walked away sadly (Mark 10:17-23). Jesus' challenge revealed the truth about the young man's law-abiding record: he loved his money more than God, thus breaking the first commandment (Exodus 20:3). And as Jesus pointed out, until he let go of this false god, he could not have eternal life (Mark 10:17, 23).

Boasting about goodness always presents a barrier to following Jesus—a false god who is *really* being served. Love of money blocked this man from following Christ; for others it may be career, relationships, security, power, or simply self-centeredness.

The next time you find yourself feeling pride in your own efforts, reevaluate your priorities. Confess your "idol worship" and give Christ first place in your life.

BIBLE READING

[17]A man came running up to Jesus, knelt down, and asked, "Good Teacher, what should I do to get eternal life?"

[18]"Why do you call me good?" Jesus asked. "Only God is truly good. [19]But as for your question, you know the commandments: 'Do not murder. Do not commit adultery. Do not steal. Do not testify falsely. Do not cheat. Honor your father and mother.'"

[20]"Teacher," the man replied, "I've obeyed all these commandments since I was a child."

[21]Jesus felt genuine love for this man as he looked at him. "You lack only one thing," he told him. "Go and sell all you have and give the money to the poor, and you will have treasure in heaven. Then come, follow me." [22]At this, the man's face fell, and he went sadly away because he had many possessions.

[23]Jesus looked around and said to his disciples, "How hard it is for rich people to get into the Kingdom of God!" [24]This amazed them. But Jesus said again, "Dear children, it is very hard to get into the Kingdom of God. [25]It is easier for a camel to go through the eye of a needle than for a rich person to enter the Kingdom of God!"

[26]The disciples were astounded. "Then who in the world can be saved?" they asked.

[27]Jesus looked at them intently and said, "Humanly speaking, it is impossible. But not with God. Everything is possible with God."

[28]Then Peter began to mention all that he and the other disciples had left behind. "We've given up everything to follow you," he said.

[29]And Jesus replied, "I assure you that everyone who has given up house or brothers or sisters or mother or father or children or property, for my sake and for the Good News, [30]will receive now in return, a hundred times over, houses, brothers, sisters, mothers, children, and property—with persecutions. And in the world to come they will have eternal life. [31]But many who seem to be important now will be the least important then, and those who are considered least here will be the greatest then."

MARK 10:17-31

Taking a Fruit Stand

PREVIEW

There are few things more frustrating than excuses. A slow driver in the left lane, perhaps. Another would be a church that doesn't care for people. You probably have a few pet peeves that would qualify as frustrating, too.

Jesus was also frustrated by people and things that didn't fulfill their purpose or potential. This passage records two accounts of his frustration. But Jesus doesn't just get bothered by these incidents—he does something about them. Today's passage exposes the misconception that Jesus was merely a soft-spoken, mild-mannered teacher. He reacted forcefully toward hypocritical religious leaders, profiteering temple merchants, and an unproductive fig tree. His words and actions were strong . . . and the number of his enemies was growing.

PERSONAL APPLICATION

In the hustle and bustle of cosmopolitan Jerusalem, true worship had given way to petty merchandising. People who came to participate in the festivals had to exchange their Roman coins for the temple money. Some of the money changers were exploiting this for their own selfish gain. What should have been *fruitful* service became selfish pursuit.

People of God who don't produce godly behavior are as useless as a fig tree that produces no fruit. Genuine fruitfulness requires genuine faith.

As you watch your powerful Lord in action, compare your life with those he castigated for their unfruitfulness and self-centeredness. What can you do to deepen your relationship with God, pushing down your roots and drawing his nourishment?

BIBLE READING

[12]The next morning as they were leaving Bethany, Jesus felt hungry. [13]He noticed a fig tree a little way off that was in full leaf, so he went over to see if he could find any figs on it. But there were only leaves because it was too early in the season for fruit. [14]Then Jesus said to the tree, "May no one ever eat your fruit again!" And the disciples heard him say it.

[15]When they arrived back in Jerusalem, Jesus entered the Temple and began to drive out the merchants and their customers. He knocked over the tables of the money changers and the stalls of those selling doves, [16]and he stopped everyone from bringing in merchandise. [17]He taught them, "The Scriptures declare, 'My Temple will be called a place of prayer for all nations,' but you have turned it into a den of thieves."

[18]When the leading priests and teachers of religious law heard what Jesus had done, they began planning how to kill him. But they were afraid of him because the people were so enthusiastic about Jesus' teaching. [19]That evening Jesus and the disciples left the city.

[20]The next morning as they passed by the fig tree he had cursed, the disciples noticed it was withered from the roots. [21]Peter remembered what Jesus had said to the tree on the previous day and exclaimed, "Look, Teacher! The fig tree you cursed has withered!"

[22]Then Jesus said to the disciples, "Have faith in God. [23]I assure you that you can say to this mountain, 'May God lift you up and throw you into the sea,' and your command will be obeyed. All that's required is that you really believe and do not doubt in your heart. [24]Listen to me! You can pray for anything, and if you believe, you will have it. [25]But when you are praying, first forgive anyone you are holding a grudge against, so that your Father in heaven will forgive your sins, too."

MARK 11:12-25

The End of the World

PREVIEW

How do you think the world will end? Will a nuclear holocaust obliterate our home planet? Will an asteroid the size of Alaska collide with the earth, causing another ice age? Or will we deplete the ozone layer so much that the world's climates will be radically changed and no longer able to support life?

In this reading, Jesus reveals something about how the world will really end. It's a horrifying finish, but Jesus assures his followers that God is in control. He also encourages his followers who will live through this time to hold fast to their faith in him. Doing so will bring a great reward at the end time. As you read, gain confidence in your heavenly Father who knows and controls the future.

PERSONAL APPLICATION

The events of the end times are still to come in world history. We know that when these events happen Christ's return will follow soon (Mark 13:26-37). Unfortunately, before his return some Christians may be deceived by false prophets who say they have received messages from God or false messiahs who claim to be God (13:5-6).

So how can we avoid being deceived? And how will we know when Christ has returned? We can look for his appearance in the clouds—one of the sure signs of his second coming (13:26; see Revelation 1:7). All people everywhere will be able to see him then.

When Jesus returns, *you will know.* In the meantime, be on your guard against false prophets and false messiahs. Don't believe what they say, because only God the Father knows when Christ will return (13:32). At the same time, be ready because he will come suddenly and unexpectedly, like a "thief in the night" (see Matthew 24:42-44; 1 Thessalonians 5:2).

BIBLE READING

²⁶"'Then everyone will see the Son of Man arrive on the clouds with great power and glory. ²⁷And he will send forth his angels to gather together his chosen ones from all over the world—from the farthest ends of the earth and heaven.

²⁸"Now, learn a lesson from the fig tree. When its buds become tender and its leaves begin to sprout, you know without being told that summer is near. ²⁹Just so, when you see the events I've described beginning to happen, you can be sure that his return is very near, right at the door. ³⁰I assure you, this generation will not pass from the scene until all these events have taken place. ³¹Heaven and earth will disappear, but my words will remain forever.

³²"However, no one knows the day or hour when these things will happen, not even the angels in heaven or the Son himself. Only the Father knows. ³³And since you don't know when they will happen, stay alert and keep watch.

³⁴"The coming of the Son of Man can be compared with that of a man who left home to go on a trip. He gave each of his employees instructions about the work they were to do, and he told the gatekeeper to watch for his return. ³⁵So keep a sharp lookout! For you do not know when the homeowner will return— at evening, midnight, early dawn, or late daybreak. ³⁶Don't let him find you sleeping when he arrives without warning. ³⁷What I say to you I say to everyone: Watch for his return!"

MARK 13:26-37

The Shock Felt around the World

PREVIEW

Whether you have ever been to a funeral or not, you are probably familiar with what a grave site looks like. That's because you have probably passed by countless cemeteries and may have even ventured to walk through a few. So imagine how dismayed you would be if you passed by a grave a couple of days after the funeral, and found that the grave was open and the body was gone.

On the third day after Jesus' crucifixion, three women go to Jesus' tomb to embalm his body with spices. But when they get there, they find an empty tomb. But then an angel tells them that Jesus is alive! As you read, rejoice with these women that Jesus has risen!

PERSONAL APPLICATION

The fact that Jesus rose from the dead is important for several reasons. First, he paid the penalty for our sin that we could never pay ourselves. His resurrection was the final act in redeeming fallen humankind from a sinful nature. Second, coming back to life proved that he is the one and only God, the author of life. No leader of any other world religion has ever come back from the grave. Third, his resurrection was a fulfillment of Old Testament prophecies about the Messiah. Jesus' resurrection was a fulfillment of God's plan for redemption. Fourth, Christ's resurrection not only fulfilled prophecies but also kept the promise he made to rise again. He proved to his followers that he is trustworthy. Fifth, his resurrection is an assurance that all believers in Christ will one day be resurrected, too.

Jesus' resurrection is a miracle in and of itself that makes him worthy of our praise. Thank and worship him for his personal sacrifice to redeem you. At the same time, thank and worship the Father for raising his Son from the grave and for designing and implementing a wonderful plan for saving humanity.

BIBLE READING

[1]The next evening, when the Sabbath ended, Mary Magdalene and Salome and Mary the mother of James went out and purchased burial spices to put on Jesus' body. [2]Very early on Sunday morning, just at sunrise, they came to the tomb. [3]On the way they were discussing who would roll the stone away from the entrance to the tomb. [4]But when they arrived, they looked up and saw that the stone—a very large one—had already been rolled aside. [5]So they entered the tomb, and there on the right sat a young man clothed in a white robe. The women were startled, [6]but the angel said, "Do not be so surprised. You are looking for Jesus, the Nazarene, who was crucified. He isn't here! He has been raised from the dead! Look, this is where they laid his body. [7]Now go and give this message to his disciples, including Peter: Jesus is going ahead of you to Galilee. You will see him there, just as he told you before he died!" [8]The women fled from the tomb, trembling and bewildered, saying nothing to anyone because they were too frightened to talk.

Then they reported all these instructions briefly to Peter and his companions. Afterward Jesus himself sent them out from east to west with the sacred and unfailing message of salvation that gives eternal life. Amen.

[9]It was early on Sunday morning when Jesus rose from the dead, and the first person who saw him was Mary Magdalene, the woman from whom he had cast out seven demons. [10]She went and found the disciples, who were grieving and weeping. [11]But when she told them that Jesus was alive and she had seen him, they didn't believe her.

[12]Afterward he appeared to two who were walking from Jerusalem into the country, but they didn't recognize him at first because he had changed his appearance. [13]When they realized who he was, they rushed back to tell the others, but no one believed them.

MARK 16:1-13

Aged to Perfection

PREVIEW

The older that people get today, the more they prefer to keep their age a secret. That's because our society values youth over age, and the potential contributions of the elderly are often ignored or dismissed as outdated and useless. That wasn't the case in Jesus' time. Age wasn't something to be embarrassed about and wasn't kept a secret. Luke's Gospel even salutes the value of the elderly by recording an incident in which two older people play an important role in Jesus' young life.

As you read this section, look for contrasts with modern views of age and youth and determine to be a person used by God, regardless of your age.

PERSONAL APPLICATION

In Simeon and Anna's culture, elders were respected, and age wasn't a strike against their usefulness. But if Simeon and Anna had lived today, their lives and testimonies probably would not have meant as much.

Despite what our society believes, the elderly still have much to contribute. As Christians, we should value them not only as human beings but also as people from whom we can learn a great deal. If you're young, invite older people to share their wisdom and experience with you. Listen carefully when they speak. Offer them your friendship, and help them find ways to continue to serve God. If you are elderly, don't believe our society's views about you. Continue serving God, however he enables you. In God's view, you are never too old to be useful.

BIBLE READING

[25]Now there was a man named Simeon who lived in Jerusalem. He was a righteous man and very devout. He was filled with the Holy Spirit, and he eagerly expected the Messiah to come and rescue Israel. [26]The Holy Spirit had revealed to him that he would not die until he had seen the Lord's Messiah. [27]That day the Spirit led him to the Temple. So when Mary and Joseph came to present the baby Jesus to the Lord as the law required, [28]Simeon was there. He took the child in his arms and praised God, saying,

[29] "Lord, now I can die in peace!
    As you promised me,
[30] I have seen the Savior
[31] you have given to all people.
[32] He is a light to reveal God to the nations,
    and he is the glory of your people Israel!"

[33]Joseph and Mary were amazed at what was being said about Jesus. [34]Then Simeon blessed them, and he said to Mary, "This child will be rejected by many in Israel, and it will be their undoing. But he will be the greatest joy to many others. [35]Thus, the deepest thoughts of many hearts will be revealed. And a sword will pierce your very soul."

[36]Anna, a prophet, was also there in the Temple. She was the daughter of Phanuel, of the tribe of Asher, and was very old. She was a widow, for her husband had died when they had been married only seven years. [37]She was now eighty-four years old. She never left the Temple but stayed there day and night, worshiping God with fasting and prayer. [38]She came along just as Simeon was talking with Mary and Joseph, and she began praising God. She talked about Jesus to everyone who had been waiting for the promised King to come and deliver Jerusalem.

LUKE 2:25-38

Lord, Master, King

PREVIEW

Sooner or later almost every person has at least one negative opinion about his or her boss. Some bosses definitely earn this reputation, while others come by it innocently through the instructions they give their employees. In this latter instance, it comes down to this: The boss has told you to do something, and you don't like it. What can you do?

You may have never thought of Jesus as a bosslike figure, but he was a leader while he was here on earth. This reading contains examples of his earthly leadership. Here he takes charge and gives orders, and gets flak for it—just as we might expect. As you read, watch Jesus lead and learn from his example.

PERSONAL APPLICATION

Many people think of Jesus as a nice man, even a great man, who taught great truths. But the problem is that these same people stop short of viewing Jesus as an authority figure. They don't think he has any right to influence even the most minuscule area of their lives. They don't understand that Jesus isn't just a nice teacher, a gentle giant, or a profound guru. He's the Creator and absolute ruler of the universe (see Colossians 1:16-20). He has all authority (see Matthew 28:18). He has the right to tell us how to live, and he has power over all forces in the universe—natural, physical, and spiritual.

Whenever you read Jesus' teachings, see them as your mandate for living. Read them as if they were directed right at you. Jesus didn't come just to inspire us, but to lay claim to us. Can you call him Lord, Master, King?

BIBLE READING

³¹Then Jesus went to Capernaum, a town in Galilee, and taught there in the synagogue every Sabbath day. ³²There, too, the people were amazed at the things he said, because he spoke with authority.

³³Once when he was in the synagogue, a man possessed by a demon began shouting at Jesus, ³⁴"Go away! Why are you bothering us, Jesus of Nazareth? Have you come to destroy us? I know who you are—the Holy One sent from God."

³⁵Jesus cut him short. "Be silent!" he told the demon. "Come out of the man!" The demon threw the man to the floor as the crowd watched; then it left him without hurting him further.

³⁶Amazed, the people exclaimed, "What authority and power this man's words possess! Even evil spirits obey him and flee at his command!" ³⁷The story of what he had done spread like wildfire throughout the whole region.

³⁸After leaving the synagogue that day, Jesus went to Simon's home, where he found Simon's mother-in-law very sick with a high fever. "Please heal her," everyone begged. ³⁹Standing at her bedside, he spoke to the fever, rebuking it, and immediately her temperature returned to normal. She got up at once and prepared a meal for them.

⁴⁰As the sun went down that evening, people throughout the village brought sick family members to Jesus. No matter what their diseases were, the touch of his hand healed every one. ⁴¹Some were possessed by demons; and the demons came out at his command, shouting, "You are the Son of God." But because they knew he was the Messiah, he stopped them and told them to be silent.   LUKE 4:31-41

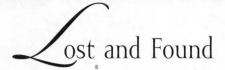

Lost and Found

PREVIEW

The start of a new year is a common occasion for making resolutions—from becoming more fit, to serving in the community, to sticking to spiritual disciplines. Our commitment is high; we can't be swayed by man or beast . . . then the second week of the year rolls along, and we begin to wonder, *Is it really worth it?*

In this reading Jesus speaks to those of us whose resolve has begun to dissolve. He demands commitment and speaks clearly about what it will take to follow him. But he does not ask us to do anything he would not do himself, and demonstrates his own commitment to people by reaching out to the lowest in society, calming John the Baptist's fears, and feeding thousands of people. As you read, consider what you can do to be more like Christ.

PERSONAL APPLICATION

To follow Jesus, sooner or later we must submit our wants and desires to his desires for us. We must stop serving ourselves and start serving him. If that means selling something, we sell it. If it means stopping a certain behavior, we stop it. If it means doing something we don't want to do, we do it. It means the end of what we want and the beginning of what Jesus wants. That is why Jesus says, "If you try to keep your life for yourself, you will lose it"—because only by giving it up to Jesus can you gain eternal life.

Is it worth it? If you have any doubt, Jesus makes a good case for doing so: "How do you benefit if you gain the whole world but lose or forfeit your own soul in the process?" (Luke 9:25). Sure, there's a price to be paid for following Jesus, but those who pay it also receive an eternal benefit.

BIBLE READING

¹⁸One day as Jesus was alone, praying, he came over to his disciples and asked them, "Who do people say I am?"

¹⁹"Well," they replied, "some say John the Baptist, some say Elijah, and others say you are one of the other ancient prophets risen from the dead."

²⁰Then he asked them, "Who do you say I am?"

Peter replied, "You are the Messiah sent from God!"

²¹Jesus warned them not to tell anyone about this. ²²"For I, the Son of Man, must suffer many terrible things," he said. "I will be rejected by the leaders, the leading priests, and the teachers of religious law. I will be killed, but three days later I will be raised from the dead."

²³Then he said to the crowd, "If any of you wants to be my follower, you must put aside your selfish ambition, shoulder your cross daily, and follow me. ²⁴If you try to keep your life for yourself, you will lose it. But if you give up your life for me, you will find true life. ²⁵And how do you benefit if you gain the whole world but lose or forfeit your own soul in the process? ²⁶If a person is ashamed of me and my message, I, the Son of Man, will be ashamed of that person when I return in my glory and in the glory of the Father and the holy angels. ²⁷And I assure you that some of you standing here right now will not die before you see the Kingdom of God."   LUKE 9:18-27

Recruiters

Preview

A huge task confronts you and you spring into action. You form committees. You buy supplies. You organize a phone-a-thon. Wait! Have you forgotten to pray?

When it came to accomplishing any task, prayer was at the top of Jesus' list. In addition to setting this example, Jesus also taught how to divide the labor—long before the days of personnel assessment profiles, project-management software, and planning calendars.

As you read this passage, understand the priority of prayer and place it at the top of your to-do list.

Personal Application

Jesus sent out seventy-two of his disciples in pairs to spread the good news about him. Despite this good start, his mission was still under-staffed. The first step he took in solving this problem was to instruct his followers to "Pray to the Lord who is in charge of the harvest, and ask him to send out more workers for his fields" (Luke 10:2). They had a huge task, and getting it done meant asking God to send more people.

Likewise, we have a huge task today in furthering the spread of the gospel. No one person, however, can save the world single-handedly. You can't be a missionary to Rwanda, live at home and minister to your family, and tell your coworkers about Christ all at once. But you can list the people and causes that matter to you and pray that God will send people to each one. You can also ask him to help you take advantage of the opportunities to share the gospel that come your way.

If you have friends and relatives who don't know Christ, pray for them. Ask God to send believers into their lives who will address their concerns, objections, and needs—people who will lead them to the Savior.

BIBLE READING

[1]The Lord now chose seventy-two other disciples and sent them on ahead in pairs to all the towns and villages he planned to visit. [2]These were his instructions to them: "The harvest is so great, but the workers are so few. Pray to the Lord who is in charge of the harvest, and ask him to send out more workers for his fields. [3]Go now, and remember that I am sending you out as lambs among wolves. [4]Don't take along any money, or a traveler's bag, or even an extra pair of sandals. And don't stop to greet anyone on the road.

[5]"Whenever you enter a home, give it your blessing. [6]If those who live there are worthy, the blessing will stand; if they are not, the blessing will return to you. [7]When you enter a town, don't move around from home to home. Stay in one place, eating and drinking what they provide you. Don't hesitate to accept hospitality, because those who work deserve their pay.

[8]"If a town welcomes you, eat whatever is set before you [9]and heal the sick. As you heal them, say, 'The Kingdom of God is near you now.' [10]But if a town refuses to welcome you, go out into its streets and say, [11]'We wipe the dust of your town from our feet as a public announcement of your doom. And don't forget the Kingdom of God is near!' [12]The truth is, even wicked Sodom will be better off than such a town on the judgment day."

LUKE 10:1-12

Let's Give Him a Hand

PREVIEW

"But what would people think?" For many of us, this question springs to our mind and even our lips more than we would like to admit. Even as we think about making a moral choice, we ponder how popular or unpopular it would be.

Those who are concerned more with the popularity than the morality of their decisions need to think twice. This reading is full of warnings that Jesus aimed primarily at Pharisees and other "experts in religious law." But they could easily apply to any person today who, like these people, is more concerned with appearances than with justice and righteousness. As you read, consider how important being popular is to you.

Jesus' lessons are to the point in other areas as well, including prayer and unbelief.

PERSONAL APPLICATION

Jesus criticized some of the Pharisees and experts in the Law harshly because they loved praise and attention (Luke 11:43). They went wrong by protecting their outward appearances while ignoring their attitudes and God's revealed desires.

Public recognition of our "religiosity" does not make us devout. We must guard against taking public admiration or honor from religious folks as proof of our own religious piety. God seeks sincere and unselfish devotion to him; this requires humility. Striving to be in the spotlight works against that. Seek God's praise and attention, not that of people.

BIBLE READING

[43]"How terrible it will be for you Pharisees! For how you love the seats of honor in the synagogues and the respectful greetings from everyone as you walk through the markets! [44]Yes, how terrible it will be for you. For you are like hidden graves in a field. People walk over them without knowing the corruption they are stepping on."

[45]"Teacher," said an expert in religious law, "you have insulted us, too, in what you just said."

[46]"Yes," said Jesus, "how terrible it will be for you experts in religious law! For you crush people beneath impossible religious demands, and you never lift a finger to help ease the burden. [47]How terrible it will be for you! For you build tombs for the very prophets your ancestors killed long ago. [48]Murderers! You agree with your ancestors that what they did was right. You would have done the same yourselves. [49]This is what God in his wisdom said about you: 'I will send prophets and apostles to them, and they will kill some and persecute the others.'

[50]"And you of this generation will be held responsible for the murder of all God's prophets from the creation of the world— [51]from the murder of Abel to the murder of Zechariah, who was killed between the altar and the sanctuary. Yes, it will surely be charged against you.

[52]"How terrible it will be for you experts in religious law! For you hide the key to knowledge from the people. You don't enter the Kingdom yourselves, and you prevent others from entering."

[53]As Jesus finished speaking, the Pharisees and teachers of religious law were furious. From that time on they grilled him with many hostile questions, [54]trying to trap him into saying something they could use against him.   LUKE 11:43-54

Division Decision

PREVIEW

What topics generate heated debate in your family? Politics, for example, is completely off-limits for some family gatherings because of the potential for misunderstandings and hurt feelings. There are many issues upon which families can disagree.

In this reading, Jesus speaks about more than mere dinnertime discussions. A person's relationship with God can—indeed, should—affect every earthly relationship. Sometimes the effect is negative and Jesus wants his followers to be prepared. As you read, think of how your Christian faith has impacted your relationships.

PERSONAL APPLICATION

Jesus came to bring strife and division, not peace. Wait—isn't Jesus supposed to be a peacemaker? Did he not say to turn the other cheek when others insult or injure us? Didn't he allow thugs to nail him to the cross? Why this talk of fighting? Why this bad news?

Jesus isn't asking us to pick fights, to be obnoxious with our views, or to brag about being enlightened until people can't stand to hear it anymore. He's merely warning us that not everyone will want to follow him. Some will accept him while others will reject him. Unlike choosing a favorite color, recognizing God's absolute authority, our sin, and Jesus' claim on our lives radically changes us. Because these changes affect many areas of great consequence, they will often ripple through the close relationships in a family.

Be patient with those who are slow to respond to God's gift of salvation or the changes he brings about in your life. Have faith that those loved ones who reject Christ may one day accept him. In the meantime endure their rejection, realizing that Christ understands what you are going through.

BIBLE READING

[49]"I have come to bring fire to the earth, and I wish that my task were already completed! [50]There is a terrible baptism ahead of me, and I am under a heavy burden until it is accomplished. [51]Do you think I have come to bring peace to the earth? No, I have come to bring strife and division! [52]From now on families will be split apart, three in favor of me, and two against—or the other way around. [53]There will be a division between father and son, mother and daughter, mother-in-law and daughter-in-law."

LUKE 12:49-53

$\mathscr{S}$urprise Party

PREVIEW

Have you ever joked about who will and will not get into heaven? Many comedians have placed famous people at the pearly gates, giving some excuse as to why they should be let in. These jokes are so popular (and often so funny) that they are heard from the pulpit, as well.

Jesus, on the other hand, paints a less-than-humorous picture about entering heaven. In this passage, he shows us the meaning of being saved and describes God's criteria for his followers—living a life that imitates Christ. As you read, match your life with his criteria.

Also look for lessons on facing criticism for the right choice; being frustrated with concern over a city; seeking honor; and the cost of following Christ.

PERSONAL APPLICATION

Many people will express great surprise when God judges the world. Some who escaped the notice of journalists and awards committees will receive great honor then; others who had great influence and authority here will have nothing to offer God (Luke 13:22-30). God doesn't care about a person's earthly popularity, status, achievements, reputation, wealth, heritage, influence, or power; he cares about a person's commitment to Christ. Many people whom God considers great get absolutely no worldly recognition.

Do not waste time trying to impress the world. Seek praise and honor instead from God alone. His approval counts for eternity.

BIBLE READING

²²Jesus went through the towns and villages, teaching as he went, always pressing on toward Jerusalem. ²³Someone asked him, "Lord, will only a few be saved?"

He replied, ²⁴"The door to heaven is narrow. Work hard to get in, because many will try to enter, ²⁵but when the head of the house has locked the door, it will be too late. Then you will stand outside knocking and pleading, 'Lord, open the door for us!' But he will reply, 'I do not know you.' ²⁶You will say, 'But we ate and drank with you, and you taught in our streets.' ²⁷And he will reply, 'I tell you, I don't know you. Go away, all you who do evil.'

²⁸"And there will be great weeping and gnashing of teeth, for you will see Abraham, Isaac, Jacob, and all the prophets within the Kingdom of God, but you will be thrown out. ²⁹Then people will come from all over the world to take their places in the Kingdom of God. ³⁰And note this: Some who are despised now will be greatly honored then; and some who are greatly honored now will be despised then."

³¹A few minutes later some Pharisees said to him, "Get out of here if you want to live, because Herod Antipas wants to kill you!"

³²Jesus replied, "Go tell that fox that I will keep on casting out demons and doing miracles of healing today and tomorrow; and the third day I will accomplish my purpose. ³³Yes, today, tomorrow, and the next day I must proceed on my way. For it wouldn't do for a prophet of God to be killed except in Jerusalem!

³⁴"O Jerusalem, Jerusalem, the city that kills the prophets and stones God's messengers! How often I have wanted to gather your children together as a hen protects her chicks beneath her wings, but you wouldn't let me. ³⁵And now look, your house is left to you empty. And you will never see me again until you say, 'Bless the one who comes in the name of the Lord!'"   LUKE 13:22-35

Who's the Boss?

PREVIEW

If you ever have had the unfortunate experience of having two bosses at work, you know that opposing supervisory forces can make the workday a continual struggle of conflicting priorities and miscommunication. Yet when it comes to values, that's the way many people live. They try to go in two directions at the same time.

God and riches can be like two bosses, each demanding your allegiance. Perhaps no other spiritual struggle is as intense as this one. It is a struggle between two needs—God and money—and where to place your faith. Some place it in money. Some place it in God. Still others try to divide their faith between the two. In this reading, Jesus lets people know that this is not possible. You must choose to serve one or the other. As you read, ask God to reveal your values, to show you where your allegiance is.

Also, look for the down-to-earth lessons found in the stories of coins; an unforgiving fellow who gets his just desserts; and a son who learns from his father what true love is.

PERSONAL APPLICATION

Money tests us at every turn. The way we earn it, the way we spend it, and the way we give it away all reveal who or what rules our heart (Luke 16:10-12). If we serve money, we will live for it and try to get it at all costs. But if we serve God, we will be honest in how we earn money, shrewd in how we spend it, and generous in how we give it. Most notably, we will be dependable with others' money.

Do riches have control over you? God wants your love and loyalty. He will not share what is rightfully his with anything or anyone. Do not fool yourself—you can't serve both God and money (16:13). Sooner or later you have to choose one over the other. Which will you choose?

BIBLE READING

¹Jesus told this story to his disciples: "A rich man hired a manager to handle his affairs, but soon a rumor went around that the manager was thoroughly dishonest. ²So his employer called him in and said, 'What's this I hear about your stealing from me? Get your report in order, because you are going to be dismissed.'

³"The manager thought to himself, 'Now what? I'm through here, and I don't have the strength to go out and dig ditches, and I'm too proud to beg. ⁴I know just the thing! And then I'll have plenty of friends to take care of me when I leave!'

⁵"So he invited each person who owed money to his employer to come and discuss the situation. He asked the first one, 'How much do you owe him?' ⁶The man replied, 'I owe him eight hundred gallons of olive oil.' So the manager told him, 'Tear up that bill and write another one for four hundred gallons.'

⁷" 'And how much do you owe my employer?' he asked the next man. 'A thousand bushels of wheat,' was the reply. 'Here,' the manager said, 'take your bill and replace it with one for only eight hundred bushels.'

⁸"The rich man had to admire the dishonest rascal for being so shrewd. And it is true that the citizens of this world are more shrewd than the godly are. ⁹I tell you, use your worldly resources to benefit others and make friends. In this way, your generosity stores up a reward for you in heaven.

¹⁰"Unless you are faithful in small matters, you won't be faithful in large ones. If you cheat even a little, you won't be honest with greater responsibilities. ¹¹And if you are untrustworthy about worldly wealth, who will trust you with the true riches of heaven? ¹²And if you are not faithful with other people's money, why should you be trusted with money of your own?

¹³"No one can serve two masters. For you will hate one and love the other, or be devoted to one and despise the other. You cannot serve both God and money."   LUKE 16:1-13

 # *How* Childish

PREVIEW

Think back to when you were a young child, perhaps five years old. Didn't it mean the world to you when an adult would take the time to listen to you? How did you feel when an adult knelt down to your level and communicated that you were important?

In a brief but important scene in this reading, Jesus takes the time to do this with a group of children. He expresses his love for them and rebukes the grown-ups who try to prohibit them from coming to him. Through this incident he also teaches the disciples and all of his followers a key truth about the kingdom of God. As you read, learn with the disciples how much little children matter to God.

PERSONAL APPLICATION

What does it mean to have the faith of a child? It means trusting in someone or something without giving it a second thought. A daughter, for example, will jump into her father's arms, knowing that he won't drop her. A son won't ponder the risks involved in going to a strange place if he knows Mom and Dad will be there, too. He will simply go. If only we would be like that with God.

Some of what God asks his people to do has no explanation or obvious benefit, but if we have the faith of a child, that should not matter. We should know that Daddy is strong enough to catch us, and we can assume that he won't take us to a bad place.

What has God asked you to do? Where has he told you to go? Take the risk of trusting God the way a child trusts his or her parents—completely and without hesitation.

BIBLE READING

[9] Then Jesus told this story to some who had great self-confidence and scorned everyone else: [10] "Two men went to the Temple to pray. One was a Pharisee, and the other was a dishonest tax collector. [11] The proud Pharisee stood by himself and prayed this prayer: 'I thank you, God, that I am not a sinner like everyone else, especially like that tax collector over there! For I never cheat, I don't sin, I don't commit adultery, [12] I fast twice a week, and I give you a tenth of my income.'

[13] "But the tax collector stood at a distance and dared not even lift his eyes to heaven as he prayed. Instead, he beat his chest in sorrow, saying, 'O God, be merciful to me, for I am a sinner.' [14] I tell you, this sinner, not the Pharisee, returned home justified before God. For the proud will be humbled, but the humble will be honored."

[15] One day some parents brought their little children to Jesus so he could touch them and bless them, but the disciples told them not to bother him. [16] Then Jesus called for the children and said to the disciples, "Let the children come to me. Don't stop them! For the Kingdom of God belongs to such as these. [17] I assure you, anyone who doesn't have their kind of faith will never get into the Kingdom of God."   LUKE 18:9-17

Happy Ending

PREVIEW

Whether watching a television show, video, or movie, or reading a book, everyone likes happy endings, where the main characters triumph over tragedy and overwhelming odds. We like to see the hero or heroine get justice or some other reward. Ultimately, we like to see evil soundly defeated and, at times, completely eliminated. We want the events to happen this way because in real life there are few happy endings. Good hardly ever seems to triumph and never seems to win out.

The bad news is that things are not going to get better—yet. In this reading, Jesus warns his followers that in the end times they will be persecuted, arrested, and killed because of him. But he also reassures them that those who remain faithful to him during the difficult times will definitely experience a happy ending. If your present struggles seem overwhelming, take hope as you read this passage—God's story has a truly happy ending.

PERSONAL APPLICATION

Jesus knew that the time would come when people would oppose both him and his disciples, even to the point of torturing and killing them. Some of his followers would even find relatives and former friends among their new enemies. Jesus told his disciples to expect this, but he also told them not to worry because God's Holy Spirit would tell them what to say and how to respond whenever they came under attack (Luke 21:14-19).

Following Christ has always entailed the risk of rejection from others. Jesus reassures us that whenever that happens, he stands right there with us, with his Holy Spirit guiding and helping us. Remember this the next time you need courage or hope, and then stand firm for Christ.

BIBLE READING

⁵Some of his disciples began talking about the beautiful stone-work of the Temple and the memorial decorations on the walls. But Jesus said, ⁶"The time is coming when all these things will be so completely demolished that not one stone will be left on top of another."

⁷"Teacher," they asked, "when will all this take place? And will there be any sign ahead of time?"

⁸He replied, "Don't let anyone mislead you. For many will come in my name, claiming to be the Messiah and saying, 'The time has come!' But don't believe them. ⁹And when you hear of wars and insurrections, don't panic. Yes, these things must come, but the end won't follow immediately." ¹⁰Then he added, "Nations and kingdoms will proclaim war against each other. ¹¹There will be great earthquakes, and there will be famines and epidemics in many lands, and there will be terrifying things and great miraculous signs in the heavens.

¹²"But before all this occurs, there will be a time of great persecution. You will be dragged into synagogues and prisons, and you will be accused before kings and governors of being my followers. ¹³This will be your opportunity to tell them about me. ¹⁴So don't worry about how to answer the charges against you, ¹⁵for I will give you the right words and such wisdom that none of your opponents will be able to reply! ¹⁶Even those closest to you—your parents, brothers, relatives, and friends—will betray you. And some of you will be killed. ¹⁷And everyone will hate you because of your allegiance to me. ¹⁸But not a hair of your head will perish! ¹⁹By standing firm, you will win your souls."

LUKE 21:5-19

Jockeying for Position

PREVIEW

Some people have trouble remaining serious at somber occasions. The weight of the moment more than escapes them—its gravity causes their minds to wander. They are oblivious to their surroundings and the importance of the event.

The disciples fall prey to a form of this as Jesus shares some difficult news. Rather than listening to what he has to say, they begin to argue about who will be the greatest in God's kingdom. Jesus' response to their arguing is amazing. He could have rebuked them for their pettiness. Instead, he tells them how to be great and then sets the example. As you read, consider how *you* may be getting in the way of God's purpose for your life. Are you focused on yourself or on doing his will?

PERSONAL APPLICATION

At Jesus' last supper with his disciples before his death, the disciples got into a lively discussion about who would be greatest in his upcoming kingdom. Why did they jockey for position at a time like this (Luke 22:24)? Did they simply not want to believe the bad news, or didn't they care? Capitalizing on their self-centeredness, Jesus explained that to be great they must serve others (22:25-27).

It's easy to criticize the disciples for their self-centeredness, but that's the way we are, too. Sometimes we have great concern for our own ascent to greatness, wealth, and prestige. But Christ commands us to do as he did by serving others.

About what desires for career advancement, better reputation, or public achievement do you dream? Rather than just serving your ambitions, look for opportunities to serve others.

BIBLE READING

[19]Then he took a loaf of bread; and when he had thanked God for it, he broke it in pieces and gave it to the disciples, saying, "This is my body, given for you. Do this in remembrance of me." [20]After supper he took another cup of wine and said, "This wine is the token of God's new covenant to save you—an agreement sealed with the blood I will pour out for you.

[21]"But here at this table, sitting among us as a friend, is the man who will betray me. [22]For I, the Son of Man, must die since it is part of God's plan. But how terrible it will be for my betrayer!" [23]Then the disciples began to ask each other which of them would ever do such a thing.

[24]And they began to argue among themselves as to who would be the greatest in the coming Kingdom. [25]Jesus told them, "In this world the kings and great men order their people around, and yet they are called 'friends of the people.' [26]But among you, those who are the greatest should take the lowest rank, and the leader should be like a servant. [27]Normally the master sits at the table and is served by his servants. But not here! For I am your servant. [28]You have remained true to me in my time of trial. [29]And just as my Father has granted me a Kingdom, I now grant you the right [30]to eat and drink at my table in that Kingdom. And you will sit on thrones, judging the twelve tribes of Israel."

LUKE 22:19-30

 **ll Aboard!**

PREVIEW

You hurry for the train, bounding along the platform. You rush through the closing doors and eagerly settle into a seat. When the conductor calls out the stops and final destination of the train, you realize in a panic that you're on the wrong one!

In a way, this is the experience of the disciples. As Jesus reaches his final destination—the cross—his disciples begin to wonder what is going on. They thought that they had signed up with a triumphant army, but they see their leader, Jesus, dying with criminals. Did they get on the wrong train? What are your expectations in your walk with Christ?

PERSONAL APPLICATION

Sometimes we expect to be rewarded too soon for following Christ. We expect congratulations (or at least grudging admiration) from coworkers and friends for our choice to do what is right. Most of all, we expect God to oversee everything with our own interests first in his mind. We can get a rude awakening when our expectations get ambushed by the exact opposite—trouble, tragedy, conflict, or disappointment. As Jesus' death on the cross shows, sometimes God's plan for us doesn't bring instant victory, justice, or reward. Suffering may precede or follow right choices.

Don't let your expectations get in the way of enjoying God's good plan for you now. He cares—you can be sure of that. Setbacks, unfairness, sufferings, and other trials enter the picture as part of it all. Exactly why, you may not know. But you can be sure that it isn't a surprise to God and that the timetable—though it may seem long—makes perfect sense to him.

BIBLE READING

[32]Two others, both criminals, were led out to be executed with him. [33]Finally, they came to a place called The Skull. All three were crucified there—Jesus on the center cross, and the two criminals on either side.

[34]Jesus said, "Father, forgive these people, because they don't know what they are doing." And the soldiers gambled for his clothes by throwing dice.

[35]The crowd watched, and the leaders laughed and scoffed. "He saved others," they said, "let him save himself if he is really God's Chosen One, the Messiah." [36]The soldiers mocked him, too, by offering him a drink of sour wine. [37]They called out to him, "If you are the King of the Jews, save yourself!" [38]A sign-board was nailed to the cross above him with these words: "This is the King of the Jews."

[39]One of the criminals hanging beside him scoffed, "So you're the Messiah, are you? Prove it by saving yourself—and us, too, while you're at it!"

[40]But the other criminal protested, "Don't you fear God even when you are dying? [41]We deserve to die for our evil deeds, but this man hasn't done anything wrong." [42]Then he said, "Jesus, remember me when you come into your Kingdom."

[43]And Jesus replied, "I assure you, today you will be with me in paradise." LUKE 23:32-43

Where Is That Pen?

PREVIEW

When was the last time you scoured the house looking for the pen that was behind your ear? Have you ever needed to ask someone for your own phone number because you couldn't remember it? Or have you ever driven to work when you were supposed to be headed to the grocery store? Lapses of attention and memory afflict everyone from time to time.

The two disciples on the road to Emmaus have one of these lapses in memory. Their lapse, however, is more serious than forgetting where they placed a pen. Fortunately, the recently risen Jesus comes along, explains where they went wrong, and sets them straight. It may seem incredible that this couple could forget Christ, but consider the times that you have "forgotten" the Savior.

PERSONAL APPLICATION

The two disciples on the road to Emmaus were depressed and hopeless. Despite others' testimony that Jesus was alive, these two still didn't believe or even grasp this fact. But when the risen Jesus met them on the road to Emmaus, he called them "foolish people" (Luke 24:25) because they found it difficult to believe the Scriptures. They had already forgotten what Jesus had told them several times before.

Sometimes our inability to enjoy the presence of Christ stems from our own disbelief of the Scriptures. We worry about life's problems despite God's promises to provide for our needs. Or we read the Bible, attend church, and even serve as Christian workers only to wonder if God is at work in the world.

Don't easily forget this truth you have learned: Jesus has defeated sin and death, and is alive today! He is with you through the Holy Spirit. Enjoy his presence.

BIBLE READING

[13]That same day two of Jesus' followers were walking to the village of Emmaus, seven miles out of Jerusalem. [14]As they walked along they were talking about everything that had happened. [15]Suddenly, Jesus himself came along and joined them and began walking beside them. [16]But they didn't know who he was, because God kept them from recognizing him.

[17]"You seem to be in a deep discussion about something," he said. "What are you so concerned about?"

They stopped short, sadness written across their faces. [18]Then one of them, Cleopas, replied, "You must be the only person in Jerusalem who hasn't heard about all the things that have happened there the last few days."

[19]"What things?" Jesus asked.

"The things that happened to Jesus, the man from Nazareth," they said. "He was a prophet who did wonderful miracles. He was a mighty teacher, highly regarded by both God and all the people. [20]But our leading priests and other religious leaders arrested him and handed him over to be condemned to death, and they crucified him. [21]We had thought he was the Messiah who had come to rescue Israel. That all happened three days ago. [22]Then some women from our group of his followers were at his tomb early this morning, and they came back with an amazing report. [23]They said his body was missing, and they had seen angels who told them Jesus is alive! [24]Some of our men ran out to see, and sure enough, Jesus' body was gone, just as the women had said."

[25]Then Jesus said to them, "You are such foolish people! You find it so hard to believe all that the prophets wrote in the Scriptures. [26]Wasn't it clearly predicted by the prophets that the Messiah would have to suffer all these things before entering his time of glory?" [27]Then Jesus quoted passages from the writings of Moses and all the prophets, explaining what all the Scriptures said about himself.   LUKE 24:13-27

eflections

PREVIEW

It is a valiant way to serve God. It does not bring any earthly reward, and the costs of serving are tremendous, emotionally and sometimes physically. This is the ministry of a soapbox preacher—one who stands in the middle of a college campus, for example, and proclaims the Word of God to sneering, mocking students. He is a modern-day John the Baptist—a lone voice crying in the wilderness.

At times, John the Baptist was probably treated like a soapbox preacher. But that did not dissuade him from completing his mission— to call the Jews to repentance, baptize Jesus, and introduce Jesus as the Messiah. As you read, learn from the courage and conviction of John the Baptist, and determine to introduce people to the Savior.

PERSONAL APPLICATION

God sent John the Baptist to identify Jesus as God's living light (John 1:8). Today, all Christians, like John the Baptist, serve to bring God's light to the world. We are not the source of God's light—we merely reflect it. Jesus Christ is the true Light. He helps us see our way to God and shows us how to walk along that path. But Christ also has chosen to shine his light through his followers to an unbelieving world. As we reflect God's moral excellence, our lives and words help guide others.

If you belong to Christ, your lifestyle, habits, words, and actions should reflect God's goodness to the people around you. Take time today to examine your life carefully. Ask God to point out any area that does not reflect his goodness. Then ask for his grace and strength, to make the needed changes in your life and to brightly reflect his light.

BIBLE READING

¹In the beginning the Word already existed. He was with God, and he was God. ²He was in the beginning with God. ³He created everything there is. Nothing exists that he didn't make. ⁴Life itself was in him, and this life gives light to everyone. ⁵The light shines through the darkness, and the darkness can never extinguish it.

⁶God sent John the Baptist ⁷to tell everyone about the light so that everyone might believe because of his testimony. ⁸John himself was not the light; he was only a witness to the light. ⁹The one who is the true light, who gives light to everyone, was going to come into the world.

¹⁰But although the world was made through him, the world didn't recognize him when he came. ¹¹Even in his own land and among his own people, he was not accepted. ¹²But to all who believed him and accepted him, he gave the right to become children of God. ¹³They are reborn! This is not a physical birth resulting from human passion or plan—this rebirth comes from God.

¹⁴So the Word became human and lived here on earth among us. He was full of unfailing love and faithfulness. And we have seen his glory, the glory of the only Son of the Father.

JOHN 1:1-14

rue Love

PREVIEW

True love has inspired countless books, poems, movie scripts, and songs. Young men and women have spent endless hours dreaming about it. Wars have been fought over it, and people have ended their lives because of losing it. How can this emotion demand so much attention and cause so much misfortune?

Unfortunately, the popular perception of true love is wrong. It is *not* romantic feelings between a man and a woman. Jesus knows the answer, and in this reading, he explains true love to the truth-seeking Pharisee, Nicodemus. Earlier, Jesus revealed his love for his Father when he cleared the temple. As you read, look for true love in action and think of how you should display your love for God.

PERSONAL APPLICATION

The entire message of the Bible comes to a focus in John 3:16: "For God so loved the world that he gave his only Son, so that everyone who believes in him will not perish but have eternal life." Did you feel the weight of every word? There is no greater love than the birth, death, and resurrection of Jesus Christ.

As seen in Jesus' sacrifice, there is a big difference between his *true* love and what we call "love." While we reserve our love for special cases and special occasions, Jesus gives his love freely to all. While we love up to a point, Jesus loves to the point of self-sacrifice. While we restrict love to those who've earned it, Jesus loves those who can never deserve it.

Where are you looking for love? Please know that God loves you unconditionally. In fact, he loves you so much that he sent his Son, Jesus, to die for you so you might be forgiven and spend eternity with him. Give your life to the one who truly loves you. Let him teach you true love so that you can truly love others.

BIBLE READING

[12]"But if you don't even believe me when I tell you about things that happen here on earth, how can you possibly believe if I tell you what is going on in heaven? [13]For only I, the Son of Man, have come to earth and will return to heaven again. [14]And as Moses lifted up the bronze snake on a pole in the wilderness, so I, the Son of Man, must be lifted up on a pole, [15]so that everyone who believes in me will have eternal life.

[16]"For God so loved the world that he gave his only Son, so that everyone who believes in him will not perish but have eternal life. [17]God did not send his Son into the world to condemn it, but to save it.

[18]"There is no judgment awaiting those who trust him. But those who do not trust him have already been judged for not believing in the only Son of God. [19]Their judgment is based on this fact: The light from heaven came into the world, but they loved the darkness more than the light, for their actions were evil. [20]They hate the light because they want to sin in the darkness. They stay away from the light for fear their sins will be exposed and they will be punished. [21]But those who do what is right come to the light gladly, so everyone can see that they are doing what God wants."   JOHN 3:12-21

Crossing the Borders

PREVIEW

"Hi, how are ya?"

"Oh, fine. How are you?"

"Fine. Nice weather we're having."

"Sure is. See ya."

If you went for months with conversations no deeper than that, you would begin to think that no one cared about you.

In this reading, Jesus has a conversation with a woman that goes way beyond small talk. When Jesus says "Hi," it's not mere chitchat—he really wants to talk. Watch how Jesus approaches this conversation and take some cues.

Jesus wants to help in a unique way—that's the theme you'll keep seeing in this reading. Watch for several examples of this in his conversations.

PERSONAL APPLICATION

In Jesus' day, prejudice was strong against women and Samaritans. In addition, this woman had a reputation for living in sin in the nearby village of Sychar. No respectable Jewish man would talk to such a woman. Then came the surprise of this woman's life: Jesus engaged her in a meaningful, no-nonsense conversation.

Not all our conversations have to be a carbon copy of this one, but all should look past race, social position, or past sins, as this one did. All should bring others a glimpse of our heavenly Father's love and offer of forgiveness, as this one did. Note that such conversations don't have to happen in a church—this one didn't.

Be prepared to share God's love through your words and everyday conversations. That is where the Good News about Christ begins.

BIBLE READING

[11]"But sir, you don't have a rope or a bucket," she said, "and this is a very deep well. Where would you get this living water? [12]And besides, are you greater than our ancestor Jacob who gave us this well? How can you offer better water than he and his sons and his cattle enjoyed?"

[13]Jesus replied, "People soon become thirsty again after drinking this water. [14]But the water I give them takes away thirst altogether. It becomes a perpetual spring within them, giving them eternal life."

[15]"Please, sir," the woman said, "give me some of that water! Then I'll never be thirsty again, and I won't have to come here to haul water."

[16]"Go and get your husband," Jesus told her.

[17]"I don't have a husband," the woman replied.

Jesus said, "You're right! You don't have a husband—[18]for you have had five husbands, and you aren't even married to the man you're living with now."

[19]"Sir," the woman said, "you must be a prophet. [20]So tell me, why is it that you Jews insist that Jerusalem is the only place of worship, while we Samaritans claim it is here at Mount Gerizim, where our ancestors worshiped?"

[21]Jesus replied, "Believe me, the time is coming when it will no longer matter whether you worship the Father here or in Jerusalem. [22]You Samaritans know so little about the one you worship, while we Jews know all about him, for salvation comes through the Jews. [23]But the time is coming and is already here when true worshipers will worship the Father in spirit and in truth. The Father is looking for anyone who will worship him that way. [24]For God is Spirit, so those who worship him must worship in spirit and in truth."

JOHN 4:11-24

Staying Power

PREVIEW

"Can't be."

"No way."

"Get outta here."

"I'll believe it when I see it."

These are some of the responses used to dismiss claims that stretch the limits of probability. When hard-to-believe statements are made, critics zoom in and strafe the landscape with dismissals, improbabilities, and proofs against. Meanwhile, a small minority might believe. Sometimes the critics are right; sometimes they are not.

In this portion of Scripture, you will see Jesus make the kinds of statements that divide the audience—not down the middle, but sharply to one side. Most disbelieve. A few hold on. This is too wild to be true. Or is it?

As you read, imagine yourself in that audience—on which side do you stand?

PERSONAL APPLICATION

Jesus' words caused many of his followers to desert him because they just couldn't accept what he said (John 6:66). Many people respond to Jesus that way. They hear the Word of God, learn a little of Jesus' teachings and actions, and decide to turn away from him. If you ask why, you will hear as many reasons as people you ask. But the bottom line is that they leave because he asks too much—the cost is too high.

What Jesus asks is sometimes difficult. But if we turn away from him, where will we go? As Peter said, "Lord, to whom would we go? You alone have the words that give eternal life" (6:68). If you feel that Jesus asks too much, ask him to change your heart. Then have the courage to keep on following in faith, as Peter did.

BIBLE READING

[53]So Jesus said again, "I assure you, unless you eat the flesh of the Son of Man and drink his blood, you cannot have eternal life within you. [54]But those who eat my flesh and drink my blood have eternal life, and I will raise them at the last day. [55]For my flesh is the true food, and my blood is the true drink. [56]All who eat my flesh and drink my blood remain in me, and I in them. [57]I live by the power of the living Father who sent me; in the same way, those who partake of me will live because of me. [58]I am the true bread from heaven. Anyone who eats this bread will live forever and not die as your ancestors did, even though they ate the manna."

[59]He said these things while he was teaching in the synagogue in Capernaum.

[60]Even his disciples said, "This is very hard to understand. How can anyone accept it?"

[61]Jesus knew within himself that his disciples were complaining, so he said to them, "Does this offend you? [62]Then what will you think if you see me, the Son of Man, return to heaven again? [63]It is the Spirit who gives eternal life. Human effort accomplishes nothing. And the very words I have spoken to you are spirit and life. [64]But some of you don't believe me." (For Jesus knew from the beginning who didn't believe, and he knew who would betray him.) [65]Then he said, "That is what I meant when I said that people can't come to me unless the Father brings them to me."

[66]At this point many of his disciples turned away and deserted him. [67]Then Jesus turned to the Twelve and asked, "Are you going to leave, too?"

[68]Simon Peter replied, "Lord, to whom would we go? You alone have the words that give eternal life. [69]We believe them, and we know you are the Holy One of God."   JOHN 6:53-69

Why Me?

PREVIEW

More than ever before, every problem demands an explanation. We want to know why the traffic is so slow today, why taxes are going up, why the job doesn't pay better. In an earlier day of fewer options, we didn't ask as many questions. But these days that's not good enough. We want to know why? who? how?

Jesus confronts that attitude in this passage. A man who has been suffering from blindness prompts the disciples to ask Jesus why. Jesus' answer sparks a controversy. Jesus knows what he's talking about, partly because he's the Son of God, and partly because he knows what it's like to suffer.

PERSONAL APPLICATION

Many people of Jesus' day believed that calamity or suffering resulted from sin. So when his disciples came upon a blind man, they put the question directly to Jesus: Who's to blame for this man's blindness? Is it his or his parents' fault? Jesus answered that no one was to blame— God allowed it in order to teach them about faith and to glorify God through the man's healing (John 9:2-3).

Jesus' lesson teaches us that we must not make assumptions about why people suffer. Sometimes we may be able to identify cause-and-effect relationships between certain choices we make and their outcomes. But we can't blame specific hurts on specific sins. God does not work the way we do. In every kind of suffering, Jesus asks that we look not for scapegoats but for ways to help those who suffer and to learn from their suffering.

When you suffer from a disease, tragedy, or disability, try not to ask, "Why did this happen to me?" or, "What did I do wrong?" Instead, ask God to give you strength for the trial and a greater reliance on him.

BIBLE READING

[1]As Jesus was walking along, he saw a man who had been blind from birth. [2]"Teacher," his disciples asked him, "why was this man born blind? Was it a result of his own sins or those of his parents?"

[3]"It was not because of his sins or his parents' sins," Jesus answered. "He was born blind so the power of God could be seen in him. [4]All of us must quickly carry out the tasks assigned us by the one who sent me, because there is little time left before the night falls and all work comes to an end. [5]But while I am still here in the world, I am the light of the world."

[6]Then he spit on the ground, made mud with the saliva, and smoothed the mud over the blind man's eyes. [7]He told him, "Go and wash in the pool of Siloam" (Siloam means Sent). So the man went and washed, and came back seeing!

[8]His neighbors and others who knew him as a blind beggar asked each other, "Is this the same man—that beggar?" [9]Some said he was, and others said, "No, but he surely looks like him!"

And the beggar kept saying, "I am the same man!"

[10]They asked, "Who healed you? What happened?"

[11]He told them, "The man they call Jesus made mud and smoothed it over my eyes and told me, 'Go to the pool of Siloam and wash off the mud.' I went and washed, and now I can see!"

JOHN 9:1-11

aithful Workers

PREVIEW

Suppose something miraculous happens to you. News of this miracle spreads quickly throughout your community, county, and state. People from miles around come to see you and the result of this incredible event. Soon, investigative reporters show up and start asking you pointed questions. The next day their stories appear under headlines containing words like *hoax* and *fraud*. There never seems to be a shortage of skeptics.

Even Jesus had to deal with skeptics. Despite the fact that he had performed many miracles, some people would not believe he was the Messiah. But, as John writes, Isaiah predicted that people would not believe. This is hard to imagine since Jesus performs one of his most amazing miracles in this reading—raising Lazarus from the dead. Some people never believe, even when the facts are undeniable.

Do you really believe that Jesus is the Messiah? How will you respond when friends, neighbors, and coworkers are skeptical about your experience with God?

PERSONAL APPLICATION

Skepticism toward Jesus' identity and claims has always been the rule, not the exception. Most people will not believe our witness about Christ. Granted, that doesn't mean we shouldn't speak. Jesus didn't stop preaching and healing the day people first said, "So what?" He stayed faithful to the task his Father had given him, regardless of how people responded. Likewise, we need to commit to do God's work faithfully, no matter how people react.

Don't be discouraged if your witness for Christ doesn't turn as many to him as you would like. You can control only your own actions, not others' responses. Be a faithful worker and continue to reach out to others for Jesus.

BIBLE READING

³⁷But despite all the miraculous signs he had done, most of the people did not believe in him. ³⁸This is exactly what Isaiah the prophet had predicted:

> "Lord, who has believed our message?
> To whom will the Lord reveal his saving power?"

³⁹But the people couldn't believe, for as Isaiah also said,

> ⁴⁰ "The Lord has blinded their eyes
>   and hardened their hearts—
> so their eyes cannot see,
>   and their hearts cannot understand,
> and they cannot turn to me
>   and let me heal them."

⁴¹Isaiah was referring to Jesus when he made this prediction, because he was given a vision of the Messiah's glory. ⁴²Many people, including some of the Jewish leaders, believed in him. But they wouldn't admit it to anyone because of their fear that the Pharisees would expel them from the synagogue. ⁴³For they loved human praise more than the praise of God.

⁴⁴Jesus shouted to the crowds, "If you trust me, you are really trusting God who sent me. ⁴⁵For when you see me, you are seeing the one who sent me. ⁴⁶I have come as a light to shine in this dark world, so that all who put their trust in me will no longer remain in the darkness."   JOHN 12:37-46

ove in Action

PREVIEW

On a cold, rainy night when you can't get to sleep, what thoughts arise? Do you think of people from your past who had a positive influence on your life? Do you remember the stories your mother or father read to you on nights like this? Or do you fantasize about your first kiss or marrying the person of your dreams?

All of these thoughts have one thing in common—love. Appropriately, this reading has a lot to do with love, especially Jesus' love for his disciples. Here Jesus demonstrates his love for them before giving them the ultimate command by which they should live. Look for Jesus' dramatic demonstration of love, and compare your love with his.

PERSONAL APPLICATION

Jesus commanded his disciples, "Just as I have loved you, you should love each other" (John 13:34). You know what happened next—Jesus died for their sins. This was the ultimate demonstration of love. As Christ's followers reflected that love, others would surely notice (13:35).

What separates Christians from the rest of the world is love. If you belong to Christ, love others as he loved you. Help people when it's not convenient. Give of your resources even when it hurts. Devote your energy to others' welfare rather than your own, and absorb hurts from others without complaining or fighting back. This kind of love does not come naturally. That is why only God's people, with the help of the Holy Spirit, can love unconditionally. This kind of love makes others sit up and notice.

BIBLE READING

²¹Now Jesus was in great anguish of spirit, and he exclaimed, "The truth is, one of you will betray me!"

²²The disciples looked at each other, wondering whom he could mean. ²³One of Jesus' disciples, the one Jesus loved, was sitting next to Jesus at the table. ²⁴Simon Peter motioned to him to ask who would do this terrible thing. ²⁵Leaning toward Jesus, he asked, "Lord, who is it?"

²⁶Jesus said, "It is the one to whom I give the bread dipped in the sauce." And when he had dipped it, he gave it to Judas, son of Simon Iscariot. ²⁷As soon as Judas had eaten the bread, Satan entered into him. Then Jesus told him, "Hurry. Do it now." ²⁸None of the others at the table knew what Jesus meant. ²⁹Since Judas was their treasurer, some thought Jesus was telling him to go and pay for the food or to give some money to the poor. ³⁰So Judas left at once, going out into the night.

³¹As soon as Judas left the room, Jesus said, "The time has come for me, the Son of Man, to enter into my glory, and God will receive glory because of all that happens to me. ³²And God will bring me into my glory very soon. ³³Dear children, how brief are these moments before I must go away and leave you! Then, though you search for me, you cannot come to me—just as I told the Jewish leaders. ³⁴So now I am giving you a new commandment: Love each other. Just as I have loved you, you should love each other. ³⁵Your love for one another will prove to the world that you are my disciples."   JOHN 13:21-35

Still in the World

PREVIEW

Some newspaper headlines can depress even entrenched optimists: crime and taxes on the rise, school test scores on the slide. But we shouldn't be surprised when we see these headlines. Bad news has been grabbing people's attention for a long time.

Even Jesus shared bad news occasionally. This passage records him talking about the hatred, grief, separation, pain, and injustice that lay ahead for his followers. But behind every dreary headline, he assures us, is a promise and a hope, realized in part now and in full later. Our reunion with Jesus is coming. The last headline is *really* good news.

PERSONAL APPLICATION

In his final prayer for the disciples, Jesus told his Father that he would send them into the world as he had been sent into the world. He asked not that the disciples be isolated from hatred and persecution but that they be protected from falling prey to the devil. He asked that God would strengthen them and teach them through the opposition they would experience. Their presence in the world would be vital, and by God's grace and power, they would thrive there (John 17:13-18).

A glance around at our painful world may make you wish for an escape. But Jesus sends you, if you follow him, into that painful world the same way that God the Father sent him. He has not left you alone. The Holy Spirit lives inside you, protecting, guiding, and teaching you. His Spirit will work through you to tell others of Jesus, ease others' pain, and further God's work.

Jesus has sent you into the world. Carry on Christ's message today, trusting God for his protection of your soul even though your body and spirit may suffer.

BIBLE READING

[6]"I have told these men about you. They were in the world, but then you gave them to me. Actually, they were always yours, and you gave them to me; and they have kept your word. [7]Now they know that everything I have is a gift from you, [8]for I have passed on to them the words you gave me; and they accepted them and know that I came from you, and they believe you sent me.

[9]"My prayer is not for the world, but for those you have given me, because they belong to you. [10]And all of them, since they are mine, belong to you; and you have given them back to me, so they are my glory! [11]Now I am departing the world; I am leaving them behind and coming to you. Holy Father, keep them and care for them—all those you have given me—so that they will be united just as we are. [12]During my time here, I have kept them safe. I guarded them so that not one was lost, except the one headed for destruction, as the Scriptures foretold.

[13]"And now I am coming to you. I have told them many things while I was with them so they would be filled with my joy. [14]I have given them your word. And the world hates them because they do not belong to the world, just as I do not. [15]I'm not asking you to take them out of the world, but to keep them safe from the evil one. [16]They are not part of this world any more than I am. [17]Make them pure and holy by teaching them your words of truth. [18]As you sent me into the world, I am sending them into the world. [19]And I give myself entirely to you so they also might be entirely yours."

JOHN 17:6-19

ecret Friends

PREVIEW

Imagine that you are the only fan in a sold-out stadium cheering for the visiting team. Couple this with the fact that the sporting event you are attending is the championship game. Even though the stadium security forces are nearby, you know that if you raise your voice to celebrate your team's score, you will be in danger. At times like this, secrecy has its advantages.

Unfortunately, secrecy can also be a trap. Peter learns this lesson the hard way as he tries but fails to hide his faith in Jesus. In this reading, Peter is not the only one to learn this lesson. Joseph of Arimathea and Nicodemus also realize that it is better to acknowledge Jesus for who he is than to deny knowing him at all. For them, however, this realization comes a little too late.

The bottom line is that secrecy has disadvantages, too, especially when it comes to faith. Secret faith is no faith at all. As you read, determine to be open and honest about your faith in Christ.

PERSONAL APPLICATION

We take a risk whenever we let others know that we follow Christ. We risk backlash—some may think less of us, some may question our judgment, some may even threaten our job or safety. Yet the time always comes when someone says, "Aren't you one of his?" Or we recognize that we must say or do something that many others will see and recognize as an act of faith in Christ.

Exposing your faith may have some disadvantages. But doing so also may help you take an important step. If you're not willing to be bold for Christ, it begs the question, *Do you really believe?*

BIBLE READING

²⁸Jesus knew that everything was now finished, and to fulfill the Scriptures he said, "I am thirsty." ²⁹A jar of sour wine was sitting there, so they soaked a sponge in it, put it on a hyssop branch, and held it up to his lips. ³⁰When Jesus had tasted it, he said, "It is finished!" Then he bowed his head and gave up his spirit.

³¹The Jewish leaders didn't want the victims hanging there the next day, which was the Sabbath (and a very special Sabbath at that, because it was the Passover), so they asked Pilate to hasten their deaths by ordering that their legs be broken. Then their bodies could be taken down. ³²So the soldiers came and broke the legs of the two men crucified with Jesus. ³³But when they came to Jesus, they saw that he was dead already, so they didn't break his legs. ³⁴One of the soldiers, however, pierced his side with a spear, and blood and water flowed out. ³⁵This report is from an eyewitness giving an accurate account; it is presented so that you also can believe. ³⁶These things happened in fulfillment of the Scriptures that say, "Not one of his bones will be broken," ³⁷and "They will look on him whom they pierced."

³⁸Afterward Joseph of Arimathea, who had been a secret disciple of Jesus (because he feared the Jewish leaders), asked Pilate for permission to take Jesus' body down. When Pilate gave him permission, he came and took the body away. ³⁹Nicodemus, the man who had come to Jesus at night, also came, bringing about seventy-five pounds of embalming ointment made from myrrh and aloes. ⁴⁰Together they wrapped Jesus' body in a long linen cloth with the spices, as is the Jewish custom of burial. ⁴¹The place of crucifixion was near a garden, where there was a new tomb, never used before. ⁴²And so, because it was the day of preparation before the Passover and since the tomb was close at hand, they laid Jesus there.   JOHN 19:28–42

The Heart of the Matter

PREVIEW

Airplane banners occasionally announce love and sometimes propose marriage. Highway billboards have been known to do the same. These are shockingly public ways to get a normally private message to the object of one's affection.

Jesus' last recorded encounter with Peter brings about one of these public declarations of love. Unlike the voluntary action of flying a banner or renting a billboard, Peter has to be coaxed into admitting his love for Jesus. As you read this passage, notice the love God has declared for you in the resurrection of his Son, Jesus.

PERSONAL APPLICATION

After Jesus rose from the dead, and shortly before he ascended into heaven, he asked Peter if he loved him (John 21:15-17). First Jesus asked if Peter's love (using the Greek word for love that means freely-given, self-sacrificial love) excelled that of the other disciples. Peter said yes, using a different word for love, the one that signifies brotherly love. Then Jesus asked again, leaving out a comparison with the others. Again Peter said yes, and again used brotherly love. Then Jesus asked Peter for a third time, this time referring to brotherly love, saying, in effect: "Are you even my friend?" Peter answered, "Lord, you know everything. You know I love you" (21:17).

Peter felt hurt at Jesus' persistence, but Jesus knew that it's all too easy to say glibly, "Sure, I love you." To face the question three times, each time pressed a little harder, forced Peter to face his true feelings and motives. A third declaration of his devotion would leave no doubt.

How would you respond if Jesus asked, "Do you truly love me? Do you *really* love me? Are you even my friend?" Be sure you can sincerely say to Jesus, "I love you. I am your friend."

BIBLE READING

[10]"Bring some of the fish you've just caught," Jesus said. [11]So Simon Peter went aboard and dragged the net to the shore. There were 153 large fish, and yet the net hadn't torn.

[12]"Now come and have some breakfast!" Jesus said. And no one dared ask him if he really was the Lord because they were sure of it. [13]Then Jesus served them the bread and the fish. [14]This was the third time Jesus had appeared to his disciples since he had been raised from the dead.

[15]After breakfast Jesus said to Simon Peter, "Simon son of John, do you love me more than these?"

"Yes, Lord," Peter replied, "you know I love you."

"Then feed my lambs," Jesus told him.

[16]Jesus repeated the question: "Simon son of John, do you love me?"

"Yes, Lord," Peter said, "you know I love you."

"Then take care of my sheep," Jesus said.

[17]Once more he asked him, "Simon son of John, do you love me?"

Peter was grieved that Jesus asked the question a third time. He said, "Lord, you know everything. You know I love you."

Jesus said, "Then feed my sheep. [18]The truth is, when you were young, you were able to do as you liked and go wherever you wanted to. But when you are old, you will stretch out your hands, and others will direct you and take you where you don't want to go." [19]Jesus said this to let him know what kind of death he would die to glorify God. Then Jesus told him, "Follow me."

JOHN 21:10-19

$\mathscr{P}$ower Source

PREVIEW

Our very way of life depends on electricity. If you don't think so, see what happens when you turn off the power in your home. You can't use your lights when it gets dark, or your TV, stereo, or computer. If you have an electric oven or if your house has electric heat, forget about cooking or staying warm. You may also want to go out and buy some ice to keep your food cold.

The church without the Holy Spirit is like a house without electrical power. That is why Jesus sends his power source—the Holy Spirit—to the church soon after his ascension. When the Spirit comes, the church is radically transformed—Peter preaches his first sermon, converting thousands; a lame beggar is healed; and Peter and John boldly face Jesus' killers. The promise Jesus gave his disciples is coming true—they have received *real* power.

PERSONAL APPLICATION

Jesus said that shortly after he ascended to heaven, the Holy Spirit would come and give his disciples power to take his message to the whole world (Acts 1:8). That's exactly what happened. First the disciples received the Holy Spirit (2:3-4). Then the Spirit gave them power that enabled them to speak in other languages and to perform miracles (2:4-12, 43; 3:6-8; 4:13). As a result, they took the message of Christ to the rest of the world (8:4).

Often, Christians try to use their own power and authority to persuade others to follow Christ. But sharing God's message should not involve slick debate or manipulation. Instead, we should share what God has done for us through the power of the Holy Spirit. Then we should depend on the Spirit for the results. The Holy Spirit works in people, helping them see that the incredible Jesus really did come to die for them, paying the penalty for their sins.

BIBLE READING

[1]On the day of Pentecost, seven weeks after Jesus' resurrection, the believers were meeting together in one place. [2]Suddenly, there was a sound from heaven like the roaring of a mighty windstorm in the skies above them, and it filled the house where they were meeting. [3]Then, what looked like flames or tongues of fire appeared and settled on each of them. [4]And everyone present was filled with the Holy Spirit and began speaking in other languages, as the Holy Spirit gave them this ability.

[5]Godly Jews from many nations were living in Jerusalem at that time. [6]When they heard this sound, they came running to see what it was all about, and they were bewildered to hear their own languages being spoken by the believers.

[7]They were beside themselves with wonder. "How can this be?" they exclaimed. "These people are all from Galilee, [8]and yet we hear them speaking the languages of the lands where we were born! [9]Here we are—Parthians, Medes, Elamites, people from Mesopotamia, Judea, Cappadocia, Pontus, the province of Asia, [10]Phrygia, Pamphylia, Egypt, and the areas of Libya toward Cyrene, visitors from Rome (both Jews and converts to Judaism), [11]Cretans, and Arabians. And we all hear these people speaking in our own languages about the wonderful things God has done!" [12]They stood there amazed and perplexed. "What can this mean?" they asked each other. [13]But others in the crowd were mocking. "They're drunk, that's all!" they said.   ACTS 2:1-13

ot-So-Free Speech

PREVIEW

Public speaking is usually listed among people's greatest fears. Yet every day, thousands of people speak in public, because they recognize that the importance of what they have to say exceeds the fear they feel.

Take Stephen, for example. His speech is brilliant. And Philip speaks well, too. So do Peter and John. We're not told if they enjoy the experiences, but we have lots of evidence that they have every reason to fear. For example, Peter and John are told by the Jewish Council never to speak of Jesus again. If they do, they will be in danger. But they ignore this threat and continue to preach. Because of Peter and John's courage and determination, the council members decide to silence them—permanently. Unlike Peter and John, Stephen never receives a warning for speaking about Jesus. Instead, his enemies stone him to death for telling the truth.

PERSONAL APPLICATION

Many of Jesus' followers were imprisoned or killed for speaking the truth about his resurrection. It was not long before the first of his followers, Stephen, was martyred. James, the brother of Jesus, was also killed because of his faith in Christ. The apostle John was exiled to an island, and tradition says Peter was crucified upside down.

The fate of Stephen and the apostles does not sound appealing. However, we should remember that they gladly died for the sake of Christ because they knew without a doubt that he was—and still is—the Messiah. This knowledge led them to speak out even under threat of death. No one could silence them.

Don't let anyone silence you, either. Speak out boldly for Jesus. Share your faith with others. If you endure persecution for your testimony, keep in mind the attitude of the apostles (Acts 5:41), and try to follow their example.

BIBLE READING

²⁷Then they brought the apostles in before the council. ²⁸"Didn't we tell you never again to teach in this man's name?" the high priest demanded. "Instead, you have filled all Jerusalem with your teaching about Jesus, and you intend to blame us for his death!"

²⁹But Peter and the apostles replied, "We must obey God rather than human authority. ³⁰The God of our ancestors raised Jesus from the dead after you killed him by crucifying him. ³¹Then God put him in the place of honor at his right hand as Prince and Savior. He did this to give the people of Israel an opportunity to turn from their sins and turn to God so their sins would be forgiven. ³²We are witnesses of these things and so is the Holy Spirit, who is given by God to those who obey him."

³³At this, the high council was furious and decided to kill them. ³⁴But one member had a different perspective. He was a Pharisee named Gamaliel, who was an expert on religious law and was very popular with the people. He stood up and ordered that the apostles be sent outside the council chamber for a while. ³⁵Then he addressed his colleagues as follows: "Men of Israel, take care what you are planning to do to these men! ³⁶Some time ago there was that fellow Theudas, who pretended to be someone great. About four hundred others joined him, but he was killed, and his followers went their various ways. The whole movement came to nothing. ³⁷After him, at the time of the census, there was Judas of Galilee. He got some people to follow him, but he was killed, too, and all his followers were scattered.

³⁸"So my advice is, leave these men alone. If they are teaching and doing these things merely on their own, it will soon be overthrown. ³⁹But if it is of God, you will not be able to stop them. You may even find yourselves fighting against God."

ACTS 5:27-39

An Open Mind

PREVIEW

Pulling off a surprise party takes the street smarts of a big-city detective and the logistical skill of an army general. Weeks of planning can crumble at any minute, but if done right, the moment of sweet surprise finally comes.

For the early church, the surprises keep coming. This reading contains some unique ones, including Philip's encounter with an Ethiopian official, Peter's vision, and Paul's conversion. Not all of the surprises are good, however—in particular, the church's persecution. But through it all, these first believers learn how powerful God is and how big their mission field has grown.

As you read, be alert for God's surprises, in the text but also in your life and church.

PERSONAL APPLICATION

The introduction of Gentiles (non-Jews) into the church was a struggle. Up until this point, all the believers were Jews. When Peter brought the news that a Gentile named Cornelius had become a believer in Christ, the believers in Jerusalem were shocked and didn't know how to respond. But Peter said that God had overcome his objections and led him to Cornelius. In fact, God had given Cornelius the Holy Spirit—proof of salvation. After Peter's colleagues heard the whole story, they praised God and accepted this new development as great news (Acts 11:2-18).

As this incident shows, conflict with other Christians may arise over important issues. When this happens, we should guard ourselves against the bias of our initial reaction. We need to listen and speak respectfully, not jump to conclusions.

Before judging the behavior of fellow believers, let them tell their side of the story. The Holy Spirit may have something important to teach you through them.

BIBLE READING

⁴Then Peter told them exactly what had happened. ⁵"One day in Joppa," he said, "while I was praying, I went into a trance and saw a vision. Something like a large sheet was let down by its four corners from the sky. And it came right down to me. ⁶When I looked inside the sheet, I saw all sorts of small animals, wild animals, reptiles, and birds that we are not allowed to eat. ⁷And I heard a voice say, 'Get up, Peter; kill and eat them.'

⁸"'Never, Lord,' I replied. 'I have never eaten anything forbidden by our Jewish laws.'

⁹"But the voice from heaven came again, 'If God says something is acceptable, don't say it isn't.'

¹⁰"This happened three times before the sheet and all it contained was pulled back up to heaven. ¹¹Just then three men who had been sent from Caesarea arrived at the house where I was staying. ¹²The Holy Spirit told me to go with them and not to worry about their being Gentiles. These six brothers here accompanied me, and we soon arrived at the home of the man who had sent for us. ¹³He told us how an angel had appeared to him in his home and had told him, 'Send messengers to Joppa to find Simon Peter. ¹⁴He will tell you how you and all your household will be saved!'

¹⁵"Well, I began telling them the Good News, but just as I was getting started, the Holy Spirit fell on them, just as he fell on us at the beginning. ¹⁶Then I thought of the Lord's words when he said, 'John baptized with water, but you will be baptized with the Holy Spirit.' ¹⁷And since God gave these Gentiles the same gift he gave us when we believed in the Lord Jesus Christ, who was I to argue?"

¹⁸When the others heard this, all their objections were answered and they began praising God. They said, "God has also given the Gentiles the privilege of turning from sin and receiving eternal life."   ACTS 11:4-18

Rules and Regulations

PREVIEW

Laws for the state of Illinois take up thirteen feet of shelf space. Add another twenty-three feet of shelving for federal laws and several more shelves containing court decisions, and you still are not done. You have city, county, and township rules to consider. If you go to school, work for a corporation, or attend church, you have even more rules to follow. It's a wonder a person doesn't need permission to take a breath.

The earliest Christians are Jewish, and they still live under the many religious rules that make up their culture. With the addition of numerous Gentile believers to the church, things get complicated. Should the Gentile Christians also follow all these rules? The solution comes straight from the truth about salvation itself.

PERSONAL APPLICATION

Paul, Peter, James, and other leaders, under the guidance of the Holy Spirit, realized that Christ saves a person by faith alone and not by observing the law (Acts 15:1-29). This conclusion, though, did not mean that the Gentile believers did not have to keep any laws. Rather, they did not have to keep the laws of Moses, including the notable rite of circumcision, in order to be saved.

We often like to add conditions to the simple mandate to believe in Christ, but we must not. The more a Christian looks like us, the better we sometimes feel about their faith. But by *looks like us* do we mean "looks like Christ," or just "looks like me"? Resist the temptation to make other Christians act just like you. The commands of Christ are all the religious rules they need, and all that most can bear.

Bible Reading

[22]Then the apostles and elders and the whole church in Jerusalem chose delegates, and they sent them to Antioch of Syria with Paul and Barnabas to report on this decision. The men chosen were two of the church leaders—Judas (also called Barsabbas) and Silas. [23]This is the letter they took along with them:

"This letter is from the apostles and elders, your brothers in Jerusalem. It is written to the Gentile believers in Antioch, Syria, and Cilicia. Greetings!

[24]"We understand that some men from here have troubled you and upset you with their teaching, but they had no such instructions from us. [25]So it seemed good to us, having unanimously agreed on our decision, to send you these official representatives, along with our beloved Barnabas and Paul, [26]who have risked their lives for the sake of our Lord Jesus Christ. [27]So we are sending Judas and Silas to tell you what we have decided concerning your question.

[28]"For it seemed good to the Holy Spirit and to us to lay no greater burden on you than these requirements: [29]You must abstain from eating food offered to idols, from consuming blood or eating the meat of strangled animals, and from sexual immorality. If you do this, you will do well. Farewell."

[30]The four messengers went at once to Antioch, where they called a general meeting of the Christians and delivered the letter. [31]And there was great joy throughout the church that day as they read this encouraging message. Acts 15:22-31

heck It Out

PREVIEW

A wise person carefully checks out certain people, places, and things before utilizing them. A new baby-sitter, a public bathroom, and a new car should definitely be checked out before being used. Some people, however, just skip this step and assume that all is OK. They like to live dangerously.

Checking things out is also a good practice for people sitting in the pews. Take the Bereans for example. They do not take everything Paul says as gospel truth. They compare what he says about Jesus with the Old Testament texts and are blessed by it.

Unfortunately, not all of Paul's audiences are as studious as the Bereans. Each one presents a different challenge—jealousy, skepticism, and apathy. As you read, learn from the way Paul handles these challenges.

PERSONAL APPLICATION

The people in Berea had more than a surface interest in the news about Christ when they heard it. They listened carefully to Paul's message, considered its merit, got out their copies of the Scriptures, and checked it all out for themselves (Acts 17:11). Always open but never careless, they verified each teaching diligently before embracing it wholeheartedly.

A preacher or teacher who gives God's true message will never contradict or explain away anything that is found in God's Word. That is why we need to think about what we hear, to evaluate sermons and teachings. If we do this and the message is true, we will benefit all the more by understanding it better and seeing more clearly how to apply it. If we do this and the message is false, we will spot the error and not follow a mistake.

BIBLE READING

¹Now Paul and Silas traveled through the towns of Amphipolis and Apollonia and came to Thessalonica, where there was a Jewish synagogue. ²As was Paul's custom, he went to the synagogue service, and for three Sabbaths in a row he interpreted the Scriptures to the people. ³He was explaining and proving the prophecies about the sufferings of the Messiah and his rising from the dead. He said, "This Jesus I'm telling you about is the Messiah." ⁴Some who listened were persuaded and became converts, including a large number of godly Greek men and also many important women of the city.

⁵But the Jewish leaders were jealous, so they gathered some worthless fellows from the streets to form a mob and start a riot. They attacked the home of Jason, searching for Paul and Silas so they could drag them out to the crowd. ⁶Not finding them there, they dragged out Jason and some of the other believers instead and took them before the city council. "Paul and Silas have turned the rest of the world upside down, and now they are here disturbing our city," they shouted. ⁷"And Jason has let them into his home. They are all guilty of treason against Caesar, for they profess allegiance to another king, Jesus."

⁸The people of the city, as well as the city officials, were thrown into turmoil by these reports. ⁹But the officials released Jason and the other believers after they had posted bail.

¹⁰That very night the believers sent Paul and Silas to Berea. When they arrived there, they went to the synagogue. ¹¹And the people of Berea were more open-minded than those in Thessalonica, and they listened eagerly to Paul's message. They searched the Scriptures day after day to check up on Paul and Silas, to see if they were really teaching the truth. ¹²As a result, many Jews believed, as did some of the prominent Greek women and many men.   ACTS 17:1-12

$\mathcal{D}$abblers Anonymous

PREVIEW

"What are your personal goals?" a corporate interviewer asked the young man hoping for his first job. "Oh," came the reply, "I'd like to dabble in sales."

"What are your long-range interests?" an interviewer asked a young woman seeking admission to medical school. "Hmm," she said, "I'd love to dabble in neurosurgery."

Dabblers are casual hobbyists, not the people stockholders want running corporate operations and not the doctors most people choose. Spiritual dabblers are hobbyists, too, and if you think a casual neurosurgeon is dangerous, note what can happen because of these folks. Some ideas are too important to dabble with, and some are too dangerous—especially those tied to the occult.

Also look for the tale of poor Eutychus. He should have left at intermission, or called for one.

PERSONAL APPLICATION

The city of Ephesus was a center for black magic and other occult practices. Some professionals made a living inventing and promoting magical formulas for wealth, happiness, and success in marriage. Most Ephesians followed superstitions and practiced sorcery. But those who believed in Christ renounced these sins and burned their occult implements in a public bonfire (Acts 19:18-19).

God clearly forbids sorcery and occult practices (see Deuteronomy 18:9-14). You cannot follow Christ and dabble in the occult, black magic, or sorcery. God's power is greater than Satan's (1 John 4:4; Revelation 20:10). Once you begin to engage in these evils superficially, however, you invite Satan to draw you in even further.

If you tend to dabble in the occult, learn a lesson from the Ephesians, and get rid of anything that could keep you trapped in such practices.

BIBLE READING

[11]"God gave Paul the power to do unusual miracles, [12]so that even when handkerchiefs or cloths that had touched his skin were placed on sick people, they were healed of their diseases, and any evil spirits within them came out.

[13]A team of Jews who were traveling from town to town casting out evil spirits tried to use the name of the Lord Jesus. The incantation they used was this: "I command you by Jesus, whom Paul preaches, to come out!" [14]Seven sons of Sceva, a leading priest, were doing this. [15]But when they tried it on a man possessed by an evil spirit, the spirit replied, "I know Jesus, and I know Paul. But who are you?" [16]And he leaped on them and attacked them with such violence that they fled from the house, naked and badly injured.

[17]The story of what happened spread quickly all through Ephesus, to Jews and Greeks alike. A solemn fear descended on the city, and the name of the Lord Jesus was greatly honored. [18]Many who became believers confessed their sinful practices. [19]A number of them who had been practicing magic brought their incantation books and burned them at a public bonfire. The value of the books was several million dollars. [20]So the message about the Lord spread widely and had a powerful effect.

ACTS 19:11–20

Opportunities That Knock

PREVIEW

What's worse than running out of gas on a busy freeway during rush hour? Being told that such problems are wonderful opportunities for character growth.

Paul has flat tires at nearly every turn. Yet each time, his delay or detour becomes an opportunity to preach, witness, and spread the Good News about Christ. Paul must have considered his itinerary to be completely in God's hands, for he doesn't complain about hunger, cold, shipwreck, snakebite, imprisonment, or the injustice of his own court case. He adjusts marvelously to change, as his last recorded speech makes clear. In an exemplary way, Paul sees each pothole as just part of the trip, which makes his life an adventure in faith.

PERSONAL APPLICATION

Paul was arrested by a Roman commander because he was the center of attention in a riot. But the reason for his arrest is not as important as how he handled this humiliation, setback, and injustice. As military officers and prominent city leaders met with King Agrippa to hear Paul's case, Paul prepared his thoughts for another speech about Jesus. He saw his troubled situation not as a cause for lodging a formal complaint with the government, but as another opportunity to present the Good News about Christ that mattered so much to him (Acts 25:23–26:32).

Every offense and injustice you suffer will test you. It will force you—as it forced Paul—to choose what to "preach" about. Will you see your humiliation only as a problem, barrier, or roadblock to your happiness? Or will you see it as an opportunity, given to you by God, to demonstrate his power and love in your life? Rather than complain at every hint of brokenness in this world, why not try to fix it? Look for ways to turn your painful experiences into an opportunity to serve God and share him with others.

BIBLE READING

[19]"And so, O King Agrippa, I was not disobedient to that vision from heaven. [20]I preached first to those in Damascus, then in Jerusalem and throughout all Judea, and also to the Gentiles, that all must turn from their sins and turn to God—and prove they have changed by the good things they do. [21]Some Jews arrested me in the Temple for preaching this, and they tried to kill me. [22]But God protected me so that I am still alive today to tell these facts to everyone, from the least to the greatest. I teach nothing except what the prophets and Moses said would happen—[23]that the Messiah would suffer and be the first to rise from the dead as a light to Jews and Gentiles alike."

[24]Suddenly, Festus shouted, "Paul, you are insane. Too much study has made you crazy!"

[25]But Paul replied, "I am not insane, Most Excellent Festus. I am speaking the sober truth. [26]And King Agrippa knows about these things. I speak frankly, for I am sure these events are all familiar to him, for they were not done in a corner! [27]King Agrippa, do you believe the prophets? I know you do—"

[28]Agrippa interrupted him. "Do you think you can make me a Christian so quickly?"

[29]Paul replied, "Whether quickly or not, I pray to God that both you and everyone here in this audience might become the same as I am, except for these chains."   ACTS 26:19-29

Privilege and Responsibility

PREVIEW

Whether or not you are a sports fan, you are undoubtedly familiar with braggadocio, or empty boasting. Many in our society—in particular athletes and their rabid fans—have made this an art form. "We're Number 1" signs and childish antics pop up everywhere. Even those who can back up their words are often full of hot air.

For those who think they are the greatest, Paul has some sobering news: You are not as great as you may think. Paul reminds us that we are all great at one thing—sinning. But that is not all that Paul has to say. The good news of Paul's letter to the Romans is that God has a great message of hope and forgiveness. Now that is something to really brag about!

PERSONAL APPLICATION

Paul knew how thoroughly kind God had been to him. He called himself and everyone else in need of Christ's forgiveness "terrible people" (Romans 2:1). That's why he had no trouble obeying God's call to travel all over the Roman Empire preaching and spreading the good news about Christ. It only made sense to him that he would share the message of God's forgiveness with others after all God had done for him (Romans 1:5).

Being a Christian is a privilege. God has taken away more of our sin than we can realize, more sin than we deserve to have forgiven. The more we appreciate the depth of this, the more we'll understand Paul's gratitude here.

If you have received Christ's forgiveness, you have an important story to tell. You don't have to be a clone of Paul, just motivated by the same gratitude, driven by the same love, committed to the same end: God's greater glory. In what way can you share the news about God's goodness today?

BIBLE READING

[5]Through Christ, God has given us the privilege and authority to tell Gentiles everywhere what God has done for them, so that they will believe and obey him, bringing glory to his name.

[6]You are among those who have been called to belong to Jesus Christ, [7]dear friends in Rome. God loves you dearly, and he has called you to be his very own people.

May grace and peace be yours from God our Father and the Lord Jesus Christ.

[8]Let me say first of all that your faith in God is becoming known throughout the world. How I thank God through Jesus Christ for each one of you. [9]God knows how often I pray for you. Day and night I bring you and your needs in prayer to God, whom I serve with all my heart by telling others the Good News about his Son.

[10]One of the things I always pray for is the opportunity, God willing, to come at last to see you. [11]For I long to visit you so I can share a spiritual blessing with you that will help you grow strong in the Lord. [12]I'm eager to encourage you in your faith, but I also want to be encouraged by yours. In this way, each of us will be a blessing to the other.

[13]I want you to know, dear brothers and sisters, that I planned many times to visit you, but I was prevented until now. I want to work among you and see good results, just as I have done among other Gentiles. [14]For I have a great sense of obligation to people in our culture and to people in other cultures, to the educated and uneducated alike. [15]So I am eager to come to you in Rome, too, to preach God's Good News.

[16]For I am not ashamed of this Good News about Christ. It is the power of God at work, saving everyone who believes—Jews first and also Gentiles. [17]This Good News tells us how God makes us right in his sight. This is accomplished from start to finish by faith. As the Scriptures say, "It is through faith that a righteous person has life."   ROMANS 1:5-17

 Little Sins?

PREVIEW

If you want to view the smallest leaves in the hardwood kingdom, look at a silk tree. Next to a maple or oak leaf, the silk tree leaflet is tiny. But despite its small leaves, the silk tree is one of the hardiest species in the world. It is a short but significant plant.

Some sins, like silk leaves, are small. But just as silk leaves are still leaves, so small sins are still sins. Paul reminds us that small acts of lying, lusting, and coveting all produce the same result as murder, adultery, and stealing—separation from God. Paul also explains how people can draw close to God and acquire joy. As you read, compare your life with Paul's inspired words and determine to root out every sin.

In addition, in this section Paul shows how two men made significant changes in the world—one for the worse, the other for the better.

PERSONAL APPLICATION

The Bible says that every person's sin has separated them from God (Romans 3:23). Most people consider some sins to be bigger than others because they have such serious consequences. For example, murder is thought to be worse than hatred, and adultery worse than lust. In one sense they are, because they hurt others. But the fact that a person commits "smaller" sins does not mean that he or she is some-how less damned. Sin is incompatible with God, who is holy and without sin. All sin, therefore, leads to death, regardless of how great or small it may seem.

Don't minimize "little" sins or overrate "big" ones. Understand and fear the effects of all sins, and ask God to help you live blamelessly before him.

BIBLE READING

[21]But now God has shown us a different way of being right in his sight—not by obeying the law but by the way promised in the Scriptures long ago. [22]We are made right in God's sight when we trust in Jesus Christ to take away our sins. And we all can be saved in this same way, no matter who we are or what we have done.

[23]For all have sinned; all fall short of God's glorious standard. [24]Yet now God in his gracious kindness declares us not guilty. He has done this through Christ Jesus, who has freed us by taking away our sins. [25]For God sent Jesus to take the punishment for our sins and to satisfy God's anger against us. We are made right with God when we believe that Jesus shed his blood, sacrificing his life for us. God was being entirely fair and just when he did not punish those who sinned in former times. [26]And he is entirely fair and just in this present time when he declares sinners to be right in his sight because they believe in Jesus.

[27]Can we boast, then, that we have done anything to be accepted by God? No, because our acquittal is not based on our good deeds. It is based on our faith. [28]So we are made right with God through faith and not by obeying the law.

[29]After all, God is not the God of the Jews only, is he? Isn't he also the God of the Gentiles? Of course he is. [30]There is only one God, and there is only one way of being accepted by him. He makes people right with himself only by faith, whether they are Jews or Gentiles. [31]Well then, if we emphasize faith, does this mean that we can forget about the law? Of course not! In fact, only when we have faith do we truly fulfill the law.

ROMANS 3:21-31

No Fear

PREVIEW

Rock climbers are a unique group of people. Some of them are extremely adventurous and like to climb without the aid of a rope. Others are a little more cautious and climb with the security a rope provides. This added confidence helps them scale the most difficult surfaces, even those that jut out and require them to hang over empty space.

In many ways, going through tough times is like climbing a sheer rock face. Trying to get through these times without God is like climbing without a rope. In this reading, Paul makes Christians aware of the "rope" that God extends to all his followers. That rope is God's promise to never let anything separate us from his love. As you read, take hope in God's rope.

PERSONAL APPLICATION

Like Paul, we face hardships in many areas of life. We may be unemployed or working under strenuous conditions. Some may be punished for doing right. Others may be going through a debilitating illness or even facing death. These experiences, or the idea of having to face them, often cause us to fear that God has abandoned us or no longer loves us. But the truth is that *nothing* can separate us from Christ's love. The fact that he died for us proves it, and this promise reminds us.

When you experience doubt about God's constant love for you, remember Paul's experience. Then reread and meditate on Romans 8:31-39. If it will help you, try memorizing verse 38: "Nothing can ever separate us from his love." Do not think that your troubles somehow mean the end of his love. You can always feel totally secure that he loves you and will be with you.

BIBLE READING

[28]And we know that God causes everything to work together for the good of those who love God and are called according to his purpose for them. [29]For God knew his people in advance, and he chose them to become like his Son, so that his Son would be the firstborn, with many brothers and sisters. [30]And having chosen them, he called them to come to him. And he gave them right standing with himself, and he promised them his glory.

[31]What can we say about such wonderful things as these? If God is for us, who can ever be against us? [32]Since God did not spare even his own Son but gave him up for us all, won't God, who gave us Christ, also give us everything else?

[33]Who dares accuse us whom God has chosen for his own? Will God? No! He is the one who has given us right standing with himself. [34]Who then will condemn us? Will Christ Jesus? No, for he is the one who died for us and was raised to life for us and is sitting at the place of highest honor next to God, pleading for us.

[35]Can anything ever separate us from Christ's love? Does it mean he no longer loves us if we have trouble or calamity, or are persecuted, or are hungry or cold or in danger or threatened with death? [36](Even the Scriptures say, "For your sake we are killed every day; we are being slaughtered like sheep.") [37]No, despite all these things, overwhelming victory is ours through Christ, who loved us.

[38]And I am convinced that nothing can ever separate us from his love. Death can't, and life can't. The angels can't, and the demons can't. Our fears for today, our worries about tomorrow, and even the powers of hell can't keep God's love away. [39]Whether we are high above the sky or in the deepest ocean, nothing in all creation will ever be able to separate us from the love of God that is revealed in Christ Jesus our Lord. ROMANS 8:28-39

atters of the Heart

PREVIEW

A perfunctory "luv ya" is about as convincing as a used-car advertisement. It is easy to pass off and too trivial to be taken seriously. You wouldn't build a relationship on a "luv ya," would you?

Like us, God does not care for or desire a "luv ya." In this reading, Paul tells the Romans that there is more to believing in Jesus than mouthing the words "Jesus is Lord." There must be a commitment of the heart as well. As you read, consider whether your faith has moved beyond words to the heart.

Also in this reading, note the lesson on God's sovereignty that Paul teaches through the illustration of clay pots. In addition, notice Paul's love for the Jews, despite their inhumane treatment of him. Read about God's mercy toward both Jews and Gentiles.

PERSONAL APPLICATION

"How do I become a Christian?" That question will receive a wide variety of answers, depending on the religious affiliation or denomination. But Romans 10:8-13 gives the true answer: If we believe in our hearts and say with our mouths that Christ is the risen Lord, we will be saved. Salvation takes no more or less work than that.

Some people try to complicate the process of becoming a Christian with additional requirements, such as belief in a cherished doctrine or certain patterns of behavior, but they should not. God has left it all marvelously simple and plainly outlined in this portion of Scripture.

Jesus will save those who truly believe in him (10:13). Don't complicate what God has made simple, especially something of such great importance as salvation. Leave doctrinal disputes and differences of opinion out of the salvation equation.

BIBLE READING

[8]Salvation that comes from trusting Christ—which is the message we preach—is already within easy reach. In fact, the Scriptures say, "The message is close at hand; it is on your lips and in your heart."

[9]For if you confess with your mouth that Jesus is Lord and believe in your heart that God raised him from the dead, you will be saved. [10]For it is by believing in your heart that you are made right with God, and it is by confessing with your mouth that you are saved. [11]As the Scriptures tell us, "Anyone who believes in him will not be disappointed." [12]Jew and Gentile are the same in this respect. They all have the same Lord, who generously gives his riches to all who ask for them. [13]For "Anyone who calls on the name of the Lord will be saved."

[14]But how can they call on him to save them unless they believe in him? And how can they believe in him if they have never heard about him? And how can they hear about him unless someone tells them? [15]And how will anyone go and tell them without being sent? That is what the Scriptures mean when they say, "How beautiful are the feet of those who bring good news!"

ROMANS 10:8-15

$\mathscr{S}$tanding Back-to-Back

PREVIEW

God's Word turns everything topsy-turvy. The first will be last, the last first. The poor will be blessed, the weary given rest. God's academy of life makes foolish people wise and worldly-wise people foolish. What we call common sense, God sometimes calls nonsense.

In this last reading of Romans, Paul's advice on how to treat "Christians who are weak in the faith" is another one of those lessons. Here Paul tells strong believers to refrain from arguing with weaker believers over issues of right and wrong. As you read, look at your life from God's perspective—upside down.

PERSONAL APPLICATION

God wants us to welcome "Christians who are weak in faith" (Romans 14:1). Exactly what kind of weaknesses do these Christians have? And what does it mean to be a "strong" Christian?

Every believer is weak in some areas and strong in others. Wherever our faith is strong, we can survive contact with sinners without falling into sin ourselves. But wherever it is weak, we must avoid contact with those activities, people, or places so we can avoid falling into sin. Thus there are differences among believers and what they regard as right and wrong.

Aside from being gracious to other believers who have different convictions, we need to be aware of our own strengths and weaknesses. Whenever we don't know whether an activity is appropriate for us we should ask, "Can I do that without sinning? Can I influence others for good, rather than being influenced by them?" Let the answers to those questions be your guide.

Take the time to ask those questions of yourself today. Then, in areas of strength, do not fear being defiled by the world. In areas of weakness, be cautious. And in the company of other Christians, be protective of the weaknesses that threaten them.

BIBLE READING

[1]Accept Christians who are weak in faith, and don't argue with them about what they think is right or wrong. [2]For instance, one person believes it is all right to eat anything. But another believer who has a sensitive conscience will eat only vegetables. [3]Those who think it is all right to eat anything must not look down on those who won't. And those who won't eat certain foods must not condemn those who do, for God has accepted them. [4]Who are you to condemn God's servants? They are responsible to the Lord, so let him tell them whether they are right or wrong. The Lord's power will help them do as they should.

[5]In the same way, some think one day is more holy than another day, while others think every day is alike. Each person should have a personal conviction about this matter. [6]Those who have a special day for worshiping the Lord are trying to honor him. Those who eat all kinds of food do so to honor the Lord, since they give thanks to God before eating. And those who won't eat everything also want to please the Lord and give thanks to God. [7]For we are not our own masters when we live or when we die. [8]While we live, we live to please the Lord. And when we die, we go to be with the Lord. So in life and in death, we belong to the Lord. [9]Christ died and rose again for this very purpose, so that he might be Lord of those who are alive and of those who have died.

[10]So why do you condemn another Christian? Why do you look down on another Christian? Remember, each of us will stand personally before the judgment seat of God. [11]For the Scriptures say,

> "'As surely as I live,' says the Lord,
> 'every knee will bow to me
>   and every tongue will confess allegiance to God.'"

[12]Yes, each of us will have to give a personal account to God.

ROMANS 14:1-12

Only God Knows

PREVIEW

Long division is a math skill that most students greatly dislike. Those who are really good at math may tolerate it, but few ever love it.

What is tolerable in the field of math is destructive in the body of Christ. No one knows this better than Paul. In this reading, Paul addresses the problem of division in the Corinthian church. What once was one church has now split into four. Paul pleads with them to stop arguing and to start getting along—a relevant message for today's church also. As you read, consider the potential for division in your church, and determine to be one who brings peace and unity in the body.

PERSONAL APPLICATION

The Corinthian church had split because the believers there thought they could judge people's motives. Individuals had rallied around certain "superstar" preachers (Paul, Peter, Apollos, and others) and had formed groups within the church based on who followed whom. The groups argued with each other over whose leader was the best Christian. But all this conflict depended on their ability to judge the hearts and motives of others—which they could not do. Paul urged them to stop judging one another, to rally around Christ, and to let God decide who served him faithfully and who did not (1 Corinthians 4:1-5).

Believers today should learn a lesson from the Corinthians. We should beware of judging others. This does not mean that we should avoid confronting those who sin (5:12-13). But we ought to stay away from judging who is a better servant for Christ. When judgments like this are made, we cast ourselves in God's role, which we do not have a right to play. Only God knows a person's heart, and only he has the right to judge.

BIBLE READING

¹Look at Apollos and me as mere servants of Christ who have been put in charge of explaining God's secrets. ²Now, a person who is put in charge as a manager must be faithful. ³What about me? Have I been faithful? Well, it matters very little what you or anyone else thinks. I don't even trust my own judgment on this point. ⁴My conscience is clear, but that isn't what matters. It is the Lord himself who will examine me and decide.

⁵So be careful not to jump to conclusions before the Lord returns as to whether or not someone is faithful. When the Lord comes, he will bring our deepest secrets to light and will reveal our private motives. And then God will give to everyone whatever praise is due.

⁶Dear brothers and sisters, I have used Apollos and myself to illustrate what I've been saying. If you pay attention to the Scriptures, you won't brag about one of your leaders at the expense of another. ⁷What makes you better than anyone else? What do you have that God hasn't given you? And if all you have is from God, why boast as though you have accomplished something on your own?

⁸You think you already have everything you need! You are already rich! Without us you have become kings! I wish you really were on your thrones already, for then we would be reigning with you! ⁹But sometimes I think God has put us apostles on display, like prisoners of war at the end of a victor's parade, condemned to die. We have become a spectacle to the entire world—to people and angels alike.   1 CORINTHIANS 4:1-9

$\mathcal{D}$amage Control

PREVIEW

The phrase "damage control" is used frequently in political circles, referring to limiting negative press coverage following a potentially damaging act or statement by a politician. The phrase could, however, easily be applied in a number of other areas. Take sex, for instance. Sex is a wonderful expression of love between a husband and wife. It is an experience that strengthens and builds the marriage relationship. Why would damage control be needed in this area?

Paul addresses this topic in his first letter to the Corinthians, warning them to avoid sex outside of marriage. Ignoring this warning today is not only spiritually harmful, but it can be physically deadly. It is important to stop the damage before it begins. As you read this passage, note the seriousness and intensity of Paul's teaching, and determine not to let sexual sin devastate your life.

PERSONAL APPLICATION

The hissing doubt of the world says that the Bible's restrictions only keep us from harmless pleasures. The world downplays the risks and plays up the pleasures, making exceptions and excuses.

Spare yourself some grief, and keep in mind the damage that sexual sin can do. It hurts God because it defies the guidelines that he so lovingly gave us. It hurts others because it breaks the commitment necessary to a relationship. And it deeply affects our personalities, which respond in anguish when we harm ourselves physically and spiritually. The destruction caused by sexual sin is so great that God urges us to *run* from it (I Corinthians 6:18).

Sex itself doesn't do any harm—sexual sin does. Preserve God's design for sex in your life, and you'll enjoy the pleasure of his Holy Spirit.

BIBLE READING

⁹Don't you know that those who do wrong will have no share in the Kingdom of God? Don't fool yourselves. Those who indulge in sexual sin, who are idol worshipers, adulterers, male prostitutes, homosexuals, ¹⁰thieves, greedy people, drunkards, abusers, and swindlers—none of these will have a share in the Kingdom of God. ¹¹There was a time when some of you were just like that, but now your sins have been washed away, and you have been set apart for God. You have been made right with God because of what the Lord Jesus Christ and the Spirit of our God have done for you.

¹²You may say, "I am allowed to do anything." But I reply, "Not everything is good for you." And even though "I am allowed to do anything," I must not become a slave to anything. ¹³You say, "Food is for the stomach, and the stomach is for food." This is true, though someday God will do away with both of them. But our bodies were not made for sexual immorality. They were made for the Lord, and the Lord cares about our bodies. ¹⁴And God will raise our bodies from the dead by his marvelous power, just as he raised our Lord from the dead. ¹⁵Don't you realize that your bodies are actually parts of Christ? Should a man take his body, which belongs to Christ, and join it to a prostitute? Never! ¹⁶And don't you know that if a man joins himself to a prostitute, he becomes one body with her? For the Scriptures say, "The two are united into one." ¹⁷But the person who is joined to the Lord becomes one spirit with him.

¹⁸Run away from sexual sin! No other sin so clearly affects the body as this one does. For sexual immorality is a sin against your own body. ¹⁹Or don't you know that your body is the temple of the Holy Spirit, who lives in you and was given to you by God? You do not belong to yourself, ²⁰for God bought you with a high price. So you must honor God with your body.

1 CORINTHIANS 6:9-20

Storybook Weddings

PREVIEW

When Lady Diana and Prince Charles were wed, there were high hopes for this romanticized couple. Their wedding was so perfect that it seemed to have been taken out of a storybook; few would have guessed the turmoil and pain their marriage would contain.

Perhaps marriages fail because people do not know how to build good relationships. Enter Paul and his first letter to the Corinthians. Paul knows the difficulty of building a successful marriage. He knows that marriage is rarely "storybook," and people should think twice before they call for the preacher. His cautious approach, however, is part of the Bible's overall celebration of love. The bottom line remains: Marriage is a gift from God.

For singles, Paul assures us that life is full and rich, and perhaps less complicated than being married. In any case, we all belong to God. Learn about marriage and about yourself in this section.

PERSONAL APPLICATION

Paul said that it was OK to marry, but he advised against it because it would lead to "extra problems" (1 Corinthians 7:28). Many people naively believe that marriage will solve several of their most pressing problems: loneliness, sexual temptation, deep emotional needs, and purpose in life. But marriage alone solves none of these uncertainties. In addition, it often brings about greater conflicts over finances, sacrificed dreams and ambitions, child rearing, personality differences, TV viewing, and a multitude of other issues.

Only Christ can satisfy our deepest needs and protect us from temptation. As wonderful as it is, marriage cannot take Christ's place.

Whether you are married or single, find your contentment in Christ. Do not expect loved ones to meet your every need, even if they love you with all their heart.

BIBLE READING

[26]Because of the present crisis, I think it is best to remain just as you are. [27]If you have a wife, do not end the marriage. If you do not have a wife, do not get married. [28]But if you do get married, it is not a sin. And if a young woman gets married, it is not a sin. However, I am trying to spare you the extra problems that come with marriage.

[29]Now let me say this, dear brothers and sisters: The time that remains is very short, so husbands should not let marriage be their major concern. [30]Happiness or sadness or wealth should not keep anyone from doing God's work. [31]Those in frequent contact with the things of the world should make good use of them without becoming attached to them, for this world and all it contains will pass away. [32]In everything you do, I want you to be free from the concerns of this life. An unmarried man can spend his time doing the Lord's work and thinking how to please him. [33]But a married man can't do that so well. He has to think about his earthly responsibilities and how to please his wife. [34]His interests are divided. In the same way, a woman who is no longer married or has never been married can be more devoted to the Lord in body and in spirit, while the married woman must be concerned about her earthly responsibilities and how to please her husband.

[35]I am saying this for your benefit, not to place restrictions on you. I want you to do whatever will help you serve the Lord best, with as few distractions as possible.   1 CORINTHIANS 7:26-35

Escape Hatches

PREVIEW

Harry Houdini will always be remembered as a master of escape. No matter what the contraption, he could free himself. Chains, locks, straitjackets, boxes, jails, and trunks could not hold Houdini. It seemed he *always* managed to find a way out.

When it comes to temptation, God wants us to be like Houdini. That's the clear teaching in this section of 1 Corinthians. God wants us to escape temptation's chains, trunks, and straitjackets, but he does not expect us to do this alone. In fact, he has given us an advantage even Houdini did not have—the Holy Spirit showing the way to escape temptation's grasp.

Paul also teaches in this section that we need to be Houdini-like with these other issues as well: false guilt; useless restrictions; silly rules; vain legalism; and the special temptation of religious pride.

PERSONAL APPLICATION

Corinthian society was much like ours today. Immorality was every-where, and the pressure on Christians to participate in it was tremen-dous. For believers surrounded and plagued by all this temptation, Paul offered these words of hope: There's *always* a way out (1 Corinthians 10:13).

At times we may feel that temptation is overpowering or impossible to resist, but God never lets that happen. Wrong desires and tempta-tions happen to everyone all the time. In every case, God provides a way out.

There are five steps you can take to avoid unnecessary temptations: (1) learn to recognize tempting circumstances; (2) stay away from every activity you know is wrong; (3) consciously choose to do only what is right; (4) ask God to help you; and (5) ask friends who love God to hold you accountable. Most importantly, whenever you are tempted, take the way out that God provides. Do not think that you have no choice. There's always a way out.

BIBLE READING

[1]I don't want you to forget, dear brothers and sisters, what happened to our ancestors in the wilderness long ago. God guided all of them by sending a cloud that moved along ahead of them, and he brought them all safely through the waters of the sea on dry ground. [2]As followers of Moses, they were all baptized in the cloud and the sea. [3]And all of them ate the same miraculous food, [4]and all of them drank the same miraculous water. For they all drank from the miraculous rock that traveled with them, and that rock was Christ. [5]Yet after all this, God was not pleased with most of them, and he destroyed them in the wilderness.

[6]These events happened as a warning to us, so that we would not crave evil things as they did [7]or worship idols as some of them did. For the Scriptures say, "The people celebrated with feasting and drinking, and they indulged themselves in pagan revelry." [8]And we must not engage in sexual immorality as some of them did, causing 23,000 of them to die in one day. [9]Nor should we put Christ to the test, as some of them did and then died from snakebites. [10]And don't grumble as some of them did, for that is why God sent his angel of death to destroy them. [11]All these events happened to them as examples for us. They were written down to warn us, who live at the time when this age is drawing to a close.

[12]If you think you are standing strong, be careful, for you, too, may fall into the same sin. [13]But remember that the temptations that come into your life are no different from what others experience. And God is faithful. He will keep the temptation from becoming so strong that you can't stand up against it. When you are tempted, he will show you a way out so that you will not give in to it.   1 CORINTHIANS 10:1-13

issing in Action

PREVIEW

Try to put together a model airplane that's missing a piece, and you will soon give up in frustration. Or if you are resourceful, you might make your own piece. But still, it will probably not fit as well as the original. Missing pieces become the most essential pieces, no matter how insignificant they may seem.

In this passage we learn that the same is true for spiritual gifts. All spiritual gifts are given by God to build up the church. But Christians tend to place more importance on some gifts and less on others. Those that are considered less important, however, are usually missed in one way or another when they are absent. As you read, think about the gifts that God has given you and how well you are using them to serve him.

PERSONAL APPLICATION

Some spiritual gifts are still thought of more highly than others. In fact, some gifts are completely discredited as real gifts. But no spiritual gift given by God should ever be considered useless. Likewise, "acceptable" or "desirable" gifts should not be put on a pedestal above others. As Paul writes, "There are different ways God works in our lives, but it is the same God who does the work through all of us. A spiritual gift is given to each of us as a means of helping the entire church" (1 Corinthians 12:6-7).

Learn to appreciate the variety of spiritual gifts that God uses to build his church. Give people with various gifts an opportunity to serve. See them all as helpers who can do something useful for God. At the same time, use the gifts God has given you to strengthen your church for the glory of Christ. Don't allow yourself or your gifts to be "missing in action."

BIBLE READING

¹And now, dear brothers and sisters, I will write about the special abilities the Holy Spirit gives to each of us, for I must correct your misunderstandings about them. ²You know that when you were still pagans you were led astray and swept along in worshiping speechless idols. ³So I want you to know how to discern what is truly from God: No one speaking by the Spirit of God can curse Jesus, and no one is able to say, "Jesus is Lord," except by the Holy Spirit.

⁴Now there are different kinds of spiritual gifts, but it is the same Holy Spirit who is the source of them all. ⁵There are different kinds of service in the church, but it is the same Lord we are serving. ⁶There are different ways God works in our lives, but it is the same God who does the work through all of us. ⁷A spiritual gift is given to each of us as a means of helping the entire church.

⁸To one person the Spirit gives the ability to give wise advice; to another he gives the gift of special knowledge. ⁹The Spirit gives special faith to another, and to someone else he gives the power to heal the sick. ¹⁰He gives one person the power to perform miracles, and to another the ability to prophesy. He gives someone else the ability to know whether it is really the Spirit of God or another spirit that is speaking. Still another person is given the ability to speak in unknown languages, and another is given the ability to interpret what is being said. ¹¹It is the one and only Holy Spirit who distributes these gifts. He alone decides which gift each person should have.   1 CORINTHIANS 12:1-11

The End Is Not Near

PREVIEW

How do you feel about the future? If you asked your neighbors that question, what do you think they would say?

Floods, earthquakes, and fires have devastated certain parts of our country and the world. Add to that the crumbling economies and civil unrest in the third world, plus increased crime rates and pollution in the West, and you have one big world mess. In light of all this, the future does not look too bright.

For those who do not know Christ, the future looks even more bleak. For Christians, however, the future holds a great deal of hope. In this reading, Paul urges the Corinthian Christians to anchor their lives in the hope of eternal life, promised by God and won by Jesus Christ. Read and be encouraged. Find your hope in Christ.

PERSONAL APPLICATION

Did you know that Christians have great hope for the future? Someday all believers will be given new bodies. Eternal life in heaven with God will cancel out death and give us a joyful, permanent home with God far better than anything we could experience here. Nothing we do for God goes unnoticed—none of it is in vain (1 Corinthians 15:51-58).

No nuclear threat, no biological menace, no political coup, no financial collapse can undo our hope for the future. Despite the worldly problems we face each day, God has a plan for us and is in control of everything.

Do not despair. No matter what the headlines say, keep your eternal future in view and keep on doing the will of God.

BIBLE READING

⁵⁰What I am saying, dear brothers and sisters, is that flesh and blood cannot inherit the Kingdom of God. These perishable bodies of ours are not able to live forever.

⁵¹But let me tell you a wonderful secret God has revealed to us. Not all of us will die, but we will all be transformed. ⁵²It will happen in a moment, in the blinking of an eye, when the last trumpet is blown. For when the trumpet sounds, the Christians who have died will be raised with transformed bodies. And then we who are living will be transformed so that we will never die. ⁵³For our perishable earthly bodies must be transformed into heavenly bodies that will never die.

⁵⁴When this happens—when our perishable earthly bodies have been transformed into heavenly bodies that will never die—then at last the Scriptures will come true:

"Death is swallowed up in victory.
⁵⁵ O death, where is your victory?
O death, where is your sting?"

⁵⁶For sin is the sting that results in death, and the law gives sin its power. ⁵⁷How we thank God, who gives us victory over sin and death through Jesus Christ our Lord!

⁵⁸So, my dear brothers and sisters, be strong and steady, always enthusiastic about the Lord's work, for you know that nothing you do for the Lord is ever useless.   1 CORINTHIANS 15:50-58

A Warm Comforter

PREVIEW

"What is your only comfort in life and in death?" The first question of the Heidelberg Catechism—one of the great documents of the church—gets right to the heart of human despair. It is a question few people can face without a frown, for real comfort is hard to come by.

Paul, of all people, knows what it is like to feel despair. After all, he has been persecuted for his faith just about everywhere he has gone. But that is not the sum of Paul's experience—he also knows God's comfort personally. Because Paul knows how good God's comfort is, he wants Christians to rest in it and feel its healing power. So he writes his second letter to the Corinthians. Find comfort as you read this passage.

PERSONAL APPLICATION

Paul had an amazing testimony about God's comfort. In Asia, Paul was near death, but God was faithful to Paul and not only comforted him through his trial but also delivered him from death (2 Corinthians 1:9-10).

Throughout history many people have asked, *Why am I suffering?* At least one of the answers (though not the only one) is this: so that the comfort you receive from God can make you a comforter to others. Being comforted means receiving strength, encouragement, and hope to deal with our troubles. The more we suffer, the more comfort God gives us. The point is that we can then comfort people who hurt. Apart from experiencing God's comfort, we don't really know how to comfort others (1:3-5).

If you are feeling overwhelmed, allow God to comfort you. Remember that every trial you endure will help you better relate to other people who are suffering. After your trial has passed, look around for other weary souls who need your compassion and God's comfort. Then minister to them by the grace and strength of our Comforter, Jesus Christ.

BIBLE READING

²May God our Father and the Lord Jesus Christ give you his grace and peace.

³All praise to the God and Father of our Lord Jesus Christ. He is the source of every mercy and the God who comforts us. ⁴He comforts us in all our troubles so that we can comfort others. When others are troubled, we will be able to give them the same comfort God has given us. ⁵You can be sure that the more we suffer for Christ, the more God will shower us with his comfort through Christ. ⁶So when we are weighed down with troubles, it is for your benefit and salvation! For when God comforts us, it is so that we, in turn, can be an encouragement to you. Then you can patiently endure the same things we suffer. ⁷We are confident that as you share in suffering, you will also share God's comfort.

⁸I think you ought to know, dear brothers and sisters, about the trouble we went through in the province of Asia. We were crushed and completely overwhelmed, and we thought we would never live through it. ⁹In fact, we expected to die. But as a result, we learned not to rely on ourselves, but on God who can raise the dead. ¹⁰And he did deliver us from mortal danger. And we are confident that he will continue to deliver us. ¹¹He will rescue us because you are helping by praying for us. As a result, many will give thanks to God because so many people's prayers for our safety have been answered.   2 CORINTHIANS 1:2-11

n a Bind

PREVIEW

Charlie Brown and Snoopy, Lois Lane and Clark Kent, Tonto and the Lone Ranger, Captain Kirk and Mr. Spock—all these are examples of relationships that augment and thrive on differences. Opposites attract, and differences can be healthy and good.

The one major exception to this rule: differences are not healthy and good in any intimate relationship between a Christian and a non-Christian. In this passage, Paul warns against forming binding relationships with people who don't know Christ. His warning is not merely a prejudice or preference. There is a real hazard in developing strong partnerships with people who have no vested interest in serving and glorifying God, so we need to beware.

PERSONAL APPLICATION

God wants us to avoid binding relationships with nonbelievers because such bonds can weaken our integrity, standards, or commitment to Christ. A partnership between a believer and a nonbeliever mismatches the values, goals, and desires of the two people involved. This doesn't mean that Christians should always avoid all relationships with non-Christians (see 1 Corinthians 5:9-10). We should definitely care for nonbelievers, showing them Christ's love. Also, a Christian who is married to a nonbelieving spouse should stay with that spouse, and not leave him or her (see 1 Corinthians 7:12-14). The bottom line, however, is that God wants us to be free to live righteous lives. Locking ourselves into personal or business relationships that could cause us to make moral compromises keeps us from doing that.

Protect your freedom to serve Christ. Don't make agreements, enter relationships, or form partnerships that could force you to do something wrong, immoral, or dishonest.

BIBLE READING

[14]Don't team up with those who are unbelievers. How can goodness be a partner with wickedness? How can light live with darkness? [15]What harmony can there be between Christ and the Devil? How can a believer be a partner with an unbeliever? [16]And what union can there be between God's temple and idols? For we are the temple of the living God. As God said:

> "I will live in them
>   and walk among them.
> I will be their God,
>   and they will be my people.
> [17] Therefore, come out from them
>   and separate yourselves from them, says the Lord.
> Don't touch their filthy things,
>   and I will welcome you.
> [18] And I will be your Father,
>   and you will be my sons and daughters,
>   says the Lord Almighty."

2 CORINTHIANS 6:14–18

Trade Secrets of a Cheerful Giver

PREVIEW

To discover the joy of giving, imagine what it would be like next Christmas if no one in your family gave you anything. Ditto for your birthday.

These examples just go to show how valuable giving really is. Imagine how foolish you would feel for doing any of the above. In a way, this is what the Corinthians were guilty of. They had made a commitment to give an offering, but when it came time to give, they changed their minds. This presented Paul with an opportunity to talk about giving and to hold the Corinthians accountable. As you read, hold *yourself* accountable for your giving habits.

PERSONAL APPLICATION

It is so easy for us to promise to give to the church or other Christian causes. But when it comes time to write out the check, our enthusiasm can quickly dwindle.

To avoid such situations, there are four steps you can take to maintain your enthusiasm when you give. First, realize that *how* you give matters more than *how much* you give. An attitude of cheerful giving is more important than the amount given. Second, budget for giving. Control your spending habits so that after you give to God, you will have enough left over to meet all of your financial obligations. That way you will not have to go back on your word in order to pay your bills. Third, realize that material wealth will not bring eternal satisfaction. Wealth can, however, be used to glorify God and lay up treasures in heaven, both of which will bring you eternal satisfaction. Fourth, give as a service to Christ, not as a way of obligating others to give back to you (otherwise it's not giving at all). If you promise to give, do it. If you can give anything at all, give it. The amount isn't the issue. The motivation and attitude is.

BIBLE READING

[1]Now I want to tell you, dear brothers and sisters, what God in his kindness has done for the churches in Macedonia. [2]Though they have been going through much trouble and hard times, their wonderful joy and deep poverty have overflowed in rich generosity. [3]For I can testify that they gave not only what they could afford but far more. And they did it of their own free will. [4]They begged us again and again for the gracious privilege of sharing in the gift for the Christians in Jerusalem. [5]Best of all, they went beyond our highest hopes, for their first action was to dedicate themselves to the Lord and to us for whatever directions God might give them.

[6]So we have urged Titus, who encouraged your giving in the first place, to return to you and encourage you to complete your share in this ministry of giving. [7]Since you excel in so many ways—you have so much faith, such gifted speakers, such knowledge, such enthusiasm, and such love for us —now I want you to excel also in this gracious ministry of giving. [8]I am not saying you must do it, even though the other churches are eager to do it. This is one way to prove your love is real.

[9]You know how full of love and kindness our Lord Jesus Christ was. Though he was very rich, yet for your sakes he became poor, so that by his poverty he could make you rich.

[10]I suggest that you finish what you started a year ago, for you were the first to propose this idea, and you were the first to begin doing something about it. [11]Now you should carry this project through to completion just as enthusiastically as you began it. Give whatever you can according to what you have. [12]If you are really eager to give, it isn't important how much you are able to give. God wants you to give what you have, not what you don't have. [13]Of course, I don't mean you should give so much that you suffer from having too little. I only mean that there should be some equality. [14]Right now you have plenty and can help them. Then at some other time they can share with you when you need it. In this way, everyone's needs will be met. [15]Do you remember what the Scriptures say about this? "Those who gathered a lot had nothing left over, and those who gathered only a little had enough."   2 CORINTHIANS 8:1-15

The Strength of Weakness

PREVIEW

The first gunshot heard at many ten-kilometer races and marathons is not for runners but for wheelchair racers. These people have taken what many would consider a disadvantage and turned it into an asset. They have taken one of life's setbacks and have turned it into a major victory.

Like wheelchair racers, Paul, too, has a physical disadvantage. He never really explains what it is, but we can tell from what he says that it is painful and crippling. Paul does not let this condition overcome him, however. Instead, he counts it to his advantage. As you read, think of your "limitations" and how you can turn them into strengths for Christ's sake.

PERSONAL APPLICATION

Today, it is not easy to find someone so willing to boast about a personal weakness as Paul was. That is because weaknesses are seen as liabilities, not assets. But God sees the situation exactly the opposite. When we are strong and confident in our abilities, we may never notice our need for God. However, when we are weak and incapable, we may realize our need for him.

Have you ever felt weak? Your human frailty—whether physical, emotional, mental, or spiritual—gives God an opportunity to display his power in your life. Admit your weaknesses, and rely on God's power to be effective in those areas. Thank him for your talent, but thank him also for your weaknesses (2 Corinthians 12:9). They will help you develop Christian character, accomplish God's work, and deepen your worship.

BIBLE READING

¹This boasting is all so foolish, but let me go on. Let me tell about the visions and revelations I received from the Lord. ²I was caught up into the third heaven fourteen years ago. ³Whether my body was there or just my spirit, I don't know; only God knows. ⁴But I do know that I was caught up into paradise and heard things so astounding that they cannot be told. ⁵That experience is something worth boasting about, but I am not going to do it. I am going to boast only about my weaknesses. ⁶I have plenty to boast about and would be no fool in doing it, because I would be telling the truth. But I won't do it. I don't want anyone to think more highly of me than what they can actually see in my life and my message, ⁷even though I have received wonderful revelations from God. But to keep me from getting puffed up, I was given a thorn in my flesh, a messenger from Satan to torment me and keep me from getting proud.

⁸Three different times I begged the Lord to take it away. ⁹Each time he said, "My gracious favor is all you need. My power works best in your weakness." So now I am glad to boast about my weaknesses, so that the power of Christ may work through me. ¹⁰Since I know it is all for Christ's good, I am quite content with my weaknesses and with insults, hardships, persecutions, and calamities. For when I am weak, then I am strong.

2 CORINTHIANS 12:1–10

Closer Than a Brother

PREVIEW

A child and a new puppy are virtually inseparable. They can spend so much time together that you would think they were a young couple in love or a mother and her newborn. Every time you turn around they are playing together, napping together, or getting in trouble together. They can become best friends.

In a sense, fellowship with Christ is like a marriage or like that relationship between a child and a puppy. It is a relationship so intimate that Christ and the Christian are—or at least should be—inseparable.

In this passage, Paul describes his close relationship with Jesus. Paul reviews his life story to remind readers of the miracles God can perform. Paul even goes so far as to say that he has been crucified with Christ and that Christ now lives in him. How close are you to Christ?

PERSONAL APPLICATION

Paul was not one of the people crucified with Christ outside Jerusalem. So what did he mean by claiming to have been "crucified with Christ" (Galatians 2:19)? Paul meant that his sinful nature had been put to death when he accepted Christ as his Savior. In essence, he had exchanged one life for another. He had given up control of his life, as well as his desire to sin, in exchange for Christ's redemption from sin and new life in the Spirit.

This spiritual reality holds true for all Christians. When we trust in Christ as Savior, God looks at us as though we had died on the cross with Jesus. Because we have been crucified with Christ, we will also be raised with him (see Romans 6:5). Now Christ lives in us, and we are spiritually alive by his power. By Christ's power we are also no longer bound by the chains of sin.

The next time you face temptation, remember that you have been crucified with Christ and that he lives in you. Then resist the temptation, confident that Christ will strengthen you and provide a way of escape as well.

BIBLE READING

[11]But when Peter came to Antioch, I had to oppose him publicly, speaking strongly against what he was doing, for it was very wrong. [12]When he first arrived, he ate with the Gentile Christians, who don't bother with circumcision. But afterward, when some Jewish friends of James came, Peter wouldn't eat with the Gentiles anymore because he was afraid of what these legalists would say. [13]Then the other Jewish Christians followed Peter's hypocrisy, and even Barnabas was influenced to join them in their hypocrisy.

[14]When I saw that they were not following the truth of the Good News, I said to Peter in front of all the others, "Since you, a Jew by birth, have discarded the Jewish laws and are living like a Gentile, why are you trying to make these Gentiles obey the Jewish laws you abandoned? [15]You and I are Jews by birth, not 'sinners' like the Gentiles. [16]And yet we Jewish Christians know that we become right with God, not by doing what the law commands, but by faith in Jesus Christ. So we have believed in Christ Jesus, that we might be accepted by God because of our faith in Christ—and not because we have obeyed the law. For no one will ever be saved by obeying the law."

[17]But what if we seek to be made right with God through faith in Christ and then find out that we are still sinners? Has Christ led us into sin? Of course not! [18]Rather, I make myself guilty if I rebuild the old system I already tore down. [19]For when I tried to keep the law, I realized I could never earn God's approval. So I died to the law so that I might live for God. I have been crucified with Christ. [20]I myself no longer live, but Christ lives in me. So I live my life in this earthly body by trusting in the Son of God, who loved me and gave himself for me. [21]I am not one of those who treats the grace of God as meaningless. For if we could be saved by keeping the law, then there was no need for Christ to die.   GALATIANS 2:11-21

The Ultimate Adoption

PREVIEW

Growing up in the White House would definitely have its perks. Every school day you would get a limo ride to and from school. In the summer you would travel the world on presidential trips with your parents. During campaign years, you would see the entire country with Mom and Dad. When you were at home, you would have more than one hundred rooms to explore. And if these benefits were not enough, you could brag a lot about what your parents did for a living.

Obviously the overwhelming majority of people have never had and never will have such privileges. But as Christians we are really better off than being a son or daughter of the president. That is because we are the children of the almighty God. As Paul reminds us in his letter to the Galatians, there is no greater privilege. What does it mean to you to be a child of the King of kings?

PERSONAL APPLICATION

Under Roman law, an adopted child was guaranteed all legal rights to his or her father's property. The child was not second-class, but equal to any other children, biological or adopted, in the father's family.

Before Christ died, we were all slaves to sin. But now that Christ has paid the penalty for our sin, we can accept his sacrifice as payment for our debt. When we do this, we are freed from the bondage of sin and are adopted into God's family. As God's adopted children, we share with Jesus all the rights of an heir.

If you belong to Christ, all he has belongs to you (Galatians 4:7). God is your heavenly Father. You can come boldly into his presence, confident that he will lovingly welcome you as his own child.

BIBLE READING

²³Until faith in Christ was shown to us as the way of becoming right with God, we were guarded by the law. We were kept in protective custody, so to speak, until we could put our faith in the coming Savior.

²⁴Let me put it another way. The law was our guardian and teacher to lead us until Christ came. So now, through faith in Christ, we are made right with God. ²⁵But now that faith in Christ has come, we no longer need the law as our guardian. ²⁶So you are all children of God through faith in Christ Jesus. ²⁷And all who have been united with Christ in baptism have been made like him. ²⁸There is no longer Jew or Gentile, slave or free, male or female. For you are all Christians—you are one in Christ Jesus. ²⁹And now that you belong to Christ, you are the true children of Abraham. You are his heirs, and now all the promises God gave to him belong to you.

⁴:¹Think of it this way. If a father dies and leaves great wealth for his young children, those children are not much better off than slaves until they grow up, even though they actually own everything their father had. ²They have to obey their guardians until they reach whatever age their father set.

³And that's the way it was with us before Christ came. We were slaves to the spiritual powers of this world. ⁴But when the right time came, God sent his Son, born of a woman, subject to the law. ⁵God sent him to buy freedom for us who were slaves to the law, so that he could adopt us as his very own children. ⁶And because you Gentiles have become his children, God has sent the Spirit of his Son into your hearts, and now you can call God your dear Father. ⁷Now you are no longer a slave but God's own child. And since you are his child, everything he has belongs to you.   GALATIANS 3:23–4:7

Planting Spiritual Fruit Trees

PREVIEW

Some people are just destined to leave things better off than they found them. Take, for instance, John Chapman—the real-life orchardist who inspired the Johnny Appleseed legend. Chapman spent forty years of his life traveling across western Pennsylvania, Ohio, and Indiana sowing apple seeds. Undoubtedly, many people benefited from the fruits of his labor.

Paul, too, spent much of his adult life sowing seeds. In this reading, he teaches the Galatians about sowing and reaping. He also teaches them how to distinguish between fruit produced by evil and fruit produced by the Holy Spirit. The difference, not surprisingly, is tremendous. As you read, note that all believers are seed-planters, tree-growers, and fruit-pickers. How's your spiritual fruit?

PERSONAL APPLICATION

Most people know the eternal consequences of living a life of sin. But we may not be aware of the immediate consequences of our sins. For instance, when we lie or bend the truth, we do not consider how our credibility will be damaged when the truth eventually gets out. A credibility problem is only the beginning of other problems that may result, such as losing others' trust and friendship, losing a job, or damaging family relationships. All of these consequences could be one kind of immoral "crop." Just think about the negative results of other sinful behaviors. They are overwhelming. By contrast, "those who live to please the Spirit will harvest everlasting life from the Spirit" (Galatians 6:8). When we do this, we will not only reap the benefits of eternal life, but we will also give the Holy Spirit the opportunity to produce good fruit in us (5:22-23).

What kind of seeds are you sowing in your life? Are you sowing to please your own desires? Or are you sowing to please God? If you are planting a selfish crop, try planting one that pleases God. Then have the patience to see how much more bountiful that crop will be in comparison to your own.

BIBLE READING

[1]Dear brothers and sisters, if another Christian is overcome by some sin, you who are godly should gently and humbly help that person back onto the right path. And be careful not to fall into the same temptation yourself. [2]Share each other's troubles and problems, and in this way obey the law of Christ. [3]If you think you are too important to help someone in need, you are only fooling yourself. You are really a nobody.

[4]Be sure to do what you should, for then you will enjoy the personal satisfaction of having done your work well, and you won't need to compare yourself to anyone else. [5]For we are each responsible for our own conduct.

[6]Those who are taught the word of God should help their teachers by paying them.

[7]Don't be misled. Remember that you can't ignore God and get away with it. You will always reap what you sow! [8]Those who live only to satisfy their own sinful desires will harvest the consequences of decay and death. But those who live to please the Spirit will harvest everlasting life from the Spirit. [9]So don't get tired of doing what is good. Don't get discouraged and give up, for we will reap a harvest of blessing at the appropriate time. [10]Whenever we have the opportunity, we should do good to everyone, especially to our Christian brothers and sisters.

GALATIANS 6:1-10

Tearing Down the Walls

PREVIEW

In November 1989, one of the most significant walls ever erected in history was torn to the ground. This barrier—the Berlin Wall—was built to keep the citizens of East Berlin from fleeing to the West. But with the collapse of Communism, the wall was no longer necessary. This once-divided people was now free to reunite. They did so in October 1990, becoming the Federal Republic of Germany.

Almost two millennia before the Berlin Wall fell, Jesus broke down the greatest barrier that ever existed through his death on the cross. Sin stood between humans and God. This, however, was not the only barrier to fall on the day of Christ's crucifixion.

PERSONAL APPLICATION

Paul wrote that Christ broke down "the wall of hostility" between Jews and Gentiles (Ephesians 2:14). The wall refers in one sense to the barrier that separated the Court of the Gentiles from the Court of Israel in the temple. In another sense, this physical wall represents the societal barrier that existed between Jews and Gentiles. Jesus did not come to affirm these barriers but to offer salvation to anyone who would believe and trust in him, including Gentiles. Thus through his death, Jew and Gentile were saved and became part of one body (2:15).

Although Christ's death should unite all believers, many Christians have erected barriers that divide God's family. Differences in doctrine, worship practices, and beliefs about acceptable behavior have severed parts of the body from one another. In addition, Christians have not been immune to prejudices, such as racism.

As followers of Christ, we should not build walls between ourselves. Rather, we should remember that Christ's death served not only to redeem us from our sin but to end discord between believers.

BIBLE READING

[11]"Don't forget that you Gentiles used to be outsiders by birth. You were called "the uncircumcised ones" by the Jews, who were proud of their circumcision, even though it affected only their bodies and not their hearts. [12]In those days you were living apart from Christ. You were excluded from God's people, Israel, and you did not know the promises God had made to them. You lived in this world without God and without hope. [13]But now you belong to Christ Jesus. Though you once were far away from God, now you have been brought near to him because of the blood of Christ.

[14]For Christ himself has made peace between us Jews and you Gentiles by making us all one people. He has broken down the wall of hostility that used to separate us. [15]By his death he ended the whole system of Jewish law that excluded the Gentiles. His purpose was to make peace between Jews and Gentiles by creating in himself one new person from the two groups. [16]Together as one body, Christ reconciled both groups to God by means of his death, and our hostility toward each other was put to death. [17]He has brought this Good News of peace to you Gentiles who were far away from him, and to us Jews who were near. [18]Now all of us, both Jews and Gentiles, may come to the Father through the same Holy Spirit because of what Christ has done for us.

[19]So now you Gentiles are no longer strangers and foreigners. You are citizens along with all of God's holy people. You are members of God's family. [20]We are his house, built on the foundation of the apostles and the prophets. And the cornerstone is Christ Jesus himself. [21]We who believe are carefully joined together, becoming a holy temple for the Lord. [22]Through him you Gentiles are also joined together as part of this dwelling where God lives by his Spirit.   EPHESIANS 2:11-22

_P_utting Anger to Bed

PREVIEW

The popularity of conflict resolution has put a damper on old-fashioned, red-eyed anger. Ranting, raving, and name-calling have almost become felonies today.

Despite this recent trend, conflict resolution is really nothing new. It has been around for a long time, even before Paul wrote his letter to the Ephesians. That is why Paul is able to give great advice in his letter for dealing with one of the main ingredients of conflict—anger. What stirs your temper?

In addition to handling anger, Paul also warns the Ephesians against illicit sex and smooth talkers who peddle fancy religious ideas. He also gives family members advice on how to relate to each other.

PERSONAL APPLICATION

Anger is a dangerous emotion, "for anger gives a mighty foothold to the Devil" (Ephesians 4:27). The Bible, however, does not tell us to avoid _being_ angry but to avoid nursing our anger (4:26-27). When we respond in anger to a situation, we sin by choosing the destructive alternative to the problem. We also open ourselves up to developing a pattern of sinful behavior that may include physical abuse and verbal attacks. If we nurse our anger into a grudge, we will become bitter, which can negatively affect all our relationships—especially the one we have with God.

Learn to control your anger without letting it rule you. When you are angry, confess your feelings to God, and ask him to help you respond to the situation as Christ would. When you are angry, follow Paul's advice and resolve your conflict before the sun goes down (4:26). Let God, not your anger, determine how you act.

BIBLE READING

²²Throw off your old evil nature and your former way of life, which is rotten through and through, full of lust and deception. ²³Instead, there must be a spiritual renewal of your thoughts and attitudes. ²⁴You must display a new nature because you are a new person, created in God's likeness—righteous, holy, and true.

²⁵So put away all falsehood and "tell your neighbor the truth" because we belong to each other. ²⁶And "don't sin by letting anger gain control over you." Don't let the sun go down while you are still angry, ²⁷for anger gives a mighty foothold to the Devil.

²⁸If you are a thief, stop stealing. Begin using your hands for honest work, and then give generously to others in need. ²⁹Don't use foul or abusive language. Let everything you say be good and helpful, so that your words will be an encouragement to those who hear them.

³⁰And do not bring sorrow to God's Holy Spirit by the way you live. Remember, he is the one who has identified you as his own, guaranteeing that you will be saved on the day of redemption.

³¹Get rid of all bitterness, rage, anger, harsh words, and slander, as well as all types of malicious behavior. ³²Instead, be kind to each other, tenderhearted, forgiving one another, just as God through Christ has forgiven you.   EPHESIANS 4:22-32

Under Construction

PREVIEW

It would be nice to renovate a room or an entire home with the click of a button or a wave of a magic wand. Imagine the time you would save, the hassle and mess you would avoid, and all the money you would have left over because it did not cost you a penny. Despite these great advantages, there is one downside to all this convenience. You would not enjoy the satisfaction that comes from achieving a difficult task through hard labor and perseverance.

The Christian life is like a home-renovation project. It is a long, tiring, and sometimes painful process. There are no buttons to push to become a mature and perfect Christian instantly. But Paul reminds the Philippians that God will see his children through this process to completion and perfection. As you read, be encouraged that God is working in you, conforming you to the likeness of his own Son (see Romans 8:29).

PERSONAL APPLICATION

God begins a process of changing believers as soon as he saves them. Through the Holy Spirit, God works on each Christian's character bit by bit. This process takes a lifetime. Signs of progress come and go, but the work is never finished. Only when Christ returns will all believers be made perfect. Meanwhile, God's work in us continues (Philippians 1:6).

If you belong to Christ, do not let life's setbacks and failures discourage you. God has promised to finish the good work he has begun in you, and in time, he will do just that. In the meantime, keep your relationship with him vital by studying his Word and spending time in prayer. Also, encourage other Christians who may be struggling with failure by reminding them of God's promise.

BIBLE READING

²May God our Father and the Lord Jesus Christ give you grace and peace.

³Every time I think of you, I give thanks to my God. ⁴I always pray for you, and I make my requests with a heart full of joy ⁵because you have been my partners in spreading the Good News about Christ from the time you first heard it until now. ⁶And I am sure that God, who began the good work within you, will continue his work until it is finally finished on that day when Christ Jesus comes back again.

⁷It is right that I should feel as I do about all of you, for you have a very special place in my heart. We have shared together the blessings of God, both when I was in prison and when I was out, defending the truth and telling others the Good News. ⁸God knows how much I love you and long for you with the tender compassion of Christ Jesus. ⁹I pray that your love for each other will overflow more and more, and that you will keep on growing in your knowledge and understanding. ¹⁰For I want you to understand what really matters, so that you may live pure and blameless lives until Christ returns. ¹¹May you always be filled with the fruit of your salvation—those good things that are produced in your life by Jesus Christ—for this will bring much glory and praise to God.

¹²And I want you to know, dear brothers and sisters, that everything that has happened to me here has helped to spread the Good News.   PHILIPPIANS 1:2-12

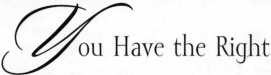ou Have the Right

PREVIEW

Perhaps no other topic today—except for salvation—is more obscured by falsehood than that of rights. Just about everyone thinks that he or she is entitled to a long list of rights not guaranteed by the Bible or the Constitution. For instance, some people believe they have the right to do illegal drugs. Others think they have the right to play their stereos loud any hour of the night. Some even believe they have the right to break the law and get away with it.

Clearly, the demand for rights has gotten out of hand in America. But Paul has an antidote for Christians caught up in or dismayed by a rights-obsessed society. His advice is to imitate Christ, who sacrificed his rights as God's own Son to save his people. As you read, consider how you can become more like Christ, our humble Lord and Savior.

PERSONAL APPLICATION

Jesus had the right to be worshiped, obeyed, and honored as God. Yet he did not lay claim to that right. Instead he lowered himself, gave up his rights, and died a humiliating death for our sins. He had more rights than anyone will ever have, and he gave them all up to save his people (Philippians 2:5-11).

All kinds of evil deeds have been committed in the name of rights. Selfish attitudes, such as "I deserve it," "It's my right," and "You have no right to stop me," have been used to justify cheating, abortion, materialism, and countless other sins.

Those who follow Christ must not only refuse to selfishly uphold their rights but avoid having selfish attitudes as well. Instead, believers should allow God to develop an attitude of humility within them.

BIBLE READING

[1]Is there any encouragement from belonging to Christ? Any comfort from his love? Any fellowship together in the Spirit? Are your hearts tender and sympathetic? [2]Then make me truly happy by agreeing wholeheartedly with each other, loving one another, and working together with one heart and purpose.

[3]Don't be selfish; don't live to make a good impression on others. Be humble, thinking of others as better than yourself. [4]Don't think only about your own affairs, but be interested in others, too, and what they are doing.

[5]Your attitude should be the same that Christ Jesus had. [6]Though he was God, he did not demand and cling to his rights as God. [7]He made himself nothing; he took the humble position of a slave and appeared in human form. [8]And in human form he obediently humbled himself even further by dying a criminal's death on a cross. [9]Because of this, God raised him up to the heights of heaven and gave him a name that is above every other name, [10]so that at the name of Jesus every knee will bow, in heaven and on earth and under the earth, [11]and every tongue will confess that Jesus Christ is Lord, to the glory of God the Father.

PHILIPPIANS 2:1-11

ot Just a Casual Acquaintance

PREVIEW

Many people use the word *know* to cover the loosest possible connections. Someone might say, "Sure, I know Joe," when in fact, Joe is a friend of a friend. Or someone might say he knows about a product because he happened to see a commercial for it the other day. Knowing about people and things hardly means anything more than having heard about them.

The meaning of the word *know* was different for Paul. It did not mean having a casual acquaintance or hearing a passing reference. In this passage, Paul explains what it means for him to know someone. And that someone he knows is Christ. As you read, think of how well you know the Savior.

PERSONAL APPLICATION

Paul accomplished a great deal, and most who know anything about him consider him a great man. But he regarded all his accomplishments to be "garbage" when compared with the greatness of knowing Christ (Philippians 3:8). One personal relationship mattered more to Paul than anything else. That's why he endured so much suffering, rejection, physical abuse, and hardship—to stay close to Christ (3:10-11).

Many priorities clamor for our time—family, job, friends, and certain goals and plans. But our relationship with Christ matters more than all of them. To know Christ is the ultimate achievement, the first priority, the best option, the highest goal. A crowded schedule in order to set aside a few minutes each day for prayer and Bible study, a friend's disapproval, a sacrifice of plans or pleasures are small prices to pay for such a reward.

Spend time getting to know your Savior. Make "knowing" Christ your highest priority.

BIBLE READING

⁴Yet I could have confidence in myself if anyone could. If others have reason for confidence in their own efforts, I have even more! ⁵For I was circumcised when I was eight days old, having been born into a pure-blooded Jewish family that is a branch of the tribe of Benjamin. So I am a real Jew if there ever was one! What's more, I was a member of the Pharisees, who demand the strictest obedience to the Jewish law. ⁶And zealous? Yes, in fact, I harshly persecuted the church. And I obeyed the Jewish law so carefully that I was never accused of any fault.

⁷I once thought all these things were so very important, but now I consider them worthless because of what Christ has done. ⁸Yes, everything else is worthless when compared with the priceless gain of knowing Christ Jesus my Lord. I have discarded everything else, counting it all as garbage, so that I may have Christ ⁹and become one with him. I no longer count on my own goodness or my ability to obey God's law, but I trust Christ to save me. For God's way of making us right with himself depends on faith. ¹⁰As a result, I can really know Christ and experience the mighty power that raised him from the dead. I can learn what it means to suffer with him, sharing in his death, ¹¹so that, somehow, I can experience the resurrection from the dead!

¹²I don't mean to say that I have already achieved these things or that I have already reached perfection! But I keep working toward that day when I will finally be all that Christ Jesus saved me for and wants me to be. ¹³No, dear brothers and sisters, I am still not all I should be, but I am focusing all my energies on this one thing: Forgetting the past and looking forward to what lies ahead, ¹⁴I strain to reach the end of the race and receive the prize for which God, through Christ Jesus, is calling us up to heaven.

PHILIPPIANS 3:4-14

Garbage In, Garbage Out

PREVIEW

In a celebrated Florida murder trial, an adolescent claimed television addiction as his defense for the crime. "The tube made him do it," his attorney argued.

Despite this argument, media programming never "makes" anyone do anything. What we put in our minds, however, does influence our actions. With this in mind, the apostle Paul advises believers in this last chapter of Philippians to meditate on truth and other pure thoughts. This includes our TV shows, movies, videos, and music. What are you doing to keep the garbage out?

PERSONAL APPLICATION

It seems nearly impossible today to think good and pure thoughts when we are constantly bombarded with immoral images, stories, and suggestions. Little entertainment today is free from profanity, "adult sexual themes," or violence. In addition, many books, magazines, and newspapers focus on the those "big three," in one way or another.

Many people defend violent, obscene, and sexually explicit media on the grounds that they do no harm. They say that watching violent television doesn't make people violent. But they miss the point. The evil lies in thinking untrue, bad, wrong, impure, ugly, coarse, and contemptible thoughts. Whether or not we become monsters, we all think monstrous thoughts. Even if all the negative thoughts never corrupt our behavior directly, our minds can still become filled with violent, evil images, and that is an evil in itself.

The situation is not hopeless, however. If you commit yourself to God and follow Paul's advice here, you can find media entertainment that is clean and even glorifying to God.

BIBLE READING

⁴Always be full of joy in the Lord. I say it again—rejoice! ⁵Let everyone see that you are considerate in all you do. Remember, the Lord is coming soon.

⁶Don't worry about anything; instead, pray about everything. Tell God what you need, and thank him for all he has done. ⁷If you do this, you will experience God's peace, which is far more wonderful than the human mind can understand. His peace will guard your hearts and minds as you live in Christ Jesus.

⁸And now, dear brothers and sisters, let me say one more thing as I close this letter. Fix your thoughts on what is true and honorable and right. Think about things that are pure and lovely and admirable. Think about things that are excellent and worthy of praise. ⁹Keep putting into practice all you learned from me and heard from me and saw me doing, and the God of peace will be with you.

¹⁰How grateful I am, and how I praise the Lord that you are concerned about me again. I know you have always been concerned for me, but for a while you didn't have the chance to help me. ¹¹Not that I was ever in need, for I have learned how to get along happily whether I have much or little. ¹²I know how to live on almost nothing or with everything. I have learned the secret of living in every situation, whether it is with a full stomach or empty, with plenty or little. ¹³For I can do everything with the help of Christ who gives me the strength I need. ¹⁴But even so, you have done well to share with me in my present difficulty.

PHILIPPIANS 4:4-14

Praying for Strangers

PREVIEW

The child away from home is always welcome to call collect, and your spouse's calls are welcome at work, even during a busy day. With people you care about, talk is precious and almost never an inconvenience. With strangers, though, it can sometimes be just the opposite.

Prayer should be like talking to a loved one. But the only way that will happen is to talk with God often and about everything. As Paul illustrates with his own example in this letter, intimate prayer even includes praying for those we do not know. As you read, think about your relationship with your heavenly Father. Have you spoken with him lately?

Also notice the other lessons in these chapters on how to have a new life in Christ, and how to stay free of legalism.

PERSONAL APPLICATION

Paul had never met the Colossian Christians, but he faithfully prayed for them (Colossians 1:9-14). He did not just pray vaguely; he prayed about specifics, asking God to cause them to grow in their understanding, wisdom, and good works so that they could know God better. Paul didn't feel timid about praying for strangers.

Needs and prayer requests fly at us from all directions. Some of the people we hear about have casual connections to us. Others we know only as names or faces. Still others have no connection to us at all. Whatever their specific needs, all have the same basic need to grow in the knowledge of God. Paul's prayer for the Colossians gives us a good pattern to follow in praying for those we do not know.

The next time you learn of a stranger's needs, do not feel overwhelmed by another prayer request. Instead, pray for that person's needs as well as for his or her growth in understanding, wisdom, and knowledge of God.

BIBLE READING

³We always pray for you, and we give thanks to God the Father of our Lord Jesus Christ, ⁴for we have heard that you trust in Christ Jesus and that you love all of God's people. ⁵You do this because you are looking forward to the joys of heaven—as you have been ever since you first heard the truth of the Good News. ⁶This same Good News that came to you is going out all over the world. It is changing lives everywhere, just as it changed yours that very first day you heard and understood the truth about God's great kindness to sinners.

⁷Epaphras, our much loved co-worker, was the one who brought you the Good News. He is Christ's faithful servant, and he is helping us in your place. ⁸He is the one who told us about the great love for others that the Holy Spirit has given you.

⁹So we have continued praying for you ever since we first heard about you. We ask God to give you a complete understanding of what he wants to do in your lives, and we ask him to make you wise with spiritual wisdom. ¹⁰Then the way you live will always honor and please the Lord, and you will continually do good, kind things for others. All the while, you will learn to know God better and better.

¹¹We also pray that you will be strengthened with his glorious power so that you will have all the patience and endurance you need. May you be filled with joy, ¹²always thanking the Father, who has enabled you to share the inheritance that belongs to God's holy people, who live in the light. ¹³For he has rescued us from the one who rules in the kingdom of darkness, and he has brought us into the Kingdom of his dear Son. ¹⁴God has purchased our freedom with his blood and has forgiven all our sins.   COLOSSIANS 1:3-14

$\mathcal{B}$ridges That Seem Too Far

PREVIEW

In 1944, Allied armies launched a disastrous mission along a narrow corridor through Holland to reach a bridge on the Rhine. The story came to be called "A Bridge Too Far."

Like the Allies' mission to reach this bridge, efforts to bridge gaps between races, social classes, and religious denominations may seem too costly and unattainable. But Paul has the solution for this impossible mission: Jesus Christ. As you read, consider the walls that separate you from others. Determine, through Christ, to tear down those walls and build bridges.

This passage also has a lot to say about successful parenting, loyal employment, and setting life goals. At the end of his letter, Paul sends greetings to friends near and far.

PERSONAL APPLICATION

Jesus does not discriminate between people on the basis of race, nationality, ethnic background, level of education, or social position. He ignores all social distinctions and accepts all people who come to him in faith (Colossians 3:11).

Looking around the world, we see that such acceptance is not the norm. People constantly make distinctions between each other on the basis of nationality, race, education level, social standing, wealth, gender, religion, and power. Cultures practice and protect these distinctions. Governments sanction them. People fight over them. But God hates distinctions.

Do not be like the world. Do not discriminate against others because of their race, gender, or socioeconomic status. Instead, pray that God will help you to love all people, and welcome them into your church community. Be like Jesus, befriending and loving those who are different from you. Never treat them as lesser people.

BIBLE READING

⁹Don't lie to each other, for you have stripped off your old evil nature and all its wicked deeds. ¹⁰In its place you have clothed yourselves with a brand-new nature that is continually being renewed as you learn more and more about Christ, who created this new nature within you. ¹¹In this new life, it doesn't matter if you are a Jew or a Gentile, circumcised or uncircumcised, barbaric, uncivilized, slave, or free. Christ is all that matters, and he lives in all of us.

¹²Since God chose you to be the holy people whom he loves, you must clothe yourselves with tenderhearted mercy, kindness, humility, gentleness, and patience. ¹³You must make allowance for each other's faults and forgive the person who offends you. Remember, the Lord forgave you, so you must forgive others. ¹⁴And the most important piece of clothing you must wear is love. Love is what binds us all together in perfect harmony. ¹⁵And let the peace that comes from Christ rule in your hearts. For as members of one body you are all called to live in peace. And always be thankful.

¹⁶Let the words of Christ, in all their richness, live in your hearts and make you wise. Use his words to teach and counsel each other. Sing psalms and hymns and spiritual songs to God with thankful hearts. ¹⁷And whatever you do or say, let it be as a representative of the Lord Jesus, all the while giving thanks through him to God the Father.   COLOSSIANS 3:9-17

Walk This Way

PREVIEW

"Monkey see, monkey do" describes the behavior of toddlers—and many grown-ups as well. Those with siblings especially pick up on new tricks and habits that they see brothers or sisters demonstrate. It's cute to see, but it's also scary for parents. They know that their children are watching them.

Paul understands this principle and has seen it applied in a more positive way. In this first letter to the church at Thessalonica, he commends the Thessalonians for their imitation of the one person everyone should strive to be like—Christ. In what ways do you imitate Christ?

PERSONAL APPLICATION

When the Thessalonian Christians turned to Christ they were dramatically changed. They gave up their idols, began serving God, and eagerly awaited Christ's return from heaven (1 Thessalonians 1:7-10). People soon noticed how they had changed, and news about them spread. No one could mistake the fact that these people believed in Jesus, because everyone could see their faith in action.

What was true then is also true now: If God is at work in your life, people will notice. Word will spread. People will see you doing "odd" things because you call Jesus Lord, and God's influence will soon be obvious to all. Whether you regard this as a blessing or a curse depends on you.

Do not underestimate the influence your good deeds can have on others. If you serve Christ, others who see the difference in you will be influenced to love and serve Christ too.

BIBLE READING

²We always thank God for all of you and pray for you constantly.
³As we talk to our God and Father about you, we think of your
faithful work, your loving deeds, and your continual anticipation
of the return of our Lord Jesus Christ.

⁴We know that God loves you, dear brothers and sisters, and
that he chose you to be his own people. ⁵For when we brought
you the Good News, it was not only with words but also with
power, for the Holy Spirit gave you full assurance that what we
said was true. And you know that the way we lived among you was
further proof of the truth of our message. ⁶So you received the
message with joy from the Holy Spirit in spite of the severe
suffering it brought you. In this way, you imitated both us and
the Lord. ⁷As a result, you yourselves became an example to all
the Christians in Greece. ⁸And now the word of the Lord is ring-
ing out from you to people everywhere, even beyond Greece, for
wherever we go we find people telling us about your faith in God.
We don't need to tell them about it, ⁹for they themselves keep
talking about the wonderful welcome you gave us and how you
turned away from idols to serve the true and living God. ¹⁰And
they speak of how you are looking forward to the coming of
God's Son from heaven—Jesus, whom God raised from the dead.
He is the one who has rescued us from the terrors of the coming
judgment.   1 THESSALONIANS 1:2-10

Just Wanted to Say Thanks

PREVIEW

At the Academy Awards in Hollywood, award-winning movie stars, producers, and artists say "thank you" to other stars, producers, and artists. Normally these people viciously compete with each other, but one night a year, they pause to recognize each other's achievements. Perhaps some express gratitude more often than this. For some, however, this is the only time they take to say thanks.

Saying thanks was not a once-a-year occasion for Paul. Rather it was a lifestyle. In the last chapter of 1 Thessalonians, Paul explains why believers should always maintain an attitude of thankfulness. When did you last thank God for his innumerable blessings?

Paul also gives practical reasons for living holy lives, especially in the area of sexual relations.

PERSONAL APPLICATION

Paul wrote that believers should "always be thankful" (1 Thessalonians 5:18). His statement can be easily misunderstood. Paul was not teaching that Christians should thank God *for* everything that happens in their lives. For instance, they should not thank God for personal sin and for the evil in the world. Evil comes from sin and from Satan, not from God. But they should thank God *in* every situation.

No matter what goes wrong or right, we can still be thankful to God for his presence and help. We have his promise that "God causes everything to work together for the good of those who love God and are called according to his purpose for them" (see Romans 8:28), so we have a reason to be thankful.

At all times, keep in mind all that God has done. Then you will have plenty of reasons to be thankful—for God, for the joys he brings, and for the spiritual growth he can bring about through trials.

Bible Reading

[12]Dear brothers and sisters, honor those who are your leaders in the Lord's work. They work hard among you and warn you against all that is wrong. [13]Think highly of them and give them your wholehearted love because of their work. And remember to live peaceably with each other.

[14]Brothers and sisters, we urge you to warn those who are lazy. Encourage those who are timid. Take tender care of those who are weak. Be patient with everyone.

[15]See that no one pays back evil for evil, but always try to do good to each other and to everyone else.

[16]Always be joyful. [17]Keep on praying. [18]No matter what happens, always be thankful, for this is God's will for you who belong to Christ Jesus.

[19]Do not stifle the Holy Spirit. [20]Do not scoff at prophecies, [21]but test everything that is said. Hold on to what is good. [22]Keep away from every kind of evil.

[23]Now may the God of peace make you holy in every way, and may your whole spirit and soul and body be kept blameless until that day when our Lord Jesus Christ comes again. [24]God, who calls you, is faithful; he will do this.

1 Thessalonians 5:12-24

old on Tight

PREVIEW

A car accident wipes out a family. Cancer strikes a young wife and mother. A poor managerial decision puts an eager, productive employee out of work. Rebel soldiers slaughter people huddled in a church. Some events in life make no sense at all. That is why we call them tragedies.

In this reading, Paul offers no easy answers for life's hardships. He does, however, offer one piece of advice that, if followed, brings real comfort and encouragement for those who are persecuted. At the same time, he warns us of the evil in this world, in particular, of those who speak falsely for God.

PERSONAL APPLICATION

God had given gifts of infinite value to the Thessalonians. Paul urged the Thessalonians to thank God for these gifts. Yet Paul also knew that they would face challenges to their belief in Christ. They would have doubts, and certain people and circumstances would encourage those doubts. Unless the Thessalonians had a firm conviction about all they had been taught, their faith would die. So Paul urged them to "stand firm and keep a strong grip on everything we taught you" (2 Thessalonians 2:15). They had the Scriptures and the letters that Paul had written to keep them on track.

As he did for the Thessalonians, God has given us a great gift—his Word. Yet it is so easy to take this gift for granted and not use it. When we stop using his gift, we make ourselves more susceptible to falsehoods. To strengthen our faith and protect ourselves from false-hoods, we need to spend time in God's Word every day.

If you do not spend time reading your Bible every day, think of things you can cut from your schedule to make time for God. If you faithfully spend time in the Word, challenge yourself to spend even more time with God.

BIBLE READING

¹³As for us, we always thank God for you, dear brothers and sisters loved by the Lord. We are thankful that God chose you to be among the first to experience salvation, a salvation that came through the Spirit who makes you holy and by your belief in the truth. ¹⁴He called you to salvation when we told you the Good News; now you can share in the glory of our Lord Jesus Christ.

¹⁵With all these things in mind, dear brothers and sisters, stand firm and keep a strong grip on everything we taught you both in person and by letter.

¹⁶May our Lord Jesus Christ and God our Father, who loved us and in his special favor gave us everlasting comfort and good hope, ¹⁷comfort your hearts and give you strength in every good thing you do and say.

³⁺¹Finally, dear brothers and sisters, I ask you to pray for us. Pray first that the Lord's message will spread rapidly and be honored wherever it goes, just as when it came to you. ²Pray, too, that we will be saved from wicked and evil people, for not everyone believes in the Lord. ³But the Lord is faithful; he will make you strong and guard you from the evil one. ⁴And we are confident in the Lord that you are practicing the things we commanded you, and that you always will. ⁵May the Lord bring you into an ever deeper understanding of the love of God and the endurance that comes from Christ.

2 THESSALONIANS 2:13—3:5

lacking Off

PREVIEW

Two work ethics are at odds in our culture today. One says that
people should work hard for a living. The other says that people
deserve the easy life. Why work when you can play, right?

These same work ethics were around during Paul's day. So Paul
addresses the real issue behind the bad work ethic—laziness. He not
only condemns the bad ethic but gives the Thessalonians an example of
what a good work ethic looks like. As you read, determine never to be
lazy in the things of God.

Also in this passage, Paul asks for prayer, guarantees the authenticity
of his letter, then says good-bye in his own special way.

PERSONAL APPLICATION

Some people in the Thessalonian church were falsely teaching that
because Christ's second coming could happen any day, people should
set aside their responsibilities, quit work, do no future planning, and
simply wait for the Lord to appear. But their lack of activity led them
into sin. These people became a burden to the church, which was
supporting them. They wasted time that could have been spent helping
others, and they gossiped (2 Thessalonians 3:6-11). They may have
thought they were being more spiritual by not working, but Paul told
them to be responsible and get back to work.

Being ready for Christ means obeying him in every area of life.
Because we know Christ is coming, we must do everything we can to
live in a way that will please him when he arrives.

Make the most of your talent and time. Cut out activities that only
distract or make it harder for you to fulfill your responsibilities.

BIBLE READING

⁶And now, dear brothers and sisters, we give you this command with the authority of our Lord Jesus Christ: Stay away from any Christian who lives in idleness and doesn't follow the tradition of hard work we gave you. ⁷For you know that you ought to follow our example. We were never lazy when we were with you. ⁸We never accepted food from anyone without paying for it. We worked hard day and night so that we would not be a burden to any of you. ⁹It wasn't that we didn't have the right to ask you to feed us, but we wanted to give you an example to follow. ¹⁰Even while we were with you, we gave you this rule: "Whoever does not work should not eat."

¹¹Yet we hear that some of you are living idle lives, refusing to work and wasting time meddling in other people's business. ¹²In the name of the Lord Jesus Christ, we appeal to such people—no, we command them: Settle down and get to work. Earn your own living. ¹³And I say to the rest of you, dear brothers and sisters, never get tired of doing good.

¹⁴Take note of those who refuse to obey what we say in this letter. Stay away from them so they will be ashamed. ¹⁵Don't think of them as enemies, but speak to them as you would to a Christian who needs to be warned.   2 THESSALONIANS 3:6-15

Clouding the Picture

PREVIEW

When in trouble, often a child's favorite trick is to divert a parent from the main issue to something else. A typical conversation may go like this: "Why were you out so late?"

"Worried about me? You worry too much, Mom. Life would be happier without so much worry. We need a family vacation. What about Disneyland?"

Spiritual speculators in the church are much like children who divert their parents' attention. Paul warns his readers not to get distracted by the false teachers who are more interested in their own reputations than in God's truth. Their religion is complex and confusing. As you read, determine to let nothing cloud God's truth and your view of Christ.

PERSONAL APPLICATION

Speculating about what the Bible may mean can make for interesting conversation, but it can also cause us to muddle the intent of God's message. We need to guard against over-spiritualizing parts of the Bible or falling in love with our own ideas about it. The Good News of salvation in Jesus Christ doesn't need new or additional "improvements" invented by clever thinkers.

The main point of Scripture is that Jesus came to save people from their sins. Let that message hold center stage in your mind and heart. Do not waste your time speculating on minute details of the Bible. You may never know the real meaning behind the detail and, at the same time, only draw attention away from the One who gave his Word to point people to him.

BIBLE READING

[3]When I left for Macedonia, I urged you to stay there in Ephesus and stop those who are teaching wrong doctrine. [4]Don't let people waste time in endless speculation over myths and spiritual pedigrees. For these things only cause arguments; they don't help people live a life of faith in God. [5]The purpose of my instruction is that all the Christians there would be filled with love that comes from a pure heart, a clear conscience, and sincere faith.

[6]But some teachers have missed this whole point. They have turned away from these things and spend their time arguing and talking foolishness. [7]They want to be known as teachers of the law of Moses, but they don't know what they are talking about, even though they seem so confident. [8]We know these laws are good when they are used as God intended. [9]But they were not made for people who do what is right. They are for people who are disobedient and rebellious, who are ungodly and sinful, who consider nothing sacred and defile what is holy, who murder their father or mother or other people. [10]These laws are for people who are sexually immoral, for homosexuals and slave traders, for liars and oath breakers, and for those who do anything else that contradicts the right teaching [11]that comes from the glorious Good News entrusted to me by our blessed God.

[12]How thankful I am to Christ Jesus our Lord for considering me trustworthy and appointing me to serve him, [13]even though I used to scoff at the name of Christ. I hunted down his people, harming them in every way I could. But God had mercy on me because I did it in ignorance and unbelief. [14]Oh, how kind and gracious the Lord was! He filled me completely with faith and the love of Christ Jesus.   1 TIMOTHY 1:3-14

$\mathcal{A}$ Bit of Practical Politics

PREVIEW

More than a million conversations a day trade news about how to win on the stock market. More than 10 million try to predict the outcome of upcoming sports events. How many conversations relate to politics—100 million? More? Too many, most people would say.

Just when you think you have had enough of politics, Paul throws his hat in the ring. But the good news about Paul's involvement in this arena is that he is not throwing mud but advocating prayer—for leaders. How often do *you* pray for your elected officials?

In addition to promoting prayer for our political leaders, Paul also discusses the standards we should uphold for church leaders.

PERSONAL APPLICATION

Paul urged Timothy to pray for civil authorities so that believers could enjoy peace and freedom, thus enabling them to live for Christ and share the gospel with others. And the reason this matters so much is that God desires all people to be saved (1 Timothy 2:4; see 2 Peter 3:9).

God wants us to take the news of Christ to others, but this won't happen if chaos and disorder have us occupied. Not everyone *will* be saved—many refuse to go through Christ's narrow gate (see Matthew 7:13; 25:31-46; John 12:44-50; Hebrews 10:26-29). But the message about Christ matters so much to God that we should pray and work for the freedom to publish it.

God's appointed means for keeping the peace resides in the hallowed halls of our civil governments, at every level. Pray often for the leaders and authorities who govern our land.

BIBLE READING

[1]I urge you, first of all, to pray for all people. As you make your requests, plead for God's mercy upon them, and give thanks. [2]Pray this way for kings and all others who are in authority, so that we can live in peace and quietness, in godliness and dignity. [3]This is good and pleases God our Savior, [4]for he wants everyone to be saved and to understand the truth. [5]For there is only one God and one Mediator who can reconcile God and people. He is the man Christ Jesus. [6]He gave his life to purchase freedom for everyone. This is the message that God gave to the world at the proper time. [7]And I have been chosen—this is the absolute truth—as a preacher and apostle to teach the Gentiles about faith and truth.

[8]So wherever you assemble, I want men to pray with holy hands lifted up to God, free from anger and controversy. [9]And I want women to be modest in their appearance. They should wear decent and appropriate clothing and not draw attention to themselves by the way they fix their hair or by wearing gold or pearls or expensive clothes. [10]For women who claim to be devoted to God should make themselves attractive by the good things they do.   1 TIMOTHY 2:1-10

Rich in More Ways than One

PREVIEW

Sharing can be a measure of love. People who love each other willingly share all they have. Conversely, when sharing becomes a chore, love is at low tide.

Just as couples in love share with one another generously, so should Christians. In this reading, Paul admonishes believers to share their wealth with those in need. But he does not stop there. He tells Christians to give happily, from the heart, and not merely out of duty to the law. How does your giving compare to Paul's admonition?

In this section, Paul also advises young leaders on how to win the respect of older people, and he reveals the source of true contentment.

PERSONAL APPLICATION

Timothy lived and ministered in Ephesus, a large and wealthy city. His church probably had many wealthy members. Paul's instructions to Timothy included the charge to teach the believers how to manage wealth (1 Timothy 6:17-19). Having a lot of money, he wrote, carries great responsibility. The wealthy must be generous, but they should not be arrogant just because they have a lot to give. They must take care not to hoard their money for security instead of finding their security in God. And they should take encouragement from the fact that their giving stores up "treasure as a good foundation for the future" (6:19).

If you have a surplus of money, the opportunities to do good with it are almost endless. Rather than keeping all of it for yourself, ask God how you can use the resources he has given you to build up treasures in heaven. If money is scarce, you can still be generous with what you have. Just be sure to ask for direction to help you share what you have wisely.

BIBLE READING

[6]Yet true religion with contentment is great wealth. [7]After all, we didn't bring anything with us when we came into the world, and we certainly cannot carry anything with us when we die. [8]So if we have enough food and clothing, let us be content. [9]But people who long to be rich fall into temptation and are trapped by many foolish and harmful desires that plunge them into ruin and destruction. [10]For the love of money is at the root of all kinds of evil. And some people, craving money, have wandered from the faith and pierced themselves with many sorrows.

[11]But you, Timothy, belong to God; so run from all these evil things, and follow what is right and good. Pursue a godly life, along with faith, love, perseverance, and gentleness. [12]Fight the good fight for what we believe. Hold tightly to the eternal life that God has given you, which you have confessed so well before many witnesses. [13]And I command you before God, who gives life to all, and before Christ Jesus, who gave a good testimony before Pontius Pilate, [14]that you obey his commands with all purity. Then no one can find fault with you from now until our Lord Jesus Christ returns. [15]For at the right time Christ will be revealed from heaven by the blessed and only almighty God, the King of kings and Lord of lords. [16]He alone can never die, and he lives in light so brilliant that no human can approach him. No one has ever seen him, nor ever will. To him be honor and power forever. Amen.

[17]Tell those who are rich in this world not to be proud and not to trust in their money, which will soon be gone. But their trust should be in the living God, who richly gives us all we need for our enjoyment. [18]Tell them to use their money to do good. They should be rich in good works and should give generously to those in need, always being ready to share with others whatever God has given them. [19]By doing this they will be storing up their treasure as a good foundation for the future so that they may take hold of real life. 1 TIMOTHY 6:6-19

trategic Retreat

PREVIEW

"I just want to" is a kid's reply
To parents begging for reasons why.

I just want to . . . experiment with drugs, find out about sex, try bungee jumping, shop till I drop. "Don't ask why," they beg, and parents say no.

For Christians who have a hard time resisting the lure of bad ideas and do not have parents around to stop them, Paul says, "Run!" Do not even give the temptation time to present its case. Just get out of there. Live boldly, Paul writes, but live wisely. A little bit of well-placed fear goes a long way. As you read, consider when you should run and when you should stand and fight.

In addition to his advice for making a hasty retreat, in these chapters Paul also encourages Christians to not be afraid of suffering and to not be ashamed of their work for the gospel.

PERSONAL APPLICATION

Paul urged Timothy to run away from anything that tempted him to do wrong (2 Timothy 2:22). Some may consider this to be cowardly, but wise people run from dangers and from enemies they cannot fight. They know their limits and respect their weak spots. When the danger involves temptation, they avoid it altogether. Running from a strong temptation makes more sense than trying to resist it.

What recurring temptation do you have difficulty resisting? Avoid any situation that tempts you in that area. Know when to run and don't be ashamed to do so. There's no point in trying to be tough and falling into sin as a result (see 1 Timothy 6:11).

BIBLE READING

[19]But God's truth stands firm like a foundation stone with this inscription: "The Lord knows those who are his," and "Those who claim they belong to the Lord must turn away from all wickedness."

[20]In a wealthy home some utensils are made of gold and silver, and some are made of wood and clay. The expensive utensils are used for special occasions, and the cheap ones are for everyday use. [21]If you keep yourself pure, you will be a utensil God can use for his purpose. Your life will be clean, and you will be ready for the Master to use you for every good work.

[22]Run from anything that stimulates youthful lust. Follow anything that makes you want to do right. Pursue faith and love and peace, and enjoy the companionship of those who call on the Lord with pure hearts.

[23]Again I say, don't get involved in foolish, ignorant arguments that only start fights. [24]The Lord's servants must not quarrel but must be kind to everyone. They must be able to teach effectively and be patient with difficult people. [25]They should gently teach those who oppose the truth. Perhaps God will change those people's hearts, and they will believe the truth. [26]Then they will come to their senses and escape from the Devil's trap. For they have been held captive by him to do whatever he wants.   2 TIMOTHY 2:19-26

The Purpose of Our Instruction

PREVIEW

Little League coaches know that very young ballplayers have to use a tee to learn how to bat before they can swing and hit pitches. Surgeons have their interns watch procedures before they let them pick up a scalpel. Parents of budding violinists endure hours of squeaks before enjoying the beautiful notes of a school orchestra. Practice makes perfect—or at least makes things better.

The same principle applies to spiritual growth. Believers cannot get better (become more like Christ) without regularly studying God's Word and applying it to their lives. That is why Paul tells Timothy about the Bible's usefulness in teaching what is true and right. As you read, evaluate your "practice" schedule.

Also in this passage, Paul gives a glimpse of the future. Life on earth does not look good for Christians, but Christ will return soon and take us to a better place.

PERSONAL APPLICATION

God gave the Bible so that people could learn to love and serve him (2 Timothy 3:16-17). A lot of the study and learning we do in life aims to make us smarter or more knowledgeable. That will happen when we study the Bible, but it's not the main reason that God gave us his Word. God wants us to change our thoughts, behavior, and character.

Some people use their knowledge of the Bible only to win arguments or to make themselves look clever. Besides missing the aim of having such knowledge, they become worse people, not better, by falling into pride (see 1 Corinthians 8:1-3).

Never flaunt your knowledge of God's Word. Study the Bible to learn how to live, not to win an argument or to show somebody up. Seek to know Christ and learn to do good.

BIBLE READING

[14]But you must remain faithful to the things you have been taught. You know they are true, for you know you can trust those who taught you. [15]You have been taught the holy Scriptures from childhood, and they have given you the wisdom to receive the salvation that comes by trusting in Christ Jesus. [16]All Scripture is inspired by God and is useful to teach us what is true and to make us realize what is wrong in our lives. It straightens us out and teaches us to do what is right. [17]It is God's way of preparing us in every way, fully equipped for every good thing God wants us to do.

[4:1]And so I solemnly urge you before God and before Christ Jesus—who will someday judge the living and the dead when he appears to set up his Kingdom: [2]Preach the word of God. Be persistent, whether the time is favorable or not. Patiently correct, rebuke, and encourage your people with good teaching.

[3]For a time is coming when people will no longer listen to right teaching. They will follow their own desires and will look for teachers who will tell them whatever they want to hear. [4]They will reject the truth and follow strange myths.

[5]But you should keep a clear mind in every situation. Don't be afraid of suffering for the Lord. Work at bringing others to Christ. Complete the ministry God has given you.

[6]As for me, my life has already been poured out as an offering to God. The time of my death is near. [7]I have fought a good fight, I have finished the race, and I have remained faithful. [8]And now the prize awaits me—the crown of righteousness that the Lord, the righteous Judge, will give me on that great day of his return. And the prize is not just for me but for all who eagerly look forward to his glorious return.

2 TIMOTHY 3:14–4:8

*W*atch Out!

PREVIEW

Phonies are not always easy to spot. Some look so real that they could fool the most suspicious and skeptical people. Phony people may even believe their own scams.

In this reading, Paul urges Titus to warn the Christians on Crete to beware of phonies. These false teachers are not concerned with truth. As you read, think of how you can determine truth from error, what is real from what is false.

In this chapter, Paul also outlines what is required of spiritual leaders, and he reminds Titus that God always tells the truth.

PERSONAL APPLICATION

Paul warned Titus about people who teach wrong doctrines (Titus 1:10-14). He told this protégé and young pastor to be harsh with these false teachers because they teach from evil motives and lead people away from Christ. Some false teachers simply have misguided opinions or a poor understanding of the Bible. Others *try* to deceive—they pretend to be sincere while hiding their cravings for money or influence over others. Jesus and the apostles repeatedly warned against such false teachers (see Mark 13:22; Acts 20:29; 2 Thessalonians 2:3-12; 2 Peter 3:3-7).

Many people think that false teaching about God makes little difference. But believing falsehoods about God, Christ, or salvation can be more fatal to your faith than drinking poison. False teachings about eternal life meddle with people's eternal destiny.

Be on guard against false spiritual teachers, and be careful of any person who claims to have spiritual truth. False teachers betray their motives by pointing people away from the Bible and toward other ideas. Test all teachings by comparing them to God's Word before letting someone teach and lead you.

BIBLE READING

[5]I left you on the island of Crete so you could complete our work there and appoint elders in each town as I instructed you. [6]An elder must be well thought of for his good life. He must be faithful to his wife, and his children must be believers who are not wild or rebellious. [7]An elder must live a blameless life because he is God's minister. He must not be arrogant or quick-tempered; he must not be a heavy drinker, violent, or greedy for money. [8]He must enjoy having guests in his home and must love all that is good. He must live wisely and be fair. He must live a devout and disciplined life. [9]He must have a strong and steadfast belief in the trustworthy message he was taught; then he will be able to encourage others with right teaching and show those who oppose it where they are wrong.

[10]For there are many who rebel against right teaching; they engage in useless talk and deceive people. This is especially true of those who insist on circumcision for salvation. [11]They must be silenced. By their wrong teaching, they have already turned whole families away from the truth. Such teachers only want your money. [12]One of their own men, a prophet from Crete, has said about them, "The people of Crete are all liars; they are cruel animals and lazy gluttons." [13]This is true. So rebuke them as sternly as necessary to make them strong in the faith. [14]They must stop listening to Jewish myths and the commands of people who have turned their backs on the truth.

[15]Everything is pure to those whose hearts are pure. But nothing is pure to those who are corrupt and unbelieving, because their minds and consciences are defiled. [16]Such people claim they know God, but they deny him by the way they live. They are despicable and disobedient, worthless for doing anything good.

TITUS 1:5-16

$\mathcal{S}$ee Figure 1

PREVIEW

Effective teaching depends on demonstration. We can find out how to do anything by just reading about it, but usually the directions or concepts do not sink in until we have seen the technique or skill demonstrated. The teacher says, "Watch me," and we learn.

Demonstrations are also useful in Christianity. Like anything else new and different, living the Christian life may be difficult to grasp and understand just by reading the instruction manual. That is why Paul advises Titus to live the Christian life in front of everyone he meets. It is a demonstration on how living for Christ is done. What do people learn about Christ when they watch you?

PERSONAL APPLICATION

Paul urged Titus to be a good example to those around him, to let his life be a living demonstration of the truth and doctrine he taught (Titus 2:7). Considering the fact that Titus was a preacher, that was quite a charge—part of his job had nothing to do with talking. As a leader, he needed to *show* the way, not just point in that direction.

Nothing communicates quite like a demonstration. It's one thing for a parent to say, "Floss your teeth," and quite another for that mom or dad to be a flosser. Seeing the living example, children will begin to learn the skill. And it's one thing for a person to say, "Christ is number one in my life," and quite another to see that statement lived out in values, choices, and commitments.

Place a great deal of emphasis on how you live, not just on what you stand for. Give attention to your habits, plans, lifestyle choices, and scheduling priorities. Bring these areas of your life under the jurisdiction of Christ so when people hear about your faith, they will have no problem understanding what you mean.

BIBLE READING

[1]But as for you, promote the kind of living that reflects right teaching. [2]Teach the older men to exercise self-control, to be worthy of respect, and to live wisely. They must have strong faith and be filled with love and patience.

[3]Similarly, teach the older women to live in a way that is appropriate for someone serving the Lord. They must not go around speaking evil of others and must not be heavy drinkers. Instead, they should teach others what is good. [4]These older women must train the younger women to love their husbands and their children, [5]to live wisely and be pure, to take care of their homes, to do good, and to be submissive to their husbands. Then they will not bring shame on the word of God.

[6]In the same way, encourage the young men to live wisely in all they do. [7]And you yourself must be an example to them by doing good deeds of every kind. Let everything you do reflect the integrity and seriousness of your teaching. [8]Let your teaching be so correct that it can't be criticized. Then those who want to argue will be ashamed because they won't have anything bad to say about us.

[9]Slaves must obey their masters and do their best to please them. They must not talk back [10]or steal, but they must show themselves to be entirely trustworthy and good. Then they will make the teaching about God our Savior attractive in every way.

[11]For the grace of God has been revealed, bringing salvation to all people. [12]And we are instructed to turn from godless living and sinful pleasures. We should live in this evil world with self-control, right conduct, and devotion to God.   TITUS 2:1-12

Taking off the Gloves

PREVIEW

Far-fetched explanations of how things work sometimes turn out to be right. The idea that the earth revolves around the sun was heresy eight hundred years ago! Silly, brainless, and hostile arguments against the truth often oppose and delay commonsense progress.

Using good judgment, we do well when we make smart choices and stay clear of stupidity, Paul writes. Pointless arguments tangle the brain, he insists. Use your best intelligence, with openness to new ideas, but do not get tangled up in nonsense. As you read, consider what you can do to stay focused on the important issues in life.

At the close of this letter, Paul also writes of more important projects that beg for attention.

PERSONAL APPLICATION

Paul warned Titus, as he warned Timothy, not to get involved in foolish and futile arguments (Titus 3:9; see 2 Timothy 2:14). Paul knew that Titus would often get into discussions about emotionally-charged topics. He knew that this pastor's study of the Scriptures and teachings about them would invite heated discussion. Thus, Paul urged Titus to choose his battles carefully and to avoid arguments that would reach no conclusion.

Some arguments lead nowhere. They concern topics that don't matter or do no one any good, even if someone does "win." We should avoid those kinds of arguments.

If you're in disagreement with someone over an issue, consider what difference it makes who's right. If it's not important, then give up arguing. Change the subject or politely excuse yourself. Make peace a prime goal even when you discuss significant matters (see Romans 12:18).

BIBLE READING

[1]Remind your people to submit to the government and its officers. They should be obedient, always ready to do what is good. [2]They must not speak evil of anyone, and they must avoid quarreling. Instead, they should be gentle and show true humility to everyone.

[3]Once we, too, were foolish and disobedient. We were misled by others and became slaves to many wicked desires and evil pleasures. Our lives were full of evil and envy. We hated others, and they hated us.

[4]But then God our Savior showed us his kindness and love. [5]He saved us, not because of the good things we did, but because of his mercy. He washed away our sins and gave us a new life through the Holy Spirit. [6]He generously poured out the Spirit upon us because of what Jesus Christ our Savior did. [7]He declared us not guilty because of his great kindness. And now we know that we will inherit eternal life. [8]These things I have told you are all true. I want you to insist on them so that everyone who trusts in God will be careful to do good deeds all the time. These things are good and beneficial for everyone.

[9]Do not get involved in foolish discussions about spiritual pedigrees or in quarrels and fights about obedience to Jewish laws. These kinds of things are useless and a waste of time. [10]If anyone is causing divisions among you, give a first and second warning. After that, have nothing more to do with that person. [11]For people like that have turned away from the truth. They are sinning, and they condemn themselves.   TITUS 3:1-11

All Things Being Equal

PREVIEW

Have you ever had the unfortunate experience of being looked down upon? Perhaps you were at a social occasion dressed a little too casually when you were snubbed. Maybe you ventured into "the wrong part of town" and were assaulted with evil stares or racial slurs. Whatever your experience may have been, one thing is certain—it hurt.

Paul's letter to Philemon deals with this issue. Here Paul writes: Respect all people. Give everyone your love, and do not regard social class, economic position, career field, or family background as a basis for judging others. Wage earners and board chairpersons are brothers and sisters in the sight of God. As you read, think of any prejudices that you may harbor.

PERSONAL APPLICATION

Onesimus was a slave who had run away from his master, Philemon. While Onesimus was on the run, he had become a Christian. What a difference his new identity would make in his relationship with Philemon. Now they were no longer just master and servant but brothers in Christ (Philemon 1:16). Because of Christ, both Onesimus and Philemon had equal status in God's family, and Paul wrote Philemon to remind him of this.

A Christian's identity as a member of God's family overrides all other distinctions. Race doesn't matter; social status doesn't matter; ethnic background doesn't matter; political label doesn't matter; gender doesn't matter—all Christians are part of the same family, equals in Christ, equally important, equally loved by God.

Don't look down on any fellow Christians. In Christ, all stand before God as your equal (see Galatians 3:28). Treat your fellow Christians as the equals they are.

BIBLE READING

[8]That is why I am boldly asking a favor of you. I could demand it in the name of Christ because it is the right thing for you to do, [9]but because of our love, I prefer just to ask you. So take this as a request from your friend Paul, an old man, now in prison for the sake of Christ Jesus.

[10]My plea is that you show kindness to Onesimus. I think of him as my own son because he became a believer as a result of my ministry here in prison. [11]Onesimus hasn't been of much use to you in the past, but now he is very useful to both of us. [12]I am sending him back to you, and with him comes my own heart.

[13]I really wanted to keep him here with me while I am in these chains for preaching the Good News, and he would have helped me on your behalf. [14]But I didn't want to do anything without your consent. And I didn't want you to help because you were forced to do it but because you wanted to. [15]Perhaps you could think of it this way: Onesimus ran away for a little while so you could have him back forever. [16]He is no longer just a slave; he is a beloved brother, especially to me. Now he will mean much more to you, both as a slave and as a brother in the Lord.

[17]So if you consider me your partner, give him the same welcome you would give me if I were coming.   PHILEMON 1:8-17

The Ultimate Power

PREVIEW

The United States of America was established so that people can have a say in how they are governed. But as soon as many of the elected officials take office, it seems that the citizens who elected them can forget about hearing from them until the next election. Perhaps, for most politicians, the will of the people is easier to forget than the power of the press. This confusion of command makes it impossible to know who really is in charge of the country—the people, the politicians, or the media.

Many who spend their time trying to figure out who is in control down here overlook the one who is in control of everything—Jesus. In this reading, the writer of Hebrews reminds readers that just because Jesus is seated in heaven does not mean that he is unaware or uninvolved in the events on earth. As you read and think of current events, remember that your sovereign and all-powerful Lord reigns.

PERSONAL APPLICATION

Sometimes the chaos, violence, immorality, and evil of this world can cloud our vision of Jesus' reign. Yet Christ does rule in heaven, and everything on earth belongs to him. He is King, even if all his subjects do not yet obey him. This is Christ's world. He has control of it.

If you want to affect the world, talk to Jesus about it. Christ's reign on earth has not yet begun, but his rule from heaven is no less real. When you are confused by present events and grow anxious about the future, remember Jesus' true position and authority. He is Lord of all, and one day he will rule on earth as he does now in heaven (see Matthew 6:10).

BIBLE READING

[1]Long ago God spoke many times and in many ways to our ancestors through the prophets. [2]But now in these final days, he has spoken to us through his Son. God promised everything to the Son as an inheritance, and through the Son he made the universe and everything in it. [3]The Son reflects God's own glory, and everything about him represents God exactly. He sustains the universe by the mighty power of his command. After he died to cleanse us from the stain of sin, he sat down in the place of honor at the right hand of the majestic God of heaven.

[4]This shows that God's Son is far greater than the angels, just as the name God gave him is far greater than their names. [5]For God never said to any angel what he said to Jesus:

"You are my Son.
Today I have become your Father."

And again God said,

"I will be his Father,
and he will be my Son."

[6]And then, when he presented his honored Son to the world, God said, "Let all the angels of God worship him." [7]God calls his angels

"messengers swift as the wind,
and servants made of flaming fire."

[8]But to his Son he says,

"Your throne, O God, endures forever and ever.
Your royal power is expressed in righteousness.
[9] You love what is right and hate what is wrong.
Therefore God, your God, has anointed you,
pouring out the oil of joy on you more than on
anyone else."

Patients of the Good Doctor

PREVIEW

Anyone who has ever had surgery knows how scary it can be. The fact that surgeons cut and stitch every day does not help, either. We still feel anxious and frightened about having our bodies opened up, even in the simplest procedures. If not for anesthesia, the operation would be indescribably painful, but even with the help of unconsciousness we know that we will be vulnerable and helpless during the procedure. And afterward, some kind of painful recovery will follow. No one can blame anyone for feeling nervous about all that.

As scary as surgery is, there is a nonphysical operation that scares some people even more. The writer of Hebrews clues us in as to who the doctor is, as well as what instrument he will be using to perform this surgery. No anesthesia is needed here, only a humble and willing heart. Are you open to spiritual surgery by the divine Surgeon?

PERSONAL APPLICATION

God uses his Word to work on our lives as a surgeon uses a scalpel (Hebrews 4:12). It cuts through our pretender's skin. It goes after the cancerous sinful growths that infect our character. It attacks our spiritually diseased condition.

For this very reason, many people fear the Bible. They fear the discomfort and pain in confronting and dealing with their spiritual problems. They fear the changes that will take place in their character and life. But changes for good should not be feared, for God removes from our character only what harms us—our sinful attitudes and behaviors.

Do not be afraid to read the Bible. Let God do corrective surgery on your thoughts, attitudes, and behaviors. Although it may be painful now, the end results will be well worth the discomfort you may experience.

BIBLE READING

[1]God's promise of entering his place of rest still stands, so we ought to tremble with fear that some of you might fail to get there. [2]For this Good News—that God has prepared a place of rest—has been announced to us just as it was to them. But it did them no good because they didn't believe what God told them. [3]For only we who believe can enter his place of rest. As for those who didn't believe, God said,

"In my anger I made a vow:
'They will never enter my place of rest,'"

even though his place of rest has been ready since he made the world. [4]We know it is ready because the Scriptures mention the seventh day, saying, "On the seventh day God rested from all his work." [5]But in the other passage God said, "They will never enter my place of rest." [6]So God's rest is there for people to enter. But those who formerly heard the Good News failed to enter because they disobeyed God. [7]So God set another time for entering his place of rest, and that time is today. God announced this through David a long time later in the words already quoted:

"Today you must listen to his voice.
Don't harden your hearts against him."

[8]This new place of rest was not the land of Canaan, where Joshua led them. If it had been, God would not have spoken later about another day of rest. [9]So there is a special rest still waiting for the people of God. [10]For all who enter into God's rest will find rest from their labors, just as God rested after creating the world. [11]Let us do our best to enter that place of rest. For anyone who disobeys God, as the people of Israel did, will fall.

[12]For the word of God is full of living power. It is sharper than the sharpest knife, cutting deep into our innermost thoughts and desires. It exposes us for what we really are. [13]Nothing in all creation can hide from him. Everything is naked and exposed before his eyes. This is the God to whom we must explain all that we have done. HEBREWS 4:1-13

Rest Assured

PREVIEW

It seems as though everything changes. Friendships, jobs, children, marriage relationships, financial security—they all change for better or for worse. Can anything or anyone be counted on to remain the same?

Yes. Today's passage invites us to step onto the solid foundation of God. If we can count on anything, we can count on him. As you read, feel both calmed by finding security in him and energized for all the changes in and around you.

Just as this passage reminds us of God's steadfastness, it also reminds us of our need to change. In addition, it presents Jesus in a new light, as High Priest.

PERSONAL APPLICATION

The original readers of this letter may have wondered, just as Christians sometimes wonder today, *Will God ever revoke his salvation?* They could rest assured, as can we, that the answer is no. God does what he says he will do, and he has promised to save all who call on him (Hebrews 6:18). He does not change his plans just because we do.

If you worry about your salvation, ask yourself whether you sincerely asked God to save you from your sins. If you did, be assured that he has done what you asked. But if you still have doubts every once in a while, remember that God is faithful. He will not abandon you.

BIBLE READING

[11]Our great desire is that you will keep right on loving others as long as life lasts, in order to make certain that what you hope for will come true. [12]Then you will not become spiritually dull and indifferent. Instead, you will follow the example of those who are going to inherit God's promises because of their faith and patience.

[13]For example, there was God's promise to Abraham. Since there was no one greater to swear by, God took an oath in his own name, saying:

[14] "I will certainly bless you richly,
   and I will multiply your descendants into countless millions."

[15]Then Abraham waited patiently, and he received what God had promised.

[16]When people take an oath, they call on someone greater than themselves to hold them to it. And without any question that oath is binding. [17]God also bound himself with an oath, so that those who received the promise could be perfectly sure that he would never change his mind. [18]So God has given us both his promise and his oath. These two things are unchangeable because it is impossible for God to lie. Therefore, we who have fled to him for refuge can take new courage, for we can hold on to his promise with confidence.

[19]This confidence is like a strong and trustworthy anchor for our souls. It leads us through the curtain of heaven into God's inner sanctuary. [20]Jesus has already gone in there for us. He has become our eternal High Priest in the line of Melchizedek.

HEBREWS 6:11-20

o More Crutches

PREVIEW

A broken leg usually means a time of walking on crutches. If the break is bad enough, getting around becomes impossible without them. Some may think this novel for a time, but the novelty soon wears off. The patient looks forward to the day when the crutches can be thrown into the closet for good.

Before Jesus came to this earth and died for everyone's sins, people depended on the crutch of animal sacrifice for forgiveness. But Christ's blood heals and frees people from sin and their dependence on spiritual crutches. Are you leaning on a crutch or on Christ?

As you read this passage, notice the comparisons between the old covenant of animal sacrifice and the new covenant with Jesus as your High Priest.

PERSONAL APPLICATION

Animal sacrifices played an important role in Israel's relationship with God. They provided a means for people to cover their sins until the coming of Christ. But these sacrifices only imitated and foreshadowed Jesus' future sacrifice. His offering paid for all sin, once and for all, and did what the animal sacrifices could only point to: *full* payment *forever* for sin.

Today, Jesus serves as our High Priest before God the Father in heaven (Hebrews 8:1-2; 9:24-28). Our hope of eternal life lies in him, and our day-to-day access to God depends on Jesus' loving intercession on our behalf.

Look to Christ for fulfillment of your spiritual needs, because he can meet them all.

BIBLE READING

[11]So Christ has now become the High Priest over all the good things that have come. He has entered that great, perfect sanctuary in heaven, not made by human hands and not part of this created world. [12]Once for all time he took blood into that Most Holy Place, but not the blood of goats and calves. He took his own blood, and with it he secured our salvation forever.

[13]Under the old system, the blood of goats and bulls and the ashes of a young cow could cleanse people's bodies from ritual defilement. [14]Just think how much more the blood of Christ will purify our hearts from deeds that lead to death so that we can worship the living God. For by the power of the eternal Spirit, Christ offered himself to God as a perfect sacrifice for our sins. [15]That is why he is the one who mediates the new covenant between God and people, so that all who are invited can receive the eternal inheritance God has promised them. For Christ died to set them free from the penalty of the sins they had committed under that first covenant.

[16]Now when someone dies and leaves a will, no one gets anything until it is proved that the person who wrote the will is dead. [17]The will goes into effect only after the death of the person who wrote it. While the person is still alive, no one can use the will to get any of the things promised to them.

[18]That is why blood was required under the first covenant as a proof of death. [19]For after Moses had given the people all of God's laws, he took the blood of calves and goats, along with water, and sprinkled both the book of God's laws and all the people, using branches of hyssop bushes and scarlet wool. [20]Then he said, "This blood confirms the covenant God has made with you." [21]And in the same way, he sprinkled blood on the sacred tent and on everything used for worship. [22]In fact, we can say that according to the law of Moses, nearly everything was purified by sprinkling with blood. Without the shedding of blood, there is no forgiveness of sins.　　　　HEBREWS 9:11-22

Your Undivided Attention, Please

PREVIEW

Toddlers are notorious for their short attention spans. Older children and especially adults, however, can fix their attention on something for quite some time. Have you ever tried to pull a ten-year-old away from a favorite video game? Or how about trying to pull an avid sports fan away from the game of the week?

It is with this kind of absorption that the writer of Hebrews says we should fix our attention on Jesus. Unlike video games and sporting events, focusing our entire attention on Jesus can benefit us in many ways, the most important of which is a deep relationship with God. As you read this passage, refocus your eyes on Christ.

This reading also teaches us some graduate-level lessons in faith and helps us to understand about the *D*-word—discipline.

PERSONAL APPLICATION

Jesus suffered tremendous humiliation, injustice, and physical pain to do God's will (Hebrews 12:2-4). Strangers arrested him for crimes he didn't commit, beat him, mocked him, and spat on him. Friends deserted him. His heavenly Father left him to die alone. He died slowly and painfully in the company of common thieves. He became an offering for our sin (see 2 Corinthians 5:21). That is the price Jesus paid to obey his heavenly Father.

The struggles you endure to follow Jesus are real. It takes energy and commitment to say no to sinful desires, to do good deeds that you don't want to do, and to discipline yourself to pray and study God's Word on a regular basis.

When you feel discouraged in your Christian life, think of Jesus and all he went through to do what God wanted. Then take heart knowing that you can do what God requires of you by his strength and grace. Stay focused on him.

BIBLE READING

¹Therefore, since we are surrounded by such a huge crowd of witnesses to the life of faith, let us strip off every weight that slows us down, especially the sin that so easily hinders our progress. And let us run with endurance the race that God has set before us. ²We do this by keeping our eyes on Jesus, on whom our faith depends from start to finish. He was willing to die a shameful death on the cross because of the joy he knew would be his afterward. Now he is seated in the place of highest honor beside God's throne in heaven. ³Think about all he endured when sinful people did such terrible things to him, so that you don't become weary and give up. ⁴After all, you have not yet given your lives in your struggle against sin.

⁵And have you entirely forgotten the encouraging words God spoke to you, his children? He said,

> "My child, don't ignore it when the Lord disciplines you,
>   and don't be discouraged when he corrects you.
> ⁶ For the Lord disciplines those he loves,
>   and he punishes those he accepts as his children."

⁷As you endure this divine discipline, remember that God is treating you as his own children. Whoever heard of a child who was never disciplined? ⁸If God doesn't discipline you as he does all of his children, it means that you are illegitimate and are not really his children after all. ⁹Since we respect our earthly fathers who disciplined us, should we not all the more cheerfully submit to the discipline of our heavenly Father and live forever?

¹²So take a new grip with your tired hands and stand firm on your shaky legs. ¹³Mark out a straight path for your feet. Then those who follow you, though they are weak and lame, will not stumble and fall but will become strong.

HEBREWS 12:1-9, 12-13

Welcome . . . Troubles?

Preview

Most people do not welcome the hard lessons of life. "Why do I have to learn this the *hard* way?" they fume. "Why couldn't I have just been able to read a good book on the topic?"

James, no stranger to trials himself, urges readers to take the most unexpected attitude when bad times descend. Although his admonishment sounds strange at first, the outcome of doing so is spiritually rewarding. As you read, consider what you are learning from your troubles.

In this passage, James also teaches us how to acquire wisdom; how to handle temptation; and how hearing God's Word and doing good works go together.

Personal Application

Be glad when you have a bad day—the experience will do you some good, James wrote (James 1:2-4). As uncomfortable as this message is, James is not saying that we should enjoy trials. Rather, he is saying that we should be glad for the good effects that trials can have on us.

A bout of suffering, usually considered a curse, can be a blessing. Suffering through trials teaches many things essential to life—such as how to have patience and endurance. Living through a trial is also the best way to build character.

When troubles come your way, welcome them as teachers, however unpleasant they may be. Take advantage of your bad circumstances by depending on God to get you through hard times. He will not only take care of you, but he will also make you a better person through it.

BIBLE READING

²Dear brothers and sisters, whenever trouble comes your way, let it be an opportunity for joy. ³For when your faith is tested, your endurance has a chance to grow. ⁴So let it grow, for when your endurance is fully developed, you will be strong in character and ready for anything.

⁵If you need wisdom—if you want to know what God wants you to do—ask him, and he will gladly tell you. He will not resent your asking. ⁶But when you ask him, be sure that you really expect him to answer, for a doubtful mind is as unsettled as a wave of the sea that is driven and tossed by the wind. ⁷People like that should not expect to receive anything from the Lord. ⁸They can't make up their minds. They waver back and forth in everything they do.

⁹Christians who are poor should be glad, for God has honored them. ¹⁰And those who are rich should be glad, for God has humbled them. They will fade away like a flower in the field. ¹¹The hot sun rises and dries up the grass; the flower withers, and its beauty fades away. So also, wealthy people will fade away with all of their achievements.

¹²God blesses the people who patiently endure testing. Afterward they will receive the crown of life that God has promised to those who love him. JAMES 1:2-12

laying Favorites

PREVIEW

Imagine yourself in a coffee shop with a bunch of your friends, having a good time laughing and talking. Suddenly, you see a disheveled person approach the table. *Oh no,* you think, *he's coming over here. What if he asks to join us?*

In this passage, James confronts the Jerusalem churchgoers for having this kind of attitude toward the poor. He reminds them that showing favoritism to the rich while neglecting or slighting the poor is wrong. As James says in a roundabout way, you cannot judge a book by its cover. When have you played favorites?

A famous passage on a chicken-and-egg question also appears: what comes first, faith or works? Get ready as well for some giant-sized lessons on one of the smallest, yet most powerful, parts of the human body.

PERSONAL APPLICATION

People of the ancient world had just as much concern for wealth and status as people do today. They wanted to be associated with rich people and undisturbed by the problems of the poor. Even some Christians would flatter the rich and dote on their needs while pushing aside poor people who came to church. James made it clear that Christians who understand their Lord live by a different standard: They dispense with the favor-the-rich custom and treat all people alike, regardless of how wealthy or impoverished they happen to be (James 2:1-4).

Jesus never showed favoritism toward rich people, and neither should we. Attempts to associate only with the financially secure betray a selfish, faithless, and uncaring attitude.

Make a point to show proper respect to all people regardless of the cut of their clothes or the size of their bank accounts.

BIBLE READING

[1]My dear brothers and sisters, how can you claim that you have faith in our glorious Lord Jesus Christ if you favor some people more than others?

[2]For instance, suppose someone comes into your meeting dressed in fancy clothes and expensive jewelry, and another comes in who is poor and dressed in shabby clothes. [3]If you give special attention and a good seat to the rich person, but you say to the poor one, "You can stand over there, or else sit on the floor"—well, [4]doesn't this discrimination show that you are guided by wrong motives?

[5]Listen to me, dear brothers and sisters. Hasn't God chosen the poor in this world to be rich in faith? Aren't they the ones who will inherit the Kingdom he promised to those who love him? [6]And yet, you insult the poor man! Isn't it the rich who oppress you and drag you into court? [7]Aren't they the ones who slander Jesus Christ, whose noble name you bear?

[8]Yes indeed, it is good when you truly obey our Lord's royal command found in the Scriptures: "Love your neighbor as yourself." [9]But if you pay special attention to the rich, you are committing a sin, for you are guilty of breaking that law.

[10]And the person who keeps all of the laws except one is as guilty as the person who has broken all of God's laws. [11]For the same God who said, "Do not commit adultery," also said, "Do not murder." So if you murder someone, you have broken the entire law, even if you do not commit adultery.

[12]So whenever you speak, or whatever you do, remember that you will be judged by the law of love, the law that set you free. [13]For there will be no mercy for you if you have not been merciful to others. But if you have been merciful, then God's mercy toward you will win out over his judgment against you.

JAMES 2:1-13

Up Close and Personal

PREVIEW

The Wild West brought about new kinds of heroes: the lone wolf, the independent pioneer, and the classic rugged individualist. No one could tame the untamed frontier like they could. They did not obey rules—they made them.

The Christian life is not an untamed frontier demanding Wild West heroes. Rather, it is a sanctuary for settlers who respect the boundaries. As you read this passage, look for the boundaries in which believers are to live.

Here James also discusses the nature of true wisdom; getting along with other people; faith and what it can do; and having the right perspective on the future. If you want to blaze a trail to God, this is a good spot from which to start.

PERSONAL APPLICATION

Getting close to God requires a transfer of ownership—a humble submission of our lives to him (James 4:7-10). Once that transaction takes place, we must continue the fight against the forces that draw us away from Christ. We must resist the devil and flee from him. We must embrace God's will and let go of our own evil desires. We must grieve our sinfulness rather than celebrate it. And we must purify ourselves.

To sign away your life won't mark you as a distinctly heroic person in most people's eyes. But it will lead to intimacy with God, and it will allow God to "lift you up" (4:10)—something he does not do for lone wolves.

BIBLE READING

[1]What is causing the quarrels and fights among you? Isn't it the whole army of evil desires at war within you? [2]You want what you don't have, so you scheme and kill to get it. You are jealous for what others have, and you can't possess it, so you fight and quarrel to take it away from them. And yet the reason you don't have what you want is that you don't ask God for it. [3]And even when you do ask, you don't get it because your whole motive is wrong—you want only what will give you pleasure.

[4]You adulterers! Don't you realize that friendship with this world makes you an enemy of God? I say it again, that if your aim is to enjoy this world, you can't be a friend of God. [5]What do you think the Scriptures mean when they say that the Holy Spirit, whom God has placed within us, jealously longs for us to be faithful? [6]He gives us more and more strength to stand against such evil desires. As the Scriptures say,

> "God sets himself against the proud,
>   but he shows favor to the humble."

[7]So humble yourselves before God. Resist the Devil, and he will flee from you. [8]Draw close to God, and God will draw close to you. Wash your hands, you sinners; purify your hearts, you hypocrites. [9]Let there be tears for the wrong things you have done. Let there be sorrow and deep grief. Let there be sadness instead of laughter, and gloom instead of joy. [10]When you bow down before the Lord and admit your dependence on him, he will lift you up and give you honor.   JAMES 4:1-10

This May Hurt a Little

PREVIEW

Few things are more frustrating than buying "quality" merchandise that falls apart as soon as you take it out of the box. Then you look inside the box and find a small slip of paper that reads: "Inspected by Number 45." Apparently, your merchandise had not been inspected closely enough. A few seconds of mild abuse by Number 45 probably would have shown this merchandise for what it was, and spared you the disappointment.

In Peter's first letter, he warns and encourages us about disappointments—how we can approach them, live through them, and be strengthened by them. They are tests or, if you will, inspections of God's merchandise—us.

Notice also in this passage a living hope, hints at what angels long to see, and the high standards for those whose faith has been tested and strengthened.

PERSONAL APPLICATION

Peter wrote of suffering several times in this letter (1 Peter 1:6-7; 3:13-17; 4:12-19; 5:9). His readers needed this discussion of trials because non-Christians misunderstood, harassed, and even physically abused Christians. Some of the opposition came from government officials, some from non-Christian individuals, and some from family members. To those abused and aching Christians, Peter wrote: "Be truly glad! There is wonderful joy ahead, even though it is necessary for you to endure many trials for a while" (1:6).

Christians are not of this world—our goals, values, and allegiance contrast and clash with society's. Thus, eventually, all believers will face trials of rejection because of their choice to follow Christ.

Accept rejection and suffering for your faith as a test. God will purify and refine you through your trials.

BIBLE READING

⁴For God has reserved a priceless inheritance for his children. It is kept in heaven for you, pure and undefiled, beyond the reach of change and decay. ⁵And God, in his mighty power, will protect you until you receive this salvation, because you are trusting him. It will be revealed on the last day for all to see. ⁶So be truly glad! There is wonderful joy ahead, even though it is necessary for you to endure many trials for a while.

⁷These trials are only to test your faith, to show that it is strong and pure. It is being tested as fire tests and purifies gold—and your faith is far more precious to God than mere gold. So if your faith remains strong after being tried by fiery trials, it will bring you much praise and glory and honor on the day when Jesus Christ is revealed to the whole world.

⁸You love him even though you have never seen him. Though you do not see him, you trust him; and even now you are happy with a glorious, inexpressible joy. ⁹Your reward for trusting him will be the salvation of your souls.

¹⁰This salvation was something the prophets wanted to know more about. They prophesied about this gracious salvation prepared for you, even though they had many questions as to what it all could mean. ¹¹They wondered what the Spirit of Christ within them was talking about when he told them in advance about Christ's suffering and his great glory afterward. They wondered when and to whom all this would happen.

¹²They were told that these things would not happen during their lifetime, but many years later, during yours. And now this Good News has been announced by those who preached to you in the power of the Holy Spirit sent from heaven. It is all so wonderful that even the angels are eagerly watching these things happen. 1 PETER 1:4-12

$\mathcal{R}$espectfully Armed

PREVIEW

A good explanation goes a long way. Think of a time when someone completely misunderstood something you did, and perhaps even asked, "Why did you do that?" Your answer made perfect sense to you. All you needed to do was enlighten the other person to your way of thinking.

Be ready to do that, Peter says in this passage. For you as a Christian, misunderstanding (but also plain curiosity) will bring questions as surely as you breathe. A good explanation will go a long way.

Other important lessons in this reading deal with obeying authority; the husband-wife relationship; and suffering for doing good.

PERSONAL APPLICATION

The idea of following Christ strikes some people as a new and radical notion. To them any Christian's faith will seem odd or curious. That is why Peter told his readers to be ready to answer questions about their faith (1 Peter 3:15).

Unfortunately, many believers feel constrained by popular assumptions that tell us to stay off the topic of religion. But we do not have to avoid the subject altogether just to stay civil. We can explain our faith to a questioner without causing conflict, especially if we are invited to do so, by conversing "in a gentle and respectful way" (3:16).

Think about why you follow Christ—why you believe and how you might explain your faith and your reasons to someone. Then the next time someone asks you why you believe, feel free to answer, gently and respectfully. Be prepared because the subject will come up eventually, especially if people catch you doing good (3:13).

BIBLE READING

¹³Now, who will want to harm you if you are eager to do good? ¹⁴But even if you suffer for doing what is right, God will reward you for it. So don't be afraid and don't worry. ¹⁵Instead, you must worship Christ as Lord of your life. And if you are asked about your Christian hope, always be ready to explain it. ¹⁶But you must do this in a gentle and respectful way. Keep your conscience clear. Then if people speak evil against you, they will be ashamed when they see what a good life you live because you belong to Christ. ¹⁷Remember, it is better to suffer for doing good, if that is what God wants, than to suffer for doing wrong!

¹⁸Christ also suffered when he died for our sins once for all time. He never sinned, but he died for sinners that he might bring us safely home to God. He suffered physical death, but he was raised to life in the Spirit.

¹⁹So he went and preached to the spirits in prison—²⁰those who disobeyed God long ago when God waited patiently while Noah was building his boat. Only eight people were saved from drowning in that terrible flood. ²¹And this is a picture of baptism, which now saves you by the power of Jesus Christ's resurrection. Baptism is not a removal of dirt from your body; it is an appeal to God from a clean conscience.

²²Now Christ has gone to heaven. He is seated in the place of honor next to God, and all the angels and authorities and powers are bowing before him.   1 PETER 3:13-22

ld-Fashioned?

PREVIEW

"You're so old-fashioned you just don't understand!" "Well, let me tell you what it was like when *I* was your age." On which side of the generation gap do you stand?

A key word in the last chapter of Peter's first epistle is *humble*. Yet it is not a word that often describes relationships between young people and their elders. Whether you are old or young, take an attitude check as you read.

Haughty leaders beware, for Peter has strong words in this passage for those who abuse their positions and responsibilities. Suffering again sets the tone, but so does the certainty of God's grace and power to carry his people through.

PERSONAL APPLICATION

The variety of ages among Christians in the early church posed a challenge. The older believers had wisdom to share; the younger ones did not always want to listen to them and follow their lead. Peter told his readers that they could solve their problem by letting the older ones humbly lead the way (1 Peter 5:3). It would take humility from *both* sides—the young would have to submit to the old, and the old would have to respect the young (5:5).

The lines of communication between older and younger generations have always had a bit of static. Humility toward each other clears up the signal. Pride breaks communication between generations, while humility opens the lines.

Look to those who are older than you for leadership and guidance. Ask them for advice. Consider their input, and when appropriate, let them lead. At the same time, never look down on the young just because they may lack the wisdom that you once lacked yourself.

BIBLE READING

[1]And now, a word to you who are elders in the churches. I, too, am an elder and a witness to the sufferings of Christ. And I, too, will share his glory and his honor when he returns. As a fellow elder, this is my appeal to you: [2]Care for the flock of God entrusted to you. Watch over it willingly, not grudgingly—not for what you will get out of it, but because you are eager to serve God. [3]Don't lord it over the people assigned to your care, but lead them by your good example. [4]And when the head Shepherd comes, your reward will be a never-ending share in his glory and honor.

[5]You younger men, accept the authority of the elders. And all of you, serve each other in humility, for

> "God sets himself against the proud,
>   but he shows favor to the humble."

[6]So humble yourselves under the mighty power of God, and in his good time he will honor you. [7]Give all your worries and cares to God, for he cares about what happens to you.

[8]Be careful! Watch out for attacks from the Devil, your great enemy. He prowls around like a roaring lion, looking for some victim to devour. [9]Take a firm stand against him, and be strong in your faith. Remember that your Christian brothers and sisters all over the world are going through the same kind of suffering you are.

[10]In his kindness God called you to his eternal glory by means of Jesus Christ. After you have suffered a little while, he will restore, support, and strengthen you, and he will place you on a firm foundation. [11]All power is his forever and ever. Amen.

1 PETER 5:1-11

Practice Makes Perfect

PREVIEW

Championship teams build their success upon the basics of their sport. The coaches routinely review the basics with the players. Good athletes practice them again and again. Great athletes strive to perfect them in their technique. Winners never forget the basics and build their game upon them like a house on a foundation.

In his second letter, Peter plays the part of the coach. He does not want Christians to forget the basics of their faith, so he reviews them in this passage. The key word here is *remember*. How's your practice schedule?

As you read, watch also for God's escape hatch and an amazing chain or fortification for your faith. And pay attention to a call to pay attention.

PERSONAL APPLICATION

Peter was concerned about his readers' faith surviving over the long run. Because Peter knew that he would die soon, he reviewed the basics of the faith to etch them into their memory (2 Peter 1:12-15). Peter wanted his readers to firmly grasp the gospel's basic message, a goal that would take repetition to achieve. He wanted them to hear again and again that Jesus had come to die for their sins, had risen on the third day, had given them eternal life, and would one day return to judge the earth. Knowing and believing those simple basics would uphold their faith and keep them strong.

From time to time, it is good to review the basics of our faith in Christ. Doing this will refresh our memory, strengthen our faith, and dispel any spiritual falsehoods we may have begun to believe.

Do you remember the basics of the faith? Whether you do or not, be sure to review the Gospels and Epistles regularly to stay spiritually sharp.

BIBLE READING

[12]I plan to keep on reminding you of these things—even though you already know them and are standing firm in the truth. [13]Yes, I believe I should keep on reminding you of these things as long as I live. [14]But the Lord Jesus Christ has shown me that my days here on earth are numbered and I am soon to die. [15]So I will work hard to make these things clear to you. I want you to remember them long after I am gone.

[16]For we were not making up clever stories when we told you about the power of our Lord Jesus Christ and his coming again. We have seen his majestic splendor with our own eyes. [17]And he received honor and glory from God the Father when God's glorious, majestic voice called down from heaven, "This is my beloved Son; I am fully pleased with him." [18]We ourselves heard the voice when we were there with him on the holy mountain.

[19]Because of that, we have even greater confidence in the message proclaimed by the prophets. Pay close attention to what they wrote, for their words are like a light shining in a dark place—until the day Christ appears and his brilliant light shines in your hearts. [20]Above all, you must understand that no prophecy in Scripture ever came from the prophets themselves [21]or because they wanted to prophesy. It was the Holy Spirit who moved the prophets to speak from God.   2 PETER 1:12-21

Totally Free

PREVIEW

"When I grow up," says many a child, "I'll do whatever I please." When they grow up, some actually try. Freedom to do anything they want looks heavenly.

Peter knows that appearances can be deceiving. In this second epistle, Peter warns his readers about the trade-off of "totally free" living. This concern that Peter addresses comes from heretics who advocate a do-what-you-like philosophy. But Peter says their teachings are really more binding than freeing. With guidance as perfect for our century as for the first, Peter provides insight into the slave-master relationship. Who is your master?

PERSONAL APPLICATION

Peter's second letter dealt with a heresy that urged Christians to sin. The heretics argued that we may as well do whatever we like because God will forgive us. They called this freedom. But Peter pointed out that freedom to do whatever we like is actually *slavery* to our sinful desires (1 Peter 2:19). He also wrote that God frees us from sin so that we can obey him rather than our sinful desires. God does not free us from the restraint to do good but from the rule of our appetites and desires.

Some people say that they want to be totally free. By this they usually mean that they do not want moral convictions or laws restraining them from doing whatever they like. In reality their desire to be totally free requires them to obey their appetites. Thus they are not totally free. Whether they realize it or not, they obey a master, too.

What or whom will you call your master? Will you follow your fleshly desires and be a slave to sin? Or will you obey God's commands and be free from sin? It is your choice. Choose wisely.

BIBLE READING

[12]These false teachers are like unthinking animals, creatures of instinct, who are born to be caught and killed. They laugh at the terrifying powers they know so little about, and they will be destroyed along with them. [13]Their destruction is their reward for the harm they have done. They love to indulge in evil pleasures in broad daylight. They are a disgrace and a stain among you. They revel in deceitfulness while they feast with you. [14]They commit adultery with their eyes, and their lust is never satisfied. They make a game of luring unstable people into sin. They train themselves to be greedy; they are doomed and cursed. [15]They have wandered off the right road and followed the way of Balaam son of Beor, who loved to earn money by doing wrong. [16]But Balaam was stopped from his mad course when his donkey rebuked him with a human voice.

[17]These people are as useless as dried-up springs of water or as clouds blown away by the wind—promising much and delivering nothing. They are doomed to blackest darkness. [18]They brag about themselves with empty, foolish boasting. With lustful desire as their bait, they lure back into sin those who have just escaped from such wicked living. [19]They promise freedom, but they themselves are slaves to sin and corruption. For you are a slave to whatever controls you. [20]And when people escape from the wicked ways of the world by learning about our Lord and Savior Jesus Christ and then get tangled up with sin and become its slave again, they are worse off than before. [21]It would be better if they had never known the right way to live than to know it and then reject the holy commandments that were given to them. [22]They make these proverbs come true: "A dog returns to its vomit," and "A washed pig returns to the mud."

2 PETER 2:12-22

The Ticking Clock

PREVIEW

When visiting another country or culture, we may discover that the sense of time is quite different from our own. What does it mean to be on time? How long should something take? Another country, another timetable. It behooves us to adjust if we want to get along.

God's sense of time is the focus of this reading. Here Peter explains that God's timing is different from that of humans. Despite the differences, however, Peter encourages readers to have patience. God is in control and has not forgotten his people. As you read, consider how you can be both watchful and relaxed.

Note that hope is held up in abundance in this reading, as is the example of Jesus.

PERSONAL APPLICATION

Some of the Christians to whom Peter wrote faced harassment and suffering for their faith. They knew that God planned an eventual judgment of the earth, when all would be put right. But they wondered, *Why was he waiting?* and *Why not do it now?* Peter told them: God has a different timetable than we do (2 Peter 3:8-9; see Psalm 90:4).

While we anxiously await God's gavel of justice to fall, God patiently waits for more people to repent. He moves with perfect timing, not slowness.

Keep waiting with Jesus for more people to repent and turn to him. Each day he delays is another opportunity for us to have compassion as he does and to give a few more people an opportunity to accept him. Use the time God's given you to spread the Good News.

BIBLE READING

³First, I want to remind you that in the last days there will be scoffers who will laugh at the truth and do every evil thing they desire. ⁴This will be their argument: "Jesus promised to come back, did he? Then where is he? Why, as far back as anyone can remember, everything has remained exactly the same since the world was first created."

⁵They deliberately forget that God made the heavens by the word of his command, and he brought the earth up from the water and surrounded it with water. ⁶Then he used the water to destroy the world with a mighty flood. ⁷And God has also commanded that the heavens and the earth will be consumed by fire on the day of judgment, when ungodly people will perish.

⁸But you must not forget, dear friends, that a day is like a thousand years to the Lord, and a thousand years is like a day. ⁹The Lord isn't really being slow about his promise to return, as some people think. No, he is being patient for your sake. He does not want anyone to perish, so he is giving more time for everyone to repent. ¹⁰But the day of the Lord will come as unexpectedly as a thief. Then the heavens will pass away with a terrible noise, and everything in them will disappear in fire, and the earth and everything on it will be exposed to judgment.

¹¹Since everything around us is going to melt away, what holy, godly lives you should be living! ¹²You should look forward to that day and hurry it along—the day when God will set the heavens on fire and the elements will melt away in the flames. ¹³But we are looking forward to the new heavens and new earth he has promised, a world where everyone is right with God.

¹⁴And so, dear friends, while you are waiting for these things to happen, make every effort to live a pure and blameless life. And be at peace with God.

¹⁵And remember, the Lord is waiting so that people have time to be saved. 2 PETER 3:3-15

Taste Test

PREVIEW

You have to develop a taste for certain foods. Though some people love it, liver, for example, gags many people on the first try. It takes a commitment to continue eating this "delicacy" before you can get over the initial taste shock.

Being a Christian involves an adjustment of appetites, John writes. Love of the right things is an acquired taste, but worth every bit of effort.

John's goal in this reading is to enlighten his readers. He does this through a message about light and dark that tells a simple truth: You can see where you are going when you walk in God's light. Otherwise you are stumbling in the dark.

PERSONAL APPLICATION

John instructed his readers to "stop loving this evil world and all that it offers you" (1 John 2:15). He listed three appeals that would drag believers down: "the lust for physical pleasure, the lust for everything we see, and pride in our possessions" (2:16). These pursuits would offer nothing of importance, and they would all fade away. Only doing God's will would have any kind of lasting effect.

To love the world and its treasures takes no effort at all—we do it naturally. That is why God tells us *not* to love it. This means that we must wean ourselves from it. We must set our sights on doing God's will, and let the world's appeals fall away in importance.

All the acts you do for Christ's sake will have lasting value—a changed life, an eternal reward, God's greater glory. Learn to love and do what God loves.

BIBLE READING

¹⁵Stop loving this evil world and all that it offers you, for when you love the world, you show that you do not have the love of the Father in you. ¹⁶For the world offers only the lust for physical pleasure, the lust for everything we see, and pride in our possessions. These are not from the Father. They are from this evil world. ¹⁷And this world is fading away, along with everything it craves. But if you do the will of God, you will live forever.

¹⁸Dear children, the last hour is here. You have heard that the Antichrist is coming, and already many such antichrists have appeared. From this we know that the end of the world has come. ¹⁹These people left our churches because they never really belonged with us; otherwise they would have stayed with us. When they left us, it proved that they do not belong with us. ²⁰But you are not like that, for the Holy Spirit has come upon you, and all of you know the truth. ²¹So I am writing to you not because you don't know the truth but because you know the difference between truth and falsehood. ²²And who is the great liar? The one who says that Jesus is not the Christ. Such people are antichrists, for they have denied the Father and the Son. ²³Anyone who denies the Son doesn't have the Father either. But anyone who confesses the Son has the Father also.

²⁴So you must remain faithful to what you have been taught from the beginning. If you do, you will continue to live in fellowship with the Son and with the Father. ²⁵And in this fellowship we enjoy the eternal life he promised us.   1 JOHN 2:15-25

he Standard

PREVIEW

Suppose you had a friend who was in serious financial trouble. What would you do for that person? Would you help bail him or her out or give financial counseling? What if your friend's problem was health related? Or worse, what if your friend was in trouble with the law? How far would you go out of your way to help this friend?

In this reading, John illustrates how far Jesus went to save us from our serious spiritual trouble—sin. Through Jesus' sacrifice, we see what true love really is. As John points out, we now have a standard against which to compare our love for others.

PERSONAL APPLICATION

Jesus loved us so much that he gave his life for us. His death on the cross to pay the penalty for our sins came as a result of his love. His selfless, sacrificial gift models how we should show love to one another (1 John 3:16).

To love someone means to be like Jesus to that person—to be selfless and to give sacrificially. Loving this way ignores all the enticements that normally compel us to be nice to people, such as the personal benefits we may gain from doing so. Also, loving others as Jesus did may not feel good all the time. This kind of love regards others' welfare above our own, and it may cost an awful lot (pride, possessions, time, money). It may cost everything.

If you truly want to reach out to others, extend to them what God extended to you: unconditional love.

BIBLE READING

¹¹This is the message we have heard from the beginning: We should love one another. ¹²We must not be like Cain, who belonged to the evil one and killed his brother. And why did he kill him? Because Cain had been doing what was evil, and his brother had been doing what was right. ¹³So don't be surprised, dear brothers and sisters, if the world hates you.

¹⁴If we love our Christian brothers and sisters, it proves that we have passed from death to eternal life. But a person who has no love is still dead. ¹⁵Anyone who hates another Christian is really a murderer at heart. And you know that murderers don't have eternal life within them. ¹⁶We know what real love is because Christ gave up his life for us. And so we also ought to give up our lives for our Christian brothers and sisters. ¹⁷But if anyone has enough money to live well and sees a brother or sister in need and refuses to help—how can God's love be in that person?

¹⁸Dear children, let us stop just saying we love each other; let us really show it by our actions. ¹⁹It is by our actions that we know we are living in the truth, so we will be confident when we stand before the Lord, ²⁰even if our hearts condemn us. For God is greater than our hearts, and he knows everything.

²¹Dear friends, if our conscience is clear, we can come to God with bold confidence. ²²And we will receive whatever we request because we obey him and do the things that please him. ²³And this is his commandment: We must believe in the name of his Son, Jesus Christ, and love one another, just as he commanded us. ²⁴Those who obey God's commandments live in fellowship with him, and he with them. And we know he lives in us because the Holy Spirit lives in us.   1 JOHN 3:11-24

Without a Doubt

PREVIEW

The news occasionally features a story that seems too incredible to be true. A construction worker has a nail driven into his skull and does not suffer any ill effects. A woman is shot six times during a robbery and lives. How can you know if these stories are really true? For the most part you cannot. You just have to trust the source.

In this reading John covers a story that some Christians sometimes doubt—their salvation. He explains to his readers how to know if they are truly saved or not. Read this passage and gain assurance.

As an added feature, John reviews Jesus' mission in coming to earth and in dying. He also throws in a sidebar on what to do if a fellow Christian is sinning.

PERSONAL APPLICATION

John wrote this letter to reassure Christians in their faith; some false teachers had given them cause to doubt that their salvation was secure.

How can we *know* we have eternal life? John tells us: trust in Jesus Christ (1 John 5:13). Jesus is God's own Son, the one who came as a human being, died to pay the penalty for our sins, and rose again. His work alone gives him the power and right to forgive all who confess their sins to him (1 John 1:9). Anyone who believes in Christ has eternal life (see John 3:16).

The next time you feel insecure about your salvation, reaffirm your trust in Christ. Then you can *know* you have eternal life, whether you feel close to God or far away.

BIBLE READING

[1]Everyone who believes that Jesus is the Christ is a child of God. And everyone who loves the Father loves his children, too. [2]We know we love God's children if we love God and obey his commandments. [3]Loving God means keeping his commandments, and really, that isn't difficult. [4]For every child of God defeats this evil world by trusting Christ to give the victory. [5]And the ones who win this battle against the world are the ones who believe that Jesus is the Son of God.

[6]And Jesus Christ was revealed as God's Son by his baptism in water and by shedding his blood on the cross—not by water only, but by water and blood. And the Spirit also gives us the testimony that this is true. [7]So we have these three witnesses—[8]the Spirit, the water, and the blood—and all three agree. [9]Since we believe human testimony, surely we can believe the testimony that comes from God. And God has testified about his Son. [10]All who believe in the Son of God know that this is true. Those who don't believe this are actually calling God a liar because they don't believe what God has testified about his Son.

[11]And this is what God has testified: He has given us eternal life, and this life is in his Son. [12]So whoever has God's Son has life; whoever does not have his Son does not have life.

[13]I write this to you who believe in the Son of God, so that you may know you have eternal life. [14]And we can be confident that he will listen to us whenever we ask him for anything in line with his will. [15]And if we know he is listening when we make our requests, we can be sure that he will give us what we ask for.

1 JOHN 5:1-15

Always Room for One More

PREVIEW

Do you remember the first time someone put you up for the night? You were away from home and a friend or relative gave you a place to sleep and the promise of a good breakfast the next morning. The bed felt different. The walls looked different from the ones in your room. You made sure that you knew where the bathroom was, just in case. Was that a sense of adventure . . . or homesickness?

In the apostle John's day, traveling teachers and missionaries spent many nights away from home. Their travels created a need for hospitality. Gaius, the person to whom John wrote this third letter, was one believer who extended hospitality to these teachers. Unfortunately, however, not all the believers back then did the same. In addition, not all of the traveling teachers preached the truth about Jesus. So John, in his second letter, warns the believers about these false teachers.

PERSONAL APPLICATION

John commended Gaius for "doing a good work for God when you take care of the traveling teachers who are passing through, even though they are strangers to you" (3 John 1:5). Traveling preachers would travel from place to place, presenting the good news about Christ to unbelievers and helping new churches get started. These ministers depended on fellow Christians to house and feed them. Believers like Gaius therefore provided a valuable ministry to ministers (1:5-8).

Today, ministers still have many needs, and like Gaius, you can help meet some of those needs. By helping ministers, you enable them to do what God has called them to do and therefore participate in their work (1:8). Don't underestimate the importance of your ministry to ministers. Anything you can do to support them through hospitality, gifts, or even words of encouragement will be welcome.

BIBLE READING

[2]Dear friend, I am praying that all is well with you and that your body is as healthy as I know your soul is. [3]Some of the brothers recently returned and made me very happy by telling me about your faithfulness and that you are living in the truth. [4]I could have no greater joy than to hear that my children live in the truth.

[5]Dear friend, you are doing a good work for God when you take care of the traveling teachers who are passing through, even though they are strangers to you. [6]They have told the church here of your friendship and your loving deeds. You do well to send them on their way in a manner that pleases God. [7]For they are traveling for the Lord and accept nothing from those who are not Christians. [8]So we ourselves should support them so that we may become partners with them for the truth.

[9]I sent a brief letter to the church about this, but Diotrephes, who loves to be the leader, does not acknowledge our authority. [10]When I come, I will report some of the things he is doing and the wicked things he is saying about us. He not only refuses to welcome the traveling teachers, he also tells others not to help them. And when they do help, he puts them out of the church.

[11]Dear friend, don't let this bad example influence you. Follow only what is good. Remember that those who do good prove that they are God's children, and those who do evil prove that they do not know God. [12]But everyone speaks highly of Demetrius, even truth itself. We ourselves can say the same for him, and you know we speak the truth.   3 JOHN 1:2-12

License Revoked

PREVIEW

Margaret can hardly wait to get her driver's license. As soon as she turns sixteen, Mom will drive her to the Department of Motor Vehicles where she will take the test and, if all goes well, get official permission to drive a Class A motor vehicle. It will mean new freedom and new responsibility.

Just as driving is a privilege, so is freedom in Christ. In this letter, Jude tells of Christians who have taken their freedom too far. He has no patience with their abuse of this privilege because they know the rules of the road and have deliberately disobeyed them.

Also in this reading you will find strong fight language for the spiritual battles we face. And our duties to one another conclude the letter.

PERSONAL APPLICATION

Jude wrote this brief letter to rebuke false teachers. These false teachers taught that Christians can live "immoral lives" because God has forgiven them (Jude 1:4). Such false teachers were wrong, and God's severe judgment awaited them (1:5-11, 14-16).

The same heresy taught back in Jude's day still flourishes today. Many people try to justify immorality and wrongdoing by appealing to God's forgiveness. But God never forgave us so that we could sin without consequence. Jesus died to free us *from* sin. He did not die to free us *to* sin.

Take care of how you use your freedom in Christ. Do not freely sin and cheapen God's forgiveness after you have indulged your appetites. Having this freedom is a privilege that comes with great responsibility. Live wisely and reverently before God.

BIBLE READING

[16]These people are grumblers and complainers, doing whatever evil they feel like. They are loudmouthed braggarts, and they flatter others to get favors in return.

[17]But you, my dear friends, must remember what the apostles of our Lord Jesus Christ told you, [18]that in the last times there would be scoffers whose purpose in life is to enjoy themselves in every evil way imaginable. [19]Now they are here, and they are the ones who are creating divisions among you. They live by natural instinct because they do not have God's Spirit living in them.

[20]But you, dear friends, must continue to build your lives on the foundation of your holy faith. And continue to pray as you are directed by the Holy Spirit. [21]Live in such a way that God's love can bless you as you wait for the eternal life that our Lord Jesus Christ in his mercy is going to give you. [22]Show mercy to those whose faith is wavering. [23]Rescue others by snatching them from the flames of judgment. There are still others to whom you need to show mercy, but be careful that you aren't contaminated by their sins.

[24]And now, all glory to God, who is able to keep you from stumbling, and who will bring you into his glorious presence innocent of sin and with great joy. [25]All glory to him, who alone is God our Savior, through Jesus Christ our Lord. Yes, glory, majesty, power, and authority belong to him, in the beginning, now, and forevermore. Amen. JUDE 1:16-25

To Be Cherished Always

PREVIEW

Some things in life just seem too good to pass up. For instance, a 30 percent-off sale at the mall always seems to happen when we have no money. At a time like this it is easy to justify spending more than we should with our credit cards. Or what about indulging in foods that are not healthy for us? Opportunities to do so always seem to come right after we have made a commitment to healthier living.

The same rule applies to sin. Just because people have made a commitment to Jesus Christ does not mean that the temptations stop. In this reading, Jesus has strong words for those who think that God's moral law has been suspended for them. He especially condemns those who have taught others the same.

Not every word in this reading is one of condemnation, however. Jesus has some encouraging words for the persecuted church as well as for the obedient church.

PERSONAL APPLICATION

In this portion of Revelation, John rebuked the Thyatiran believers for tolerating sexual immorality in their church (Revelation 2:20). The false prophetess Jezebel taught them to regard it lightly, but it was not a light matter at all.

The temptation to minimize the problems of sexual immorality has never been greater. Virtually *everyone* regards sexual choice as a freedom and right of adulthood. If "two consenting adults" can't be free to decide to have sex, then who can? Or so the reasoning goes. Yet God invented sex to be an intimate bond between husband and wife *only* (see Genesis 2:24). The fact that we can easily corrupt it gives us all the more reason to guard its purity closely.

Cherish your sexuality as you would a precious gem. How you express it matters a great deal. Keep yourself pure for the sake of Christ and the purpose for which he created you.

BIBLE READING

[18]"Write this letter to the angel of the church in Thyatira. This is the message from the Son of God, whose eyes are bright like flames of fire, whose feet are like polished bronze:

[19]"I know all the things you do—your love, your faith, your service, and your patient endurance. And I can see your constant improvement in all these things. [20]But I have this complaint against you. You are permitting that woman—that Jezebel who calls herself a prophet—to lead my servants astray. She is encouraging them to worship idols, eat food offered to idols, and commit sexual sin. [21]I gave her time to repent, but she would not turn away from her immorality. [22]Therefore, I will throw her upon a sickbed, and she will suffer greatly with all who commit adultery with her, unless they turn away from all their evil deeds. [23]I will strike her children dead. And all the churches will know that I am the one who searches out the thoughts and intentions of every person. And I will give to each of you whatever you deserve. [24]But I also have a message for the rest of you in Thyatira who have not followed this false teaching ('deeper truths,' as they call them—depths of Satan, really). I will ask nothing more of you [25]except that you hold tightly to what you have until I come.

[26]"To all who are victorious, who obey me to the very end, I will give authority over all the nations. [27]They will rule the nations with an iron rod and smash them like clay pots. [28]They will have the same authority I received from my Father, and I will also give them the morning star! [29]Anyone who is willing to hear should listen to the Spirit and understand what the Spirit is saying to the churches."

REVELATION 2:18-29

*F*alling Down and Wanting To

PREVIEW

Suppose you won a Nobel or a Pulitzer prize, or some equally presti-
gious honor. Would you feel worthy to receive such an award? What
would you do with all the praise and acclaim? Suppose then, after the
shock wore off, you had it revoked. "Not worthy of it after all," the
committee decided. How *then* would you feel?

In this reading the award winners do something that would be
considered unusual in our culture. They willingly give back their awards
without anyone asking them to do so.

PERSONAL APPLICATION

In his vision of heaven around God's throne, John saw the twenty-four
elders cast their crowns before God and worship him, proclaiming the
Lord to be "worthy . . . to receive glory and honor and power" (Revelation 4:11). God's awesome greatness compelled them to cast their
crowns at the feet of Jesus. And why shouldn't they? Jesus has done
more to be worthy of the glory, honor, and power he claims than
human beings can ever comprehend. Is not Jesus' birth proof enough of
that?

Those who find it difficult to accept God's authority or claim of glory
have the wrong god in mind. They have forgotten the total sacrifice he
made when Jesus, the Creator of all, came down to earth as a tiny baby
in the home of a simple Jewish couple. Their concept of God does not
match the reality of his victory over sin and death, either.

Give God the glory and honor he deserves. Take your "crown"—
your claim to fame, or whatever your "glory" may be—and cast it at
Jesus' feet by praising him. Fall down and worship, as the twenty-four
elders did. What could make more sense at such a time as this?

BIBLE READING

[1]Then as I looked, I saw a door standing open in heaven, and the same voice I had heard before spoke to me with the sound of a mighty trumpet blast. The voice said, "Come up here, and I will show you what must happen after these things." [2]And instantly I was in the Spirit, and I saw a throne in heaven and someone sitting on it! [3]The one sitting on the throne was as brilliant as gemstones—jasper and carnelian. And the glow of an emerald circled his throne like a rainbow. [4]Twenty-four thrones surrounded him, and twenty-four elders sat on them. They were all clothed in white and had gold crowns on their heads. [5]And from the throne came flashes of lightning and the rumble of thunder. And in front of the throne were seven lampstands with burning flames. They are the seven spirits of God. [6]In front of the throne was a shiny sea of glass, sparkling like crystal.

In the center and around the throne were four living beings, each covered with eyes, front and back. [7]The first of these living beings had the form of a lion; the second looked like an ox; the third had a human face; and the fourth had the form of an eagle with wings spread out as though in flight. [8]Each of these living beings had six wings, and their wings were covered with eyes, inside and out. Day after day and night after night they keep on saying,

"Holy, holy, holy is the Lord God Almighty—
the one who always was, who is, and who is still to come."

[9]Whenever the living beings give glory and honor and thanks to the one sitting on the throne, the one who lives forever and ever, [10]the twenty-four elders fall down and worship the one who lives forever and ever. And they lay their crowns before the throne and say,

[11] "You are worthy, O Lord our God,
to receive glory and honor and power.
For you created everything,
and it is for your pleasure that they exist and were created."
REVELATION 4:1–11

A Time to Die

PREVIEW

It is easy to get caught up in the grimy details of our lives. We can become so mired in our problems that we fall in with the complainers. Then something convicting happens. We hear that someone else has suffered or died for believing in Christ. Suddenly our suffering seems paltry by comparison, and we ponder the question: What would we do in a situation like that?

This reading provides a vivid picture of those who have suffered for Christ and are patiently waiting in heaven for God to bring about justice. The news they receive is both good and bad—more will die for their faith. But God will judge the earth justly, and their deaths will be avenged.

PERSONAL APPLICATION

After the Lamb (Christ) broke the fifth seal, John saw the souls of martyrs who had died for telling others about Christ. These martyrs had been killed "for the word of God and for being faithful in their witness." They cried out to God for justice, asking when God would avenge their blood. Jesus told them to wait a little while longer, until they were joined by the others who had yet to be killed for their faith (Revelation 6:9-11).

In contrast to these saints, we seem to care more about getting justice for the petty inequities we suffer. A traffic ticket, a snide remark, or an accusation of bad motives can set us off on a holy crusade. How poorly those causes compare to the cause of these men and women who had entrusted themselves to Jesus.

Rest assured that God is perfectly just and good. He does not forget when a child of his suffers for doing right. He keeps accounts and will one day settle them. Wait for God to bring about justice instead of taking it into your own hands.

BIBLE READING

[9]And when the Lamb broke the fifth seal, I saw under the altar the souls of all who had been martyred for the word of God and for being faithful in their witness. [10]They called loudly to the Lord and said, "O Sovereign Lord, holy and true, how long will it be before you judge the people who belong to this world for what they have done to us? When will you avenge our blood against these people?" [11]Then a white robe was given to each of them. And they were told to rest a little longer until the full number of their brothers and sisters—their fellow servants of Jesus—had been martyred.

[12]I watched as the Lamb broke the sixth seal, and there was a great earthquake. The sun became as dark as black cloth, and the moon became as red as blood. [13]Then the stars of the sky fell to the earth like green figs falling from trees shaken by mighty winds. [14]And the sky was rolled up like a scroll and taken away. And all of the mountains and all of the islands disappeared. [15]Then the kings of the earth, the rulers, the generals, the wealthy people, the people with great power, and every slave and every free person—all hid themselves in the caves and among the rocks of the mountains. [16]And they cried to the mountains and the rocks, "Fall on us and hide us from the face of the one who sits on the throne and from the wrath of the Lamb. [17]For the great day of their wrath has come, and who will be able to survive?"

REVELATION 6:9-17

tanding Firm

PREVIEW

News programs occasionally report about a person who took a stand for right against a tremendous injustice or wrong. Although the person's crusade may seem hopeless, he or she continues to stand on conviction. And sometimes this person even wins.

In this reading, two prophets stand up against the world for God's message. Their mission is life-and-death, for themselves and for those to whom they preach.

PERSONAL APPLICATION

The two witnesses were opposed for telling everyone about sin, repentance, and the coming judgment. The opposition came from everyone, not just a large majority or a powerful few. The opposition included violence. As soon as God withdrew his protection from the two witnesses, the people killed them and then celebrated their death (Revelation 11:10). Even though the witnesses were right, no one listened.

Being the only spokesperson for God's point of view doesn't make that point of view wrong. The majority may very well be wrong, every single one of them. If so, it doesn't do you any good to be wrong right along with them. And if you try, the most you can hope for is to have some company in your failure, but what consolation is that? In the case of the two witnesses, virtually the entire *world* was wrong.

Stand up for what is right no matter how few people share your convictions. Those who have closed their minds to God's Word will have to answer for themselves. God's truth will stand on its own, even if you're the only one defending it.

BIBLE READING

[3]"And I will give power to my two witnesses, and they will be clothed in sackcloth and will prophesy during those 1,260 days."

[4]These two prophets are the two olive trees and the two lampstands that stand before the Lord of all the earth. [5]If anyone tries to harm them, fire flashes from the mouths of the prophets and consumes their enemies. This is how anyone who tries to harm them must die. [6]They have power to shut the skies so that no rain will fall for as long as they prophesy. And they have the power to turn the rivers and oceans into blood, and to send every kind of plague upon the earth as often as they wish.

[7]When they complete their testimony, the beast that comes up out of the bottomless pit will declare war against them. He will conquer them and kill them. [8]And their bodies will lie in the main street of Jerusalem, the city which is called "Sodom" and "Egypt," the city where their Lord was crucified. [9]And for three and a half days, all peoples, tribes, languages, and nations will come to stare at their bodies. No one will be allowed to bury them. [10]All the people who belong to this world will give presents to each other to celebrate the death of the two prophets who had tormented them.

[11]But after three and a half days, the spirit of life from God entered them, and they stood up! And terror struck all who were staring at them. [12]Then a loud voice shouted from heaven, "Come up here!" And they rose to heaven in a cloud as their enemies watched.   REVELATION 11:3-12

Pay Now or Pay Later

PREVIEW

"No money down! No payments for a year! Zero percent financing!" Sound familiar? You know the deal. You also know that they are not going to give you something for nothing, so you had better find out what the catch is. Somewhere down the line, you will pay for that too-good-to-be-true offer.

In this passage, John tells of a bad deal that many will make with the beast from the sea in the end times. At first the deal looks good, but that is because the real payment—the eternal consequences—has not yet come due. As you read, determine not to fall for Satan's sales pitch.

The rest of this reading contains a retelling of the Christmas story and a heavenly war. Michael and the other angels fight for God, while Satan enlists the help of a strange beast. The battle is on.

PERSONAL APPLICATION

Those who worshiped the beast suffered the consequences (Revelation 14:9-12). At first it appeared that Satan had offered a better way—just take this mark, worship the beast, and all will be well; you'll be able to buy food for your family. But the price was eternal punishment.

Satan often comes along to deceive us, and the only way to avoid falling into his trap is to trust and obey God. Satan will try to make his way seem more attractive, easier, less painful, and more pleasurable than God's. But just beyond Satan's attractive, painless solution lies a more painful consequence.

When God's way seems to exact a price, trust in his plans for your future. Though you may pay a short-term price for obeying God, trust that he will reward you greatly for your obedience. You can be sure that the reward will be well worth the sacrifice.

BIBLE READING

⁹Then a third angel followed them, shouting, "Anyone who worships the beast and his statue or who accepts his mark on the forehead or the hand ¹⁰must drink the wine of God's wrath. It is poured out undiluted into God's cup of wrath. And they will be tormented with fire and burning sulfur in the presence of the holy angels and the Lamb. ¹¹The smoke of their torment rises forever and ever, and they will have no relief day or night, for they have worshiped the beast and his statue and have accepted the mark of his name. ¹²Let this encourage God's holy people to endure persecution patiently and remain firm to the end, obeying his commands and trusting in Jesus."

¹³And I heard a voice from heaven saying, "Write this down: Blessed are those who die in the Lord from now on. Yes, says the Spirit, they are blessed indeed, for they will rest from all their toils and trials; for their good deeds follow them!"

¹⁴Then I saw the Son of Man sitting on a white cloud. He had a gold crown on his head and a sharp sickle in his hand.

¹⁵Then an angel came from the Temple and called out in a loud voice to the one sitting on the cloud, "Use the sickle, for the time has come for you to harvest; the crop is ripe on the earth." ¹⁶So the one sitting on the cloud swung his sickle over the earth, and the whole earth was harvested.

¹⁷After that, another angel came from the Temple in heaven, and he also had a sharp sickle. ¹⁸Then another angel, who has power to destroy the world with fire, shouted to the angel with the sickle, "Use your sickle now to gather the clusters of grapes from the vines of the earth, for they are fully ripe for judgment." ¹⁹So the angel swung his sickle on the earth and loaded the grapes into the great winepress of God's wrath. ²⁰And the grapes were trodden in the winepress outside the city, and blood flowed from the winepress in a stream about 180 miles long and as high as a horse's bridle.   REVELATION 14:9-20

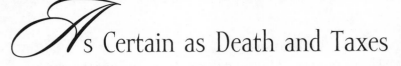s Certain as Death and Taxes

PREVIEW

Nothing seems more certain than death and taxes. Everyone knows that he or she will die someday. It is a given, a nasty fact of life. Although not everyone will admit or think about that for too long. Another fact every adult U.S. citizen knows is that on April 15, they have to have their income-tax forms completed and in the mail. Despite the fact that they have had significant sums of money taken from each of their paychecks throughout the year, they may owe more. So they have to pay up.

One thing is more certain than death and taxes—Christ's return. In this reading John tells his readers to be prepared today for Christ's second coming because preparing tomorrow may be too late. For those who heed John's warning, there is a wonderful blessing. As you read, consider what you must do to be prepared.

PERSONAL APPLICATION

Christ will return "as unexpectedly as a thief!" (Revelation 16:15; see 1 Thessalonians 5:1-6). His return will take everyone completely by surprise, and it will mark the beginning of the final judgment (Revelation 16:1-21). There will be no more opportunities to turn to God.

The certainty of tomorrow's sunrise falls somewhat shy of 100 percent. When God's plan calls for it, tomorrow will not come—Christ will. Many people will have planned to get their act together that day, to stop their indulgences and start living prudently on that day, to do what they knew they ought to have done before that day. Their one more chance will not materialize. Christ will have returned to judge the earth, and only those who awaited his return—only those who *already* submitted their lives to him—will be prepared.

Be ready when Christ returns. If you have not accepted him as your Savior and Lord, today may be your last opportunity to respond to the invitation he has been holding out for two thousand years.

BIBLE READING

¹²Then the sixth angel poured out his bowl on the great Euphrates River, and it dried up so that the kings from the east could march their armies westward without hindrance. ¹³And I saw three evil spirits that looked like frogs leap from the mouth of the dragon, the beast, and the false prophet. ¹⁴These miracle-working demons caused all the rulers of the world to gather for battle against the Lord on that great judgment day of God Almighty.

¹⁵"Take note: I will come as unexpectedly as a thief! Blessed are all who are watching for me, who keep their robes ready so they will not need to walk naked and ashamed."

¹⁶And they gathered all the rulers and their armies to a place called Armageddon in Hebrew.

¹⁷Then the seventh angel poured out his bowl into the air. And a mighty shout came from the throne of the Temple in heaven, saying, "It is finished!" ¹⁸Then the thunder crashed and rolled, and lightning flashed. And there was an earthquake greater than ever before in human history. ¹⁹The great city of Babylon split into three pieces, and cities around the world fell into heaps of rubble. And so God remembered all of Babylon's sins, and he made her drink the cup that was filled with the wine of his fierce wrath. ²⁰And every island disappeared, and all the mountains were leveled. ²¹There was a terrible hailstorm, and hailstones weighing seventy-five pounds fell from the sky onto the people below. They cursed God because of the hailstorm, which was a very terrible plague.   REVELATION 16:12-21

Greed Is Not Good

PREVIEW

Books on business management sell quite well, and for good reason: all businesses—large, medium, and small—compete in a brutal marketplace where nice guys really do finish last. Every competitive edge makes a difference. Every competitive edge soon becomes obsolete, too, which only quickens the pace, raises the stakes, and deepens the businessperson's commitment to finding a sure way to make more money.

John's vision in this passage is disheartening to anyone who is greedy for wealth. Here, the mother of all material wealth, Babylon, is destroyed. But the bad news for businesspeople, or merchants, is good news for those who love God more than wealth. As you read, determine to focus on God and his plan, not on money.

PERSONAL APPLICATION

The greed demonstrated by the merchants in John's vision is nothing new. People have always exploited sinful human desires, such as greed, lust, and pride, for money. They view human vices as opportunities to make a living or even to get rich. They reason, "As long as people want this, why not give it to them?" But those who love God hate evil. They do not want to encourage it in others any more than they want it ruling their own lives. They don't see people's greed and evil desires as opportunities to exploit, but as sad facts of human nature that need to be brought under the lordship of Christ.

Honor God in your business dealings. Avoid the temptation to take advantage of people's vices to enrich yourself. If you make or sell goods or services, uphold God's glory in it all. No one can undermine your business ethics if you care most about their effects on other people.

BIBLE READING

[1]After all this I saw another angel come down from heaven with great authority, and the earth grew bright with his splendor. [2]He gave a mighty shout, "Babylon is fallen—that great city is fallen! She has become the hideout of demons and evil spirits, a nest for filthy buzzards, and a den for dreadful beasts. [3]For all the nations have drunk the wine of her passionate immorality. The rulers of the world have committed adultery with her, and merchants throughout the world have grown rich as a result of her luxurious living."

[4]Then I heard another voice calling from heaven, "Come away from her, my people. Do not take part in her sins, or you will be punished with her. [5]For her sins are piled as high as heaven, and God is ready to judge her for her evil deeds. [6]Do to her as she has done to your people. Give her a double penalty for all her evil deeds. She brewed a cup of terror for others, so give her twice as much as she gave out. [7]She has lived in luxury and pleasure, so match it now with torments and sorrows. She boasts, 'I am queen on my throne. I am no helpless widow. I will not experience sorrow.' [8]Therefore, the sorrows of death and mourning and famine will overtake her in a single day. She will be utterly consumed by fire, for the Lord God who judges her is mighty."

[9]And the rulers of the world who took part in her immoral acts and enjoyed her great luxury will mourn for her as they see the smoke rising from her charred remains. [10]They will stand at a distance, terrified by her great torment. They will cry out, "How terrible, how terrible for Babylon, that great city! In one single moment God's judgment came on her."   REVELATION 18:1-10

ission Accomplished

PREVIEW

There are not too many things in this world that feel better than reaping the fruits of your long, hard labor. For parents, their labor is rewarded when their children grow up and become good, productive members of society. For college students, this is receiving a diploma on graduation day. For sports teams, this is winning the championship.

One day our labor to believe in and follow Christ will also come to fruition. In this reading, John describes the reward God will give his followers for their faithfulness. He will take us to our heavenly home—the new Jerusalem. Living here for eternity will be worth every sacrifice made, every prayer offered, every trial endured, and every persecution suffered. As you read, rejoice in Christ's victory and determine to remain faithful to him.

PERSONAL APPLICATION

At the end of history, God will destroy the old heaven and earth and create new and perfect ones. Those who died in their sins will be cast into the "lake that burns with fire," separated from God forever (Revelation 21:8). In sharp contrast, those who have been covered with Christ's blood will enter God's Holy City to live with him in eternal joy. Inside that city the people will hear Jesus say, "[God] will remove all of their sorrows, and there will be no more death or sorrow or crying or pain. For the old world and its evils are gone forever" (21:4). Actually, the end of history is also a beginning—the beginning of God's perfect world.

Everyone longs for a perfect world, one that is without suffering, death, or sadness. In this perfect world, we also long for fulfilling love and justice. All of this seems like an impossible fantasy. But here it is— God's promised future for all who love him.

BIBLE READING

¹Then I saw a new heaven and a new earth, for the old heaven and the old earth had disappeared. And the sea was also gone. ²And I saw the holy city, the new Jerusalem, coming down from God out of heaven like a beautiful bride prepared for her husband.

³I heard a loud shout from the throne, saying, "Look, the home of God is now among his people! He will live with them, and they will be his people. God himself will be with them. ⁴He will remove all of their sorrows, and there will be no more death or sorrow or crying or pain. For the old world and its evils are gone forever."

⁵And the one sitting on the throne said, "Look, I am making all things new!" And then he said to me, "Write this down, for what I tell you is trustworthy and true." ⁶And he also said, "It is finished! I am the Alpha and the Omega—the Beginning and the End. To all who are thirsty I will give the springs of the water of life without charge! ⁷All who are victorious will inherit all these blessings, and I will be their God, and they will be my children. ⁸But cowards who turn away from me, and unbelievers, and the corrupt, and murderers, and the immoral, and those who practice witchcraft, and idol worshipers, and all liars—their doom is in the lake that burns with fire and sulfur. This is the second death."

⁹Then one of the seven angels who held the seven bowls containing the seven last plagues came and said to me, "Come with me! I will show you the bride, the wife of the Lamb."

¹⁰So he took me in spirit to a great, high mountain, and he showed me the holy city, Jerusalem, descending out of heaven from God. ¹¹It was filled with the glory of God and sparkled like a precious gem, crystal clear like jasper. ¹²Its walls were broad and high, with twelve gates guarded by twelve angels. And the names of the twelve tribes of Israel were written on the gates. ¹³There were three gates on each side—east, north, south, and west. ¹⁴The wall of the city had twelve foundation stones, and on them were written the names of the twelve apostles of the Lamb.

REVELATION 21:1-14

Topical Index